The Wiley Handbook of Contextual Behavioral Science

The Wiley Handbook of Contextual Behavioral Science

Edited by

**Robert D. Zettle,
Steven C. Hayes, Dermot Barnes-Holmes,
and Anthony Biglan**

WILEY Blackwell

Library of Congress Cataloging-in-Publication data applied for

HB ISBN: 9781118489567

A catalogue record for this book is available from the British Library.

Cover image: Eye spots on the outer hindwings of a giant owl butterfly, Caligo idomeneus, La Selva Reserve, Amazon Basin, Ecuador. Photo © Wild Horizons/UIG via Getty Images

Set in 10/12pt Galliard by SPi Global, Pondicherry, India
Printed and bound in Malaysia by Vivar Printing Sdn Bhd

1   2016

Contents

List of Contributors

Mark Alavosius, University of Nevada, Reno, United States

Rob Archer, Director, The Career Psychologist, London, United Kingdom

Laura Backen Jones, Oregon Research Institute, United States

Dermot Barnes-Holmes, Ghent University, Belgium

Yvonne Barnes-Holmes, Ghent University, Belgium

Anthony Biglan, Oregon Research Institute, United States

Frank W. Bond, Goldsmith College, University of London, United Kingdom

Robert Brockman, Institute for Positive Psychology and Education, Australian Catholic University, Australia

Joseph Ciarrochi, Institute for Positive Psychology and Education, Australian Catholic University, Australia

Christine Cody, Oregon Research Institute, United States

Lisa Coyne, Suffolk University, United States

Mark R. Dixon, Southern Illinois University, United States

James Duguid, Institute for Positive Psychology and Education, Australian Catholic University, Australia

Paul E. Flaxman, University of London, United Kingdom

Mairéad Foody, National University of Ireland Maynooth, Ireland

Evan M. Forman, Drexel University, United States

Steven C. Hayes, University of Nevada, Reno, United States

James D. Herbert, Drexel University, United States

Peter Hitchcock, Drexel University, United States

Ramona Houmanfar, University of Nevada, Reno, United States

Sean Hughes, Ghent University, Belgium

Ian Hussey, Ghent University, Belgium

Todd B. Kashdan, Center for the Advancement of Well-Being, George Mason University, United States

Deirdre Kavanagh, Ghent University, Belgium

Jean Lee, Oregon Research Institute, United States

Michael E. Levin, Utah State University, United States

April Lightcap, University of Oregon, United States

Jason Lillis, Brown Alpert Medical School, Providence, Rhode Island, United States

Joda Lloyd, Goldsmith College, University of London, United Kingdom

Douglas M. Long, University of Nevada, Reno, United States

Carmen Luciano, University of Almeria, Spain

Ciara McEnteggart, Ghent University, Belgium

Jean-Louis Monestès, Epsylon Lab, Montpellier and Mental Health Service, University of Reunion, France

Carol Murphy, National University of Ireland Maynooth, Ireland

Donny Newsome, Fit Learning, Reno, Nevada, United States

Philip Parker, Institute for Positive Psychology and Education, Australian Catholic University, Australia

Brandon T. Sanford, University of Nevada, Reno, United States

Baljinder Sahdra, Institute for Positive Psychology and Education, Australian Catholic University, Australia

Brooke M. Smith, Utah State University, United States

Thomas G. Szabo, Florida Institute of Technology, United States

Niklas Törneke, Therapist in Private Practice, Kalmar, Sweden

Michael P. Twohig, Utah State University, United States

Matthieu Villatte, Evidence-Based Practice Institute, Seattle, Washington, United States

Koa Whittingham, School of Psychology, University of Queensland, Australia

Kelly G. Wilson, University of Mississippi, United States

Robert D. Zettle, Wichita State University, United States

1

Examining the Partially Completed Crossword Puzzle

The Nature and Status of Contextual Behavioral Science

Steven C. Hayes, Robert D. Zettle, Dermot Barnes-Holmes, and Anthony Biglan

The purpose of this volume is to describe contextual behavioral science (CBS) – its nature, origins, status, and future. The parts of the handbook deal in succession with its foundational assumptions and strategies, basic work in language and cognition, contextual approaches to clinical interventions and assessment, and extensions of CBS across settings and populations. Although presented sequentially, the chapters are deliberately interwoven: Philosophical issues arise in the basic science chapters, basic science issues appear in the intervention chapters, and so on. They form a kind of intellectual and practical web or network (thus the term "reticulated" for the overall strategy) that taken as a whole describes CBS and its current status, as well as providing some good hints about where this tradition may be going.

It is in the nature of books that topics need to be presented in a linear fashion. CBS did not develop that way in a historical sense, however. For example, the work on functional contextualism did not precede the work on relational frame theory (RFT), which then preceded the development of acceptance and commitment therapy (ACT). CBS rather developed more the way one might attack a complex crossword puzzle – sometimes successfully pursuing clues in one part of the puzzle led to hints for how to move forward in other parts; sometimes advancements were made in a corner of the puzzle that would be disconnected from anything else for a long time. Sometimes these leaps and jumps were strategic; sometimes they were more like a random walk, driven by whim and circumstance. But always the goal was the overall puzzle: How to create a behavioral science more worthy of the challenge of the human condition.

A puzzle of that kind is one that in all likelihood will challenge behavioral science for some time, so although progress has clearly been made over the last few decades, what CBS is deliberately focused on is how to create a knowledge development strategy that is sustainable and progressive over the long haul. What CBS brings to the table is a principle-focused, communitarian strategy of reticulated scientific and practical development, grounded in functional contextualistic philosophical assumptions,

The Wiley Handbook of Contextual Behavioral Science, First Edition. Edited by Robert D. Zettle, Steven C. Hayes, Dermot Barnes-Holmes, and Anthony Biglan.

and applied at all levels of analysis in behavioral science. This vision builds on the historical fact that CBS gradually gathered together different kinds of professionals who were pursuing clues in one part of the puzzle with an eye toward what it suggested for how to advance in other parts. What once was an implicit strategy driven merely by breadth of interests has blossomed into a more conscious strategy of constructing a coherent intellectual and practical web of knowledge by proceeding in an interrelated and communitarian way all at once. Having a web of knowledge as a scientific product is what all forms of behavioral science aspire to, but CBS has adopted that end point as an analytic approach at the operational level, challenging all of the professionals involved to be always responsible for the whole of it when approached within common functional contextualistic assumptions. That is the deeper sense in which CBS is a communitarian and contextualistic *strategy* of reticulated scientific and practical development.

The CBS approach is quite different than a bottom-up strategy, in which basic scientists alone are given all of the duties of constructing principles of high precision and scope that can be applied by practitioners to complex human behavior. It is also different than technological applied work that leaps into the evaluation of applied ideas without a concern for basic principles or the scope of theories. That is one of the major differences between CBS and purely technologically oriented approaches. In a CBS approach, clinicians sometimes need to be responsible themselves for developing psychological principles, and "bench" scientists sometimes need to be responsible for learning how to apply the principles they have derived. This occurs both in the laboratories and the clinics of those who straddle that applied/basic divide, and across the crossword puzzle of content domains. Clinicians are working on social stigma or the empowerment of indigenous peoples; educators are working on relational fluency and the development of intellect; therapists are working on prevention or extending the flexibility of organizations; basic scientists are writing about evolutionary epistemology or are extending implicit measures to clinics. Over time that approach seems to be expanding the CBS community itself, not just in terms of size, where its growth has been rapid, but also in terms of its focus and professional interconnections. Cognitive scientists and evolutionary biologists are part of the CBS community, for example, and their students and colleagues are being drawn into the same communitarian approach. The list of professions, disciplines, and groups heavily involved in CBS is already long and continues to grow: social workers, psychiatrists, occupational therapists, nurses, prevention scientists, coaches, behavior analysts, educators. Development is broad at the level of language communities and nations as well, bringing new sensitivities and a diversity of topics driven by culture, intellectual traditions, and social needs. About half of the current members of the Association for Contextual Behavioral Science are outside of North America, 20 chapters exist for countries outside of the United States, and 26 special interest groups pursue issues across the full range of behavioral science topics.

Now that a substantial body of interrelated work exists, it may seem to have emerged, in retrospect, from a coherent and predictable process. Students especially should not be deceived. Science is not only nonlinear, it is not predictable. Science is the behavior of scientists and as such it is sometimes systematic and is at other times an unsystematic social enterprise. It is ultimately self-organizing based on its purpose and knowledge criteria, but it is also constantly devolving and beginning anew. There is no reason to think that this naturally unsystematic or, at times, even chaotic quality will, or should, change. Simply because a body of work exists does not mean that it is finished, or that it could have only have turned out that way, or that developers had this end in mind all along.

Advancing an existing body of work requires the same kinds of risks and leaps that were required in its creation. Students may imagine or even be told that their scientific forbears knew what they were doing, saw a future, and then pursued it systematically. This can be a very inspiring story when it is applied to scientific heroes, but it is a secretly discouraging narrative because students in general do not see into the future and they often wait in vain for the touch of the muses they have been told visited their mentors. There is no such division between academic and practitioner generations – the apparent difference is an illusion imposed by the asymmetry of the impact of the known past versus unknown future on verbal processes. The purposive tales that surround established bodies of work are mostly reconstructions and reinterpretations, integrated into a coherent account that downplays or even hides from view the social, emotional, or accidental sources of progress that characterized the development of the tradition in real time.

CBS has moved forward fed not just by scientific studies and findings, and logical extensions of theories and principles, but also by personal commitments, leaps of intuition, friendships and alliances, the yearning to be of use, and by the "egos" of individual scientists, who, like most humans, seek to be heard and proven right in some way. While a mere verbal warning is unlikely to stem the tendency for scientific and clinical traditions to devolve into the safety of social agreement, we do not want this moment to pass without pleading with young scientists especially to accept nothing on faith. We would also urge them to politely refuse the appeals of the establishment to take anything as a given or as obvious, and thus as something that needs to be agreed to without further consideration. It does not matter if the establishment making this appeal is cognitively oriented or behaviorally oriented; psychological or biological in its approach; contextualistic or mechanistic in its assumptions. It does not matter if the establishment includes the very authors of this book. Doubt everything and hold it lightly – even doubt itself. Let CBS grow and change based on its successes, but be careful of adaptive peaks that could prevent this field from continuing to push toward its ultimate goals. The young, and others willing to take risks, will push this field forward, but not if they are turned into applauders or passive recipients of knowledge.

This book has a clear organization – which we will describe while that warning is fresh in our minds. In Part I of the book, edited primarily by Steven C. Hayes, we explore the idea that CBS is a strategy of scientific development, that is based on a core set of philosophical assumptions, and that is nested within multidimensional, multilevel evolution science as a contextual view of life. Chapter 3 (Levin, Twohig, & Smith), provides an overview of CBS; chapter 4 (Biglan & Hayes) provides a similarly broad summary for functional contextualism. Chapter 5 (Wilson) deals with the variety of terms and principles in a CBS approach, cautioning against the tendency for scientists and practitioners alike to reify and ontologize them. Chapter 6 (Long & Sanford) explores the reflective implications of a functional contextualistic approach for the actions of scientists themselves – essentially applying a psychological flexibility model to the doing of science itself. In chapter 7, the final chapter of Part I, Monestès examines the contribution of CBS to the study of human evolution, focusing especially on the role of human language.

In Part II, edited primarily by Dermot Barnes-Holmes, RFT is described and linked to other aspects of CBS. Hughes and D. Barnes-Holmes begin in chapter 9 by laying out the basic account and then continuing in chapter 10 to extend its implications for the study of human language and cognition as a whole. In chapter 11, Y. Barnes-Holmes, Kavanagh, and Murphy explore the implications of RFT for education and special education, and, in chapter 12, the final chapter of Part II, Törneke, Luciano, Y. Barnes-Holmes, and Bond relate RFT to the understanding and treatment of human suffering.

Part III, edited primarily by Robert D. Zettle, explores contextual approaches to clinical interventions and assessment. Chapter 14 (Herbert, Forman, & Hitchcock), provides an overview of the defining, distinguishing, and common features of contextual approaches to psychotherapy. Villatte uses RFT and CBS principles in chapter 15 to help understand the in-session actions of both therapists and clients. Chapter 16 (Ciarrochi, Zettle, Brockman, Duguid, Parker, Sahdra, & Kashdan) explores a pragmatic approach to psychological assessment, extending the implications of functional contextualism to the nature and quality of measurement. Levin and Villatte consider the role of laboratory-based intervention studies and experimental psychopathology studies in a CBS approach in chapter 17. In chapter 18, the final chapter of Part III, Y. Barnes-Holmes, Hussey, McEnteggart, D. Barnes-Holmes, and Foody examine the relationship between RFT and middle-level terms in ACT.

Part IV, edited primarily by Anthony Biglan, examines extensions of CBS into a range of nonclinical topics and areas. In chapter 20, Backen Jones, Whittingham, Coyne, and Lightcap examine CBS and parenting; in chapter 21 Szabo & Dixon examines CBS in education. Bond, Lloyd, Flaxman, and Archer describe the extension of ACT and the concept of psychological flexibility to the workplace in chapter 22. In chapter 23, Levin, Lillis, and Biglan consider the possibility of community-wide strategies for promoting psychological flexibility. Biglan, Lee, and Cody extend CBS thinking to the evolution of capitalism in chapter 24. In chapter 25, the final chapter of this part, Alavosius, Newsome, Houmanfar, & Biglan apply CBS to the environment.

Trends in CBS

This volume presents a partially completed crossword puzzle. It is one in which vast regions of the puzzle remain unaddressed. The future of CBS remains to be written, but there are a number of basic and applied topics that are beginning to be worked on now that seem imminent. In the epilogue we will look ahead as best we can, but at this point it seems most worthwhile to characterize the broad trends that will be evident as you read this volume.

At one time it was possible to think of CBS merely as an overarching term for ACT, RFT, and their relationship. Those days are quickly passing away, as this volume shows. RFT is being linked to modern work in cognitive science (DeHouwer, Barnes-Holmes, & Moors, 2013), ACT methods are being linked to principles drawn from evolution science (Wilson, Hayes, Biglan, & Embry, 2014), and a variety of evidence-based contextual interventions are being linked to psychological flexibility and other core CBS concepts (Hayes, Villatte, Levin, & Hildebrandt, 2011). RFT is guiding clinical work directly (Törneke, 2010; Villatte, Villatte, & Hayes, 2015) and psychological flexibility is being applied to larger and larger systems. We can see the beginnings of a contextual behavioral neuroscience, and a broader integration with contextual approaches to biology more generally (e.g., Barnes-Holmes et al., 2005; Fletcher, Schoendorff, & Hayes, 2010; Wilson et al., 2014). CBS is beginning to develop more contextual models of assessment and its evaluation, turning away from the elemental realist ontological assumptions that reside inside psychometric theory (Borsboom, Mellenbergh, & van Heerden, 2003) toward such methods as experience sampling (Bolger, Davis, & Rafaeli, 2003) or radically functionalist concepts such as treatment utility (Hayes, Nelson, & Jarrett, 1987). RFT is developing methods that make clearer and clearer the differences between functional and structural models of cognition, and between relational and associative models of language and cognition (Hughes, Barnes-Holmes, & DeHouwer, 2011). A good example is the maturation of the Implicit Relational Assessment Procedure (IRAP) and its underlying theory, as this volume will demonstrate. Applied methods are now springing directly from RFT concepts more broadly, not just the middle-level terms of psychological flexibility (e.g., Cassidy, Roche, & Hayes, 2011; Rehfeldt & Barnes-Holmes, 2009) – a process that seems likely to continue.

These and other trends show that CBS is broadening and deepening. Although it came from behavior analysis, it is no longer tightly tied to behavior analysis as we have known it historically, and CBS is no longer just about ACT and RFT. Instead, CBS is about putting functional contextualistic assumptions into behavioral science writ large and building the bridges to allies and fellow travelers that are needed to make progress as measured against the grand aspiration of this tradition: creating a behavioral science more adequate to the challenge of the human condition.

References

Barnes-Holmes, D., Regan, D., Barnes-Holmes, Y., Comins, S., Walsh, D., Stewart, I., … Dymon, S. (2005). Relating derived relations as a model of analogical reasoning: Reaction times and event related potentials. *Journal of the Experimental Analysis of Behavior, 84*, 435–452.

Bolger, N., Davis, A., & Rafaeli, E. (2003). Diary methods: Capturing life as it is lived. *Annual Review of Psychology, 54*, 579–616.

Borsboom, D., Mellenbergh, G. J., & van Heerden, J. (2003). The theoretical status of latent variables. *Psychological Review, 110*, 203–219.

Cassidy, S., Roche, B., & Hayes, S. C. (2011). A relational frame training intervention to raise intelligence quotients: A pilot study. *The Psychological Record, 61*, 173–198.

DeHouwer, J., Barnes-Holmes, D., & Moors, A. (2013). What is learning? On the nature and merits of a functional definition of learning. *Psychonomic Bulletin & Review, 20*, 631–642.

Fletcher, L. B., Schoendorff, B., & Hayes, S. C. (2010). Searching for mindfulness in the brain: A process-oriented approach to examining the neural correlates of mindfulness. *Mindfulness, 1*, 41–63.

Hayes, S. C., Nelson, R. O., & Jarrett, R. (1987). Treatment utility of assessment: A functional approach to evaluating the quality of assessment. *American Psychologist, 42*, 963–974.

Hayes, S. C., Villatte, M., Levin, M., & Hildebrandt, M. (2011). Open, aware, and active: Contextual approaches as an emerging trend in the behavioral and cognitive therapies. *Annual Review of Clinical Psychology, 7*, 141–168.

Hughes, S., Barnes-Holmes, D., & DeHouwer, J. (2011). The dominance of associative theorising in implicit attitude research: Propositional and behavioral alternatives. *The Psychological Record, 61*, 465–498.

Rehfeldt, R. A., & Barnes-Holmes, Y. (2009). *Derived relational responding: Applications for learners with autism and other developmental disabilities*. Oakland, CA: New Harbinger.

Törneke, N. (2010). *Learning RFT: An introduction to relational frame theory and its clinical application*. Oakland, CA: New Harbinger.

Villatte, M., Villatte, J., & Hayes, S. C. (2015). *The language of psychotherapy*. New York: Guilford.

Wilson, D. S., Hayes, S. C., Biglan, T., & Embry, D. (2014). Evolving the future: Toward a science of intentional change. *Behavioral and Brain Sciences, 34*, 1–22.

Part I

Contextual Behavioral Science
Nature, Strategy, and Current Status

Steven C. Hayes

2

Why Contextual Behavioral Science Exists

An Introduction to Part I

Steven C. Hayes

The first part of this volume focuses on the big picture: What is contextual behavioral science (CBS), how does it differ from other approaches, and what are some of the contemporary issues involved in the progress of CBS? In a way it is historically backwards to speak first of CBS as a tradition or approach because, as it was lived, the sense that an approach was building came late. The first use of the term "contextual behavioral science" was after the beginning of this millenium – whereas the work and choices that lead to this distinct approach occurred decades earlier.

There are five chapters in this part that cover key features of CBS as a philosophical and strategic system. As a way of setting a context for them, a brief historical introduction seems warranted.

Most of the core elements of CBS were not assembled in an identifiably sequential way, but one aspect was. CBS emerged out of a content-focused issue: How can behavioral psychology address the issue of human language and cognition? In a historical sense that content issue led to a cascade of issues that are now central to the identity of CBS. The cascade was chaotic and included an interrelated set of basic developments, applied developments, and (perhaps most central of all), philosophical and strategic developments. But it had a core: understanding language and cognition from a contextual behavioral point of view.

Some day, that story may be told as it was lived. That day is not today – our purposes here are more summative and intellectual – but perhaps I can be forgiven a brief bit of history that sets the stage for the issues explored in this part (and in this book). Because this is early history, many of the citations are to my own work, which I note and apologize for in advance. It is unavoidable when dealing with these earliest days.

In 1972 or 1973, the late Willard Day, founder and editor of the journal *Behaviorism*, visited the Psychology Department at West Virginia and gave a colloquium on the importance to a behavioral perspective of understanding verbal behavior "as it actually occurs; as it is actually displayed by human beings." A student in the audience, I took him to mean that we needed an analysis that was profoundly useful in predicting and controlling this kind of behavior. He was not arguing that

The Wiley Handbook of Contextual Behavioral Science, First Edition. Edited by Robert D. Zettle, Steven C. Hayes, Dermot Barnes-Holmes, and Anthony Biglan.

such an account existed: Rather his claim was that it was essential to the very survival of behavioral thinking that such an account be brought into existence.

To explain why this thundered down upon me, you need to understand the mood of the times. Behavior analysis seemed to many of those inside of it to be incredibly fresh and exciting. It was subtle and challenging – not at all like the cartoons that nonbehavioral people often made of it. It had nothing to do with eliminating consideration of private experiences – rather it was focused on a functional understanding of these events. Day had written (1969), for example, about how close behaviorism was to phenomenology. Skinner (1948) had written a utopian novel, *Walden Two*, which had led me to become a behaviorist in the first place. He had explicitly overthrown the Watsonian prohibitions against introspection and the study of private events (Skinner, 1945). This was an exciting new form of behaviorism that could begin to speak to the deepest challenges of the human condition.

At the same time, however, behaviorism was under severe attack. Just a year or two earlier the movie *A Clockwork Orange* had conflated behavior modification with involuntary aversive conditioning. Skinner's (1971) *Beyond Freedom and Dignity* had just appeared and was immediately and falsely taken to mean that behavioral science would try to eliminate freedom and dignity in order to create progress. Somehow, the cultural elite declared, behaviorism would create a society of robots.

To behavior analysts, the ones who felt the beating heart of a new way forward that would speak to issues of love, community, compassion, and purpose, it all felt so unfair. People did not understand. Aversive conditioning? Robots?

Willard Day's colloquium thundered down in that context. Behavioral folks needed to explain how to *foster* freedom and dignity. We had to do so in a fashion that avoided the "mental way stations" that sometimes lurk inside such terms and that can block our ability to understand how to live better lives and to support the growth and prosperity of others. Doing great things in understanding human complexity required that we understand language as it actually occurs. The very survival of behavioral thinking was at stake.

Sitting there, before I stood up to leave the room, I made a mental promise. If it could be done, I would find a way.

The search for an adequate behavioral approach to the challenge of human language and cognition occurred within what we now think of as the contextualistic wing of behavior analysis. There was nothing particularly creative or risky about having functional contextual philosophical commitments guide this search – it is just what a functionally and contextually oriented behavior analyst would do.

It dawned on me only slowly that even many behavior analysts were not in agreement about these philosophical commitments, and that, in order to proceed with clarity, the philosophical approach needed to be explicated. That process of refinement had two aspects.

As I began to search for a solution as a young academic, it became obvious that an interest in language and cognition meant that behavior analysts were going to be studying how one kind of action impacted another. Later on, RFT would explain more fully how and why that happened, but from the beginning it was apparent that studying language in a pragmatic way led naturally to a thorny issue of how to think about behavior–behavior relationships. From a contextualistic point of view, that in itself raised profound questions. If language and cognition were important, they were important because of the relations they established with other actions. At the same time, allowing actions to assume the role of independent variables in an experimental analysis would essentially create a form of mentalism that would fundamentally undermine the pragmatic commitments of behavior analysis.

These issues were addressed in detail in the mid-1980s (Hayes & Brownstein, 1986). By explicating the dangers of such mentalism to a behavioral view of the purposes of behavioral science, a kind of bracket was drawn around the pursuit of an adequate account of language and cognition. No, thoughts were not independent variables, but yes, relationships among behaviors need to be understood. The solution was that they needed to be understood *in context*. The pragmatic demands of prediction and influence as goals demanded nothing less, because only context could be changed directly.

The work on contextualism (Hayes, Hayes, & Reese, 1988) and the distinctive nature of functional contextualism (Biglan & Hayes, 1996; Hayes, 1993) embedded this issue of behavioral causes into a larger set of assumptions about the proper unit of analysis in a contextual behavioral account. The purposes of functional contextualism were distinguished from the purposes of other forms of contextualism such as social constructionism. The assumptions of a contextual world view were stated.

Why CBS Gradually Distinguished Itself from Traditional Behavior Analysis

What this philosophical work did was to specify how contextualism linked to radical behaviorism, but it also began to distinguish the two. This process was not merely an act of translation, as if functional contextualism was nothing more than a matter of avoiding the unfortunate terms Skinner sometimes chose that made it almost impossible for him to be heard without distortion. It was an exercise in extension and explication. Prediction and control was replaced by prediction and influence – a small, but needed, step. Precision, scope, and depth were added as key outcome dimensions. The social nature of science was made more foundational. The psychological level of analysis was defined. The truth criterion was carefully specified. The a-ontological nature of evolutionary epistemology was laid out. (These points are not referenced here because there is no need – the story is well told in this part of the book.)

The work on contextualism laid the foundation for CBS is a particular form of behavior analysis, with a particular set of assumptions and purposes. Gradually, this philosophical work allowed intuitive extensions of Skinnerian thinking construed as a form of radical pragmatism to be replaced by deliberate extensions founded on a clear and stated set of assumptions.

One reason this philosophical work was so necessary is that Skinner himself was not clear. Behavior analysis contained (and does to this day) two very different ideas about psychology. Unfortunately, both of those ideas were in Skinner's work, and their contradictions were neither noticed nor resolved.

Consider, for example, the only place Skinner ever clearly defined "behavior." In his treatment of the topic in the *The Behavior of Organisms*, Skinner (1938) defined behavior as "the movement of an organism or of its parts in a frame of reference provided by the organism itself or by various external objects or fields of force" (p. 6). This is an entirely topographical definition. It is deeply mechanistic. It carried no sense of function. Its only link to context was the frame of reference needed to define movement. It is impossible to use such a definition to directly address thoughts, or feelings, or urges. None of these are "movements."

But wait. A few lines later Skinner (1938) defined behavior as "the functioning of an organism which is engaged in acting upon or having commerce with the outside world" (p. 6). This is an entirely different approach. It is functional and explicitly contextual. It treats behavior and the context in which it occurs as an integrated phenomenon. It contains nothing that we cannot apply with equal relevance to thoughts, or feelings, or urges. Two fundamentally different definitions; same paragraph.

Over and over again the same problem occurs in the canonical works of behavior analysis. On the one hand, Skinner (1953) criticized the idea that understanding stimuli required "metaphysical speculations on what is 'really there' in the outside world" (p. 138) and said:

> Responses to some forms of stimulation are more likely to be "right" than responses to others, in the sense that they are more likely to lead to effective behavior … but any suggestion that they bring us closer to the "real'" world is out of place. (p. 139)

On the other hand, Skinner (1953) defined stimuli formally rather than functionally when he spoke of "those energy changes at the periphery which we designate as stimuli" (p. 449). Two fundamentally different views of stimuli; same book.

The end result was predictable. Yes, behavior analysis contained a vigorous community of functional and contextually oriented behavioral scientists and practitioners. But it also contained a large (perhaps even larger) community of reductionistic elemental realists who disliked contextualistic thinking. These inconsistencies (see Hayes et al., 1988 for a more detailed list) initially drove the need for clarity about functional contextualism, but over the long run they were part of what drove CBS into its own association, with its own journal and conference.

Behavior analysis as an organized field ultimately could not adequately house CBS. That is a painful sentence to write after decades of trying to reach another conclusion. Nevertheless, it needs to be said and be explained.

First and foremost it could not do so because behavior analysis as a field is philosophically divided. I have just suggested that this division occurred because its founder was philosophically unclear, but, regardless of why it is the case, it is the case. No objective observer could fail to agree.

Beyond issues of philosophical clarity, CBS eventually needed its own identity because the substantive work that needed to be done and cooperative alliances that needed to be built could not happen without fundamentally altering Skinnerian ideas, approaches, and cultural traditions. That proved to be impossible to do within traditional behavior analysis. Thus, as CBS as a research strategy developed, the need to define CBS as a distinct area grew.

An example is contained in the creation of relational frame theory (RFT) as a behavioral approach to language and cognition and its subsequent empirical progress. About the same time that acceptance and commitment therapy (ACT) was emerging (Hayes, 1984; 1987), and contextualism was being explicated (Hayes & Brownstein, 1986), RFT as a behavioral account of stimulus equivalence and derived relational responding finally took shape (Hayes, 1986, first published as Hayes, 1991).

It was immediately apparent that relational framing led to new forms of behavioral regulation (Hayes, Devany, Kohlenberg, Brownstein, & Shelby, 1987; Wulfert & Hayes, 1988). Relational framing could create reinforcers, augment or diminish their impact, alter classically conditioned stimuli, or establish forms of stimulus control that did not fit any other previously identified forms. This was both exciting and horrible news. It was exciting because a vast set of new research questions opened up, many of which led directly to questions of central importance to mainstream psychology. It was horrible because the hard-won knowledge about direct contingencies that behavioral psychology had spent a good part of a century creating now had to be reworked with verbal humans. Decades of difficult experimental and conceptual work lay ahead. It was not possible to do that work inside the animal learning tradition, insofar as nonhuman animals have not yet been clearly shown to do the core elements of relational framing with sufficient robustness for it to be used as a preparation.

The criticisms of RFT within behavior analysis were immediate and vigorous (e.g., see the criticisms published in the *Analysis of Verbal Behavior*, volume 19, 2003), but they were not intellectually telling (Hayes, Barnes-Holmes, & Roche, 2003). What followed, unfortunately, was a response that avoided conflict at the cost of progress. To explain what I mean, here was the conclusion of our response to several of these early criticisms (Hayes et al., 2003, p. 53):

> If behavior analysis, as a field, is to face the challenge that RFT presents, the following questions will need to be answered: 1. Are we satisfied that an operant is a basic behavioral process? 2. If so, can we define and empirically identify operant behavior? 3. If we can, can we define and empirically identify traditional relational responding (based on formal properties of relata) as operant behavior? 4. If so, can we define and empirically identify arbitrarily applicable relational responding (as defined in our book) as operant behavior? 5. If so, is it the case empirically that this relational operant modifies stimulus functions established by other learning processes?
>
> If the answer is "Yes" to each of these questions, then the field as a whole will have to deal with the wide-ranging and revolutionary implications that arise from this relational operant. Behavior analysis will have unquestionably entered the "post-Skinnerian" era because, in effect, behavioral psychology will have to re-examine the impact of a wide variety of behavioral processes in verbal organisms that have hitherto provided the bedrock upon which our science is built. Stepping up to this challenge is exactly what RFT attempts to do, but stepping up to the challenge of these five questions is something that the entire field of behavior analysis can no longer comfortably avoid.

In the more than 10 years since, not a single article has appeared in a behavior analytic journal providing data that suggest that relational operants do not exist. Well-crafted arguments about the logical impossibility of relational frames are also absent. Instead, the challenge of RFT to the hegemony of Skinnerian thinking about verbal behavior has largely been met in traditional behavior analysis by a refusal to engage with the issues.

ACT further created the need for CBS as a distinct tradition. Clinical domains are excellent areas in which to explore ideas about language and cognition. Part of the need for a contextualistic account of language and cognition came because clinical psychologists needed basic accounts that worked. If they did not exist, they needed to be created.

This very idea changed the research strategy of behavior analysis. Instead of a bottom-up approach, in which basic principles would suggest applications (a word that etymologically means "to bring into contact with" as if the primary issue is bringing foundational principles into contact with complexity), CBS adopted a strategy in which all parties were responsible for progress. So-called "applied" workers might need to bring clinical realities "into contact with" the search for high precision/high scope ways of speaking about phenomena – not just the other way around. In other words, practitioners might have the responsibility to drive basic developments that serve their needs, not merely learn how to make use of whatever basic developments have occurred. The mutual interest of basic and applied professionals in progress in a pragmatic approach to language and cognition fundamentally altered the dynamic inside behavior analysis. Animal laboratories were immediately much less important, for example. That was a bitter pill for basic behavior analysis to swallow.

The centrality of a psychotherapy approach in CBS also challenged behavior analysis in another way. As board-certified behavior analysts were established throughout the United States to do professional work with those struggling with developmental disabilities, there was less room for traditional psychotherapy work within the institutional confines of applied behavior analysis, which became more and more dominated by developmental disabilities and autism.

The radical pragmatism of functional contextualism created another kind of disconnect with traditional behavior analysis in the willingness to use terms that are useful in some areas and not others. This is evident in the embrace of the use of "middle-level" terms: high scope, but lower precision terms that orient the field toward domains. This issue first appeared in an article that attempted a detailed analysis of the term "spirituality" (Hayes, 1984). The core of the argument was that we needed to take seriously terms that carved out domains in which distinctive functional accounts applied, even if the terms literally contradict behavioral assumptions. Said in another way, if "meaning is use," then we cannot look in the dictionary for approved behavioral terms, because such an approach violates a behavioral perspective on language. Yes, taken literally, the term "spirituality" contradicts the monistic assumptions of behavioral psychology, but when it is examined functionally there appear to be good reasons for the term, based on relational learning and sense of self.

That article (Hayes, 1984) proved to be prescient in areas such as perspective-taking and deictic framing, as well as acceptance-based psychotherapy. Much of what later becomes CBS was foreshadowed there, 30 years ago. Ironically, the core step was to take seriously a phenomenon that literally contradicts behavioral assumptions. That is a step that even today most behavior analysts are unwilling to make.

As ideas about functional contextual approaches to language and cognition began to take shape, and functional contextual thinking itself became clearer, a more radically pragmatic perspective on theory and conceptualization emerged. If truth was getting things done, we needed to be more catholic about concepts because sometimes highly technical accounts were needed, and sometimes accounts were needed that merely oriented analysts to a domain.

It was only when all of these elements (and more) came together, that it was possible to stop and look back and notice what was happening. The abandonment of bottom-up behavior analysis and the embrace of a reticulated research program happened because intuitively useful steps were taken. The rationale for these steps came later. Creating a new approach to language and cognition changed how behavioral principles were thought about, researched, and applied. The pragmatic embrace of multiple ways of speaking opened up new ways to think about theories and models.

As CBS has consciously formed as a scientific tradition, that clarity has gradually broadened the vision of the field. CBS is moving into applied forms of RFT, education, attitude change, and other areas. CBS has in the last half dozen years consciously placed itself under the umbrella of multidimensional and multilevel evolution science (Hayes, Barnes-Holmes, & Wilson, 2012; Wilson, Hayes, Biglan, & Embry, 2014a; 2014b), beginning to fulfill a long hoped for vision (Skinner, 1981). This has in turn linked CBS to other evolutionary ideas such as those of Elinor Ostrom (Wilson, 2014). It has begun to build a bridge to cognitive science as well (DeHouwer, 2011).

The Chapters in Part I

The chapters in Part I lay out the nature of CBS and situate it in its larger intellectual context. Chapter 3, by Levin, Twohig, and Smith, provides a point-by-point overview of CBS and its features. Chapter 4, by Biglan and Hayes, does a deep dive into functional contextualism – its nature, linkage to pragmatism, and its scientific implications. Wilson thinks through the implications of middle-level terms in chapter 5. In chapter 6 Long and Sanford explore the strategic impact of applying CBS thinking to the behavior of scientists. Monestès, in chapter 7, shows both that the theoretical and metatheoretical features of CBS fit spectacularly well with evolution science and that CBS's historical and contextual approach to language and cognition alters how we think about human evolution itself.

These chapters are dominantly strategic and philosophical. They are meant to ground the more substantive chapters in the parts that follow into a set of philosophical assumptions and strategic choices that are named and clarified. Metaphorically, this part allows the reader's feet to be firmly placed in core analytic choices, so that, as the book explores how CBS researchers and practitioners deal with human language and cognition, or how CBS approaches issues of human suffering and human prosperity, there can be a greater appreciation of the overall attempt.

The purpose of CBS is to make progress toward a psychology more worthy of the challenge of the human condition. This book will allow the reader to assess whether any progress is being produced within the tradition defined by this first part of the book.

References

Biglan, A., & Hayes, S. C. (1996). Should the behavioral sciences become more pragmatic? The case for functional contextualism in research on human behavior. *Applied and Preventive Psychology: Current Scientific Perspectives, 5*, 47–57.

Day, W. F. (1969). Radical behaviorism in reconciliation with phenomenology. *Journal of the Experimental Analysis of Behavior, 12*, 315–328.

DeHouwer, J. (2011). Why the cognitive approach in psychology would benefit from a functional approach and vice versa. *Perspectives on Psychological Science, 6*, 202–209.

Hayes, S. C. (1984). Making sense of spirituality. *Behaviorism, 12*, 99–110.

Hayes, S. C. (1986, June). *What is a verbal stimulus?* Invited address presented to the Summer Institute on Verbal Relations, Behaviorists European Summer Academy, Bad Kreuznach, West Germany.

Hayes, S. C. (1987). A contextual approach to therapeutic change. In N. Jacobson (Ed.), *Psychotherapists in clinical practice: Cognitive and behavioral perspectives* (pp. 327–387). New York, NY: Guilford.

Hayes, S. C. (1991). A relational control theory of stimulus equivalence. In L. J. Hayes & P. N. Chase (Eds.), *Dialogues on verbal behavior* (pp. 19–40). Reno, NV: Context Press.

Hayes, S. C. (1993). Analytic goals and the varieties of scientific contextualism. In S. C. Hayes, L. J. Hayes, H. W. Reese, & T. R. Sarbin (Eds.), *Varieties of scientific contextualism* (pp. 11–27). Reno, NV: Context Press.

Hayes, S. C., Barnes-Holmes, D., & Roche, B. (2003). Behavior analysis, relational frame theory, and the challenge of human language and cognition: A reply to the commentaries on *Relational Frame Theory: A Post-Skinnerian Account of Human Language and Cognition*. *Analysis of Verbal Behavior, 19,* 39–54.

Hayes, S. C., Barnes-Holmes, D., & Wilson, K. G. (2012). Contextual behavioral science: Creating a science more adequate to the challenge of the human condition. *Journal of Contextual Behavioral Science, 1,* 1–16.

Hayes, S. C., & Brownstein, A. J. (1986). Mentalism, behavior–behavior relations and a behavior analytic view of the purposes of science. *The Behavior Analyst, 9,* 175–190.

Hayes, S. C., Devany, J. M., Kohlenberg, B. S., Brownstein, A. J., & Shelby, J. (1987). Stimulus equivalence and the symbolic control of behavior. *Mexican Journal of Behavior Analysis, 13,* 361–374.

Hayes, S. C., Hayes, L. J., & Reese, H. W. (1988). Finding the philosophical core: A review of Stephen C. Pepper's *World Hypotheses. Journal of the Experimental Analysis of Behavior, 50,* 97–111.

Skinner, B. F. (1938). *The behavior of organisms,* New York, NY: Appleton-Century-Crofts.

Skinner, B. F. (1945). The operational analysis of psychological terms. *Psychological Review, 52,* 270–276.

Skinner, B. F. (1948). *Walden two.* Oxford, England: Macmillan.

Skinner, B. F. (1953). *Science and human behavior.* New York, NY: The Free Press.

Skinner, B. F. (1971). *Beyond freedom and dignity.* New York, NY: Bantam Books.

Skinner, B. F. (1981). Selection by consequences. *Science, 213,* 501–504.

Wilson, D. S. (2014). Introducing PROSOCIAL: Using the science of cooperation to improve the efficacy of your group. *Evolution: This View of Life.* Retrieved from http://www.this viewoflife.com/index.php/magazine/articles/introducing-prosocial-using-the-science-of-cooperation-to-improve-the-effic

Wilson, D. S., Hayes, S. C., Biglan, T., & Embry, D. (2014a). Collaborating on evolving the future. *Behavioral and Brain Sciences, 34,* 44–61.

Wilson, D. S., Hayes, S. C., Biglan, T., & Embry, D. (2014b). Evolving the future: Toward a science of intentional change. *Behavioral and Brain Sciences, 34,* 1–22.

Wulfert, E., & Hayes, S. C. (1988). Transfer of a conditional ordering response through conditional equivalence classes. *Journal of the Experimental Analysis of Behavior, 50,* 125–144.

3

Contextual Behavioral Science
An Overview
Michael E. Levin, Michael P. Twohig, and Brooke M. Smith

To begin a discussion of scientific strategy inside a pragmatic approach to the behavioral sciences, it is worth stepping back and appreciating the scope of challenges faced as a society. The prevalence of human suffering is staggering, with almost half of the population meeting criteria for a psychological disorder in their lifetimes (Kessler et al., 2005) and many more struggling with difficulties in functioning and major life stressors (e.g., divorce, bereavement, trauma, unemployment). Prejudice and discrimination continue to occur toward a broad range of marginalized groups (Pager & Shepherd, 2008). Armed conflicts and other large-scale forms of violence continue (Themnér & Wallensteen, 2013), rates of obesity are growing (Ogden et al., 2006), and challenges related to pollution and depletion of environmental resources exist, such as diseases due to climate change (Friel et al., 2011). Although these issues are multifaceted, for each human behavior is both a core contributor and an agent for change.

The scope, significance, and difficulty of addressing these challenges highlight how crucial it is to be strategic about behavioral science and its applications. Creating a progressive and pragmatic science requires careful consideration of each of the key facets adopted in a scientific approach (i.e., philosophical assumptions, theory, and methods), and equally, if not more importantly, *how all of these facets can be integrated to best meet one's scientific and applied goals*. This chapter provides an overview of the approach to behavior science described in this volume: contextual behavioral science (CBS). In the sections to follow, each of the core facets of CBS will be presented as well as considering how they interact in the service of building a progressive approach to science that helps address the breadth and depth of human struggles and potential.

Contextual Behavioral Science in Context: A Brief History

CBS initially developed out of the effort to apply behavior analysis to the types of complex human behavior and contexts addressed in clinical psychology (i.e., clinical behavior analysis; Dougher & Hayes, 2000) while simultaneously developing the

The Wiley Handbook of Contextual Behavioral Science, First Edition. Edited by Robert D. Zettle, Steven C. Hayes, Dermot Barnes-Holmes, and Anthony Biglan.
© 2016 John Wiley & Sons, Ltd. Published 2016 by John Wiley & Sons, Ltd.

needed basic knowledge to do so in a coherent fashion. Although CBS shares many similarities with and is historically rooted in the contextual wing of behavior analysis, it has also diverged from traditional behavior analysis over the years. This divergence includes a greater emphasis on modern behavioral accounts of language and cognition (Dougher, Twohig, & Madden, 2014), a willingness to use less technical "middle-level" terms when useful (e.g., referring to "values" in therapist protocols instead of "motivative augmentals"), a reticulated versus purely bottom-up program of knowledge development, and an expanded set of research methods, particularly in the area of group level statistics (Vilardaga, Hayes, Levin, & Muto, 2009).

As is evident throughout this book, CBS is historically very closely connected to both acceptance and commitment therapy (ACT; Hayes, Strosahl, & Wilson, 2011) and relational frame theory (RFT; Hayes, Barnes-Holmes, & Roche, 2001), having been the scientific foundation for these programs of research (Hayes, Levin, Plumb, Boulanger, & Pistorello, 2013). However, as this book also illustrates, CBS represents a larger movement seeking to help improve scientific strategy within the behavioral sciences writ large; supporting an open, collaborative, diverse and nonhierarchical scientific/professional culture; and building bridges to some forms of evolutionary science (Wilson, Hayes, Biglan, & Embry, 2014a; 2014b) and cognitive science (DeHouwer, 2011), as well other areas. CBS is defined by its unique integration of a specific philosophy of science, an approach to theory building, and a set of research methods.

In the inaugural issue of the Journal of Contextual Behavioral Science, Hayes, Barnes-Holmes, and Wilson (2012) define CBS this way:

> Contextual Behavioral Science (CBS) is a principle-focused, communitarian strategy of reticulated scientific and practical development. Grounded in contextualistic philosophical assumptions, and nested within multi-dimensional, multi-level evolution science as a contextual view of life, it seeks the development of basic and applied scientific concepts and methods that are useful in predicting-and-influencing the contextually embedded actions of whole organisms, individually and in groups, with precision, scope, and depth; and extends that approach into knowledge development itself so as to create a behavioral science more adequate to the challenges of the human condition. (p. 2)

This definition encompasses issues with many subtopics, several of which need to be discussed in order to understand this broad definition. It is to these issues and subtopics that we now turn.

Philosophy of Science

Every theoretical approach to psychology, and behavioral science more broadly, contains within it certain philosophical assumptions about the nature of reality, what the proper units of analysis are, what it means to know something, and how science ought to be conducted. Assumptions are pre-analytic, meaning they create a foundation on which analysis can be built, but they cannot be proven or disproven using that same analysis (Hayes, 1998). Oftentimes, assumptions go unstated and unrecognized; yet, they are the lens through which the world, and the role of science within it, is viewed. They form the basis of our theories, inform the methods we use, determine how we interpret our results, and dictate the very questions we ask. In order for these various components of scientific endeavor to form a coherent framework that can be maintained over time, it is critical for scientists to be clear about and accountable to the assumptions they bring to bear on matters of ontology, epistemology, and the goals of science (Hayes et al., 2012).

CBS is grounded in a specific philosophy of science known as functional contextualism (Hayes, Hayes, & Reese, 1988; see chapter 4 in this volume; Biglan, 2015). "Contextualism" is a term originating with Pepper (1942) who meant it to apply to forms of pragmatism. Pepper delineated four basic worldviews, or ways in which people tend to organize their understanding of the world through simple commonsense root metaphors. These views provide a convenient way in which to understand the nature of the world (i.e., its ontological assumptions) and the criteria by which "truth" is determined (i.e., its epistemological assumptions). Of these, two are most relevant to behavioral sciences: mechanism (also termed "elemental realism"), which is characteristic of many approaches, and contextualism, variants of which are inherent in radical behaviorism, CBS, and behavior analysis (Hayes et al., 1988), and other forms in social constructionism, postmodernism, and hermeneutics, among other areas (Hayes, Hayes, Reese, & Sarbin, 1993).

The root metaphor of mechanism is the commonsense machine. As with all machines, the world is understood to be composed of fundamental parts, with certain relations between them, propelled by a force, all of which fit together as an assemblage to make up a whole. The parts, relations, and forces are assumed to have an ontological reality; in other words, they are real things that exist in the universe. With an actual machine, these parts may be levers, pistons, and bolts, and the force may be electricity or steam-power. Within psychology, theories identify parts, such as "self-efficacy," cognitions, or the hippocampus, while the forces driving these parts may be "motivation," "drive," "information," or the electricity behind action potentials. These parts and forces form the basic units of analysis, and each can be analyzed independent of the others and their context. The truth criterion of mechanism is correspondence between the model of the world and the world as it *actually* is (Pepper, 1942). Thus, a theory is considered true to the degree its predictions match the data (Hayes et al., 1988).

Contextualism takes as its root metaphor the ongoing act-in-context, or the behavior of a whole organism, considered within, and inseparable from, its historical and situational context (Hayes et al., 1988; 2012). The parts are understood only in relation to one another and to the whole; none of the parts have meaning by themselves. Instead, meaning emerges through the relationship of the various parts. An example of such a contextualistic approach within psychology is Skinner's three-term contingency. The contingency itself is the basic unit of analysis, and each of its parts, antecedent, behavior, and consequence, have meaning only in their interrelationship. A consequence is defined by its effect on behavior, behavior by the consequences it produces, and antecedents by the behaviors that occur in their presence and the consequences those behaviors produce.

Contextualism is monistic; all legitimate elements of scientific analysis are physical in that they are in some way observable (note this still includes internal events like cognition). From a contextual perspective, internal events such as cognitions and emotions are no different than external events merely because they are private:

behavior is "any and all actions of the whole organism" (Hayes et al., 2012). The ongoing act-in-context is the fundamental unit of analysis, and the parts derived from this whole can be derived in any number of ways. The way in which the parts are derived is based *not* on the purported ontological reality of those parts, as in mechanism, but instead depends upon the utility of analysis relevant to the goal of analysis. Truth is pragmatically determined by "successful working": an analysis is true to the degree that it meets its analytic goal or set of goals. What distinguishes functional contextualism from other forms (such as the descriptive contextualism of the social constructionists) is its goal of *prediction and influence of behavior with precision, scope, and depth.*

Prediction is a goal shared by both functional contextualism and mechanism. However, while mechanists seek to construct an accurate model of part of the world, nothing guarantees that these models will lead to an ability to influence behavior. A disconnection between prediction and influence occurs frequently when mechanistic models are entirely composed of dependent variables – a model might specify, for example, how thought relates to emotion without including any independent variables. In the absence of independent variables that might be directly changed and tested, influence cannot be assessed. In contrast, functional contextualism considers prediction-and-influence of behavior to be a single unitary goal and thus any model or theory without directly manipulable variables is considered to be flawed, even before empirical tests are made. The emphasis on precision (limited number of terms to account for a given event), scope (breadth of application of technical terms), and depth (coherence across levels of analysis), ensures an application of prediction-and-influence that is both broad and deep. The divergences of functional contextualism from more commonly held mechanistic assumptions and adoption of a functional contextual philosophy of science has a number of implications for the CBS approach to theory and research methods.

Implications of CBS for Theory

Focus on Environmental Causes

Consistent with a functional contextual approach to science, environmental variables (i.e., historical and current contextual variables that are external to and control the occurrence/function of behavior) are considered central to any analysis of behavior. This is for pragmatic, and not ontological, reasons. If the goal of CBS is prediction *and* influence, then the science needs to focus on elements of the world that can be directly manipulated to influence behavior (Hayes & Brownstein, 1986). This makes nonenvironmental variables poor choices for CBS scientists as analytic end points because they are difficult or impossible to change directly. Examples include cognition, emotion, behavior, and, in practical terms, many of the details of underlying biology. Because environmental variables encompass most of those that can be directly manipulated, this approach will emphasize such variables as "causes." It is not that these other types of variables are unimportant in behavioral sciences, they are just not pragmatically useful to refer to as causes for those interested in the prediction and influence of behavior.

It is important that the events selected as independent variables are separate (i.e., external) to the behaviors to be influenced, because influence must emanate from outside the behavioral system of an individual. The scientist exists outside this behavioral system and, thus, can only directly control events in that domain (Hayes & Brownstein, 1986). Once an environmental event has affected a given behavior, this behavior may affect many others – actions do influence actions – but for pragmatic reasons the particular causal chain under analysis must always begin with historical and situational events, and the source of whatever behavior–behavior relations are found is also assumed to be environmental. To leave out environmental context is to leave the analysis incomplete and without variables that can be manipulated to make prediction and influence possible. This is why CBS is careful about behavior–behavior relations. For example, suppose it is found that thinking "nobody likes me" is related to isolating from others. Rather than explain the isolation on the basis of the thought, a contextual behavioral scientist will examine the social and linguistic contingencies that lead both to the thought and to the ability of such thoughts to acquire behavior regulatory functions. It is easy to lose sight of the environmental beginnings of a causal chain and the contexts that govern behavior–behavior relations, and instead to see internal or other behavioral events as themselves being causal.

Functional Contextual View of Private Events

From a CBS perspective, internal events are viewed as actions of the individual to predict and influence, even though they may be observable only by an audience of one. Thus, CBS looks at the contexts that evoke private experiences and how context affects relations between internal events and other behaviors. Some of the conceptual work within CBS has offered ways to address aspects of private experience scientifically within a consistent philosophical approach (e.g., Hayes, 1984) – avenues that have since been successfully explored experimentally (e.g., McHugh & Stewart, 2012).

Whether and how to address internal events within behavioral psychology has been a topic of much debate. Historically, this dates back to the debates between methodological and radical behaviorism (Moore, 2013). Methodological behaviorists argued that science should be objective to the extent that only overtly and publicly observable actions should be legitimate elements of study; thus their unwillingness to include an analysis of private behaviors (especially those not publicly observable under any conditions, such as thinking). These distinctions worked for some aspects of basic behavioral science, but quickly showed limitations once complex human behavior was considered, as some events were difficult to interpret without including private events within the analysis (Dougher, 2013).

Radical behaviorists welcomed the incorporation of private events into their analyses in principle, provided the contingencies for self-observation were sufficiently tight (Moore, 2013; Skinner, 1974); that is part of what made radical behaviorism "radical." This opening was seldom taken advantage of experimentally, however, because both public and private actions were argued to emerge from the same set of contingencies. For example, fear and overt avoidance would both emerge from aversive conditioning – but nothing central and additional would likely be added by studying fear.

CBS adopts the monistic perspective of a radical behavioral approach. From a functional contextual viewpoint, instead of defining behavior as a publicly observable event, behavior is anything the organism does, whether public or private. What makes a CBS approach different is that the analysis of verbal behavior suggests that, with human beings, overt behavior and private events may be influenced by different sets of contingencies maintained by the social/verbal community. Thus, for example, how the individual relates to fear can influence overt avoidance behavior. This makes the analysis of private experience not just possible but necessary to the analysis of complex human behavior. We will return to this topic after examining a CBS approach to verbal events.

Role of Behavioral Principles in Theory

Behavioral principles are descriptions of reliable relationships between action and its context that are designed to have both high precision and high scope in supporting the prediction and influence of behavior. For example, reinforcement specifies how a history of consequences that occur in the context of an action can increase the probability of it occurring again in the future. Using high precision and high scope principles as the building blocks of theory helps ensure the development of models that are parsimonious, broadly applicable, supported at a more basic level of analysis, and oriented toward manipulable variables that predict and influence behavior. For those reasons, functional contextualists seek theories that are grounded in basic behavioral principles. In a CBS approach, theories are "analytic, abstractive" meaning that they are taken to be supersets of functional analyses, rather than hypothetico-deductive exercises in model building.

As more basic research is conducted, our understanding of behavioral principles is elaborated and theoretical models can be refined and improved to better predict and influence behavior. Some very basic parameters about the principle of reinforcement that were discovered in the laboratory now guide applied work. For example, research shows that maintenance and relapse once reinforcement has been removed is impacted significantly by the temporal timing, magnitude, and frequency of reinforcers (Madden, 2013), and so on. This basic information has led to some very useful and relatively easy to use technologies such as *time in/time out* (Friman, 2009). Similar attempts have been made within CBS, particularly in addressing private events, but they are based in particular on the extension of behavioral principles to language and cognition.

Role of a Basic Account of Verbal Processes in Theory

CBS is distinct from other wings of behavioral psychology in its emphasis on verbal/symbolic processes as an additional important stream of behavioral influence, and its particular focus on an empirical, behavioral account of language and cognition, RFT. In general, RFT and research into related areas such as stimulus equivalence and rule-governed behavior, show that while verbally capable humans are sensitive to environmental contingencies, they can also be heavily influenced by verbal processes in orderly ways (Hayes et al., 2001). Unlike various mainstream cognitive and cognitive-behavioral perspectives, however, CBS maintains a contextual approach to language and cognition, in which thoughts and feelings are not causal.

RFT research shows that there are multiple sets of contextual events that influence the way verbally capable humans respond to stimulus events. One set is shared with nonhuman animals: the contingencies that influence operant conditioning, classical conditioning, and social learning processes. Within the domain of language and cognition, two additional sets apply. Because RFT will be described in some detail elsewhere in the volume, only an overview of the differences that impact CBS research strategy will be provided here.

The core of language and cognition, according to RFT, is the learned ability to form mutual relationships among events, to combine these into networks, and to change the functions of related events as a result. One context, the relational context, regulates the first two defining features that make up the arbitrary relationships that exist in human language. This context helps define the meaning of verbal events based on the relational frames (same, different, opposite, and so on) that apply between events.

For example, suppose someone yells "Look! A bat!" The context under which the sound "bat" is heard would affect whether a stick of wood or a flying animal is brought to mind. The relational context selects the relations of similarity, difference, and so on, that apply. A second context, the functional context, helps define the psychological functions that are transformed by the resulting relational network. The word "Look!" is such a functional context – it could evoke looking and approach if said near a cave on a bat-observing expedition; it could evoke fear and ducking if said in the first row of seats near home plate after a batter swings.

Research on RFT has helped define some of the parameters of these verbal and nonverbal influences. It is these details of analysis that make CBS accounts differ both from traditional behavioral accounts or mainstream cognitive accounts.

Verbal relations are sensitive to many of the same learning parameters as overt actions, but the details of this analysis alter the details of applied methods rationalized by it. For example, viewing verbal events as learned helps explain why trying to get rid of cognitive relations is often unwise – there is no process called "unlearning." The memory of a trauma, say, is quite likely to reoccur when back in the context where the trauma occurred, or situations that are similar to it, or stimuli occur that are related to it only verbally. Deliberately trying to get that memory not to occur (e.g., by thinking of something else) only elaborates the relational network relevant to it.

Similarly, relations that are trained, and then are extinguished, will resurge when verbal relations learned later are also extinguished (e.g., Wilson & Hayes, 1996; cf. Epstein, 1996). Thus, even verbal reactions that are at very low strength can reoccur – it is important not to expect verbally accessed parts of one's history to "disappear."

Regardless of the relational response that occurs, however, the functional context can often be altered such that different responses occur despite the derived relational context (e.g., Valdivia, Luciano, & Molina, 2006). For example, in some contexts thinking "I can't do it" might contribute to quitting a difficult task (such as a context of literal meaning, in which the individual relates to his thought as true or false based purely on the socially supported coherence of a verbal network), while in other contexts it might not (for example, a context in which an individual relates to his thought as just another thought evoked by history). To return to our trauma example, even though the memory of a traumatic event occurs, it may or may not evoke escape or avoidance depending on the functional context that is present. If the memory and the emotion it elicits occurs in the context of self-judgment it may have a very different impact than if it occurs in the context of self-compassion or curiosity. Distinguishing direct contingency, relational, and functional contexts are thus important because they offer varying avenues to follow clinically.

An example exists in the area of motivation. The traditional behavioral account of motivation is to consider these events to be "establishing operations" – events that make certain consequences more or less reinforcing (Michael, 1993). The conditions under which events were argued to function as establishing stimuli were quite limited, however, and were largely linked to classical conditioning analyses. It is now known that many events acquire their motivational properties verbally by being in relational networks with consequences and bringing some of their perceptual functions into the present (Ju & Hayes, 2008). This helps explain the impact of CBS interventions in areas such as values clarification.

Use of Middle-Level Terms

One of the defining feature of CBS is the pragmatic use language. Although CBS strongly emphasizes basic behavioral principles including RFT in theory building, it also recognizes the potential limitations in using a strictly technical, basic language as the theoretical analysis is scaled up to more applied levels and specific domains of complex human behavior. Part of this is practical, given the additional barriers a highly technical account presents for dissemination to applied interventionists. Another reason is that basic principles are by their nature very precise abstractions designed to have high scope. Although this gives a starting point and foundation in moving to more applied and domain specific theories, these principles alone are likely to be too broad in many instances to be a complete, stand-alone theory without additional conceptual elaboration.

Middle-level terms are explicitly not technical terms. Middle-level terms serve to orient individuals toward domains in which sets of functional analyses provide guidance in how to apply technical concepts. For example, the relevance of knowledge of how verbal processes can increase the positive reinforcing functions of particular behavior through motivative and formative augmentals might be referenced using the middle-level term "values." Middle-level terms need to be well defined and increasingly linked to basic principles but it is not necessary that they currently be fully understood technically. Their function is not merely shorthand or user friendliness – it is to orient the listener to a domain.

This has always been part of behavior analysis – CBS merely underlines their importance and utility. For example, calling an action "aggressive" does not mean that aggression is a technical term, nor that aggression is fully understood via basic behavioral principles. Aggression is a middle-level term that specifies a domain that can then begin to be addressed through existing accounts (e.g., through changes in reinforcability produced by aversive stimulation).

Analytic Abstractive Theory Versus Hypothetico-Deductive Theory

CBS has developed high precision/high scope technical concepts, such as relational frames and their defining features, which can be used in traditional functional analysis, but has also emphasized the development of theories that are simply supersets of functional analyses. Relational frame theory is a theory of that kind. This contrasts with the hypothetico-deductive models often used in mechanistic approaches, which typically postulate hypothetical causal constructs that are inferred and not directly observable or manipulable (e.g., cognitive schema), and that are verified by their correspondence to descriptions.

Practical Clinical Models

In much the same way, middle-level terms can be drawn together into practical clinical models. They do not have the same degree of precision as formal theories, but, in a CBS approach, ways of speaking can emerge that are considered in reference to their own purpose and context. Examples include the psychological flexibility model of psychopathology (Hayes et al., 2012), the flexible connectedness model of human relationships (Vilardaga, Estévez, Levin, & Hayes, 2012), or the concept of experiential avoidance as a psychological pathogen (Hayes, Wilson, Gifford, Follette, & Strosahl, 1996). For example, the concept of experiential avoidance is an abstracted theoretical concept developed through a more general observation of the tendency of a variety of problem behaviors to serve a verbally established escape/avoidance function related to internal experiences.

A metaphor often used in describing the utility of such models is that they are similar to a computer operating system, while the basic principles upon which they are ultimately based is like the source code (Vilardaga et al., 2009). To use the system, practitioners may only need to use the "operating system" without having to fully understand all of the basic programming upon which it is based. Middle-level terms and practical clinical models both exemplify the functional contextual emphasis on using different ways of speaking to meet practical goals; when conducting applied work it may sometimes be more effective to use a middle-level term but, when refining the precision, coherence, and depth of the theoretical model, a focus on more basic and technical terms may be more effective.

The ultimate goal is not necessarily to have a basic account of complex human behavior, but to have an account that better serves prediction and influence of behavior. Anything that improves the prediction and influence of behavior is on the right track. When terms are used that have high scope but lower levels of precision (e.g., middle-level terms; descriptions of applied techniques) in a reticulated model the challenge is to increase their precision by the use of technical analysis. That is a challenge to middle-level terms and other concepts, but it is also a challenge to basic terms. For example, if cognitive defusion methods are effective, it is the job of behavioral principles, RFT, or other basic accounts to help explain why. Suggesting that a middle-level term, or an applied technique for that matter, that has known benefits in prediction and influence is unscientific because the basic account has not yet been fully developed, turns that task on its head in a way that could easily hamper progress inside a reticulated development strategy. Such a rigidly bottom-up approach is not consistent with the functional contextual approach to scientific analysis which suggests that all parties are ultimately responsible for progress across all domains and levels. Important innovations at an applied level are opportunities to further grow the basic research to explore these new phenomena. When that occurs, the basic developments need to be allowed to challenge middle-level terms as well. For example, when detailed knowledge exists of the conditions under which transformations of stimulus functions occurs through relational framing, the less precise orienting terms of "defusion" may need to be revised or even abandoned in favor of other terms that orient listeners to the implications and applications of this knowledge. This balance of basic and applied research within an overall process of theory building, united by a common pragmatic goal, is a core part of CBS and leads directly to its integrated approach to methods that is described in the next section.

While there are many middle-level terms in behavioral science, six interrelated processes of change are particularly pertinent to CBS: acceptance, defusion, being present, self as context, values, and committed action (Hayes et al., 2011). These six processes were developed both out of applied advances and out of general functional contextual thinking about how language and cognition affect human behavior (both in terms of psychopathology and psychological health/change). Some of these processes focus more on reducing excessive/maladaptive contextual control related to thoughts and feelings (acceptance, defusion, self as context), while others focus more on increasing contact with other sources of behavioral control (being present), or using cognitive processes, in interaction with other behavioral principles and techniques, to increase effective behavior change (values, committed action). Each one of these terms has a specific definition, which is easily understandable and disseminable, that can guide applied work.

Implications of CBS for Research Methods

One of the defining features of CBS is its reticulated strategy in which research on basic principles, theory building/testing, and applied interventions are simultaneously conducted in an organized, integrated, web-like fashion such that findings in each area build off and inform the others. This approach to scaling knowledge across levels of analysis is a natural result of the analytic abstractive approach to theory building and focus on developing models with high scope and precision that guide prediction and influence. For the reticulated strategy to work, applied workers need to care about basic issues and basic workers need to care about applied issues. In practice this has happened in CBS because of an application of a mutual interest model of basic and applied relations, in which both parties are focused on the same general topical area (e.g., the impact of language on behavior). Reticulated development allows the field to focus on both theory testing and pragmatic issues in applied methods, examining a range of behaviors and levels of analysis, and maintaining an open, supportive professional community. To provide further context in describing these methodological features, examples will be provided from the ACT and RFT literature as relevant.

Mutual Interest Model of Basic and Applied Research

As previously illustrated, prediction and influence of behavior with precision, scope, and depth requires an emphasis on basic principles and a scaling of these principles into analytic abstractive theories. This requires close collaboration between basic and applied researchers such that basic principles are available and updated as needed to address applied concerns, while work in applied domains highlights areas for continued basic research. Fitting with the communitarian approach in CBS, this is best achieved by basic and applied researchers sharing a particular domain of interest with common goals, though not necessarily fully overlapping.

The connection between ACT and RFT illustrates this mutual interest model in which a shared interest in developing a new behavioral account of language and cognition led to growth in both basic and applied areas simultaneously, each influencing the other. For example, we described earlier how seeing cognition as learned led early in the days of ACT and RFT to concern over applied methods that seemed to be calling for "unlearning." Similarly, early clinical work on sense of self led to predictions about possible cognitive relations underlying this sense (Hayes, 1984) which later in turn lead to developments in RFT (e.g., McHugh, Barnes-Holmes & Barnes-Holmes, 2004; McHugh & Stewart, 2012). Such developments in RFT informed new therapeutic techniques and potential theoretical refinements (Dymond & Roche, 2013), for example, research on the relational frames involved in perspective-taking altered ACT "self-as-context" interventions (Foody, Barnes-Holmes, Barnes-Holmes, & Luciano, 2013). Similarly, developments in ACT values interventions highlighted areas for further RFT research such as work on motivative augmentals (Ju & Hayes, 2008). As RFT continues to develop, additional opportunities for mutual interest collaborations are presented, such as in the areas of implicit cognition, developmental disabilities, organizational behavior management, and education (Dymond & Roche, 2013).

Focus on Theory Testing in Applied Methods

Another illustration of the CBS reticulated approach is its emphasis on theory testing in applied research. When interventions are based on analytic abstractive theoretical models and basic principles, any test of the intervention implicitly also tests the theory and basic research. This is taken further in CBS research through an emphasis on process of change analyses, laboratory-based methods, and moderator and contextual analyses.

Examining theoretical processes of change is strongly emphasized in CBS. This provides a means to examine whether (a) the intervention targeted the process it was designed/theorized to, (b) whether changes in the process predicted behavior change, and (c) whether changes in the process accounted for (i.e., mediated) intervention effects on behavior change. Each of these features provides critical information for theory development and basic research. Assuming there is not a method issue, if an intervention impacts a putative process of change, but changes in the process are not predictive of changes in outcome, it suggests the theory needs to be revised (i.e., changing the process does not change the outcome). Similarly, if changes in the process do not account for the impact of the intervention, it suggests that there may be other processes of change playing a role in intervention effects. Alternatively, if an intervention does not impact the process of change, it suggests that the intervention needs refinement. Finally, if an intervention impacts the outcome, but not the process of change, it suggests an issue with this process of change (both that the intervention does not successfully target it and that targeting it is not necessary for producing behavior change). Because these processes of change are tightly linked to basic principles, their success or failure based on observed patterns of outcome can provide useful directions for additional basic research.

As an example, mediational and process of change analyses have consistently been emphasized within the ACT outcome literature. Consistent with the theoretical model and treatment approach, outcome studies have demonstrated ACT has a greater impact on psychological flexibility processes relative to most comparison conditions, changes in psychological flexibility relate to improvements in outcomes, and, most importantly, changes in psychological flexibility mediate (i.e., statistically account for) treatment effects (Ruiz, 2010).

Another illustrative example is in the use of laboratory-based methods in CBS, which, due to their high level of experimental control, provide a number of opportunities to bridge basic research, theoretical models, and applied research and interventions (see chapter 17 in this volume). Researchers can develop analogues to clinical interventions to further explore their connection to basic principles. For example, a study compared repeated exposure to a directly conditioned aversive stimulus relative to exposure to a stimulus with only derived aversive functions, which could serve to further clarify how cognitive processes outlined in RFT might interact with exposure-based methods (Roche, Kanter, Brown, Dymond, & Fogarty, 2008). Laboratory-based methods can also be used to test theoretical predictions related to how independent and combined intervention components function or how they impact processes of change. For example, comparing an acceptance-based intervention versus acceptance and values on persistence in a painful task (Branstetter, Cushing, & Douleh, 2009) may provide insight into how these two therapeutic processes/components interact to affect behavior. Similarly, a number of laboratory-based studies have been conducted on specific ACT technologies and components, which not only tested the potential impact on behavioral outcomes, but also more specific theoretical questions such as how do these components differ from other therapeutic processes, do components have a greater impact on overt behavior or internal distress, and are metaphors and experiential exercises more effective than simple instruction (Levin, Hildebrandt, Lillis, & Hayes, 2012).

Another set of CBS research methods focuses on moderators and contextual factors. For example, as the technology has developed, CBS researchers have increasingly begun using ecological momentary assessment (EMA) techniques (e.g., Kashdan et al., 2014; Vilardaga, Hayes, Atkins, Bresee, & Kambiz, 2013). EMA involves completing repeated assessments throughout the day, providing valuable information regarding the context in which behavior occurs and how variables interact over time. This research seeks to identify functional relationships regarding when and how context predicts, and can influence, behavior.

In a related line of research, moderation analyses are also emphasized to study how contextual variables affect the impact of interventions. Although this is an area on which ACT has focused less research efforts, a growing number of studies have begun to identify moderators including degree of experiential avoidance (e.g., Masuda et al., 2007) and level of distress (e.g., Fledderus, Bolmeijer, Pieterse, & Schreurs, 2012). Further examination of moderators, particularly those that orient to contextual factors which inform intervention adaptations, is important for future development.

The breadth of research methods commonly used to test the theoretical model within applied research is another key feature of CBS. Although CBS is historically rooted in behavior analysis, one of its distinctions is in an expanded use of group level methods, in addition to single subject approaches (Vilardaga et al., 2009). The use of a variety of group level methodologies, such as mediational analyses, component research, and EMA, serves to more fully test the precision, scope, and depth of the theoretical model.

Focus on Pragmatic Goals in Applied Methods

The implications of functional contextualism echo all the way down to the notably pragmatic focus of research within CBS intervention development. Traditionally, behavioral sciences have prioritized internal validity as a first step in intervention testing, conducting well-controlled randomized trials to determine efficacy, essentially, prioritizing whether the analysis was "true," in that threats to internal validity were minimized while sensitivity to detecting treatment effects was maximized (e.g., reduced heterogeneity, increased experimental control). This naturally led to delaying research on effectiveness (whether it works in less controlled and more naturalistic settings/populations) and implementation issues (how to train and maintain fidelity and competence with intervention providers), often until after several years and a significant investment of time and money in efficacy testing.

From a CBS perspective, although internal validity is important, an analysis is ultimately "correct" in that it can successfully be applied to predict and influence behavior. Thus, there is a much greater emphasis in CBS on conducting research on effectiveness, training, and dissemination early and throughout intervention development/testing. For example, one of the very first clinical trials of ACT was an effectiveness study testing the impact of an ACT training on clinical outcomes among providers with a heterogeneous caseload (Strosahl, Hayes, Bergan, & Romano, 1998). Said in another way, external validity in CBS can be and often is placed early in the research agenda.

In addition to testing effectiveness, CBS emphasizes addressing pragmatic implementation and dissemination issues in intervention design. The use of middle-level theoretical terms is one reflection of this, as training in and adoption of CBS interventions was recognized to be more likely and effective if the burden of learning technical terms was minimized. As another example, there has been growing interest in CBS in developing a diverse array of innovative implementation methods including self-help and Web-based interventions (e.g., Fledderus et al., 2011; Levin, Pistorello, Hayes, & Seeley, 2014), phone-based counseling (e.g., Bricker, Mann, Marek, Liu, & Peterson, 2010), worksite wellness programs (see chapter 22 in this volume) and public health approaches (see Biglan, 2015; chapter 23 in this volume), among others.

Studying Behavior across Content Domains and Levels of Analysis

To adequately test the scope and depth of the theoretical model and basic principles it is important to examine whether they apply across a broad range of behaviors that are hypothesized to share similar functions, and across levels of analysis (e.g., biology, psychology, behavior of groups/communities). For example, the basic principles and implications of RFT have been tested across a variety of areas and levels including education, intelligence, language development, perspective-taking, implicit cognition, developmental disorders, psychopathology, organizations, and neurophysiology, among other areas (Dymond & Roche, 2013). This approach can help identify the boundaries of a model, identifying areas for further technical and applied development.

In addition to testing scope and depth, this expanded interest in various areas of human behavior also reflects the pragmatic focus of CBS. Issues that have been historically understudied in much of the behavioral sciences, such as how to develop more effective, nurturing communities and scale principles to a public health level (see Biglan 2015; chapter 23 in this volume), also represent some of the most pressing challenges facing society. CBS takes an active responsibility toward focusing prediction-and-influence efforts on addressing such issues.

Embedding the Psychological Level of Analysis into Functional and Contextual Biological and Cultural Knowledge

As discussed in other chapters in this part of the book, functional, contextual behavioral thinking has always thought of itself as part of evolution science. Skinner, for example, argued repeatedly that behavior had to be understood as a combination of three forms of "levels of variation and selection" (1981, p. 502): contingencies of survival, rein-forcement, and cultural evolution. CBS seeks a unified fabric of science – that is what the goal of "depth" promises. Modern evolution science is looked to by CBS authors as a way to examine and integrate cultural and biological factors in a functional and contextual way, so that behavioral science knowledge can be woven into a single coherent fabric (e.g., Hayes & Sanford, 2014; Wilson et al., 2014a; 2014b). Thus, for example, when biological factors are considered, they will not be treated as independent variables that impact behavior but rather as aspects of functional, contextual systems that evolved within and across lifetimes.

Maintaining an Open, Diverse, and Supportive Community

The Association for Contextual Behavioral Science (ACBS) represents the results of an ongoing effort to develop a diverse and inclusive community of scientists, practi-tioners, and other professionals interested in behavioral science. The community is organized in an open and nonhierarchical format, meaning that everyone's opinions are valued and sought after, rotating leadership is elected through majority vote, there are minimal governance rules placed on members, and free sharing of resources is a norm and highly supported. For example, practitioners are not required to receive certification to practice or even train others in ACT. Similarly, individuals are free to practice ACT, but to call it a different name if they so choose. Resources including treatment protocols, measures, worksheets, and other tools are often freely available within ACBS. The community seeks to promote diversity and assist disadvantaged groups, for example, through a developing nations fund that sup-ports practitioners in such countries to attend ACT trainings and conferences. Diversity is promoted at another level through a tradition of inviting scholars to the annual conference from a variety of areas outside the ACBS community, including some of the strongest critics of CBS research programs, where their thoughts are actively sought out and engaged in open dialogues. Organization dues are open to whatever each individual wants to pay, based on their values related to ACBS. Overall, this approach to community building has resulted in a large association of over 7,000 members, including notable growth among individuals outside the United States, and arguably has contributed substantially to the rapidly growing dissemination of ACT and RFT. This open and supportive community has also served to promote innovations by a variety of professionals in areas including training methods, applications to new problems, and novel intervention methods (e.g., Luoma & Vilardaga, 2013; Polk & Schoendorff, 2014).

Summarizing CBS

As a whole, CBS can be defined by its functional contextual philosophy and the implications of this philosophy for theory and how to approach research and practice. The pragmatic focus on prediction and influence of behavior as a shared goal and criterion for "truth" naturally leads to features including an emphasis on manipulable, contextual factors, analytic abstractive theory building, and a reticulated approach to research in which basic science, theory development, and a diverse array of applied methods are highly integrated and constantly informing each other.

Considering the Boundary Conditions and Defining Features of CBS

CBS is defined by its philosophical assumptions and approach to behavioral science, not by its domain. Thus, focusing on acceptance, mindfulness, values, experiential avoidance, or other processes relevant to ACT, does not necessarily make such research CBS. This is exemplified by some programs of research on mindfulness in which the emphasis is on identifying causal biological mechanisms (e.g., Kilpatrick et al., 2011) and models emphasizing behavior–behavior relations (e.g., Rasmussen & Pidgeon, 2011) over manipulable variables.

CBS as a model of scientific strategy has the potential to inform and help bridge behavioral sciences including psychology, behavior analysis, evolution science, cognitive science, and a range of other basic and applied sciences. Research that is more or less consistent with the defining features and assumptions of CBS can be conducted in any of these domains. As CBS becomes more prevalent and expansive, challenges will include keeping research consistent with most of the core tenets of CBS and being able to differentiate between CBS and non-CBS programs of research.

Although clear lines are difficult to draw at the level of broader scientific strategy, it may be useful as a scientific community to further consider the boundary conditions that define what is and is not CBS as a field. Defining CBS by content issues, such as those relevant to ACT, risks inclusion of programs that do not include a critical analysis of more basic scientific assumptions and the exclusion of new domains that emerge from the CBS agenda. Defining CBS by a short set of basic assumptions, such as functional contextualism, risks losing track of the more refined but also critical details such as analytic abstractive theory building or the reticulated approach to knowledge development. Being too strict and conservative with regards to criteria might limit the expansion of CBS and stand in direct contrast with its open and diverse community.

By its very nature, CBS is a multifaceted and interrelated system and set of assumptions, thus making it difficult at times to clearly identify and discriminate it from non-CBS research programs. Research programs are likely to vary to the degree to which they overlap with the core tenets of CBS. Given all of this, one strategy might be to develop a list of key, unique features of CBS that could be used to consider the degree to which any given program of research fits with this approach to science. Such a list has not yet been provided (though see Hayes, 2008 and Vilardaga et al., 2009 for initial attempts within the areas of clinical psychology and behavior analysis) and should be fully developed as an iterative process within the scientific community.

As a step in this direction a preliminary list was collected through a discussion on CBS email listservs, which was then further developed and refined. As a way to support further conversation and elaboration of such criteria, and to summarize the features of CBS discussed in this chapter, a preliminary list of questions/criteria one might consider in identifying CBS research is presented. These criteria are separated into philosophy, theory, and methods to reflect the three main facets of CBS, with "CBS consistent" responses included in *italics*.

CBS Philosophical Assumptions

- What is the goal? (*Prediction-and-influence of behavior* vs. prediction of behavior, accurate classification of behavior, etc.)
- What is the unit of analysis? (*Behavior in context* vs. behavior–behavior relations, brain–behavior relations, etc.)
- What is the criterion for "truth"? (*Successful working* vs. correspondence with reality)
- What is the ontological stance? (*Constructs are useful* vs. constructs are "real")
- Are philosophical assumptions clearly recognized and stated? (*Yes* or no)

CBS Theory

- How is behavior defined and categorized? (*By the function of behavior and its relationship with context* vs. its form/topography)
- What is the relationship between basic research and theoretical models? (*Analytic abstractive theory with close ties to basic principles* vs. hypothetico-deductive theory, or theory based only on applied research, clinical experience, metaphorical extension [e.g., like a computer], etc.)
- Does the theory consider all aspects of an action, including the verbal, historical, cultural, genetic, and/or biological context, as it is useful for prediction and influence?
- Are middle-level terms used when appropriate to guide the application of technical terms to specific domains of complex behaviors?
- How are middle-level terms approached? (*They are used, revised, and discarded as needed based on their ongoing contribution to prediction-and-influence of behavior* vs. middle-level terms are reified)
- Are manipulable variables emphasized in the model?
- What variables are causal in the model? (*Contextual/environmental variables* vs. behaviors, cognitions, biological mechanisms, hypothetical constructs, etc.)
- How are behavior–behavior relations approached? (*In relation to the manipulable contextual factors that govern them* vs. without considering context)
- Does the theory demonstrate, or at least strive toward, precision, scope, and depth?

CBS Methods

- What is the relationship of basic science and applied science? (*Mutual interest model with both areas collaborating on a shared goal* vs. being disconnected, unrealized mutual obligations, etc.)
- Do researchers use a range of methods (including single subject and group level) as needed to meet analytical goals and test research questions?
- Are research questions/designs relevant to multiple levels of analysis such as efficacy of the intervention, utility of the theoretical model, and depth/scope of basic principles?

- Does research test the precision, scope, and depth of the theoretical model?
- Are researchers interested/willing to study behavior across content domains and levels (individuals, organizations, communities) in so far as it serves to further work on basic principles, theory building/testing, and applied goals?
- Are behavior change interventions closely linked to theory and basic principles?
- Are behavior change interventions tested in terms of how they work (i.e., processes of change) and not just whether they work?
- Does the research program focus on identifying contextual factors in analyzing behavior and examining moderators of interventions?
- Does research study *the functional role of context in maintaining/changing behavior* vs. only whether variations in context predict behavior, absent any focus on influence?
- Does the research program emphasize pragmatic issues (i.e., dissemination/implementation, training, external validity, treatment utility) early and throughout intervention development?
- Is the professional community open, supportive, nonhierarchical, and diverse?
- Is behavioral knowledge at the psychological level embedded into biological or cultural knowledge within multidimensional and multilevel evolution science as a contextual approach?

Conclusion

This chapter began with highlighting the importance of considering scientific strategy. In closing, it is worth returning to the question "What type of scientific strategy do we need?" From a CBS point of view, a strategy is needed that emphasizes how to influence behavior, not just reliably predict it. CBS researchers assume that a strategy is needed that combines a variety of research methods and levels of analysis, using that integration to move science forward, rather than keeping methods and domains in separate silos. CBS puts theory at the forefront of research questions, rather than just testing the efficacy of intervention packages. It considers a scientific analysis correct only if it helps to meet scientific goals, and focuses on variables that can be manipulated. In these ways, CBS offers one potential answer for how to develop a progressive approach to behavioral science that might better meet the challenges faced by society and opportunities for further growth. This volume is an extended examination of the degree to which these answers provide a plausible scientific guide.

References

Biglan, A. (2015). *The nurture effect: How the science of human behavior can improve our lives and our world*. Oakland, CA: New Harbinger.

Branstetter, A. D., Cushing, C., & Douleh, T. (2009). Personal values and pain tolerance: Does a values intervention add to acceptance? *Journal of Pain, 10,* 887–892.

Bricker, J.B., Mann, S.L., Marek, P.M., Liu, J. & Peterson, A.V. (2010). Telephone-delivered acceptance and commitment therapy for adult smoking cessation: A feasibility study. *Nicotine & Tobacco Research, 12,* 454–458.

DeHouwer, J. (2011). Why the cognitive approach in psychology would benefit from a functional approach and vice versa. *Perspectives on Psychological Science, 6,* 202–209.

Dougher, M. J. (2013). Behaviorisms and private events. *The Behavior Analyst, 36,* 223–227.

Dougher, M. J., & Hayes, S. C. (2000). Clinical behavior analysis. In M. J. Dougher & S. C. Hayes (Eds.), *Clinical behavior analysis* (pp. 11–26). Reno, NV: Context Press.

Dougher, M., Twohig, M. P., & Madden, G. J. (2014). Basic and translational research on stimulus–stimulus relations. *Journal of the Experimental Analysis of Behavior, 101,* 1–9.

Dymond, S. & Roche, B. (2013). *Advances in relational frame theory: research and application.* Reno, NV: Context Press.

Epstein, R. (1996). *Cognition, creativity, and behavior: Selected essays,* Westport, CT: Praeger.

Fledderus, M., Bolmeijer, E.T., Pieterse, M.E., & Schreurs, K.M.G. (2011). Acceptance and commitment therapy as guided self-help for psychological distress and positive mental health: A randomized controlled trial. *Psychological Medicine, 42,* 485–495.

Foody, M., Barnes-Holmes, Y, Barnes-Holmes, D., & Luciano C. (2013). An empirical investigation of hierarchical versus distinction relations in a self-based ACT exercise. *International Journal of Psychology and Psychological Therapy, 13,* 373–388.

Friel, S., Bowen, K., Campbell-Lendrum, D., Frumkin, H., McMichael, A.J., & Rasanathan, K. (2011). Climate change, noncommunicable diseases, and development: The relationships and common policy opportunities. *Annual Review of Public Health, 32,* 133–147.

Friman, P. C. (2009). Time-out, time-in, and task-based grounding. In W. T. O'Donohue & J. E. Fisher (Eds.), *General principles and empirically supported techniques of cognitive behavior therapy* (pp. 655–662). Hoboken, NJ: John Wiley & Sons Inc.

Hayes, S.C. (1984). Making sense of spirituality. *Behaviorism, 12,* 99–110.

Hayes, S.C. (1998). The value of visiting foreign intellectual islands: The example of the cognitive-behavioral debate. *The Behavior Therapist, 21,* 139–141.

Hayes, S.C. (2008). Climbing our hills: A beginning conversation on the comparison of acceptance and commitment therapy and traditional cognitive behavioral therapy. *Clinical Psychology: Science and Practice, 5,* 286–295.

Hayes, S. C., Barnes-Holmes, D., & Roche, B. (2001). *Relational frame theory: A post-Skinnerian account of human language and cognition.* New York, NY: Kluwer/Plenum.

Hayes, S. C., Barnes-Holmes, D., & Wilson, K. G. (2012). Contextual behavioral science: Creating a science more adequate to the challenge of the human condition. *Journal of Contextual Behavioral Science, 1,* 1–16.

Hayes, S. C., & Brownstein, A. J. (1986). Mentalism, behavior–behavior relations, and a behavior-analytic view of the purposes of science. *The Behavior Analyst, 9,* 175–190.

Hayes, S. C., Hayes, L. J., & Reese, H. W. (1988). Finding the philosophical core: A review of Stephen C. Pepper's *World hypotheses: a study in evidence. Journal of the Experimental Analysis of Behavior, 50,* 97.

Hayes, S. C., Hayes, L. J., Reese, H. W., & Sarbin, T. R. (Eds.). (1993). *Varieties of scientific contextualism.* Oakland, CA: Context Press/New Harbinger.

Hayes, S. C., Levin, M. E., Plumb, J., Boulanger, J., & Pistorello, J. (2013). Acceptance and commitment therapy and contextual behavioral science: Examining the progress of a distinctive model of behavioral and cognitive therapy. *Behavior Therapy, 44,* 180–198.

Hayes, S. C., & Sanford, B. (2014). Cooperation came first: Evolution and human cognition. *Journal of the Experimental Analysis of Behavior, 101,* 112–129.

Hayes, S. C., Strosahl, K. D., & Wilson, K. G. (2011). *Acceptance and commitment therapy: The process and practice of mindful change.* New York, NY: Guilford.

Hayes, S. C., Wilson, K. W., Gifford, E. V., Follette, V. M., & Strosahl, K. (1996). Experiential avoidance and behavioral disorders: A functional dimensional approach to diagnosis and treatment. *Journal of Consulting and Clinical Psychology, 64,* 1152–1168.

Ju, W. C., & Hayes, S. C. (2008). Verbal establishing stimuli: Testing the motivative effect of stimuli in a derived relation with consequences. *The Psychological Record, 58,* 339–363.

Kashdan, T. B., Goodman, F. R., Machell, K. A., Kleiman, E. M., Monfort, S. S., Ciarrochi, J., & Nezlek, J. B. (2014). A contextual approach to experiential avoidance and social anxiety: Evidence from an experimental interaction and daily interactions of people with social anxiety disorder. *Emotion, 14*, 769–781.

Kessler, R. C., Berglund, P., Demler, O., Jin, R., Merikangas, K. R., & Walters, E. E. (2005). Lifetime prevalence and age-of-onset distributions of DSM-IV disorders in the national comorbidity survey replication. *Archives of General Psychiatry, 62*, 593–602.

Kilpatrick, L.A., Suyenobu, B. Y., Smith, S. R., Bueller, J. A., Goodman, T., Creswell, J. D., … Naliboff, B. D. (2011). Impact of mindfulness-based stress reduction training on intrinsic brain connectivity. *Neuroimage, 56*, 290–298.

Levin, M. E., Hildebrandt, M., Lillis, J., & Hayes, S. C. (2012). The impact of treatment components suggested by the psychological flexibility model: A meta-analysis of laboratory-based component studies. *Behavior Therapy, 43*, 741–756.

Levin, M. E., Pistorello, J., Hayes, S. C. & Seeley, J. (2014). Feasibility of a prototype web-based acceptance and commitment therapy prevention program for college students. *Journal of American College Health, 62*, 20–30.

Luoma, J. B., & Vilardaga, J. P. (2013). Improving therapist psychological flexibility while training acceptance and commitment therapy: A pilot study. *Cognitive Behaviour Therapy, 42*, 1–8.

Madden, G. J. (2013). *APA handbook of behavior analysis, vol. 1: Methods and principles.* Washington, DC: American Psychological Association.

Masuda, A., Hayes, S. C., Fletcher, L. B., Seignourel, P. J., Bunting, K., Herbst, S. A., … Lillis, J. (2007). The impact of acceptance and commitment therapy versus education on stigma toward people with psychological disorders. *Behaviour Research and Therapy, 45*, 2764–2772.

McHugh, L., Barnes-Holmes, Y., & Barnes-Holmes, D. (2004). Perspective-taking as relational responding: A developmental profile. *The Psychological Record, 54*, 115–144.

McHugh, L., & Stewart, I. (Eds.) (2012). *The self and perspective taking: Contributions and applications from modern behavioral science.* Oakland, CA: New Harbinger.

Michael, J. (1993). Establishing operations. *The Behavior Analyst, 16*, 191–206.

Moore, J. (2013). Methodological behaviorism from the standpoint of a radical behaviorist. *The Behavior Analyst, 36*, 197–208.

Ogden, C. L., Carroll, M. D., Curtin, L. R., McDowell, M. A., Tabak, C. J., & Flegal, K. M. (2006). Prevalence of overweight and obesity in the United States, 1999–2004. *Journal of the American Medical Association, 295*, 1549–1555.

Pager, D., & Shepherd, H. (2008). The sociology of discrimination: Racial discrimination in employment, housing, credit, and consumer markets. *Annual Review of Sociology, 34*, 181–209.

Pepper, S. C. (1942). *World Hypotheses: A Study in Evidence.* Berkeley, CA: University of California Press.

Polk, K. L., & Schoendorff, B. (2014). *The ACT Matrix: A new approach to building psychological flexibility across setting and populations.* Reno, NV: Context Press.

Rasmussen, M. K., & Pidgeon, A. M. (2011). The direct and indirect benefits of dispositional mindfulness on self-esteem and social anxiety. *Anxiety, Stress, & Coping, 24*, 227–233.

Roche, B., Kanter, J. W., Brown, K. R., Dymond, S., & Fogarty, C. C. (2008). A comparison of "direct" versus "derived" extinction of avoidance. *The Psychological Record, 58*, 443–464.

Ruiz, F. J. (2010). A review of acceptance and commitment therapy (ACT) empirical evidence: Correlational, experimental psychopathology, component and outcome studies. *International Journal of Psychology and Psychological Therapy, 10*, 125–162.

Skinner, B.F. (1974). *About behaviorism.* New York, NY: Vintage Books.

Skinner, B. F. (1981). Selection by consequences. *Science, 213*, 501–504.

Strosahl, K. D., Hayes, S. C., Bergan, J., & Romano, P. (1998). Assessing the field effectiveness of acceptance and commitment therapy: An example of the manipulated training research method. *Behavior Therapy, 29*, 35–64.

Themnér, L., & Wallensteen, P. (2013). Armed conflict, 1946–2012. *Journal of Peace Research, 50*, 509–521.

Valdivia, S., Luciano, C., & Molina, F. J. (2006). Verbal regulation of motivational states. *The Psychological Record, 56*, 577–595.

Vilardaga, R., Estévez, A., Levin, M. E., & Hayes, S. C. (2012). Deictic relational responding, empathy and experiential avoidance as predictors of social anhedonia: Further contributions from relational frame theory. *The Psychological Record, 62*, 409–432.

Vilardaga, R., Hayes, S. C., Atkins, D. C., Bresee, C., & Kambiz, A. (2013). Comparing experiential acceptance and cognitive reappraisal as predictors of functional outcome in individuals with serious mental illness. *Behaviour Research and Therapy, 51*, 425–433.

Vilardaga, R., Hayes, S. C., Levin, M., & Muto, T. (2009). Creating a strategy for progress: A contextual behavioral science approach. *The Behavior Analyst, 32*, 105–133.

Wilson, D. S., Hayes, S. C., Biglan, T., & Embry, D. (2014a). Evolving the future: Toward a science of intentional change. *Behavioral and Brain Sciences, 34*, 1–22.

Wilson, D. S., Hayes, S. C., Biglan, T., & Embry, D. (2014b). Collaborating on evolving the future. *Behavioral and Brain Sciences, 34*, 44–61.

Wilson, K., & Hayes, S. C. (1996). Resurgence of derived stimulus relations. *Journal of the Experimental Analysis of Behavior, 66*, 267–281.

4

Functional Contextualism and Contextual Behavioral Science

Anthony Biglan and Steven C. Hayes

This chapter describes functional contextualism, the philosophical foundation of the contextual behavioral science approach. We first describe the historical context for the development of functional contextualism, beginning with the general philosophy of pragmatism or contextualism and Skinner's use of this framework in the development of behavior analysis. We delineate the key features of functional contextualism, contrast it with the other major philosophical frameworks that are discernible in the behavioral sciences, and discuss why following the functional contextualist strategy makes it more likely that the behavioral sciences will contribute to the improvement of human well-being. The chapter discusses the implications of functional contextualism for the integration of the behavioral and biological sciences and for the study of private events. We briefly examine the implications of a functional contextualist framework for a variety of areas of the human sciences, including evolution, organizational research, public health, economics, and dissemination and implementation research. Finally, we discuss how functional contextualism is leading to a unique view of the role of values in human society.

Pragmatism: What is True is What Works

Functional contextualism is one variant of the general philosophical tradition of pragmatism or contextualism (Hayes, Hayes, Reese, & Sarbin, 1993). The development of the philosophy of pragmatism is generally attributed to Charles Peirce, William James, Oliver Wendell Holmes, and John Dewey. In his history of pragmatism, Louis Menand succinctly summarizes the main features of this way of thinking:

> They all believed that ideas are not "out there" waiting to be discovered, but are tools – like forks and knives, and microchips – that people devise to cope with the world in which they find themselves. They believed that ideas are produced not by individuals, but by groups of individuals – that ideas are social. They believed that ideas do not develop according to some inner logic of their own, but are entirely dependent, like germs, on

The Wiley Handbook of Contextual Behavioral Science, First Edition. Edited by Robert D. Zettle, Steven C. Hayes, Dermot Barnes-Holmes, and Anthony Biglan.
© 2016 John Wiley & Sons, Ltd. Published 2016 by John Wiley & Sons, Ltd.

their human carriers and the environment. And they believed that since ideas are provisional responses to particular and unreproducible circumstances, their survival depends not on their immutability but on their adaptability. (2001, p. xii)

Menand identifies two major influences on the development of pragmatism, the American Civil War and evolutionary theory. The Civil War, which lasted from 1861 to 1865, led to the deaths of 620,000 men. In terms of the current population, that is equivalent to six million Americans dying. Menand argues that the war shook the faith of many Americans in the verities that had driven the North and South to this disastrous war. Who is right about literal "truth" can become less interesting in the context of catastrophic quarrels about that issue – which is why more pragmatic perspectives can be strengthened culturally by seemingly irresolvable human conflict.

The second influence was the theory of evolution. Up until Darwin propounded his theory, the primary way of thinking about causation involved the push or pull of a causal agent (Menand, 2001; Smith, 1986). It is a natural and adaptive function of humans to notice when an antecedent event affects another event. We see it when a tool, such as a lever, is used to move a rock. Indeed, humans are so accustomed to inferring causation of this sort that the Latin phrase *post hoc ergo propter hoc* (after this, therefore because of this) has come to be used to point out that this is often fallacious reasoning.

The notion that a phenomenon could be affected by events that followed it is far less obvious in our day-to-day experience. Darwin discerned this influence on the evolution of species and it has since been recognized as an influence on behavior, gene expression, symbolic processes, and cultural evolution (Wilson, Hayes, Biglan, & Embry, 2014; Jablonka & Lamb, 2006). The process involves selection by consequences. The characteristics of species have been shaped by the contribution that those characteristics made to the survival of the organism. Put another way, environments with features in which a particular trait furthered the survival of the organism caused the trait in question to be more likely to be reproduced and spread in the population.

Once you begin thinking about how particular variants of a species arose because of their success in a given environment and how behaviors are selected by their success in achieving needed outcomes, it is a natural next step to think about your ideas and analyses in terms of their success in achieving a goal. This is the basic insight of the philosophy of pragmatism. The early pragmatists were quite clear in this area. Peirce, for example, said "there is no distinction of meaning so fine as to consist in anything but a possible difference of practice" (1878/1983, p. 145). James similarly said, "truth in our ideas means their power to 'work'" (1907/1981, p. 165).

Selection by consequences calls for us to evaluate our ideas by the degree to which they enable us to achieve our goals. Evolutionary thinking encourages a focus on the success of organisms' features – including their behavior – in aiding survival or other outcomes that contribute to survival. In this context, pragmatic thinking can be thought of as a generalization of this principle. One can examine virtually anything that an organism does in terms of the organism's success. This is true regarding the actions of groups or organizations.

Human verbal capacities add a consideration that goes beyond the degree to which genetically driven phenotypes or behaviors contribute to success. For verbally able humans, it is possible to state what might be done and to evaluate the truth of a statement in terms of the outcome. Moreover, it is possible to describe what has been done and what its consequences have been. It is also possible to make generalizations about the value of verbally stated principles or theories, though the generalizations are also statements whose truth can be evaluated in terms of the success it does or does not deliver.

The Unique Event in Context

Evolution encourages us to focus on specific circumstances before we make generalizations – if we make them at all. For example, Coleman and Wilson (1998) describe how phenotypic variation among sunfish occurs in a single lake. Slightly different contexts within the lake led to selection of different features.

This way of thinking may seem odd to those of us accustomed to thinking of science as having as its central aim the development of laws with broad scope. Such an orientation may be more important for biological and behavioral sciences than for physical sciences. Mechanical and chemical relations tend to be the same across a broad range of background conditions. That is much less true of behavior. Think about a specific behavior, such as brushing your teeth. It may be useful to speak of the class of behaviors called brushing our teeth, but every single occasion of this behavior is unique.

If we take seriously the notion that each behavioral event is unique, how do we make sense of the world? Part of the answer is by classifying events into classes based on the success of those classifications in achieving some goal. In the case of behavioral research, Skinner developed the concept of the operant by proposing that we group behaviors based on their having the same functional relationship to antecedents and consequences (Skinner, 1935) and then assess the usefulness of these groupings with experimental analysis. For example, asking someone to turn up the heat but then doing it yourself might be considered members of the same response class of "raising the temperature" because they both work to accomplish this end. The utility of gathering these into a single operant class is shown by functional covariation. It might be shown, for example, by the increased likelihood of both when temperatures fall, or the increased likelihood of turning it up yourself when others are absent.

The designation of a set of behaviors as a "functional response class" simply means that they are thought to function in the same way. The test of this claim is our ability to predict and influence events. A "class" is not in the world separate from our verbal behavior, it is in our verbal behavior enabling us to function in and with the world.

Thus, functional contextualists like to start with the unique event in context and build up to general principles if it works to have such general principles. The drive for general principles should not trump the possibility that one could find a very useful principle in a particular context that cannot be generalized and should not eliminate the possibility that some variation is assumed and will not yield to an experimental analysis.

The Pragmatism of B. F. Skinner

The immediate predecessor and most important influence on functional contextualism was the work of B. F. Skinner. While one might think that the most important influence on Skinner's pragmatism was the American pragmatists, the historian

Laurence Smith (1986) documents that he was more directly influenced by Ernst Mach, who in turn was influenced by James.

Among the examples of Skinner's pragmatic thinking is his statement that science is "a corpus of rules for effective action" (1957, p. 235). Regarding scientific knowledge, Skinner said "There is a special sense in which it could be 'true' if it yields the most effective action possible" (1974, p. 235).

The pragmatic nature of Skinner's approach is illustrated by the way he developed the concept of the operant in an early paper entitled, "The Generic Nature of the Concepts of Stimulus and Response" (1935). He examined various ways in which these concepts had been conceptualized. The most common method was to describe stimuli and responses in terms of the physical properties. A response was defined by physical movement through space. A stimulus might be defined by its color, texture, intensity, size, etc. But these physicalistic ways of defining stimulus and response could lead to every instance of a stimulus and response relationship being treated as a separate entity. Skinner argued that that the most useful way of approaching this problem was to define classes of stimuli and response based on their ability to produce "orderliness of changes in the correlation" between stimuli and responses (Skinner, 1935/1999, p. 517). Thus, the operant was to be defined in terms of a class of responses that could be shown to be consistently related to a class of stimuli. The flexibility of this unit was a critical innovation. It meant that the variety of ways a rat might press a lever to obtain pellets could be treated as a single unit, provided that the consistent relationship could be shown; in the same way a much more complex behavior, such as a student studying for exams as a function of social approval, could be treated as an operant, provided that social approval could be shown to reliably affect studying.

The success of the Skinnerian strategy was demonstrated by its success in yielding precise and generalizable principles about the influences on behavior and the many effective interventions that have been developed based on those principles. Indeed, over the past 50 to 60 years, behavioral scientists have developed numerous family, school, community, and organizational interventions that make use of principles regarding the selection of behavior by its consequences (Biglan, 2003; 2015).

Skinner was clear about the link between truth and successful working: "[Scientific knowledge] is a corpus of rules for effective action, and there is a special sense in which it could be 'true' if it yields the most effective action possible. ... [A] proposition is 'true' to the extent that with its help the listener responds effectively to the situation it describes" (Skinner, 1974, p. 235). A particularly bold move made by Skinner contributed to our thinking about scientific knowledge and led to his philosophy of science, radical behaviorism: He applied contingency thinking to the scientist doing science. He argued that knowing is situated behavior; it is behavior in context (Skinner, 1945; 1957). Looked at in this way, the very act of a scientist in saying that something is true, can be viewed as behavior occurring in a context – behavior that leads to reinforcing outcomes or not.

When even the behavior of the scientist was viewed as an act-in-context something interesting happened in behavioral thinking – scientific restrictions installed by early behaviorists, such as the prohibition against introspection, fell away. Far from being merely an extreme form of behaviorism, Skinner's radical behaviorism declared that the distinction between scientifically valid and nonvalid observations could not be equated with the distinction between publicly observed actions and private events (e.g., thoughts and feelings) that are directly observed by an audience of one.

Watson (1924; e.g., p. 14) claimed behavior as the subject matter of psychology and defined it by its form: Behavior was muscle movements and glandular secretions. Watson suggested that, even if mental or other nonmovement activities existed, they could not constitute the subject matter of a scientific psychology because public agreement as to their occurrence was impossible. In contrast, Skinner (1945) defined scientifically valid observations as those under the control of a history of speaking based on contact with stimulus events rather than on audience factors, states of reinforceability, and so on. These contingencies could be tight even when the events were private or loose even when the events were public.

The latter effect is easily demonstrated. Suppose the following slide is flashed on the screen for a bit less than a second:

Blonds have
more
more fun

If asked to write down what they saw, the vast majority of observers will write down "blondes have more fun." That inaccurate observation is controlled by the familiarity of the phrase, not by the words on the screen. The observation is scientifically "subjective," even though it is publicly observable. Conversely, a person taught to carefully notice the world within might report thoughts or feelings in a scientifically valid way. This is why Skinner said that radical behaviorism "does not insist upon truth by agreement and can therefore consider events taking place in the private world within the skin. It does not call these events unobservable" (Skinner, 1974, p. 16). This fundamental change in behaviorism is often not known or understood by those outside of the tradition because Skinner did not move to investigations of thinking and feeling, arguing that they were unnecessary for scientific understanding of overt activity (Skinner, 1953). That position has changed in CBS because RFT suggests that relational framing alters other behavioral processes, but our point here is that applying pragmatic analysis to the behavior of analysts leads in unexpected directions.

Functional Contextualism

Skinner can be interpreted in a variety of ways, and, in recent years, *functional contextualism* has emerged as way to describe an interpretation of Skinner's approach to the study of behavior that is based on an epistemological commitment to pragmatism (Biglan & Hayes, 1996; Hayes, 1995). The explicit goal of functional contextualism is the prediction and influence of the behavior of individuals or the actions of groups or organizations. Prediction-and-influence is single goal. That is, the goal is not only to identify variables that predict behavior, but to identify variables that can be shown to *influence* the behavior in question. It is sometimes written as "prediction-and-influence" to emphasis this fact.

Skinner spoke of "prediction and control." Functional contextualists have adopted the phrase "prediction and influence" for at least three reasons (Biglan & Hayes,

1996; Hayes & Wilson, 1995). First, the term *control* suggests an exclusive and nonprobabilistic influence. Yet behavior is multiply determined; a variable we identify as influencing behavior is never its only influence. For example, food may function as a reinforcer of a particular behavior, but its impact depends in part on whether the organism is food-deprived. Second, control in behavior theory sometimes means the absence of variability, which is a different construct. Third, control may connote coercive control of other people's behavior. Given the not entirely unwarranted stereotype in the history of behavior modification of unwanted behavior control, the term "influence" seems both more accurate and less likely to prompt rejection of the approach out of fears of unwanted "behavior control" (see Biglan, 1995 for a discussion of the issues involved in the protection of individual rights in the context of a science of behavioral influence).

Precision

Precision is the degree to which the events referred to by concepts used to predict and influence behavior are unambiguous and unambiguously related one to the other. This combination of factors means that a given phenomenon can be explained in a very limited number of ways when concepts are precise. For example, the concept of reinforcement is precise in the sense that only events that can be shown to increase the probability of behavior when they are made contingent on the behavior can be said to be reinforcers. Moreover, the relationship among variables is highly reliable. If examining the impact of attention on a given child's tantrums, a limited set of things might be said. The effect of that contingency might be reinforcing, punishing, or neither, but it cannot be all three based on the preferences of the analyst.

A theory that is not precise is one in which the referents of concepts are ambiguous or ambiguously related to each other. For example, some cognitive concepts have been criticized because they fail to distinguish between occurrent events, such as having a thought and constructs that simply characterize a behavioral tendency (Biglan, 1987). The concept of intention is an example. A person might be said to have an intention because of a specifically stated intention to do something, but the term may also be used to explain behavior, when no specific intentional events are specified or measured (e.g., the intention is inferred from the behavior). Both senses may useful in analyzing behavior but they are distinct processes.

One example from contextual behavioral science work may help to clarify what we mean by precision. Theory of mind is the ability to attribute beliefs, intents, desires, knowledge, and other "mental states" to oneself and others and to understand that others have beliefs, desires, and intentions that differ from one's own (Premack & Woodruff, 1978). This is useful for designating this important tendency in human behavior. However, relational frame theory research on deictic relations has provided a more precise analysis of some of the processes by which humans are able to infer the mental states of others (Barnes-Holmes, McHugh, & Barnes-Holmes, 2004). The analysis also exemplifies the CBS focus on prediction and influence. While theory of mind research has elucidated an important aspect of human functioning and has shown that lack of these skills is a critical deficit for people with autism, the RFT work on deictics has elucidated manipulable variables that influence the development of the perspective-taking skills that underpin theory of mind (McHugh & Stewart, 2012).

Scope

Scope means an analysis is relevant to a broad range of phenomena. For example, the concept of reinforcement has been shown to account for changes in behavior of humans and nonhumans across an extraordinarily broad range of behaviors. Broad scope is sought for pragmatic reasons: Analyses that can apply to a broad range of phenomena are simply more useful in many instances. However, functional contextualists do not assume that scope will necessarily be found. Scope is an aspiration, not an a priori declaration. Pragmatists start with the unique act-in-context and work toward generalizable relations – if they can be found.

The commitment of behavioral psychology to high scope concepts is apparent in the search for behavioral principles. Concepts with high precision and low scope are not *principles*. For example, it is quite likely that pointing a gun at people and asking for their money will lead them to provide it. This is a highly precise observation but it has no scope. It would likely not apply to charitable giving, the likelihood of using money to purchase useful products, to loans, to investing, or many other uses of money. The objection many psychologists have of *influence* as an analytic goal is often a disguised concern over scope. "I am not that interested in prediction and influence," goes the refrain. "I seek understanding." Functional contextualists reply, "We agree that understanding is important, but prediction and influence, *with precision, scope, and depth*, is what we mean by understanding."

Depth

Depth means that the analysis is consistent with well-established and useful accounts at other levels of analysis. For example, the principles of reinforcement should not be contradicted by findings about brain functioning. This too is a pragmatic goal: a unified fabric of science is a particularly useful form of science. Wilson, Hayes, Biglan, and Embry (2014) provide an example using an evolutionary framework that shows the degree to which our understanding of phenomena ranging from genetic evolution through behavioral, symbolic, and cultural evolution can be understood in terms of the principles of variation and selection.

Alternative Strategies: Mechanism and Organicism

Most behavioral science research does not occur in the context of an explicit philosophical or theoretical framework. Our ways of thinking about science and our common practices are usually implicit and unexamined. Pragmatism, and specifically functional contextualism, is far from the dominant philosophical framework underpinning the behavioral sciences. Pragmatism needs to be explicit to be effective because it is too unusual to be fully intuitive, at least initially.

At least two other frameworks commonly characterize behavioral science research: *mechanism* and *organicism*. They both fit more with commonsense assumptions and as a result, are often implicit.

Philosopher Stephen Pepper articulated generic features of strategies for under-standing the world. He argued that perspectives on the world can often be understood in terms of their "world hypotheses." By this he meant that each strategy proposed an all-encompassing way of thinking about how to understand our world by using an analogy to a commonsense metaphor. In this sense, they might be thought of as very general paradigms.

Each world hypothesis has a root metaphor and a truth criterion. The root metaphor is a way of thinking about phenomena. For contextualism, the root metaphor is the unique act-in-context. How should we think about phenomena? Think of them in terms of their relation to their context. The truth criterion is the standard by which we assess the validity of our analysis. For contextualism, the truth criterion is "success-ful working." That is, a contextual analysis is held to be true or valid if it helps you to achieve some goal. The goal for functional contextualism, by declaration, is prediction and influence with precision, scope, and depth. But many other forms of contextual-ism are defined by the specific goals they pursue (Hayes, 1993).

For mechanism, the root metaphor is the machine. "Mechanistic" as a term is sometimes used as an epithet, suggesting that a person is unfeeling or robot-like. For that reason, the term "elemental realism" is also used as a synonym for this approach.

How do analysts understand the world in mechanism, or elemental realism? They do so by identifying the machine parts, their interrelations, and the forces involved in those relations. Pepper characterized the truth criterion of mechanism as "predictive verification." An analysis is valid to the extent that a description of the interrelation-ships of parts matches real world examples of the phenomenon. For example, many cognitive theories of human behavior involve models of the relationships between cognitions and other aspects of behavior. The *theory of reasoned action* (Ajzen & Fishbein, 1980; Fishbein, 1979) postulates that behavior can be predicted from people's stated intentions. These, in turn, can be predicted by knowing someone's attitude toward a behavior and that person's beliefs about the norms relevant to it. Multiple studies have validated the theory and such models have been shown to accurately predict intentions and behavior (e.g., Albarracín, Johnson, Fishbein, & Muellerleile, 2001; Webb, Joseph, Yardley, & Michie, 2010).

The development of philosophy of science in psychology was heavily influenced by mechanistic thinking due to its success in the physical sciences (Hatfield, 2002; Smith, 1986). Given the unquestioned advances in the physical sciences in the past 200 years, it is not surprising that behavioral sciences would have attempted to emulate the mech-anistic approach. Much of that success rested on the careful specification of the parts of the world under study and the analysis of how they interacted. In physics and chemistry, the mechanical relations among objects and their influence on each other could be described with great precision and scope. And the analyses yielded models that could guide effective action on the world. These mechanical models were developed through a process of *predictive verification* in which theoretical models were tested against sam-ples of the phenomenon of interest and were accepted or rejected on the basis of how accurately they predicted observed phenomena in experimental research.

For organicism, the root metaphor is the process of organic development, such as the growing plant (Hayes, Hayes, Reese, & Sarbin, 1993). Developmental stage models in psychology are examples of organicist analyses. They seek to describe the orderly changes from one stage to the next. The truth criterion for organicism is coherence: "When a network of interrelated facts converges on a conclusion, the coherence of this network renders this conclusion 'true'" (Hayes, Hayes, & Reese, 1988, p. 100). In contrast to functional contextualism, this framework does not necessarily seek to identify variables that influence the changes from one stage to the next.

Why a Contextual Strategy is Valuable

Functional contextualists make no claim that prediction-and-influence with precision, scope, and depth is the one true goal for science. The goal is simply declared and it is freely admitted that scientists might choose to pursue other goals. Such choices cannot be defended, in the sense that one can prove one set of goals superior to another, because accomplishment of goals provides the metric for truth in a pragmatic account. The foundational nature of goals is itself an example of a pragmatic orientation. One could say only that the pursuit of one goal was superior to another by showing that pursuing one led to better outcomes than another. But in this case, one would have to define the goal that made one outcome "better" than another, and that itself would be a choice that could be defended only in terms of some other goal, ad infinitum.

We can say, however, that prediction-and-influence with precision, scope, and depth can contribute to certain useful societal outcomes. Elsewhere, we have argued that a scientific strategy focusing on identifying variables that allow us to predict – and influence – phenomena may make a greater contribution over time to our ability to manipulate the world than would a strategy that makes the predictive validity of its models the priority (Biglan & Hayes, 1996). Certainly the empirical progress that has been made on the development of treatment (Hayes, Luoma, Bond, Masuda, & Lillis, 2006) and preventive interventions (National Research Council & Institute of Medicine, 2009) testifies to the value of focusing on identifying environmental influences on behavior.

Over the past 10 years there has been explosive growth in the number of behavioral scientists and practitioners who have adopted this framework. The Association for Contextual Behavioral Science was only created in 2006 and now has over 7,300 members worldwide. This growth also reflects the success of the approach to some degree in developing an effective science of behavior change.

There are concrete reasons that a contextual approach to behavior promises to be more productive of practical interventions over time than strategies that focus on building models of the relationships among psychological and behavioral variables. In the physical sciences, mechanistic analyses result quite naturally in the ability to take practical action. Knowing the relationship between parts of the physical world usually gives direct information about how to use one part to affect the other. Think, for example, about the principles involved in applying electrical changes to semi-conducting materials. Detailed understanding of that process has led to the development of modern electronics. Physicists John Bardeen, William Shockley, and Walter Brattain won the 1956 Nobel Prize in Physics for their discovery of point contact transistors based on physical knowledge of that kind – a discovery that literally changed the world in the flow of inventions and applications that resulted, from the modern computer to today's media.

Yet when we turn to behavior as a subject matter we encounter a complication. Prior to scientific study of behavior, we were accustomed to assuming that when a person did something, the cause was inside them. When asking, "Why did he do it?" the answers that come to mind are often of that kind: "Because he wanted to; because he planned it; because he was conscientious." Our prescientific way of talking about the internal determinants of behavior led behavioral scientists to devote a great deal of attention to the study of possible internal causes of behavior. Theories about personality and attitudes are two good examples.

Originally personality theory sought to identify traits and to show that they predicted people's behavior. And in fact certain traits are highly predictive of behavior. For example, the trait of conscientiousness, which involves a person being very thorough, organized, and efficient, is associated with people succeeding in a broad range of activities (Goldberg, 1990). Similarly, substantial evidence indicates that a person's attitudes toward an activity (e.g., smoking) predicts whether that person will smoke (National Cancer Institute, 2008).

But there is a problem translating these findings into practical ways to influence behavior. Unlike a lever that can lift a heavy weight or a transistor that can change states via electrical charges, traits and attitudes cannot be directly manipulated. In recent years we have learned that conscientiousness can be nurtured by teaching habits of organization and by reliably reinforcing conscientious behaviors (Lapierre & Hackett, 2007; Wiegand & Geller, 2005). But these events are in the environment of the person, not in their personality.

The point is that, in order to take effective action to influence behavior, we must alter some aspect of the context of that action: broadly conceived, the person's environment. As evidence has accumulated about the ways that environments affect behavior and as principles about the selection of behavior have been successfully applied to the remediation of behavior problems, behavioral scientists have increasingly focused on understanding the context that influences behavior.

In sum, if we are interested in the human sciences contributing to the ability of human societies to improve human well-being, then the focus on prediction and influence may be critical because it leads directly to a focus on identifying manipulable variables. This contrasts with philosophical strategies such as mechanism and organicism, which may provide accurate accounts of relations among variables but do not necessarily identify influences that we can exploit directly in efforts to evolve more nurturing cultures.

Indeed, in our view, this pragmatic orientation is a major reason why the behavioral sciences have made so much progress in identifying what can be done to dramatically improve the human condition (Biglan, 2015; Komro, Flay, Biglan, & The Promise Neighborhoods Research Consortium, 2011; National Research Council & Institute of Medicine, 2009). The fruits of this effort are not yet widely visible. But the pragmatic focus on identifying environmental factors that predict and influence our behavior are providing practical tools to influence the further evolution of societies toward greater well-being for all (Biglan & Embry, 2013).

The Material Causality of the Body

Functional contextualism has implications for how we think about biological causes. Evolutionists encourage us to think about both proximate and ultimate causes of phenotypes (Wilson, 2007). For example, the proximate cause of a lizard having a sandy color may be its genes or epigenes, but the ultimate cause involves the contribution of that color to survival in a given environment (Wilson, 2007).

This way of thinking is relevant to neuroscience and other forms of biological research on behavior. Recent advances in neuroscience tell us a great deal about the neural functioning that subserves behavior; the same elaboration of knowledge is occurring in the area of epigenetics. In a meaningful sense, these processes can be considered proximate causes of behavior. However, from a functional contextualist perspective, our ability to influence behavior depends on our ability to alter the environment that affects both the organism and behavior. Thus, functional contextualists focus on the history (ontogenetic and phylogenetic) that gave rise to such biological processes.

Because neurons are physical and develop over time there is a tendency to miss or dismiss this issue. In fact we know very little about how to use neuroscience knowledge to produce direct methods of influencing behavior. Physical interventions exist – for example, progress is being made on creating vaccines that reduce the reinforcing effects of substances such as cocaine or nicotine (Volkow & Skolnick, 2012) – but administrating a vaccine is an environmental event and its precise impact on biology is often little known. The environmental events that lead to changes in neurophysiology are often poorly studied (it is much better in the area of epigenetics).

As a practical matter, while our growing understanding of biological functioning will undoubtedly sharpen our understanding of behavior, our ability to take effective action to influence it will largely involve altering the environment. Until it is known how to alter neural pathways or the epigenome in a precise fashion without the use of environmental manipulation the primary utility of these biological measures for behavioral science will be as dependent variables, which can validate environmental interventions or pinpoint moderators of the impact of interventions. For example, there is a subgroup of aggressive children who are most affected by an intervention like the Good Behavior Game (GBG), which reinforces elementary school students for on-task, cooperative behavior (Embry, 2002). It has been hypothesized that this may be due to differences between aggressive and nonaggressive children in reward sensitivity (Lochman & Dodge, 1994). Neuroscience research that pinpointed neural processes involving reward sensitivity might more precisely identify a subgroup of children who benefit from the GBG. That might lead to new ways to intervene with this subset of children. However, those interventions would most likely be more refined environmental manipulations. In this sense the identification of neural systems that subserve environmental effects might first contribute to the goal of predicting and influencing behavior by specifying a subgroup of children for whom the intervention was likely to work or did work. The same can be said for epigenetic effects, which already hint at environmental signatures in such areas as the methylation patterns involved in regulating genes involved in stress responses. It is not helpful to behavioral sciences to view biological knowledge as a substitute for contextual behavioral knowledge, because it could undermine our ability to predict and influence important classes of action. If our ultimate goal as a society is to increase the prevalence of well-being in the population, is it possible that we are currently putting too little of our scientific resources into learning how to evolve environments that nurture the development of prosocial behavior? The solution to this conundrum is not to avoid biological measures, but to actively harness them to pragmatic ends.

Private Events

Some behavior analysts tend to restrict their attention to observable behavior that is defined by its physical dimensions (e.g., Johnston & Pennypacker, 1993). Yet a functional contextualist orientation encourages us to analyze behavior in the terms of our ability to predict and influence it, regardless of where it "resides." Skinner (1945) argued that there is no reason why we cannot analyze behavioral events that we cannot publicly access. He provided a schema for understanding how the verbal community establishes a person's ability to describe internal events, even though others have no direct access to them. They do this based on collateral evidence (e.g., someone's observable emotional behavior) or environmental events (e.g., injury). Until recently however, behavior analysts have done very little research based on this analysis.

This has changed with the advent of relational frame theory research. As Part II of this volume attests, a large, growing body of research shows that the human ability to derive and arbitrarily apply relations is critical to understanding human behavior. Arbitrary applicable relational responding involves the ability to derive relations, ultimately without direct training in a given instance, among stimuli that have not previously participated in direct training.

The relational response is not inferred but often emerges directly in overt behavior. For example, Dougher, Goldstein, and Leight (1987) have shown that the influence of a stimulus on physiological measures of arousal can be altered by teaching a person to distinguish a set of three stimuli in terms of "greater than" and "less than" relations among arbitrary stimuli. A stimulus that participants learned was "greater than" one stimulus and "less than" another was then paired with shock. The stimulus that by derivation is "greater than" this target stimulus produces greater arousal than the target itself, which has been paired with shock. No such effect has been shown with nonverbal organisms, which would generally show less arousal to both stimuli that were not directly paired with shock.

Behavior analysis has progressed greatly in understanding environmental influences on behavior, but most progress has involved manipulating behavioral consequences. Account of the alteration of stimuli functions has been largely restricted to direct conditioning. RFT research has shown that for verbally able humans the functions of stimuli alter through their participation in relational frames. This implies that the functions of most stimuli for verbally able humans are due to the relation of one stimulus to others as a function of the person's relational responding.

From the standpoint of cognitive accounts of behavior, RFT provides a precise and empirically supported account of the contingencies that select cognitive processes. Whereas much cognitive research has focused on the role that cognitive events have in affecting other behavior, RFT's functional contextualist strategy provides an account of how cognitive events get established developmentally and, perhaps more importantly, how the relationships between verbal behavior and other behavior are established and regulated. Rather than assuming that covert verbal behavior has an inexorable impact on what people do, RFT and ACT research has shown that the relationship between thoughts and feelings and other behavior depends on the context. It is itself manipulable: Contexts, such as those promoting mindfulness or dispassionate observation, can reduce the influence of thoughts. For example, encouraging smokers to accept rather than struggle with cigarette cravings reduces the likelihood that the cravings will drive them back to smoking (Gifford et al., 2004).

Analysis is Itself an Act in Context

A detailed focus on the unique act in context has led some to point out that the scientist's behavior is itself an act in context (Gifford & Hayes, 1999; Skinner, 1957; see also chapter 6 in this volume). This idea raises the possibility of an empirical science of scientific research. For a functional contextualist, the goal would be the same as for the study of any other behavior, namely the prediction and influence of scientists' behavior. One effect of this line of research might be to develop a more precise and thorough analysis of the contingencies that select scientific behavior. Of particular relevance are consequences such as grant funding, tenure, and peer approval. The promotion of effective scientific behavior might be better if we understood the variables that predict and influence it.

It is worth mentioning one odd implication of viewing analysis as itself an act-in-context. Issues of epistemology (how we know what we know) become the core focus of functional contextual philosophy of science, while issues of ontology (whether what we know is real and what the real categories are) become uninteresting or irrelevant. Claiming that something works "because it is real" adds nothing to workability. Since there is no difference that does not make a difference, questions of ontology are simply put aside within a functional contextual approach. This is not due to idealism or dualism but rather reflects the practical imperative of a contextualistic approach.

We see this a-ontological position as central to functional contextualism or to any philosophy of science based on evolutionary epistemology. It is admittedly an initially surprising implication for those pursuing a monistic, naturalistic account of phenomena. However, the a-ontological nature of functional contextualism is helpful in undermining appeals that go beyond experience. The principled disinterest in ontological truth and the enthusiastic interest in pragmatic truth are echoed in clinical procedures in CBS, such as in the emphasis on defusion and workability in ACT, and the willingness to use technical and nontechnical terms in CBS in different contexts for different purposes.

Another way to speak about a disinterest in ontology is to note that the ultimate basis of "truth" in pragmatism necessarily involves nonverbal knowing. Hayes (1997) explains the reasons for this in detail. In brief, in pragmatism if a statement works in accomplishing a goal, it is "true." But in response to the question, "How do you know it works," an unsophisticated contextualist will be tempted to answer by verbal statements about the impact of the statement. This is fine for a while as helpful information is likely to be obtained but the ultimate flaw in this approach is that it appeals to a correspondence-based theory of truth, not to a pragmatic one. It is as if the analyst is trying to answer the question by saying "I know because it *really* has this impact." That is correspondence, not successful working.

Some use "ontology' to refer merely to an explicit specification of concepts to be used in a domain, and the relationship between then. If that is all that is meant by the term, there is no necessary conflict with contextualism. If, however, one means the more traditional philosophical definition of what categories exist or can be said to exist in the world and the correspondence between analyses of the world and these categories, then there is a major conflict caused by the decontextualized truth criterion being employed. As Barnes-Holmes (2000) put it, "if the scientific activity of the behavioral pragmatist is the product of a behavioral history, then he or she can never claim to have found an ontological truth, because a different or more extended history may have produced a different truth" (p. 198).

If something works, pragmatically it ultimately rises above purely verbal knowledge. If science discovers a new food source, a full belly helps to prove its truth; if a cure for a deadly disease is found, its truth partly becomes evident through the breath, look, or smile of one who is cured. There is nothing dualistic about nonverbal workability but it is silent about the verbal issue of reality.

Evolutionists try to avoid the implication of an evolutionary epistemology by failing to apply their own concepts to themselves. Campbell (1959), conducting a detailed analysis of how organisms come to know, specifically drew a line there: "no effort is made to justify 'my own' knowledge processes" (p. 157). He was well aware of the inconsistency but justified it on the grounds that it avoided solipsism (p. 157). Nearly 30 years later (1987) he acknowledged that a comprehensive pragmatist position is implied by a consistent application of evolutionary principles. The same dodge has been attempted by pragmatic philosophers but in every case it inserts contradictory assumptions into contextualism (e.g., see Barnes-Holmes, 2000, and his detailed criticism of the dodge attempted by Quine, 1974; for additional discussion on this point see Hayes and Long, 2013).

In this and every other area we have examined,

> The core analytic assumptions of the philosophy of science underlying CBS are merely the assumptions implicit in variation and selective retention, as modified by the verbal purpose established by RFT. Truth is merely what works, but scientists are free to say, "Works toward what?" when considering their own verbal practices because that sets the criteria for selection. (Hayes & Long, 2013, p. 21)

In this context we see no advantage in failing to be thoroughgoing about the assumptions underlying CBS, even if an a-ontological position is implied.

Implications of Functional Contextualism for Other Areas of Science

It is clear that functional contextualism originated in psychology. Yet scientists working in any area could choose to adopt a goal of prediction and influence with precision, scope, and depth. Next we describe what value that might have for many areas of human sciences.

Evolution

Above we noted the influence of evolutionary theory on the development of pragmatism. There are several specific links between evolutionary thinking and functional contextualism (Wilson et al., 2014). As we suggested, contextualist thinking was influenced by the emphasis in evolutionary theory on the outcome or success of any given phenotype.

Evolutionary thinking focuses on understanding phenomena in terms of variation and selective retention (Wilson et al., 2014). Implicitly, the goal of an evolutionary analysis is to identify relations between phenotypes and the environmental variables that select phenotypes. This is consistent with the functional contextualist perspective.

Would the explicit adoption of the functional contextualist framework contribute to evolutionary science?

Flexible units. As noted in our discussion of Skinner's concept of the operant, the functional contextualist approach encourages the creation of concepts based on their usefulness for prediction and influence. Until very recently, however, evolutionary thinking has been dominated by gene-centric approach, such as a focus on the "selfish gene" (Dawkins, 1976) or insistence that selection only takes place at the level of genes. This lack of flexibility about the kinds of units that could be studied in terms of variation and selection ruled out consideration of selection of other units. The possibility that selection could happen at the group level was obscured, for example: it has taken 40 years for this type of selection to become more acceptable as a scientific target (Sober & Wilson, 1999). The restriction over multilevel selection has impeded productive analysis of the development of altruism, cooperation not associated with kin selection, and the evolution of human organizations, including the entire capitalist system (e.g., Biglan & Cody, 2013).

Application. The practical implications of evolutionary thinking might also be more fully explored if functional contextualism were explicit. It is understandable that evolutionists have hesitated to address the implications of evolution for human well-being, given the excesses of the eugenics movement and related thinking about social Darwinism (Ramsden, 2006). But a comprehensive focus on prediction and influence in variation and selection at multiple levels from genetic and epigenetic selection through behavior, symbolic processes, and organizations, provides a more precise understanding of selection at all of these levels. And, it has the potential to exploit knowledge about selecting consequences to influence further evolution in the interest of human well-being (Wilson et al., 2014). This evolution can include the selection of safeguards against human exploitation (Biglan, 1995).

The productive interplay in multilevel and multidimensional selectionist analyses. As flexible multilevel and multidimensional analyses have proceeded, some interesting aspects of the interplay among these levels and dimensions have been suggested. In particular, it now seems quite possible that behavioral evolution influenced genetic evolution. Specifically, it has been suggested that the Cambrian explosion, which involved sudden and massive increases in speciation, may have been due to the evolution of the ability of organisms to have their behavior selected by its consequences (Ginsburg & Jablonka, 2010; Schneider, 2012). The theory is that once environmental consequences could shape organisms' behavior, the range of environments in which a species could survive expanded. But once organisms gained advantages in a particular environment through their ability to adapt behavior, variants of a species whose behavior was selected by operant consequences in a given environment could evolve genetic adaptations that gave them increasingly better chances of surviving. That is, operant conditioning may have provided the scaffolding enabling the subsequent progression of genetic evolution.

Functional contextualism and evolutionary psychology. Wilson et al. (2014) criticized the theory of massive modularity that has dominated evolutionary psychology. According to this view, the primary way in which evolution has influenced human behavior is in the selection of cognitive "modules" that account for human capacities such as language. From that perspective, human behavior is pretty much the result of evolved capacities that are invariant across people and situations; the behavior of the individual in a given situation is a function of these invariant capacities.

Wilson et al. (2014) argue that this view ignores the evidence that behavior, including symbolic processes, varies in a given situation and is selected by consequences in that situation. They compare these two views to the innate and adaptive components of the immune system. For some pathogens, we have evolved a system of macrophages that defend against threats to the organism that have been common for thousands of years. However, the immune system also has an adaptive component that itself is an evolutionary system for selecting and reproducing as many as 100 million antibodies that the macrophages do not immediately eliminate. Similarly, human behavior, including symbolic processes, can involve the genetically evolved modular capacity to have behavior selected by immediate consequences – the latter selection process of operant conditioning being analogous to the adaptive component of the immune system.

The functional contextualist strategy is relevant to this analysis. Specifically, while viewing human behavior as a function of the massive modularity of inherited cognitive functions could provide an appealing mechanistic account of human behavior, it does not provide an adequate focus on influencing behavior. Of course it could have turned out that massive modularity was correct, in which case our ability to modify human behavior and cultural evolution would seem rather limited. But the point is that an analysis that is not relentlessly seeking prediction *and influence*, but is instead satisfied with an account that purports to explain behavior, is unlikely to find influences that can be exploited to influence beneficial behavioral and cultural evolution. Wilson et al. (2014) go on to describe numerous examples of beneficial interventions that have been developed as a result of pursuing the possibility that behavior and cultural practices are selected by their consequences.

Organizations

As chapter 22 in this volume indicates, a functional contextualist strategy is already being applied to the study of business and organizations. That work has primarily centered on the ways that organizations and their members can be helped to function more effectively by increasing the psychological flexibility of organization members (e.g., Hayes, Bond, Barnes-Holmes, & Austin, 2006).

What has received less attention is the evolutionary process by which the practices of organizations are selected by consequences in the organization's environment. Chapter 24 in this volume presents a functional contextualist analysis of the evolution of organizations as a function of selection by the economic consequences of their practices. However, empirical analyses of these relationships are currently lacking. Given the massive impact of for-profit corporations on the well-being of humans (e.g., Biglan, 2011; Biglan & Cody, 2013; Biglan & Embry, 2013), analyses of contingencies that select problematic versus beneficial practices are badly needed. Only by pinpointing the consequences that select corporate practices can we develop policies to influence these practices. In a sense it is widely understood that in a capitalist system economic consequences are critical to for-profit entities. But when the Chief Justice of the Supreme Court avers that unlimited campaign contributions to candidates do not influence the actions of elected officials (*McCutcheon v. Federal Election Commission*, 2014), it is clear that, at least in the United States, we are far from an effective analysis of capitalism.

Public Health

Broadly conceived, public health focuses on reducing the incidence and prevalence of disease. In addition to targeting physical illnesses, it targets so-called mental illness and any behavior or environmental condition that can influence physical or psychological well-being. Public health is already a fairly pragmatic field. Public health researchers and advocates readily adopt programs, policies, and practices that affect incidence and prevalence.

Would its explicit embrace of functional contextualism enhance its effectiveness? In this case there may be mutual benefits from consilience between functional contextualism and public health. Thus far, functional contextualists have worked mostly on the analysis of individual behavior. Skinner once observed:

> It is true that we could trace human behavior not only to the physical conditions which shape and maintain it but also to the causes of those conditions and the causes of those causes, almost ad infinitum but we need take analysis only to the point at which "effective action can be taken." (1974, p. 210)

However, as the proximal environmental conditions that shape human behavior have become increasingly clear, it becomes important to take effective action to alter proximal conditions that harm human well-being. For example, it is now well established that coercive social interactions in families influence the development of aggressive social behavior and a host of related problems (Dishion & Snyder, in press). And it is also clear that family poverty is a risk factor for coercive family interactions (e.g., Conger, Patterson, & Ge, 1995). Thus, a thoroughly effective effort to prevent aggressive social behavior and related problems requires that we reduce family poverty in order to reduce the *prevalence* of coercive interactions in families.

The public health community is beginning to target this problem. However, far more attention goes to poverty's impact on well-being than to policies that affect poverty and the strategies that might lead to changing those policies (e.g., Brooks-Gunn, Duncan, & Aber, 1997; Duncan & Murnane, 2011). To affect poverty we need a functional contextual analysis of policies that contribute to it and the variables that influence adoption and maintenance of policies affecting poverty. In particular, a selectionist analysis of the way in which corporate practices that exacerbate poverty are selected by profits would point to policies that could influence whether corporations continue to advocate for policies harmful to families (e.g., Biglan & Cody, 2013; Biglan & Embry, 2013).

Economics

Could functional contextualism also strengthen the degree to which economics contributes to human well-being? One way it could do so would be to sharpen the focus of economists on identifying manipulable variables and encourage experimental analyses of the impact of those variables. Behavioral economics is already doing that but macroeconomic research tends to focus only on prediction. Interrupted time series designs may often be possible. For example, more precise estimates of the impact of minimum wage on employment could be obtained through natural experiments in which state and local implementation of minimum wage laws are evaluated in terms of their impact on family income and unemployment, through comparisons of the time series in locations that do and do not implement increases in the minimum wage. The recent interest in applying evolutionary theory to economics provides an opening to such analyses via a coherent contextualistic approach (Wilson, Gowdy, & Rosser, 2013).

Dissemination and Implementation Research

As the corpus of evidence-based prevention and treatment programs has grown, sectors of the behavioral science community have begun to turn to the problem of how these interventions can be widely and effectively disseminated (Glasgow, 2008; Glasgow, Vogt, & Boles, 1999). One hope has been that empirically based strategies would be identified that would guide the dissemination and implementation of programs. Thus far, progress has been slow. Space constraints do not permit a thorough discussion of research in this area or of the complexities making this a daunting task. However, a functional contextualist perspective does suggest an approach to this research that could increase the chances of progress.

Inspired by the success of randomized trials in identifying interventions that affect targeted outcomes, it is natural to expect to use randomized trials to develop effective dissemination and implementation strategies. But an accurate history of the development of treatment and prevention strategies would show that these strategies emerged from considerable work with individuals that involved learning how to change the context for a specific behavior. Randomized trials commenced only when we had generalizable principles that could be tested with multiple cases.

As Glasgow (2008) has argued, our knowledge of how to get individuals and organizations to adopt evidence-based interventions is sufficiently crude in most cases that we are not yet ready to submit implementation strategies to randomized trials. We would do better to study the individual provider organization and gain an understanding of the functional influences on practices. Such work may lack the prestige of randomized trials, but it may be essential for gaining an understanding of the major influences on adoption and implementation.

Recall that contextualists begin with the unique act-in-context. That would seem to be an important starting place for this problem. Consider the diversity of treatment and preventive interventions to be disseminated, the range of individuals and organizations that would be implementing them, the variety of ways in which such interventions would be funded. How likely is it that we can begin with a set of prescriptions that would work for this enormous diversity of cases? And consider multiple levels which must be dealt with – from the individual up to the corporation.

A more productive strategy may be to treat each case as unique, search for the factors that might be manipulated to predict and influence implementation, and test strategies using interrupted time series experiments (Biglan, Ary, & Wagenaar, 2000).

Cultural Evolution

Ultimately the human sciences will contribute to human well-being by influencing the further evolution of societies (Wilson et al., 2014). In the past 50 years, we have learned more about the factors that influence behavior and health than was learned in the whole of human history before this time (Biglan, 2015). Most of what we have learned involves the way that families, schools, workplaces, and media affect behavior. This knowledge is slowly disseminating through societies, largely because of the spread of evidence-based programs, policies, and practices. The result should be an increase in the prevalence of nurturing families, schools, workplaces, and communities and thus a reduction in the incidence and prevalence of antisocial behavior and related problems such as drug abuse, early childbearing, depression, and even cardiovascular disease (Biglan, Flay, Embry, & Sandler, 2012). As stated above, this progress is largely due to the fact that behavioral scientists have searched for manipulable variables affecting development.

Further progress depends to a great extent on identifying manipulable variables that affect the adoption, implementation, and maintenance of existing evidence-based practices. It also depends upon functional contextualist analyses of the factors influencing practices of the larger system of corporate, governmental, and nongovernmental organizations (e.g., Biglan & Embry, 2013).

Functional Contextualism and Human Values

It is often said that science contains no values (Allchin, 1988). For many scientists, science produces facts that cannot be translated into values. From this standpoint, behavioral scientists cannot say how people should behave; they can tell us only what conditions influence people to behave in certain ways. When taken to the extreme, this view can lead to behavioral scientists remaining mute regarding the values their society might embrace and to be unwilling, as scientists, to advocate for particular values.

Sam Harris (2011) has criticized this view. He argues that believing science has no implications for our values has led many educated people to conclude we should accept virtually any behavioral or cultural practice. He argues that science can tell us "what we *should* do and *should* want – and therefore what *other people* should do and should want in order to live the best lives possible" (2011, p. 27). He claims that a concern for human well-being "is the only intelligible basis for morality and values" (pp. 27–28) and that "'morality'… really relates to the intentions and behaviors that affect the well-being of conscious creatures" (p. 32).

His position is an interesting one. Judging from other aspects of his writings, Harris would seem to reject the a-ontological position functional contextualism leads to. For example, Harris insists there is no God, whereas a functional contextualist would argue that talk about the existence of God is situated behavior that might be evaluated in terms of its contribution to prediction and influence. With respect to values, functional contextualists would argue (or acknowledge) that their choice to pursue prediction and influence is not a choice dictated by scientific findings. Indeed choosing this goal is foundational to engaging in the scientific activity of functional contextualists.

The difference between these two positions is subtle but important. If the insistence that there is no God is made on ontological grounds – as an issue of existence – then it is inconsistent with pragmatism. But a wide variety of values can be advocated on pragmatic grounds, once even a single value is embraced.

Functional contextualists have examined this issue as it applied to themselves. From a functional contextualist perspective at least two values are built into functional contextual science. Hayes (2006) notes that, at a minimum, functional contextualists embrace the value of prediction and influence. As with all ultimate goals in pragmatism, this choice cannot be defended. It is simply what a community of investigators has chosen to pursue. As any form of contextualism cannot proceed without clarity about the goals of the analysis, this choice suggests something larger that makes it important: the recognition that goals are fundamental to pragmatism. This means that not only do functional contextualists value their specific goals, they value valuing itself. Thus, functional contextualists have two explicit values: valuing values and valuing scientific knowing, defined in terms of prediction and influence with precision, scope, and depth.

From there, additional values spring up empirically. Hayes provides an example: If physicians value health, they will value clean water, simply because there is no way to be healthy without it. In the same way, CBS research itself suggests that psychological flexibility is a kind of "psychological clean water."

Psychological flexibility is defined as changing or persisting in behavior to serve chosen values, based on what the situation affords. "Based on what the situation affords" means "given the prevailing contingencies" and refers to the situated nature of effective action. Said another way, psychological flexibility is a kind of effectiveness: one that is value focused and situated.

Once we embrace the importance of values and prediction-and-influence, the effectiveness inherent in psychological flexibility makes the specific skills that enable psychological flexibility into kinds of implicit values on empirical grounds (Hayes, 2006). They are ongoing qualities of patterns of action that foster and enable values. For example, acceptance and defusion seem pivotal in promoting people's contact with their present experience and in reducing the degree to which literal, temporal, and evaluative language overrides responding to the contingencies in the present moment (what the situation affords). Increasingly, evidence shows that people who cannot accept their thoughts and feelings, and who are unable to get out from under the influence of their thoughts and feelings over their actions, are less likely to act in the service of their values (Bond et al., 2011). Hayes (2006) suggests that, by embracing the value of being psychologically flexible (i.e., living consistently within a set of chosen values), we will then by nature value acceptance and defusion.

Taking an accepting, nonjudgmental approach to your own life means taking a kinder and more loving stance toward oneself. For example, if people have many negative evaluations of themselves, acceptance and defusion imply that they will view these evaluations as evaluations only, not as reality, and will accept that they have those evaluations but they don't struggle to avoid them and indeed view having these evaluations with compassion for themselves.

Acceptance and compassion have always been defining features of love in the most general *agape* sense of that term. Thus, love emerges as an implicit value in the work of functional contextualists who have developed acceptance and commitment therapy (see Part IV of this volume). This is not because love is a scientific or philosophical goal a priori in functional contextualism but because on empirical and conceptual grounds we find it is foundational for effective psychological functioning.

RFT and ACT research extends that perspective socially but demonstrates the utility of thinking about the sense of self having three facets: the conceptualized self, self as an ongoing process of knowing, and a transcendent sense of self (Hayes, Barnes-Holmes, & Roche, 2001). The transcendent sense of self emerges in part from seeing that you observe from a consistent context, namely I/HERE/NOW. Hayes (1984) argued that this sense of self results from the social demand to make verbal reports based on a self-perspective which over time leads to a transcendent quality because perspective-taking is a context of reporting, it is not itself the typical object of reporting. Hayes (1984) suggested that a context of perspective-taking lines up well with the traditional qualities said to result from a sense of spirituality.

This in turn does two things. First, spirituality becomes an implicit value in the work of functional contextualists because on empirical and conceptual grounds it appears to be foundational for psychological flexibility. Acceptance and defusion require this sense of self; from this perspective one can look at, rather than through, one's thoughts and feelings and can defuse from them: This sense of self is necessary for taking a loving and kind stance towards oneself.

Second, research on perspective-taking suggests that for humans to have a perspective on their own experience they must have a perspective on others' experiences. The developing person learning to abstract I/HERE/NOW must do so in the context of discriminating that others are not here, but there, are often not here now, and are never I. Thus, verbal development also involves learning to see the world from the perspective of others. As a result, self-kindness demands compassion toward others.

CBS research builds on these basic ideas. Three psychological functions empirically underpin the human tendency to care about others (Vilardaga, Estévez, Levin, & Hayes, 2012): perspective-taking, empathy, and psychological flexibility. People with all three of these skills or behavioral tendencies are more likely to care about other people (Vilardaga et al., 2012). Consider each skill in turn. If a person can take the perspective of another, they will see what the other person sees and experiences. In essence they will have some skill in seeing the world from the other person's perspective. By itself, however, this skill could lead to a variety of outcomes. Understanding what another experiences and thinks could be as valuable to a con artist as a loving parent. If, in addition, a person has an empathic response when they perceive what another is feeling (a kind of transformation of function of perspective-taking), they are more likely to experience some of the feelings that the other person is feeling. If empathy is defined simply as having the feelings of the other, it may have a variety of effects. For example, experiencing the extreme distress of another may evoke tremendous distress and avoidance. This is where psychological flexibility – and specifically experiential avoidance – becomes important. If a person is avoidant of feeling this type of distress, their reaction to experiencing another's distress may not be supportive of the other person. For example, they may have the well-documented response of attributing the problem to the behavior of the other person in ways that are consistent with the thesis that "this could never happen to me." However, if they are willing to have whatever feelings come up, they may able to take action to assuage the feelings of the other.

As these elements come into play, thinking shifts from a philosophical perspective to an empirical one. The value of prediction and influence is chosen and implies the importance of valuing values and their achievement. That in turn sets up the importance of psychological flexibility, and the processes that contribute to it. But that in turn, emphasizes the importance – individually and socially – of a kind of spiritual awareness and loving approach. This is an extended example of how functional contextualism begins outside of an empirical system with specific goals that make a pragmatic approach possible, but that choice soon leads to a much larger set of values.

When you couple this line of thinking with emerging evidence about the fundamental importance of nurturing environments for human well-being (Biglan,

2015; Biglan et al., 2012), it is reasonable to conclude that the promotion of psychological flexibility is in the interest of advancing human well-being. If you embrace the goal of prediction-and-influence of human behavior, you are functionally embracing the goals of valuing and success in living those values. From that small beginning a set of concerns emerges that focuses on how to better care for, and indeed love, others, even when in the presence of their distress, and act to care for them because you have become better able to experience the distress that you feel when you are aware of what they feel.

Conclusion

The heart and soul of CBS is functional contextualism. Functional contextualism is an extension and reworking of scientific pragmatism, adding in the importance of stated goals to the deliberate use of variation and selective retention, stating a particular goal that defines this tradition, and then relentlessly applying the result to the analysis of content phenomena and of the analytic process itself. CBS is intensely interested in pragmatic truth linked to its stated goals, *and nothing else*. That is the guiding hand of functional contextualism on this scientific tradition.

References

Ajzen, I., & Fishbein, M. (1980). *Understanding attitudes and predicting social behaviour*. Englewood Cliffs, NJ: Prentice-Hall.

Albarracín, D., Johnson, B. T., Fishbein, M., & Muellerleile, P. A. (2001). *Theories of reasoned action and planned behavior as models of condom use: a meta-analysis*. CHIP Documents, Paper 8. Retrieved from http://digitalcommons.uconn.edu/chip_docs/8

Allchin, D. (1988). Values in science and in science education. In B. J. Fraser and K. G. Tobin (Eds.), *International handbook of science education* (pp. 1083–1092). New York, NY: Kluwer Academic.

Barnes-Holmes, D. (2000). Behavioral pragmatism: no place for reality and truth. *The Behavior Analyst, 23*, 191–202.

Barnes-Holmes, Y., McHugh, L., & Barnes-Holmes, D. (2004). Perspective-taking and theory of mind: A relational frame account. *The Behavior Analyst Today, 5*, 15–25.

Biglan, A. (1987). A behavior-analytic critique of Bandura's self-efficacy theory. *The Behavior Analyst, 10*, 1–15.

Biglan, A. (1995). Choosing a paradigm to guide prevention research and practice. *Drugs and Society, 8*, 149–160.

Biglan, A. (2003). Selection by consequences: One unifying principle for a transdisciplinary science of prevention. *Prevention Science, 4*, 213–232.

Biglan, A. (2011). Corporate externalities: A challenge to the further success of prevention science. *Prevention Science, 12*, 1–11.

Biglan, A. (2015). *The nurture effect: How the science of human behavior can improve our lives and our world*. Oakland, CA: New Harbinger.

Biglan, A., Ary, D., & Wagenaar, A. C. (2000). The value of interrupted time-series experiments for community intervention research. *Prevention Science, 1*, 31–49.

Biglan, A., & Cody, C. (2013). Integrating the human sciences to evolve effective policies. *Journal of Economic Behavior & Organization, 90*, S152–S162.

Biglan, A., & Embry, D. D. (2013). A framework for intentional cultural change. *Journal of Contextual Behavioral Science, 2*, 95–104.

Biglan, A., Flay, B. R., Embry, D. D., & Sandler, I. N. (2012). The critical role of nurturing environments for promoting human well-being. *American Psychologist, 67*, 257–271.

Biglan, A., & Hayes, S. C. (1996). Should the behavioral sciences become more pragmatic? The case for functional contextualism in research on human behavior. *Applied and Preventive Psychology, 5*, 47–57.

Bond, F. W., Hayes, S. C., Baer, R. A., Carpenter, K. C., Guenole, N., Orcutt, H. K., … Zettle, R. D. (2011). Preliminary psychometric properties of the Acceptance and Action Questionnaire – II: A revised measure of psychological flexibility and acceptance. *Behavior Therapy, 42*, 676–688.

Brooks-Gunn, J., Duncan, G. J., & Aber, J. L. (1997). *Neighborhood poverty. Volume 2: Policy implications in studying neighborhoods.* New York, NY: Russell Sage Foundation.

Campbell, D. T. (1959). Methodological suggestions from a comparative psychology of knowledge processes. *Inquiry, 2*, 152–182.

Campbell, D. T. (1987). Evolutionary epistemology. In G. Radnitzky & W. Bartley (Eds.), *Evolutionary epistemology, rationality, and the sociology of knowledge* (pp. 48–89). La Salle, IL: Open Court.

Coleman, K., & Wilson, D. S. (1998). Shyness and boldness in pumpkinseed sunfish: Individual differences are context-specific. *Animal Behaviour, 56*, 927–936.

Conger, R. D., Patterson, G. R., & Ge, X. (1995). It takes two to replicate: A mediational model for the impact of parents' stress on adolescent adjustment. *Child Development, 66*, 80–97.

Dawkins, R. (1976). *The selfish gene.* New York, NY: Oxford University Press.

Dishion, T. J., & Snyder, J. (Eds.). (in press). *Handbook on coercive relationship dynamics.* New York, NY: Oxford University Press.

Dougher, M. J., Goldstein, D., & Leight, K. A. (1987). Induced anxiety and pain. *Journal of Anxiety Disorders, 1*, 259–264.

Duncan, G. J., & Murnane, R. (2011). *Whither opportunity? Rising inequality, schools, and children's life chances.* New York, NY: Russell Sage Foundation.

Embry, D. D. (2002). The Good Behavior Game: A best practice candidate as a universal behavioral vaccine. *Clinical Child and Family Psychology Review, 5*, 273–297.

Fishbein, M. (1979). A theory of reasoned action: Some applications and implications. *Nebraska Symposium on Motivation, 27*, 65–116.

Gifford, E. V., & Hayes, S. C. (1999). Functional contextualism: A pragmatic philosophy for behavioral science. In W. O'Donohue & R. Kitchener (Eds.), *Handbook of behaviorism* (pp. 285–327). San Diego, CA: Academic Press.

Gifford, E. V., Kohlenberg, B. S., Hayes, S. C., Antonuccio, D. O., Piasecki, M. M., Rasmussen-Hall, M. L., & Palm, K. M. (2004). Applying a functional acceptance based model to smoking cessation: An initial trial of acceptance and commitment therapy. *Behavior Therapy, 35*, 689–705.

Ginsburg, S., & Jablonka, E. (2010). The evolution of associative learning: A factor in the Cambrian explosion. *Journal of Theoretical Biology, 266*, 11–20.

Glasgow, R. E. (2008). What types of evidence are most needed to advance behavioral medicine? *Annals of Behavioral Medicine, 35*, 19–25.

Glasgow, R. E., Vogt, T. M., & Boles, S. M. (1999). Evaluating the public health impact of health promotion interventions: The RE-AIM framework. *American Journal of Public Health, 89*, 1322–1327.

Goldberg, L. R. (1990). An alternative "description of personality": The big-five factor structure. *Journal of Personality and Social Psychology, 59*, 1216–1229.

Harris, S. (2011). *The moral landscape: How science can determine human values.* New York, NY: Simon & Schuster.

Hatfield, G. (2002). Psychology, philosophy, and cognitive science: Reflections on the history and philosophy of experimental psychology. *Mind & Language, 17*, 207–232.

Hayes, S. C. (1984). Making sense of spirituality. *Behaviorism, 12*, 99–110.

Hayes, S. C. (1993). Analytic goals and the varieties of scientific contextualism. In S. C. Hayes, L. J. Hayes, H. W. Reese, & T. R. Sarbin (Eds.), *Varieties of scientific contextualism* (pp. 11–27). Reno, NV: Context Press.

Hayes, S. C. (1995). Why cognitions are not causes. *The Behavior Therapist, 18*, 59–60.

Hayes, S. C. (1997). Behavioral epistemology includes nonverbal knowing. In L. J. Hayes & P. M. Ghezzi (Eds.), *Investigations in behavioral epistemology* (pp. 35–43). Reno, NV: Context Press.

Hayes, S. C. (July 2006). *Outline of functional contextualism.* Paper presented at the World Conference on ACT, RFT, and Contextual Behavioral Science, London, England.

Hayes, S. C., Barnes-Holmes, D., & Roche, B. (2001). Relational frame theory: A post-Skinnerian account of human language and cognition. New York, NY: Kluwer/Plenum.

Hayes, S. C., Bond, F., Barnes-Holmes, D., & Austin, J. (Eds.). (2006). *Acceptance and mindfulness at work: Acceptance and commitment therapy, relational frame theory, and organizational behavior management.* Binghamton, NY: Haworth.

Hayes, S. C., Hayes, L. J., & Reese, H. W. (1988). Finding the philosophical core: a review of Stephen C. Pepper's *World hypotheses: A study in evidence. Journal of the Experimental Analysis of Behavior, 50*, 97–111.

Hayes, S. C., Hayes, L. J., Reese, H. W., & Sarbin, T. R. (Eds.). (1993). *Varieties of scientific contextualism.* Oakland, CA: Context Press/New Harbinger.

Hayes, S. C., & Long, D. (2013). Contextual behavioral science, evolution, and scientific epistemology. In B. Roche & S. Dymond (Eds.). *Advances in relational frame theory: Research and application* (pp. 5–26). Oakland, CA: New Harbinger/Context Press.

Hayes, S. C., Luoma, J. B., Bond, F. W., Masuda, A., & Lillis, J. (2006). Acceptance and commitment therapy: Model, processes and outcomes. *Behaviour Research and Therapy, 44*, 1–25.

Hayes, S. C., & Wilson, K. G. (1995). The role of cognition in complex human behavior: A contextualistic perspective. *Journal of Behavior Therapy and Experimental Psychiatry, 26*, 241–248.

Jablonka, E., & Lamb, M. J. (2006). *Evolution in four dimensions: Genetic, epigenetic, behavioral, and symbolic variation in the history of life.* Cambridge, MA: MIT Press.

James, W. (1981). *Pragmatism.* Indianapolis, IN: Hackett. (Original work published 1907).

Johnston, J. M., & Pennypacker, H. S. (1993). *Strategies and tactics of behavioral research.* New York, NY: Erlbaum.

Komro, K. A., Flay, B. R., Biglan, A., & The Promise Neighborhoods Research Consortium (2011). Creating nurturing environments: A science-based framework for promoting child health and development within high-poverty neighborhoods. *Clinical Child and Family Psychology Review, 14*, 111–134.

Lapierre, L. M., & Hackett, R. D. (2007). Trait conscientiousness, leader-member exchange, job satisfaction and organizational citizenship behaviour: A test of an integrative model. *Journal of Occupational and Organizational Psychology, 80*, 539–554.

Lochman, J. E., & Dodge, K. A. (1994). Social-cognitive processes of severely violent, moderately aggressive, and nonaggressive boys. *Journal of Consulting and Clinical Psychology, 62*, 366–374.

McCutcheon v. Federal Election Commission. 572 U.S. Supreme Court (2014).

McHugh, L., & Stewart, I. (2012). *The self and perspective taking: contributions and applications from modern behavioral science.* Oakland, CA: New Harbinger.

Menand, L. (2001). *The metaphysical club.* New York, NY: Macmillan.

National Cancer Institute (2008). *The role of the media in promoting and reducing tobacco use.* Tobacco Control Monograph No. 19 (Vol. NIH Pub. No. 07-6242). Bethesda, MD: U.S.

Department of Health and Human Services, National Institutes of Health, National Cancer Institute.

National Research Council & Institute of Medicine (2009). *Preventing mental, emotional, and behavioral disorders among young people: progress and possibilities.* Committee on Prevention of Mental Disorders and Substance Abuse among Children, Youth, and Young Adults: Research Advances and Promising Interventions. Washington, DC: The National Academies Press.

Peirce, C. S. (1983). How to make our ideas clear (selected excerpts). In M. White (Ed.), *The age of analysis: 20th century philosophers* (pp. 143–153). New York, NY: Meridian. (Original work published 1878).

Premack, D., & Woodruff, G. (1978). Does the chimpanzee have a theory of mind? *Behavioral and Brain Sciences, 1*, 515–526.

Quine, W. V. (1974). *The roots of reference.* La Salle, IL: Open Court.

Ramsden, E. (2006). *Confronting the stigma of perfection: Genetic demography, diversity and the quest for a democratic eugenics in the post-war United States.* Working Papers on the Nature of Evidence: How Well Do "Facts" Travel? No. 12/06. London, England: London School of Economics.

Schneider, S. M. (2012). *The science of consequences: How they affect genes, change the brain, and impact our world.* Amherst, NY: Prometheus Books.

Skinner, B. F. (1935). The generic nature of the concepts of stimulus and response. *The Journal of General Psychology, 12*, 40–65.

Skinner, B. F. (1945). The operational analysis of psychological terms. *Psychological Review, 52*, 270–276.

Skinner, B. F. (1953). *Science and human behavior.* New York, NY: Simon & Schuster.

Skinner, B. F. (1957). *Verbal behavior.* New York, NY: Appleton-Century-Crofts.

Skinner, B. F. (1974). *About behaviorism.* New York, NY: Random House.

Skinner, B. F. (1999). In *Cumulative Record.* V. G. Laties and A. C. Catania (Eds.). Acton, MA: Copley. (Original work published 1935).

Smith, L. D. (1986). *Behaviorism and logical positivism: a reassessment of the alliance.* Stanford, CA: Stanford University Press.

Sober, E., & Wilson, D. S. (Eds.). (1999). *Unto others: The evolution and psychology of unselfish behavior.* Boston, MA: Harvard University Press.

Vilardaga, R., Estévez, A., Levin, M. E., & Hayes, S. C. (2012). Deictic relational responding, empathy, and experiential avoidance as predictors of social anhedonia: Further contributions from relational frame theory. *The Psychological Record, 62*, 409–432.

Volkow, N. D., & Skolnick, P. (2012). New medications for substance use disorders: Challenges and opportunities. *Neuropsychopharmacology, 37*, 290–292.

Watson, J. B. (1924). *Behaviorism.* New York, NY: Peoples Institute.

Webb, T., Joseph, J., Yardley, L., & Michie, S. (2010). Using the internet to promote health behavior change: A systematic review and meta-analysis of the impact of theoretical basis, use of behavior change techniques, and mode of delivery on efficacy. *Journal of Medical Internet Research, 12*, e4.

Wiegand, D. M., & Geller, E. S. (2005). Connecting positive psychology and organizational behavior management: Achievement motivation and the power of positive reinforcement. *Journal of Organizational Behavior Management, 24*, 3–25.

Wilson, D. S. (2007). *Evolution for everyone: How Darwin's theory can change the way we think about our lives.* New York, NY: Delacorte Press.

Wilson, D. S., Gowdy, J. M., & Rosser, J. B. (Eds.). (2013). Evolution as a general theoretical framework for economics and public policy (Special issue). *Journal of Economics and Behavioral Organization, 90*.

Wilson, D. S., Hayes, S. C., Biglan, A., & Embry, D. D. (2014). Evolving the future: Toward a science of intentional change. *Behavioral and Brain Sciences, 37*, 395–416.

5

Contextual Behavioral Science
Holding Terms Lightly
Kelly G. Wilson

Terms are merely ways of speaking. If I use the term "salt" at the dinner table in a request, it solves the problem of too little salt on my meal because someone at the other end of the table passes me the salt – not the pepper, not the potatoes, not the salad. The salt. Using the word "salt" at the dinner table, in conjunction with a generic form of request, such as "Pass the _____, please" organizes my dinner mates' behavior in a way that gets me the salt and allows us to all get along in a congenial fashion.

Scientific terms, and systems of terms, are not different than that in kind. Skinner, in *About Behaviorism*, describes scientific theories as "a corpus of rules for effective action, and there is a special sense in which it could be 'true' if it yields the most effective action possible" (1974, p. 235). Terms are components of theories that can be evaluated in light of their efficacy in organizing the behavior of scientists towards their specified goals. Within CBS, truth is an incoherent concept considered independently of effective action toward some specified goal.

Precision and Scope in CBS

Scientific terms do differ from ordinary speech in several regards. Whereas ordinary speech can be very precise, it often is not. For example, "pass the salt" is quite precise. But other examples are far less so. If you were to ask a friend why he did not come to yoga yesterday, he might reply "I didn't feel like it." The conditions that precipitated "not feeling like it" and actually not coming are entirely vague. One could imagine a thousand scenarios that might precipitate this outcome, an argument with a spouse, an illness, an injury, weariness from work, and so on. Scientific ways of speaking require a higher level of precision. The reasons are several. Scientific ways of speaking are intended to generate general principles, not just descriptions of one particular event. The doing of science relies heavily on replicability of findings. Thus, the language which I use to describe an experiment must be sufficiently precise that someone else could, in principle, reproduce the conditions I organized and thereby reproduce the effects I found.

The Wiley Handbook of Contextual Behavioral Science, First Edition. Edited by Robert D. Zettle, Steven C. Hayes, Dermot Barnes-Holmes, and Anthony Biglan.

Experimental science is not about singular events, but instead about classes of events. That was one of the starting points of behavior analysis (Skinner, 1935) and it means that some degree of scope is necessary in terms and systems of terms. To the extent that we can create systems of terms that help us to interact effectively with a broader range of phenomena, while retaining some level of precision, we ought to prefer such terms. The principle of parsimony suggests that we ought not to multiply terms unnecessarily. Given two theoretical accounts of equivalent explanatory force, we ought to prefer the simpler account. The addition of terms must, as the pragmatists suggest, cash out in the form of broader, more precise, and more useful explanations.

There is a tension between complexity and level of explanatory force. We prefer simpler analyses, but not so much so that we will give up important areas of inquiry by our tight hold on the simplicity of theoretical formulation. Likewise, there is often a tension between precision and scope. If we narrow our range of inquiry, precision is often more easily obtainable. A bread recipe is highly precise but it applies to a tiny range of phenomena. Big, broadly applicable, internally coherent theoretical systems are inherently more challenging than theories of narrow bands of phenomena. For example, generating a highly precise theory of memory and recall is a simpler task than the one set for itself by contextual behavioral science, which proposes "the development of a coherent and progressive science of human action that is more adequate to the challenges of the human condition" (Association for Contextual Behavioral Science, 2014, n.p.). Taking on such a broad challenge is uncommon, but not unheard of in the history of psychology.

CBS was in many regards birthed in two major professional organizations. The initial debates around the underlying philosophy of science occurred at the Association for Behavior Analysis International (ABAI). Not only were underlying philosophical views of some ABAI members challenged but, simultaneously, a crop of new terms were introduced. Likewise, early presentations of acceptance and commitment therapy at the then Association for the Advancement of Behavior Therapy raised considerable controversy. These were highly developed professional and scientific organizations that already had well-established sets of theoretical terms. What could provide justification for the introduction of new terms? Skepticism about the introduction of new terms is healthy, but exploring the limits of systems is likewise healthy.

A CBS Metaphor from the History of Acceptance and Commitment Therapy

Acceptance and commitment therapy is the most researched and tested application of contextual behavioral science. But ACT was not always called ACT. It was originally called *comprehensive distancing*. It was a nice enough name, but it had a problem: near universal misunderstanding. The name seemed to imply that we should take a step back from difficult thoughts and emotions in order to get away from them or perhaps to get a more "realistic" view.

However, neither avoidance nor objectivity was the purpose of distancing in proto-ACT. Back then, I had to use a metaphor to explain the intended meaning. If I held my hand pressed tightly to my face covering my eyes, and then described hands to you, I would say that they are black and stretch out in all directions as far as the eye can see. Hands exert pressure on the face. And that is what hands are like. If I were to move my hand a dozen inches from my face, I could describe it again: pink and white skin with varying patterns, tendons in a radial pattern across the back, lumpy meandering blue tubes running just beneath the skin, five wiggly articulated fingers, one set opposed to the others, each with a hard nail on one side at the tip and a richly articulated swirling pattern on the skin of the other side, and, by the way, I have two of them connected to my arms and to me!

The distance from the hand does not take me out of contact with the hand. In fact, this change in perspective, this stepping back, allows a much fuller, richer contact with the hand. I could now do things with both my hands and my eyes that were impossible before. I might also see how some aspects of the hand were really artifacts of the press of the hand against my face – blackness stretching out indefinitely in all directions. And I would not just learn more about my hand, but also about myself, about the world surrounding that hand, and, perhaps, a meta-lesson about the power of multiple perspectives that can vastly change understanding.

In the best of worlds, we might recognize that this possibility lurks in each and everything about which we are completely certain. This is not to say that one view, up close, is a poorer or less important view, or that the stepped-back view is somehow privileged. The lesson of distancing is that we should hold all of our conclusions lightly and remain open to other ways of seeing so that we can select the ways of seeing that serve different purposes at different times. If we want to screen out a very bright light, some version of a hand, up close, will solve the problem nicely. If I want to touch the face of a child, the hand extended suits my purpose. Comprehensive distancing was abandoned years ago as a name because it needed to be explained. And a name that requires a page to explain is ultimately a poor name.

In ACT, we step back from thoughts to see them in a more articulated way, to see their connections to other patterns of action, how they fit and don't fit, how they function in our lived experience. For example, a thought like "I am socially awkward and should minimize talking to people at the party." This rule, followed, might function to momentarily solve the problem of anxiety, but might prevent improvement in the problem of few social relations – success in one problem-solving context, failure in another.

Taking a Step Back from Skinner

In a certain sense the entire CBS theoretical and philosophical project was part of a step back from our most central and immediate historical intellectual antecedent, B. F. Skinner's radical behaviorism. It was not a step back to distance us from Skinner or his enormous contribution. Rather, it was a step back to view that body of work through a philosophical and metatheoretical lens. In particular, we looked at radical behaviorism as a form of contextualism (Hayes, Hayes, & Reese, 1988; Pepper, 1942).

In 1945 Skinner contributed a paper to a symposium on operationism called "An Operational Analysis of Psychological Terms" (Skinner, 1945). This paper looms large among Skinnerians and is often referred to simply as "The '45 Paper." The paper is worthy of such reverence. If you understand the analysis of "meaning" Skinner takes in the '45 paper, you can readily understand the functional contextual analysis he is making in books like *Verbal Behavior* (1957), *About Behaviorism* (1974) and *Beyond Freedom and Dignity* (1971), which have been frequently and grossly misunderstood.

What was radical about Skinner's 1945 approach to operational analysis was that he applied the same analysis to the behavior of the scientist in the use of psychological terms as he applied to the behaving organism in an experiment. To understand the behavior of scientists, we need to understand the behavior in terms of its functional relation to context. When asked about the appropriate operational definition that captured the meaning of psychological terms Skinner's response was as follows:

> Meanings, contents, and references are to be found among the determiners, not the properties, of a response ... To be consistent the psychologist must deal with his own verbal practices by developing an empirical science of verbal behavior. He cannot, unfortunately, join the logician in defining a definition, for example, as a "rule for the use of a term" (Feigl); he must turn instead to the contingencies of reinforcement which account for the functional relation between a term, as a verbal response, and a given stimulus. This is the "operational basis" for his use of terms; and it is not logic but science. (1945, p. 277)

Skinner proposes here that if we want to specify the meaning of a term, we need to specify the antecedent conditions which occasion the use of the term and the reinforcing contingencies that produced, refined, and maintain that use. Skinner's suggestion, not entirely well received by his more conventional colleagues, was that psychology could make real progress by making functional analyses of its own terminology.

A frequent response to the fuzziness of psychological terms, certainly often attempted in clinical psychology, has been to work ever harder to achieve consistent categorization (see, for example, the *Diagnostic and Statistical Manual for Mental Disorders*) and operational analyses that rely on publicly observable data. However, a contextual view offers an alternative to obsessively constrained categorization. Before we specify the category with excruciating detail, it is worth considering the goodness of the category itself. Within an elemental realist paradigm, cataloguing the world of real things is self-justified by its correspondence to reality. Traditional concepts of measurement and conceptual categorization are based fundamentally on this ontological claim (Borsboom, Mellenbergh, & van Heerden, 2003).

Within a CBS framework, coherent or consistent categorizing and cataloging is insufficient to justify use of a term. We assume that human-derived relational responding is sufficiently flexible that a near infinite number of categories *could* be generated. As soon as we consider the formulation of categories within the context of the goals of the analysis, however, the proliferation of categories is constrained to those that further the purpose of the analysis. Distinctions made that do not further the goals of the analysis are *distinctions without a difference*.

The Fruits of Stepping Back from Skinner

When the nascent CBS movement stepped back from Skinner several features of that work became apparent.

1   There was a clear practical, functional contextual theme running through Skinner's work that could be distinguished from other contextual views (Hayes, 1993) and from the more elemental realist wing of behavior analysis.
2   Within a contextual view, terms are parts derived from the whole. The validity of these abstracted parts, their *truth value*, could only be determined within particular

problem-solving contexts. Truth is local in functional contextualism. Breadth of applicability is not assumed – it is strictly an empirical matter.

3   Skinner's radical behavioral system of terms, while enormously productive in many problem-solving contexts, had been less effective in others.

4   In particular, traditional behavior analysis had made relatively small contributions to the laboratory experimental analysis of human cognition, emotion, and motivation, among other complex human behavioral patterns.

5   The absence of a large contribution by radical behaviorism was particularly visible in the relatively small influence of behavior analysis in applied realms where control of direct-acting contingencies was limited. For example, traditional behavior analysts played a small role in the traditional clinic or counseling center, where psychologists, social workers, and counselors have access to perhaps an hour of the client's week, and virtually no access to contingencies at home, work, and in social settings.

Scientific Generativity across Problem-Solving Contexts

This is not to say that early behavior analytic principles were not powerful. Basic behavioral principles, derived from the laboratory study of animal learning provide an example of a set of theoretical terms that had both tremendous precision and scope.

Consider the following small handful of terms that emerged from operant behavioral labs in the last century: discriminative stimuli, operant responses, consequential stimuli, and establishing operations sufficient to make those consequences effective. Not only did these terms and their investigation produce an enormous body of laboratory-based data, the language of the four-term contingency led very early on to the development of applied theories about human difficulties (e.g., Bijou, 1976). For example, individuals with intellectual disabilities, once thought completely incapable of learning, were demonstrated to be teachable given the proper organization of contingencies (Matson & Andrasik, 1983). This small set of terms led to large bodies of data in both laboratory and in a number of applied settings. The most notable applied contributions were in settings where the persons intervening had a great deal of control over contingencies. In institutions, among children, and in hospital settings, applied behavioral technologies transformed lives and continue to do so.

While respectful of the many contributions to principles of learning terms derived from the laboratory have made, those prolific terms failed to produce an equivalent evidence base in the realm of complex human behavior. Ultimately, the body of evidence, both in the laboratory and in applied settings, decides the fate of scientific theories, not the assertions of theoreticians. In fact, this is a distinguishing feature of science. Authority is not equivalent to truth. Over time, at least, "truth" is determined by the weight of evidence.

Expanding Behavioral Terminology

There has always been recognition within CBS, and radical behaviorism before CBS, of the problem of unconstrained proliferation of terms in psychology. At one extreme, psychology as a whole contains an enormously diverse and diffuse proliferation of terms. The 1930s and 1940s can be thought of as the era of big theories in psychology. Several behavioral schools shared a grand vision for psychology. Some within these theoretically integrated research efforts examined narrow bands of psychological phenomena, such as memory, motivation, and emotion. However, as a group, they were not satisfied with theories that were restricted to these narrow areas. The likes of Clark Hull, Edward Tolman, and B. F. Skinner aspired to big theories that explained all behavior under a coherent integrated framework. The major theorists of the era of big theories were quite interested in philosophy of science and metatheoretical issues that spanned the various sciences (Smith, 1986). As an example, Skinner's 1945 paper was part of a larger symposium that also included original contributions from the experimental psychologist and psychology historian E. G. Boring; Nobel prize-winning physicist P. W. Bridgman; philosopher Herbert Feigl, a member of the Vienna Circle; and Carroll C. Pratt, a scholar of the logic of psychology (Boring, Bridgman, Feigl, Pratt, & Skinner, 1945).

Most of the big behavioral theories collapsed as integrated schools of psychology in the 1950s and 1960s. Researchers continued to run experiments and produce orderly data, to get academic posts, grants, publish, attract students, be well recognized in their subspecialty area, and well regarded at their home institutions. But the big theories of the earlier part of the century ceased to be a central organizing force. What was left in their wake was a fractionated discipline with little ambition to put psychology together as an integrated whole. For most of psychology, big theory ceased even as a self-proclaimed ambition, whereas such ambitions were prominent in the intellectual antecedents of contemporary experimental psychology. Not only were there not many contenders for an integrated psychological theory, there were not even integrated theories of small subspecialties in psychology. For example, there was and still is no integrated theory of memory. Memory is sliced into parts and different theories contend within these fractions of a fraction of the psychological universe, each theory with its own set of psychological terms.

There is an exception among the big theories emerging from the last century. Skinner's radical behaviorism continued, and continues to this day, as a contender for integrated psychological theory. In contrast to the extraordinary proliferation of terms within experimental psychology as a whole, significant segments of the radical behavioral community have resisted the inclusion of new terminology even when current theoretical formulations failed to deliver a substantial evidence base.

Nowhere is this so evident as in the area of verbal behavior. Skinner's system, however, coherent and eloquent, never produced a large and expansive body of experimental evidence. His analysis of verbal behavior was published in its full form in 1957 in *Verbal Behavior*. However, the broadest outlines of his 1957 treatment were apparent as early as the 1945 paper on operationism. The size of the experimental analysis of human behavior, including both laboratory and applied experiments, pales next to the enormous body of work that came from his analysis of the four-term operant contingency. Although Skinner expressed ambition for an analysis that encompassed virtually every area of serious human concern (e.g., Skinner, 1953), the terms he so carefully crafted simply lacked the necessary scope to support a large body of experiments in all of these domains. The bulk of radical behavioral writing in areas of complex human behavior is interpretive, not experimental.

Criteria for Inclusion of New Variables

The Association for Behavioral and Cognitive Therapies (ABCT) was originally called the Association for the Advancement of Behavior Therapy. Behavior therapy emerged from a commitment to "operationally defined learning theory and conformity to well-established experimental paradigms" (Franks & Wilson, 1974, p. 7). When learning theory failed to provide experimentally and clinically prolific ways of speaking about cognitive phenomena, new ways of speaking were created, and "cognitive behavior therapy" (CBT) largely replaced behavior therapy (Beck, Rush, Shaw, & Emery, 1979; Mahoney, 1974; Meichenbaum, 1977), eventually even in the name of the society itself. These new ways of speaking began in clinical theories of cognition, but they soon borrowed from information-processing theories that were based on computers as machine models of human thinking. For example, Beck said that

> Although there have been many definitions of cognitive therapy, I have been most satisfied with the notion that cognitive therapy is best viewed as the application of the cognitive model of a particular disorder with the use of a variety of techniques designed to modify the dysfunctional beliefs and faulty information processing characteristic of each disorder. (Beck, 1993, p. 194)

Most of the developers of these new theories were elemental realists (Hayes, 2004) and thus the criteria they apply to new terms are the ability to marshal evidence for the correspondence between terms and measures of events. Those criteria provide very little brake on the development of new terms and indeed it is not uncommon to hear that CBT has no real commitment to behavioral terms over any other kind.

CBS, as a group, shares the vision of the behavioral theories of the 1930s and 1940s. CBS retains the skepticism of traditional behavior analysis in the addition of terms and sets several criteria for making decisions about adding variables and about letting go of variables. Some are "rules of the game" that are related to the nature of functional contextualism and our underlying philosophy of science. Some, like parsimony, are widely shared with most scientific systems, but workability is the most characteristic. It is the absolute bedrock of CBS. *Whereas elemental realist positions have a basis in the antecedent conditions of the world, the only foundation in CBS is the consequence of our analyses.*

Choose variables that are abstractive analytic. CBS is an abstractive analytic method, as contrasted with a hypothetico-deductive method. In a contextual system, the whole is considered to be primary and parts abstracted from the total event field under observation. Since the variables are abstracted from the whole of that which is observed, both dependent and independent variables are in principle observable (though not necessarily publicly observable). Within behavior analysis, the psychological level of analysis is taken to be the behavior of whole organisms in and with a context, where behavior constitutes the dependent variable of the analysis and the context in which the behavior is situated is the independent variable. There is nothing in CBS that would prevent an analyst from proposing patterns of neurological activities as a dependent variable and the contexts which predict and influence those patterns as the independent variable, but what is found there might need to be reworked at the level of the whole organism. Within CBS one might also reasonably resort to an appeal to variables that are in principle observable but not currently being observed, such as physiological variables or reinforcement histories. However, the best way from a functional contextual point of view to check the workability of all proposed variables is to bring them into the realm of current observation and to show their relevance to dependent outcomes by experimental manipulation (see Wilson, 2001).

So, for example, a behavior pattern might be argued to result from a particular sort of hypothesized reinforcement history, but a demonstration that allows prediction and influence through the creation of such a history is the gold standard for experimental confirmation. Likewise, if we postulated that contextual events impacted behavior that was mediated by some neurobiological change, we would want, straight away, to bring all aspects of the interaction, context, neurobiology, and behavioral outcome into the realm of direct observation, investigation, and, ultimately, experimental analyses. Underspecified or even unspecified hypotheticals are the hiding places of incomplete analyses.

Given the flexibility of human-derived relational responding, there are a myriad of ways that an event field could be parsed and a nearly infinite number of terms that might emerge from such an effort. What restrains the proliferation of terms within contextual behavioral science?

In order to examine these constraints, we need to examine the stated goals of CBS, since the *truth value* of the terms is always related to the goals of the analysis. Because it is, in principle, possible for contextual behavioral science to have virtually any goal, we will take as our starting point the only organizational effort to explicate a goal against which the truth-value of terms could be evaluated. Fortunately, as an organized area of work CBS has been quite clear about its goals:

> Founded in 2005 (incorporated in 2006), the Association for Contextual Behavioral Science (ACBS) is dedicated to the advancement of functional contextual cognitive and behavioral science and practice so as to alleviate human suffering and advance human well being. (Association for Contextual Behavioral Science, 2014)

Scope. The problem of the scope of terms and sets of terms can be thought of as the capacity of a set of terms to effectively organize scientist behavior across many problem-solving contexts. In part, early CBS efforts were a response to the failure of traditional behavior analysis to organize the behavior of scientists with regard to the topic of complex human behavior either in highly controlled laboratory settings or in many clinical and applied settings. In CBS, we should prefer terms with maximal scope. We should prefer sets of terms that allow us to speak, measure, and organize experiments on as broad an array of phenomena as possible, constrained only by the goals of the analysis. A good example from traditional behavior analysis is the principle of reinforcement. The probability of a pattern of responding can be made more or less likely depending upon the consequences that follow the response. The principle of reinforcement has remarkable scope. It has allowed for problem solving across multiple contexts, but, as we have seen, not without limit.

Precision. Precision can be thought of as the lynchpin in understanding the meaning of middle-level terms. Precision in the use of terms, within a CBS system, does not ultimately mean the precision with which a term refers to a phenomenon of interest. Rather, precision refers to the precision with which we can specify antecedents and consequences for the use of the term (see Skinner, 1945). Many of the terms familiar from traditional behavior analysis have high levels of precision, and CBS terms such as those from relational frame theory (RFT) have kept pace. Saying something is an example of a discriminative stimulus or an example of combinatorial mutual entailment can be captured under a relatively tight and reproducible set of antecedents and consequences that represent both necessary and sufficient conditions for the use of the term. Terms used in lay language can be much more challenging. If a friend were to say "I've been down lately," any number of conditions might hold. The person could mean that their physical energy was low. They could mean that they were down financially. Or, they might mean that their mood had been low.

Depth. Depth refers to the coherence of well-developed ways of speaking across fields of analysis. Psychology is such a field but it is embedded in a larger fabric of science. The consilience being explored between CBS and evolution science (Hayes & Sanford, 2014; Wilson et al., 2014) is an example. In this exchange, both behavioral and evolutionary science are enriching one another. Depth can be thought of as a special kind of scope. Just as scope across a range of behavioral areas is pragmatically useful, an increasingly unified fabric of sciences simplifies scientific questions and enables social cooperation across disciplines. Such cooperation makes it more likely that findings in one field can influence and enrich other related disciplines.

Generativity. Generativity has not often been talked about explicitly in CBS writings but it is key to a pragmatic approach. Generativity can be thought of in two senses: a theory can generate a large body of interpretive accounts; a theory can generate a large body of experiments and empirical extensions. Of the two, the second is most important pragmatically speaking. Experiments and empirical extensions are among the most potent scientific tool we possess – we need terms to propel us forward. Although Skinner's four-term contingency analysis had tremendous scope in generating interpretive analyses in the area of complex human behavior, it did not generate a similar body of experimental analyses and empirical extensions. Finding the limit of the ability of a set of terms to generate experiments can be viewed as an indicator of the limits of the usefulness and therefore the truth-value of those terms. If important phenomena lay outside this zone of generated experiments, new terms may be needed in order to expand the scope of the analysis.

Scope, depth, and generativity as a guide to middle-level terms. CBS is at its heart a nonhierarchical view of science. So, for example, a neuroscience understanding of behavior is not more "fundamental" or more "basic" than a behavioral analysis. This feature has a long history in functional views of behavior (Skinner, 1950). In fact, greedy reductionism has been forcefully argued against for many decades on both a logical and practical basis (Jessor, 1958). A more coherent contextual way to understand a neuroscience analysis versus a behavioral analysis is that these are different problem-solving contexts that require different sets of terms.

CBS is a reticulated model of doing science in that particular sense. It would be incorrect to say that basic terms are foundational in a CBS approach. No problem-solving context is foundational. As suggested above, the only foundation in CBS is the consequence of the analysis. Instead, analysts are responsible for the interconnections between knowledge domains and approaches. This responsibility does not come from assuming the primacy of one kind of account over another, but instead comes from the interest in scope and depth as aspects of the truth criteria embraced in CBS.

Middle-level terms are "middle level" in the sense that they are more precise than lay language, but less precise than technical ways of speaking. This difference explains what is "middle" in middle-level terms, but scope, generativity, and depth carry the keys to understanding when and why we might be willing to give up a degree of precision in the service of fostering progress in areas in which a more precise account is either not currently viable, not readily accessible, or not readily understandable within important problem-solving contexts. Middle-level terms orient listeners to important domains in which more precise accounts are not yet fully constructed or understandable – provided such terms are not reified they can foster reticulated theoretical, experimental, and practical development.

Generativity and basic versus applied theories. In a traditional "bottom-up" behavioral approach, basic theories are supposed to generate applied solutions. What is usually unstated is what to do when basic theories are unavailable. The line between basic and applied theories is much more ambiguous from a CBS perspective. In a contextual behavioral approach, theories organize the behavior of scientists, not the world; they are true to the extent that they organize the behavior of scientists for the most effective action possible. That is, theories should allow for the maximum level of prediction and influence with precision, scope, and depth in furtherance of our goals. Although as an entire enterprise CBS is aimed ultimately at the alleviation of human suffering and the promotion of human well-being, particular scientists may be only peripherally involved in science that is directly influential towards those ends.

Some very tightly controlled laboratory research involves patterns of responding that are models for complex human responding, but are topographically very different than usual behaviors in usual settings. For example, in an RFT study, subjects may be asked to link arbitrarily configured visual stimuli with other arbitrary visual stimuli, and subsequently to be tested on the extent to which mutual entailment, combinatorial entailment, and transformation of stimulus function occur (Hayes, Barnes-Holmes, & Roche, 2001). The theoretical terms that organize the training, testing, and evaluation in this very basic science might reasonably be called *basic theory*. However, we need to be cautious about thinking that the "basicness" is a property of the terms or of the theory in which they are embedded. Rather, a good basic theory is a theory that effectively organizes the behavior of scientists within these highly controlled experimental settings. Basic, highly abstracted, highly controlled laboratory studies are a particular problem-solving context.

Sometimes theoretical terms can be developed and refined in highly controlled laboratory settings and then work equally well in other problem-solving contexts. The principle of reinforcement provides an excellent example. The principle of reinforcement has been extraordinarily useful in both the most tightly controlled laboratory settings and also in a number of applied settings. The development of functional analyses and the use of positive reinforcement transformed the care of individuals with intellectual disabilities. In addition, there is a rich history of experimental evidence showing the utility of this concept in many, many applied settings, including education, workplace safety, and addiction treatment, among many others.

Examples like the principle of reinforcement that allow for problem solving across multiple contexts are exemplar principles. In fact, when we find principles that function across contexts it is difficult to say whether the principle is an example of basic or applied science. The ambiguity is enhanced by the fact that some applied settings are able to create extremely high levels of experimental control (Hanley, Iwata, & McCord, 2003). The pragmatic utility of successful bottom-up terms, like reinforcement, has sometimes led to a misunderstanding of the role of theory – as if an account must be bottom-up to be legitimate. From a contextual behavioral point of view the key issue is not how "basic" the theories are upon which applied methods are built. It is how useful particular theories are in their targeted problem-solving contexts, and the degree to which analytic goals are met (e.g., scope, depth, generativity).

New Terms in CBS

In what follows, we will use as case studies two sets of terms within CBS in the light of central CBS philosophical and metatheoretical guidelines to explore the territory laid out above. We will examine the six-process psychological flexibility model, and then will briefly consider relational frame theory, an arguably basic terminological system. Finally, we will discuss a few emerging terminological systems within CBS and their potential to meet CBS theoretical and philosophical challenges.

The Psychological Flexibility Model: Precision, Scope, Depth, and Generativity across Problem-Solving Contexts

The psychological flexibility model is a six-process model that is described on its positive side as a model for psychological growth, development, and effective action. The elements include six interdependent repertoires. These repertoires and the contexts that generate and maintain them include

1 Acceptance processes: Can an individual cultivate an openness to difficult experience in the service of valued living?
2 Defusion processes: Can an individual engage their own verbal products without being inflexibly controlled by them and while remaining sensitive to the impact of behavior on valued patterns of living?
3 Present moment processes: Can an individual bring attention to the current external and internal environment to bear in a moment-by-moment way with the dual qualities of focus and flexibility?
4 Self processes: Can the person make contact with a sense of self that is not identical with verbally constructed stories about self and can they cultivate the capacity to see themselves and events around them from multiple perspectives?
5 Values processes: Can the individual generate a verbally constructed, extended, and evolving pattern of desired activity?
6 Commitment processes: Can an individual, upon recognizing their own pattern of behavior as it diverges from patterns described as valued patterns, return to that valued behavioral pattern?

Precision. The six-process model was the first CBS model generally spoken of as incorporating middle-level terms. These terms orient clinicians to important domains but it is much more difficult to specify the conditions under which "acceptance" might be appropriately used than, say, "discriminative stimulus." We cannot speak of precision within a CBS system without considering the particulars of problem-solving contexts, however. The scope of a functional analysis of behavior could in principle extend out into ever broader contexts. Functional contextualism offers a stopping point, however: the point at which prediction and influence is possible.

Likewise, there is no absolute metric for precision that exists out in the world, in the event field itself. Consistent with Skinner, precision is not a property to be found within the term itself. Rather precision must consider the particulars of the problem-solving contexts in which the term is to be used.

Middle-level terms have sometimes been criticized for a lack of precision, but we must ask "in what sense?" If I had a shoe store, I might find myself in the context of solving the problem of which size shoes to sell a person. Imagine I brought in my brand new super duper foot-measuring device. Rather than those imprecise gadgets that you put your foot on, my device is a giant foot micrometer that could measure to tenths of a millimeter. While it might be possible to more precisely measure the length of a foot, this precise device would make no difference in the fitting of shoes, since they only come in half sizes. Similarly, the usefulness of the psychological flexibility model cannot be assessed inside a decontextualized conceptualization of precision. Middle-level terms earn their keep in the areas of scope, depth, and generativity, not precision.

Scope. The psychological flexibility model was aimed broadly at a general dimensional approach to understanding human suffering. The first of these dimensions explored in depth was experiential avoidance (the flipside of acceptance). In a heavily cited paper, Hayes and colleagues offered experiential avoidance as a functional diagnostic dimension and explored its applicability across different psychological diagnoses and also the ways that it allowed for interpretation of sensibilities from a wide variety of therapeutic schools (Hayes, Wilson, Gifford, Follette, & Strosahl, 1996). However, though experiential avoidance was argued to be a key functional dimension, it was soon apparent that it could not describe the emerging ACT model in full. The broader six-process model was an attempt to flesh out a set of dimensions that could describe the intended breadth of the approach. The psychological flexibility model has subsequently been applied to an extraordinary range of clinical phenomena both in physical and mental health contexts (Ruiz, 2012). Across a large range of contexts, both in terms of difficulties treated and context in which interventions occurred, the model has proved to readily applied.

Depth. A good example of depth is provided by the way that psychological flexibility principles that explain ACT appear to cohere with ideas of variation and selective retention that explain evolutionary development in other domains (Wilson et al., 2014). Acceptance and defusion help increase behavioral variability; values and committed action help select and retain behavioral variants; perspective-taking and contact with the now help consciously link variation and selection to the present context.

Generativity. The psychological flexibility model has not only been generative in the interpretations of behavioral problems, growth, and development. The model has generated many book-length explorations of the model and a plethora of interventions that are aimed at increasing particular processes and combinations of processes.

Importantly, these developments have not merely been interpretive. The psychological flexibility model has also amassed a large body of data. Generating component interventions has likewise generated a large number of experimental analyses of components. These studies form a bridge between highly controlled laboratory studies and real world problem-solving contexts.

The introduction of the six-process model generated a good deal of attention. Google scholar shows nearly 3,000 citations since the model was introduced a decade ago, 625 in the last year alone. The concept of experiential avoidance, which was the first and perhaps best-developed clinical concept, adds about another 6,000 citations. The last decade has witnessed an upsurge in the generation of methods to measure other aspects of psychological flexibility including measures of values (e.g., Smout, Davies, Burns, & Christie, 2014), committed action (e.g., McCracken, 2013), defusion (e.g., McCracken, DaSilva, Skillicorn, & Doherty, 2013) as well as a variety of broader measures of psychological flexibility. Recent studies indicate that psychological flexibility adds to existing measures and concepts (Gloster, Klotsche, Chaker, Hummel, & Hoyer, 2011). Scores of studies have examined the relationships between psychological flexibility concepts and other commonly used concepts in applied psychology and physical medicine, including general psychological distress, depression, anxiety, pain, diabetes (e.g., Chawla & Ostafin, 2007). Often, in longitudinal studies, measures of psychological flexibility concepts predict future psychopathology, above and beyond current levels (e.g., Sharp, Kalpakci, Mellick, Venta, & Temple, 2015) and do so better than alternative concepts and measures (e.g., Kashdan, Barrios, Forsythe, & Steger, 2006).

Various measures of psychological flexibility and its component processes have been used to examine mechanisms of action in randomized clinical trials of both ACT (Bricker, Wyszynski, Comstock, & Heffner, 2013; Zettle, Rains, & Hayes, 2011) as well as other forms of therapy (e.g., Arch, Wolitzky-Taylor, Eifert, & Craske, 2012). Indeed, the psychological flexibility model, in whole and in parts, has begun to be adopted outside of ACT and CBS (Hayes, Villatte, Levin, & Hildebrant, 2011). On the whole, one could argue on the strength of the evidence base, the psychological flexibility model has been a highly generative scientific model.

Relational Frame Theory: Precision, Scope, Depth, and Generativity across Problem-Solving Contexts

The earliest CBS efforts to understand "rule-governed behavior" led ultimately to the conclusion that basic four-term contingency analyses were adequate to allow for interpretation of complex human behavior, but not for demonstrating prediction and influence of a sufficiently wide range of complex human behavior involving verbal events. Relational frame theory was an attempt to solve that problem. RFT added a relatively small set of key terms.

Precision. Relational frame theory contains five essential terms and three essential elements abstracted from the event field of complex human behavior. First, it contains mutual entailment and combinatorial mutual entailment. These terms describe essential symbolic relations among stimuli. Second is the concept of transformation of psychological function, describing the impact of verbal stimuli. Third, and finally, relational frame theory contains terms for two sorts of contextual control: C_{rel}, a context controlling which relation among stimuli is brought to bear on an array of stimuli, and C_{func}, a context controlling which psychological functions will be transformed. The conditions for the use each of these terms is highly specified in the sense that these terms can be applied unambiguously to the variety of experiments and preparations covered by the theory (Hayes et al., 2001). These terms led to additional concepts such as names of particular kinds of framing, or verbal tasks (e.g., pragmatic verbal analysis) but in general RFT is composed of a limited and highly precise set of terms.

Scope. RFT was developed as a general way of speaking about fundamental aspects of complex human behavior. The scope of the intended target of this analysis is apparent in the scope of the initial book length treatment of relational frame theory (Hayes et al., 2001) that covered areas as divergent as psychotherapy, psychopathology, self, and spirituality. RFT was never intended as a theory for and about laboratory experiments. It was a theory of human language and cognition.

Depth. The linkage of RFT terms and analyses to well-researched areas such as evolution science (Hayes & Sanford, 2014), or cognitive science (e.g., DeHouwer, 2011) shows that a notable level of consilience exists between RFT and relevant studies and approaches in sister sciences. This has obviously increased over time, experimentally (Barnes-Holmes et al., 2004) and interpretively as RFT methods and concepts begin to be explored and used.

Generativity. RFT has arguably been extremely generative. It has generated a large body of highly controlled laboratory studies including very tightly controlled studies demonstrating basic processes such as mutual and combinatorial entailment across a wide variety of different relations (such as opposition, hierarchy, equivalence; Dymond & Roche, 2013). It has also generated highly controlled experiments demonstrating prediction and influence over behavior of considerable social or clinical import such as prejudice and stigma (Dixon, Zlomke, & Rehfeldt, 2006; Watt, Keenan, Barnes, & Cairns, 1991; Weinstein, Wilson, & Drake, 2008), the expansion of fear learning (Dougher, Hamilton, Fink, & Harrington, 2007; Roche, Kanter, Brown, Dymond, & Fogarty, 2008) and secure sense of self (Luciano et al., 2011). Finally it has provided not only a rich body of interpretations of complex human behavior (Hayes et al., 2001; Törneke, 2010) but has led to new applied methods, such as ways of increasing intellectual performance (Cassidy, Roche, & Hayes, 2011) or improving perspective taking (McHugh & Stewart, 2012).

It is worth noting, however, that the linkage between RFT concepts and a broad range of clinical phenomena has been notably slower that psychological flexibility concepts. Several impressive interpretive attempts have been mounted (Hayes et al., 2001; Törneke, 2010) and individuals have argued that an experimental version of such a system is possible (e.g., Villatte, Villatte, & Hayes, in press). Successful clinical and analogue experiments driven by RFT concepts are also beginning to appear (e.g., Luciano et al., 2011). Nevertheless, it is undeniable that the progress of RFT concepts inside the clinic has been notably slower overall than the progress of psychological flexibility concepts. This is true both in terms of the development of clinical applications and also in terms of empirical analyses of change processes within clinical trials.

Some RFT-focused researchers and clinicians, such as Niklas Törneke, Carmen Luciano, and Yvonne Barnes-Holmes, have pursued analytic strategies involving far less reliance on the six-process psychological flexibility model and have suggested more focus on traditional behavioral principles in combination with relational frame theory (personal communications). These researchers could well be right: In the long run, RFT as a ground for clinical innovation may outstrip middle-level terms currently being used and may do so with added precision. It is also possible that new terms will need to be generated that will help guide RFT applications. However, it is not where researchers place their bets on future progress that is critical to the present discussion – it is seeing that this issue is empirical, contextual, and pragmatic, not one of ontology or essence.

One form of criticism of psychological flexibility concepts that reveals some degree of essentialism, is the idea that particular flexibility concepts bear no point-to-point correspondence to behavioral principles or to RFT concepts. There is, however, no a priori requirement of point-to-point correspondence. If such point-to-point correspondence were required, the terms of RFT might be required to correspond in a point-to-point way with traditional behavioral analyses. RFT exists precisely because that project proved unmountable as an experimental program. What is required is a concern for useful reticulation – the creation of useful interconnections between aspects of a broad research and application approach. But that criterion cuts in both ways.

Consider a well-established concept and set of procedures such as, say, defusion. At one level, defusion is merely a name for procedures that change the functional altering effects of human language. Said in another way, fusion and defusion are terms for the degree to which rules or other verbal formula transform stimulus functions to a greater or lesser degree. As with defusion, it is quite possible to link the various flexibility ideas fairly well to RFT principles. Even if that were not the case, it is a mistake to treat this issue as one of a failure of flexibility concepts. If defusion cannot be disassembled into RFT relevant ideas, this could equally well be argued to be a failure in scope of RFT concepts, rather than a failure in the depth of flexibility concepts. RFT principles are designed to explain complex human behavior involving language and cognition. Thus, reticulation is a challenge to all, basic and applied alike. Reticulation does not mean that terms are fully reducible, one to the other. It means they interrelate in a coherent and fruitful way.

Terms across Problem-Solving Contexts: The CBS Way

We can think about a variety of problem-solving contexts relevant to scientists: of tightly controlled laboratory experiments, of population-based studies, of measurement, of clinical and other applied experiments, of analogue studies bridging basic and applied realms. We must also consider the accessibility of terms and systems of terms to other problem-solving contexts, however: the context of disseminating interventions to clinicians and other applied specialists not trained deeply in CBS; the context of recipients of care; and so on.

There is no implicit or explicit dictate in CBS that terms that are useful in one problem-solving context must be *reducible* to terms in another problem-solving context. Scope and depth rather underline the useful relationship among terms.

Not all means of speaking need be measured according to their ability to generate experiments. Clinical contexts often involve solving problems that have nothing to do with creating experiments. In therapy I might, in speaking to a troubled couple, ask that they listen to one another with their hearts. I might quote literature: "the heart has its reasons that reason does not understand." No experiment will likely come from this way of speaking – but if it is useful, if the couple listens to one another in a kinder way, we would call these "true" ways of speaking. Terms that orient clinicians to how and when use such language may be useful and may generate experiments.

As an example, consider the ACT matrix (Polk & Schoendorff, 2014). It is a conceptual system that is incredibly easy to understand and teach. It seems to be a simple route to understanding change in ACT for both clients and clinicians. But it was not originally conceived to be a scientific model. It was a clinical model, developed for use in applied group interventions. Mindfulness is another term widely used within CBS scientists and practitioners. It has some of the same properties. None of these terms are at odds with existing sets of terms with well-established bodies of evidence but their range of use is quite different. The scientific productivity of these ways of speaking is ultimately an empirical matter. For example, though not broadly explored thus far in the CBS community, it is clear that some ways of speaking about mindfulness have moved mindfulness from a tradition-based practice into the realm of experimental science. Again, the criteria for evaluation are not matters of essence, rather of outcome.

A recent development in functional analytic psychotherapy (FAP; Kohlenberg & Tsai, 1991) provides a new and interesting case study in and of itself. FAP, boiled down to its essentials, can be thought of in the following way. Many human difficulties are either directly generated by, or made worse by, or potentially improved by more or less adaptive interpersonal functioning. The FAP therapist assumes that, though formally diverse, interpersonal patterns that are causing clients trouble in their lives will eventually show themselves in the relationship between the therapist and the client. Early on FAP identified client interpersonal patterns that were maladaptive (Clinically Relevant Behaviors 1) and adaptive (Clinically Relevant Behaviors 2). The FAP therapist's job was to reinforce CRB2s and to teach clients to recognize and extinguish CRB2s. On the face of it, few would argue that more adaptive interpersonal repertoires and fewer maladaptive interpersonal repertoires would solve a lot of problems. However, this formulation has not produced a large body of experimental evidence or evidence of any other sort really. Recently, FAP theorists have reformulated the model in terms of increasing client awareness, courage, and love (see discussion in Kanter, Holman, & Wilson, 2014). FAP therapists still use the CRB1 and CRB2 formulation. However, the awareness, courage, and love model has lent itself almost immediately to lines of experimental research that were not clear before its use. This research has not yet reached publication, however, it is easily imaginable how such a formulation could lend itself to measurement studies, experimental analogue studies of component processes, and direct process research within FAP randomized clinical trials. This small reorganization in principles could potentially generate a host of studies after years of languishing experimentally with the previous formulation. Whether these new FAP middle-level terms will survive examination within a CBS framework or not is yet to be seen. However, as the CBS system has become clearer, we can suggest the criteria by which the inclusion of such terms might be guided: Do these new terms increase scope, depth, and generativity? Do they bring focus to centrally important areas of human functioning? Do they comport with behavioral principles as extended by RFT? Do they link to CBS' embeddedness in the larger body of evolution science?

Summary

Terms are tools, and any tool must be evaluated relative to the job being done. Understanding the pragmatic basis of truth is not a free for all, because the goals of analysis limit the range of useful terms. The task is to be clear about the goals of analysis and to hold terms to account for their utility within the broader discipline, and with the contexts in which they will be applied. We must be prepared to allow ways of speaking to serve and to be prepared to let them go when they do not. CBS is ultimately a practical matter and all of our work must be held ultimately to the test of whether, and to what extent, it has served the improvement and enrichment of our own lives and of the lives we serve.

References

Association for Contextual Behavioral Science (2014). Home page. Retrieved from http://contextualscience.org/acbs

Arch, J. J., Wolitzky-Taylor, K. B., Eifert, G. H., & Craske, M. G. (2012). Longitudinal treatment mediation of traditional cognitive behavioral therapy and acceptance and commitment therapy for anxiety disorders. *Behaviour Research and Therapy, 50*, 469–478.

Barnes-Holmes, D., Staunton, C., Barnes-Holmes, Y., Whelan, R., Stewart, I., Commins, S., ... Dymond, S. (2004). Interfacing relational frame theory with cognitive neuroscience: Semantic priming, the implicit association test, and event related potentials. *International Journal of Psychology and Psychological Therapy, 4*, 215–240.

Beck, A. T. (1993). Cognitive therapy: Past, present, and future. *Journal of Consulting and Clinical Psychology, 61*, 194–198.

Beck, A. T., Rush, A. J., Shaw, B. F., & Emery, G. (1979). *Cognitive therapy of depression.* New York, NY: Guilford.

Bijou, S. W. (1976). *Child development: The basic stage of early childhood.* New York, NY: Prentice-Hall.

Boring, E. G., Bridgman, P. W., Feigl, H., Pratt, C. C., & Skinner, B. F. (1945). Rejoinders and second thoughts. *Psychological Review, 52*, 278–294.

Borsboom, D., Mellenbergh, G. J., & van Heerden, J. (2003). The theoretical status of latent variables. *Psychological Review, 110*, 203–219.

Bricker, J., Wyszynski, C., Comstock, B., & Heffner, J. L. (2013). Pilot randomized controlled trial of web-based acceptance and commitment therapy for smoking cessation. *Nicotine and Tobacco Research, 15*, 1756–1764.

Cassidy, S., Roche, B., & Hayes, S. C. (2011). A relational frame training intervention to raise intelligence quotients: A pilot study. *The Psychological Record, 61*, 173–198.

Chawla, N., & Ostafin, B. (2007). Experiential avoidance as a functional dimensional approach to psychopathology: An empirical review. *Journal of Clinical Psychology, 63*, 871–890.

DeHouwer, J. (2011). Why the cognitive approach in psychology would benefit from a functional approach and vice versa. *Perspectives on Psychological Science, 6*, 202–209.

Dixon, M. R., Zlomke, K. M., & Rehfeldt, R. A. (2006). Restoring Americans' nonequivalent frames of terror: An application of relational frame theory. *The Behavior Analyst Today, 7*, 275–289.

Dougher, M. J., Hamilton, D., Fink, B., & Harrington, J. (2007). Transformation of the discriminative and eliciting functions of generalized relational stimuli. *Journal of the Experimental Analysis of Behavior, 88*, 179–197.

Dymond, S., & Roche, B. (Eds.). (2013). *Advances in relational frame theory: Research and application.* Oakland, CA: New Harbinger.

Franks, C. M., & Wilson, G. T. (1974). *Annual review of behavior therapy: Theory and practice.* New York, NY: Brunner/Mazel.

Gloster, A. T., Klotsche, J., Chaker, S., Hummel, K. V., & Hoyer, J. (2011). Assessing psychological flexibility: What does it add above and beyond existing constructs? *Psychological Assessment, 23*, 970–982.

Hanley, G. P., Iwata, B. A., & McCord, B. E. (2003). Functional analysis of problem behavior: a review. *Journal of Applied Behavior Analysis, 36*, 147–185.

Hayes, S. C. (1993). Analytic goals and the varieties of scientific contextualism. In S. C. Hayes, L. J. Hayes, H. W. Reese, & T. R. Sarbin (Eds.), *Varieties of scientific contextualism* (pp. 11–27). Reno, NV: Context Press.

Hayes, S. C. (2004). Acceptance and commitment therapy, relational frame theory, and the third wave of behavior therapy. *Behavior Therapy, 35*, 639–665.

Hayes, S. C., Barnes-Holmes, D., & Roche, B. (2001). *Relational frame theory: A post-Skinnerian account of human language and cognition.* New York, NY: Plenum.

Hayes, S. C., Hayes, L. J., & Reese, H. W. (1988). Finding the philosophical core: A review of Stephen C. Pepper's *World Hypotheses*. *Journal of the Experimental Analysis of Behavior, 50*, 97–111.

Hayes, S. C., & Sanford, B. (2014). Cooperation came first: Evolution and human cognition. *Journal of the Experimental Analysis of Behavior, 101*, 112–129.

Hayes, S. C., Villatte, M., Levin, M., & Hildebrandt, M. (2011). Open, aware, and active: Contextual approaches as an emerging trend in the behavioral and cognitive therapies. *Annual Review of Clinical Psychology, 7*, 141–168.

Hayes, S. C., Wilson, K. W., Gifford, E. V., Follette, V. M., & Strosahl, K. (1996). Experiential avoidance and behavioral disorders: A functional dimensional approach to diagnosis and treatment. *Journal of Consulting and Clinical Psychology, 64*, 1152–1168.

Jessor, R. (1958). The problem of reductionism in psychology. *Psychological Review, 65*, 170–178.

Kanter, J. W., Holman, G., & Wilson, K. G. (2014). Where is the love? Contextual behavioral science and behavior analysis. *Journal of Contextual Behavioral Science, 3*, 69–73.

Kashdan, T. B., Barrios, V., Forsyth, J. P., & Steger, M. F. (2006). Experiential avoidance as a generalized psychological vulnerability: Comparisons with coping and emotion regulation strategies. *Behaviour Research and Therapy, 44*, 1301–1320.

Kohlenberg, R. J., & Tsai, M. (1991). *Functional analytic psychotherapy*. New York, NY: Plenum.

Luciano, C., Ruiz, F. J., Torres, R. M. V., Martin, V. S., Matinez, O. G., & Lopez, J. C. (2011). A relational frame analysis of defusion interactions in acceptance and commitment therapy: A preliminary and quasi-experimental study with at-risk adolescents. *International Journal of Psychology and Psychological Therapy, 11*, 165–182.

Mahoney, M. J. (1974). *Cognition and behavior modification*. Cambridge, MA: Ballinger.

Matson, J. L., & Andrasik, F. (1983). *Treatment issues and innovations in mental retardation*. New York, NY: Springer.

McCracken, L. (2013). Committed action: An application of the psychological flexibility model to activity patterns in chronic pain. *The Journal of Pain, 14*, 828–835.

McCracken, L. M., DaSilva, P., Skillicorn, B., & Doherty, R. (2013). The Cognitive Fusion Questionnaire: A preliminary study of psychometric properties and prediction of functioning in chronic pain. *The Clinical Journal of Pain, 30*(10), 894–901.

McHugh, L., & Stewart, I. (Eds.) (2012). *The self and perspective taking: Contributions and applications from modern behavioral science*. Oakland, CA: New Harbinger.

Meichenbaum. D. H. (1977). *Cognitive-behavior modification: An integrative approach*. New York, NY: Plenum.

Pepper, S. C. (1942). *World hypotheses: A study in evidence*. Berkeley, CA: University of California Press.

Polk, K. L., & Schoendorff, B. (Eds.) (2014). *The ACT Matrix: A new approach to building psychological flexibility across settings and populations*. Oakland, CA: Context Press/New Harbinger.

Roche, B., Kanter, J. W., Brown, K., Dymond, S., & Fogarty, C. (2008). A comparison of "direct" versus "derived" extinction of avoidance. *The Psychological Record, 58*, 443–464.

Ruiz, J. R. (2012). Acceptance and commitment therapy versus traditional cognitive behavioral therapy: A systematic review and meta-analysis of current empirical evidence. *International Journal of Psychology and Psychological Therapy, 12*, 333–357.

Sharp, C., Kalpakci, A., Mellick, W., Venta, A., & Temple, S. C. (2015). First evidence of a prospective relation between avoidance of internal states and borderline personality disorder features in adolescents. *European Child & Adolescent Psychiatry, 24*, 283–290.

Skinner, B. F. (1935). On the generic nature of the concepts of stimulus and response. *Journal of General Psychology, 12*, 40–65.

Skinner, B. F. (1945). The operational analysis of psychological terms. *Psychological Review. 52*, 270–276.

Skinner, B. F. (1950). Are theories of learning necessary? *Psychological Review, 57*, 193–216.

Skinner, B. F. (1953). *Science and human behavior*. New York, NY: The Free Press.

Skinner, B. F. (1957). *Verbal behavior*. East Norwalk, CT: Appleton-Century-Crofts.

Skinner, B. F. (1971). *Beyond freedom and dignity*. New York, NY: Knopf.

Skinner, B. F. (1974). *About behaviorism*. New York, NY: Knopf.

Smith. L. D. (1986). *Behaviorism and logical positivism: A reassessment of the alliance*. Stanford, CA: Stanford University Press.

Smout, M., Davies, M., Burns, N., & Christie, A. (2014). Development of the Valuing Questionnaire (VQ). *Journal of Contextual Behavioral Science, 3*, 164–172.

Törneke, N. (2010). *Learning RFT: An introduction to relational frame theory and its clinical applications*. Oakland, CA: Context Press/New Harbinger.

Villatte, M., Villatte, J., & Hayes, S. C. (in press). *Mastering the clinical conversation*. New York, NY: Guilford.

Watt, A., Keenan, M., Barnes, D., & Cairns, E. (1991). Social categorization and stimulus equivalence. *The Psychological Record, 41*, 33–50.

Weinstein, J., Wilson, K. G., & Drake, C. E. (2008). A relational frame theory contribution to theories of social categorization. *Behavior and Social Issues, 17*, 39–64.

Wilson, K. G. (2001). Some notes on theoretical constructs: Types and validation from a contextual-behavioral perspective. *International Journal of Psychology and Psychological Therapy, 1*, 205–215.

Wilson, D. S., Hayes, S. C., Biglan, T., & Embry, D. (2014). Collaborating on evolving the future. *Behavioral and Brain Sciences, 34*, 44–61.

Zettle, R. D., Rains, J. C., & Hayes, S. C. (2011). Processes of change in acceptance and commitment therapy and cognitive therapy for depression: A mediational reanalysis of Zettle and Rains (1989). *Behavior Modification, 35*, 265–283.

6

Pragmatism and Psychological Flexibility in the Research Context
Applying Functional Contextualism to Scientific Methodology
Douglas M. Long and Brandon T. Sanford

With its foundational commitment to a pragmatic vision of scientific progress, contextual behavioral science (CBS) expands the usual scope of problems addressed in discussions of scientific methods as well as the principles employed in solving them. Whereas a researcher's personal psychology and cultural context have traditionally been viewed as nonscientific sources of bias, CBS sees purposeful engagement with social and emotional processes as an essential ingredient of scientific progress, since science is a name for particular contextualized actions of scientists. This perspective informs an understanding of the inadequacy of current efforts to support research integrity and progressivity across sciences, and motivates the application of behavior change principles for cultural change within scientific communities (e.g., Biglan & Embry, 2013). In this chapter we will discuss how and why principles of psychological flexibility and behavior analysis can be extended "into knowledge development itself so as to create a behavioral science more adequate to the challenges of the human condition" (Hayes, Barnes-Holmes, & Wilson, 2012).

We intend to provide an example of how this can occur by providing an introductory guide to the application of psychological flexibility principles within the CBS community. While time will tell whether or not this extension of behavioral principles into knowledge development serves scientific progress, this has nonetheless become an important feature of the CBS culture.

Philosophical Context

What does it mean to say that science is progressive and what are the methods by which scientific progress is achieved? Decades of philosophical analysis have given rise to divergent understandings of scientific progress. Below we shall discuss two of those understandings – *realism* and *pragmatism* – which provide general views of progress that arguably have divergent implications for methodological thinking and standards

The Wiley Handbook of Contextual Behavioral Science, First Edition. Edited by Robert D. Zettle, Steven C. Hayes, Dermot Barnes-Holmes, and Anthony Biglan.
© 2016 John Wiley & Sons, Ltd. Published 2016 by John Wiley & Sons, Ltd.

by which theories are evaluated (Cacioppo, Semin, & Berntson, 2004; Fishman, 1999; Long, 2013). An appreciation of CBS's roots in philosophical pragmatism shall then inform our extension of behavioral principles into knowledge development.

Realism and the Problem of Conceptual Biases

Realism views progress as the gradual convergence of science upon an increasingly accurate representation of objective truth (e.g., Hacking, 1983; McMullian, 1984). Attempting to remove human preferences and biases from knowledge development, methodologists have traditionally construed science as an application of logical and statistical procedures to empirical observations (Moore, 2010). For example, the falsification of theories whose empirical predictions fail to comport with observed data has been thought to push scientific knowledge "closer to the truth" through a process of elimination (e.g., Meehl, 1978; Popper, 1959). Falsification has encountered problems, however, because a strictly logical process of theory elimination relies upon premises that may themselves be false (Duhem, 1954; Quine, 1951) and competing mathematical models that fit the data equally well can always be found (MacCallum, Wegener, Uchino, & Fabrigar, 1993; Scarr, 1985).

Because of the need to supplement logical and mathematical procedures in guiding theory development, increasing attention has been paid to the role of a theory's conceptual attributes such as depth, simplicity, scope, and coherency (Laudan, 1996; Meehl, 1992). Conceptual standards serve to resolve ambiguities in statistical models (Forster, 2000) and to guide the allocation of laboratory resources by influencing what questions are asked and what answers can be entertained as plausible (Laudan, 1977). For example, Hayes and colleagues (2012) heavily weight the standard of conceptual scope by advocating for the development of a core set of principles that are useful across a broad range of populations and contexts. This push for scope seems likely to result in a body of knowledge very different from the products of a research agenda focused on developing unique principles for topographically defined circumstances (e.g., Omer & Dar, 1992).

A realist might ask whether concepts with greater applied scope somehow provide more *accurate* depictions of reality; but pragmatists might embrace conceptual scope because it makes efficient use of practical and cognitive resources. The ambiguity over such issues is challenging to a realist view of scientific progress because it acknowledges that conceptual standards are human choices that antedate discovery claims. Skeptics of realism have pointed to historical examples of useful theories that were shaped by conceptual standards that now seem bizarre – such as coherency with doctrines of the Catholic Church (Kuhn, 1957; Laudan, 1981). Psychologist Sandra Scarr (1985) has pointed out that such conceptual biases continue to be found in modern science. After documenting the role gender biases play in shaping mathematical models of human behavior she concluded that "we do not discover scientific facts, we invent them" (p. 499).

Responding to such skepticism, realists have advanced what is known as the "no miracles" argument for realism (Boyd, 1983; Putnam, 1978). The argument goes that successful theories must somehow correspond to a real world that exists independently of human conceptual preferences or the successes of science would appear to be miraculous. The task of the realist methodologist then is to specify procedures to minimize the extent to which human psychology and conceptual biases produce deviations from an accurate depiction of reality. To this end, realist methodologists have advocated for a metascientific inquiry wherein actuarial methods applied to theoretical developments across history would extract the common conceptual characteristics of successful theories (Faust, 1984; Meehl, 1983; 1992). Though interesting, this exercise would face a challenge in distinguishing between sciences and nonsciences as well as between the scientific and nonscientific activities of scientists. Data collection would itself require a clear definition of scientific method – the very thing that this exercise is meant to inform.

Our purpose here is not to argue against realism as such but to point out that science cannot hold itself up by its own bootstraps. The identification of historical episodes of interest for the Faust/Meehl metascientific enterprise would on some level require a pre-analytic commitment to a set of intellectual values – just as chess moves cannot be evaluated unless we choose to treat "checkmate" as important. Observations of this sort draw attention once again to the context of human scientific activity as determinative of its meaning and import. This appreciation of science as a contextualized human action is part of what has motivated the CBS emphasis on philosophy of science and attention to pragmatism in particular.

Pragmatism and the Ownership of Intellectual Values

Pragmatism offers an alternative view of scientific progress and has been espoused in different forms over the last century at least (James, 1907/2003; Misak, 2007). A pragmatist's version of scientific progress is a matter of problem-solving effectiveness (Laudan, 1977), where problems are defined by the values of the scientist and can be construed either narrowly (e.g., improving a school's performance) or broadly (e.g., creating world peace). For a pragmatist, it does not matter whether or not a theory corresponds with any sort of metaphysical truths about the world. Rather than aiming to represent a reality free from the conceptual lenses of human preferences, theories are meant to guide human behavior in predicting and influencing events (Skinner, 1969).

Responding to the "no miracles" argument for realism, pragmatism rejects entirely the assumption of representationalism – the notion that our language represents the world (Rorty, 1979). In its place, pragmatists tend to adopt the Darwinian notion of selection by consequences – extended to the survival of behaviors as well as to organisms (Skinner, 1981) – as an explanation for science's success. Theories, like organisms, compete with one another. Those that are best adapted to their circumstances continue on, while others are abandoned. The circumstances that determine a theory's success are multifaceted: social, economic, empirical, and conceptual. Over time, scientific communities form around shared criteria for theory selection (Long, 2013). These criteria are enforced to maximize the problem-solving effectiveness of theories, helping scientists to better fulfill their goals.

The particular form of pragmatism underpinning CBS, known as *functional contextualism*, has as its goal the prediction and influence of behavioral interactions with principles characterized by conceptual precision, scope, and depth (Biglan & Hayes, 1997; Hayes, 1993). Within a pragmatic tradition like CBS, the "truth" or "warranted assertability" of any theory depends at least in part upon the goals and abilities of the researchers and their intended audiences. This is not to say that "anything goes." What this does entail, however, is that the explicit identification of shared values and theory selection criteria is essential to the formation of a progressive scientific community (Hayes, 1993).

Conceptual preferences in theory development are only problematic biases if they are not made explicit and self-consistent. If they are clearly stated and owned they become intellectual values. If advocates take responsibility for their coherence and impact, they can become part and parcel of serious scientific work. Functional contextualism, for example, is explicitly committed to the conceptual preference of ultimately restricting causal status to manipulable environmental variables. This is not meant to contradict causal claims made about cognitions and emotions within other systems of thought (Hayes & Wilson, 1995). Rather, this is a conceptual commitment that is particularly attractive to researchers who value the production of principles that can serve clinicians or others in changing behavior, such as occurs in practical settings (Hayes, Long, Levin, & Follette, 2013). Values such as "helping people" or "making a difference" are often what bring people to a career in psychology – functional contextualists are willing to elevate the accomplishment of such goals to a foundational status.

Our point in contrasting realism and pragmatism is not to advance one position over the other, but to highlight one way in which these views can shape the behaviors of researchers (e.g., Cacioppo et al., 2004). Whereas realist researchers have tended to exclude or minimize the psychology of the scientist in methodological discussions, pragmatists see science fundamentally as a form of cooperative social behavior – an extension of human psychology and culture (Hayes & Long, 2013). Pragmatically speaking, the aim of methodological writing within CBS (or any pragmatic science tradition) is to set a verbal context that evokes behaviors that are effective in advancing scientific progress. As such, we must view as incomplete any account of research methodology that excludes a discussion of the social and psychological contexts necessary to sustain effective research behaviors. In this approach, scientific methodology necessarily includes such questions as: How do scientific communities form? What sustains them? How do scientists go about identifying intellectual values and acting consistently with these? What problem behaviors get in the way and what can be done to get researchers back on track? How can researchers choose research topics that will make a profound difference in the success and well-being of others? Before turning our attention to how CBS has addressed such questions, we shall discuss how sciences in general have grappled with problem behaviors of scientists.

Behavioral Barriers to Scientific Progress

We have suggested that the identification of shared values and conceptual standards is an important contextual element of a pragmatically progressive scientific community. Just as research communities benefit from stating their shared values, problematic sources of influence on theory development also require attention. This is not merely an intellectual exercise. Contingencies that shape problematic behaviors such as plagiarism, misrepresentation of data, failures to conduct research carefully, or failures to publish worthwhile findings, not only slow empirical progress, but also have real costs for real individuals. In a different direction, contingencies that reduce creativity, support unquestioned conformity with current received views, result in a failure to pursue important questions or in the punishment of young scientists when they innovate, tend to slow innovation and risk taking. It is worth reviewing here some examples of both of these classes of researcher actions. Doing so will provide a context for our extension of contextual behavioral principles to scientific communities.

Lack of care, unethical behavior, and poor follow through. A salient contemporary example of misguided research behavior is that of Deiderik Stapel, a prominent social psychologist who was recently implicated in extensive misconduct over the period of several years (Tilburg University, 2011). Stapel's transgressions were of the most egregious type in science, including the complete fabrication of data suspected to have been used in over 30 publications involving several unwitting doctoral students and professional colleagues. While large-scale fraud such as this appears to be rare, unethical behavior as a whole is unfortunately more common. A recent meta-analysis spanning scientific disciplines suggested that approximately 2% of researchers report having fabricated, falsified, or otherwise modified results to improve the outcome, with over 33% reporting other questionable research practices such as: failing to publish data which conflicted with one's previous research, withholding details of methodology or results in papers or proposals, using inadequate or inappropriate research designs, or the premature termination of a study by a company (Fanelli, 2009). Alarmingly, this same study reported that approximately 14% of researchers had personal knowledge of the fabrication, falsification, or inappropriate modification of research results by colleagues.

Apart from the starkest offenses there is a vast ethical gray area wherein researchers must regularly make decisions regarding the removal of outliers, the flexibility of a statistical procedure's underlying assumptions, the appropriateness of inclusion and exclusion criteria, or the determination of adequate statistical power. Overly liberal decision-making can make findings difficult to replicate and interpret, wasting the time, effort, and resources of future scientists. Misleading research may diminish the impact of the dissemination of scientific results (Ryan, 1998) and may put clients at risk of ineffective treatment.

There have been several proposals as to how to best protect research integrity. Proposals that seek to identify instances of fraud include a movement towards the replication of findings (Pashler & Wegenmakers, 2012; Winerman, 2013), increasing the availability of raw data used in publications (Wicherts, 2011; Simonsohn, 2013), and the improvement of standards for acceptance to scientific journals (Katelaris, 2011). Additionally, there are now well-established statistical procedures by which fraudulent data can be detected (Evans, 2001; Al-Marzouki, Evans, Marshall, & Roberts, 2005). While these approaches may serve to be effective in limiting the extent to which resources are wasted as a result of misleading publications, they are not likely to be effective in preventing misconduct – except perhaps in the already rare cases of the outright creation of data. Furthermore, subtle threats to research integrity such as those described in the ethical gray area are nearly impossible to detect.

The approach most commonly advocated for in the prevention of scientific misconduct is increasing the amount of ethics education scientists receive (e.g., Zigmond & Fischer, 2002). The call for increasing amounts of ethics education has been echoed widely across disciplines (Alberts & Shine, 1994; National Institute of Medicine, 2002; Steneck, 2006). Unfortunately, there are data suggesting that ethics education does not reliably improve the behavior of scientists. Anderson and colleagues (2007) conclude that, "In general, respondents who received training in research integrity differed little in their subsequent reported behavior from those with no training in research integrity" (p. 857). This conclusion is consistent with findings on the impact of didactic professional development programs more generally. For example, we know that didactic instruction focused on intellectual understanding appears to be ineffective in changing the practices of professionals such as doctors, nurses, therapists, and teachers (Fixsen, Naoom, Blasé, Friedman, & Wallace, 2005).

In a sense, research ethics education follows a "just say no" rationale analogous to the failed Drug Abuse Resistance Education program for adolescents (DARE; Ennet, Tobler, Ringwalt, & Flewelling, 1994; Lynam et al., 1999). Ironically, DARE programs that appealed to rationally oriented information demonstrated the greatest gains in knowledge but produced the smallest gains in attitudinal and behavioral change (Bruvold, 1993). In addition to being intuitive and easy to advocate for, such programs appear to be effective because of the relatively low base-rates of the behaviors they are intended to prevent (Lynam et al., 1999). Ethics education seems to be quite similar. Advocating thorough and comprehensive ethics education has the look and feel of a solution, even if it is inert. Before considering a way forward, we shall first turn our attention to another class of problem behaviors.

Failures to innovate or to notice chance events that could produce progress. Behavioral barriers to scientific progress can occur even for researchers acting with the best intentions. Overly conservative decision-making and rigid attachment to dominant theories and methods can result in failures to innovate, failures to capitalize on serendipitous events, and failures to pursue data that challenges widely held ideas. For example, much methodological training has emphasized hypothesis testing driven by relations among preconceived theoretical constructs (Marx, 1976). While such an approach is not without its merits, capitalizing on chance findings throughout the research process may serve to inform new theory developments or entirely new lines of research (Sivak, 2009; Steinberg, 2011). For example, Steinberg's (2011) work on a failed cholesterol drug led him to explore the role of inhibiting cholesterol synthesis in a group of patients with a rare genetic disorder, resulting in the development of an effective dietary intervention. Had the scientist adhered too strongly to the original hypothesis or the specific research domain, the results of the initial experiment would likely have gone nowhere. Sir Alexander Fleming's discovery of penicillin's antibacterial properties occurred completely by accident and initial attempts by others at replicating Fleming's observations were failures (Henderson, 1997). While in retrospect we might view Fleming's behavior as persistence through adversity, this might not have been so clear at the time. Scientists must tolerate a great deal of uncertainty while walking the fine line between effective persistence and ineffective perseveration.

Ineffective perseverance in pursuing new ideas, or perseverative embrace of older ideas that are proving unhelpful, can be promoted by many research practices, such as through the habitual use of statistical procedures without consideration of whether their assumptions are met (Borsboom, 2005; Cronbach & Shavelson, 2004). Unhealthy perseveration is perhaps most noticeable, however, during major theoretical shifts. The historical tendency for scientists to perseverate in pursuit of supporting evidence for existing theories was famously described by Thomas Kuhn in his *Structure of Scientific Revolutions* (1970). Kuhn described *paradigms* as tools that inform what questions are asked as well as the methods and answers that are viewed as reasonable. As a research agenda continues, if increasingly adequate solutions are not discovered the paradigm itself may come into question – polarizing advocates of the current paradigm with those advancing alternatives. The current controversies regarding overreliance of researchers upon the American Psychiatric Association's diagnostic categories are demonstrative of this phenomenon (Kupfer, First, & Regier, 2002). While the recent movement within the National Institute of Health to promote translational research may be a welcomed change (Jenks, 2012; Woolf, 2008), this could also create an economic incentive to continue research guided by established theories rather than new paradigms.

Finding a Functional Contextual Way Forward

Because scientists are highly trained and intelligent individuals there is a tendency to believe that didactic training should be sufficient for supporting research integrity. Researchers are expected to live up to a standard of behavior beyond that of other professionals because "scientists *are* different, or at least they should be" (Zigmond & Fischer, 2002, p. 234). The promotion of scientific progress is not aided by assumptions that scientists are somehow special or different with a vantage point, "perched on the epicycle of Mercury" (Skinner, 1974, p. 234). From a functional contextual viewpoint, promoting research integrity requires attention to the contingencies in which it occurs. Revisiting our previous example, Deiderik Stapel noted in his confession of misconduct that in "modern science there was a lot of pressure to publish research and competition was high" (cf. Wise, 2011). In an era where the phrase "publish or perish" is trumpeted as a cultural norm, it is no surprise that the repertoire of an otherwise intelligent individual would become so restricted as to produce publications from a fabricated data set. Our speculation here is not meant to morally excuse such behavior, but to promote a contextual understanding in hope of contributing to a cultural shift in how scientific integrity is supported.

While our attention to the psychological attributes of the scientist is nothing new (e.g., Bernard, 1865/1957), we hope that the functional contextual approach goes a step further by effectively highlighting manipulable variables that can bring about the desired behaviors of scientists. A functional contextual analysis must begin with some discussion of the possible contingencies at play in producing and sustaining the behaviors of interest. In this view, science can roughly be understood as a form of human cooperation shaped and supported by social resource allocation that has been sustained through the evolutionarily selection of groups better adapted to their circumstances (Hayes & Long, 2013). The effective allocation of limited social resources (e.g., attention, status, wealth, etc.) is essential since the ultimate aims of scientific endeavors may be extremely distal or never directly contacted by the scientists. In the first class of problematic behaviors described above, the scientist's behavior may be so strongly guided by social reinforcement that this is pursued at a cost to the processes the social community is intending to support. In response to this, methodological and procedural rules have been enforced by the community. Unfortunately, one unintended but natural consequence of such rule governance can be the narrowing of a scientist's behavioral variability to the detriment of the more broad agenda of improving the human condition (e.g., Hayes & Ju, 1997) – as in the second class of problem behaviors described above.

Cultural traditions commonly form in order to organize and maintain a research community around a shared vision for progress and to avoid the pitfalls we have just discussed. These are expressed in both subtle and major ways: as familiar sayings or phrases in lab meetings, as social traditions at conferences, and in the arrangement of contingencies within institutions and organizations. Such occurrences are common within any research community but have rarely been documented or recognized as methodologically important.

Because our focus is on how functional contextualism and CBS lead to a different way of thinking about scientific methodology, we will use as an example of our meaning the cultural practices that appear to be developing inside the CBS community. We intend to use the psychological flexibility model as the structure within which to consider these, because that model is one of the primary and most robust scientific products of CBS, but we could equally well apply relational frame theory (RFT) principles, evolutionary principles, or behavioral principles in structuring examples of a contextual approach to scientific methods taken to be the actions of scientists.

Psychological Flexibility and Enhancement of Research Practices

In what follows, we shall provide an account of some cultural features of the CBS community that seem important to its functioning as a research tradition, and we will link these features to some examples of researcher behavior such as those we've just considered. While this account will by no means be systematic or exhaustive it shows how certain basic ideas about the context of scientific work have been applied by an entire research community. We are not arguing that these methods are correct, or that this is the way to get better research – those are empirical questions. Rather our purpose is to show that contextual perspectives lead to the establishment of characteristic cultural practices as a matter of supporting pragmatically progressive research. Because we will be exploring various cultural practices, few of which are written down in scientific articles, the reader will have to tolerate a fair amount of informality in this section. In essence, part of what we are doing in this section of the chapter is telling stories about major CBS laboratories and figures. In most cases we will not slow down the reading by explaining in detail who these people are, trusting that serious students will know and skeptical readers can readily find out. We apologize in advance for the "in group" feel this might convey, but trust the reader will understand that these choices are in the service of readability and our larger intellectual purpose in this chapter.

The psychological flexibility (PF) model shall serve as our analytic framework (Hayes, Strosahl, & Wilson, 2012). This model forms the basis of acceptance and commitment therapy (ACT), which has shown applied utility in the prediction and influence of a variety of problem behaviors such as depression, worksite stress, anxiety, and substance use, amongst others (Hayes, Luoma, Bond, Masuda, & Willis, 2006). It is an extension of certain evolutionary ideas, such as the need to create healthy variability, situated in context, that can be selected by chosen criteria and retained by practice and cultural support. Aside from its foundations in functional contextualism and evolutionary epistemology, the primary reason for our emphasis on the PF model in this chapter is historical. It is widely known in CBS and thus we believe has both an implicit and explicit role in the creation of CBS research strategy.

Psychological flexibility principles as applied to the research process can regularly be found in listservs, professional conferences, and lab gatherings. Indeed, founders of the Association for Contextual Behavioral Science (ACBS) have argued that the association itself "has been organized in a way that is consciously linked to the psychological flexibility model and to the evolution of prosocial groups" (Hayes, Barnes-Holmes, & Wilson, 2012, p. 14). Thus, examining these issues from the point of view of PF seems warranted. This is merely a device, however, since any principles related to behavior change, social psychology, or the evolution of groups may be prescriptively applied to the behaviors of scientists so long as they orient the reader to manipulable contextual variables.

The PF model consists of six core overlapping and interacting processes that can be intervened upon in order to support individuals in persisting or changing behavior in the service of chosen values. We shall briefly introduce each process as it is discussed, and reference more comprehensive accounts for readers who wish to delve deeper (e.g., Hayes, Strosahl, & Wilson, 2012). As we discuss CBS culture below, we shall introduce PF processes with examples of how they have been applied, as well as with invitations for the reader to examine how this approach might be relevant to his or her research behaviors.

Values

While scientists investigate exciting topics, the process of data collection and analysis is often rather mundane and requires painstaking attention to detail. When combined with the fact that there are no guarantees that the result of this process will provide clear conclusions, the prospect of engaging with research can begin to seem arduous or even depressing. Creating a verbal context that supports a sense of meaning in day-to-day research activities is accomplished through interventions that target values. In the psychological flexibility model, values are defined as "freely chosen, verbally constructed consequences of ongoing, dynamic, evolving patterns of activity, which establish predominant reinforcers for that activity that are intrinsic in engagement in the valued behavioral pattern itself" (Wilson & DuFrene, 2009, p. 66). For example, scientists may hope their work will contribute to a future society that is more peaceful and healthy; perhaps there is something valuable about the process of learning and exploring; and so on. Whatever values are chosen for oneself or for a community, this sense of purpose is arguably extremely important to the scientific process.

The values process can be targeted on multiple levels – within a professional organization, a research lab, or within an individual. Commonly values processes are engaged with verbal prompts that orient the listener to the relationship between the scientific behavior to be done and the associated value. Doing so arguably helps to sustain research behaviors by transferring the stimulus functions of the value to the behavior itself – in behavioral terms scientific values can serve as motivative and formative augmentals for scientific behavior. Seen that way, values work is a process by which the hard work of research can become more intrinsically reinforcing – hopefully lessening the possibility of excessive focus on extrinsic reinforcers such as financial or social gains. It may also guide decision-making by providing a sense of direction through otherwise ambiguous circumstances as might be encountered in the case of unexpected findings or roadblocks to research.

Examples within the CBS community. The Association for Contextual Behavioral Science (ACBS) has not only stated its overall mission as one of alleviating human suffering and advancing human well-being, but has also committed itself to "open and low cost methods of connecting with this work so as to keep the focus on benefit to others" (ACBS, 2014a). This value has shaped several major features of the organization such as the use of a values-based dues system in which individuals pay what they think membership is worth to them in the context of what they can afford, or free access to the *Journal of Contextual Behavioral Science* (JCBS) included with membership.

The collaborative creation of a lab values statement is another way in which a shared sense of meaning can be established. Many CBS research labs have made their values statements publicly available online, providing a fertile source of examples for this chapter. These manifestos often state lab values both in terms of the intellectual content mission of analyzing of complex behaviors, and through identifying valued interpersonal processes that support the development of lab members. This is colorfully exemplified by Kelly Wilson's lab manifesto identifying "world domination through peace, love, and understanding," as the lab's motto (Wilson, 2014). Another example can be found from the lab of Lisa Coyne: "We value empiricism, and strive always to be open to what the data tell us. We value creating a community of scientists who help each other, and can have free and open discourse" (Coyne, 2014). Many CBS labs have annual rituals in which each member states their values behind their lab participation for the year.

Thus, in a CBS approach part of the scientific method is asking scientists and scientists in training such questions as "Why do you want to be a researcher?" or "What makes this work meaningful to you?" There are no right or wrong answers to such a values discussion. Some members of the community or the individual research laboratory may have deeply personal reasons for engaging with research – such as honoring the memory of a lost family member or friend – while others may have more intellectual values in mind. Some members may not yet have any idea of how to discuss their values. Researchers enter into values discussions for the purpose of empowering their day to day work with a sense of curiosity, engagement, and interest. In that context, even the most mundane task has a larger sense of meaning and purpose.

Acceptance

Committing yourself to a valued agenda of knowledge development also means making yourself vulnerable to fear, sadness, boredom, anxiety, and the full rollercoaster of emotions that can accompany a research project. Research can often take many months or even years to complete and comes with no guarantee of significant outcomes. Even if interesting results are produced, the investment of countless hours in the project comes with an opportunity cost such as the cost of time not spent with family and friends. In a psychological flexibility model, *experiential avoidance* is defined as persistent and rigid attempts to control and reduce the form or frequency of private events such as thoughts, emotions, memories, bodily sensations, and urges even when doing so causes behavioral harm (Hayes, Wilson, Gifford, Follette, & Strosahl, 1996). As an alternative, the PF model targets the acceptance process to build "the voluntary adoption of an intentionally open, receptive, flexible, and nonjudgmental posture with respect to moment-to-moment experience" (Hayes, Strosahl, & Wilson, 2012, p. 272). Thus, part of the scientific method viewed from a CBS perspective is to help scientists be more willing to bring themselves into contact with uncertainty, anxiety, sadness, and so on in the service of following through on a line of research and dealing with unexpected outcomes. Acceptance may also help researchers deal with the social pressures of research – such as when presenting evidence that potentially conflicts with widely accepted beliefs within a scientific community.

Examples within the CBS community. The PF process of acceptance can be targeted in a research lab in multiple ways. It is helpful for the research team to create opportunities for nonjudgmental acknowledgment of the emotional components of research or costs being incurred and to provide social support for healthy choices. As Kelly Wilson's lab manifesto puts it, "The lab is built on the core assumption that there is no joy or sorrow, no burden or blessing, which is not improved by sharing ... Being in the lab means sharing your joys and sorrows" (Wilson, 2014). The establishment of an accepting social context is not just a matter of improving quality of life, but of maintaining the effectiveness of the work group. Amy Murrell's lab mission statement notes that "Sometimes (in order to make this a more effective workgroup) painful things might need to be pointed out, either to you or to others. This can be done in an honest and gentle way" (Murrell, 2014).

A lab can also promote PF by communicating social acceptance of lab members who have struggled to produce research results or who have chosen to contribute to the field in other ways. Acceptance can also be targeted through the communication of interest in null findings or research results that conflict with current theories favored by a community. For example JCBS has made a public commitment that "papers reporting null findings are also welcome if their methodology is sound and their power sufficient" (JCBS, 2014, p. 3). There are active plans for a new form of paper session at the ACBS World Conference: a series of papers demonstrating technological or conceptual failures, with the only requirement on the audience being that all speakers get a standing ovation, regardless of how painful the results may be. In large and small ways, creating a context of social acceptance seems important in order to support researchers in making the bold and risky research decisions that scientific progress sometimes requires.

CBS cultural practices are also based on the idea that ideas are shared, even though this increases the likelihood that others will get the credit for idea. Unhealthy competition undermines the long-term productivity of the group as a whole in animal models (Muir, 1985; 1996) and evolutionary principles suggest the same for human beings (e.g., Wilson, 2012). For example, in ACBS recognized trainers sign a values statement that they will freely share training innovations with other trainers and will refrain from making proprietary claims, even though this openness creates some degree of uncertainty.

Defusion

If we are to test the utility of a theory, we must fully immerse ourselves in it – allowing it to shape our experiences and expectations. We come to treat the theory's verbal constructions as though they are real and use them to guide our decision-making and resource allocation. This can shape our behaviors in very useful ways – narrowing our attention to persist through long and grueling statistical procedures to find relationships between variables that we would not have otherwise expected. At the same time, this "fusion," or blending of our direct experiences with verbally constructed ones, can produce rigid rumination, overattachment to finding the "right" answers, and insensitivity to other stimuli of importance. The unintentional tendency to interpret ambiguous data as consistent with preconceived notions has been well documented in the literature on confirmation bias (Nickerson, 1998). In the PF model, overattachment to verbally constructed experience is targeted through the process of defusion, which aims to reduce cognition's "automatic effect on behavior such that other sources of behavioral regulation can better participate in the moment," and to promote "a stance of voluntary cognitive flexibility" (Hayes, Strosahl, & Wilson, 2012, p. 245). In addition to loosening the grip of preconceived interpretations of data, defusion may be beneficial in preventing excessive attachment to procedural rules that can suffocate innovation.

Examples within the CBS community. Defusion can be promoted in part through recognition of the natural tendency for scientists to become overly attached to their theories. This is part of what motivates CBS's emphasis on training researchers to have an awareness of our position in history, noting that science is littered with abandoned theories that were once highly valued (e.g., Kuhn, 1957). Even modern science continues to struggle with the reification of theoretical constructs (e.g., Kupfer, First, & Regier, 2002). So as to not exclude CBS from this lineage, prominent ACT researchers have been known at ACBS conferences to quip, "ACT is wrong. Let's hope there's something better in 10 years." Furthermore, the phrase "hold it lightly" is used to remind the CBS community to not become rigidly fused with any particular theoretical model (Hayes, Barnes-Holmes, & Wilson, 2012).

Support for a more flexible and defused use of language can easily be integrated into the normal lab process of giving and receiving feedback about research practices. After viewing a presentation and agreeing that a series of empirical predictions is completely reasonable, a lab member might playfully add, "and of course, maybe this is all wrong." Importantly however, defusion is best supported not through contradictory statements alone, but through a broadening of behavioral responses in the presence of a theoretical model. For example, CBS researcher Takashi Muto once pointed out during a lab meeting while spending a sabbatical year in Reno that the popular visual representation of the PF model resembled the shell of a turtle – leading to a number of humorous observations about turtles, as well as to the creation of new clinical tools (see Hayes, Strosahl, & Wilson, 2012, p. 131).

Humor is an excellent tool for creating a context of defusion, as this inherently involves taking a step back from verbal constructs and relating to them in a more flexible way. ACBS has supported this at an organizational level by inviting conference attendees to compose skits and songs reflecting on their experiences with CBS training, research, and clinical work. This tradition of ACBS "Follies" events exemplifies, "one of our CBS values – remembering to hold ourselves and the work lightly" (ACBS, 2014b) and has been described as "a geeky contextual behavioral Monty Python, crossed with Saturday Night Live, Whose Line is it Anyway, and the Voice!" (Batten, 2014).

Present Moment Awareness

The content of the PF processes described herein can become stale – as part of a story of how things once were, or as part of the constantly growing to-do list. Fostering psychological flexibility processes in a research context requires an ongoing commitment that is renewed in each moment. For example, the utility of a lab values manifesto comes more from the collaborative values clarification process than it does from the physical document that is produced. Though it may be tempting to treat the document as a finished product, it should be periodically revised. The ability to refocus on the processes of importance in each moment without unnecessary entanglement with stories about the past or future is essential. In the PF model, the process of present moment awareness is discussed as the skillful and intentional allocation of attention, which is important because "the ability to allocate our attention with both focus and flexibility gives us the best chance to be shaped by, and to shape, the world around us" (Hayes, Strosahl, & Wilson, 2012, p. 202).

Examples within the CBS community. Part of present moment awareness is about bringing oneself more directly into contact with the contingencies that one chooses to treat as important. Within a research lab or professional organization, this occurs most obviously through systematic data collection and analysis. Discussing the extension of PF principles to the operations of ACBS, Hayes, Barnes-Holmes, and Wilson noted that "this connection needs to be actively monitored and modified based on results" (2012, p. 14). Greater contact with valued contingencies can be further promoted through supplementing self-report measures with direct behavioral observations, and through including applied work as part of researcher training (e.g., Hayes, Barlow, & Nelson-Gray, 1999). Both of these practices are intended to encourage greater pragmatic contextual sensitivity in the process of principle development.

Interpersonally, present moment awareness can be promoted through regular mindfulness exercises at the beginning of lab meetings. Such contemplative practices can help to prevent burnout (Shapiro, Astin, Bishop, & Cordova, 2005) and can also provide an opportunity for improving the quality of lab member relationships. In a discussion of the lab commitment to "showing up and being there," John Forsyth's lab manifesto emphasizes that "it is the halfhearted things you do while juggling other things that wear you out. When advanced team members interact they are not just physically present, they are wholeheartedly present" (Forsyth, 2006).

Self

Perhaps the most pernicious of pitfalls occurs when a researcher's behaviors come to be predominantly organized in the service of being right and looking good. While there is much to be gained by taking part in a spirited intellectual debate, entanglement with "winning" or "losing" can draw energy away from engagement with more valued activities. From a PF viewpoint, academic contexts can unfortunately support an over-identification with social status and intellectual content, letting us lose contact with the whole person who is more than the sum of his or her parts. Verbally constructed stories about ourselves and others – whether positive or negative – can guide our perceptions of events as well as our decision-making in ways that are needlessly restrictive. By targeting this self-process through verbal prompts for perspective taking with others and oneself, the PF model aims to build a more flexible sense of self that rests in the ever-present process of observing and experiencing, rather than in the changing contents of consciousness. The hope is that this flexibility will empower people to make values-consistent choices, even if doing so means "looking bad" or "being wrong."

Examples within the CBS community. In a world where careers are built through the identification of ideas with names, it is no wonder that personal attachment with signifiers of social status can interfere with collaboration and creativity (Hayes, 1998). In his advice to new graduate students Charles Lord conveyed the familiar saying, "you *are* your vita," and added that as a new academic you should, "alter your perspective so that you derive your professional self-respect entirely from what is on that document" (Lord, 2004, p. 10). Such a verbal context is likely to promote achievement but it is also likely to promote relentless defense against perceived failure – which could readily extend to the point of engaging in ethically dubious research behaviors such as those documented above. From a PF perspective, we suggest instead that "you are your vita, and you are not your vita."

It is important both to develop a professional image, and to see oneself as much more than just that. One way to foster this flexible sense of self in a research lab is to invite lab members to share information about their activities and roles in other areas of life. Some research labs have gone so far as to establish a tradition of welcoming children and pets into the workplace (e.g., Oregon Research Institute, 2014). Kelly Wilson's lab manifesto notes that "seeing a baby sitting on my lap during a lecture or rolling around on the floor during lab will be common and welcome" (Wilson, 2014). Such practices not only aim to maintain a more broad and flexible sense of self, but prompt for awareness of the diversity contained within one's colleagues.

Committed Action

As responsibilities pile up it can be easy to begin to view a career like one does a to-do list where each project is just another task to be checked off before you can *really* start living your life and doing the things you value. Aside from contributing to burnout, treating the process of science as simply a means to an end may lend itself to a loosening of academic integrity (Hayes, 1998). Arranging for prompts and social reminders about values can help individuals and organizations find creative opportunities to act in more values-consistent ways. The PF model defines committed action as "a values-based action that occurs in a particular moment in time and that is deliberately linked to creating a pattern of action that serves the value" (Hayes, Strosahl, & Wilson, 2012, p. 328).

Examples within the CBS community. Using a shared calendar to publicly make commitments and track progress on self-assigned projects can be a helpful way of orienting lab members to how closely they have been sticking to their chosen values. Such reminders of the passage of time are important, as it is often easier to invest time in trivial tasks with known outcomes than it is to take steps toward more meaningful projects with unknown outcomes. In the proper context, reminders of the finitude of life can serve to promote more values-consistent behavior (Burke, Martens, & Faucher, 2010). In his advice to new graduate students, Steve Hayes suggests "suppose unknown to you, you only have two or three research studies allotted to you before you die. Do you want to spend one on *that*?" (1998, p. 3).

Sometimes living consistently with values can be more a matter of *how* you approach a task than of the task itself. For example, orienting a new research assistant to your lab can be about more than just gaining more hands for your project. It can be about connecting with a new person and helping them to grow and explore new interests. As John Forsyth's lab manifesto puts it: "We are devoted to better the lives of others. This translates into our daily (lab) lives from the way we greet and thank each other sincerely, to the way we are open, patient, and caring with one another" (Forsyth, 2006).

Scientists need reminders that we can make any moment meaningful through how we choose to treat it. ACBS has established a tradition of inviting conference attendees to choose ribbons that they can fasten to the bottom of their name badges. These ribbons contain phrases such as "your values are showing," and "be here now, and there then." Though small and slightly comical, these ribbons can provide reminders for people to look for opportunities for valued engagement with one another. What is more, the ribbons themselves are an example of ACBS taking action in line with its value of creating a scholarly community that is "mutually supportive" and "effective in producing valued outcomes" (ACBS, 2014a).

Conclusion

In this chapter we have aimed to show how seeing science as a matter of contextually situated action can considerably expand the number of events that are part of the "scientific method." We have explored how the psychological flexibility model – a set of principles developed through CBS research – has been applied in a reticulated fashion onto the CBS research culture in many ways, large and small. This has been motivated in part by pragmatic philosophical assumptions that guide methodology toward a focus on the psychological context of science, and also by recognition of current inadequacies in the prevention of scientific misconduct. While the focus of this chapter has been primarily conceptual, it is worth noting preliminary empirical support for the utility of the psychological flexibility model in relation to academic and workplace behaviors. For example, in addition to reducing educator stress (Jeffcoat & Hayes, 2012), psychological flexibility interventions have been observed to increase workplace innovation (Bond & Bunce, 2000) and increase the implementation of empirically based practices (Varra, Hayes, Roget, & Fisher, 2008).

There seems to be no reason not to develop an empirical metascience based on functional contextual assumptions and principles. This chapter shows in outline form how that might be organized with psychological flexibility concepts, but it is just one example of such an application of CBS ideas to the context of research. There is no reason that RFT ideas could not be applied to empirical studies of how to describe research results in ways that foster their creative applications. Likewise, social support structures might be examined for their role in increasing attention to detail while performing research. By applying CBS thinking to science itself, a contextual approach to scientific methodology can be crafted that has a chance to be extended beyond CBS labs and into other sciences.

References

Alberts, B., & Shine, K. (1994). Scientists and the integrity of research. *Science, 266,* 1660–1661.

Al-Marzouki, S., Evans, S., Marshall, T., & Roberts, I. (2005). Are these data real? Statistical methods for the detection of data fabrication in clinical trials. *British Medical Journal, 331,* 267–270.

Anderson, M. S., Horn, A. S., Risbey, K. R., Ronning, E. A., Vries, R. D., & Martinson, B. C. (2007). What do mentoring and training in the responsible conduct of research have to do with scientists' misbehavior? Findings from a national survey of NIH-funded scientists. *Academic Medicine, 82,* 853–860.

Association for Contextual Behavioral Science (ACBS). (2014a, May). Home page. Retrieved from http://contextualscience.org/acbs

Association for Contextual Behavioral Science (ACBS). (2014b, June). *Program – World Conference 12 – Minneapolis*. Retrieved from http://contextualscience.org/wc12_program

Batten, S. (2014, June). *Program – World Conference 12 – Minneapolis*. Retrieved from http://contextualscience.org/wc12_program

Bernard, C. (1957). *An introduction to the study of experimental medicine*. New York, NY: Dover Publications. (Original work published 1865).

Biglan, A., & Embry, D. D. (2013). A framework for intentional cultural change. *Journal of Contextual Behavioral Science, 2*, 95–104.

Biglan, A., & Hayes, S. C. (1997). Should the behavioral sciences become more pragmatic? The case for functional contextualism in research on human behavior. *Applied and Preventive Psychology, 5*, 47–57.

Bond, F. W., & Bunce, D. (2000). Mediators of change in emotion-focused and problem-focused worksite stress management interventions. *Journal of Occupational Health Psychology, 5*, 156–163.

Borsboom, D. (2005). *Measuring the mind: Conceptual issues in contemporary psychometrics*. Cambridge, England: Cambridge University Press.

Boyd, R. N. (1983). On the current status of the issue of scientific realism. *Erkenntnis, 19*, 45–90.

Bruvold, W. H. (1993). A meta-analysis of adolescent smoking prevention programs. *American Journal of Public Health, 83*, 872–880.

Burke, B. L., Martens, A., & Faucher, E. H. (2010). Two decades of terror management theory: A meta-analysis of mortality salience research. *Personality and Social Psychology Review, 14*, 155–195.

Cacioppo, J. T., Semin, G. R., & Berntson, G. G. (2004). Realism, instrumentalism, and scientific symbiosis: Psychological theory as a search for truth and the discovery of solutions. *American Psychologist, 59*, 214.

Coyne, L. W. (2014, June). *Early Childhood Research Clinic*. Retrieved from http://www.suffolk.edu/college/departments/14061.php

Cronbach, L. J., & Shavelson, R. J. (2004). My current thoughts on coefficient alpha and successor procedures. *Educational and Psychological Measurement, 64*, 391–418.

Duhem, P. (1954). Physical theory and experiment. In P. Duhem, *The aim and structure of physical theory* (pp. 180–195). Princeton, NJ: Princeton University Press.

Ennett, S. T., Tobler, N. S., Ringwalt, C. L., & Flewelling, R. L. (1994). How effective is drug abuse resistance education? A meta-analysis of Project DARE outcome evaluations. *American Journal of Public Health, 84*, 1394–1401.

Evans, S. (2001). Statistical aspects of the detection of fraud. In S. Lock, F. Wells, & M. Farthing (Eds.), *Fraud and misconduct in medical research* (3rd ed., pp. 186–204). London: BMJ Publishing.

Fanelli, D. (2009). How many scientists fabricate and falsify research? A systematic review and meta-analysis of survey research. *PLoS ONE, 4*, e5738.

Faust, D. (1984) *The limits of scientific reasoning*. Minneapolis, MN: University of Minnesota Press.

Fishman, D. B. (1999). *The case for pragmatic psychology*. New York, NY: New York University Press.

Fixsen, D. L., Naoom, S. F., Blasé, K. A., Friedman, R. M., & Wallace, F. (2005). *Implementation research: A synthesis of the literature*. Tampa, FL: National Implementation Research Network.

Forster, M. R. (2000). Key concepts in model selection: Performance and generalizability. *Journal of Mathematical Psychology, 44*, 205–231.

Forsyth, J. P. (2006, January). *Lab values statement – the manifesto*. Retrieved from http://www.albany.edu/adrp/

Hacking, I. (1983). Experimentation and scientific realism. *Philosophical Topics, 13*, 71–87.

Hayes, S. C. (1993). Analytic goals and the varieties of scientific contextualism. In S. C. Hayes, L. J. Hayes, H. W. Reese, & T. R. Sarbin (Eds.), *Varieties of scientific contextualism* (pp. 11–27). Oakland, CA: New Harbinger/Context Press.

Hayes, S. C. (1998). Thirteen rules of success: A message for students. *The Behavior Therapist, 21*, 47–49.

Hayes, S. C., Barlow, D. H., & Nelson-Gray, R. O. (1999). *The scientist practitioner: Research and accountability in the age of managed care*. Boston: Allyn & Bacon.

Hayes, S. C., Barnes-Holmes, D., & Wilson, K. G. (2012). Contextual behavioral science: Creating a science more adequate to the challenge of the human condition. *Journal of Contextual Behavioral Science, 1*, 1–16.

Hayes, S. C., & Ju, W. (1997). The applied implications of rule-governed behavior. In W. O'Donohue (Ed.), *Learning and Behavior Therapy* (pp. 374–391). New York: Allyn & Bacon.

Hayes, S. C., & Long, D. M. (2013). Contextual behavioral science, evolution, and scientific epistemology. In B. Roche & S. Dymond (Eds.), *Advances in relational frame theory: Research and application*. Oakland, CA: New Harbinger.

Hayes, S. C., Long, D. M., Levin, M. E., & Follette, W. C. (2013). Treatment development: Can we find a better way? *Clinical Psychology Review, 33*, 870–882.

Hayes, S. C., Luoma, J. B., Bond, F. W., Masuda, A., & Lillis, J. (2006). Acceptance and commitment therapy: Model, processes and outcomes. *Behaviour Research and Therapy, 44*, 1–25.

Hayes, S. C., Strosahl, K. D., & Wilson, K. G. (2012). *Acceptance and commitment therapy: The process and practice of mindful change*. New York, NY: Guilford.

Hayes, S. C., & Wilson, K. G. (1995). The role of cognition in complex human behavior: A contextualistic perspective. *Journal of Behavior Therapy and Experimental Psychiatry, 26*, 241–248.

Hayes, S. C., Wilson, K. G., Gifford, E. V., Follette, V. M., & Strosahl, K. (1996). Experiential avoidance and behavioral disorders: A functional dimensional approach to diagnosis and treatment. *Journal of Consulting and Clinical Psychology, 64*, 1152.

Henderson, J. W. (1997). The yellow brick road to penicillin: a story of serendipity. *Mayo Clinic Proceedings, 72*, 683–687.

James, W. (2003). *Pragmatism: A new name for some old ways of thinking*. New York, NY: Barnes & Noble. (Original work published 1907).

Jeffcoat, T., & Hayes, S. C. (2012). A randomized trial of ACT bibliotherapy on the mental health of K-12 teachers and staff. *Behaviour Research and Therapy, 50*, 571–579.

Jenks, S. (2012). New NIH center broadens scope of translational research. *Journal of the National Cancer Institute, 104*, 728–731.

Journal of Contextual Behavioral Science (JCBS) (2014). *Author information pack*. Retrieved from http://www.journals.elsevier.com/journal-of-contextual-behavioral-science

Katelaris, A. (2011). Research fraud – where to from here? *Medical Journal of Australia, 194*, 619.

Kuhn, T. S. (1957). *The Copernican revolution: Planetary astronomy in the development of western thought*. Cambridge, MA: Harvard University Press.

Kuhn, T. S. (1970). *The structure of scientific revolutions* (2nd ed.). Chicago, IL: Chicago University Press.

Kupfer, D. J., First, M. B., & Regier, D. A. (2002). *A research agenda for DSM V*. Washington, DC: American Psychiatric Association.

Laudan, L. (1977). *Progress and its problems: Towards a theory of scientific growth*. Berkeley, CA: University of California.

Laudan, L. (1981). A confutation of convergent realism. *Philosophy of Science, 28*, 19–49.

Laudan, L. (1996). Demystifying underdetermination. In L. Laudan (Ed.), *Beyond positivism and relativism* (pp. 29–54). Boulder, CO: Westview.

Long, D. M. (2013). Pragmatism, realism, and psychology: Understanding theory selection criteria. *Journal of Contextual Behavioral Science, 2*, 61–67.

Lord, C. G. (2004). A guide to PhD graduate school: How they keep score in the big leagues. In J. M. Darley, M. P. Zanna, & H. L. Roediger III (Eds.), *The compleat academic: A career guide* (2nd ed., pp. 3–15). Washington, DC: American Psychological Association.

Lynam, D. R., Milich, R., Zimmerman, R., Novak, S. P., Logan, T. K., Martin, C., … Clayton, R. (1999). Project DARE: No effects at 10-year follow-up. *Journal of Consulting and Clinical Psychology, 67*, 590–593.

MacCallum, R. C., Wegener, D. T., Uchino, B. N., & Fabrigar, L. R. (1993). The problem of equivalent models in applications of covariance structure analysis. *Psychological Bulletin, 114*, 185.

Marx, M. H. (1976). Formal theory. In M. H. Marx & F. E. Goodson (Eds.), *Theories in contemporary psychology* (2nd ed., pp. 234–260). New York, NY: Macmillan.

McMullian, E. (1984). A case for scientific realism. In J. Leplin (Ed.) *Scientific realism* (pp. 8–40). Berkeley, CA: University of California Press.

Meehl, P. E. (1978). Theoretical risks and tabular asterisks: Sir Karl, Sir Ronald, and the slow progress of soft psychology. *Journal of Consulting and Clinical Psychology, 46*, 806–834.

Meehl, P. E. (1983). Subjectivity in psychoanalytic inference: The nagging persistence of Wilhelm Fliess's Achensee question. In J. Earman (Ed.), *Minnesota studies in the philosophy of science: Vol. X, testing scientific theories* (pp. 349–411). Minneapolis, MN: University of Minnesota Press.

Meehl, P. E. (1992). The miracle argument for realism: An important lesson to be learned by generalizing from Carrier's counterexamples. *Studies in History and Philosophy of Science, 23*, 267–282.

Misak, C. (Ed.). (2007). *New pragmatists*. Oxford, England: Oxford University Press.

Moore, J. (2010). Philosophy of science, with special consideration given to behaviorism as the philosophy of the science of behavior. *The Psychological Record, 60*, 137–150.

Muir, W. M. (1985). Relative efficiency of selection for performance of birds housed in colony cages based on performance in single bird cages. *Poultry Science, 64*, 2239–2247.

Muir, W.M. (1996). Group selection for adaptation to multiple-hen cages: Selection program and direct responses. *Poultry Science, 75*, 447–458.

Murrell, A. (2014, June). *UNT Contextual Psychology Group mission*. Retrieved from http://psychology.unt.edu/dr-amy-murrell/unt-contextual-psychology-group-mission

National Institute of Medicine. (2002). *Integrity in scientific research: Creating an environment that promotes responsible conduct of research*. Washington, DC: National Research Council.

Nickerson, R. S. (1998). Confirmation bias: A ubiquitous phenomenon in many guises. *Review of General Psychology, 2*, 175–220.

Omer, H., & Dar, R. (1992). Changing trends in three decades of psychotherapy research: The flight from theory into pragmatics. *Journal of Consulting and Clinical Psychology, 60*, 88–93.

Oregon Research Institute. (2014, June). *Who we are: Work hard, play hard!* Retrieved from http://www.ori.org/about_ori/who_we_are

Pashler, H., & Wagenmakers, E. J. (2012). Editors' introduction to the special section on replicability in psychological science: A crisis of confidence? *Perspectives on Psychological Science, 7*, 528–530.

Popper, K. R. (1959). *The logic of scientific discovery*. London, England: Hutchinson.

Putnam, H. (1978). What is realism? In H. Putnam, *Meaning and the moral sciences* (pp. 140–153). London, England: Routledge and Kegan Paul.

Quine, W. V. (1951). Main trends in recent philosophy: Two dogmas of empiricism. *The Philosophical Review, 60,* 20–43.

Rorty, R. (1979). *Philosophy and the mirror of nature.* Princeton, NJ: Princeton University Press.

Ryan, K. J. (1998). Research fraud and public trust. *Forum for Applied Research and Public Policy, 13,* 50–56.

Scarr, S. (1985). Constructing psychology: Making facts and fables for our times. *American Psychologist, 40,* 499–512.

Shapiro, S. L., Astin, J. A., Bishop, S. R., & Cordova, M. (2005). Mindfulness-based stress reduction for health care professionals: results from a randomized trial. *International Journal of Stress Management, 12,* 164.

Simonsohn, U. (2013). Just post it: The lesson learned from two cases of fabricated data detected by statistics alone. *Psychological Science, 24,* 1875–1888.

Sivak, J. (2010). The Charles F. Prentice Award Lecture 2009: Crystalline lens research and serendipity in science. *Optometry and Vision Science, 87,* 622–630.

Skinner, B. F. (1969). *Contingencies of reinforcement: A theoretical analysis.* New York, NY: Appleton-Century-Crofts.

Skinner, B. F. (1974). *About behaviorism.* New York, NY: Knopf.

Skinner, B. F. (1981). Selection by consequences. *Science, 213,* 501–504.

Steinberg, D. (2011). Chance and serendipity in science: Two examples from my own career. *Journal of Biological Chemistry, 286,* 37895–37904.

Steneck, N. H. (2006). Fostering integrity in research: Definitions, current knowledge and future directions. *Science and Engineering Ethics, 12,* 53–74.

Tilburg University (2011). Interim report regarding the breach of scientific integrity committed by prof. D.A. Stapel. *Tilburg University,* 1–21.

Varra, A. A., Hayes, S. C., Roget, N., & Fisher, G. (2008). A randomized control trial examining the effect of acceptance and commitment training on clinician willingness to use evidence-based pharmacotherapy. *Journal of Consulting and Clinical Psychology, 76,* 449–458.

Wicherts, J. M. (2011). Psychology must learn a lesson from fraud case. *Nature, 480,* 7.

Wilson, D. S. (2012). Consilience: Making contextual behavioral science part of the United Ivory Archipelago. *Journal of Contextual Behavioral Science, 1,* 39–42.

Wilson, K. G. (2014, April). *The Mississippi Center for Contextual Psychology lab manifesto.* Retrieved from http://www.kellygwilson.com/Manifesto.html

Wilson, K. G., & DuFrene, T. (2009). *Mindfulness for two: An acceptance and commitment therapy approach to mindfulness in psychotherapy.* Oakland, CA: New Harbinger s.

Winerman, L. (2013). Interesting results: Can they be replicated? *Monitor on Psychology, 44,* 38.

Wise, J. (2011). Extent of Dutch psychologist's research fraud was "unprecedented." *British Medical Journal, 343,* d7201.

Woolf, S. H. (2008). The meaning of translational research and why it matters. *Journal of the American Medical Association, 299,* 211–213.

Zigmond, M. J., & Fischer, B. A. (2002). Beyond fabrication and plagiarism: The little murders of everyday science. *Science and Engineering Ethics, 8,* 229–234.

7

A Functional Place for Language in Evolution

The Contribution of Contextual Behavioral Science to the Study of Human Evolution

Jean-Louis Monestès

Selection, the central process of evolution, is common to evolutionary sciences and to behavior analysis (Catania, 2001; Cziko, 1995; Donahoe, 2012). Based on this overlap, behavior analysts long ago argued for a marriage between behavior science and evolutionary sciences (e.g., Skinner, 1981). It never occurred.

One of the main reasons appears to be the limited place granted to behavior in many approaches to evolutionary sciences, at least historically. In the hands of well-known evolutionists, behavior is often considered simply as the phenotypic expression of the genome, and as a dependent rather than an explicative variable (e.g., Maynard Smith & Szathmary, 2000). A second reason might be that the behavioral approach has had a hard time "when dealing with species for which a theory of mind seems essential" (Kokko & Jennions, 2010, p. 293). As a consequence, traditional behavior analysis has not been able to propose a convincing hypothesis for the processes and role of language in human evolution.

Recently, however, there have been dramatic changes, both in evolutionary sciences and in behavior analysis, in these two areas. Thus, the time seems right to re-examine the relationship between evolutionary sciences and behavioral perspectives.

In evolutionary sciences, the place of behavior is being actively reconsidered. Epigenetic inheritance allows for a fresh look at the role of behavior as an important variable in evolution (Danchin, Giraldeau, Valone, & Wagner, 2004; Jablonka & Lamb, 2005; Mameli, 2004; Pigliucci & Muller, 2010). In addition, multilevel and multidimensional approaches to evolution are now being seriously considered, in which the processes of variation and selective retention act simultaneously on different dimensions of selection (gene, epigenes, behavior, culture, symbolic events) as well as on the individual and group levels (e.g., Jablonka & Lamb, 2014). Contextual behavioral science (CBS) is shedding light on language mechanisms in a convincing manner that is linking behavioral principles to evolutionarily plausible accounts of language and cognition (e.g., Hayes & Sanford, 2014). Specifically, empirical evidence in support of relational frame theory (Hayes, Barnes-Holmes, & Roche, 2001)

The Wiley Handbook of Contextual Behavioral Science, First Edition. Edited by Robert D. Zettle, Steven C. Hayes, Dermot Barnes-Holmes, and Anthony Biglan.
© 2016 John Wiley & Sons, Ltd. Published 2016 by John Wiley & Sons, Ltd.

appears to be underlining the importance of language in human evolution, by showing how language transforms the relations between humans and their environment.

It is a central argument of this chapter that language has become a true inheritance stream responsible for a large part of human evolution. Among other gifts, language gives human beings a kind of intentionality that alters their place in nondirectional evolution in its broad sense.

This chapter first describes behavior as a central driving force in evolution, and then discusses the major influence of the specific kind of behavior called "language" on human evolution. Both series of arguments suggest that CBS has an important role to play among the evolutionary sciences.

The Central Role of Behavior in Evolution

A Generalized Selectionist Approach

Selection occurs in any complex system capable of both variation and transmission of adapted patterns. In the life sciences, selection occurs simultaneously on several dimensions, each contributing to the differential selection not just of genes, but also of epigenes, behaviors, symbolic events, and culture; in other words, on any inherited variant. This chapter will first introduce the selectionist model application at the behavioral level, the core subject of this chapter, and will then turn to the implications of multidimensional and multilevel approaches to evolution.

Selection at the behavior level. Selection by consequences is a mechanism which biological evolution and operant conditioning share in common (Skinner, 1981). One of the major contributions of behavior analysis to psychology is the way it highlighted the importance of consequences on the actions of organisms. In biological and behavioral evolution, "cause," in a sense, works backward. One needs to focus on what happens after the event being considered, be it behavior or other phenotypic expressions, in order to understand how actions and gene/epigene systems become strengthened. The consequences of behavior become the causes of its subsequent occurrence, in the same way as an organism's adaptation to its current environment sets its capacity to reproduce and transmit its genetic and epigenetic organization.

Natural selection at all levels automatically emerges as soon as three conditions are fulfilled: variation, selection, and heritability. At the behavioral level, the primary unit of analysis is the operant, and the study is done at the ontogenetic level. Behavioral variation is ubiquitous, such as individuals varying within populations. Even two occurrences of the apparently same action, with exactly the same consequences, are seldom identical. For example, a door can be opened with left or right hand, facing it or not, pushing vigorously or slowly, and so on. Second, as adaptation to the environment determines each organism's survival, the different consequences of behaviors will determine their future. For behaviors, the reinforcement process corresponds to the survival criterion in natural selection. Depending on their consequences, behaviors differentially reproduce, that is, their future probability varies, much as the genetic pool of an organism is transmitted to the next generation through the number of offspring it breeds (Donahoe, 2012).

CBS broadens the unit of analysis of behavior science by fully taking into account the context of occurrence. "History, circumstances, and consequences are aspects of the act itself in a functional sense" (Hayes, Barnes-Holmes, & Wilson, 2012, p. 3). The act and its context are not fully separable in a contextual approach of behavior. Hence, context – considered both historically and situationally – represents a part of the selection unit in a selectionist and contextual view of behavior. In the present chapter, the ongoing situated act-in-context is taken as the unit of analysis for the selectionist approach of behavior. As such, the ongoing act-in-context can be selected, and can "reproduce" (can be repeated), provided that the context retains enough common characteristics with the initial context in which behavior first occurred and was reinforced.

Multidimensional and multilevel selection. Natural selection has been proposed to address problems in various fields, such as epistemology, economics, psychology, anthropology, or medicine (Cziko, 1997). A selectionist approach can be adopted at any level of analysis, as soon as a system is capable of variation and selective persistence.

In the study of species' evolution the hypothesis of a unique effect of selection at the organism level has been prevailing for a long time. However, the question of the level on which selection operates – gene, cell, organism, or group – has been an issue in evolutionary sciences from its earliest days. Multilevel selection proposes that selection operates simultaneously at different levels so as to maximize survival and reproductive success of the concerned unit of selection. Contextual conditions determine the balance that exists between levels. Disadvantageous behavioral patterns for one individual in the context of within-group competition may favor group members in the context of between-group competition.

Cooperation is one of the best examples of this mechanism: Altruistic behavior is selectively disadvantageous within groups but may be favored at group level, if groups whose individuals cooperate are more prone to survive and reproduce (Wilson, Van Vugt, & O'Gorman, 2008; Wilson & Wilson, 2008). Thus, different levels of selection can act simultaneously, and patterns selected at one level can impact other levels, depending on the specific context of selection.

Evolutionary sciences are beginning to leave an era in which the gene was considered to be virtually the only mechanism by which heritable changes could appear and be transmitted across generations. Well developed multidimensional approaches have been proposed, for example by Jablonka and Lamb (2005; 2014) who argue that four inheritance systems play a role in evolution: genetic, epigenetic, behavioral, and symbolic (see also Danchin & Wagner, 2010; Danchin et al., 2011). Variations exist in each system and can be selected and transmitted when adapted to the environment. Ultimately, each of these dimensions may have an effect on evolution. The last three systems – epigenetic, behavioral, and symbolic – insert a new principle into Darwinian theory: Changes during organisms' lifetime can also play a role in evolution, and consequently behavior takes a central role in evolutionary processes. In part this is because behavioral and symbolic changes can persist directly across lifetimes in the form of cultural adaptations and then be transmitted to the next generation; in part it is because they alter the conditions under which genes are expressed and are selected on the basis of phenotypic variation.

Evolutionary sciences and CBS study how environmental regularities bring about changes in organisms and populations. However, the influence of the environment is nondistinctive: it does not influence only genes, or only behaviors, at an individual or group scale. It operates on everything, simultaneously, in a "unified fabric of evolutionary development" (Hayes & Sanford, 2014, p. 116). Evolution constitutes a unique process to which any dimension (genetic and epigenetic, behavioral, and symbolic) contributes regardless of the relevant configuration on which the environment acts (cell, organism, group).

Behavior as a Driving Force in Evolution

Beyond selection at the ontogenetic level, behavior increasingly appears to be a central driving force at the phylogenetic level, even if it has long been considered as a simple phenotypic expression of the genome. Behaviors enhance their own transmission across generations, have a direct action on gene expression as shown by epigenetic studies, and finally contribute to their own evolution by modifying the environment.

Behaviors enhance their own replication. With the arrival of selection by consequences through operant learning, the behaviors of organisms were more able to change at an ontogenetic level. Slow behavioral adaptations by means of genetic variation and selection cycles across generations were no longer needed for an organism to adapt to its environment. Operant learning brought plasticity to behaviors and gave rise to a much broader variety of behaviors. Within this behavioral diversity, different patterns of interaction with the environment were tested. Eventually, individuals who found a "Good Trick" (Dennett, 1991) survived and reproduced more than those who did not discover this efficient behavior. Consequently, operant learning created a new selection pressure. Individuals exhibiting behaviors very far from the Good Trick could then be adversely selected, leading to behavior being selected across generations, provided that the determinant part of the environment stays the same (but see the section "Context and the behavioral evolutionary loop"), thus transforming a learned behavior into a genetically transmitted one. In fact, learning itself may have been selected because it allows just such rapid phenotypic adjustments, which would eventually be selected at genetic level. Generally speaking, this effect (the selection of genetic constitutive variations that substitute for facultative variations), called the Baldwin effect (Simpson, 1953), enhances the ability to respond rapidly and efficiently to new stimuli. The final result is that "species with plasticity will tend to evolve faster" (Dennett, 1991, p. 186), because the adapted behaviors will tend to enhance their own reproduction in the succeeding generations. Through this process, ultimately, behaviors stand as a true selection process for themselves, accelerating the evolution of species. In addition to the epigenetic modulation of DNA, the Baldwin effect represents one of the central arguments to state that "genes are followers, not necessarily leaders, in phenotypic evolution" (West-Eberhard, 2003, p. 158).

Behaviors directly modulate DNA. Epigenetics is the study of gene expression modifications mediated by environmental variations or developmental noise acting at the ontogenetic level. These modifications can result from environmental events or from the organism's behaviors. Dietary choices, niche selection, and niche transformation are among the behaviors that can be responsible for modifications of gene expression. To date, the main mechanisms studied to apprehend phenotypic expression variation are DNA methylation and histone acetylation, and RNA-mediated genetic control of gene expression, but these are only some of a much larger set of such epigenetic processes (Jablonka & Lamb, 2005).

A remarkable characteristic of epigenetic modifications is their role as an inheritance system in its own right. To a degree, changes in genetic expression through methylation and RNA-mediated control are transmissible across generations without any change in nucleotide sequences. Expression of cellular DNA can be transformed by epigenetic processes that are transmitted to daughter cells during mitosis, and at times across generations due to modifications in gametes. These modifications of gene expression can extend across several generations even when the original cause is withdrawn. For example, Dias and Ressler (2014) conditioned male mice to fear a specific odor, and looked for changes two generations later. Through epigenetic changes in sperm, offspring showed an increased behavioral sensitivity to the odor conditioned two generations before, without having encountered it in their own lifetimes.

The fact that genes can be differentially expressed across different contexts, even across generations, alters the role of genes, environment, and behavior in determining the organism's fate. If genes are differentially expressed in different contexts impacted by behavior, behavior assumes a far more central role in the biological evolution of the organisms emitting these behaviors. An organism's behaviors can have consequences for offspring, even if the descendants never reproduce these behaviors and live in a very different environment.

Like learning, epigenetic mechanisms help organisms who are confronted to various and ever changing environments that forbid an exhaustive programming at genome level. Epigenetic mechanisms allow rapid biological adjustments, far quicker than gene selection across sexual reproduction. Learning processes also allow adaptation to environments new to the species. The combination of both provides an ontogenetic regulation mechanism that fosters rapid biological adjustments. Behavioral plasticity is conveyed by learning processes that in turn mediate gene expression plasticity, so that learning processes serve as an interface between organism and environment, driving changes in both.

Context and the behavioral evolutionary loop. Each of an organism's behaviors occurs in a precise context, and CBS proposes that "history, circumstances, and consequences are aspects of the act itself in a functional sense" (Hayes et al., 2012, p. 3). This point explains why CBS chooses the ongoing situated act-in-context as a unit of analysis. In addition, at a psychological level of analysis, one has to focus on the situated actions of whole organisms (Hayes, 1993), and to consider behaviors as interactions in and with a context (including other organisms), that is considered both historically and situationally (Hayes & Sanford, 2014).

Most studies of behavior and learning processes conduct that analysis at the organism level. The study of reactions to stimuli, and ontogenetic transformation of behaviors according to their consequences, brought precise and reliable knowledge on respondent and operant learning, respectively. However, it is also the case that the environment itself changes, in part due to operant behavior that "operates" on it. This has been less studied, even though any change in the environment can have tremendous importance for the evolution of organisms and the further modification of their behavior. In a larger evolutionary context, considering the effects of consequences on the organism should go hand in hand with consideration of the environmental modification that results from the organism's behaviors.

In a hypothetical example, imagine that a chimpanzee finds edible termites after pulling away a strip of tree bark. The reinforcing effectiveness of eating termites would determine the future probability of pulling away bark strips from trees. As the behavior appearred more frequently, the chimpanzee would find more termites, and its behavior would continue to be reinforced. The repetition of this behavior in its ecological niche, however, could produce large-scale environmental changes that would lead the termites to become scarcer due to exhaustion of the supply of trees in which termites could grow. Pulling barks away would then be less and less reinforced, and would progressively extinguish. The conditions leading to extinction of the behavior were created by the very success of the behavior that was driven to extinction. The consequences of the behavior changed the environment in such a way that, in return, the environment itself caused the extinction of the very behavior that initially modified it.

In most research on learning processes in the laboratory, environmental modifications are not much considered. Indeed, in most such experiments, these modifications are controlled so that they cannot appear. However, in the natural environment it is commonplace, as pointed in the previous example, for the future of behavior controlled by consequences to be impacted by changes in the long-term probability of consequences coming from the environment that are partly organized by the behavior itself. Among other things, this means that taking environmental changes into account is essential to understand the long-term role of behavior in an evolutionary context. Such a systemic approach does not represent a different domain of study; rather, given the central place of the environment in the selection of behaviors, a systemic approach helps capture the act-in-context in its whole complexity at a psychological level.

The point of view defended here is that behaviors are at the center stage of evolution because they modify the very context in which actions appear (see also Odling Smee, Laland, & Feldman, 2003). In a sense, operant behaviors change themselves, in a sort of evolutionary loop.

This behavioral evolutionary loop is amplified when an important part of the environment consists of other organisms also capable of rapid adaptation to environmental changes through learning. A behavioral evolutionary loop – the modification of behavioral evolution by means of the consequences this very behavior creates – is considerably enhanced in the case of consequences produced by other organisms with similar learning abilities. When social creatures behave in the presence of others, behavioral consequences may often be mediated by the social context and the actions of others. The behavior of others changes in relation to my actions, and others would be sensitive to the changes they create in my behavior. A kind of social interlocking system can emerge, in which behavioral evolutionary loops exist as a natural result of complementary social contingencies. Consequently, the diversity and maintenance of consequences to my behavior will be broader and more robust than in an environment deprived of organisms with learning abilities. As a highly social species, humans emit behaviors in systems in which the evolutionary loop is common and notably influential.

The Crucial Role of Language in Human Evolution

Behavior plays a central role in evolution because it is a true unit on which selection operates, because it modulates DNA expression, and because it contributes to its own selection. In human species, symbolic behaviors and language constitute a very special category of behaviors, which dramatically changes evolution, and which due to patterns of retention can function as inheritance streams in its own right (Jablonka & Lamb, 2006; 2014). Language brings modification for each step of the selection process: It selects behaviors, it modifies the value of the stimuli potentially responsible for their selection, it increases variation in behaviors, and it changes their retention and inheritance. Finally, language can give rise to behaviors that are seemingly incompatible with the process of evolution itself. CBS helps capture the modifications language engenders on human evolution by studying the mechanisms operating at the core of language and symbolic behavior.

CBS Definition of Language

CBS relies on relational frame theory (RFT; Hayes, Barnes-Holmes, & Roche, 2001) to apprehend language. RFT proposes a special learned unit, arbitrarily applicable derived relational responding, to account for language in human species. Derived relational responding has three specific properties. First, when a human being is taught a relation between a stimulus A and a stimulus B (e.g., A=B), they are also taught, initially through multiple exemplars, to derive the inverse relation (e.g., B=A). This mutual entailment property permits any verbal stimulus to "stand for" or "refer to" any other stimulus, providing that they have been put in an equivalence relation. The second property of derived relational responding is combinatiorial entailment, meaning simply that mutually entailed relations combine into networks of relations. When at least three stimuli are set in an equivalence relation by pairs (e.g., A=B, B=C), relationships are derived between the two stimuli which were not previously related (e.g., A=C, C=A). Eventually, when trained to derive relations between stimuli, human beings learn to do it independently from the intrinsic properties of stimuli, under the control of arbitrary relational cues (Blackledge, 2003). The last property of arbitrarily applicable derived relational responding is transformation of stimulus functions. If you are bitten by a piranha (A), and then I inform you that piranhas are *characidae* (A=B), and then, in presence of another fish you are told that this fish is a *characidae* (C=B), you might be scared of this one as well because of the combinatorial relational (A=C) and the transformation of emotional functions from A or C, even though you never had any direct experience with this animal, and the only new stimuli in your environment are the words you heard. Transformations of stimulus functions are under the control of functional cues that select the relevance of specific functional dimensions. These properties (contextually controlled mutual and combinatorial entailment; contextually controlled transformation of stimulus functions) are argued to apply to all words and symbols we use. The easiest example is a relationship of equivalence. When any event is set into an equivalence relationship with a word or symbol, the word acquires some stimulus properties of that event, and "stands for" that event.

How Language Selects Behaviors

Language is so pervasive among humans that it is very difficult to act without any occurrence of language being automatically involved. Although arbitrarily applicable derived relational responding emerges originally as a result of specific social contingencies (e.g., Luciano, Gómez-Becerra, & Rodríguez-Valverde, 2007), as it develops it helps people predict and control their environment in ways that are impossible to avoid. As a symbolic system, and because of the properties presented above, language dramatically impacts the selection processes impinging on human beings.

Language changes how stimuli select behaviors. A beefsteak has a reinforcing value for any animal that eats meat, at least when they are food deprived. No doubt a piece of steak consumed today would have had much the same reinforcing value for our pre-verbal ancestors. However, a piece of beefsteak consumed today may also evoke verbal health or ecological concerns (such as worries over cholesterol, or objections to the amount of land and water needed to raise cattle, and so on) that could undermine or even eliminate its reinforcing value for some contemporaries. The steak's taste and nutrients have not changed as compared to a similar steak eaten by our ancestors. What is different is the relational network that surrounds meat. The punitive value of steak was not acquired by eating: it was acquired by language. Stimulus functions, originally appetitive, were transformed: meat now reminds consumers of the risk of heart attacks, or occasions guilt about polluting the planet. Through arbitrarily applicable derived relational responding and the transformation of functions, stimuli can acquire virtually any stimulus function. Quoting Epictetus, "What upsets people is not things themselves but their judgments about the things." RFT explains how these "judgments" are built and are contextually regulated. The comprehension of the behavioral processes responsible for these symbolic effects alters our views of the role of behavior, including verbal behavior, in the evolution of humans.

Due to the symbolic functions afforded by derived relational responding, verbal organisms evolve in a sort of parallel reality populated with the verbally derived significance of events in addition to the intrinsic properties of the events they interact with. In a very specific way, behaviors can be selected by these symbolic functions, even though they may never have any direct consequences for the organism. Stimuli select actions due to what they represent, not to what they are directly. In other words, symbolic stimuli can select behaviors based on the derived functions they embody.

Language as a selection variable for behaviors. In addition to the modifications of usual sources of behavioral selection, language can constitute a stream of selection in its own right. In many cases, behaviors are controlled by language alone. Rule-governed behavior (Hayes, 1989) can be defined as behavior, either verbal or nonverbal, that is under the control of verbal antecedents (Catania, 1991; Zettle & Hayes, 1982). One type of rule-governed behavior is "pliance" – rules that are followed because of a history of socially mediated consequences for the correspondence between a rule and relevant action (Hayes, Zettle, & Rosenfarb, 1989). The social approval engaged by pliance can totally mask other effects – to the point that the person becomes insensitive to the direct consequences of their behaviors (Catania, Shimoff, & Matthews, 1989, 1990; Hayes, Brownstein, Zettle, Rosenfarb, & Korn, 1986; Monestès, Villatte, Stewart, & Loas, 2014; Shimoff & Catania, 1998). An example occurs when actions are engaged because doing so is "right" or "proper." Such an appeal to verbal consequences can maintain behaviors even when these behaviors are ineffective or even deleterious to the organism.

Due to the derivation of stimulus functions, verbal stimuli can gain a punishing or reinforcing value from the relational networks in which they participate. This happens, for example, when I thank you for your help in moving my washing machine. Verbal stimuli become factors of selection in these circumstances capable of modifying the probability and frequency of the behaviors they follow, with the particularity that this source of selection is always available, inexhaustible and, to some degree, can be self-administrated.

Language Creates an Explosion of Behavior Variation

Variation is one of the pillars of evolutionary processes. Without variation, any differential selection or adaptation to environment modifications is impossible. At the biological level, variation is so important that it is itself selected. The transmission of noncoding DNA, representing 98% of the human genetic pool (Elgar & Vavouri, 2008) highlights the importance of the source of variation. Some of this so-called "dead space" is regulating the active genome thus creating orders of magnitude more variation from which new patterns can emerge and be selected (Jablonka & Lamb, 2014). Sexual selection provides another example: asexual reproduction is inheritantly less variable, which is why organisms capable of both sexual and asexual reproduction shift to the former strategy in the case of drastic changes in the environment (e.g., Nevalainen & Luoto, 2013).

At the behavioral level, variation also plays a paramount role, although it received less attention than the variables responsible for selection (Dewitte & Verguts, 1999). The very existence of learning abilities points to the determinant role of variation in behavior. In addition, the capacity for variation has been demonstrated as a true dimension of behavior, which contributes to new patterns of response (Grunow & Neuringer 2002), and which can also be reinforced (Neuringer, 2002; Page & Neuringer, 1985). The high frequency of variation in behavior topography is one of the reasons why function is targeted by behavior science: Behaviors with different topographies can have an identical function and be functionally equivalent (Kantor, 1938).

Regardless of the unit of selection (e.g., gene or behavior), variability is so decisive that it is systematically selected, even though in the abstract one would think that the tendency to select perfectly adapted patterns would lead to transmission of successful patterns without variation. With regard to language, the three properties of derived relational responding – mutual entailment, combinatorial entailment, and transformation of functions – create an explosion of variation in verbal organisms' behaviors. With mutual and combinatorial entailment, one can derive four relations after being taught only two relations between three stimuli. Generally speaking, when someone is taught X relations, they derive X^2. The three properties of derived relational responding also apply to relations between relations, which allows the creation of thousands of derived relations after being initially taught only eight object–sign relations, for example (Hayes & Long, 2013). In addition, since relations among stimuli are not restricted to equivalence but can comprise a wide variety of other types of relations, such as comparison or conditionality, verbal networks can ultimately award the opposite function, from reinforcing to punishing, for example. This creates an exponential increase of behavior variation in relation to any stimulus: Since stimuli may acquire new functions by mean of derivation and transformation, they can evoke behavior that would never appear otherwise. In the context of large relational networks, such as exists in any educated human, the number of possible derived relations or functions (and thus sources of variation) is literally incalculable.

Finally, language itself is capable of tremendous variation. Because the stimuli composing language are arbitrary, they can be endlessly transformed and blended to create new linguistic configurations, which eventually split, much as distinct species appear through the geographical separation of several individuals. Linguistic stimuli can also be combined and associated to form new meanings, detached from direct experience, as is the case in fiction, poetry, metaphor, or science. These possibilities linked to language variation likely played a central role in the enrichment of humans' incredibly broad repertoire. Although the famous discovery of the Blombos perforated shell beads in South Africa (Henshilwood, d'Errico, Vanhaeren, Van Niekerk, & Jacobs, 2004) moved the early signs of symbolic activity back to 75,000 years ago, the spreading of symbolic activity around 40,000 years ago corresponds to a period of prodigious explosion of behavior diversity which has continued to become more complex since.

Modification of Behavioral Heritability through Language

Before language, transmission of behaviors between individuals relied on such processes as imitation, or inducing others to contact environments in which actions would be shaped. Imitation and social learning represents a faster means of behavior transmission than genetic inheritance, but suffers from serious limitations: A unity of time and location is required between the organism who emits the behavior and the one who reproduces it. At times a strict environmental configuration is necessary to allow the occurrence of the behavior. For lithic reduction to be transmitted through imitation, an individual who doesn't know how to use a hammerstone needs to meet someone who does, and the relevant stones must be available around them. With derived relational responding and the possibility to symbolize stimuli and behaviors by mean of vocal sounds or drawn signs, behavior transmission is fundamentally altered and enhanced. The ability to use arbitrary language stimuli withdraws the obligatory encounter between the model and the learner. Verbal stimuli can be transmitted across time and space, whatever the context, which dramatically increases the possibility of behavioral transmission, horizontally between contemporaries, and also vertically across generations. Finally, written forms of language, which appeared more recently in human history, allows for retention for an almost infinite duration and without volume limitations, that is, independently from human memory capacities. This form of heritability nowadays has been fleshed out in books, tapes, digital media, and the like. Relatively speaking, such media are extremely reliable, allowing for essentially perfect reproduction and conservation of information, resulting in an accumulation of perfectly transmitted behaviors.

Intuitively, one could think that such a large and perfect transmission of behaviors would result in the diminution of behavior variation. On the contrary, transmission of behaviors by means of language contributes to the variation of behaviors and to the appearance of new behaviors. The invention of currency around 4000 BCE in Sumer constitutes a good example of this phenomenon. Globular envelopes were used to lock up clay tokens representing, for example, a number of sheep confided to a shepherd. Progressively, these envelopes were engraved on their surface to replace tokens, and then flattened out. These tablets were then exchanged, giving rise to trade instead of the prevailing barter (Herrenschmidt, 2007). Without the symbolization allowed by derived relational responding, currencies and trade would never have appeared, and nor would a large part of human behavior.

Evolution Has No Purpose but Humans Do

When observing a perfectly adapted organ, such as an eye or a wing, the first conclusion that comes to mind is that such a perfect adaptation cannot be anything but designed. According to the famous assertion by William Paley, if something perfectly fits its environment, that design implies a designer, and a goal to be reached, a designed function or a plan. This teleological argument has long been disproved, notably by Darwin himself (see also Gould, 1989; 1996; 2000), and the consensus among evolution scientists is that evolution has no goal, and is nondirectional.

This point is rather difficult to apprehend since the selection of the most adapted patterns easily and mistakenly leads to the conclusion that adaptation, or progress, constitute the final goals of evolution. This is a mistake at the level of process: There is no goal, and no place for teleology in evolution.

While this viewpoint is agreed upon among evolutionists in the life sciences, the nonteleological argument is more difficult to accept for psychologists, and that for a simple reason: Human beings seem to act with intentionality. This leaves us with a puzzle: How can a species, an outcome of the evolution process, emit goal-directed behaviors if there is no goal for evolution?

Relational frame theory allows CBS to deal with verbal purpose and intention, without questioning the nondirectionality of evolution. For a verbal organism, "verbal time is the past as the constructed future in the present" (Hayes, 1992, p. 114). Contrary to nonverbal organisms, a constructed future exists for humans in the form of "before … after" or "if … then" relational framing, which can influence present behaviors. Derived relational learning allows stimuli to control behavior even when these stimuli are absent. With derived relational responding, behaviors' functions cannot be analyzed by exclusively considering past experiences: The analysis must also include a temporal extension because such temporal extensions are themselves part of human language and cognition (Hayes & Long, 2013).

Intentionality and goal-directed behaviors do exist in the human repertoire. However, in order to avoid circularity, "the theory must explain how purposiveness of this type has come into existence at this stage of evolution without using the very notion of purposiveness that is being explained" (Maxwell, 2010, p. 266). The RFT proposition reaches this condition. Although verbal organisms can emit goal-directed behaviors, language, the very condition for these behaviors to occur, did not appear for a purpose. Derived relational responding results from selection at both phylogenetical and ontogenetical scale and is, as such, the product of nondirectional evolution.

On a phylogenetic scale, several hypotheses have been proposed to explain language evolution within a selectionist account, one of the most convincing being that symbolic behavior evolved as an extension of human cooperation (Hayes & Sanford, 2014; see also Tomasello, 2008). At an ontological scale, RFT states that arbitrarily applied relational responding is an operant (Hayes, Fox et al., 2001; Hayes, Gifford, & Wilson, 1996), and is the product of a multi-exemplar training history (Healy, Barnes-Holmes, & Smeets, 2000). As such, arbitrary applied relational responding is selected without a goal, but according to its consequences. RFT fleshes out Dennett's (1995) intuition that "intentionality doesn't come from on high; it percolates from below, from the initially mindless and pointless algorithmic processes that gradually acquire meaning and intelligence as they develop" (p. 205). The fact that human beings can set goals for their behaviors does not imply that evolution is goal-directed. At the evolutionary scale, the possibility for human beings to act in a goal-oriented manner is a by-product. Actually, human capacity for goal-directed behaviors conversely helps to understand why humans grant intention to processes which do not have any: how can one possibly imagine that evolution is nondirectional when most of our actions are?

Analyzing the possibility for human beings to act with intention and in a goal-directed manner raises a fundamental question: Can human beings now set a purpose for their evolution when evolution writ large has none? Goal-directedness alters a great many things in the application of evolutionary principles to human action. For example, although derived relational responding was likely selected in part due to its resulting increase in variability, CBS researchers in acceptance and commitment therapy target the psychological rigidity (and thus the *decrease* in variability) that results when avoiding emotions or following rules dominates over other sources of behavioral regulation. Goal setting as a by-product of evolution can promote social ills (e.g., seeking comfort or ease can lead to ecological issues that threaten life on a planetary scale) but it can also lead to the deliberate use of selectionist ideas for social good (Wilson, 2007).

Contextual behavioral perspectives are useful in part because they empower us to consider how best to use evolutionary processes to promote human welfare. That is what is occurring in psychotherapy, or any applied domain. Everything is possible, and evolution does not care about the direction human beings will choose. Humanity has to take this responsibility.

Conclusion

Appreciating the global role of behavior in evolution erases the division between hard and soft science. Due to its influence on the environment, on DNA expression, on its own replication, and at different levels of selection, behavior plays a central role in the evolution of complex organisms. From a CBS perspective, language, because it changes the selection processes and represents a true selection force, a variation stream, and a prolific medium of symbolism, is at the very heart of human evolution. All these reasons put "contextual behavioral approaches into the center of evolution science itself" (Hayes & Sanford, 2014, p. 114).

Based on the comprehension of language and symbolic behavior that relational frame theory brings, contextual behavioral science has a role to play in the study of human evolution as it has shaped us so far, and will help predict and influence our future evolution. In the words of Skinner (1988), "the whole story will eventually be told by the joint action of the sciences of genetics, behavior, and culture" (p. 83). It appears that the time has come for joint action between CBS and the evolutionary sciences, in order to address the challenges the human race is facing, such as overpopulation and environmental destruction. Such a common action is already on its way (Wilson, Hayes, Biglan, & Embry, 2014).

In these times of unequalled rapid and massive information transfer, scientists have the responsibility to fully understand the tremendous influence of language on our behaviors. Since evolution gave us the opportunity to act with intentionality, it is up to us to use this possibility to the greatest effect, in the interests of humankind itself.

Acknowledgments

The author thanks Steven C. Hayes (University of Nevada, USA), Etienne Danchin (CNRS, Toulouse, France), and Eva Jablonka (Tel Aviv University, Israel) for their comments on initial versions of this chapter.

References

Blackledge, J. T. (2003). An introduction to relational frame theory: Basics and applications. *The Behavior Analyst Today, 3,* 421–433.

Catania, A. C. (1991). Glossary. In I. H. Iversen & K. A. Lattal (Eds.), *Experimental analysis of behavior. Part 2* (pp. G1–G44). Amsterdam, the Netherlands: Elsevier.

Catania, A. C. (2001). Three varieties of selection and their implications for the origins of language. In G. Györi (Ed.), *Language evolution: Biological, linguistic and philosophical perspectives* (pp. 55–71). New York, NY: Peter Lang.

Catania, A. C., Shimoff, E., & Matthews, B. A. (1989). An experimental analysis of rule-governed behavior. In S. C. Hayes (Ed.), *Rule-governed behavior. Cognition, contingencies, and instructional control.* (pp. 119–150). New York, NY: Plenum.

Catania, A. C., Shimoff, E. H., & Matthews, B. A. (1990). Properties of rule-governed behaviour and their implications. In D. E. Blackman & H. Lejeune (Eds.), *Behaviour analysis in theory and practice* (pp. 215–230). London, England: Erlbaum.

Cziko, G. (1995). *Without miracles. Universal selection theory and the second Darwinian revolution.* Cambridge, MA: MIT Press.

Danchin, É., Charmantier, A., Champagne, F. A., Mesoudi, A., Pujol, B., & Blanchet, S. (2011). Beyond DNA: Integrating inclusive inheritance into an extended theory of evolution. *Nature Reviews Genetics, 12,* 475–486.

Danchin, É., Giraldeau, L. A., Valone, T. J., & Wagner, R. H. (2004). Public information: From nosy neighbors to cultural evolution. *Science, 305,* 487–491.

Danchin, É., & Wagner, R. H. (2010). Inclusive heritability: Combining genetic and non-genetic information to study animal behavior and culture. *Oikos, 119,* 210–218.

Dennett, D. C. (1991). *Consciousness explained.* Boston, MA: Little, Brown.

Dennett, D. C. (1995). *Darwin's dangerous idea: Evolution and the meanings of life.* London, England: Allen Lane.

Dewitte, S., & Verguts, T. (1999). Behavioral variation: A neglected aspect in selectionist thinking. *Behavior and Philosophy, 27,* 127–145.

Dias, B. G., & Ressler, K. J. (2014). Parental olfactory experience influences behavior and neural structure in subsequent generations. *Nature Neuroscience, 17,* 89–96.

Donahoe, J. W. (2012). Reflections on behavior analysis and evolutionary biology: A selective review of evolution since Darwin – the first 150 years. *Journal of the Experimental Analysis of Behavior, 97,* 249–260.

Elgar, G., & Vavouri, T. (2008). Tuning in to the signals: Noncoding sequence conservation in vertebrate genomes. *Trends in Genetics, 24,* 344–352.

Gould, S. J. (1989). *Wonderful life: The Burgess Shale and the nature of history.* New York, NY: Norton.

Gould, S. J. (1996). *Full house: The spread of excellence from Plato to Darwin.* New York, NY: Harmony Books.

Gould, S. J. (2000). *The lying stones of Marrakech.* New York, NY: Three Rivers Press.

Grunow, A., & Neuringer, A. (2002). Learning to vary and varying to learn. *Psychonomic Bulletin & Review, 9,* 250–258.

Hayes, S. C. (Ed.). (1989). *Rule-governed behavior: Cognition, contingencies, and instructional control.* New York, NY: Plenum.

Hayes, S. C. (1992). Verbal relations, time, and suicide. In S. C. Hayes & L. J. Hayes (Eds.), *Understanding verbal relations* (pp. 109–118). Reno, NV: Context Press.

Hayes, S. C. (1993). Nature-nurture: Two-headed arrows and wrong-headed questions. In S. C. Hayes, L. J. Hayes, H. W. Reese, & T. R. Sarbin (Eds.), *Varieties of scientific contextualism* (pp. 316–319). Reno, NV: Context Press.

Hayes, S. C., Barnes-Holmes, D., & Roche, B. (2001). *Relational frame theory: A post-Skinnerian account of human language and cognition.* New York, NY: Plenum.

Hayes, S. C., Barnes-Holmes, D., & Wilson, K. G. (2012). Contextual behavioral science: Creating a science more adequate to the challenge of the human condition. *Journal of Contextual Behavioral Science, 1*, 1–16.

Hayes, S. C., Brownstein, A. J., Zettle, R. D., Rosenfarb, I. S., & Korn, Z. (1986). Rule-governed behavior and sensitivity to changing consequences of responding. *Journal of the Experimental Analysis of Behavior, 45*, 237–256.

Hayes, S. C., Fox, E., Gifford, E. V., Wilson, K. G., Barnes-Holmes, D., & Healy, O. (2001). Derived relational responding as learned behavior. In S. C. Hayes, D. Barnes-Holmes, & B. Roche (Eds.), *Relational frame theory: A post-Skinnerian account of human language and cognition* (pp. 21–49). New York, NY: Plenum.

Hayes, S. C., Gifford, E. V., & Wilson, K. G. (1996). Stimulus classes and stimulus relations: Arbitrarily applicable relational responding as an operant. In T. R. Zentall & P. M. Smeets (Eds.), *Stimulus class formation in humans and animals* (pp. 279–299). Amsterdam, the Netherlands: Elsevier.

Hayes, S. C., & Long, D. (2013). Contextual behavioural science, evolution, and scientific epistemology. In B. Roche & S. Dymond (Eds.), *Advances in relational frame theory: Research and application* (pp. 5–26). Oakland, CA: New Harbinger/Context Press.

Hayes, S. C., & Sanford, B. T. (2014). Cooperation came first: Evolution and human cognition. *Journal of the Experimental Analysis of Behavior, 101*, 112–129.

Hayes, S. C., Zettle, R. D., & Rosenfarb, I. (1989). Rule following. In S. C. Hayes (Ed.), *Rule governed behavior: Cognition, contingencies, and instructional control* (pp. 191–220). New York, NY: Plenum.

Healy, O., Barnes-Holmes, D., & Smeets, P. M. (2000). Derived relational responding as generalized operant behavior. *Journal of the Experimental Analysis of Behavior, 74*, 207–227.

Henshilwood, C., d'Errico, F., Vanhaeren, M., Van Niekerk, K., & Jacobs, Z. (2004). Middle Stone Age shell beads from South Africa. *Science, 304*, 404.

Herrenschmidt, C. (2007). *Les trois écritures: langue, nombre, code.* Paris, France: Gallimard.

Jablonka, E., & Lamb, M. J. (2005). *Evolution in four dimensions: Genetic, epigenetic, behavioral, and symbolic variation in the history of life.* Cambridge, MA: MIT Press.

Jablonka, E., & Lamb, M. J. (2014). *Evolution in four dimensions: Genetic, epigenetic, behavioral, and symbolic variation in the history of life* (2nd ed.). Cambridge, MA: MIT Press.

Kantor, J. R. (1938). The nature of psychology as a natural science. *Acta Psychologica, 4*, 1–61.

Kokko, H., & Jennions, M. D. (2010). Behavioral ecology: The natural history of evolutionary biology. In M. A. Bell, W. F. Eanes, & D. F Futuyma (Eds.), *Evolution since Darwin: The first 150 years* (pp. 291–318). Sunderland, MA: Sinauer.

Luciano, C., Gómez-Becerra, I., & Rodríguez-Valverde, M. (2007). The role of multiple-exemplar training and naming in establishing derived equivalence in an infant. *Journal of Experimental Analysis of Behavior, 87*, 349–365.

Mameli, M. (2004). Nongenetic selection and nongenetic inheritance. *British Journal for the Philosophy of Science, 55*, 35–71.

Maxwell, N. (2010). *Cutting God in half and putting the pieces together again: A new approach to philosophy.* London, England: Pentire Press.

Maynard Smith, J., & Szathmary, E. (2000). *The origins of life: From the birth of life to the origin of language.* Oxford, England: Oxford University Press.

Monestès, J. L., Villatte, M., Stewart, I., & Loas, G. (2014). Rule-based insensitivity and delusion maintenance in schizophrenia. *The Psychological Record, 64*, 329–338.

Neuringer, A. (2002). Operant variability: Evidence, functions, and theory. *Psychonomic Bulletin & Review, 9*(4), 672–705.

Nevalainen, L., & Luoto, T. P. (2013). Sedimentary chydorid (Cladocera) ephippia in relation to lake ecological quality in the Austrian Alps. *Journal of Limnology, 72*, 52–61.

Odling-Smee, F. J., Laland, K., & Feldman, M. W. (2003). *Niche construction: The neglected process in evolution.* Princeton, NJ: Princeton University Press.

Page, S., & Neuringer, A. (1985). Variability as an operant. *Journal of Experimental Psychology: Animal Behavior Processes, 11*, 429–452.

Pigliucci, M., & Muller, G. B. (2010). *Evolution, the extended synthesis*. Cambridge, MA: MIT Press.

Shimoff, E., & Catania, A. C. (1998). The verbal governance of behavior. In K. A. Lattal, M. Perone, & I. H. Iversen (Eds.), *Handbook of human operant behavioral research methods* (pp. 371–404). New York, NY: Plenum.

Simpson, G. G. (1953). The Baldwin effect. *Evolution, 7*, 110–117.

Skinner, B. F. (1981). Selection by consequences. *Science, 213*, 501–504.

Skinner, B. F. (1988). Genes and behavior. In G. Greenberg & E. Tolbach (Eds.), *Evolution of social behavior and integrative levels* (pp. 77–83). Hillsdale, NJ: Erlbaum.

Tomasello, M. (2008). *Origins of human communication*. Cambridge, MA: MIT Press.

West-Eberhard, M. J. (2003). *Developmental plasticity and evolution*. New York, NY: Oxford University Press.

Wilson, D. S. (2007). *Evolution for everyone: How Darwin's theory can change the way we think about our lives*. New York, NY: Delta.

Wilson, D. S., Hayes, S. C., Biglan, T., & Embry, D. (2014). Evolving the future: Toward a science of intentional change. *Behavioral and Brain Sciences, 34*, 1–22.

Wilson, D. S., Van Vugt, M., & O'Gorman, R. (2008). Multilevel selection theory and major evolutionary transitions implications for psychological science. *Current Directions in Psychological Science, 17*, 6–9.

Wilson, D. S., & Wilson, E. O. (2008). Evolution "for the good of the group." *American Scientist, 96*, 380–389.

Zettle, R. D., & Hayes, S. C. (1982). Rule-governed behavior: A potential theoretical framework for cognitive behavior therapy. In P. C. Kendall (Ed.), *Advances in cognitive behavioral research and therapy* (pp. 73–118). New York, NY: Academic Press.

Part II

Relational Frame Theory

Dermot Barnes-Holmes

8

Relational Frame Theory

Finding Its Historical and Intellectual Roots and Reflecting upon Its Future Development: An Introduction to Part II

Dermot Barnes-Holmes, Yvonne Barnes-Holmes, Ian Hussey, and Carmen Luciano

The following two chapters (9 and 10) by Hughes and Barnes-Holmes in this part of the CBS handbook provide a very detailed and systematic review of relational frame theory (RFT) and its evidence. As such, there seems little point in recapitulating some of that work in this opening chapter of Part II. Furthermore, the subsequent two chapters provide examples of how RFT has been applied in the domains of educational (chapter 11, Barnes-Holmes, Kavanagh, & Murphy) and clinical psychology (chapter 12, Törneke, Luciano, Barnes-Holmes, & Bond). The current part therefore provides a comprehensive overview of the basic and applied wings of RFT. By way of narrative or commentary, this opening chapter aims to provide a particular perspective, perhaps somewhat controversial at the present time, on the history and future development of the account itself.

We begin here by asking the question: What are the historical and intellectual roots of RFT? The seminal volume contains a narrative by Steve Hayes, which addresses the origins of the theory from the personal perspective of the person who first conceptualized the account (Hayes, Barnes-Holmes, & Roche, 2001). However, we are asking a broader and perhaps more fundamental question here. Why did Steve come up with RFT at that time? Or, in other words, what was the confluence of historical and intellectual variables that led him to do so, and subsequently supported the theory's development and continued growth to this day? Here is our view on the matter.

Placing RFT in the Wider Context of CBS

For us, RFT is Darwinian, in the sense that it seeks to explain the development of a complex system (i.e., human language and cognition) through a focus on selection by consequences. The theory also seems to comport with Wittgenstein's argument that human language is a type of social game (rather than a "cognitive" representational

The Wiley Handbook of Contextual Behavioral Science, First Edition. Edited by Robert D. Zettle, Steven C. Hayes, Dermot Barnes-Holmes, and Anthony Biglan.
© 2016 John Wiley & Sons, Ltd. Published 2016 by John Wiley & Sons, Ltd.

system). Perhaps, more obviously, RFT is also Skinnerian, in that it explicitly draws on the concept of the operant as a unit of analysis. And, last but not least, it is Sidmanian in that it draws upon the insight that derived equivalence relations provide a functional analysis of symbolic meaning. If you bring each of these historical and intellectual influences together, they lead almost inexorably to RFT. We truly are, as the old cliché goes, standing on the shoulders of giants.

Put in this historical context, one can easily appreciate how a young Steve Hayes who was on a mission "to understand how language is actually used" (Hayes et al., 2001, p. vii), and was struggling to find a clear functional definition of a verbal stimulus, produced an account of human language and cognition that we now know as RFT. Add to this, a young English PhD student who read Steve's first manuscript on RFT (on a much delayed train ride between Bangor in North Wales and London), and who was obsessed with conducting basic experimental analyses of human cognition from a behavior-analytic perspective. And voila – you have a theory and an international research program. Well, perhaps not quite the latter, at least not at that point, but fast forward almost 15 years and you have what is affectionately now known as the "Purple Book" (Hayes et al., 2001). And fast forward almost another 15 years and few would deny that we have some momentum, internationally, in advancing RFT as a modern behavioral theory of human language and cognition.

Okay, so far so good. We can all sit back and congratulate ourselves on what a great job we have done – or can we? To be frank, we don't think so. Despite the advances and achievements that have clearly been made over the past 25 years or so, we have grown increasingly concerned that RFT is not being seen as a work in progress, and it is in danger of becoming ossified as "The Purple Book." While other volumes and reviews of RFT research may follow, it is critical that they do more than merely genuflect at the tabernacle containing the 2001 treatise. Of course, there is still a great deal of important *empirical* work to do that falls directly out of the original text. Nevertheless, there is no basis for complacency – if RFT does not continue to grow *conceptually*, in our opinion, it will die prematurely.

The other concern we have is the perception within the CBS community that RFT researchers should work away as "the unseen elves in the basement" whose duty is to provide a basic science that underlies acceptance and commitment therapy (ACT; e.g., Bond, Hayes, & Barnes-Holmes, 2006). In terms of simple PR, this is a disastrous metaphor – what young researcher looking to build a career in academic psychology aspires to be a small green servant who lives in an intellectual basement? Strategically, at a community level, it is even worse because the metaphor appears to dictate the research agenda that the elves must follow as they serve up basic science results to their (applied) lords and masters. In our view, the reality of the relationship between ACT and RFT is quite different and is summarized as follows (see also chapter 18 in this volume for a more detailed treatment of this issue).

Many readers of this book will recognize that research on ACT has grown exponentially in recent years. Similarly, research on RFT has also grown considerably, but certainly not at the same pace as research on ACT. The difference in growth is understandable given that funding and other resources are typically more widely available for applied research, particularly randomized controlled trials, than for basic (experimental) research in psychology. One consequence of these differential growth patterns is that new concepts and theoretical terms have emerged in the ACT literature that are difficult to interpret from an RFT perspective, and are certainly of limited value in conducting basic (functional) experimental analyses of human psychopathology (hereafter referred to as psychological suffering). The emergence of the "hexaflex" in the ACT literature, for example, has proposed concepts such as "acceptance," "cognitive defusion," and "being present" (along with the core concept of psychological flexibility) as central to psychological well-being. Unfortunately, these concepts have proven difficult, if not impossible, to pin down in terms of relatively precise functional analyses. This limitation has been widely recognized in clearly acknowledging that the hexaflex is composed of "middle-level" terms, which are more theoretically specific and clinically useful than folk-psychological terms (e.g., mindfulness and self-awareness), but nonetheless do not provide the precision, scope, and depth associated with well-defined functional concepts (e.g., reinforcement, stimulus-generalization, and derived transformation of functions). There are no immediate grounds for concern here, however, because this "tension" between the basic and applied sciences is expected and supported within the functional approach itself. For example, in a recent article, Hayes, Barnes-Holmes, and Wilson (2012) argued:

> We should not expect RFT labs to provide an account that will apply point to point with existing clinical models. For example, while excellent progress has been made in the deictic basis of sense of self, the same cannot yet be said for acceptance. Fortunately, a reticulated approach does not demand this. As basic findings are extended, entirely new middle level terms may emerge and existing ones will fall away or be supported only in part. For example, cognitive control over behavior may be shown to be related to, say, the distinction between relational framing that is relatively brief and immediate versus extended and elaborated ... These new basic findings may provide a way to think about the issues engaged by concepts like "fusion" and "defusion" even if there is no point correspondence. (p. 8)

Indeed, it appears that the foregoing argument has been reflected recently in a renewed interest in attempting to connect RFT concepts and analyses to human psychological suffering with the publication of texts written explicitly for clinicians (e.g., Törneke, 2010; Villatte, Villatte, & Hayes, in press). While such books are indeed welcome and will hopefully orient clinical psychologists and applied researchers toward the importance of functional analyses of human language in understanding and treating psychological suffering, the critical ingredient will involve developing and maintaining vibrant and productive programs of basic RFT research in this domain. Above and beyond further empirical research, however, it is critical that RFT continues to develop conceptually if it is to connect in a meaningful way with clinical and applied psychology generally. To be frank, in our view, RFT is not sufficiently developed conceptually, at the present time, to step up to the challenge of reticulating in a highly productive and useful way with the needs and concerns of our applied colleagues.

In making this argument, we are not suggesting that RFT "nerds" should be left alone to get on with arcane, abstruse, or obscurantist research replete with A1s, B1s, and C1s, and yet another derived transformation of function that occurs, unsurprisingly, through a relational network. And, we are not suggesting that we simply import previous RFT research into reasonably receptive areas of mainstream psychology. This latter strategy we have labeled, rather cynically perhaps, "I bring you C" research. By this, we mean conducting RFT studies that were originally done more or less 10 to 20 years ago, but using mainstream group designs in areas such as fear or evaluative conditioning. In effect, this work involves showing transfer effects across three or more stimuli (A–B–C), rather than just one or two stimuli (A–B), as is typical in mainstream conditioning work. In the short term, RFT may gain some traction in mainstream psychology with this strategy, but in the longer term it is an intellectually bankrupt move.

As noted earlier, we are arguing that RFT research should not continue with A1–B1–C1 studies alone. Certainly, this early research was instrumental in establishing *new* functional analytic-abstractive "units of analysis" (e.g., relational frames, relational networks, etc.). However, in our view, we need to move beyond merely "proving" that these units of analysis "exist," and begin to harness the full power and potential of RFT as a theory of human language and cognition. To appreciate the point we are making here, let us revisit the concept of a unit of analysis in behavioral psychology.

Units of Analysis

All mature sciences have basic, mutually agreed upon units of analysis (e.g., proteins, cells, genes, elements, atoms, and fields). In general, the basic strategy is to identify relatively simple units that allow the research scientist to construct and deconstruct complexity. Behavioral psychology, consistent with a bottom-up approach to science, is built upon generally agreed units of analysis. One of the most fundamental of such units is the discriminated operant. Typically, this is understood as an overarching, spatio-temporal, contextually defined analytic unit. A well-worn example is the presence versus absence of a light in an operant chamber that comes to control the probability of a response class, such as lever pressing. The discriminated operant is not defined by any one element in and of itself, but by the relations among the three elements together (i.e., antecedent, behavior, consequence) that occur in an appropriate motivational context. Critically, the unit of analysis that is the operant can be used to analyze relatively simple behaviors or more complex psychological events. For example, a food-deprived rat pressing a lever for food in the presence of a light can be understood as an operant response, as could a child's temper tantrums to escape a demanding task, or an individual's panic attacks to escape a socially threatening situation.

In applying the concept of the operant to the analysis of any particular behavior, it is important to specify the functional response class upon which both the discriminative stimulus and the reinforcers operate. In dealing with relatively simple responses this can be a straightforward task. For example, lever presses are relatively easily defined and measured in an operant chamber, but when tackling more complex behaviors the identification of the response unit becomes more challenging – not only conceptually, but also empirically. Nowhere else is this more apparent than in the struggle that behavioral psychology has had in the domain of human language and cognition. Skinner's (1957) attempt to do this in *Verbal Behavior* aimed to provide a conceptual operant analysis of the units of human language in terms of mands, tacts, intraverbals, and so on. Although progress was certainly made with this conceptual analysis, particularly in the arena of developmental disabilities, its lack of success in leading to a vibrant program of experimental research, not to mention in the broader clinical domain, has been well documented (Dymond, O'Hora, Whelan, & O'Donovan,

2006). One could argue that the key problem was that *Verbal Behavior* failed to identify the key response classes involved in human language and cognition, which can be categorized as genuinely symbolic or referential (see Barnes-Holmes, Barnes-Holmes, & Cullinan, 2000). It was not until Sidman (1971) developed the concept of the equivalence relation that an operant analysis of the symbolic properties of human language and cognition was made possible (see also Sidman, 1994). The subsequent emergence of relational frame theory provided a scientific unit of analysis of the symbolic properties of language that was deliberately and self-consciously operant in nature – that is the relational frame (Hayes et al., 2001).

Relating as a Unit of Analysis

The critical point about RFT is that the functional response unit involves relating, rather than pressing a key or pointing at a stimulus. That is, once relational framing as an operant has been established, operant contingencies now impact on the response unit of relating rather than functional classes composed of lever pressing or pointing at particular stimuli (see Hayes & Barnes, 1997). As has been noted previously, conceptualizing an operant response class as involving the act of relating requires a thorough and radical functional understanding of the operant (Barnes-Holmes & Barnes-Holmes, 2000). To put it bluntly, one cannot think of the operant in topographical terms, and fully appreciate the functionality of the RFT definition of symbolic verbal behavior. By way of example, it is easy to think of lever pressing in topographical terms because you can visually see a discrete key press in time. That is, it "looks like" what it is. The act of relating, however, involves a number of discrete events spread out in space and time (i.e., it is an overarching, spatio-temporal unit of analysis). Nevertheless, the temptation to deconstruct the response of relating into more visually discrete units such as looking, pointing, and key pressing can be almost irresistible for more topographically minded researchers.

One of the core problems, as we see it, with a lot of RFT research to date is a failure to fully appreciate the operant nature of the analysis. We have been so mesmerized by the extent to which relational framing appears to provide so-called "unreinforced," "emergent," "derived," or "untaught" behaviors that we have rarely asked questions about the relative strengths or probabilities of the operant units of relational framing themselves. In one sense, this blind-sightedness is understandable because demonstrating a relational frame in the laboratory requires training and derivation of untaught relations. Indeed, RFT studies are carefully crafted, for the most part, to ensure that derived responses cannot be explained by histories of reinforcement or other well-established behavioral principles, such as primary stimulus generalization, higher order respondent conditioning, etc. Although such demonstration research is undoubtedly important, rarely does it lead to questions about the persistence, probability, or strength of a particular pattern of relational responding. Instead, the concepts and methods invite a binary or dichotomous way of thinking about relational frames: In the highly rarefied environment of the research laboratory, frames are either demonstrated or they are not.

This research strategy is entirely consistent with the requirement that specific properties of relational framing should be observed in the absence of direct or programmed reinforcement contingencies. In the natural environment, however, novel or emergent relational responses occur rarely without reinforcement by a listener or other variables, such as achieving internal verbal coherence. In this sense, there appears to be a disjoint between studying language as relational framing in the laboratory and studying language as it occurs in the natural environment. At some point, therefore, it seems important to draw a line under the need to engage in nothing but demonstration work, and to accept that RFT could provide reasonably adequate units of analysis for the study of human language and cognition in the real world.

Of course, we recognize that demonstration and analytic RFT research may be best thought of as existing on a continuum. That is, there are clear examples of pure demonstration studies and others that appear to be more analytic. For example, most of the early RFT research involved demonstrations of predicted entailment and transformation effects (e.g., Dymond & Barnes, 1995; Roche & Barnes, 1997; Steele & Hayes, 1991). On balance, other studies have also involved demonstrating these types of effects, but have begun to address specific analytic questions. For instance, some researchers have sought to determine if it is possible to separate mutually and combinatorially entailed derived relations using delayed feedback (Healy, Barnes-Holmes, & Smeets, 2000). And, others have analyzed the relative extent to which derived fear and derived avoidance responses persist during periods of extinction (Luciano et al., 2013). And yet others have attempted to analyze the early verbal histories that RFT predicts are instrumental in establishing specific relational frames (e.g., Barnes-Holmes, Barnes-Holmes, Smeets, Strand, & Friman, 2004; Luciano, Gomez Beccera, & Rodriguez, 2007). What seems important now, however, is to fully recognize the need for an active program of analytic research, to develop a systematic framework for organizing this research, and to move forward with the empirical challenges this will entail.

At this point, it seems useful to reflect upon recent developments in RFT that extend beyond the previously discussed phase of demonstration research. Nowhere else is this clearer, in our view, than in the development of the Implicit Relational Assessment Procedure (IRAP) and the Relational Elaboration and Coherence (REC) model (Barnes-Holmes, Barnes-Holmes, Stewart, & Boles, 2010; Barnes-Holmes, Murphy, Barnes-Holmes, & Stewart, 2010; Cullen, Barnes-Holmes, Barnes-Holmes, & Stewart, 2009; Hughes, Barnes-Holmes, & Vahey, 2012). In making this argument, we are not suggesting that the development of a measure of so-called "implicit cognition" was critical; rather the attempt to develop a methodology for measuring natural verbal relations, or relational framing "in flight," was the important move. In other words, the initial intention was to shift the focus, both empirically and conceptually, from establishing and demonstrating relational frames in the laboratory, to measuring the strength, probability, or persistence of relational framing that had been established by prior histories. Unfortunately, however, the research began with "frames in flight" and then became focused on "implicit cognition." We recognize that this work has been valuable on a number of fronts, but in our view it has also served to undermine the ongoing development of RFT as a basic scientific enterprise. It seems time to return, therefore, to the original focus of attempting to analyze the dynamics of relational framing in flight. In doing so, the line will be firmly drawn, and we will have crossed the Rubicon from pure demonstration to analytic research.

A Multidimensional Multilevel Framework for the Analysis of Relational Framing

In making this shift, it seems useful to propose a conceptual framework that will help to guide future research on the dynamics of relational framing. Toward this end, we have begun to conceptualize these dynamics in a three-dimensional space,[1] involving degrees of derivation, complexity, and coherence in arbitrarily applicable relational responding (see Figure 8.1). As an aside, we recognize that additional dimensions are involved, hence we use the term multidimensional (rather than three-dimensional). For example, relational flexibility is assumed to be inherent in each of the three dimensions, in that relational responses, be they relatively simple or complex, coherent or incoherent, or derived only a few or many times, may be relatively flexible or inflexible (e.g., more or less sensitive to current contextual variables). And it seems likely that such differential degrees of relational flexibility will yield possible differences in the strength, persistence, or probability of the relevant response classes in future contexts (O'Toole & Barnes-Holmes, 2009). Furthermore, as we explain below, levels of behavioral development are also an important part of the conceptual framework that we are proposing. For present purposes, however, we will focus on the three dimensions illustrated in Figure 8.1.

Broadly speaking, derivation refers to the extent to which a particular pattern of relational responding has occurred in the past; complexity refers to the various ways in which patterns of relational responding may differ in terms of properties such as number of stimuli, relations, transformation of functions, and varieties of contextual control; and coherence refers to the extent to which a particular pattern of relational

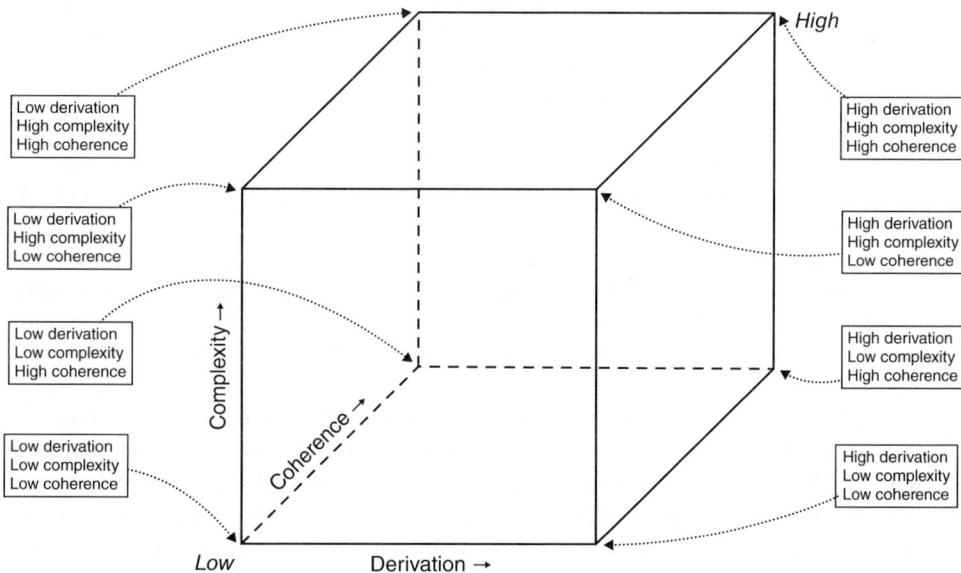

Figure 8.1   A graphical representation of the interaction among three key dimensions of arbitrarily applicable relational responding as conceptualized within the multidimensional multilevel (MDML) analytic framework.

responding yields relatively consistent consequences. More informally, derivation refers to how "well practiced" a verbal response has become. Given that the first time a derived response is emitted it is by definition highly derived (i.e., novel or emergent), level of derivation reduces as it becomes more practiced. The term complexity is relatively intuitive in that it refers to the intricacy or density of a pattern of relational responding. For example, all things being equal, a mutually entailed relational response is less complex than a combinatorially entailed response. Finally, the concept of coherence also seems intuitive because it refers to the extent to which an instance of relational responding yields a predictable consequence. For example, if you are told that A is bigger than B, you would expect to be told that you are correct if you concluded that B is smaller than A.

Although each of these three dimensions has been discussed previously in the RFT literature, the proposed framework suggests a shift toward considering the dynamic and interactive nature of these dimensions. That is, they should be seen as codefining or covarying with each other. For example, a relatively complex relational network, such as a story, may require less derivation, appear more coherent, and seem less complex with repeated exposures to the network. Critically, these three dimensions apply to at least five different levels of behavioral development, such as (a) the relational response, (b) the relational frame, (c) the relational network, (d) the relating of relations, and (e) the relating of relational networks.

For illustrative purposes, let us focus on derivation. At the level of the relational response, for example, each time a person infers or reasons that if A is the same as B then B must be the same as A, that particular (mutually entailed) response reduces in derivation or novelty. This point has been made before in the context of the REC model, but what has often been missed in previous writings is a full appreciation of the fact that derivation (and indeed complexity and coherence) also varies at other levels of behavioral development. For example, derivation may also be seen as reducing at the level of the relational frame itself. That is, each time an individual is exposed to an exemplar of a particular relational frame (e.g., A=B=C, therefore C=A; D=E=F, therefore F=D, etc.), the overarching pattern of entailed relations may be seen as becoming less and less novel or derived. In other words, as the frame itself strengthens or becomes more and more practiced, the relational responding becomes less and less derived from the original or initial source of exemplars that served to establish that frame. The same general logic applies to other levels of behavioral development, such as the relating of relations. For example, research has shown that children improve in their ability to relate relations with increasing age, suggesting that multiple exposures to such tasks reduce the derivation involved in the overarching pattern of relating relations itself (see Stewart & Barnes-Holmes, 2004, for a summary).[2]

The critical point is that because derivation, complexity, and coherence are seen to operate and interact at multiple levels of behavioral development, the resulting framework generates a plethora of potential units of analysis. As articulated here, the framework yields 15 analytic units (i.e., three dimensions multiplied by five levels of behavioral development). And, perhaps most importantly of all, each of these units may be conceptualized as a verbal or relational response class that may enter into a discriminated operant, thus allowing for direct manipulation via appropriately arranged environmental contingencies of reinforcement. It is this analytic tool that we have labeled a multidimensional multilevel (MDML) conceptual framework.

To appreciate the potential of this framework it seems useful to consider just one example of how it facilitates an RFT analysis of human suffering. Imagine two socially anxious individuals, a man who "freezes" or panics in the moment when first seeing an audience he is about to address, versus a woman who experiences intense anxiety as a result of ruminating the day before a public talk about the many possible ways in which she could perform badly. It might be tempting to think of the first example as involving a largely nonverbal, respondent or Pavlovian response, whereas the latter clearly involves extended or complex verbal or relational responding. According to the MDML framework, however, these two examples both involve verbal behavior, but may be conceptualized as located in different areas of the three-dimensional space illustrated in Figure 8.1. For instance, one could argue that the man's "freezing" response is in fact relational and likely involves low complexity, low derivation, and high coherence. The woman's rumination-based anxiety is more obviously relational, but may be conceptualized as involving high complexity, high derivation, and high coherence. Note that in this example, complexity and derivation differ across the two examples, but coherence does not (because in both cases, the relational responding is consistent with many other examples of "socially anxious" behaviors in the histories of the two individuals).

The MDML framework thus conceptualizes virtually all such clinically relevant behaviors as verbal, but explains the clear differences in terms of multiple dimensions (a more complete analysis may also refer to different levels of behavioral development but this would require a detailed treatment of the MDML, which is beyond the scope of the current introductory chapter). Within the MDML, therefore, there is no simplistic dichotomy between verbal and nonverbal behavior based on whether a response is derived versus controlled by direct acting contingencies. Rather, all units of analysis within the MDML remain verbal response classes even when they are impacted upon by direct contingencies of reinforcement (see O'Hora, Barnes-Holmes, & Stewart, 2014, for a relevant empirical example). In effect, the MDML serves to highlight the intensely operant but wholly verbal nature of RFT, with a focus on the impact of direct acting contingencies on its (verbal) operant units of analysis, from the most simple or basic relational responses to the most complex contextually controlled interactions among complex relational networks. In one sense, this is RFT "super-stylie" but only time will tell if we have "gone too far" with this particular conceptual analysis. In any case, we are happy to let the data guide us in this regard.

As an aside, it is also worth noting that in the language of ACT's hexaflex model, both examples of social anxiety outlined above might be seen as involving "fusion" with thoughts and feelings about social embarrassment, etc., and thus verbal processes are involved in both instances. We are certainly comfortable with such a claim, but would point out that the MDML analysis we offer here provides a degree of analytic precision that the concept of fusion, and other middle-level terms do not (see chapter 18 in this volume). As such, we believe that the MDML has the potential to generate basic experimental analyses of behaviors that are possibly relevant to the phenomena to which fusion refers, without those analyses being driven directly by the middle-level concept itself (see Luciano et al., 2014). In our view, this would be a healthy and productive way to help realize the CBS ambition to establish and maintain a reticulating relationship between RFT and ACT.

Conclusion

We have only just begun to explore how the MDML framework may be applied to clinical (and educational) domains, but it is looking very promising, leading us to new insights and ways of thinking about human suffering and its treatment. As noted earlier, we believe that RFT as articulated in the "Purple Book" is not sufficiently well developed to reticulate in a highly productive and sophisticated way with applied research and practice. In short, the problem with reticulation is a problem with RFT, not just ACT (or other applied wings of CBS). As we view the years that lie in front of us, therefore, we as RFT researchers feel the intense pressure of producing a version of RFT that can in fact step up to that challenge. The challenge will not be met simply by writing interpretations of human suffering and its treatment in RFT terms as articulated in the "Purple Book" or in more recent volumes. Nor will the challenge we face be addressed simply by building links with other scientific traditions, such as cognitive psychology, neuroscience, evolutionary science, social anthropology, etc. This outreach work will certainly be important strategically and politically, and also scientifically, but we must not mistake political or strategic progress per se, for empirical and conceptual progress in the basic science of human language and cognition within CBS itself. In short, CBS must do that work, because no one else will do it for us. We hope that this introduction and the four chapters that follow will help the reader begin to see the enormity and importance of that challenge, but in so doing this part will also provide at least a glimmer of hope that it may just be possible to deliver what RFT was originally designed to do.

Notes

1   It is important to note the distinction between the well-established defining properties of a relational frame (i.e., mutual entailment, combinatorial entailment, and the transformation of function) and the dimensions that we discuss here. The former provide the definition of one specific analytic unit (the relational frame), whereas the latter provide the dynamic units that we hope will facilitate the analysis of relatively simple and complex instances of human language and cognition.

2   The concept of derivation may be used in two ways within RFT. First, it may indicate that arbitrarily applicable relational responding is *derived* from a history of operant learning, or multiple-exemplar training. That is, the ability to engage in such relational responding is derived from a *continuously growing* source of prior learning. When derivation is used in this first sense, it may be seen as increasing across repeated instances because the source of the derivation (i.e., the generalized operant class itself) grows with every reinforced exemplar. The second way in which derivation may be employed within RFT is in the sense that derived relational responding involves "arriving at a conclusion" based on a relation, subset of relations, or multiple exemplars of such relations. More informally, it involves, "reasoning," "inferring," or "deducing" from a *limited* source of prior learning. Critically, it is only in the second sense that derivation may be interpreted as decreasing across multiple instances of a particular pattern of arbitrarily applicable relational responding. For example, if an individual is told that A is the same as B and then derives for the first time that B is the same as A, the latter relational response is entirely derived from the former. Once the latter response is emitted and reinforced in some way, the next time it occurs it is less derived because it is based to some degree on a direct history of reinforcement, rather

than "abstract reasoning" from a limited source (i.e., from the specified A-same-as-B rela-tion). A similar type of analysis may be applied to other levels of relational responding. For example, the first time that a young child responds in accordance with a specific relational frame, the frame itself may be seen as derived entirely from the previously reinforced mul-tiple exemplars. Once derived, however, the frame as a relational response unit may con-tinue to be reinforced across subsequent exemplars and thus becomes less and less derived from the *original* or *initial* source of exemplar training. This reduction in derivation, from the original source, seems important because it may facilitate novel forms of derivation at more complex levels of relational responding, such as the relating of derived relations to derived relations (see Stewart & Barnes-Holmes, 2004). In other words, reductions in the dimension of derivation at one level may lead to increases in derivation at other levels, thus supporting our use of the label, *multidimensional multilevel* framework, to capture the highly dynamic nature of RFT that we are outlining here.

References

Barnes-Holmes, D. & Barnes-Holmes, D. (2000). Explaining complex behavior: Two perspec-tives on the concept of generalized operant classes. *The Psychological Record, 50*, 251–265.

Barnes-Holmes, D., Barnes-Holmes, Y., & Cullinan, V. (2000). Relational frame theory and Skinner's *Verbal Behavior*: A possible synthesis. *The Behavior Analyst, 23*, 69.

Barnes-Holmes, D., Barnes-Holmes, Y., Stewart, I., & Boles, S. (2010). A sketch of the Implicit Relational Assessment Procedure (IRAP) and the Relational Elaboration and Coherence (REC) model. *The Psychological Record, 60*, 527–542.

Barnes-Holmes, D., Murphy, A., Barnes-Holmes, Y., & Stewart, I. (2010). The Implicit Relational Assessment Procedure (IRAP): Exploring the impact of private versus public contexts and the response latency criterion on pro-white and anti-black stereotyping among white Irish individuals. *The Psychological Record, 60*, 57–66.

Barnes-Holmes, Y., Barnes-Holmes, D., Smeets, P. M., Strand, P., & Friman, P. (2004). Establishing relational responding in accordance with more-than and less-than as general-ized operant behavior in young children. *International Journal of Psychology and Psychological Therapy, 4*, 531–558.

Bond, F. W., Hayes, S. C., & Barnes-Holmes, D. (2006). Psychological flexibility, ACT and organizational behavior. In S. C. Hayes, F. W. Bond, D. Barnes-Holmes, & J. Austin (Eds.), *Acceptance and mindfulness at work: Applying acceptance and commitment therapy and relational frame theory to organizational behavior management* (pp. 25–54). Binghamton, NY: Haworth Press.

Cullen, C., Barnes-Holmes, D., Barnes-Holmes, Y., & Stewart, I. (2009). The Implicit Relational Assessment Procedure (IRAP) and the malleability of ageist attitudes. *The Psychological Record, 59*, 591–620.

Dymond, S., & Barnes, D. (1995). A transformation of self-discrimination response functions in accordance with the arbitrarily applicable relations of sameness, more-than, and less-than. *Journal of the Experimental Analysis of Behavior, 64*, 163–184.

Dymond, S., O'Hora, D., Whelan, R., & O'Donovan, A. (2006). Citation analysis of Skinner's *Verbal Behavior*: 1984–2004. *The Behavior Analyst, 29*, 75–88.

Hayes, S. C., & Barnes, D. (1997). Analyzing derived stimulus relations requires more than the concept of stimulus class. *Journal of the Experimental Analysis of Behavior, 68*, 235–270.

Hayes, S. C., Barnes-Holmes, D., & Roche, B. (Eds.). (2001). *Relational frame theory: A post-Skinnerian account of human language and cognition.* New York, NY: Plenum.

Hayes, S. C., Barnes-Holmes, D., & Wilson, K. G. (2012). Contextual behavioral science: Creating a science more adequate to the challenge of the human condition. *Journal of Contextual Behavioral Science, 1*, 1–16.

Healy, O., Barnes-Holmes, D., & Smeets, P. M. (2000). Derived relational responding as generalized operant behavior. *Journal of the Experimental Analysis of Behavior, 74*, 207–227.

Hughes, S., Barnes-Holmes, D., & Vahey, N. (2012). Holding on to our functional roots when exploring new intellectual islands: A voyage through implicit cognition research. *Journal of Contextual Behavioral Science, 1*, 17–38.

Luciano, C., Gomez Beccera, I., & Rodriguez, M. (2007). The role of multiple exemplar training and naming in establishing derived equivalence in an infant. *Journal of the Experimental Analysis of Behavior, 87*, 349–365.

Luciano, C., Valdivia-Salas, S., Ruiz, F. J., Rodríguez-Valverde, M., Barnes-Holmes, D., Dougher, M., ... Gutierrez, O. (2013). Extinction of aversive eliciting functions as an analog of exposure to conditioned fear: Does it alter avoidance responding? *Journal of Contextual Behavioral Science, 2*, 120–134.

Luciano, C., Valdivia-Salas, S., Ruiz, F. J., Rodríguez-Valverde, M., Barnes-Holmes, D., Dougher, M. J., ... Gutierrez-Martínez, O. (2014). Effects of an acceptance/defusion intervention on experimentally induced generalized avoidance: A laboratory demonstration. *Journal of the Experimental Analysis of Behavior, 101*, 94–111.

O'Hora, D., Barnes-Holmes, D., & Stewart, I. (2014). Antecedent and consequential control of derived instruction-following. *Journal of the Experimental Analysis of Behavior, 102*, 66–85.

O'Toole, C. & Barnes-Holmes, D. (2009). Three chronometric indices of relational responding as predictors of performance on a brief intelligence test: The importance of relational flexibility. *The Psychological Record, 59*, 119–132.

Roche, B., & Barnes, D. (1997). A transformation of respondently conditioned stimulus function in accordance with arbitrarily applicable relations. *Journal of the Experimental Analysis of Behavior, 67*, 275–300.

Sidman, M. (1971). Reading and auditory-visual equivalences. *Journal of Speech and Hearing Research, 14*, 5–13.

Sidman, M. (1994). *Stimulus equivalence: A research story*. Boston, MA: Authors Cooperative.

Skinner, B. F. (1957). *Verbal behavior*. Appleton-Century-Crofts, New York.

Steele, D. L., & Hayes, S. C. (1991). Stimulus equivalence and arbitrarily applicable relational responding. *Journal of the Experimental Analysis of Behavior, 56*, 519–555.

Stewart, I., & Barnes-Holmes, D. (2004). Relational frame theory and analogical reasoning: Empirical investigations. *International Journal of Psychology and Psychological Therapy, 4*, 241–262.

Törneke, N. (2010). *Learning RFT: An introduction to relational frame theory and its clinical application*. Oakland, CA: Context Press.

Villatte, M., Villatte, J. L., & Hayes, S. C. (in press). *Mastering the clinical conversation: Language as intervention*. New York, NY: Guilford.

9

Relational Frame Theory
The Basic Account
Sean Hughes and Dermot Barnes-Holmes

Introduction

Imagine that you are a relative newcomer to the world of psychological science and that you have managed to find an Archimedean point from which to survey the contemporary landscape of the discipline. Taking a look around, you will observe a rich, vibrant and active country fragmented into a series of "intellectual communities" or subdisciplines such as health, social, and cognitive psychology, not to mention clinical, personality, and neuropsychology. Although you may notice that individuals are increasingly forging new connections with their counterparts from other areas, more often than not, these communities are interested in their own sets of questions and independently engaged in the development of their own methods and theories. One of the consequences of this fragmented approach is a massive proliferation of competing theories and models about highly specific phenomena that often appeal to radically different concepts or "analytic units." At the same time, any attempt or interest in the development of "overarching" theories that cannot only account for highly specific events, but also connect entire subdisciplines, has reduced to a trickle (although see Anderson, 2013; Garcia-Marques & Ferreira, 2011; Posner & Rothbart, 2007 for recent attempts). Thus, unlike the biological sciences, we have no widely accepted theory like natural selection that applies to, and binds, seemingly unrelated areas (e.g., language, cognition, and emotion) in a relatively coherent or parsimonious way. Nor do we have overarching accounts such as Newtonian or quantum mechanics that, when combined, enable us to predict a wide range of outcomes, from the actions of a single individual to the behavior of entire groups or societies. No periodic table has emerged that specifies the basic psychological "units" of analysis, how these units relate to one another, or accommodate the movement from simple to increasingly complex behaviors. In short, psychology appears to be more a collection of "loosely related study areas than a coherent, unified and evolving science" (Yanchar & Slife, 1997, p. 235).

Interestingly, and parallel to these developments, citizens of another intellectual country known as contextual behavioral science (CBS) have also sought to understand human language and cognition. Drawing on nearly a half century's worth of empirical findings, they have identified what they believe to be the core functional

The Wiley Handbook of Contextual Behavioral Science, First Edition. Edited by Robert D. Zettle, Steven C. Hayes, Dermot Barnes-Holmes, and Anthony Biglan.
© 2016 John Wiley & Sons, Ltd. Published 2016 by John Wiley & Sons, Ltd.

"unit" from which the rich diversity of human psychological life springs forth. Even more surprisingly, a rising tide of scientific studies indicate that this basic unit (termed arbitrarily applicable relational responding or AARR) allows for a whole host of complex behaviors to be predicted and influenced with precision, scope, and depth. These findings have led to the development and subsequent refinement of a functional-contextual account of human language and cognition known as relational frame theory (RFT; Hayes, Barnes, & Roche, 2001). Unlike many other theoretical enterprises in modern psychology (which tend to focus on specific features or aspects of a relevant domain), RFT operates with a relatively ambitious and extremely broad goal in mind: to develop an inductive, monistic, and functionally rooted account of language and cognition that can speak to topics as diverse as the origins of language and the emergence of self, to factors responsible for human suffering, intelligence, reasoning, and evaluation. One need only thumb through the pages of this book to see how RFT has brought new insights, and also new controversies, wherever it has led.

Over the next two chapters we hope to provide an accessible introduction to the foundations, nature, and implications of this new theory. We will illustrate how a deceptively simple idea (that AARR is a learned operant acquired early on in our development) has transformed our ability to predict and influence many complex human behaviors. Indeed, within the space of two decades, RFT researchers have linked relational responding to the development of language, reasoning, and inference, as well as self and perspective-taking, implicit cognition, developmental disorders, psychopathology, intelligence, and organizational behavior. These basic findings have been used to inform progress in applied areas such as health psychology, clinical psychology, social psychology, consumer psychology, and neuropsychology. They have also led to the development of programs for teaching and remediating linguistic/cognitive deficits, directly informed the treatment of psychopathology, influenced how we approach the behavior of organizations, and stimulated new connections with cognitive and evolutionary science.

Given the sheer scope of what RFT sets out to achieve and the explosion of research and theorizing that has taken place over the last two decades, we have had to divide our story into two halves. In this chapter our main aim is to introduce the reader to the origins of, as well as arguments and evidence for, RFT. In Section 1 we trace the study of AARR to its historical roots and explain why this phenomenon has occupied the attention of behavioral scientists for over 40 years now. This section will also provide a general introduction to RFT and highlight how the ability to frame events relationally unlocks an incredible degree of flexibility when adapting to the physical and social world around us. In Section 2 we take a closer look at some of the core assumptions that underpin this account. We explain precisely what RFT researchers mean when they claim that AARR is a learned operant behavior and chart how this ability is acquired early in infancy and rapidly scales in complexity. Section 3 examines the main "families" or types of relational responses that have been empirically examined to date and discusses their respective similarities and differences, while Section 4 demonstrates how the ability to AARR develops over time, is amenable to change, and falls under different forms of stimulus control. In the final section (Section 5) we highlight a number of features of relational responding that will become important when linking RFT to language and cognition later on. Although RFT remains the subject of continued debate, we believe that it provides an important theoretical and empirical advance for behavior analysis in particular and scientific psychology more generally.

This basic treatment of the theory will provide the necessary foundation for much of what is discussed in chapter 10 in this volume. In the second half of our story we take the reader on a journey through the RFT literature, stopping to consider some of the key empirical and conceptual developments that have shaped our understanding of human language and cognition. Doing so will reveal how RFT has stimulated a rich, vibrant, and progressive program of research, generated a host of new procedures, and raised novel questions in the process. Readers who are primarily interested in how RFT has been interfaced with specific aspects of psychological science might benefit from proceeding directly to the next chapter. However, those looking for a more technical understanding of this account and to better appreciate its origins, assumptions, and aims should begin their journey here.

Section 1: Background to the Development of Relational Frame Theory

Throughout much of the past century, the question of what makes humans unique has occupied considerable attention within the behavioral sciences. In the behavior analytic tradition, for example, it was assumed that those learning principles identified in nonhumans could stretch to, and account for, much of complex human behavior (see Dymond, Roche, & Barnes-Holmes, 2003; Hayes, 1987; Hayes, Barnes-Holmes, & Roche, 2001). This "continuity assumption" served as an "intellectual rudder" and guided much work in the field, with researchers focusing on nonhumans in order to identify general learning principles that could predict and influence the behavior of our own species. In many respects, this bottom-up strategy was a successful one, yielding concepts that apply equally to humans and nonhumans alike (e.g., reinforcement, punishment, generalization, discrimination, extinction, recovery, and habituation). However, when researchers turned their attention to complex human behavior, a number of important findings emerged, findings that hinted at learning processes or principles that may be unique to, or largely elaborated in, some species relative to others. Indeed, early evidence from three different research domains highlighted that humans consistently respond in ways that are not readily observed elsewhere in the animal kingdom.

Language

Surprisingly, and unlike much of nonhuman behavior, language refused to submit to an analysis in direct contingency terms, and attempts to do so faced numerous conceptual and empirical problems. For instance, Skinner (1957) devised a direct contingency account that defined verbal behavior as that which is "reinforced through the mediation of other persons" (p. 2), and "where the 'listener' must be responding in ways that have been conditioned precisely in order to reinforce the behavior of the speaker" (p. 225). However, this definition and the interpretive analysis that it occasioned were criticized on several grounds (see Gross & Fox, 2009; Hayes, Barnes-Holmes, & Roche, 2001; Leigland, 1997). Referring to verbal behavior as that which is reinforced via social mediation turned out to be too general a statement and one that made it difficult to distinguish verbal from any other social behavior. For example, according to Stewart and Roche (2013):

> In an operant experiment, for example, the behavior of the organism under investigation is reinforced by an experimenter who has been explicitly trained to do so. Thus, by Skinner's definition, the behavior of nonhumans in these experiments qualifies as verbal. (p. 52)

In other words, given that organisms were already engaging in verbal behavior in the laboratory, it proved difficult to isolate the latter in order to study it. The above definition was also argued to be nonfunctional because it was based on the history of a second organism (the listener) rather than the organism of interest (the speaker). This introduced a scenario whereby the history of the listener needed to be studied in order to understand the behavior of the speaker, and in no other area of behavioral thinking were functional response classes defined in this way. Rather behavior was (and still is) defined as a function of an organism's learning history and current contextual factors. The above definition also led to a paradoxical situation in which the behavior of the speaker was considered to be verbal, while the behavior of the listener was not, downplaying the importance of verbal comprehension relative to production. Finally, a number of authors pointed out that children learn thousands of words as well as a variety of "linguistic rules" that are often combined in the absence of direct instruction or experience (Chomsky, 1959; for a discussion see Barnes-Holmes & Murphy, 2007). Thus it seemed that a direct contingency approach failed to account adequately for two of language's core properties (generativity and flexibility).

While Skinner's analysis stimulated a number of empirical and practical applications in the domain of developmental disabilities, its volume and scope over the past 50 years has been limited (e.g., Dymond & Alonso-Álvarez, 2010; although see Greer, 2008; Sautter & LeBlanc, 2006; Schlinger, 2008, 2010). This interpretive analysis failed to equip researchers with a means to predict and influence a comprehensive range of verbal behaviors and did not translate into a rising cycle of research and analysis capable of stimulating new and important empirical questions about language itself.

Rule-Following

Lines of fracture between human and nonhuman behavior started to emerge elsewhere as well. A growing body of work on rule-following revealed that humans and nonhumans adapt to the same set of environmental regularities in dramatically different ways. Much of this research employed intermittent schedules of reinforcement wherein an organism was exposed to a learning task that sometimes reinforced high and (at other times) low rates of responding (Baron & Galizio, 1983; Lowe, 1979; Shimoff, Catania, & Matthews, 1981). Although nonhumans successfully completed such tasks, they often adjusted to contingencies in ways that differed to their human counterparts. Evidence suggested that these interspecies differences were due to the deployment of (covert) self-generated rules on the part of humans and that the effects of these rules could be (a) augmented when they were explicitly stated prior to the task, or (b) eliminated when steps were taken to minimize their impact on subsequent performance (see Hayes, Brownstein, Zettle, Rosenfarb, & Korn, 1986). Research on human operant behavior also revealed that people become insensitive to subsequent changes in the environment once their behavior comes under instructional control (Hayes, Brownstein, Haas, & Greenway, 1986), while developmental studies showed that preverbal infants respond in strikingly similar ways to nonhumans (unlike more verbally sophisticated children who respond in ways that mirror adults; Bentall, Lowe, & Beasty, 1985; Vaughan, 1985).

Overall, this work led to two important conclusions. The first was that humans frequently formulate verbal rules about contingencies in the wider world and that these rules are deployed in order to regulate how they respond to those contingencies (i.e., humans were interacting with the world through a "verbal lens"; Hayes, 1989b). The second was that – like language – rule-governed behavior stubbornly refused to be analyzed in direct contingency terms (see Barnes-Holmes, O'Hora et al., 2001; O'Hora & Barnes-Holmes, 2004). For instance, Skinner (1969) suggested that rules or instructions could be defined as discriminative stimuli that "specify" a contingency between antecedents, responses, and consequences. Thus when a father gives his son the following instruction, "Clean your room now and I will give you some pocket money later," the son is likely to tidy his room because a contingency has been specified between cleaning and receiving a reward. The problem for Skinner was this definition failed to clarify how rules or instructions come to function as "contingency specifying stimuli," especially when the individual has never received direct training for following such instructions in the past. Nor did it explain why rules or instructions come to act "as though" they were discriminative stimuli in the absence of an appropriate history of differential reinforcement (Schlinger & Blakely, 1987).

To illustrate, imagine that a friend hears that you intend to vacation in Europe next summer and remarks, "When you visit Paris make sure to climb the Eiffel Tower." Schlinger (1993) correctly pointed out that it is (a) the act of visiting Paris, and not this statement that evokes or sets the occasion for climbing the Eiffel Tower, and that (b) this climbing response was not established in the same way as other discriminative stimuli. Although Schlinger offered a more accurate description of instructions as "function-altering stimuli," he did not outline the history of reinforcement that is necessary for stimuli to alter the operant and/or respondent properties of other stimuli. In short, the rule-governed behavior literature seemed to suggest that a key feature was missing from a sophisticated functional analysis of such behavior. It would only be with the discovery of derived stimulus relating (O'Hora, Barnes-Holmes, Roche, & Smeets, 2004) that researchers would be able to articulate how stimuli acquire the "specifying" or "function-altering" properties of instructions. It is to this topic that we now turn.

Stimulus Equivalence

The discovery of a phenomenon known as stimulus equivalence further cemented the idea that humans were able to respond in ways that could not be explained in direct contingency terms. Although the concept of equivalence had long attracted the attention of philosophers (e.g., Aristotle in "De Memoria et Reminiscentia," 1941) and behavioral researchers (e.g., Hull, 1934; Jenkins & Palermo, 1964), it was only after a pioneering set of studies by Murray Sidman in the 1970s that this "symbolic" type of behavior was subject to careful and systematic scrutiny (Sidman, 1971; 2000; 2009). Interest in this phenomenon stemmed from a rather puzzling finding: When participants are exposed to a series of conditional discriminations, the stimuli involved in those discriminations are spontaneously related in ways that were never directly trained or instructed. Consider an early study designed to teach a group of institutionalized teenage boys with severe developmental disabilities how to read (Sidman, 1971). The author found that when the boys were taught to select pictures (B) in the presence of certain spoken words (A) and to select written words (C) in the presence of those same spoken words (A) they did something entirely unexpected. Although they had never been trained to relate written words (C) and pictures (B), they could now do so. That is, they not only showed evidence of having learned the directly trained relations between A and B as well as A and C, but also responded in a number of untrained ways that traditional learning theories could not readily explain (e.g., they related B to C). Sidman proposed that this type of training caused the written words, spoken words, and pictures to become interchangeable or equivalent to one another, and as a result, he labeled this effect "stimulus equivalence." Researchers quickly realized that stimulus equivalence represented "something new" – a type of behavior in which humans could respond to stimuli and events as if they were related in the absence of any direct reinforcement or instruction. Even more interesting was the fact that these "derived" or "emergent" relations between stimuli were entirely unexpected and should not have occurred according to direct contingency accounts. For instance, an explanation of equivalence in terms of stimulus generalization seemed problematic given that the stimuli involved in those relations – printed words, spoken words, and pictures – bore no physical resemblance to one another. Nor could such outcomes be explained away as respondents or operants because they emerged in the absence of such a history of learning. Rather, it seemed as if stimuli had become "symbols" that were mutually substitutable, even though (in many cases) they had never been paired with, or directly related to, each other in the past. These early assumptions proved to be accurate and over the ensuing four decades an extensive literature emerged suggesting that stimulus equivalence could be obtained with a wide variety of stimuli, populations, and procedures (for a review see Sidman, 1994; 2000; 2009). This work also revealed that when pigeons, rats, chimpanzees, and baboons were exposed to training procedures like that outlined above they consistently failed to produce outcomes similar to those observed in their human counterparts (Brino, Campos, Galvão, & McIlvane, 2014; Dugdale & Lowe, 2000; Lionello-DeNolf, 2009; although see Hughes & Barnes-Holmes, 2014; Zentall, Wasserman, & Urcuioli, 2014). Thus stimulus equivalence seemed to represent a type of behavior that was highly elaborated in, or unique to, some species and absent in others.

Summary

The difficulty in accounting for language in direct contingency terms, combined with the striking difference between human and nonhuman operant behavior and the discovery of stimulus equivalence, led many researchers to the same conclusion: While most organisms adapt to the environment via direct contact with contingencies, humans appear to respond in ways that are inherently symbolic, flexible, and generative. Yet this finding introduced an additional set of questions: What type of learning history do people need in order to act as if stimuli are related in the absence of reinforcement or instruction? How and when do these relational abilities emerge and what role do they play in basic human language, rule-following, and stimulus equivalence? Could they also play a role in other psychological phenomena such as perspective-taking and self, analogical reasoning, as well as "fast" and "slow" cognition? In order to provide an answer to these questions, we first need to delve a little deeper into research on stimulus equivalence. As we shall see, work in this area set the stage for experimental methodologies and conceptual insights that would lead to a better understanding of derived stimulus relating – and by implication – human language and cognition.

Stimulus Equivalence: An Overview

According to Sidman (2000), in order for a behavior to qualify as an instance of stimulus equivalence, it must first demonstrate three core properties, which he termed (a) reflexivity, (b) symmetry, and (c) transitivity. The most basic of these is *reflexivity* which refers to the fact that – within an equivalence relation – each stimulus must be conditionally related to itself. For example, people should select spoken words (A) in the presence of spoken words (A), written words (B) in the presence of written words (B), and pictures (C) in the presence of pictures (C). *Symmetry* requires that the relationship between stimuli also be reversible, so that when a person is taught to select the written word D-O-G (B) in the presence of a spoken word "*DOG*" (A) he or she will also select the spoken word (A) in the presence of the written word (B) (i.e., responding as if "A is the same as B" leads to the derived relation "B is the same as A"). *Transitivity* refers to the fact that when two or more relations are trained, a novel set of derived relations also tend to emerge. Thus if people are taught to choose the written word D-O-G (B) in the presence of a spoken word "*DOG*" (A) and a picture of a dog (C) in the presence of the spoken word (A), a novel relation between the written word (B) and picture (C) will subsequently emerge. It is worth noting that this example actually involves combined symmetry and transitivity, which has been interpreted as providing a simple or abbreviated test for an equivalence relation (see Figure 9.1). A final feature of

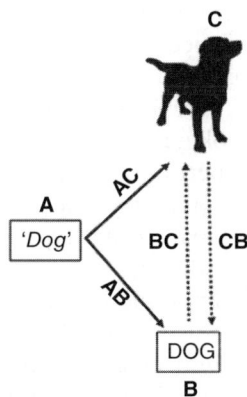

Figure 9.1   A visual illustration of an equivalence relation between the spoken word "*DOG*" (A), the written word D-O-G (B) and a picture of a dog (C). The solid arrows (AB and AC) designate relations between stimuli that are explicitly taught while the dashed arrows (BC and CB) indicate derived relations that emerge without any training or instruction. Note that testing only the B–C and C–B relations has sometimes been used as an abbreviated method for assessing equivalence responding (e.g. Devany, Hayes, & Nelson, 1986).

stimulus equivalence is the transfer of stimulus functions. Many researchers have found that when a function is explicitly trained to one member of an equivalence class, that same function may then transfer to the other members of the equivalence class without further training. For instance, if a fear-eliciting function is established for an actual dog (through the receipt of a bite) a child may come to respond with fear whenever they are presented with the written word D-O-G or the spoken word "*DOG*" (for related findings see Dougher, Perkins, Greenway, Koons, & Chiasson, 2002; Rodríguez-Valverde, Luciano, & Barnes-Holmes, 2009; Smyth, Barnes-Holmes, & Forsyth, 2006).

While stimulus equivalence generated a considerable amount of empirical and theoretical interest in its own right, it also set the stage for an entirely new possibility: If humans can derive that arbitrary stimuli such as spoken words, written words, and pictures are the same, then can they also derive other types of relations as well? In other words, are humans capable of responding in even more complex ways that extend above and beyond equivalence? If so, would these other types of *derived stimulus relations* also be reflexive, symmetrical, and transitive, and lead to transfers of function? After nearly three decades of work we now know that most humans are capable of deriving arbitrary relations among stimuli and events without direct training or instruction to do so. We also know that equivalence is just the tip of the iceberg and that people can derive relations between stimuli in a near infinite number of ways. For instance, stimuli can be related as the same (e.g., "*Hound is the same as dog*"; Cahill et al., 2007) or opposite to one another (e.g., "*Good is the opposite of Evil*"; Dymond, Roche, Forsyth, Whelan, & Rhoden, 2008), as well as hierarchically ("*Cat is a type of mammal*"; Gil, Luciano, Ruiz, & Valdivia-Salas, 2012), comparatively ("*Fruit is better than candy*"; Vitale, Barnes-Holmes, Barnes-Holmes, & Campbell, 2008), deictically ("*I am not you*"; McHugh & Stewart, 2012), and temporally ("*March comes before May*"; O'Hora et al., 2008) related. While these findings propelled our understanding of human learning forward, they also introduced an unavoidable conceptual problem: Many relational responses are difficult, if not impossible, to describe using the terms that Sidman originally devised in the context of stimulus equivalence. Comparative relations, for example, are not symmetrical. If an elephant is bigger than a mouse, it does not follow that a mouse is bigger than an elephant (in fact, a mouse is smaller than an elephant). The same goes for causal relations. If "smoking causes cancer" and "cancer causes death," only some, but not all, of the properties of equivalence apply. Transitivity applies in that smoking causes death, but symmetry does not (given that cancer does not cause smoking). Thus causal (and many other types of derived) relations are nonreflexive, asymmetrical, transitive, and connected. In other words, it quickly became apparent that humans were capable of relating stimuli in a vast number of different ways and that a new set of terms was needed that could adequately account for all possible derived relations that might emerge between and among stimuli. These technical terms would need to be broad enough so that they could not only describe the effects observed within the equivalence literature, but also encompass the properties of any other type of relation as well. Toward this end, researchers from a theoretical background known as relational frame theory have identified what they believe to be a small but powerful set of terms that meet these various requirements. In the following section, we provide a general introduction to this account and consider these technical terms in greater detail.

Relational Frame Theory: An Overview

At its core, RFT argues that language, rule-following, and stimulus equivalence are all instances of a type of operant behavior known as arbitrarily applicable relational responding (AARR; Barnes-Holmes, Luciano, & Barnes-Holmes, 2004a, b; Dymond & Roche, 2013; Hayes, Barnes-Holmes, & Roche, 2001; Rehfeldt & Barnes-Holmes, 2009). According to this perspective, "relating" is a type of behavior and involves *responding to one event in terms of another*. While nonhumans and humans can both respond relationally to stimuli and events, the latter rapidly develop a more complex type of behavior (AARR) that fundamentally alters how they interact with the world around them. In what follows, we examine how RFT carves this type of operant behavior into two different varieties (nonarbitrarily and arbitrarily applicable) and discuss how the latter may not only provide an explanation for stimulus equivalence, but for other types of derived stimulus relations as well.

Nonarbitrarily Applicable Relational Responding (NAARR)

Mammals, birds, fish, and insects can all be trained to respond to the relations between and among stimuli in the environment. However, for many different species, these relational responses appear to be characterized by two key properties: (a) they are rooted in a prior history of direct experience and (b) they are defined by the physical features of the to-be-related stimuli themselves (Giurfa, Zhang, Jenett, Menzel, & Srinivasan, 2001; Harmon, Strong, & Pasnak, 1982; Reese, 1968). RFT refers to this type of behavior as an instance of nonarbitrarily applicable relational responding (or NAARR) because the organism is relating stimuli based on their formal or physical properties. Properties such as color, shape, quantity, and size are considered "nonarbitrary" because they are based on the physical characteristics of the stimuli, unlike arbitrary or arbitrarily applicable properties, that are determined by social convention. To illustrate the concept of NAARR more clearly, imagine that a pigeon is exposed to a learning task in which a sample stimulus (e.g., a red circle) is presented at the top of a computer screen and two comparison stimuli (e.g., a red and a green circle) are presented at the bottom of the screen. On trials where a red circle serves as a sample stimulus, selecting the red circle from the available comparisons is reinforced, and whenever a green circle is the sample, selecting the green circle from the available comparisons is reinforced. Training continues in this way across a wide spectrum of different colors and shapes. Once the bird is consistently correct across a large number of trials it is then presented with a number of entirely novel stimuli (that were never directly reinforced in the past). Research suggests that the pigeon will continue to select a shape from the bottom of the screen that is physically identical to a shape at the top of the screen even when that particular response was never previously reinforced (Frank & Wasserman, 2005). Now consider a series of studies wherein adult rhesus monkeys (Harmon et al., 1982) or marmosets (Yamazaki, Saiki, Inada, Iriki, Watanabe, 2014) are trained to select the taller of two items that differ only in terms of their respective height. When subsequently presented with a previously "correct" item (i.e., a stimulus that was taller than its comparison stimulus) as well as a novel item that is even taller, they consistently select the latter, despite reinforcement for choosing the former at an earlier point in time. These studies, in addition to many others, suggest that animals can respond to the nonarbitrary (i.e., physical) relationship that exists between stimuli. In the above examples, pigeons related shapes based on their physical similarity to one another, while rhesus monkeys or marmosets responded to the comparative relationship between items that differed in their respective height (both providing examples of NAARR).

Arbitrarily Applicable Relational Responding (AARR)

RFT argues that while humans and nonhumans can both show NAARR, the former are typically exposed to a set of contingencies by the socio-verbal community that results in the development of a more advanced type of relating known as AARR. This behavior is not based on the physical relationship that exists between stimuli, but rather on the ability to derive relations between stimuli and events independently of their physical characteristics and in the absence of any direct training or instruction to do so.

As an example, imagine that I show you three identically sized coins and tell you that "*Coin A* is worth far less than *Coin B* which is, in turn, worth far less than *Coin C*." I then give you the option to select any of the three coins and your hand immediately gravitates toward the third option. It is likely that the selection of Coin C occurs after you have derived a number of untrained relations between the various stimuli (e.g., that "Coin C is worth far more than A or B" and that "Coin A is worth far less than B or C"). What is remarkable here is that you can respond to the relation between stimuli despite the fact that (a) you have never encountered these items in the past, and (b) the three coins do not differ in any physical way. According to RFT, this example showcases an instance of AARR in which stimuli are arbitrarily related along a comparative dimension (worth). In a similar way the equivalence phenomenon discovered by Sidman can also be viewed as an instance of AARR, but one in which stimuli are arbitrarily related based on their sameness or similarity.

As we have seen above, the terms originally devised by Sidman to describe simple instances of AARR fail to accommodate the different properties of relational responses at increased levels of complexity. Thus a more generic set of terms was needed that could account for all possible derived relations that might be established between and among events. With this in mind, RFT argues that all derived stimulus relations (including equivalence) are characterized by three core properties known as (a) mutual entailment, (b) combinatorial entailment, and (c) the transformation of stimulus functions.

Mutual entailment. The first of these properties (*mutual entailment*), like the concept of symmetry, refers to the inherent bidirectionality or "reversibility" of stimulus relations, so that if A is related to B, people will also respond as if B is related to A. However, unlike symmetry, mutually entailed relations are not always symmetrical. If a person learns that the word for "woman" (A) is the same as the word for "vrouw" (B), they will likely respond as if the word "vrouw" (B) is the same as the word "woman" (A). Yet if they learn that a medicine in the blood (A) prevents cancer (B), they will not derive that cancer (B) prevents medicine in the blood (A). Thus while symmetry represents a subtype of mutual entailment in which derived and directly trained relations are the same, other mutually entailed relations are also possible that are not equivalent in nature.

Combinatorial entailment. The second property of derived stimulus relating is known as *combinatorial entailment*. This term refers to the fact that when two stimulus relations combine, a number of novel untrained relations tend to emerge. For instance, if A is related to B and B is related to C, then people will also respond as if A is related to C and C is related to A without any training or instructions to do so. Once again, it is important to note that while combinatorial entailment bears similarity to the concepts of "transitivity" and "equivalence," it actually extends beyond both of them. To illustrate, imagine that you spend a summer in Europe and learn that the Croatian word for apple (A) is "jabuka," (B) while in Spain it is "manzana" (C). In this instance, you will likely respond to a jabuka (B) as being the same as a manzana (C) and a manzana (C) as the same as a jabuka (B). Now imagine that the following year you decide to travel to Canada where you are informed that a quarter (A) is worth more than a dime (B), and that a dime (B) is worth more than a nickel (C). In this instance, it is unlikely that you will treat these three coins as interchangeable or equivalent to one another. Rather a *bigger-than* relation will be derived between the quarter (A) and nickel (C) while a *smaller-than* relation will be derived between the nickel (C) and quarter (A). Therefore, while transitivity represents a subtype of combinatorial entailment based on similarity, other types of combinatorial relations are possible that are nonequivalent in nature.

Transformation of stimulus functions. The third and final property of derived stimulus relating, known as the *transformation of stimulus functions*, is particularly important from an RFT perspective because it is the process by which stimuli and events come to acquire, change, and lose their psychological properties. This term refers to the finding that when stimuli are related to one another – and the functions of one of those stimuli is modified in some way – the corresponding functions of other stimuli in that relation will spontaneously change without any training or instruction to do so. Critically, the transformation of functions always depend on the nature of the relation established between and among stimuli (e.g., Cahill et al., 2007; Dymond & Barnes, 1995; Gil et al., 2012; Smyth et al., 2006; Whelan, Barnes-Holmes & Dymond, 2006). As we pointed out above, when symmetry (*X–same–Y*) and equivalence relations are formed (*X–same–Y*; *Y–same–Z*) and a function is then established for one of those stimuli (X), corresponding functions may subsequently *transfer* to the other stimuli in that relation as well (e.g., Y and Z). Imagine, for example, that a symmetry relation is formed between the word "poisonous" (X) and a novel liquid (Y) and a second relation is then established between novel liquid (Y) and a gas (Z). The formation of an equivalence relation between these three stimuli may lead to a transfer of functions from X to Y and Z, such that people respond with fear and attempt to avoid all contact with both substances, despite having never encountered either in the past. On the other hand, when nonequivalent relations are formed, the functions of a stimulus may not simply transfer but rather be *transformed* through those relations. Now imagine that an opposition relation is established between the word "poisonous" (X) and a liquid (Y) and a second opposition relation is then established between the liquid (Y) and a gas (Z). Unlike before, the liquid (Y) will not evoke fear and avoidance (given that it is opposite to "poisonous"), while gas (Z) might (given that the combinatorially entailed relation is one of similarity between X and Z). In other words, while *transfers* of function constitute a subtype of *transformations* of functions (in which the psychological properties of a stimulus are broadly similar for stimuli in that relation), other types of derived stimulus relations can involve complex changes in functions (for the first empirical demonstration of a transformation of functions see Dymond and Barnes, 1995).[1]

Contextual Control over AARR

If humans have the capacity to arbitrarily relate any stimulus to any other stimulus and substitute one for the other, then why does this ability not lead to complete and utter chaos? For example, why do people not try to eat the word "apple," lick the words "ice cream" off a page, or even swat the word "fly" from a book? RFT proposes that the way in which people relate stimuli (and transform functions through those relations) is under the control of stimuli in the past or present environment known as contextual cues. While certain types of contextual cues specify how stimuli are related (e.g., "A *same as* B" or "A *causes* B"), others specify the psychological properties that are transformed through those relations (e.g., "A *tastes* disgusting" or "B *feels* soft"). RFT researchers usually refer to the former as "relational cues" (or C_{rels} for short) given that they specify how stimuli and events should be related. These cues can be used to relate stimuli in a near infinite number of ways, from relations based on similarity or opposition to those based on hierarchy, comparison, deictics, temporality, and/or causality. At the same time, responding can also be controlled by "functional cues" (or C_{funcs}) in the environment that specify the type of psychological properties that are transformed in accordance with stimulus relations. For example, the verbal stimulus "ice cream" could in principle evoke many of the psychological properties of actual ice cream (such as its taste, smell, appearance, or its coolness) based on the equivalence relation between the word and the food-item. If, however, someone asks you to *picture* ice cream, the visual properties of ice cream would likely predominate. Likewise, in the sentence "imagine what ice cream tastes like," the expression "*tastes like*" may serve as a functional cue that is responsible for the fact that only the gustatory and not other functions of ice cream predominate (e.g., what it looks like).

RFT argues that all mutually and combinatorially entailed relations are under some form of contextual control, without which different patterns of relational responding could not be observed. If AARR was not brought under the control of relational cues, for example, then all types of relations would apply to all events, resulting in chaotic and useless responses or "relational gridlock." Likewise, if the transformation of functions were not restrained via functional cues, stimuli and events would collapse functionally in useless ways. For example, if all the functions of one stimulus in an equivalence relation were to transfer to another stimulus, then the two stimuli would merge and become indistinguishable in a psychological sense (e.g., a child would attempt to eat the word "candy" or an adult would try to drive the word "car"). Thus relational and functional cues may be seen as the metaphorical "scaffolding of relating," specifying the manner in which stimuli should be related and functions transformed.

Summary

Relational frame theory is built upon a relatively simple idea: that a learned operant behavior known as arbitrarily applicable relational responding represents the basic functional "unit" from which phenomena like meaning, rule-governed behavior, and stimulus equivalence spring forth. The concept of AARR may appear to be difficult (and it is definitely technical), but most of its components have already been described. *Relational responding* refers to the ability to respond to relations between stimuli rather than just responding to each stimulus separately and RFT distinguishes between two classes of such behavior (NAARR and AARR). On the one hand, many different species can respond in novel ways based on the physical relationship that exists between previously encountered stimuli. In the language of RFT, such behaviors are defined as instances of *nonarbitrarily applicable* relational responding or NAARR. On the other hand, humans quickly learn how to (a) relate stimuli in ways that do not depend on their physical properties and (b) the stimuli involved in those relations often become related to each other in ways that were never explicitly trained. In the language of RFT, such outcomes are defined as instances of *arbitrarily applicable* relational responding or AARR. A behavior is defined as an instance of AARR whenever it shows evidence of mutual entailment, combinatorial entailment, and the transformation of function. RFT proposes that the manner in which stimuli are mutually and combinatorially related, as well as the psychological properties transformed in accordance with those relations, always depends on two different types of contextual control. The first (relational cues) specifies how stimuli are related while the second (functional cues) specify which functions are to be transformed through those relations.

Why is AARR So Important?

Over the past 40 years AARR has captured the imagination of behavioral scientists due to its symbolic, flexible, and generative properties. From the beginning researchers realized that this type of behavior was inherently *generative*. Providing humans with a small set of direct experiences consistently causes them to act as if those stimuli are related to one another in a staggering number of novel and untrained ways. Indeed, there is an exponential increase in the number of untrained relations as more and more stimuli are related, so that by the time eight stimulus relations are trained, people can – in principle – act as if those stimuli are related in several thousand untrained ways. Thus AARR represents a type of behavior that rapidly accelerates learning as more and more stimuli are related. A second reason why AARR has attracted so much attention within the functional tradition is that it equips humans with an unparalleled degree of *flexibility* when interacting with the world around them. The aforementioned properties of relational responding allow organisms to better adjust to their environments, because relating itself becomes a part of the environment that increases the scope of the organism's interactions with it. For instance, once an individual has learned how to respond in an arbitrarily applicable fashion, they can relate any stimulus to any other stimulus in a near infinite number of ways. They can relate stimuli with no physical resemblance (like spoken words, written words, and pictures) and these relations can come to control how they subsequently respond. People can also act as if stimuli have acquired, changed, or lost their psychological properties without the need to directly contact contingencies in the environment. To illustrate, suppose that a person learns that a novel item (A) is less than a second item (B) and that B is less than a third item (C). Thereafter, B is repeatedly paired with electrical shocks. Evidence indicates that people will display greater fear toward C than B and more fear to B than A, despite the fact that C and A were never paired with shock and that none of the stimuli share any physical similarity (Dougher, Hamilton, Fink, & Harrington, 2007). Moreover, if people learn that they can avoid being shocked by repeatedly pressing a button when they see B, they will also press that same button when they see A and C (Auguston & Dougher, 1997). Finally, when avoidance of C is subsequently extinguished, participants will spontaneously stop avoiding A and B as well (Roche, Kanter, Brown, Dymond, & Fogarty, 2008; but see Luciano et al., 2013; 2014; Vervoort, Vervliet, Bennett, & Baeyens, 2014). Functionally speaking, it seems unlikely that this behavior is a simple case of stimulus generalization given that the three items bear no physical resemblance to one another. At the same time, it does not appear to be an instance of classical conditioning seeing as B and C were never paired with aversive events, nor an instance of operant conditioning given that fear or avoidance responding in the presence of certain stimuli was never reinforced in the past. Put another way, when organisms respond not only to external events but come to relate those events in different ways, the possibilities of manipulating and changing the world are dramatically increased.

In short, the generativity and flexibility of AARR, combined with its potential to scale in complexity, finally equipped researchers with a means to tackle psychological phenomena in way that was sorely lacking in the past (e.g., Skinner, 1957). Researchers quickly realized that two core features of AARR (generativity and flexibility) are also two core features of human language. For instance, the ability to derive relations between arbitrary stimuli closely mirrors the symbolic or referential nature of language, wherein spoken and written words share few physical properties with their referents, yet people respond to each of those stimuli as though they are equivalent (e.g., shouting "SNAKE" on an airplane might elicit many of the same fear responses as seeing a snake on an airplane). Likewise, the ability to derive a large number of relations between stimuli from a limited number of experiences also mirrors the remarkable generativity that lies at the heart of language (Hayes, Barnes-Holmes, & Roche, 2001). These theoretical observations were bolstered by empirical support on several fronts. Whereas verbally able humans form derived stimulus relations with remarkable ease, their nonhuman counterparts have yet to demonstrate such relations convincingly or unequivocally (Hughes & Barnes-Holmes, 2014; Lionello-DeNolf, 2009). Individuals with verbal deficits also demonstrate impairments in their ability to respond in relationally complex ways (Barnes, McCullagh, & Keenan, 1990; O'Connor, Rafferty, Barnes-Holmes, & Barnes-Holmes, 2009) and providing remedial training in AARR can serve to address those deficits (Murphy, Barnes-Holmes, & Barnes-Holmes, 2005; Persicke, Tarbox, Ranick, & St. Clair, 2012; Walsh, Horgan, May, Dymond, & Whelan, 2014). At the same time, the ability to derive stimulus relations repeatedly correlates with cognitive and linguistic skills (Cassidy, Roche, & Hayes, 2011; O'Hora et al., 2008; O'Toole & Barnes-Holmes, 2009). The development of AARR initially emerges in infancy but develops gradually around the same time as verbal abilities (Luciano, Gomez-Becerra, & Rodriguez-Valverde, 2007) while brain-imaging studies reveal that derived relations produce similar patterns of neural activation to semantic processes (Barnes-Holmes et al., 2005; see also Whelan & Schlund, 2013).

As we shall see in the next chapter, the influence of AARR (and the history of learning that gave rise to it) is also argued to play a role in other domains such as perspective-taking (McHugh & Stewart, 2012), implicit and explicit cognition (Hughes, Barnes-Holmes, & Vahey, 2012), problem-solving (Stewart, Barrett, McHugh, Barnes-Holmes, & O'Hora, 2013), analogical reasoning (Lipkens & Hayes, 2009), as well as fears, phobias, avoidance, and anxiety (Hayes, Strosahl, & Wilson, 1999). For now though let us turn to the origins of AARR and examine how this operant behavior may be learned early on in our development.

Section 2: On the Origins and Properties of AARR

In the first section of the chapter we briefly discussed the research leading up to the development of RFT and provided an introduction to the theory itself. In Section 2 we take a closer look at the various assumptions that underpin this functional account of human language and cognition. We will show how the ability to frame events relationally is a type of operant behavior that is under both antecedent and consequential stimulus control. In effect, we argue that this operant is (a) generalized and purely functionally defined, (b) relational, and (c) arbitrarily applicable, but nonarbitrarily applied. In what follows we unpack each of these points in greater detail.

What is a Generalized and Functionally Defined Operant?

The concept of a generalized and functionally defined operant has often been used within the behavior analytic tradition to interpret or explain complex behaviors. When researchers speak of a functionally defined operant they are simply emphasizing the following point: that the core property of any operant (generalized or not) is the correspondence between a class of responses defined by its consequences and the variety of responses generated by these consequences. In other words, operant response classes are defined according to their functional effects as opposed to what any response within that class looks like (i.e., its topography). To illustrate this point, consider the act of powering on your computer. You may press the power button with your right finger, left hand, nose, a stick, or so forth. Although each of these responses appear different they are all button presses and qualify as members of the same operant class because they all share a common function (i.e., they all lead to the same consequence). The need to draw attention to the functional nature of operant classes arises from the fact that, in everyday life, the topographical and functional properties of operants often overlap, and it easy to confuse one with the other. In the above example, the operant of "powering on a computer" may be defined as the effect of activity on a certain button, but almost every such response involves the person using their right index finger. While that same button may also be activated in a variety of ways (e.g., by accidentally dropping something on it) these responses are often ignored for practical purposes. And even if they were included, there is some notional limit to the range of topographies or movements that could possibly depress the button. The key point to appreciate here is that operant classes are defined functionally in terms of their effects rather than topographically based on what a given response looks like.

RFT puts this topography versus function issue squarely and unavoidably on the table (Barnes-Holmes & Barnes-Holmes, 2000; Healy, Barnes-Holmes, & Smeets, 2000). It argues that in many cases the stimuli and responses that comprise an operant class have very few topographical features in common. For instance, it is possible to train people to emit entirely random sequences of numbers during an experiment by providing feedback on the randomness of a numerical string that participants had emitted on the previous trial. By definition, the functional class of "random number sequences" cannot be formed on the basis of what the stimuli look like because each of those stimuli vary in their topographical features. Yet this operant response class can still be trained (see Neuringer, 2002). While many other instances of generalized operants have now been identified (e.g., identity matching; Sidman, 2000; learning set;

Harlow, 1959), the most well known is arguably generalized imitation (Baer & Deguchi, 1985; Catania, 1998; Horne & Erjavec, 2007).

Generalized imitation refers to a specific functional relation: namely one between a model, an imitator, and a history of differential consequences for imitating. Although humans may be evolutionarily prepared to imitate the actions of other members of our species (Meltzoff, 2005), we seem to acquire a more general class of "do-what-other-people-do" as an operant behavior. Dinsmoor (1995) described the operative process as follows:

> When a number of correspondences have been reinforced between the actions of an observer and the actions of a model, the correspondence itself may become a governing factor in the relation between the two actions, extending to new topographies of behavior. (pp. 264–265)

In other words, when the "correspondence" between the behavior of a model and the behavior of an imitator has been repeatedly reinforced, entirely novel responses may be imitated without the need for further reinforcement. Imagine, for example, that a father sets out to teach his child a range of behaviors (e.g., clapping, dancing, sharing) using a sock-puppet. If only one specific imitative response was ever trained (e.g., clapping) it is unlikely that generalized imitation would emerge, no matter how long the training lasted. However, if the relevant properties of the context are varied (e.g., the father engages in a range of different actions), consistent reinforcement is delivered for imitative responses, and increasingly novel and/or difficult responses are gradually introduced, then the functional class of generalized imitation will likely be acquired. A wide range of response topographies can now be substituted for the topographies used in the initial training, leading to a robust imitative repertoire. For instance, if a novel behavior is produced by the puppet (e.g., cleaning), the child may imitate this behavior despite the fact that this imitative response was never reinforced in the past. At this point the operant class is said to be generalized in that it contains imitative responses above and beyond those that were differentially reinforced. It is also functionally defined insofar as the stimuli and responses in that class bear no topographical similarity to one another – they are united by their common function.

AARR is a Generalized and Functionally Defined Operant

RFT argues that AARR is a generalized operant class that is established in a broadly similar way. Through early natural language interactions, human infants are exposed to a wide variety of stimuli, populations, and contexts in which differential consequences are provided for responding to the relationship that exists between stimuli. This functional relation is initially based on the nonarbitrary properties of the stimuli involved, but exposure to a sufficient number of exemplars of varying topography serves to abstract or "wash out" these irrelevant factors and brings the functional relation under the control of arbitrary contextual cues. These cues can be applied in such a way that stimuli can be related regardless of their physical relationship to one another. When different types of relating have been abstracted and brought under the control of contextual cues that extend beyond the physical properties of the related events, relational responding is said to be *arbitrarily applicable*.

To illustrate this point more clearly, imagine that you are attempting to teach your infant son how to name a number of objects around the house. You will likely begin by pointing at an item (e.g., a toy bear), uttering its name in the presence of your son, and then reinforcing any orientating response that he makes toward the item (i.e., hear the word *bear* → look at the bear). At the same time, you will also present the item to your son and then model or reinforce appropriate responses (see the bear → say the word *bear*). Both of these interactions will take place in the presence of contextual cues and – in natural language interactions – these cues typically take the form of questions such as "What is this?" or "What is the name of that?" In the language of RFT, you are directly reinforcing bidirectional responding in both directions to an object and its name in the presence of a contextual cue. Importantly, this training will not stop here: You and others in the social community (teachers, friends, family) will likely engage in the same exercise with your son across a vast spectrum of different objects, from toys ("Where is your bike?"), to people ("Who is that?"), food ("This is an apple"), and properties of the environment ("That is called the sun … what is that called?"), and do so in a wide variety of different contexts: at the park, home, at the shopping mall, school, and so on. Although the particular stimuli, people, and contexts change across time, the functional relation between those stimuli is always held constant: Reinforcement is provided for relational responding in both directions and in the presence of arbitrary contextual cues. Gradually, after a sufficient number of exemplars, the generalized response pattern of object–word symmetry is abstracted from the topography of particular objects or events and comes under the control of contextual cues, thus establishing *derived* symmetry (i.e., being able to derive the untaught response when trained in only one direction) with any new word–object pair.

In other words, through a history of multiple exemplar training (MET), your son learns a type of generalized bidirectional responding that no longer depends on the physical features of the stimuli involved and that leads to the mutually entailed response being emitted in the absence of direct reinforcement. Now when you present him with a novel object and a vocal stimulus he has never encountered before (e.g., a laptop and the label "laptop"), he will respond in a bidirectional manner without any reinforcement for doing so (e.g., he will point to the laptop when asked "Where is the laptop?" and answer with "laptop" when asked "What is this?"). According to RFT, this functional relation between an object and word constitutes an instance of mutual entailment in which stimuli are related on the basis of their arbitrary similarity to one another. In other words, your son has learned to treat a word and its referent as functionally similar in certain contexts.

A history of MET also allows for more complex relational responses to emerge. For instance, imagine a second scenario where you and your son examine a picture book containing many different items and you come across an entirely new stimulus: a picture of an African lion as well as the written word "lion" printed on the opposite page. Given the prior history of reinforcement for bidirectional responding in the presence of contextual cues, pointing toward the picture and saying "This is a lion" will likely lead your son to emit a number of mutually entailed responses (e.g., asking "What is that?" will result in him saying "lion" while simply saying "Where is the lion?" will lead him to point toward the appropriate picture). At the same time a second mutually entailed relation may be trained between the spoken and written words such that you utter the word "lion" in the presence of your son and then reinforce any orientating response that he makes toward the written word (i.e., hear the sound *lion* → look at the word lion). You will also orientate your son toward the written word (by pointing to it) and then modelling or reinforcing an appropriate response (see the word lion → emit the sound *lion*). Once again, these relational responses will be trained in all directions in the presence of certain contextual cues. For example, you will likely reinforce pointing toward the written word lion whenever your son sees a picture of a lion, pointing toward the picture whenever he sees the written word, and saying *lion* whenever he sees the written word or picture. In the language of RFT, your son is being exposed to a set of contingencies which reinforce bidirectional responding to the arbitrary relation between *two or more* stimuli. This same interaction will take place across a staggering number of different objects, words, and sounds in a variety of contexts. Although each of these relational responses may be reinforced initially, with sufficient training your son will come to emit the mutually and combinatorially entailed relations without any further training or instructions to do so. Thus, for example, when you relate a new picture of a zebra with the sound *zebra*, and the sound with the written word "zebra," your son may respond to those stimuli as being related in a number of untrained ways (i.e., he will show evidence of mutual and combinatorial entailment).

The take-home message here is that the ability to respond to the relation between stimuli can be discriminated, abstracted, and brought under arbitrary contextual control. In much the same way that training generalized imitation across multiple exemplars can lead to the abstraction of the functional relation between the model and observer, training humans to respond relationally across exemplars can lead to a situation in which relating itself (rather than the properties of the stimuli involved) becomes the important factor. In order for this to occur, the organism must be exposed to a sufficient number of exemplars that allows it to discriminate between the relevant features of the relation (responding to one event in terms of another based on a contextual cue) and the irrelevant features (the actual physical properties of the objects being related). As relational responding is freed through abstraction from the formal properties of related events, it comes under the control of relational and functional cues (C_{rels} and C_{funcs}) that serve as discriminative stimuli for the relevant relational response. When such cues are presented, the individual's prior history of relational learning can be brought to bear on any arbitrarily chosen set of stimuli, regardless of their nonarbitrary properties or the nonarbitrary relations between them. Moreover, while these bidirectional relations between stimuli are initially reinforced in both directions (e.g., "A is related to B" and "B is related to A") the entailed or derived relations quickly come to be emitted without any further reinforcement for doing so (e.g., people will relate B to A whenever they learn that "A is related to B"). Thus, RFT suggests that the well-established concept of the operant can be extended to relational responding in order to explain one of the key generative features of human language. Indeed, from an RFT perspective, AARR is the behavioral process that underlies the symbolic nature of language and we will return to this point in chapter 10 in this volume.

For now it is worth noting that a history of differential reinforcement for bidirectional responding across multiple exemplars (MET) may also give rise to many other patterns of relational responding. Comparative relations provide a ready illustration. A parent might present a child with two boxes of toys, one with more toys than the other, and reinforce the selection of the box with more items in the presence of contextual cues such as "Which box has more toys?" or "Give daddy the box with more toys." They may also reinforce the selection of the physically smaller object in the presence of cues such as "Which box has less toys?" or "Give daddy the box with less toys." This training continues across many different exemplars that vary in their physical quantity and across many different contexts. However, in each case the functional relation of responding comparatively to the stimuli based on their physical properties is held constant. When the child begins to respond correctly to novel stimuli based on their physical size, relational training may shift to entirely arbitrary stimuli and continue until responding comes under the control of cues other than the physical dimensions of the stimuli involved. For instance, the parent may present their child with a nickel (which is physically larger than a penny), a penny and a dime (which is physically smaller than a nickel or a penny) and ask "Which coin is worth the most?" The child may initially respond to the stimuli based on their nonarbitrary or physical properties and select the nickel because it is physically larger than either a penny or a dime. Such a response will likely fail to produce social reinforcement in that the parent may respond with "No – the nickel is not worth the most." Given a sufficient number of trials, responding may thus be brought under the control of arbitrary contextual cues (e.g., the word *most*), such that the child now responds to the coins based on their conventional value rather than their physical size (i.e., the child selects the dime which is physically the smallest but monetarily the largest). The child may subsequently respond to foreign currencies in a functionally similar manner (i.e., by asking what individual coins are worth rather than assuming that larger coins are worth more than smaller coins). As we shall see in Section 3, this type of training may also provide the basis for responding in accordance with distinction, opposition, hierarchy, spatial, and many other types of derived stimulus relations as well.

Summary

In short, RFT argues that AARR is a learned operant behavior that emerges via a protracted history of differential reinforcement across multiple exemplars and is characterized by three important properties: (a) it is generalized, (b) relational, and (c) arbitrarily applicable but nonarbitrarily applied. These three features do not undermine the argument that AARR is an operant behavior nor do they require that we invent a new type of operant to accommodate this phenomenon. However, they do require us to be conceptually precise in our understanding of what constitutes an operant (for a detailed discussion of this issue see Barnes-Holmes & Barnes-Holmes, 2000). AARR is *generalized* insofar as it is defined functionally in terms of its effects rather than the topography or form of any given stimulus or response. It is *relational* insofar as it is an operant that involves responding to one event in terms of another.

Section 3: The Rich Complexity of AARR

In the previous section we argued that AARR represents a type of generalized operant behavior in which stimuli are related under the control of contextual cues that have themselves been abstracted through a history of differential reinforcement and brought to bear so that stimuli can be related to one another without regard to their physical properties. And as we outlined in Section 1, once this ability to AARR has been acquired, people can relate stimuli and events in a near infinite number of ways, from relations based on sameness or coordination (e.g., "*Hound is the same as dog*") to those that involve comparison (e.g., "*Italian is better than French cuisine*"), opposition ("*night is opposite to day*"), temporality ("*summer comes before winter*"), hierarchy ("*sunflowers are a type of flower*"), analogy ("*I'm right as rain*"), and deictics ("*I am sitting here in this chair now*").

In the language of RFT, these different patterns of AARR are known as *relational frames*. This term is based on the metaphor of a "picture frame" and is used to convey the idea that people interact with the world by "framing events relationally." In much the same way that a picture frame can hold a variety of images regardless of what those images actually look like (e.g., family photos, vacation images, or classical art), people can arbitrarily relate stimuli regardless of what they look, smell, feel, taste, or sound like. The key point to remember here is that "relational frames" are not hypothetical entities or mediating mental mechanisms used to account for behavior. Rather they are convenient labels for a specific type of AARR that: (a) shows the contextually controlled properties of mutual entailment, combinatorial entailment, and transformation of functions, (b) is due to a history of relational responding relevant to the contextual cues involved, and (c) is not based solely on a direct history of learning or the nonarbitrary characteristics of stimuli/responses. In other words, the terms *AARR* and *derived stimulus relating* are generic labels that are used to describe a type of generalized operant behavior while the terms *relational frames* or *relational framing* describe specific instances of that behavior (e.g., "stimuli were related in a frame of coordination, comparison, distinction ..." and so forth). Over the past decade a wide variety of relational frames have been identified and subjected to an experimental analysis. In what follows, we shine a light on this work, discuss the main "families" of relational frames, and focus on the defining characteristics that distinguish one frame from another. While this treatment is not an exhaustive one (for a more detailed overview see Luciano, Rodrigquez, Manas, & Ruiz, 2009), it will serve to demonstrate some of the more common frames and how they may be combined to establish various classes of events.

Coordination

This relational frame is perhaps the most commonly known and ubiquitous pattern of relational responding and involves relating stimuli on the basis of identity, sameness, or similarity. Broadly speaking, stimuli within coordination relations are arbitrarily related under the control of cues such as "is" or some functional equivalent (e.g., "same as," "similar to," "like," "equals," or "means"). Thus, if an individual learns via experience or instruction that the English word "emergency" is the same as the French word "urgence," she will act as if "urgence" is the same as "emergency," even though this latter relationship has never been directly instructed. If she is then taught that "urgence" is the same as the German word "notfall," she will show evidence of mutual and combinatorial entailment (e.g., she will act as if "emergency" is the same as "notfall," "notfall" the same as "emergency," and "notfall" the same as "urgence"). Coordination appears to be the simplest arbitrarily applicable relational response and the one upon which many other relational frames are built.

Transformations of function in accordance with coordination relations are observed when a response trained in the presence of one stimulus also occurs in the presence of other stimuli that participate in that derived relation. Moreover, and unlike many other types of relational frames, the function acquired by each stimulus in the relation will be broadly similar (i.e., a transfer rather than a transformation will take place). Consider the above example in which a coordination relation was formed between the English word *emergency*, the French word *urgence*, and the German word *notfall*. Once this relation has been established a person who visits France and hears loud shouts of "urgence" (or "notfall" during a vacation to Germany) may come to experience heighted arousal or fear. They may also use those same words in those same countries to attract help from others. Now imagine that a coordination relation is established between three novel stimuli (A, B, C) and a musical mood induction technique is used to generate happy or sad affective states in the presence of B. People may report feeling happy or sad in the presence of A and C as well. Experimental evidence for the transfer of functions via coordination relations has now been obtained across a variety of populations and procedures (e.g., Barnes-Holmes, Barnes-Holmes, Smeets, & Luciano, 2004; see also Barnes-Holmes, Barnes-Holmes, Smeets, Cullinan, & Leader, 2004; Cahill et al., 2007; Dymond et al., 2008; Dymond, Schlund, Roche, & Whelan, 2014; Gannon, Roche, Kanter, Forsyth, & Linehan, 2011; Gómez, López, Martín, Barnes-Holmes, & Barnes-Holmes, 2007; Munnelly, Martin, Dack, Zedginidze, & McHugh, 2014; Rodríguez-Valverde et al., 2009). Accumulating evidence suggests that when other contextual cues are absent, people tend to relate stimuli in ways that involve lower levels of relational complexity. This can be seen on the matching-to-sample (MTS) task that typically yields evidence of equivalence responding until other relational cues are introduced that specify alternative relationships between stimuli and events (see also Hughes, De Houwer, & Barnes-Holmes, 2014). Thereafter more complex relations may emerge (e.g., Dougher et al., 2007; also see Hughes et al., 2012).[2]

Opposition

A second and more complex frame is that of opposition that involves arbitrarily relating stimuli under the control of cues such as "opposite," or "completely different." Whereas coordination involves the abstraction of a particular dimension along which stimuli may be equated (*"sun is the same as sol"*), the latter requires the abstraction of a dimension along which stimuli may be differentiated. That is, frames of opposition involve stimuli being related in ways that differ in direction (and to the same degree) from some reference point along a specified continuum. Along the physical dimension of temperature, for example, cool is the opposite of warm, and cold is the opposite of hot. Stimuli can also be framed in opposition along a variety of arbitrary dimensions as well (e.g., "odd is the opposite of even," "work is the opposite of play," and "easy is opposite to difficult"). Three points are worth noting here. First, the relevant dimension along which stimuli are related may or may not be specified in frames of opposition. If you are told that "cold is the opposite of hot" then the dimension of temperature is clearly implied and yet you can also relate A as the opposite of B without any such dimension being stipulated. Second, transformations of function through opposition relations lead to different outcomes at the mutual and combinatorial levels. While mutually entailed opposition relations involve opposition (*"Dog–opposite–Cat"* entails that *"Cat–opposite–Dog"*), combinatorially entailed opposition relations involve coordination (*"Cat–opposite–Dog–opposite–Tiger"* entails that *"Cat–same–Tiger"*). One implication is that frames of opposition should only develop after frames of coordination have been successfully acquired (see Barnes-Holmes, Barnes-Holmes, & Smeets, 2004 for evidence to this effect). Third, because these frames involve opposition at the mutually entailed level and coordination at the combinatorially entailed level, the transformations of functions that occur within these frames lead to stimuli acquiring different functions depending on their location within the relation. If a child is told, for example, that a type of candy (A) tastes disgusting and that candy (A) is opposite to candy (B) and candy (B) is opposite to candy (C) he may rapidly approach and consume candy (B) and yet avoid any contact with (A) or (C). Stated more precisely, mutually entailed opposition relations between an aversive (A) and neutral stimulus (B) may lead to the latter acquiring appetitive functions. A second mutually entailed opposition relation between (B) and another neutral stimulus (C) may lead to the latter acquiring aversive functions (see Dymond & Barnes, 1996; Dymond et al., 2008; Roche, Linehan, Ward, Dymond, & Rehfeldt, 2004; Whelan & Barnes-Holmes, 2004a, 2004b; Whelan, Cullinan, & O'Donovan, 2005).

Distinction

Similar to coordination and opposition, frames of distinction involve relating stimuli along (a) some physical or arbitrary dimension that is (b) under the control of cues such as "different," "dissimilar," and "is not the same" (e.g., "a star is different than a planet" or "freedom is not the same as justice"). Critically, however, these frames are characterized by a number of properties that distinguish them from their counterparts. One such property is their lack of specificity: Whereas all of the relations in frames of coordination and opposition are specified, this is not the case for those that comprise frames of distinction. If you are told that "Toyota" is the same as "Honda," and "Honda" is the same as "Nissan," you can determine what the mutual and combinatorially entailed relations are between each of these stimuli. Likewise, if you learn that "good" is opposite to "evil," which is in turn opposite to "honest," you can also determine the derived relations between these stimuli as well. Yet if are told that "Google" is different to McDonalds," and "McDonalds" is different to "Apple," you cannot determine what the relation is between "Google" and "Apple" (they may be different or they may be the same). In other words, frames of distinction involve relating stimuli that differ in degree along some continuum. Transformations of function through distinction relations may also demonstrate greater levels of variability than other frames given this lack of specificity. To illustrate, imagine that fear-eliciting properties are established for a Pokémon character in the laboratory by repeatedly pairing it with a shock. Thereafter a mutually entailed distinction relation is established between this character and a second Pokémon (B) and another such relation is established between Pokémon (B) and a third Pokémon (C). While participants may naturally come to fear Pokémon A, they could respond in a wide variety of ways toward (B) and (C) (e.g., these stimuli could elicit more or less fear than A and be rated as more or less negative, neutral, or positive than each other or A). Frames of distinction have attracted considerably less attention in the literature relative to their coordination, opposition, and comparative counterparts. While no study has established this pattern of relational responding where it was previously absent, a number of studies have examined this frame as it relates to clinical and cognitive phenomena (see Dixon & Zlomke, 2005; Foody, Barnes-Holmes, Barnes-Holmes, & Luciano, 2013; O'Toole & Barnes-Holmes, 2009; Roche & Barnes, 1996).

Comparison

The family of comparative frames involve responding to events in terms of a quantitative or qualitative relation along some specified dimension. This relating is usually under the control of contextual cues such as "heavier/lighter," "better/worse," "larger/smaller." Many specific subtypes of comparative frames exist and each is defined (in part) by the dimensions along which the relation applies (size, attractiveness, speed, and so on). For example, if I say that "an elephant is bigger than a lion," and "a lion is bigger than a mouse," then the stimuli can be compared along the dimension of size, and you can derive that "an elephant is bigger than a mouse" and that "a mouse is smaller than an elephant." However, I could also tell you that a "lion is faster than an elephant and an elephant is faster than a mouse," in which case the same stimuli can be compared along the dimension of speed, and you can derive that "the lion is faster than the mouse and the mouse is slower than the lion." In other words, comparative relations are specified at the mutual and combinatorially entailed levels. This specification increases when the dimension along which stimuli are being related is quantified. For instance, if I told you that "an elephant is three times the size of a lion and a lion is three times the size of a mouse," you could derive that the elephant is exactly six times bigger than the mouse and that the mouse is six times smaller than the elephant.

When stimuli participate in comparative frames they may acquire similar or entirely different functions depending on how they are related. Imagine you learn that a certain stimulus (A) is less than (B), which is in turn less than (C), and that (A) signals that you are about to receive a monetary reward. You may experience more arousal when you see B and even greater arousal when you see C despite the fact that neither stimulus signaled reward in the past. In this case a transformation of function through a comparative relation has led to stimuli acquiring similar (eliciting) functions that vary in their respective magnitude. Now imagine that you are told that a new house is more valuable than an old shack and that a mansion is more valuable than a house. You may come to evaluate the shack negatively, the house neutrally, and the mansion positively. In this case, a transformation of function through comparative relations has led to stimuli acquiring different (evaluative) functions from one another. Comparative relations have been the subject of significant empirical scrutiny, both historically in the animal literature (e.g., transposition represents an instance of nonarbitrary comparative relating; Reese, 1968), and more recently with comparative framing in human infants and adults (Barnes-Holmes, Barnes-Holmes, Smeets, Strand, & Friman, 2004; Berens & Hayes, 2007; Cassidy et al., 2011; Dougher et al., 2007; Munnelly, Freegard, & Dymond, 2013; Murphy & Barnes-Holmes, 2009; Vitale, Campbell, Barnes-Holmes & Barnes-Holmes, 2012; Whelan et al., 2006).

Spatial Relations

This family of frames involves the abstraction of a spatial dimension along which stimuli may be related and often comes under the control of cues such as "here/there," "in/out," "front/back," and so on (e.g., "Walter is in the lab," "Bart is on his skateboard"). These frames share many similarities to comparative relations insofar as they involve responding to events in terms of their directional displacement along a specified (spatial) dimension. Moreover, they typically imply or specify how stimuli should be related with regard to a reference point and this characteristic makes them quite specific. For example, if you are told that "Arnold's gym" faces the back of "Rocky's café," you could order the fronts and backs of both premises in a linear sequence (back door of the gym, front door of the gym, back door of the café, front door of café). This is because front and back doors are relative to each premises, and knowing the orientation of the two buildings implies a number of additional relations between these stimuli. While spatial relations have been tangentially examined in the context of deictic framing (McHugh & Stewart, 2012; Weil, Hayes, & Capurro, 2011), empathy (Vilardaga, 2009) and clinical phenomena (Vilardaga, Estévez, Levin, & Hayes, 2012; Villatte, Monestès, McHugh, Freixa i Baqué, & Loas, 2010), they have yet to be subjected to an experimental analysis in and of themselves or instantiated in organisms where previously absent or weak.

Temporal Relations

This family of frames also shares many similarities to comparative relations insofar as they involve responding to events in terms of their directional displacement along a specified (temporal) dimension. Such relations often come under the control of cues such as "before/after," "now/then," and "soon/later" (e.g., "night comes before day," "cover your eyes now as the eclipse will start soon"). Critically, these frames differ in important ways from those discussed above. According to RFT, the experience and construction of time differs for organisms with and without a history of AARR. For the latter time is simply change – the transition from "one totality to another in which the second totality now stands on, evolved from, or in some sense includes the first" (Hayes, 1992, p.112). From this perspective, organisms without the ability to AARR experience change in a unidirectional manner, from a now to a new now or from this to a new this, but never from a new this to an old this. To illustrate, consider a pigeon in an operant chamber whose behavior (key pecking) is reinforced in the presence of a green light. First, there was an observed green light, then a peck on a key, then food was eaten. Later there was an observed green light, then a peck on a key, and the food was eaten. Still later there was an observed green light, then a peck on a key, and the food was eaten. In this scenario the pigeon directly experiences a sequence of events or an orderly procession from one act to another. Thus for the bird (and other organisms without a history of AARR) time is:

> *the past as the future in the present.* Based on a history of change ("past") the animal is responding in the present to present events cuing change to other events. It is not the literal future that is part of the psychology of the animal – it is the past *as* the future. (Hayes, 1992, p. 113)

In other words, the only future that such an organism knows is the past that it has experienced.

This no longer applies when organisms learn how to respond in an arbitrarily applicable fashion. Once this ability has been acquired people can temporally frame stimuli and events in ways that are independent of their prior experience (e.g., "I'm going to heaven after I die" or "My life will be so much better after I kill myself"). Such relations lead to time being framed as a bidirectional dimension along which events can be ordered and sequenced, so that consequences in the distant past ("My grandfather and father both died from smoking before I was born"), present ("My exam takes place now"), or far future ("Eating healthy now will increase my likelihood of living to old age") can exert an influence on how we behave. In other words, for an organism with the ability to engage in AARR, time is the *past as the constructed future in the present*. Based on a history of deriving temporal sequences among events ("past"), the organism is responding in the present by constructing a spatial relation between two or more stimuli. It is not the literal future that is part of the psychology of the organism – it is the past *as* the future, but in this case the future is constructed on the basis of their ability to AARR (Hayes, 1992, p. 114). In other words, AARR influences the overarching experience of time so that the past can now be reconstructed and the future imagined, planned for, and contemplated whenever stimuli are framed as coming before or after, now or then, and sooner or later than one another.

Several properties of this type of framing are worth noting. Similar to coordination and opposition relations, temporal frames are typically specified in nature, so that knowing "*March comes before April*" and "*April comes before May*," allows you to derive that "*March comes before May*" and "*May comes after March*." However, transformations of function through temporal frames are often unlike those seen in their counterparts. In the case of comparative relations, transformation of functions usually involve a change in the physical properties of responses to the transformed stimuli (e.g., responding with greater fear when you see a spitting cobra than a wasp). Yet transformations of function through temporal relations usually result in the presence or absence of the response as a whole (e.g., people usually have dessert *after* rather than *before* dinner, or put on their clothes *after* rather than *during* a shower). To illustrate, imagine that two temporal relations were established in the laboratory (e.g., A1–*before*–B1–*before*–C1 and A2–*after*–B2–*after*–C2) and that C1 occasions an unpleasant electric shock whenever A1 is selected before B1 and B1 is selected before C1. Also imagine that C2 occasions a reward (e.g., money) whenever it is selected after B2 and B2 is selected after A2. Participants may come to respond with fear toward C1 (and evaluate C2 positively) only when the aforementioned sequences are emitted. In this case, the presence versus absence of fear or evaluative responding depends on how stimuli are temporally related to each other.

Unfortunately, evidence of temporal framing and the history of learning needed to establish it is currently scarce. This class of relations has received far less attention than other frames in the RFT literature, with existing work focused on their implications for intelligence and rule-following, as well as their experimental induction in adult populations (e.g., O'Hora et al. 2004; O'Hora, Peláez, & Barnes-Holmes, 2005; O'Hora et al., 2008; O'Toole & Barnes-Holmes, 2009). It remains to be seen how these frames are initially established in the natural environment, how the unidirectional experience of change comes to be abstracted, and the bidirectional dimension of time constructed. Given their potential role in suicide (Hayes, 1992) and delayed gratification (Mischel & Ayduk, 2004), for example, closer attention to temporal relations certainly seems warranted.

Deictics

Another family of frames is those that specify a relation between stimuli from the perspective of the speaker. Growing evidence suggests that these deictic frames are comprised of three main types of relations: (a) spatial (HERE–THERE), (b) temporal

(NOW–THEN), and (c) interpersonal (I–YOU). Whereas coordination, distinction, and comparative relations emerge based on what people learn about stimuli that are physically similar, dissimilar, or quantitatively different along some dimension, deictics are somewhat different. They are not abstracted from a nonarbitrary or physical referent, but rather from the invariance of the speaker's perspective: Framing events deictically can only be achieved with regard to a specific perspective or point of view. Although people are exposed to a history of reinforcement for relating in different ways across a wide variety of stimuli, situations, and settings, it is the constant division between the speaker (who is always HERE and NOW) and the to-be-related stimuli (that are THERE and THEN) that provides the environmental consistency upon which deictic relations are abstracted and arbitrarily applied. For instance, during and throughout their early interactions with the socio-verbal community, children will learn to respond to and ask questions like the following: "What are you doing here?," "What am I doing now?," "What will you do there?," and so on. The physical environment in which such questions are asked and answered will differ from occasion to occasion, but the patterns of interpersonal (I–YOU), spatial (HERE–THERE), and temporal relations (NOW–THEN) will be applied consistently, and, as is the case with other relational frames, these patterns will be abstracted over time.

Deictic framing represents one of the most active areas in the RFT literature at present. This class of relations has been found to emerge during early to middle childhood (McHugh, Barnes-Holmes, & Barnes-Holmes, 2004) and has been experimentally engineered where previously absent or weak (Rehfeldt, Dillen, Ziomek, & Kowalchuk, 2007; Weil et al., 2011). Deictics have also been implicated in a wide range of social and clinical phenomena, from social anhedonia (Villatte, Monestès, McHugh, Freixa i Baqué, & Loas, 2008) to schizophrenia, (Villatte et al., 2010), empathy and stigma (Vilardaga, 2009), Theory of Mind (Barnes-Holmes, McHugh, & Barnes-Holmes, 2004), deception (McHugh, Barnes-Holmes, & Barnes-Holmes, 2007), false beliefs (McHugh, Barnes-Holmes, Barnes-Holmes, & Stewart, 2006), pathological altruism (Vilardaga & Hayes, 2012), intelligence (Gore, Barnes-Holmes, & Murphy, 2013), and the sense of self (for a detailed treatment of deictic framing see Barnes-Holmes, Hayes, & Dymond, 2001; McHugh & Stewart, 2012).

Hierarchy

This family of frames refers to the fact that different relations can be related to one another in a hierarchical fashion and typically comes under the control of contextual cues such as "is attribute/part/member of," or "belongs to" (e.g., "Croissant is a type of pastry and pastries are a type of food"). This type of framing may be characterized by a number of properties. One such property is transitive class containment; that is, the relations between the members of a category are transitive. For instance, if C is a member of B, and B is a member of A, then C is a member of A (e.g., all Irish Setters are dogs, and all dogs are animals; therefore, all Irish Setters are animals; Slattery, Stewart, & O'Hora, 2011). These frames also involve asymmetrical relations that emerge between and among members or categories of the same hierarchy. For instance, if category A contains category B, then category B does not necessarily contain category A (e.g., "motor vehicles" contain "cars," but "cars" do not contain all "motor vehicles").

Like so many other families of frames it seems plausible that hierarchical framing is also based, in part, on an appropriate history of NAARR. For instance, a child might learn, in one context, to relate objects based on whether they are physically part of other things (e.g., "Your toe is part of your foot") and in another, to relate objects based on whether they contain other things (e.g., "The toy box contains your ball, your teddy, and your building blocks"). Given a sufficient number of exemplars across a variety of settings and situations, this behavior may come under the control of contextual cues that are abstracted and applied arbitrarily to stimuli regardless of their physical relationship to one another. For example, if you are told that A contains B and B contains C, then you can derive that A contains C and C is contained by A, without any specific information about the actual physical properties of the stimuli involved or how they are actually contained. A transformation of function may occur in accordance with this relational frame if you are told that C is a highly toxic substance, in that you might be more willing to pick up A rather than B because two containers afford more protection than just one.

It is important to recognize that hierarchical framing can involve increasingly complex interactions among frames. For instance, a more complete example of hierarchical framing, than the simple one provided above, might be as follows: container A contains two separate containers, B and X, and each of these containers contains two substances; B contains C and D, and X contains Y and Z. In this case, A contains all other elements within the network, but B contains only C and D and X contains only Y and Z. Thus a difference relation may be derived between B and X (because they are separate containers) but frames of coordination may be derived between C and D and between Y and Z, because each pair is housed within the same container (see Figure 9.2). Now imagine that I tell you that C and D are both inert substances but both Y and Z are highly toxic. You might be relatively willing to pick up container A and container B, but less willing to pick up container X.

Hierarchical relational frames and the complex networks and transformation of functions that may emerge in accordance with them are ubiquitous in natural verbal behavior. Family or kinship relations provide a ready example. Imagine, for instance, that a friend informs you about a new television show about an American family known as the Simpsons. One part of the family is from Shelbyville and is aggressive, while the other part of the family is from Springfield and is funny. Thereafter, she tells you that Homer is from Springfield and Herbert is from Shelbyville, and upon hearing this, you may derive that Homer will be funny and Herbert aggressive. In the above example, the functions established for stimuli at one level of the hierarchy (i.e., the functions of aggressive and funny established for Springfield and Shelbyville) will alter the functions of subordinate class members (Homer is from Springfield and now funny, while Herbert is from Shelbyville and now aggressive) and superordinate class members (the Simpsons family is partly funny and partly aggressive).

The key point here is that a range of different relational frames can come to participate in hierarchical relational networks and this often leads to different transformations

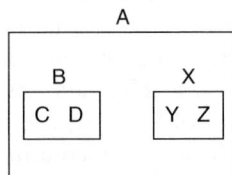

Figure 9.2   A graphical representation of one possible hierarchical relational network.

of function depending on how stimuli are related within those hierarchies. Take the previous example. When members of the Simpson clan are hierarchically framed according to their age, Homer may participate in a frame of coordination with his wife Marge, be comparatively higher than their children Bart, Maggie, and Lisa (who participate in a frame of coordination with each other), and comparatively lower than his father Abe. If you learn that old age is typically evaluated negatively then you may come to like Bart, Maggie, and Lisa more than Homer and Marge, and the latter stimuli more than Abe. At the same time, those stimuli could also be framed hierarchically with respect to gender, so that two superordinate classes of stimuli ("males" and "females"), which are part of the same hierarchy (gender), are framed in opposition to one another, while the members of those subordinate classes are framed on the basis of coordination (e.g., Bart is the same as Homer and Abe, who are all distinct from Marge, Lisa, and Maggie). If you then learn that girls are evaluated more positively than boys, an entirely different pattern of contextually controlled transformation of function will likely take place, with Marge, Lisa, and Maggie liked more than Homer, Bart, and Abe. These two hierarchical relations could also be combined so that stimuli are framed according to age and gender, leading to a more complex transformation of (evaluative) functions than before. The key point here is that complex hierarchical relational networks can involve different relations, and the manner in which those relations are hierarchically related will dictate how functions are transformed within and between those relations.

Similar to their spatial and temporal counterparts, hierarchical relations have received comparatively less attention than other families of relational frames (Gil, Luciano, Ruiz, & Valdivia-Salas, 2014; Gil et al., 2012; Griffee & Dougher, 2002; Slattery et al., 2011; Slattery & Stewart, 2014), and have not been established in populations where such abilities are absent or weak. Nor has the importance of specific frames for the development of hierarchical relating been explored in the developmental literature (although for a discussion on how this might be achieved see Luciano et al., 2009). Given the importance of these frames for complex behaviors such as category learning (Murphy, 2002), evaluation (Hughes et al., (in press)) and problem-solving (Stewart et al., 2013), future work will need to pay closer attention to this pattern of relational responding.

Summary

In the previous section we highlighted a number of relational frames that have occupied the attention of RFT researchers over the past two decades. It seems important to repeat that these frames are not mediating mental or physical constructs, but simply labels that are used to talk about specific instances of a generalized operant behavior (AARR). Whenever researchers speak of a *relational frame* they are speaking of an organism, who, given the proper historical and situational context, is relating stimuli independently of their physical properties and under the control of contextual cues that have previously been abstracted and are now being arbitrarily applied.

Research conducted over the last 20 years has refined our understanding of relational framing and the history of learning needed to produce these outcomes. This work has shown that stimuli can be related in many different ways, including coordination, opposition, distinction, comparison, deictics, temporality, and hierarchy. Indeed, a number of frames such as deictics, hierarchy, and temporality were only tentatively discussed by Hayes, Barnes-Holmes, and Roche (2001) in the original RFT book and yet these frames have now received empirical support have been implicated in a wide range of social and cognitive phenomena. Likewise, frames that were only ever examined with adult populations have now been established *ab initio* in the laboratory for organisms that previously lacked those abilities (infants and children). A common thread running through much of this work is that relational frames tend to emerge in line with RFT's predictions (i.e., via a systematic transition from nonarbitrary to arbitrary responding based on multiple-exemplar training with novel stimuli).

Despite these developments, a number of important issues still need to be addressed. Whereas coordination, comparison, opposition, and deictic relations have been subjected to tightly controlled experimental analyses, their temporal, spatial, hierarchical, and causal counterparts have not enjoyed such attention. Only a handful of studies have examined these relations and often only tangentially in the context of other relational frames. Thus it still remains to be determined, for example, to what extent temporal and causal frames overlap functionally and whether it is better to consider them as largely separate or tightly connected. Likewise, we are only beginning to understand the manner and order in which different frames emerge in the natural environment (Luciano et al., 2009) as well as the role that specific frames play in maintaining and undermining other patterns of relational responding (Foody et al., 2013). It seems probable that relational repertoires like coordination and opposition need to be acquired prior to the emergence of comparison and more complex frames such as deictics, hierarchy, or causality. At present, many of these questions still await an answer. What has become clear, though, is that the aforementioned families of relational frames, while certainly important, are by no means the only ways in which humans can relate. Several researchers have started to model other types of frames such as those involved in mathematical relations (McGinty et al., 2012; Ninness et al., 2006; 2009). If RFT is correct, the number of relational frames is limited only by the creativity of the "relational" community that trains them.

Section 4: Evidence for AARR as a Learned Operant Behavior

So far we have argued the ability to respond in an arbitrarily applicable fashion unfolds through on-going interaction with the socio-verbal community (i.e., it is a type of behavior that can be generated, maintained, modified, or eliminated). If this assumption is correct, then AARR should demonstrate the same characteristics as any other operant: It should evolve gradually over time; be amenable to change and fall under the control of antecedent and consequential stimuli. In the following sections, we submit these theoretical claims to closer inspection and determine whether they hold up in the face of recent empirical evidence.

Development of AARR

Learning is an inherently developmental concept. As organisms interact with regularities in the environment, their actions gradually evolve and change (De Houwer, Barnes-Holmes, & Moors, 2013). If AARR is an instance of generalized operant behavior then it should also develop over time as well. At this point it is important to realize that any experiment that sets out to examine the development of AARR using adults or psychology students will involve relational performances that are almost certainly based on a prior history of relating. In such cases, the formation or modification of relational responses will be based on a rich and protracted history of relational learning. Consequently, these studies fail to provide strong evidence for the RFT view that AARR is established, in the first instance, as generalized operant behavior. Rather this requires that researchers shift their attention to the study of organisms with a limited or nonexistent history of AARR such as human infants and nonhuman animals. So far this analytic strategy has met with varying levels of success.

Development in humans. On the one hand, attempts to chart the emergence of AARR during the earliest stages of human development have proven fruitful. Studies indicate that the ability to engage in AARR is initially absent, but gradually grows in complexity, with mutually entailed coordination relations emerging first, followed by combinatorially entailed coordination, and noncoordination relations. For instance, several authors have found that infants are capable of receptive mutual entailment by 17 months, productive mutual entailment at 19 months, followed quickly by combinatorial entailment at 23 months (Lipkens, Hayes, & Hayes, 1993). Others have found that coordination relations can emerge even earlier when infants are provided with repeated training in symmetrical responding across multiple exemplars (Luciano et al., 2007). Recent work with young children has sought to assess the development of AARR in a different way: by testing for the absence of certain patterns of relational responding and then establishing those very repertoires in the laboratory. Consider, for example, the work of Barnes-Holmes, Barnes-Holmes, Smeets, Strand, and Friman, 2004. Prior to their studies a number of children were selected that had yet to learn how to respond in accordance with comparative or opposition relations. During the task they were shown a number of identically sized paper circles (referred to as "coins") and asked to pick the coin(s) that would buy as many sweets as possible. In Experiment 1 comparative relations were trained such that children were presented with three coins (A, B, C) and told:

> If this coin (experimenter points to the first coin – A) buys less sweets than this coin (experimenter points to coin B), and this coin (experimenter points to B again) buys less sweets than this coin (Experimenter points to coin C), which coin would you choose to buy as many sweets as possible?

In Experiment 2 opposition relations were trained. Children were once again shown three coins and told:

> If this coin (D) buys few sweets, and is opposite to this coin (C), and if this coin (C) is opposite to this coin (B), and if this coin (B) is opposite to this coin (A), which would you choose to buy as many sweets as possible?

After a protracted history of reinforcement for bidirectional responding across multiple exemplars, the children demonstrated evidence of derived opposition and comparative relating. In other words, they could relate any coin to any other coin in any direction, even when entirely novel coins and experimenters were introduced (see also Rehfeldt & Barnes-Holmes, 2009). This capacity to generate coordination, opposition, and comparative frames *ab initio* has now been replicated on numerous occasions (e.g., Barnes-Holmes, Barnes-Holmes, & Smeets, 2004; Berens & Hayes, 2007; Gorham, Barnes-Holmes, Barnes-Holmes & Berens, 2009; Smeets & Barnes-Holmes, 2005; see also Barnes et al., 1990; Peláez, Gewirtz, Sanchez, & Mahabir, 2000).

Similar attempts to engineer deictic relations in young children have revealed that such relations are typically absent until four years of age (Barnes-Holmes, McHugh, & Barnes-Holmes, 2004; McHugh, Barnes-Holmes, Barnes-Holmes, Stewart, & Dymond, 2007) and that their development can be accelerated via a similar history of learning as outlined above (Heagle & Rehfeldt, 2006), even in developmentally delayed populations who typically show deficits in this domain (Rehfeldt et al., 2007; Weil et al., 2011). As noted in the previous section, much of this work has focused on understanding perspective-taking, false belief, and deception as repertoires of derived relational responding and has employed cross-sectional developmental methodologies (see McHugh & Stewart, 2012). In each case, a clear developmental profile has emerged suggesting that the fluency of deictic relating is initially poor but quickly improves as a function of age. Comparable findings have also been obtained with tasks that require participants to relate derived relations to other derived relations (see chapter 10 in this volume for more details), which is evident in adults and nine-year-old children, but absent or weak in five-year-old preschoolers (Carpentier, Smeets, & Barnes-Holmes, 2002; 2003; Pérez, García, & Gómez, 2011). When taken together, these findings support the notion that AARR is a generalized operant behavior that emerges through a protracted history of bidirectional training with multiple exemplars. This ability appears to be acquired in the earliest stages of infancy and rapidly scales in complexity, starting with mutual and combinatorial entailment based on coordination, and moving to comparative, opposition, deictic, and other patterns of relating during early to middle childhood. Providing normally developing infants or young children (as well as their developmentally delayed counterparts) with MET appears to facilitate the development of relational abilities that were previously weak or absent.

Development in nonhumans. Researchers have also looked to nonhumans as another potential window into the emergence of AARR and much of this work has centered around the search for symmetry and equivalence responding in rats, pigeons, sea lions, dogs, chimpanzees, bonobos, and baboons (for an overview see Lionello-DeNolf, 2009). While evidence has been obtained for symmetry and acquired equivalence responding in nonhumans, these performances can often be explained in ways that (a) do not involve AARR, (b) are only present in a subsection of the sample, or (c) are emitted with unacceptably low levels of accuracy (e.g., Dugdale & Lowe, 2000; Hayes, 1989a; Lionello-DeNolf, 2009). A number of authors have recently countered that these failures to observe symmetry and equivalence stem from properties of the procedures used and that nonhumans are in fact capable of such performances under a set of highly specific conditions (Frank & Wasserman, 2005; Galvão et al., 2005; McIlvane, Serna, Dube, & Stromer, 2000; Urcuioli, 2008; Zentall et al., 2014). It is worth noting that RFT has always remained agnostic to the possibility that AARR is a uniquely human capacity and it has never been argued that derived stimulus relating is forever beyond the grasp of other species. Rather, RFT has simply viewed this claim as an empirical rather than purely theoretical one (Dymond et al., 2003). What has emerged over the past 40 years is that so called associative symmetry and acquired-equivalence effects in nonhumans may arise, at least in part, from a functionally different history of learning to the generalized operant behavior of AARR displayed by their human counterparts (see Barnes & Roche, 1996; Hughes & Barnes-Holmes, 2014). Moreover, and as the evidence currently stands, it seems likely that there is also some "glass ceiling" in terms of relational complexity, contextual control, and generalizability that humans are capable of that is not evident elsewhere in the animal kingdom. For instance, other species have yet to show evidence for derived stimulus relating under nonequivalent contextual control and do not seem to respond to stimuli as being opposite, more than/less than, hierarchically, temporally, or casually related in an *arbitrarily applicable* fashion. Nor does it seem likely that they can relate derived relations to other derived relations and form increasingly complex networks of stimulus relations.

Nonetheless, investigations conducted with nonhumans under controlled conditions could provide a very useful platform for studying the early development of derived stimulus relating. Animal preparations and populations offer an opportunity to ask questions about AARR that cannot be answered with humans for ethical and practical reasons. This work could help us disentangle the history of learning involved in establishing and manipulating relational responding as a generalized operant behavior (e.g., Kastak & Shusterman, 2002; McIlvane, 2014). It could also provide information about the type, amount, and order of training that is required before relational responding becomes abstracted and generalizes to novel stimuli. Furthermore, it remains to be seen whether this advanced type of relational learning stretches across many different evolutionary branches or whether it is unique to a small number of species. The requirement for certain environmental or evolutionary conditions to be present before complex forms of AARR emerge also remains to be seen (Hayes & Long, 2013).

Flexibility of AARR

One of the hallmarks of operant behavior is its amenability to change. Accumulating evidence indicates that flexibility is a property of AARR as well. We now know that derived stimulus relations can be modified (even after they have formed) and that the relationships established between those stimuli may be altered individually or collectively depending on contextual factors. Imagine, for example, that a researcher establishes a coordination relation between three stimuli (A, B, C) and then modifies how all of those stimuli are related at a later point in time. A consistent finding is that novel relations will be derived that are in-line with these altered relations (e.g., O'Connor, Barnes-Holmes, & Barnes-Holmes, 2011). Yet if that same researcher only alters a small subset of the baseline relations then some of the derived relations will change, while others will remain intact (Cahill et al., 2007; Carr & Blackman, 2001; Dixon, Rehfeldt, Zlomke, & Robinson, 2006; Pilgrim & Galizio, 1995; Roche, Barnes, & Smeets, 1997; Watt, Keenan, Barnes, & Cairns, 1991; although see Garotti & De Rose, 2007; Pilgrim, Click, & Galizio, 2011; Smeets, Barnes-Holmes, Akpinar, & Barnes-Holmes, 2003). These findings suggest that relating one event to another and combining relations among events are flexible behaviors under environmental control.

The fact that relating can come under different types of contextual control could also be seen as additional support for its flexibility. As we have seen, relating stimuli and events in the presence of contextual cues dramatically alters how people behave. After learning that the written word "poison" (A) is the same as a picture containing a unknown symbol (B) and that the latter is the same as the spoken word "G-I-F" (C), people will likely avoid consuming any items that contain images of B or that are labeled with C. However, if they subsequently learn that symbol (B) is the opposite of poison (A) and that GIF (C) is the opposite of (B) then they may approach the latter, but avoid substances labeled with the former stimulus. These relational responses are said to be flexible insofar as they vary systematically according to how stimuli are related, so that opposition relations (Dymond et al., 2008) can give rise to different outcomes to their comparative (Dougher et al., 2007), distinction (Foody et al., 2013), hierarchical (Gil et al., 2012), and temporal counterparts (O'Hora et al., 2004). In effect, derived stimulus relations themselves appear to be a type of relational flexibility.

AARR Falls under Antecedent Stimulus Control

A third property of operant behavior is that it falls under the control of the antecedent conditions that precede it. An extensive literature now indicates that AARR is also sensitive to antecedent stimulus control like any other operant. This is evident from the fact that a wide range of relational cues can be engineered in the laboratory and subsequently used to control how people relate stimuli and events to one another (as described in Section 3).

AARR Falls under Consequential Stimulus Control

The fourth (and perhaps defining) property of an operant response class is that it is influenced by contingent consequences. Once again, AARR appears to fall under similar types of stimulus control. Consider the work of Wilson and Hayes (1996). In this study participants were exposed to a learning phase that was designed to establish three four-member coordination relations. They were then exposed to a second learning task that dismantled these relations and reorganized the stimuli involved into three new coordination relations. When the authors subsequently punished any response that was in line with this second set of relations, a resurgence of the previously established coordination relations was observed (for similar findings see Healy et al., 2000). This resurgence effect is exactly the same as that seen elsewhere in the behavior analytic literature and refers to the fact that when an operant response ceases to produce reinforcement, or begins to produce punishment, responding becomes increasingly variable and earlier topographies tend to re-emerge (e.g., Doughty & Oken, 2008; Epstein, 1985; Lieving & Lattal, 2003). This work also highlights that "derived stimulus relations are extraordinarily difficult to break up, even with direct, contradictory training. … Once relations are derived, they never really seem to go away. You can add to them, but you cannot eliminate them altogether" (Pankey & Hayes, 2003, p. 315).

Further evidence that derived relational responding may be under consequential control was provided by Leonhard and Hayes (1991). In their study participants were first exposed to a MTS task designed to establish equivalence responding. They were then split into two different groups. The first group received a set of test trials that were entirely consistent with the previously formed equivalence relations, while the second group received a large number of trials that were inconsistent with those relations. Results revealed that these inconsistent trials significantly reduced mutual and combinatorial entailment in the second group. The authors also found that when all of the participants were subsequently trained and tested using novel stimuli and a normal MTS procedure, individuals from the second group continued to display significantly reduced levels of equivalence responding. These findings further support the argument that AARR is exquisitely sensitive to its consequences. Requiring people to relate stimuli in ways that are unspecified, inconsistent, or incoherent with their prior learning history serves to punish immediate and future instances of relational responding (see also Quinones & Hayes, 2014; Vitale et al., 2008).

At the same time a number of authors have found that the delivery of delayed consequences for responding can disrupt the emergence of mutual and combinatorially entailed relations (Healy, Barnes, & Smeets, 1998; Healy et al., 2000). For example, in Experiment 1 of the latter study, participants were exposed to a number of training and testing trials designed to establish two different coordination relations. Following this first cycle of training and testing they were provided with feedback about their performance on the task. While half of the participants received feedback that was consistent with the previously established relations (accurate), the other half received feedback that was inconsistent with those relations (inaccurate). Both groups were then exposed to another round of training and testing involving a novel set of stimuli. This cycle of training and testing, using novel sets of stimuli for each cycle, continued until a participant responded in-line with the feedback across three consecutive stimulus sets. Once this stability criterion was reached, feedback was switched from accurate to inaccurate (or vice versa), and training and testing continued, using novel stimulus sets, until the performance once again reached the stability criterion. Results revealed that two contrasting patterns of AARR emerged as a function of the type of feedback (delayed consequences) provided. When feedback was accurate, participants responded in ways that were consistent with combinatorially entailed relations and when that feedback was inaccurate, they responded in ways that contradicted those same relations. In their final experiment, Healy and colleagues once again delivered accurate or inaccurate performance-contingent feedback. However, this time one type of feedback was provided following tests for mutual entailment and the other type of feedback following tests for combinatorial entailment. The authors found that derived stimulus relations, as behavioral units, could be "fractured" or "broken down" into component operants by appropriate reinforcement contingencies. In other words, they found that it is possible to separate and recombine mutually and combinatorially entailed relations by manipulating the type of feedback (consequences) that participants received – a finding that is broadly consistent with other studies (e.g., Gomez, Barnes-Holmes, & Luciano, 2001; 2002; Pilgrim & Galizio, 1995; Roche et al., 1997; Smeets et al, 2003). When taken together, these various lines of inquiry provide firm support for the notion that AARR is a generalized operant that is sensitive to consequential control.

Summary

Twenty years' worth of data in the areas of development, flexibility, antecedent and consequential control support RFT's claims that AARR is a form of learned operant behavior. Confirmatory evidence for this claim has now been obtained across a variety of normative and developmentally delayed samples, stimulus modalities, settings, procedures, age groups, and relational frames. At the same time – and to the best of our knowledge – no contradictory evidence has been offered that seriously conflicts with the above account. What has become clear though is that derived relational responding represents a type of human performance that cannot be contained experimentally without raising serious ethical concerns. It develops so early and powerfully that researchers are often limited in their ability to test the processes that produce AARR in humans and to manipulate its emergence in systematic ways. Hopes that nonhuman animals would provide an alternative means for addressing these questions were seriously dampened by the finding that AARR is extremely difficult to observe elsewhere in the animal kingdom. Debate raged (and continues to do so) around the ability of other species to show even the most rudimentary properties of derived stimulus relating (mutual and combinatorial entailment) to the point that developmental research with infants and children (despite its methodological and ethical issues) has yielded greater insight into the operant nature of AARR.

Section 5: Important Additional Features of AARR

Since the first book-length treatment of RFT by Hayes and colleagues (2001) a number of important features of AARR have increasingly attracted theoretical and empirical attention. These concern the influence of coherence in shaping how people frame events relationally, the complexity of the relational response itself, and the number of times that it has been derived in the past. In chapter 10 in this volume we will discuss the role that coherence, complexity, and derivation play in fast and slow cognition. But for now, let us examine these various features of AARR in greater detail.

Relational Coherence

As we have just seen, the ability to frame events relationally is a learned operant behavior that can be shaped, modified, or eliminated by contingencies of reinforcement or punishment. RFT argues that an important set of contingencies that serve to guide AARR in general are those in which social consequences are delivered to ensure that people frame in an internally consistent or coherent fashion. An individual is said to be responding *coherently* when all of the elements in a derived relation are related in a manner that is consistent with what was previously learned. In contrast, incoherent responding refers to instances in which derived relations are not consistent with what was previously learned. Imagine, for example, that a friend tells you "an airplane is bigger than a car" and "a car is bigger than a mouse," "but a mouse is bigger than an airplane." You will quickly realize that stimuli are combinatorially entailed within this comparative relation in a manner that is incoherent with the mutually entailed relations and come to question the veracity of your friend's statement. In other words,

> when one's story does not cohere, the socio-verbal environment generally demands the story be changed until it is logically consistent. Stories that are consistent are generally reinforced (or set the stage for other reinforceable behaviors), while inconsistent stories typically result in no reinforcement or outright punishment. After lengthy exposure to these differential consequences, telling coherent stories increase in likelihood and incoherent storytelling becomes aversive. (Blackledge, Moran, & Ellis, 2009, p. 243)

RFT proposes that from the cradle to the grave and in nearly every interaction in between, the socio-verbal community reinforces coherent (and punishes incoherent) relational responding, to the extent that coherence itself quickly becomes a type of conditioned reinforcer for most individuals.

To date, only a handful of studies have examined the impact of relational coherence in the laboratory. Early work in this vein reported that people tend to revert back to previously learned, coherent ways of relating whenever they are faced with a situation in which they have to respond in an inconsistent fashion (e.g., Leonhard & Hayes, 1991; Pilgrim & Galizio, 1995; Wilson & Hayes, 1996). More recently, work has focused on how people react to relationally ambiguous contexts. For instance, learning that "Bill is more honest than George" and "Hillary is more honest than George" does not allow us to derive a coherent relation between Bill and Hillary: It may be that Bill is more honest than Hillary or vice versa.

Quinones and Hayes (2014) recently sought to determine if people will respond in coherent or incoherent ways when faced with such ambiguous scenarios. In their first experiment, two comparative relations were established (A1 less than B1, A1 greater than C1; and A2 greater than B2, C2 less than A2) and participants were tested to determine if they would respond to B1 and C1 (as well as B2 and C2) as being the same/different and as being greater/less than one another. While the first relation is unambiguous (i.e., B1 is greater than C1 and thus B1 and C1 are different) the second relation is ambiguous (B2 and C2 may be the same or different). Consistent with past work, the authors found that people tend to derive coherent relations when presented with an unambiguous relation and yet responded idiosyncratically when presented with ambiguous relations (see also Vitale et al., 2008; 2012). That is, individuals who related B2 as different to C2 consistently related B2 as either greater or less than C2. In contrast, people who related B2 as the same as C2 responded randomly when they were asked to relate those same stimuli as either greater or less than each other. In a second experiment, participants received non-arbitrary multiple exemplar training that was designed to bias responding toward either "same" or "different" when confronted with an ambiguous stimulus relation. In line with Experiment 1, participants biased toward "different" produced consistent B2–C2 comparative responses, whereas those participants who were biased toward "same" responding produced idiosyncratic performances. When taken together, these findings suggest that an individual's learning history may bias them to respond in specific ways when confronted with ambiguous stimulus relations. Interestingly, even when participants responded idiosyncratically to the comparative relation, this pattern cohered with another response pattern (i.e., treating the B2 and C2 stimuli as the same). In this sense, a given instance of inconsistent responding may in fact be part of an overarching pattern of coherent relational responding, thus highlighting the potential power of coherence to function as a type of conditioned reinforcer for AARR itself.

Interestingly, while recent work has begun to unpack the relationship between coherence and AARR, evidence to support the claim that the former acts as a conditioned reinforcer for the latter remains extremely limited (Wray, Dougher, Hamilton, & Guinther, 2012). The fact that this question has yet to be subjected to a systematic analysis is somewhat surprising given that it is a popular assumption in the RFT literature and one that underpins many of the claims made about clinical (Barnes-Holmes, Barnes-Holmes, Cochrane, McHugh, & Stewart, 2004), cognitive

(Hughes et al., 2012), and social phenomena (Roche, Barnes-Holmes, Barnes-Holmes, Stewart, & O'Hora, 2002). Future work in this area will need to articulate precisely when and how coherence functions as a reinforcer for AARR and examine its potential role in other psychological domains as well (Blackledge et al., 2009; Gawronski, 2012; Quinones & Hayes, 2014).

Relational Complexity

A second feature of AARR is the complexity of the relational response involved. As we have seen throughout this chapter, stimulus relations can vary in their complexity and be arranged along a continuum from low to high. Stimuli can be related to one another in a vast number of ways, from simple mutually entailed relations between single stimuli to combinatorial relations involving multiple stimuli, to the relating of stimulus relations to other relations, to the complex relating of entire relational networks to other networks. Not only can stimulus relations vary in their complexity, but so too can the type and number of functions transformed according to those relations. For example, mutually or combinatorially entailed relations between stimuli may involve single functions being transformed based on a relation between one stimulus and another, whereas the relating of complex networks of relations to other networks may involve a vast array of stimulus functions being modified in accordance with those relations.

Given that relational responses, like all behaviors, unfold across time, it appears that (all things being equal) more complex responses take additional time and are emitted with less accuracy relative to their less complex counterparts. To illustrate, consider the concept of nodal distance that refers to the number of nodes that link any two stimuli in a set of trained conditional relations. Interestingly, the time taken to respond in accordance with an equivalence relation increases and the accuracy of those responses decreases when the nodal distance within the equivalence class grows (Fields & Moss, 2007; Tomanari, Sidman, Rubio, & Dube, 2006; Wang, McHugh, & Whelan, 2012). Critically, however, when other relations above and beyond equivalence are involved, the complexity of a relation will be dictated not only by nodal distance, but by the number and type of relations involved (O'Hora, Roche, Barnes-Holmes, & Smeets, 2002; Steele & Hayes, 1991). Indeed, some work now indicates that, as the number and type of relations increase, the speed and accuracy of responding decreases relative to responses that are at lower levels of complexity (see Barnes-Holmes et al., 2005; Hyland, Smyth, O'Hora, & Leslie, 2014; Reilly, Whelan, & Barnes-Holmes, 2005; Vitale et al., 2008).

Levels of Derivation

Relations can not only vary in their complexity, but also in the degree to which they have been previously derived or inferred in the past. As noted above, derivation refers to the finding that once a set of relations between stimuli is directly trained, a number of additional untrained relations also emerge and allow for the transformation of functions. To illustrate, consider a situation where a participant has just been trained to select B when given A and C when given B. Thereafter, and upon testing, a series of untrained relations are evident (e.g., selecting A when given C or C when given A).

In this learning situation, the first instance in which the person derives the relation between A and C may be defined as a "high derivation" response given that the history of deriving that particular response is minimal. Alternatively, imagine that the same person is then provided with an ever increasing number of opportunities to derive or infer the relation between those same stimuli. Across each of these successive derivation opportunities the resulting response may come to be increasingly defined as involving "low" levels of derivation, in the sense that the relating becomes less and less novel or emergent. Note that, according to RFT, deriving or inferring may well decline, with repeated instances, even when some form of programmed reinforcement is not provided for each derived response because derivation itself is "rewarded" by contacting increased relational coherence (see Hayes, Fox et al., 2001, pp. 42–43).

It also appears that the extent to which a response has been derived in the past will influence its probability of being emitted quickly and accurately in the future. For instance, the speed with which participants derive coordination, comparative, and opposition relations becomes significantly faster with each successive opportunity to derive (O'Hora et al., 2002; Roche et al., 2004; Steele & Hayes, 1991). Likewise, an overarching history of derivation may facilitate the emergence of more accurate relational performances within and across stimulus sets (Healy et al., 2000; Roche et al., 2004; Saunders & Green, 1999; Sidman, 1994; Wang et al., 2012; Wulfert & Hayes, 1988).

It should be noted here that the concept of "levels of derivation" in RFT may be applied to multiple levels of analysis. Imagine, for example, that a young child is trained to relate A *same as* B and B *same as* C and is then tested for the C *same as* A combinatorially entailed relation. The first time the child produces this relational response the level of derivation would be defined as high, but if the child derives that response many times thereafter, derivation is seen as dropping to lower and lower levels. Now imagine that the child is trained and tested for the same relational frame, but using a new set of stimuli (train D *same as* E and E *same as* F; test F *same as* D). Once again, the first time the child derives the F–D relation, derivation for that particular response would be defined as high, and would then be seen as dropping with each successive F–D relational response. Critically, however, at the level of the relational frame itself (in this case coordination), derivation would also be defined as dropping from responding with the A–B–C stimulus set to the D–E–F set. In other words, the level of deriving the frame of coordination itself may be seen as reducing across multiple stimulus sets as the deriving becomes less and less novel across those sets. The same general logic applies to more complex patterns of AARR. Thus, for example, the first time a child derives a relation of coordination between two frames of coordination (C *same as* A is the same as F *same as* D) derivation will be high for both the particular relating-relations response and the act of relating derived relations itself. If relating-relations is then "practiced" across other novel sets of stimuli, the level of derivation or inference involved in relating-relations would be seen as reducing across those sets. This view of AARR helps to make sense of the fact that complex relational responding, such as relating-relations, appears to be relatively weak in children aged 4–5 but thereafter appears to grow in strength as they are provided with more and more opportunities to derive such complex relational responses (see Stewart & Barnes-Holmes, 2004).

As noted in the introduction to this part of the handbook, the recent focus on relational coherence, complexity, and levels of derivation in RFT is serving to inject a much needed emphasis on the role of reinforcement contingencies in understanding AARR. Indeed, we believe that this refocusing will be quite transformative in terms of moving RFT forward over the coming years, in that it will encourage researchers to identify the functional units of analysis that are being selected and strengthened or weakened as individuals interact with their verbal communities and the world around them. In time, we hope that the need for middle-level terms, such as defusion, acceptance, and even psychological flexibility itself, that currently abound in the applied wing of CBS, may be replaced with (or perhaps better supported by) RFT concepts that are far more closely tied to (experimental) functional analyses of the behavioral units that are actually selected by manipulable environmental variables.

Summary

On the one hand, it appears that humans search for and create consistency between and among derived stimulus relations involving arbitrary stimuli. Once the ability to engage in AARR emerges "it is maintained by *coherence* ... when relational networks are internally coherent, we feel confident that we understand. Because such understanding often predicts an ability to control events, coherence becomes a proxy variable for instrumental success" (Hayes, 2002, p. 104). On the other hand, it seems that the *complexity* of a relational response and the degree to which it has been previously *derived* can vary along a continuum from low to high. Like the concept of the relational frame discussed above, complexity and derivation are not hypothetical constructs or mental mechanisms: They are simply properties of AARR that will be more or less evident in different contexts. Specifically, it appears that the complexity of a relational response, as well as the degree to which it has been previously derived in the past, influences the probability that it will be emitted with speed and accuracy in the future. Responses characterized by an extensive history of derivation and low levels of complexity appear to be emitted with relatively greater speed/accuracy than their more complex and less derived counterparts (see Hughes et al., 2012 for a detailed treatment). Coherence, complexity, and derivation seem to play an important role in many areas of psychological science, an idea upon which we shall expand in chapter 10 in this volume.

Conclusion

Throughout this chapter we sought to provide an accessible introduction to, and a state-of-the-art report on, RFT and the empirical work that it has stimulated over the past two decades. At the core of this account lies a relatively simple claim with far-reaching consequences – namely that a generalized operant behavior known as arbitrarily applicable relational responding is learned early on in our development and provides the behavioral foundation for human language and cognition. So far our story has focused on the background, origins, and nature of AARR and largely left its role in human language and cognition untouched. We adopted this strategy so that the various components of AARR could be carefully considered and the empirical basis for this account examined before we demonstrate how it has been interfaced with specific aspects of psychological science. Let us now turn our attention, in the next chapter, to how this ability to frame events relationally provides the basis upon which many complex human behaviors are built.

Notes

1   An alternative term that captures the property of reflexivity does not appear to be necessary. Furthermore, some researchers have questioned the utility of reflexivity as a defining property of AARR because such responding may be based upon either derived stimulus relations or formal similarity (Steele & Hayes, 1991; see also Barnes, 1994). In any case, this issue is not important in the context of the current chapter and thus requires no further discussion.
2   Note that a near infinite range of stimuli (including spoken or written words, symbols, sounds, etc.) may come to function as contextual cues controlling the arbitrary relating of stimuli and events. Although the most common examples will be highlighted throughout this section, it is important to appreciate that the coordination of these words with many other words and phrases generates an almost infinite array of substitute stimuli that will also control a given pattern of relational responding. For instance, it is possible to establish nonsense words, arbitrary shapes, sounds, and tastes as contextual cues within the laboratory that function in the same as words such as "is," "opposite," "more/less than," "belongs to," and so forth. As always, the importance of a stimulus ultimately lies in its function rather than a particular topography.

References

Anderson, N. H. (2013). Unified psychology based on three laws of information integration. *Review of General Psychology, 17*, 125–132.

Aristotle. (1941). De memoria et reminiscentia (J. I. Beare, trans.). In R. McKeone (Ed.), *The basic works of Aristotle* (pp. 607–617). New York, NY: Random House.

Auguston, E. M., & Dougher, M. J. (1997). The transfer of avoidance evoking functions through stimulus equivalence classes. *Journal of Behavioral Therapy and Experimental Psychiatry, 28*, 181–191.

Baer, D. M., & Deguchi, H. (1985). Generalized imitation from a radical-behavioral viewpoint. In S. Reiss & R. R. Bootzin (Eds.), *Theoretical issues in behavior therapy* (pp. 179–217). New York, NY: Academic Press.

Barnes, D. (1994). Stimulus equivalence and relational frame theory. *The Psychological Record, 44*, 91–124.

Barnes, D., McCullagh, P., & Keenan, M. (1990). Equivalence class formation in non-hearing impaired children and hearing impaired children. *Analysis of Verbal Behavior, 8*, 1–11.

Barnes, D., & Roche, B. (1996). Relational frame theory and stimulus equivalence are fundamentally different: A reply to Saunders' commentary. *The Psychological Record, 46*, 489–507.

Barnes-Holmes, D., & Barnes-Holmes, Y. (2000). Explaining complex behavior: Two perspectives on the concept of generalized operant classes. *The Psychological Record, 50*, 251–265.

Barnes-Holmes, D., Barnes-Holmes, Y., Smeets, P. M., Cullinan, V., & Leader, G. (2004). Relational frame theory and stimulus equivalence: Conceptual and procedural issues. *International Journal of Psychology and Psychological Therapy, 4*, 181–214.

Barnes-Holmes, D., Cochrane, A., Barnes-Holmes, Y., Stewart, I., & McHugh, L. (2004). Psychological acceptance: Experimental analyses and theoretical interpretations. *International Journal of Psychology and Psychological Therapy, 4*, 517–530.

Barnes-Holmes, D., Hayes, S. C., & Dymond, S. (2001) Self and self-directed rules. In S. C. Hayes, D. Barnes-Holmes, & B. Roche (Eds.), *Relational frame theory: A post-Skinnerian account of human language and cognition* (pp. 119–139). New York, NY: Kluwer/Plenum.

Barnes-Holmes, D., Luciano, C., & Barnes-Holmes, Y. (2004). Relational frame theory: Definitions, controversies, and applications I. *International Journal of Psychology and Psychological Therapy, 4*, 177–394.

Barnes-Holmes, D., Luciano, C., & Barnes-Holmes, Y. (2004). Relational frame theory: Definitions, controversies, and applications II. *International Journal of Psychology and Psychological Therapy, 4*, 443–622.

Barnes-Holmes, D., & Murphy, C. (2007). Addressing the generativity of language: A late reply to Chomsky. In B. S. Mesmere (Ed.), *New autism research developments* (pp. 175–196). New York, NY: Nova Science Publishers.

Barnes-Holmes, D., O'Hora, D., Roche, B., Hayes, S. C., Bissett, R. T., & Lyddy, D. (2001). Understanding and verbal regulation. In S. C. Hayes, D. Barnes-Holmes, & B. Roche (Eds.), *Relational frame theory: A post-Skinnerian account of human language and cognition* (pp. 103–117). New York, NY: Kluwer/Plenum.

Barnes-Holmes, D., Staunton, C., Whelan, R., Barnes-Holmes, Y., Commins, S., Walsh, D., … Dymond, S. (2005). Derived stimulus relations, semantic priming, and event-related potentials: Testing a behavioral theory of semantic networks. *Journal of the Experimental Analysis of Behavior, 84*, 417–430.

Barnes-Holmes, Y., Barnes-Holmes, D., McHugh, L., & Hayes, S. (2004). Teaching derived relational responding with young children. *Journal of Early and Intensive Behavior Intervention, 1*, 56–90.

Barnes-Holmes, Y., Barnes-Holmes, D., & Smeets, P. M. (2004). Establishing relational responding in accordance with opposite as generalized operant behavior in young children. *International Journal of Psychology and Psychological Therapy, 4*, 559–586.

Barnes-Holmes, Y., Barnes-Holmes, D., Smeets, P. M., & Luciano, C. (2004). The derived transfer of mood functions through equivalence relations. *The Psychological Record, 54*, 95–114.

Barnes-Holmes, Y., Barnes-Holmes, D., Smeets, P. M., Strand, P., & Friman, P. (2004). Establishing relational responding in accordance with more-than and less-than as generalized operant behavior in young children. *International Journal of Psychology and Psychological Therapy, 4*, 531–558.

Barnes-Holmes, Y., McHugh, L., & Barnes-Holmes, D. (2004). Perspective-taking and Theory of Mind: A relational frame account. *The Behavior Analyst Today, 5*, 15–25.

Baron, A., & Galizio, M. (1983). Instructional control of human operant behavior. *The Psychological Record, 33*, 495–520.

Bentall, R. P., Lowe, C. F., & Beasty, A. (1985). The role of verbal behavior in human learning: II. Developmental differences. *Journal of the Experimental Analysis of Behavior, 43*, 165–181.

Berens, N. M., & Hayes, S. C. (2007). Arbitrarily applicable comparative relations: Experimental Evidence for relational operants. *Journal of Applied Behavior Analysis, 40*, 45–71.

Blackledge, J. T., Moran, D. J., & Ellis, A. E. (2009). Bridging the divide: Linking basic science to applied psychotherapeutic interventions – a relational frame theory account of cognitive disputation in rational emotive behavior therapy. *Journal of Rational-Emotive & Cognitive-Behavior Therapy, 27*, 232–248.

Brino, A. L., Campos, R. S., Galvão, O. F., & McIlvane, W. J. (2014). Blank-comparison matching-to-sample reveals a false positive symmetry test in a capuchin monkey. *Psychology & Neuroscience, 7*(2), 193–198.

Cahill, J., Barnes-Holmes, Y., Barnes-Holmes, D., Rodríguez-Valverde, M., Luciano, C., & Smeets, P. M. (2007). The derived transfer and reversal of mood functions through equivalence relations II. *The Psychological Record, 57,* 373–389.

Carpentier, F., Smeets, P. M., & Barnes-Holmes, D. (2002). Matching functionally-same relations: Implications for equivalence–equivalence as a model for analogical reasoning. *The Psychological Record, 52,* 351–312.

Carpentier, F., Smeets, P. M., & Barnes-Holmes, D. (2003). Equivalence-equivalence as a model of analogy: Further analyses. *The Psychological Record, 53,* 349–372.

Carr, D., & Blackman, D. E. (2001). Relations among equivalence, naming, and conflicting baseline control. *Journal of the Experimental Analysis of Behavior, 65,* 245–247.

Cassidy, S., Roche, B., & Hayes, S. C. (2011). A relational frame training intervention to raise intelligence quotients: A pilot study. *The Psychological Record, 61,* 173–198.

Catania, A. C. (1998). *Learning* (4th ed.). Upper Saddle River, NJ: Prentice Hall.

Chomsky, N. (1959). A review of B.F. Skinner's *Verbal behavior. Language, 35,* 26–58.

De Houwer, J., Barnes-Holmes, D., & Moors, A. (2013). What is learning? On the nature and merits of a functional definition of learning. *Psychonomic Bulletin & Review, 20,* 631–642.

Devany, J. M., Hayes, S. C., & Nelson, R. O. (1986). Equivalence class formation in language – able and language-disabled children. *Journal of the Experimental Analysis of Behavior, 46,* 243–257.

Dinsmoor, J. A. (1995). Stimulus control: II. *The Behavior Analyst, 18,* 253–269.

Dixon, M. R., Rehfeldt, R. A., Zlomke, K. M., & Robinson, A. (2006). Exploring the development and dismantling of equivalence classes involving terrorist stimuli. *The Psychological Record, 56,* 83–103.

Dixon, M. R., & Zlomke, K. M. (2005). Using the precursor to the relational evaluation procedure (PREP) to establish the relational frames of sameness, opposition, and distinction. *Revista Latinoamericana de Psicología, 37,* 305–316.

Dougher, M. J., Hamilton, D., Fink, B., & Harrington, J. (2007). Transformation of the discriminative and eliciting functions of generalized relational stimuli. *Journal of the Experimental Analysis of Behavior, 88,* 179–197.

Dougher, M., Perkins, D. R., Greenway, D., Koons, A., & Chiasson, C. (2002). Contextual control of equivalence-based transformation of functions. *Journal of the Experimental Analysis of Behavior, 78,* 63–94.

Doughty, A. H., & Oken, G. (2008). Extinction-induced response resurgence: A selective review. *The Behavior Analyst Today, 9,* 27–34.

Dugdale, N., & Lowe, C. F. (2000). Testing for symmetry in the conditional discriminations of language trained chimpanzees. *Journal of the Experimental Analysis of Behavior, 73,* 5–22.

Dymond, S., & Alonso-Álvarez, B. (2010). The selective impact of Skinner's *Verbal behavior* on empirical research: A reply to Schlinger (2008). *The Psychological Record, 60,* 355–360.

Dymond, S., & Barnes, D. (1995). A transformation of self-discrimination response functions in accordance with the arbitrarily applicable relations of sameness, more-than, and less-than. *Journal of the Experimental Analysis of Behavior, 64,* 163–184.

Dymond, S., & Barnes, D. (1996). A transformation of self-discrimination response functions in accordance with the arbitrarily applicable relations of sameness and opposition. *The Psychological Record, 46,* 271–300.

Dymond, S., & Roche, B. (Eds.), (2013). *Advances in relational frame theory: Research and application.* Oakland, CA: New Harbinger.

Dymond, S., Roche, B., & Barnes-Holmes, D. (2003). The continuity strategy, human behavior, and behavior analysis. *The Psychological Record, 53,* 333–347.

Dymond, S., Roche, B., Forsyth, J. P., Whelan, R., & Rhoden, J. (2008). Derived avoidance learning: Transformation of avoidance response functions in accordance with same and opposite relational frames. *The Psychological Record, 58,* 269–286.

Dymond, S., Schlund, M. W., Roche, B., & Whelan, R. (2014). The spread of fear: Symbolic generalization mediates graded threat-avoidance in specific phobia, *The Quarterly Journal of Experimental Psychology, 67,* 247–259.

Epstein, R. (1985). Extinction-induced resurgence: Preliminary investigations and possible applications. *The Psychological Record, 35,* 143–153.

Fields, L., & Moss, P. (2007). Stimulus relatedness in equivalence classes: Interaction of nodality and contingency. *European Journal of Behavior Analysis, 8,* 141–159.

Foody, M., Barnes-Holmes, Y., Barnes-Holmes, D., & Luciano, C. (2013). An empirical investigation of hierarchical versus distinction relations in a self-based ACT exercise. *International Journal of Psychology & Psychological Therapy, 13,* 373–388.

Frank, A. J., & Wasserman, E. A. (2005). Associative symmetry in the pigeon after successive matching-to-sample training. *Journal of the Experimental Analysis of Behavior, 84,* 147–165.

Galvão, O.F., Da Silva Barros, R., Dos Santos, J. R., De Faria Brino, A. L., Brandao, S., Lavratti, C. M., … McIlvane, W. J. (2005). Extent and limits of the matching concept in Cebus apella: A matter of experimental control? *The Psychological Record, 55,* 219–232.

Gannon, S., Roche, B., Kanter, J., Forsyth, J. P., & Linehan, C. (2011). A derived relations analysis of approach-avoidance conflict: Implications for the behavioral analysis of human anxiety. *The Psychological Record, 61,* 227–252.

Garcia-Marques, L., & Ferreira, M. (2011). Friends and foes of theory construction in psychological science: Vague dichotomies, unified theories of cognition, and the new experimentalism. *Perspectives on Psychological Science, 6,* 192–201.

Garotti, M., & De Rose, J. C. (2007). Reorganization of equivalence classes: Evidence for contextual control by baseline reviews before probes. *The Psychological Record, 57,* 87–102.

Gawronski, B. (2012). Back to the future of dissonance theory: Cognitive consistency as a core motive. *Social Cognition, 30,* 652–668.

Gil, E., Luciano, C., Ruiz, F.J., & Valdivia-Salas, V. (2012). A preliminary demonstration of transformation of functions through hierarchical relations. *International Journal of Psychology and Psychological Therapy, 12,* 1–19.

Gil, E., Luciano, C., Ruiz, F. J., & Valdivia-Salas, S. (2014). A further experimental step in the analysis of hierarchical responding. *International Journal of Psychology and Psychological Therapy, 14,* 137–153.

Giurfa, M., Zhang, S., Jenett, A., Menzel, R., & Srinivasan, M. V. (2001). The concepts of "sameness" and "difference" in an insect. *Nature, 410,* 930–933.

Gomez, S., Barnes-Holmes, D., & Luciano, M. C. (2001). Generalized break equivalence I. *The Psychological Record, 51,* 131–150.

Gomez, S., Barnes-Holmes, D., & Luciano, M. C. (2002). Generalized break equivalence II: Contextual control over a generalized pattern of stimulus relations. *The Psychological Record, 52,* 203–220.

Gómez, S., López, F., Martín, C. B., Barnes-Holmes, Y., & Barnes-Holmes, D. (2007). Exemplar training and a derived transformation of functions in accordance with symmetry and equivalence. *The Psychological Record, 57,* 273–294.

Gore, N., Barnes-Holmes, Y., & Murphy, G. (2013). The relationship between intellectual functioning and relational perspective-taking. *International Journal of Psychology and Psychological Therapy, 10,* 1–17.

Gorham, M., Barnes-Holmes, Y., Barnes-Holmes, D., & Berens, N. (2009). Derived comparative and transitive relations in young children with and without autism. *The Psychological Record, 59,* 221–246.

Greer, R. D. (2008). The ontogenetic selection of verbal capabilities: Contributions of Skinner's verbal behavior theory to a more comprehensive understanding of language. *International Journal of Psychology and Psychological Therapy, 8,* 363–386.

Griffee, K., & Dougher, M. J. (2002). Contextual control of stimulus generalization and stimulus equivalence in hierarchical categorization. *Journal of the Experimental Analysis of Behavior, 78*, 433–447.

Gross, A. C., & Fox, E. J. (2009). Relational frame theory: An overview of the controversy. *The Analysis of Verbal Behavior, 25*, 87–98.

Harlow, H. E. (1959). Learning set and error factor theory. In S. Koch (Ed.), *Psychology: A study of a science* (Vol. 2, pp. 492–537). New York, NY: McGraw-Hill.

Harmon, K., Strong, R., & Pasnak, R. (1982). Relational responses in tests of transposition with rhesus monkeys. *Learning and Motivation, 13*, 495–504.

Hayes, S. C. (1987). Upward and downward continuity: It's time to change our strategic assumptions. *Behavior Analysis, 22*, 3–6.

Hayes, S. C. (1989a). Nonhumans have not yet shown stimulus equivalence. *Journal of the Experimental Analysis of Behavior, 51*, 385–392.

Hayes, S. C. (Ed.). (1989b). *Rule-governed behavior: Cognition, contingencies, and instructional control*. New York, NY: Plenum.

Hayes, S. C. (1992). Verbal relations, time, and suicide. In S. C. Hayes & L. J. Hayes (Eds.), *Understanding verbal relations* (pp. 109–118). Reno, NV: Context Press.

Hayes, S. C. (2002). Acceptance, mindfulness, and science. *Clinical Psychology: Science and Practice, 9*, 101–106.

Hayes, S. C., Barnes-Holmes, D., & Roche, B. (Eds.). (2001). *Relational frame theory: A post-Skinnerian account of human language and cognition*. New York, NY: Plenum.

Hayes, S. C., Brownstein, A. J., Haas, J. R., & Greenway, D. E. (1986). Instructions, multiple schedules, and extinction: distinguishing rule-governed from scheduled-controlled behavior. *Journal of the Experimental Analysis of Behavior, 46*, 137–147.

Hayes, S. C., Brownstein, A. J., Zettle, R. D., Rosenfarb, I., & Korn, Z. (1986). Rule-governed behavior and sensitivity to changing consequences of responding. *Journal of the Experimental Analysis of Behavior, 45*, 237–256.

Hayes, S. C., Fox, E., Gifford, E. V., Wilson, K. G., Barnes-Holmes, D., & Healy, O. (2001). Derived relational responding as learned behavior. In S. C. Hayes, D. Barnes-Holmes, & B. Roche (Eds.), *Relational frame theory: A post-Skinnerian account of human language and cognition* (pp. 21–49). New York, NY: Plenum.

Hayes, S.C., & Long, D. (2013). Contextual behavioral science, evolution, and scientific epistemology. In S. Dymond & B. Roche (Eds.), *Advances in relational frame theory: Research & application* (pp. 5–26). Oakland, CA: New Harbinger.

Hayes, S. C., Strosahl, K., & Wilson, K. G. (1999). *Acceptance and commitment therapy: An experiential approach to behavior change*. New York, NY: Guilford.

Heagle, A. I., & Rehfeldt, R. A. (2006). Teaching perspective-taking skills to typically developing children through derived relational responding. *Journal of Early and Intensive Behavior Intervention, 3*, 1–34.

Healy, O., Barnes, D., & Smeets, P. M. (1998). Derived relational responding as an operant: The effects of between-session feedback. *The Psychological Record, 48*, 511–536.

Healy, O., Barnes-Holmes, D., & Smeets, P. M. (2000). Derived relational responding as generalized operant behavior. *Journal of the Experimental Analysis of Behavior, 74*), 207–227.

Horne, P. J., & Erjavec, M. (2007). Do infants show generalized imitation of gestures? *Journal of Experimental Analysis of Behavior, 87*, 63–87.

Hughes, S., & Barnes-Holmes, D. (2014). Associative concept learning, stimulus equivalence, and relational frame theory: Working out the similarities and differences between human and non-human behavior. *Journal of Experimental Behavior Analysis, 101*, 156–160.

Hughes, S., Barnes-Holmes, D., & Vahey, N. (2012). Holding on to our functional roots when exploring new intellectual islands: A voyage through implicit cognition research. *Journal of Contextual Behavioral Science, 1*, 17–38.

Hughes. S., De Houwer, J. & Barnes-Holmes, D. (in press). *The Moderating Impact of Distal Regularities on the Effect of Stimulus Pairings: A Novel Perspective on Evaluative Conditioning.* Experimental Psychology.

Hull, C. L. (1934). The concept of the habit–family hierarchy and maze learning: Part 1. *Psychological Review, 41*, 33–52.

Hyland, J.M., Smyth, S., O'Hora, D.P. & Leslie, J.C. (2014). The effect of before and after instructions on the speed of sequential responding. *The Psychological Record, 64*, 311–319.

Jenkins, J. J., & Palermo, D. S. (1964). Mediation processes and the acquisition of linguistic structure. In U. Bellugi & R. Brown (Eds.), *The acquisition of language* (pp. 141–169). Monographs of the Society for Research in Child Development, 29.

Kastak, C. R., & Schusterman, R. J. (2002). Sea lions and equivalence: Expanding classes by exclusion. *Journal of the Experimental Analysis of Behavior, 78*, 449–465.

Leigland, S. (1997). Is a new definition of verbal behavior necessary in the light of derived relational responding? *The Behavior Analyst, 20*, 3–10.

Leonhard, C., & Hayes, S. C. (1991, May). *Prior inconsistent testing affects equivalence responding.* Paper presented at the meeting of the Association for Behavior Analysis, Atlanta.

Lieving, G. A., & Lattal, K. A. (2003). Recency, repeatability, and reinforcer retrenchment: An experimental analysis of resurgence. *Journal of the Experimental Analysis of Behavior, 80*, 217–233.

Lionello-DeNolf, K. M. (2009). The search for symmetry: 25 years in review. *Learning & Behavior, 37*, 188–203.

Lipkens, G., & Hayes, S. C. (2009). Producing and recognizing analogical relations. *Journal of the Experimental Analysis of Behavior, 91*, 105–126.

Lipkens, G., Hayes, S. C., & Hayes, L. J. (1993). Longitudinal study of derived stimulus relations in an infant. *Journal of Experimental Child Psychology, 56*, 201–239.

Lowe, C. F. (1979). Determinants of human operant behaviour. In M. Zeiler & P. Harzem (Eds.), *Advances in the analysis of behavior: Volume 1. Reinforcement and the organisation of behavior* (pp. 159–192). Chichester, England: Wiley.

Luciano, C., Gómez-Becerra, I., & Rodríguez-Valverde, M. (2007). The role of multiple-exemplar training and naming in establishing derived equivalence in an infant. *Journal of Experimental Analysis of Behavior, 87*, 349–365.

Luciano, C., Rodrigquez, M., Manas, I., & Ruiz, F. (2009). Acquiring the earliest relational operants: Coordination, difference, opposition, comparison, and hierarchy. In R. A. Rehfeldt & Y. Barnes-Holmes (Eds.), *Derived relational responding: Applications for learners with autism and other developmental disabilities* (pp. 149–172). Oakland, CA: New Harbinger.

Luciano, C., Valdivia-Salas, S., Ruiz, F. J., Rodríguez-Valverde, M., Barnes-Holmes, D., Dougher, M. J., & Gutierrez, O. (2013). Extinction of aversive eliciting functions as an analog of exposure to conditioned fear: Does it alter avoidance responding? *Journal of Contextual Behavioral Science, 2*, 120–134.

Luciano, C., Valdivia-Salas, S., Ruiz, F. J., Rodríguez-Valverde, M., Barnes-Holmes, D., Dougher, M. J., … Gutierrez-Martínez, O. (2014). Effects of an acceptance/defusion intervention on experimentally induced generalized avoidance: A laboratory demonstration. *Journal of the Experimental Analysis of Behavior, 101*, 94–111.

McGinty, J., Ninness, C., McCuller, G., Rumph, R., Goodwin, R., Kelso, G., … Kelly, E. (2012). Training and deriving precalculus relations: A small group web-interactive approach. *The Psychological Record, 62*, 225–242.

McHugh, L., Barnes-Holmes, Y., & Barnes-Holmes, D. (2004). Perspective-taking as relational responding: A developmental profile. *The Psychological Record, 54*, 115–144.

McHugh, L., Barnes-Holmes, Y., & Barnes-Holmes, D. (2007). Deictic relational complexity and the development of deception. *The Psychological Record, 57*, 517–531.

McHugh, L., Barnes-Holmes, Y., Barnes-Holmes, D., & Stewart, I. (2006). Understanding false belief as generalized operant behavior. *The Psychological Record, 56*, 341–364.

McHugh, L., Barnes-Holmes, Y., Barnes-Holmes, D., Stewart, I., & Dymond, S. (2007). Deictic relational complexity and the development of deception. *The Psychological Record, 57,* 517–531.

McHugh, L., & Stewart, I. (2012). *The self and perspective taking: Contributions and applications from modern behavioral science.* Oakland, CA: New Harbinger.

McIlvane, W. J. (2014). Associative concept learning in animals by Zentall, Wasserman, and Urcuioli: A commentary. *Journal of the Experimental Analysis of Behavior, 101,* 161–164.

McIlvane, W. J., Serna, R. W., Dube, W. V., & Stromer, R. (2000). Stimulus control topography coherence and stimulus equivalence: Reconciling test outcomes with theory. In J. C. Leslie & D. E. Blackman (Eds.), *Experimental and applied analysis of human behavior* (pp. 85–110). Reno, NV: Context Press.

Meltzoff, A. N. (2005). Imitation and other minds: The "Like Me" hypothesis. In S. Hurley & N. Chater (Eds.), *Perspectives on imitation: From cognitive neuroscience to social science* (Vol. 2, pp. 55–77). Cambridge, MA: MIT Press.

Mischel, W., & Ayduk, O. (2004). Willpower in a cognitive-affective processing system: The dynamics of delay of gratification. In R. F. Baumeister & K. D. Vohs (Eds.), *Handbook of self-regulation: Research, theory, and applications* (p. 99–129). New York, NY: Guilford.

Munnelly, A., Freegard, G., & Dymond, S. (2013). Constructing relational sentences: Establishing arbitrarily applicable comparative relations with the relational completion procedure. *The Psychological Record, 63,* 751–768.

Munnelly, A., Martin, G., Dack, C., Zedginidze, A., & McHugh, L. (2014). The transfer of social exclusion and inclusion functions through derived stimulus relations. *Learning & Behavior, 42,* 270–280.

Murphy, C., & Barnes-Holmes, D. (2009). Derived more–less relational mands in children diagnosed with autism. *Journal of Applied Behavior Analysis, 42,* 253–268.

Murphy, C., Barnes-Holmes, D., & Barnes-Holmes, Y. (2005). Derived manding in children with autism: Synthesizing Skinner's verbal behavior with relational frame theory. *Journal of Applied Behavior Analysis, 38,* 445–462.

Murphy, G. L. (2002). *The big book of concepts.* Cambridge, MA: MIT Press.

Neuringer, A. (2002). Operant variability: Evidence, functions, and theory. *Psychonomic Bulletin and Review, 9,* 672–705.

Ninness, C., Barnes-Holmes, D., Rumph, R., McCuller, G., Ford, A., Payne, R., … Elliott, M. (2006). Transformation of mathematical and stimulus functions. *Journal of Applied Behavior Analysis, 39,* 299–321.

Ninness, C., Dixon, Barnes-Holmes, D., Rehfeldt, R.A., Rumph, R., McCuller, G., … Ninness, S. (2009). Deriving and constructing reciprocal trigonometric relations: A web-interactive training approach. *Journal of Applied Behavior Analysis, 43,* 191–208.

O'Connor, J., Barnes-Holmes, Y., & Barnes-Holmes, D. (2011). Establishing contextual control over symmetry and asymmetry performances in typically-developing children and children with autism. *The Psychological Record, 61,* 287–312.

O'Connor, J., Rafferty, A., Barnes-Holmes, D., & Barnes-Holmes, Y. (2009). The role of verbal behavior, stimulus nameability, and familiarity on the equivalence performances of autistic and normally developing children. *The Psychological Record, 59,* 53–74.

O'Hora, D., & Barnes-Holmes, D. (2004). Instructional control: Developing a relational frame analysis. *International Journal of Psychology and Psychological Therapy, 4,* 263–284.

O'Hora, D., Barnes-Holmes, D., Roche, B., & Smeets, P. M. (2004). Derived relational networks and control by novel instructions: A possible model of generative verbal responding. *The Psychological Record, 54,* 437–460.

O'Hora, D., Pelaez, M., & Barnes-Holmes, D. (2005). Derived relational responding and performance on verbal subtests of the WAIS-III. *The Psychological Record, 55*(1), 155.

O'Hora, D., Pelaez, M., Barnes-Holmes, D., & Amesty, L. (2005). Derived relational responding and human language: Evidence from the WAIS-III. *The Psychological Record, 55*, 155–174.

O'Hora, D., Pelaez, M., Barnes-Holmes, D., Rae, G., Robinson, K., & Chaudhary, T. (2008). Temporal relations and intelligence: Correlating relational performance with performance on the WAIS-III. *The Psychological Record, 58*, 569–584.

O'Hora, D., Roche, B., Barnes-Holmes, D., & Smeets, P. M. (2002). Response latencies to multiple derived stimulus relations: Testing two predictions of relational frame theory. *The Psychological Record, 52*, 51–76.

O'Toole, C., & Barnes-Holmes, D. (2009). Three chronometric indices of relational responding as predictors of performance on a brief intelligence test: The importance of relational flexibility. *The Psychological Record, 59*, 119–132.

Pankey, J., & Hayes, S. C. (2003). Acceptance and commitment therapy for psychosis. *International Journal of Psychology and Psychological Therapy, 3*, 311–328.

Pelaez, M., Gewirtz, J. L., Sanchez, A., & Mahabir, N. M. (2000). Exploring stimulus equivalence formation in infants. *Behavior Development Bulletin, 9*, 20–25.

Pérez, V., García, A., & Gómez, J. (2011). Facilitation of the equivalence–equivalence response. *Psicothema, 23*, 407–414.

Persicke, A., Tarbox, J., Ranick, J., & St. Clair, M. (2012). Establishing metaphorical reasoning in children with autism. *Research in Autism Spectrum Disorders, 6*, 913–920.

Pilgrim, C., Click, R., & Galizio, M. (2011). A developmental analysis of children's equivalence-class formation and disruption. *Acta de Investigacion Psicologica, 1*, 55–76.

Pilgrim, C., & Galizio, M. (1995). Reversal of baseline relations and stimulus equivalence: I. Adults. *Journal of the Experimental Analysis of Behavior, 63*, 225–238.

Posner, M. I., & Rothbart, M. K. (2007). Research on attention networks as a model for the integration of psychological science. *Annual Review of Psychology, 58*, 1–23.

Quinones, J. L., & Hayes, S. C. (2014). Relational coherence in ambiguous and unambiguous relational networks. *Journal of the Experimental Analysis of Behavior, 101*, 76–93.

Reese, H. W. (1968). *The perception of stimulus relations: Discrimination learning and transposition*. New York, NY: Academic Press.

Rehfeldt, R. A., & Barnes-Holmes, Y. (2009). *Derived relational responding: Applications for learners with autism and other developmental disabilities*. Oakland, CA: New Harbinger.

Rehfeldt, R. A., Dillen, J. E., Ziomek, M. M., & Kowalchuk, R. E. (2007). Assessing relational learning deficits in perspective-taking in children with high functioning autism spectrum disorder. *The Psychological Record, 57*, 23–47.

Reilly, T., Whelan, R., & Barnes-Holmes, D. (2005). The effect of training structure on the latency responses to a five-term linear chain. *The Psychological Record, 55*, 233–249.

Roche, B., & Barnes, D. (1996). Arbitrarily applicable relational responding and human sexual categorization: A critical test of the derived difference relation. *The Psychological Record, 46*, 451–475.

Roche, B., & Barnes, D., & Smeets, P. M. (1997). Incongruous stimulus pairing contingencies and conditional discrimination training: Effects on relational responding. *Journal of the Experimental Analysis of Behavior, 68*, 143–160.

Roche, B., Barnes-Holmes, Y., Barnes-Holmes, D., Stewart, I., & O'Hora, D. (2002). Relational frame theory: A new paradigm for the analysis of social behavior. *The Behavior Analyst, 25*, 75–91.

Roche, B. T., Kanter, J. W., Brown, K. R., Dymond, S., & Fogarty, C. C. (2008). A comparison of "direct" versus "derived" extinction of avoidance responding. *The Psychological Record, 58*, 443–464.

Roche, B., Linehan, C., Ward, T., Dymond, S., & Rehfeldt, R. (2004). The unfolding of the relational operant: A real-time analysis using electroencephalography and reaction time measures. *International Journal of Psychology & Psychological Therapy, 4*, 587–603.

Rodríguez-Valverde, M., Luciano, C., & Barnes-Holmes, D. (2009). Transfer of aversive respondent elicitation in accordance with equivalence relations. *Journal of the Experimental Analysis of Behavior, 92*, 85–111.

Saunders, R. R., & Green, G. (1999). A discrimination analysis of training-structure effects on stimulus equivalence outcomes. *Journal of the Experimental Analysis of Behavior, 72*, 117–137.

Sautter, R. A., & LeBlanc, L. A. (2006). Empirical applications of Skinner's analysis of verbal behavior with humans. *The Analysis of Verbal Behavior, 22*, 35–48.

Schlinger, H. D. (1993). Separating discriminative and function-altering effects of verbal stimuli. *The Behavior Analyst, 16*, 9–23.

Schlinger, H. D. (2008). The long goodbye: Why B. F. Skinner's *Verbal Behavior* is alive and well on the 50th anniversary of its publication. *The Psychological Record, 58*, 329–337.

Schlinger, H. D. (2010). The impact of Skinner's *Verbal Behavior*: A response to Dymond and Alonso-Alvarez. *The Psychological Record, 60*, 361–368.

Schlinger, H., & Blakely, E. (1987). Function-altering effects of contingency-specifying stimuli. *The Behavior Analyst, 10*, 41–45.

Shimoff, E., Catania, A. C., & Matthews, B. A. (1981). Uninstructed human responding: Sensitivity of low-rate performance to schedule contingencies. *Journal of the Experimental Analysis of Behavior, 36*, 207–220.

Skinner, B. F. (1957). *Verbal behavior.* Englewood Cliffs, NJ: Prentice Hall.

Skinner, B. F. (1969). *Contingencies of reinforcement: A theoretical analysis.* Englewood Cliffs, NJ: Prentice Hall.

Sidman, M. (1971). Reading and auditory-visual equivalences. *Journal of Speech and Hearing Research, 14*, 5–13.

Sidman, M. (1994). Equivalence relations and behavior: A research story. Boston, MA: Authors Cooperative.

Sidman, M. (2000). Equivalence relations and the reinforcement contingency. *Journal of the Experimental Analysis of Behavior, 74*, 127–146.

Sidman, M. (2009). Equivalence relations and behavior: An introductory tutorial. *The Analysis of Verbal Behavior, 25*, 5–17.

Slattery, B., & Stewart, I. (2014). Hierarchical classification as relational framing. *Journal of the Experimental Analysis of Behavior, 101*, 61–75.

Slattery, B., Stewart, I., & O'Hora, D. (2011). Testing for transitive class containment as a feature of hierarchical classification. *Journal of the Experimental Analysis of Behavior, 96*, 243–260.

Smeets, P. M., & Barnes-Holmes, D. (2005). Establishing equivalence classes in preschool children with many-to-one and one-to-many training protocols. *Behavioural Processes, 69*, 281–293.

Smeets, P. M., Barnes-Holmes, Y., Akpinar, D., & Barnes-Holmes, D. (2003). Reversal of equivalence relations. *The Psychological Record, 53*, 91–120.

Smyth, S., Barnes-Holmes, D., & Forsyth, J. P. (2006). A derived transfer of simple discrimination and self-reported arousal functions in spider fearful and non-spider fearful participants. *Journal of the Experimental Analysis of Behavior, 85*, 223–246.

Steele, D. L., & Hayes, S. C. (1991). Stimulus equivalence and arbitrarily applicable relational responding. *Journal of the Experimental Analysis of Behavior, 56*, 519–555.

Stewart, I., & Barnes-Holmes, D. (2004). Relational frame theory and analogical reasoning: Empirical investigations. *International Journal of Psychology and Psychological Therapy, 4*, 241–262.

Stewart, I., Barrett, K., McHugh, L., Barnes-Holmes, D., & O'Hora, D. (2013). Multiple contextual control over non-arbitrary relational responding and a preliminary model of pragmatic verbal analysis. *Journal of the Experimental Analysis of Behavior, 100*, 174–186.

Stewart, I., & Roche, B. (2013). Relational frame theory: An overview. In S. Dymond & B. Roche (Eds.), *Advances in relational frame theory: Research and application* (pp. 51–71). Oakland, CA: New Harbinger.

Tomanari, G. Y., Sidman, M., Rubio, A. R., & Dube, W. V. (2006). Equivalence classes with requirements for short response latencies. *Journal of the Experimental Analysis of Behavior, 85,* 349–369.

Urcuioli, P. J. (2008). Associative symmetry, "anti-symmetry," and a theory of pigeons' equivalence-class formation. *Journal of the Experimental Analysis of Behavior, 90,* 257–282.

Vaughan, M. E. (1985). Repeated acquisition in the analysis of rule-governed behavior. *Journal of the Experimental Analysis of Behavior, 44,* 175–184.

Vervoort, E., Vervliet, B., Bennett, M., & Baeyens, F. (2014). Generalization of human fear acquisition and extinction within a novel arbitrary stimulus category. PLoS ONE, *9*(5), e96569.

Vilardaga, R. (2009). A relational frame theory account of empathy. *The International Journal of Behavioral Consultation and Therapy, 5,* 178–184.

Vilardaga, R., Estévez, A., Levin, M. E., & Hayes, S. C. (2012). Deictic relational responding, empathy, and experiential avoidance as predictors of social anhedonia: Further contributions from relational frame theory. *The Psychological Record, 62,* 409–432.

Vilardaga, R., & Hayes, S. C. (2012). A contextual behavioral approach to pathological altruism. In B. Oakley, A. Knafo, G. Madhavan, & D. S. Wilson (Eds.), *Pathological altruism* (pp. 31–48). New York, NY: Oxford University Press.

Villatte, M., Monestès, J. L., McHugh, L., Freixa i Baqué, E., & Loas, G. (2008). Assessing deictic relational responding in social anhedonia: A functional approach to the development of Theory of Mind impairments. *International Journal of Behavioral Consultation and Therapy, 4,* 360–373.

Villatte, M., Monestès, J. L., McHugh, L., Freixa i Baqué, E., & Loas, G. (2010). Adopting the perspective of another in belief attribution: Contribution of relational frame theory to the understanding of impairments in schizophrenia. *Journal of Behavior Therapy and Experimental Psychiatry, 41,* 125–134.

Vitale, A., Barnes-Holmes, Y., Barnes-Holmes, D., & Campbell, C. (2008). Facilitating responding in accordance with the relational frame of comparison: Systematic empirical analyses. *The Psychological Record, 58,* 365–390.

Vitale, A., Campbell, C., Barnes-Holmes, Y., & Barnes-Holmes, D. (2012). Facilitating responding in accordance with the relational frame of comparison II: Methodological analysis. *The Psychological Record, 62,* 663–675.

Walsh, S., Horgan, J., May, R. J., Dymond, S., & Whelan, R. (2014). Facilitating relational framing in children and individuals with developmental delay using the Relational Completion Procedure. *Journal of the Experimental Analysis of Behavior, 101,* 51–60.

Wang, T., McHugh, L., & Whelan, R. (2012). A test of the discrimination account in equivalence class formation. *Learning and Motivation, 43,* 8–13.

Watt, A., Keenan, M., Barnes, D., & Cairns, E. (1991). Social categorization and stimulus equivalence. *The Psychological Record, 41,* 33–50.

Weil, T. M., Hayes, S. C., & Capurro, P. (2011). Establishing a deictic relational repertoire in young children. *The Psychological Record, 61,* 371–390.

Whelan, R., & Barnes-Holmes, D. (2004a). Empirical models of formative augmenting in accordance with the relations of same, opposite, more-than, and less-than. *International Journal of Psychology and Psychological Therapy, 4,* 285–302.

Whelan, R., & Barnes-Holmes, D. (2004b). The transformation of consequential functions in accordance with the relational frames of same and opposite. *Journal of the Experimental Analysis of Behavior, 82,* 177–195.

Whelan, R., Barnes-Holmes, D., & Dymond, S. (2006). The transformation of consequential functions in accordance with the relational frames of more-than and less-than. *Journal of the Experimental Analysis of Behavior, 86*, 317–335.

Whelan, R., Cullinan, V., & O'Donovan, A. (2005). Derived same and opposite relations produce association and mediated priming. = Mismas Relaciones derivadas y Opuestas Producen la Asociación y la Preparación Mediada. *International Journal of Psychology & Psychological Therapy, 5*, 247–264.

Whelan, R., & Schlund, M. W. (2013). Reframing relational frame theory research: Gaining a new perspective through the application of novel behavioral and neurophysiological methods. In S. Dymond & B. Roche (Eds.), *Advances in relational frame theory: Research and application* (pp. 73–96). Oakland, CA: New Harbinger.

Wilson, K. G., & Hayes, S. C. (1996). Resurgence of derived stimulus relations. *Journal of the Experimental Analysis of Behavior, 66*, 267–281.

Wray, A. M., Dougher, M. J., Hamilton, D. A., & Guinther, P. M. (2012). Examining the reinforcing properties of making sense: A preliminary investigation. *The Psychological Record, 62*, 599–622.

Wulfert, E., & Hayes, S. C. (1988). Transfer of a conditional ordering response through conditional equivalence classes. *Journal of the Experimental Analysis of Behavior, 50*, 125–144.

Yamazaki, Y., Saiki, M., Inada, M., Iriki, A., & Watanabe, S. (2014). Transposition and its generalization in common marmosets. *Journal of Experimental Psychology: Animal Learning and Cognition, 40*, 317–326.

Yanchar, S. C., & Slife, B. D. (1997). Pursuing unity in a fragmented psychology: Problems and prospects. *Review of General Psychology, 1*, 235–255.

Zentall, T. R., Wasserman, E. A., & Urcuioli, P. J. (2014). Associative concept learning in animals. *Journal of the Experimental Analysis of Behavior, 101*, 130–151.

10

Relational Frame Theory
Implications for the Study of Human Language and Cognition
Sean Hughes and Dermot Barnes-Holmes

Introduction

Stop for a moment and imagine a childhood version of yourself, standing in your parents' garden on a warm summer's day. In your left hand lies a small green acorn, and in the right is a watering can filled to the brim. You scoop a little earth from the ground, bury the acorn, cover it up, and then splash some water over the soil. Every summer you return to the exact same spot and carefully tend to the seed, watching as it inches out of the ground and blooms into a small sapling and then a young tree. Now imagine many years later you return to your parents' garden and in the place of a seed stands a large oak whose roots are buried deep in the soil. You can see that its weather-worn trunk stretches up from the ground and reaches into the sky, and then splits into a dense tangle of branches, that each strike out in a different direction.

In many ways this metaphor reflects how researchers interested in relational frame theory (RFT) have approached the study of human language and cognition over the past two decades. In place of an acorn, they have planted the seed of a simple idea (that the ability to frame events relationally is a learned operant behavior) and have provided the necessary conditions (rigorous empirical scrutiny) for that seed to flourish and bloom into a progressive research program. The roots of this work are buried in a philosophical framework (functional contextualism) that specifies the assumptions, goals, and values of the researcher, and, by implication, the principles, theories, and methodologies that they draw upon. The weather-worn trunk reflects the transformation of the simple idea into an empirically grounded account (RFT) that describes how an advanced type of relational learning is acquired early on in our development and how that ability quickly grows in scale and complexity. For RFT researchers, this ability to frame events relationally is the common trunk from which many complex human behaviors spring forth. While these branches may certainly look different (given that they are characterized by different properties, types, and combinations of relational frames) they are each extensions of the same behavioral "trunk" or process. When conceptualized in this way, we see that RFT is a research enterprise whose roots (philosophy) ground and support its trunk (theory) which in turn splits into a variety of branches (basic and applied research).

The Wiley Handbook of Contextual Behavioral Science, First Edition. Edited by Robert D. Zettle, Steven C. Hayes, Dermot Barnes-Holmes, and Anthony Biglan.
© 2016 John Wiley & Sons, Ltd. Published 2016 by John Wiley & Sons, Ltd.

If the learned ability to relationally frame is the functional "seed" from which language and cognition grow, then this simple idea should give birth to research and application in domains where language and cognition are of known relevance. For instance, RFT should unlock new insights into analogical and metaphorical reasoning, rule-following, perspective-taking, thinking (fast and slow), problem-solving, and adapting in various ways to our social, physical, and verbal worlds. At the same time, it should also provide the basis for new approaches to psychological development, language interventions, and psychotherapy, not to mention ways for dealing with the (problematic) behavior of social groups, organizations, and societies. The handbook you are now reading is a testament to how RFT has met these challenges head on over the past two decades and delivered on many fronts. While other chapters in this section focus their attention on those branches of RFT which are yielding the most fruit and are growing at the greatest speed (education, psychopathology) our aim is different: To take in the canopy as a whole and describe how much of the richness of human psychology may stem from a limited set of explanatory principles. Given the sheer scope of the RFT literature we do not intend to review every empirical finding but rather to paint a picture of the theory in broad strokes, stopping to consider current themes and issues that are shaping research in this area (for book-length treatments see Dymond & Roche, 2013; Hayes, Barnes-Holmes, & Roche, 2001; Rehfeldt & Barnes-Holmes, 2009; Törneke, 2010).

In Section 1 we consider how the ability to relationally frame sets the stage for the emergence of language and how the former's generative and flexible nature accounts for much of the latter's utility. This section will also highlight how relational framing rapidly increases in both scale and complexity, expanding from the relating of individual stimuli to the relating of relational networks to other networks. As we shall see in Section 2, this leap in complexity gives rise to phenomena such as analogical and metaphorical reasoning, as well the ability to generate and follow rules or instructions. In Section 3 we turn our attention to the notion of "cognition" and consider how different types and properties of relational framing play a role in perspective-taking, intelligence, and implicit cognition. In Section 4 we conclude by providing a brief overview of the key achievements of RFT research to date. We hope that our brief synopsis will not only set the stage for those topics considered in the following chapters, but showcase a living, breathing research enterprise that has come a long way in a very short period of time. In each section we highlight current issues and emergent themes in the RFT literature and offer suggestions for future research in this area. We also describe how this theory sometimes connects with, and at other times departs from, alternative approaches in psychological science. However, by specifying variables that facilitate prediction-and-influence, RFT seems to extend beyond alternative accounts, providing a comprehensive, theoretically unified, empirically grounded, and practically applicable account of complex human behavior.[1]

Section 1: RFT and Language

A "language" (from the Latin root *lingua* or "tongue") is often considered to be a "system of symbols and rules that enable us to communicate," "symbols being things that stand for other things" (words) while "rules specify how words are ordered to form sentences" (Harley, 2013, p. 5). Although philosophers, psychologists, and linguists continue to debate the very definition of this phenomenon one thing is clear: From the cradle to the grave and nearly every day in between, humans are bathed in a sea of language. From early childhood they swim in conversation and weave stories about the past, present, and future. By adulthood they use written and spoken words to control their own and other people's behavior and to transmit information within and between generations. Throughout much of the past century scholars have sought to better understand the social, biological, and neural factors that underpin this ability, as well as to identify its core properties, structure, and function. During this time language has been conceptualized and studied in a wide variety of ways, from functional (behavioral), mental (computational), and statistical perspectives (connectionist models), to biological (physiological methods) and anthropological (cultural and cross-cultural) approaches.

As we saw in chapter 9, early efforts within the behavior-analytic tradition to extrapolate from the learning principles identified in nonhumans to the verbal behavior of our own species failed – amongst other things – to provide a satisfactory explanation for linguistic generativity or productivity (Chomsky, 1959; Skinner, 1957; although see Barnes-Holmes, Barnes-Holmes, and Cullinan, 2000). This contributed – in part – to the historical shift away from functional analyses of behavior–environment interactions and towards accounts interested in the mental mechanics of language. Researchers increasingly switched their focus to the mental level of analysis and began postulating hypothetical or "computational" mechanisms to explain how language was acquired and used. Emphasis on historical and environmental factors took a backseat to questions about the neural (Christiansen & Chater, 2008) and genetic architecture (Pinker & Jackendoff, 2005) that is assumed to realize and transmit these mechanisms within and between successive generations (see also Berwick, Friederici, Chomsky, & Bolhuis, 2013; Christiansen & Kirby, 2003). Although there are nontrivial differences across such accounts they typically conceptualize language *mechanistically* as being similar to a machine, composed of discrete parts that interact and are subject to specific operating conditions. At the same time, they often conceptualize language *mentalistically* as being mediated by a specific set of mental or computational processes which facilitate linguistic comprehension and production. This has resulted in an emphasis on the structural properties of language (morphology, syntax, and phonology) as well as the mental mechanisms and knowledge representations necessary for its development and operation (for a far more detailed treatment see Altmann, 2001; Berwick et al., 2013; Chomsky, 2011; Harley, 2013; Traxler, 2012).

Language at the Functional Level of Analysis

Critically, and despite frequent suggestions to the contrary, the empirical and conceptual analysis of language within the behavior-analytic tradition did not flicker and die with Chomsky's critique of Skinner's work. Over the intervening years, research on rule-governed behavior, stimulus equivalence, and derived stimulus relating pointed to possible behavioral processes that were missing from Skinner's direct contingency account, processes that seemed unique to, or at least largely elaborated in, our own species relative to others (see chapter 9). A new functional approach to language and cognition began to take shape, one that was philosophically and conceptually rooted in, and yet extended far beyond, Skinner's original account. This work did not, and could not, ape developments at the mental level of analysis due to its scientific goals, values, and assumptions. Rather this work sought to better understand how the social and physical environment shapes and maintains *verbal behavior*.[2] Questions about the mental mechanics of language were substituted for those that focused on those ongoing streams of organism–environment interactions, considered both historically and situationally, that would facilitate the prediction-and-influence of this phenomenon. For instance, what type of behavior are we talking about when we refer to "verbal behavior" and what are the environmental factors of which it is a function? How can we account for its generativity, flexibility, and symbolic nature in purely functional (nonmental) terms? Could a limited set of learning principles and behavioral processes really account for the movement from simple to increasingly complex verbal behavior in a coherent and parsimonious manner? Was this ability genetically hardwired or acquired through ongoing interaction in and with the environment, and, if the latter is true, then how precisely does it develop?

Language as RFT researchers see it. Drawing on over four decades of research, RFT has begun to offer answers to these and a host of related questions (see Dymond & Roche, 2013). According to this perspective, in order to understand verbal behavior we first need to understand a learned, generalized, and contextually controlled type of operant behavior known as arbitrarily applicable relational responding (AARR). This is because the former is argued to be an instance of the latter. As we discussed in chapter 9, *relating* refers to a generalized pattern of behavior that involves responding to at least one stimulus in terms of at least one other stimulus. Many different species can relate stimuli based on their formal or physical properties and these behaviors are defined as *nonarbitrarily applicable relational responses* or NAARR. Critically, however, humans display all the hallmarks of a more advanced type of relational behavior that allows for stimuli to be related regardless of their physical properties and in ways that were never reinforced in the past. These latter outcomes are defined as instances of AARR and demonstrate three core properties known as mutual entailment, combinatorial entailment, and the transformation of function. There are many different patterns of AARR, or relational framing, and each is a type of operant behavior that is learned through ongoing interactions in and with the socio-verbal community.

The origins of verbal behavior. The earliest examples of such interactions begin in childhood and are designed to establish the most rudimentary form of AARR – namely mutually entailed coordination relations between one stimulus (e.g., a word) and another (e.g., its referent). As we saw in chapter 9, this usually involves uttering the name of an object in the presence of an infant and then reinforcing orientating responses towards that item (i.e., hear word → look for object). At other times the object itself is presented to the child and appropriate auditory responses reinforced (i.e., see object → say word). Both of these interactions will take place in the presence of contextual cues, and in natural language interactions these cues typically take the form of questions such as "*What is this?*" or "*Where is the…?*"

In the language of RFT, bidirectional responding to an object and its name is being differentially reinforced in the presence of a contextual cue. Each and every day children encounter thousands of training exemplars with feedback for these and other relational responses. Although the stimuli, people, and contexts involved in training bidirectional responding change across time, the functional relation between the object and its referent is always held constant: The child's relational responding is reinforced in both directions and in the presence of arbitrary contextual cues.

> Eventually after a sufficient number of exemplars, the generalized response pattern of object–word symmetry is abstracted away from the topography of objects and brought under the control of contextual cues so that mutual entailment (i.e., being able to derive the untaught response when trained in only one direction) with any new word–object pair becomes possible. (Stewart & Roche, 2013, p. 59)

A child with this repertoire can now derive an untaught bidirectional relation from a trained relation, irrespective of the physical features of the word–object pair. For instance, presenting the child with a novel object (zebra) and relating that object to a word she has never encountered before ("zebra") in the presence of certain contextual cues will lead her to respond in a bidirectional manner. This occurs because the cues coupled with a history of unidirectional responding is highly predictive of reinforcement for bidirectional responding (e.g., she will point to the zebra when asked "Where is the zebra" and answer with "zebra" when asked "What is this?"). In the language of RFT, this bidirectional relation between an object and word represents an instance of mutually entailed coordination wherein a word is treated as functionally similar to its referent. In everyday language we could say that the child has learned how to name.

This history of multiple exemplar training (MET) sets the stage for more complex and varied types of relational responses to emerge and develop, such as the ability to relate mutually entailed relations to other mutually entailed relations (i.e., to combinatorially entail). For instance, once a history of reinforcement for bidirectional responding in the presence of arbitrary contextual cues is in place, pointing towards a picture of a flower (A) and saying "*This is a bloem*" will likely cause the child to emit a number of mutually entailed responses (e.g., asking "*What is that?*" will result in her saying the word *bloem* (B) while simply saying "*Where is the bloem*" will lead her to point towards the picture of the flower (A)). In addition, a second relation may also be established between the spoken word *bloem* (B) and a new stimulus (the written word BLOEM (C)) by uttering the spoken word (B) and then reinforcing orientating responses towards the written word (C) (i.e., hear spoken word → look at written word). In many cases, caregivers will also orientate the child towards the written word (C) (e.g., by pointing to it) and then model or reinforce appropriate responses (see the written word → emit the spoken word). Once again, these relational responses will be trained in both directions in the presence of certain contextual cues across different situations, stimuli and populations. Following sufficient exemplars and training, the child will come to emit not only mutual but combinatorially entailed relations without any further reinforcement. Now when a new picture (A) is related to a spoken word (B) which is in turn related to a written word (C) the child will respond to those stimuli in ways that were never directly trained or instructed. For instance, she will act as if the picture is the same as the written word, the spoken word is the same as the picture, and as if the written word is the same as the spoken word and picture. In the language of RFT, the child has been exposed to a set of contingencies that reinforce bidirectional responding to the arbitrary relation between *two or more* stimuli (i.e., she has learned how to combinatorially entail). In everyday language we could say that the child has learned how to treat pictures, written, and spoken words as mutually substitutable stimuli that "stand" for one another.

Expansion of linguistic abilities. The complexity of relational responding rapidly accelerates once children learn how to mutually and combinatorially entail relations between large numbers of stimuli in ways that extend above and beyond coordination. While the precise order and sequence in which relations are learned has yet to be empirically determined it appears that children initially learn how to AARR in accordance with sameness or coordination relations (Lipkens, Hayes, & Hayes, 1993; Luciano, Gómez-Becerra, & Rodríguez-Valverde, 2007). Thereafter they quickly learn how to relate stimuli in a vast number of different ways, responding to objects and events on the basis of frames of distinction ("A is different to B"), opposition ("A is opposite to B"), comparison ("A is heavier than B"), hierarchy ("A is part of B"), temporality ("A comes after B"), causality ("A causes B"), conditionality ("A is a condition for B"), and deictics ("A is mine and B is yours") to name but a few. Research indicates that these frames are typically established via a similar history of MET as described above and appear to emerge in a logical and interdependent fashion, starting simple and growing in complexity (e.g., Barnes-Holmes, Barnes-Holmes, Smeets, Strand, & Friman, 2004; Berens & Hayes, 2007; Carpentier, Smeets, & Barnes-Holmes, 2003; Gorham, Barnes-Holmes, Barnes-Holmes, & Berens, 2009; see also Rehfeldt & Barnes-Holmes, 2009).

The scale and complexity of these relations grows even further as (a) more and more stimuli come to be related via direct training or derivation and (b) children learn how to relate entire relations to other relations under contextual control. These "networks" of relations are themselves comprised of multiple relational frames and continue to grow in complexity as children interact with the wider socio-verbal community. To illustrate, consider only a fraction of the possible relations which surround a given word in everyday use, such as "laptop." This stimulus is part of many hierarchical relations, such as the relational network "noun," or "electronic devices." Other terms are in a hierarchical relation with it, such as "hard drive" or "screen." It enters into many comparisons: It is better than a calculator, bigger than a watch, heavier than a feather. It is the same as computer, but different to a house, and so on.

> The participation of the word "laptop" in these relations is part of the training required for the verbal community to use the stimulus "laptop" in the way that it does. Even the simplest verbal concept quickly becomes the focus of a complex network of stimulus relations in natural language use. (Hayes et al., 2001, p. 40)

In other words, as a child continues to interact with the socio-verbal community entire relations are combined in increasingly complex ways to form an elaborate and ever-growing network of related stimuli. According to RFT, the expansion of this network likely begins in infancy when we first learn to frame words and objects in coordination with one another and continues throughout the rest of our lives.

> As children grow into adulthood, continued verbal interactions produce an increasingly complex and multi-relational network involving vast numbers of different objects and events and the relations between them … everything we encounter and think about, including ourselves, our thoughts and emotions, our prospects, other people, and our environment, becomes part of this elaborate verbal relational network. (Stewart & Roche, 2013, p. 66)[3]

The Generative and Flexible Nature of Relational Framing

The ability to relationally frame is quite simply a game changer. Learning how to relate stimuli and events in an arbitrarily applicable fashion equips humans with an extraordinarily efficient and generative means of interacting with the world around them. Once a sophisticated repertoire of framing is in place, any stimulus, regardless of what it looks, smells, tastes, sounds, or feels like, can be related to any other stimulus in a near infinite number of ways. Arbitrary symbols such as written and spoken words, mathematical and scientific notation, pictures and images can be related to each other as well as physical objects in the environment, transforming the psychological properties of those stimuli. Indeed, the flick of a wrist, a grunt, raised eyebrow, frown, or virtually any discrete event may become a "verbal stimulus" when it participates in a relational network with other stimuli and has its functions altered as a result. Thus, from an RFT point of view, when we speak of the capacity for stimuli to "stand for" or "symbolize" other stimuli in the environment we are actually speaking of the participation of those stimuli in derived stimulus relations. It is this type of generalized contextually controlled operant which endows language with its characteristic symbolism and flexibility.

The generative implications of AARR are also spectacular. A single specified relation between two sets of related events might give rise to myriad derived relations in an instant. To illustrate, imagine you are informed that the word *money* is the same as *geld* which in turn is the same as *dinero*. From these two directly trained relations (*money–geld* and *geld–dinero*) you can derive four additional untrained relations (*money–dinero, dinero–money, geld–money*, and *dinero–geld*). Now imagine a second scenario in which three more stimuli are related to one another (*argent, soldi*, and *pengar*). Once again, four new relations will be derived, and when the first relation is related to the second, 16 new relations can be derived between and among stimuli. Indeed, the generativity of AARR is such that by the time that eight stimulus relations are established, several thousand derived relations can emerge "because every stimulus and relationship between and among stimuli can be related one to the other in all directions" (Hayes, 2012). Put simply, the ratio of derived to trained relations seems to grow exponentially as humans learn to relate increasing numbers of stimuli in increasingly complex ways. This may help to explain how humans develop a repertoire of tens of thousands of interrelated verbal stimuli without the need for the socioverbal community to directly reinforce those relations in all directions.[4]

At the same time, when stimuli participate in derived relations they can acquire entirely new functions, or have their existing functions spontaneously modified or extinguished. For instance, establishing a coordination relation between the words *emergency, noodgeval*, and *akut* may result in a transfer of function from the former to the latter, such that people will respond in broadly similar ways in the presence of these respective stimuli. They may shout *noodgeval* when threatened during a trip to Belgium, or quickly orientate towards someone screaming *akut* while in Sweden. However, learning that the word *veiligheid* is opposite to *emergency* which is in turn opposite to *säkerhet* will not occasion similar patterns of behavior as above. Rather these stimuli will acquire novel functions in accordance with the derived relations in which they participate (i.e., both words may be taken to mean "safety"). Thus, from an RFT point of view, the transformation of function through derived stimulus relations may account for much of language's productivity (i.e., how novel words, sentences, and solutions to problems are "generated" in the absence of direct reinforcement) (for more see Stewart, McElwee, & Ming, 2013).

Empirical links between derived stimulus relating and language. Evidence for a strong relationship between language and the ability to derive relations between stimuli has emerged on several fronts. First, verbally trained humans appear to derive with remarkable ease and sophistication. Yet several decades of work suggests that their nonhuman (and arguably nonverbal) counterparts find it difficult to demonstrate even the most rudimentary properties of such behavior (Hughes & Barnes-Holmes, 2014; Lionello-DeNolf, 2009; Zentall, Wasserman, & Urcuioli, 2014). Second, the capacity to derive relations develops and grows in complexity around the same time as children start to show evidence of language (Luciano et al., 2007), while brain-imaging studies indicate that relational responding produces similar patterns of neural activity as seen when humans perform linguistic tasks (Barnes-Holmes et al., 2005; Whelan, Cullinan, & O'Donovan, 2005). Third, individuals with linguistic deficits demonstrate impairments in their ability to derive relations between stimuli (Barnes, McCullagh, & Keenan, 1990) and providing remedial training in how to do so leads to corresponding improvements in linguistic skills (Murphy & Barnes-Holmes, 2010a, 2010b; Persicke, Tarbox, Ranick, & St. Clair, 2012; Rosales & Rehfeldt, 2007; Walsh, Horgan, May, Dymond, & Whelan, 2014; see also Rehfeldt & Barnes-Holmes, 2009; Stewart, McElwee, et al., 2013). Finally, the fluency and flexibility of derived stimulus relating in normally developing populations consistently correlates with performance on other linguistic tasks (O'Hora et al., 2008; O'Toole & Barnes-Holmes, 2009; Whelan et al., 2005) while training designed to improve the former leads to corresponding improvements in the latter (e.g., Cassidy, Roche, & Hayes, 2011).

Critically, an empirical relationship does not indicate that derived stimulus relations depend upon language or that such relations are mediated by language, although some researchers have adopted this position for theoretical reasons (e.g., Greer & Longano, 2010; Horne & Lowe, 1996). Nor does it indicate that language depends upon derived stimulus relations, although others have gravitated towards this interpretation as well (see Sidman, 1994). Rather, when two dependent variables are correlated, one conservative strategy is to determine whether both variables are reflective of the same basic underlying psychological process. It could be that the correlation between linguistic ability and derived stimulus relations occurs because both are instances of the same general behavioral process (i.e., AARR). If the two do overlap at the level of behavioral process, then questions about human language may also be questions about derived stimulus relations, and vice versa. This is the basic empirical and theoretical strategy that RFT researchers have adopted over the past 20 years (i.e., that the ability to "language" and derived relations between stimuli are both instances of a learned, generalized, and contextually controlled type of operant behavior known as arbitrarily applicable relational responding).

Summary. At its core, RFT argues that, during our early development, we effectively "learn how to language": We are provided with a history of learning which involves learning how to respond relationally to stimuli based on aspects of the context that specify the relation. Thus, when we speak of language or verbal behavior we are actually referring to *"the action of framing events relationally."* Stimuli such as spoken or written words, mathematical or scientific notation, as well as pictures and signs become "verbal stimuli" when they participate in relational networks with contextual cues, the latter of which help establish the meaning or psychological functions of the stimuli for the language user. Likewise, a speaker is said to *"speak with meaning"* whenever they frame events relationally and produce sequences of verbal stimuli as a result. A listener is said to *"listen with understanding"* whenever they respond as a result of framing events relationally. Thus verbal meaning and understanding do not reflect the operation or outcome of some mediating mental event but rather constitute a type of contextually controlled operant behavior.

Section 2: From Simplicity to Complexity – Analogies, Metaphors, Rules, and Instructions

So far we have offered a broad introduction to language from an RFT point of view. We have defined this phenomenon as the act of relational framing, described how it is established during infancy, and highlighted how its generativity and productivity arise from the ability to AARR. An important test for any psychological theory of language, however, is the extent to which it allows the researcher to predict and influence increasingly complex verbal behaviors, such as the ability to create and comprehend analogies, metaphors, rules, or instructions. In what follows we demonstrate how RFT accommodates each of these phenomena by making just one small leap in conceptual complexity – namely from the notion that stimuli can be related, to the idea that relations themselves can be related to other relations.

Analogical Reasoning

Analogies refer to the relating of two situations or analogues based on a common set of relationships that exist between and among their constituent elements. The core idea is that knowledge is transferred from a more familiar or better understood analogue (termed the base) to a second analogue (termed the target).

> By "better understood" we mean that the person has prior knowledge about functional relations within the source analog – beliefs that certain aspects of the source have causal, explanatory, or logical connections to other aspects ... This asymmetry in initial knowledge provides the basis for analogical transfer (i.e., the source is used by the person to generate inferences about the target). (Holyoak, 2012, p. 234)

To illustrate this more clearly, consider the analogy: "*Blizzard is to snowflake as army is to soldier.*" Here you transfer what you currently know about the source relation (blizzards and snowflakes) to the target relation (army and soldiers) by assessing the relationship within and between these two domains (i.e., that armies are comprised of soldiers in much the same way that blizzards are comprised of snowflakes). In this way, analogical reasoning represents a means by which existing knowledge about stimuli and events in one area can be used to guide behavior towards novel stimuli in new contexts.

The ability to generate and understand analogies is thought to be one of the most important and sophisticated aspects of human intelligence and the former is argued to be central to the development of the latter (e.g., Sternberg, 1977). Analogies are important vehicles for communicating in educational and scientific settings, they facilitate problem-solving (Barnett & Ceci, 2002), underpin creativity (Mayer, 1999), aid scientific discovery (Holyoak & Thagard, 1995), play a prominent role in certain psychotherapies (Hayes, Strosahl, & Wilson, 1999) and frequently predict academic success (Kuncel, Hezlett & Ones, 2004). According to RFT, analogical reasoning is a

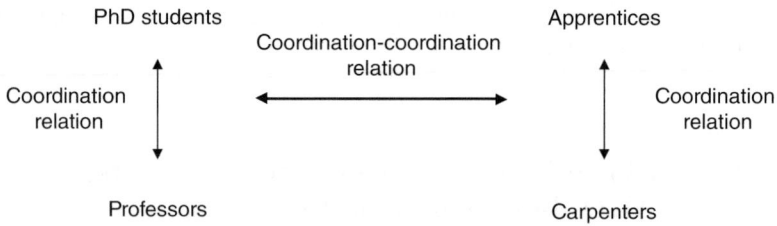

Figure 10.1   The analogy denoted as "PhD students:professors::apprentices:carpenters" and the relations between and among those elements.

complex or "higher-order" instance of AARR wherein entire stimulus relations are related to one another (Stewart, Barnes-Holmes, Hayes, & Lipkens, 2001; Stewart, Barnes-Holmes, & Weil, 2009). In other words, two relations are deemed to be analogous (i.e., related analogically) if the trained or derived relations in the "base" relation are placed in a frame of coordination with the trained or derived relations in the "target" relation.

To illustrate this more clearly, take a look at Figure 10.1. This relational network can be described in analogical terms as "PhD students are to professors as apprentices are to carpenters" and denoted as A:B::C:D. In the language of RFT, this analogy consists of an overarching coordination relation between two other arbitrary coordination relations. On the one hand, a contextual cue ("*are to*") serves to establish that the words "PhD students" and "professors" are coordinated along some unspecified dimension. For many individuals this relation is likely based on the fact that students and professors are members of the same general class of stimuli known as "academics" (although in principle this relation could also be based on other properties of the stimuli involved such as their occupational status, expertise, age, and so on). On the other hand, the above cue also serves to establish a second coordination relation between the words "apprentice" and "carpenter," and for many people, this relation is likely based on the fact that both are members of a general stimulus class known as "tradesmen" (although once again this relation may be based on other stimulus properties such as their skill or age). Finally, another contextual cue ("as") serves to establish an overarching coordination relation between the two relations outlined above (i.e., "PhD students are to professors" (coordination relation) "as" (coordination relation) "apprentices are to carpenters" (coordination relation)). This overarching relation specifies that the similarity between students and professors in the first relation is the same as the similarity between an apprentice and carpenter in the second relation (i.e., it involves an abstraction of a similarity between similarities).

Several points are worth noting here. First, analogies do not require that stimuli within the first or second relation be related on the basis of coordination; they can also be related in a variety of different ways. For instance, the contextual cue "is to" in the following analogies, "*dark is to light as laugh is to cry*" or "*spring is to season as August is to month*," specifies that stimuli are related in opposition or hierarchically with one another. Nevertheless, in most analogies, the former relation is nearly always framed in coordination with the latter relation via the contextual cue "as." Second, the contextual cue that controls how stimuli are related in the "base" relation always controls how stimuli are related in the "target" relation. Thus if the contextual cue specifies a distinction relation for the "base" ("*baby is to adult*") it will do so for the "target" (as *"puppy is to dog"*); if it specifies a hierarchical relation for the "base" (*"stem is to flower"*) it will do so for the "target" (as *"trunk is to tree"*) and so on. Third, the relations within analogies can often be traced back to the physical or non-arbitrary properties of the stimuli involved. Consider the following analogy: "*a planet is to a star as an electron is to an atomic nucleus.*" In this case, the arbitrary coordination relation between the words "planet" and "star" is based, to some extent, on the coordination of physical properties shared by the actual stimuli with which the words are coordinated (e.g., the former are usually smaller than and orbit the latter). Likewise, the arbitrary coordination relation between the words "electron" and "atomic nucleus" is based on the shared physical properties between these two stimuli (e.g., the former are usually smaller than and orbit the latter). Although the two coordination relations and the overarching coordination relation between them is entirely arbitrary in nature (there are no physical similarities shared by the words or between the words and the objects that they refer to), they can readily be traced back to shared nonarbitrary features. Put simply, the contextual cue ("is") specifies that just as planets share some nonarbitrary properties with stars so do electrons with atomic nuclei. In this way, nonarbitrary stimulus features may influence the derivation of coordination relations (see Stewart, Barnes-Holmes, Roche, & Smeets, 2002). Finally, an individual's history of learning will influence the pattern of derived relations that will take place within a given analogy. In the above example, for instance, you might abstract the category (i.e., celestial and atomic particles) first and only abstract the nonarbitrary properties (e.g., size and shape) thereafter.

Accumulating evidence supports the notion that coordinate framing of derived relations provides a good model of analogical reasoning (e.g., Barnes, Hegarty, & Smeets, 1997; Barnes-Holmes et al., 2005; Carpentier, Smeets, & Barnes Holmes, 2002; Carpentier, Smeets, Barnes-Holmes, & Stewart, 2004; Lipkens & Hayes, 2009; Ruiz & Luciano, 2011). Much of this work has focused on the history of learning that gives rise to the creation and solution of analogies in the laboratory. In a seminal study, Barnes et al. (1997) provided the first RFT model of analogical reasoning as the derivation of equivalence relations between equivalence relations or "equivalence–equivalence" responding. In this experiment participants were exposed to a learning task designed to establish a number of coordination relations between arbitrary stimuli. A matching-to-sample (MTS) task presented a "sample" stimulus in the middle of the screen (e.g., A1) and reinforced the selection of one of four "comparison" stimuli at the bottom of the screen (e.g., B1, B2, B3, and B4). In this way participants learned via training that stimuli were related on the basis of coordination (e.g., A1-same-B1) and distinction (e.g., A1 different from B2, B3, or B4). Thereafter, a test for mutual and combinatorial entailment was administered to see if derived stimulus relations emerged as expected. In the final section of the task participants were exposed to an "analogy test" that was similar in many ways to the learning task they encountered before but with one key difference: This time the task was comprised of two different types of trials known as similar–similar or different–different trials. During the former the sample stimulus in the middle of the screen was always a compound of a combinatorially entailed relation of sameness (e.g., B1C1) while the comparison stimuli at the bottom of the screen were either a compound stimulus formed by a combinatorially entailed relation of sameness (B3C3) or distinction (A3C4). Different–different trials were similar but this time the sample stimulus was a combinatorially entailed relation of distinction. In the language of RFT, this "analogy test" was designed to see if participants would relate two derived coordination or distinction relations to each other in accordance with a frame of coordination (i.e., relationally frame one relation as being coordinated with another relation). This is precisely what the authors found, with adults as well as 9- and 12-year-old children readily passing the analogical test when provided with sufficient training (see also Pérez, García, & Gomez, 2011; Ruiz & Luciano, 2012).

Numerous studies have now extended this analysis by examining analogical reasoning in different age groups, with different measures, relations, and domains. For instance, Carpentier and colleagues (2002, 2003) found that five-year old children, unlike their nine-year-old and adult counterparts, experience considerable difficulties when exposed to a similar task as above and only demonstrated such performances when provided with extensive training. These results mirror the developmental divide observed in the analogical literature between children in early and late childhood (Sternberg & Rifkin, 1979) and suggest that the ability to create analogies emerges in parallel with the overall ability to frame events relationally. A number of RFT researchers have also sought to devise a more sophisticated means of experimentally establishing analogies using a task known as the Relational Evaluation Procedure (REP; Stewart, Barnes-Holmes, & Roche, 2004).

In yet other research, relating derived relations, as a model of analogy, was measured using reaction times and event-related potentials (ERPs). This work demonstrated that analogical responses that were lower (similar–similar) relative to higher in complexity (different–different) were emitted with greater speed and were underpinned by different patterns of neural activity in the left-hemispheric prefrontal regions (Barnes-Holmes et al., 2005). Interestingly, this pattern of neural activity mirrors that seen elsewhere in the neurocognitive literature (Luo et al., 2003) and suggests that similar brain regions are recruited when people AARR in this way or solve analogies. More recently, Lipkens and Hayes (2009) demonstrated that the coordinated relating of opposition and comparative relations could also be used to engineer analogies in the laboratory. At the same time, they found that directly training an analogy between two relations allowed participants to derive a number of untrained analogies between novel events. Finally, Ruiz and Luciano (2011) extended the RFT model of analogy by training and testing "cross-domain" analogies which they defined as the relation of relations in separate relational networks. Whereas the work discussed thus far focused on within-domain analogies ("*curing a stomach tumor is like curing a lung tumor*"), cross-domain analogies involve the transfer of knowledge from one domain to a completely unrelated domain ("*curing a stomach tumor is like capturing an enemy fortress*"). The authors found that such analogies could be established via a history of MET and that performance during their experimental procedure strongly correlated with that on a standard measure of analogical reasoning.

Summary and future directions. Taken together, the above work suggests that the ability to create and solve analogies arises from the coordinated relating of derived relations. This type of higher-order relational responding allows for entire classes of responses to impact other classes, providing one potential explanation for the generativity seen in human language and cognition. Although RFT researchers have made rapid strides in this domain many questions still need to be addressed. First, can transformations of functions through analogical frames be experimentally modelled (see Stewart, Barnes-Holmes, Roche, & Smeets, 2002), and is it possible to engineer this type of relational responding where it was previously absent or weak? Work in this area has typically focused on establishing instances of analogical reasoning in the laboratory using adults and children who could already analogically frame (but see Carpentier et al., 2002). A stronger demonstration would involve establishing analogical reasoning in cases where it was previously absent. Second, the role of nonarbitrary stimulus properties in analogical reasoning also requires attention (Stewart, Barrett, McHugh, Barnes-Holmes, & O'Hora, 2013) as does the role of analogical reasoning in psychopathology and psychotherapy (Foody et al., 2014). Third, applied researchers will need to determine if the above work can be translated into educational and intellectual interventions that directly target and remediate deficits in analogical framing in normative and developmentally delayed populations (see Persicke et al., 2012; Stewart et al., 2009). Those same researchers could take such educational strategies one step further and determine whether advanced training in analogical reasoning actually promotes other types of behaviors such as creativity or intelligence. We will return to this issue later in the chapter.

Metaphorical Reasoning

Metaphors represent a subclass of analogies that rapidly transfer a characteristic that is highly evident in one event (usually termed the "vehicle") to a different event ("target"). They are like "linguistic chauffeurs," who ferry information about a known domain to an unknown or less known domain, and, as a result, change how we respond to the latter based on what we know about the former. Metaphors are woven into the very fabric of language and are essential for effective communication. For instance, we speak of relationships as "train-wrecks," political debates as taking place "in arenas" where "one side battles the other," exams as being "a walk in the park," or novel insights as requiring "thinking outside the box." Our parents are "dependable as a rock," brothers are "pig-headed," and even the world can be seen as a stage, "all the men and women merely players who have their exits and their entrances."

According to RFT, this "rapid transfer of a characteristic" from the vehicle to the target refers to the transformation of function that occurs when entire relations are related to other relations. Interestingly, metaphors seem to be characterized by a number of properties that distinguish them from their analogical counterparts. Foremost amongst these is the role that nonarbitrary or physical properties of stimuli (or the relationship between stimuli) play in analogies and metaphors. Analogies can, but need not be, based on the physical relations that exist between and among stimuli: RFT studies like those highlighted above indicate that people can analogically respond in ways that do not depend on the physical properties of the stimuli involved. However, the psychological effects of metaphors are mainly due to the physical properties of stimuli involved in the relating of relations (see Stewart & Barnes-Holmes, 2001, for a detailed discussion).

To illustrate, consider the metaphor: "*surfing the net*" which implies that using the Internet is similar to surfing waves in the ocean. In the language of RFT, this metaphor involves two separate relational networks that are (a) framed in coordination with one another and which (b) involve a physical dimension or relation that (c) modifies and transforms the functions of stimuli participating in those relational networks. In the above example, we have specified two events (surfing waves of water and surfing information on the Internet) that participate in separate relational networks and which are characterized by a variety of psychological functions. The above statement serves to arbitrarily frame those stimuli as coordinated with one another. In many ways this metaphor is functionally similar to the type of analogies described previously: "surfing" (A) is to "water" (B) as "surfing" (C) is to "the Internet" (D). However, it is characterized by a number of properties that suggest a definition in terms of metaphor may be more apt. For instance, the focus on surfing is transferred from the domain of watersports, where it is physically applicable, to that of the Internet, where it is metaphorically applicable (i.e., a transformation of function from actual surfing to information retrieval). Stated more precisely, the coordinated relating of two relational networks leads to the functions of stimuli in the "vehicle" relation (surfing in the ocean) transforming the functions of the "target" relation (surfing the Internet). For example, through the metaphor a person may derive that just as surfing in the ocean is an enjoyable but effortful exercise so too is swimming through the vast ocean of information that exists on the Internet. In other words, the effectiveness of a metaphor depends, in large part, upon the discrimination of formal stimulus dimensions that provide the ground for the metaphor, such as the perceptual/functional similarity between surfing in the ocean and "surfing" currents of information.

Analogies and metaphors also tend to differ in their directionality. At their most basic, both involve two events (A and B) that are related in the following fashion: "A is (like) B." In the case of many analogies, the position of the A and B terms may be swapped and the result is still meaningful. For example, in the analogy "*an atom is like the solar system*" swapping the order of A and B yields a valid and understandable analogy (*the solar system is like an atom*). In the language of RFT, analogies involve a coordination relation between derived relations and reversing the order in which these relations are coordinated often yields broadly similar transformations of function. However, in the case of metaphor, if the A and B terms are swapped, the phrase loses it metaphorical quality: While the statement "*my father is a pig*" makes sense the reverse does not ("*a pig is my father*"). Metaphors such as this work because the A and B terms have a property in common that is obvious and stereotypical in the case of B (pigs) but not A (fathers). Furthermore, for the metaphor to work from a listener's perspective, the father in question must possess, if only weakly, some of the functions of actual pigs, such as being slightly overweight, displaying poor eating habits, and generally being quite messy. In the language of RFT, two relational networks are framed in coordination with one another (fathers and pigs), but comparative or hierarchical relations also seem to be involved in the transformation of functions that gives the metaphor its linguistic power. In the above metaphor we could consider "pig" as the superordinate category and its dominant properties (e.g., poor eating habits) as subordinate categories with which the target may be coordinated (my father eats like a pig). In other words, metaphors lead us to relate a target (father) and vehicle (pig) in a hierarchical fashion, and thus the direction of the metaphor is not readily reversible. In this way, the unidirectional, hierarchical relating of derived relations may be an important means of functionally distinguishing metaphors from analogies.

Future directions. Surprisingly, the distinction between *creating* versus *comprehending* metaphors, as well as the difference between metaphors and analogy has yet to be empirically modelled in the laboratory. Nor has metaphor been subjected to empirical scrutiny within the RFT literature since its original theoretical treatment well over a decade ago. This is despite the fact that RFT provides clear, testable predictions about the origins and properties of metaphorical reasoning, its relationship to analogical reasoning, not to mention technologies for establishing this ability where previously absent or weak (see Persicke et al., 2012). The same goes for functionally similar phenomena such as allegory, anecdote, simile, parable, storytelling, and humor, which also seem to involve the relating of relations to other relations, but under different forms of contextual control (Stewart et al., 2001). Thus a rich, deep vein of research with seemingly wide-scale implications for many areas of psychological science has yet to be mined.

A functionally understood account of metaphor will not only convey theoretical benefits (by deepening our understanding of complex relational responding) but also offer practical value for those working in the applied wings of CBS. For many years now, clinicians and scholars have recognized that metaphors are effective tools for combating human suffering (e.g., Hayes et al., 1999; McCurry & Hayes, 1992; Orsillo & Batten, 2005). Within the ACT literature, for example, metaphors have been argued to "promote the deliteralization of psychological content in a way that allows a person to experientially step out of their existing language system, and thus be less susceptible to the effects of 'cognitive fusion,' wherein certain types of unhelpful transformations of functions occur" (Foody et al., 2014, p. 14). To illustrate this more clearly, consider the following metaphor which is frequently used in clinical settings: "*struggling with anxiety is like struggling in quicksand*." In this case, two relations (struggling with anxiety versus struggling with quicksand) are coordinated via the contextual cue "is like" which results in the transformation of functions (struggling in the context of a difficult situation) from the domain of quicksand, where it is physically applicable, to that of anxiety, where it is metaphorically applicable.

> In other words, quicksand is the prototypical context in which the salience of struggling is highlighted and coordinating this with anxiety serves to highlight the futility of struggling there also, a fact that was not previously salient to the client. The salience of the futility of struggling is, therefore, only abstracted via the contextual cue for coordination between the two contexts. (Foody et al., 2014, p. 17)

An avalanche of ACT studies have emerged over the past decade and have drawn upon metaphors (amongst other clinical tools) to address a wide spectrum of psychological problems. If we are to better understand the effectiveness of existing (and create new) metaphors in clinical contexts then we will need to subject RFT's account of this phenomenon to far closer empirical scrutiny. For instance, an experimental analysis of metaphor will need to be offered and the role of noncoordinate frames (causal, hierarchical, and comparative) accounted for. Given that metaphors play a critical role in experimental analogues of (McMullen et al., 2008) and acceptance-based interventions targeting psychopathology (e.g., Bach & Hayes, 2002; Twohig, Hayes, Masdua, 2006) these questions will need to be asked and answered soon. This work may require that we pay special attention to the role of deictic frames in particular. Clinical metaphors are usually employed to produce a shift in perspective in the client's view of their own psychological suffering (e.g., seeing struggling with anxiety as the problem rather than the solution). The next logical step then is to explore the role of deictics and other relational frames in (clinical) metaphors. Other researchers could also consider how explicit training in the use of metaphors stimulates scientific creativity, improves educational outcomes, as well as our capacity to solve social problems and make real-world decisions (Thibodeau & Boroditsky, 2011). Still others could examine how AARR gives rise to "unstated metaphors." For instance,

> when we say "I shot down his argument," or "He couldn't defend his position," or "She attacked my theory," we are alluding to an unstated metaphor that argument is war. Similarly, to say "Our marriage is at a crossroads," or "We've come a long way together," or "He decided to bail out of the relationship" is to assume metaphorically that love is a journey. (Pinker, 2006, p. 2)

Summary. In short, analogies and metaphors are woven into the very fabric of language and RFT provides a functional account of their origins and properties. While several branches of this research literature have bloomed and flourished (analogy) others will need careful cultivation in the coming years (metaphor), especially given their practical utility in clinical and educational domains. Finally, the foregoing analysis highlights how the basic ideas of RFT can yield tangible benefits for those in the applied wing of CBS. This theory not only explains how metaphors acquire their psychological power but also suggests methods for developing effective clinical metaphors that can alter the way in which people frame events in the world around them.

Rules and Instructions

The ability to generate and apply rules to our own behavior (as well as that of others) is a fundamental avenue through which humans adapt to the world around them. Self or socially generated rules allow us to set and achieve goals (O'Hora & Maglieri, 2006), delay immediate gratification, and even deal with events before they occur (e.g., "*Mow my lawn next month and I will pay you afterwards*"; Doll, Jacobs, Sanfey, & Frank, 2009). Rules or instructions allow us to respond to consequences that are extremely abstract in nature (e.g., "*only honest people go to Heaven*") as well as indirectly profit from other people's experiences. For instance, a person can respond to the rule "*If you drink bleach, you will die*" without having to engage in the behavior of drinking bleach or encountering the consequence of dying. More generally, rules such as moral principles, laws, commands, religious prescriptions, norms, and customs serve as the bedrock upon which many social and cultural groups are formed and function (Baumeister, 2008) while grammatical and syntactical rules provide the "scaffolding" that binds language together (Hayes et al., 2001; McHugh & Reed, 2008). Interestingly, this ability to generate and follow rules also has a dark side. In some cases rules rapidly accelerate the rate at which we adapt to the world around us while in others they have precisely the opposite effect, undermining our sensitivity to changes in the wider world and producing undesirable consequences that could have otherwise been avoided (e.g., Hayes, Brownstein, Zettle, Rosenfarb, & Korn, 1986; Shimoff, Catania, & Matthews, 1981; also see Törneke, Luciano, & Valdivia Salas, 2008). For several years now, contextual behavioral scientists have argued that this capacity to become "locked into" or "stuck" in maladaptive patterns of rule-following plays a key role in psychopathology, from addiction ("*I need to smoke in order to cope*"), to self-harm ("*I always cut myself when I do poorly at school*"), as well as suicide ("*My pain will stop after I kill myself*") and schizophrenia (see Hayes et al., 1999; Luoma, Kohlenberg, Hayes, Bunting, & Rye, 2008). In the domain of addiction, for example, it may be that gamblers following the rule "*My bad luck is bound to change*" continue to bet despite the aversive outcomes that result from following that rule (i.e., losing increasingly large sums of money; Dixon, Hayes, & Aban, 2000). Likewise, a person addicted to alcohol may emit the rule "*I will feel better after drinking*" and this may be effective in the short run. But when this rule persists over time, drinking continues, social and interpersonal problems fail to go away, and thoughts and feelings about poor life outcomes may actually increase (Törneke et al., 2008).

RFT and instructional control. Naturally, an RFT account of rule-following has the concept of AARR at its core. According to this perspective, rules or instructions represent complex networks of relations that serve to modify the psychological properties of stimuli in those networks (Barnes-Holmes, Hayes, & Dymond, 2001; O'Hora & Barnes-Holmes, 2004; Törneke et al., 2008). In previous sections we described how relational frames are elaborated into relational networks that themselves are related and applied to the nonarbitrary environment. Rule-governed behavior is a subset of such behavior and refers to the coordination of behavior with a verbally specified contingency that often makes reference to antecedent, behavioral, and consequential events.

To illustrate, imagine that you are about to hike through some mountains in southern Canada for the first time and a friend from the region warns you about a species of snake that lives in the area. He tells you that the stripes on this snake's back are red, yellow, and black and that "*If red touches yellow then you're a dead fellow but if red touches black then you're okay Jack.*" Several days later a snake with red and yellow stripes crosses your path and you start to sweat, experience fear, and quickly walk in the opposite direction. RFT provides an analysis of how your behavior comes under instructional control by examining "the relational frames involved and the cues that occasion the derivation of those relations, as well as the psychological functions transformed through those relations and the cues that occasion those transformations of function" (Stewart, 2013, p. 274). For instance, the instruction gains its psychological power because words like "red," "yellow," "snake," and "dead" participate in coordination relations with other stimuli and events (e.g., the word "snake" with actual snakes, the word "dead" with dead organisms and so on). But coordination relations are not enough. If the instruction consisted simply of "snake, yellow, red, black, dead, ok, Jack" it would not make much sense – it would not specify that snakes with red/yellow stripes are the antecedent in the presence of which one should escape (the behavior), nor that avoiding death would be the consequence of doing so.

According to RFT, the person following the instruction must respond to the *relations between* the words contained in the statement, not merely those words themselves. In effect, it is the relating of words via relational cues which leads to stimuli acquiring new or changing their existing psychological properties. In the above example, conditional cues such as "if," "then," and temporal cues such as "before," "after" specify the order of events and their contiguous relationship to one another. Interpersonal cues ("you") specify the individual towards whom the rule is directed. At the same time, functional cues such as "dead" and "ok" alter the functions of the snake such that the listener is more likely to avoid it in one context and disregard it in another. In other words, this relational network leads to a transformation of functions wherein the functions of the snake are altered depending on the relationship between the colors on its back. Once you hear the above instruction, you will likely avoid all contact with a red/yellow striped snake and readily approach or disregard his red and black striped cousin. According to RFT, people are said to "understand" a rule or instruction whenever their behavior falls under the control of derived relations such as those outlined here. They can prescribe rules for themselves as well as others and identify whether they are following those rules by assessing the extent to which their behavior coordinates with that rule (for more see D. Barnes-Holmes et al., 2001; O'Hora & Barnes-Holmes, 2004).

If rule-following is an instance of AARR then we should be able to model such behavior in the laboratory; demonstrate that it develops over time, is amenable to change, and is sensitive to its antecedents and consequences. We should also be able to establish this behavior where it was previously absent or weak. Over the past decade a number of studies have started to tackle these and related questions. For instance, we now know that instructional control can be experimentally modelled under laboratory conditions. Much of this work has involved the formation of relational cues meaning "same," "different," "before," and "after." During a subsequent "instruction-following" test participants are presented with a number of trials that contain arbitrary stimuli (nonsense words and colored shapes) along with the aforementioned cues. On each trial, the contextual cues were used to establish coordination (e.g., *A1–same–B1–same–C1; A2–same–B2–same–C2; A3–same–B3–same–C3*) and temporal relations between stimuli (e.g., *C3–before–C2–before–C1*). Prior to the study participants were informed that each stimulus corresponds to a certain key on the keyboard and that they should press those keys based on what they see during a given trial. If RFT is correct, and instruction-following is a type of behavior that is under the control of derived stimulus relations, then participants should press the keys in the order specified by those relations (e.g., press the key corresponding to C3 before the key corresponding to C2 and so on). Furthermore, they should also do this for entirely novel sets of stimuli that were never differentially reinforced in the past and that bear no resemblance to one another. Results suggest that participants readily pass such a test (O'Hora, Barnes-Holmes, Roche, & Smeets, 2004), that responding in line with such "instructions" falls under the control of its antecedents and consequences (O'Hora, Barnes-Holmes, & Stewart, 2014), and that instructed behavior may demonstrate the same functional properties as directly experienced and derived performances (Dymond, Schlund, Roche, De Houwer, & Freegard, 2012). Several researchers have begun to establish rule-following in populations where such an ability was previously absent (e.g., with developmentally delayed children; Tarbox, Zuckerman, Bishop, Olive, & O'Hora, 2011; see also Tarbox, Tarbox, & O'Hora, 2009).

Pliance, tracking, and augmenting. RFT researchers have also distinguished between three different kinds of contingencies that produce rule-following, labelled these contingencies plys, tracks, and augmentals and linked them to variety of clinical phenomena (Törneke et al., 2008). Pliance is defined as rule-governed behavior under the control of a history of socially mediated reinforcement for coordination between behavior and antecedent verbal stimuli (e.g., when a child cleans his or her bedroom after being told by a parent "*You will only get pocket-money once your chores are complete*"). Tracking is defined as rule-governed behavior under the control of a history of coordination between the rule and the way the environment is arranged independently of the delivery of the rule (e.g., enjoying a clean room after being told that "*Cleaning your room will make you feel great*"). Finally, augmenting is defined as behavior that alters the degree to which stimuli in instructions function as reinforcers or punishers. These latter type of contingencies have been further subdivided into two varieties. Motivative augmentals temporarily alter the degree to which previously established consequences function as reinforcers or punishers (e.g., "*Wouldn't a tender steak and some crispy fries taste great right now?*"). Formative augmentals establish reinforcing or punitive functions for a stimulus in the first instance (e.g., "*Do you want this slip of paper – it is last week's winning lottery ticket?*"). A number of studies have sought to provide experimental analogues of these different types of instructions (Ju & Hayes, 2008; O'Hora et al., 2014; Valdivia, Luciano, & Molina, 2006) and show that they play an important role in phenomena such as depression (McAuliffe, Hughes, & Barnes-Holmes, 2014) and schizophrenia (Monestès, Villatte, Stewart, & Loas, 2014).

Summary and future directions. Taken together, the above work reveals that rules and instructions exert a powerful influence over our current actions and future behavior. From an RFT perspective, when we use words like "rules" and "instructions" we are referring to relational networks that typically specify a temporal antecedent; the topography of a response; the appropriate context for the response; the type of consequences that will be contacted; and when those consequences are delivered (e.g., "*If I study for my exams now I will be in with a good chance of getting a job later*"). They do so without the need for people to directly experience the events involved or even encounter the stimuli that they refer to.[5] Although the foregoing account of rule-governed behavior is well over 20 years old much work still remains to be done. First and foremost, some conceptual spring-cleaning seems in order. Nontechnical terms such as "rules" and "instructions" may need to be jettisoned in favor of alternatives with less historical baggage. One possibility is that researchers refer to this class of behavior as "complex relational regulation." Although the complexity of the networks involved in such regulation can vary, many will usually involve transformations of functions in accordance with networks composed of coordination, conditional, temporal, and deictic relations. The advantage of this definition is that it avoids the use of terms (rules and instructions) which are used in numerous ways both inside and outside of behavioral psychology. Adopting the concept of "complex relational regulation," however, simply encourages the researcher to distinguish between more or less complex forms of verbal regulation (for a related discussion see D. Barnes-Holmes et al., 2001; O'Hora & Barnes-Holmes, 2004).

Second, a systematic experimental analysis of the current and historical factors that serve to establish, maintain, and modify this type of behavior is sorely needed. The same goes for the origins of complex relational regulation in infancy and the potential role that other relational frames (spatial and hierarchy) play in this process. Few interventions exist for establishing this repertoire in people who do not already display it and only a handful of studies have sought to remediate this ability where previously weak or absent. Researchers will need to identify how verbal regulation transitions from the basic to complex forms seen typically in adults, such as the ability to derive rules that specify long-delayed (e.g., death) or highly abstract consequences (e.g., going to heaven or hell) (see Tarbox et al., 2009). Third, future work will need to focus on the potential factors that increase or decrease the probability of rule-following. RFT researchers have long argued that rules may be stated and understood and yet not followed because (a) the behavior specified by the rule is not in the behavioral repertoire of the listener, (b) the rule-giver lacks credibility, or (c) lacks authority and ability to mediate reinforcement. The plausibility of the rule may also be called into question because it is contradictory or incoherent with the individual's prior learning history. These and other moderators such as the accuracy, type, and source of the rule as well as the role of relational complexity, derivation, and coherence in their formation, persistence, and change will need to be subjected to closer inspection in the coming years. Fourth, concepts like plys, tracks, and augmentals, while certainly popular in the CBS literature, are not strictly speaking technical terms for RFT and have often enjoyed more theoretical than empirical support. Future work will need to provide more precise functional analyses of these different types of verbal stimuli, demonstrate that they actually give rise to functionally distinct outcomes, and determine their role in different social, clinical, and cognitive phenomena. Take, for example, the clinical domain. If plys and tracks can decrease our sensitivity to reinforcement contingencies, and thus, by implication, increase the likelihood of certain psychopathologies, would training flexibility in deploying and discarding such rules serve to undermine human suffering? Fifth, RFT and ACT researchers have focused more on the *maladaptive* role that rules play in everyday life and less on their *adaptive* role in goal-setting, motivation, persuasion, morality, delayed gratification, and social cognition (although see O'Hora & Maglieri, 2006). Thus greater attention should be paid to the positive consequences of this type of behavior.

Conclusion

In the preceding section we focused our attention on those areas of RFT that have made the greatest strides in the domain of language since Hayes et al.'s seminal text in 2001. The intervening years have served to further solidify the relationship between AARR and language, with research supporting the former's role in analogical and metaphorical reasoning as well as instructional control. Nearly 15 years on we can confidently say that RFT has taken significant steps towards a naturalistic, functional-analytic account of human language. Evidence indicates that we have identified the environmental regularities and history of learning necessary to predict and influence the development and change of verbal behavior with relative precision, scope, and depth. These variables have allowed us to devise interventions that can remediate linguistic deficits in developmentally delayed populations or accelerate those same abilities in their typically developing counterparts (see chapter 11 in this volume). This program of research has also stimulated new insight into the powerful role that language plays in human suffering and the need for psychotherapeutic approaches that target how one frames events relationally (see chapter 12 in this volume).

However, we have only begun to scratch the surface of where an RFT approach to language may eventually take us. For instance, while the theory has had much to say on issues such as (generative) grammar, allegory, anecdotes, parables, storytelling, and humor, these topics still await empirical scrutiny. The same goes for other important classes of verbal behavior such as persuasion, rhetoric, and logic (Roche, Barnes-Holmes, Barnes-Holmes, Stewart, & O'Hora, 2002). At the same time, RFT has made clear, testable assumptions about language development, from the probability of speech errors and novel utterances to the relationship between verbal comprehension and production. This is also true for child-directed speech, degenerate stimulus input, and the role of AARR in U-shaped grammatical development (e.g., Cullinan & Vitale, 2009; Hayes et al., 2001; McHugh & Reed, 2008; Stewart et al., 2013). A functional analysis of these and related topics would not only cement our understanding of verbal behavior but also provide further evidence that RFT can adequately account for the generative and productive nature of human language. Finally, complex relational regulation represents a novel intellectual country that RFT researchers are only starting to explore. Charting this new domain will require methodological innovation that enables researchers to better generate and manipulate relational networks, capture their impact on behavior, and remediate such abilities in educational and developmental contexts.

Section 3: RFT and Human Cognition

The philosophical and conceptual swing from the functional to mental level of analysis during the 1960s was not limited to the domain of language. With the advent of cognitive psychology, researchers began to draw upon a different philosophical framework (mental mechanism), with its own root (computer or neural net) and causal metaphors (links-in-a-chain). The result was a focus on the action of mental mechanisms which were suggested to be independent from, and yet instantiated by, physical systems in the environment (e.g., computers or brains). These mental processes and representations became an explanatory intermediary between environment and behavior, invoked in order to understand phenomena such as learning, perceiving, recognizing, and remembering, reasoning, decision-making, problem-solving, feeling, attending, and being creative. Collectively, these behaviors were repackaged under the rubric of "cognition" which referred "to all the processes by which the sensory input is transformed, reduced, elaborated, stored, recovered, and used ... cognition is involved in everything a human being might possibly do ... every psychological phenomenon is a cognitive phenomenon" (Neisser, 1967, p. 4). Behavior was now treated as an indication, manifestation, or expression of physiological and/or neurological processes taking place inside the person or mediating mental processes such as expectations, desires, intentions, attributions, attitudes, and feelings which took place somewhere "outside of the physical world in which information is represented and processed independently of the physical system in which it is implemented" (De Houwer, 2011, p. 202). These mental events were assumed to operate on environmental input (bottom-up processing), were said to be influenced by other mental events such as knowledge and expectation (top-down processing), or some combination of the two. Approached in this way, the purpose of psychological science became twofold. The goal of research was to identify the basic mental processes which mediate between input (environment) and output (behavior) in order to better predict the behavioral effect of interest. The second was to identify the operating conditions that were both necessary and sufficient for those mental processes to successfully function (e.g., Bargh & Ferguson, 2000).[6]

Cognition at the functional level of analysis. Shifting to the functional level of analysis requires that we adopt a strikingly different perspective, one in which cognition is conceptualized *as* behavior. The metaphor of an information processing machine or neural net is set to the side along with questions about the mental mechanisms and operating conditions which mediate between environment and behavior. Instead of searching for mechanisms or processes that underlie perception, attention, and memory, decision-making, emotion, and thought, the question becomes "What are the functional relations between behavior and environment that give rise to, sustain or undermine those actions which people refer to as involving thinking, remembering, attending, being creative, or intelligent?" Although it is true that early behaviorists focused exclusively on *public* behaviors and excluded *private events* from legitimate analysis, this is not the case for their contemporary counterparts, who arrange behavior along a single continuum from public (e.g., ticking a box that indicates a particular dislike) to private (e.g., thinking or feeling that I do not like a particular person without saying so out loud). By referring to cognitive phenomena like thinking, remembering, and reasoning as behaviors, functional researchers seek to emphasize that (a) it is the task of psychology to predict-and-influence these events and that (b) public or private events can only be influenced by manipulating the environment external to that behavior. In other words, CBS views both public and private behaviors, and possible interactions between the two, as dependent variables (i.e., outcomes for which we must find a cause) and environmental regularities external to the behavior(s) of interest as independent variables (i.e., the causes of behavior). This strategy of treating private events as behavior – and thus as a dependent variable – is adopted in order to achieve CBS's central goal of prediction-and-influence (for an excellent discussion see Hayes & Brownstein, 1986).

Cognition as the RFT researcher sees it. This conceptualization of (public vs. private) behavior, combined with a focus on environmental moderators rather than mental mediators, has led to the popular misconception that functional researchers are disinterested in – or incapable of – dealing with psychological phenomena such as language or cognition (e.g., Bargh & Ferguson, 2000). Yet nothing could be further from the truth. Functional accounts have sought to provide a naturalistic explanation for the emergence and development of phenomena such as self and perspective-taking, implicit cognition and intelligence. RFT, for example, argues that cognition is not a mental event that mediates between environment and behavior; rather it is a behavioral event (AARR), and, as such, there is no reason that the study of cognition cannot be carried out at the functional level of analysis. Put simply, arbitrarily applicable relational responses are what "minds" are full of, and when we speak of "cognitive" phenomena we are referring to complex instances of relational framing that are more or less evident under different environmental conditions. It is to this topic that we now turn.

Self and Perspective-Taking

The "self" represents one of the most ubiquitous and enduring concepts in psychological science. Since the earliest days of the discipline researchers have appealed to the notion of "self" as a causal or explanatory factor when accounting for complex human behavior. For instance, we are said to "self-determine" and "self-regulate" (Deci & Ryan, 1985), have a host of "self-perceptions" (Laird, 2007), and act in ways that are either "self-enhancing" or "self-defeating" (Sedikides & Gregg, 2008). Our "self-beliefs," "self-esteem," and "self-concepts" are argued to shape our thoughts and feelings (Greenwald & Farnham, 2000) while our "self-discipline," "self-control," and "self-efficacy" influence how we behave towards ourselves and others (Zimmerman, 2000). The self plays an important role in psychodynamics, humanism, and positive psychology as well as in several psychotherapeutic approaches including ACT (Hayes et al., 1999). Much of this work has been conducted at the mental level of analysis, and, as such, the self has usually been conceptualized as a mediating mental agent or motivational force which makes decisions and causes action (see Baumeister, 2010).

Self-discrimination. Interestingly, and despite its nontechnical status, researchers operating at the functional level of analysis have also referred to the "self," often describing behavior as being under "self-control," or as being "self-monitored," "self-reinforced," or "self-discriminated." However, rather than posit the self as a mediating mental mechanism, these researchers have sought to better understand the wider class of "self-related" behaviors and their environmental determinants. Early work in this area focused on the idea that self-awareness involves responding to one's own respond-ing. For instance, Skinner (1974) argued that "there is a difference between behaving and reporting that one is behaving or reporting the causes of one's behavior" (pp. 34–35). Thus he defined self or self-awareness functionally and argued that it emerges from a history of reinforcement or punishment for accurately labeling controlling environmental antecedents or consequences of one's behavior or physiology (for more see Lattal, 2012).

RFT expands upon this account in several key ways. Foremost amongst these is that it distinguishes between two fundamentally different types of self-discrimination. The first is displayed by many different organisms and involves simply behaving with regards to the individual organism's own behavior. This can be observed in the labo-ratory by exposing nonhumans to reinforcement schedules that generate different patterns of responding and then administering a second task which requires them to correctly discriminate between those different behaviors (e.g., Reynolds & Catania, 1962; Shimp, 1983). These experiments suggest that even organisms without the ability to AARR can discriminate their own behavior when contingencies are appro-priately arranged. The second type of self-discrimination is grounded in the ability to AARR and involves behaving *verbally* with regard to our own behavior. According to this perspective, the ability to frame events relationally "serves to transform the highly limited forms of self-awareness seen with non-humans into an extremely complex form of behavior requiring a separate and special treatment in its own right" (Stewart, 2013, p. 274). To illustrate, consider the work of Dymond and Barnes (1994). In their study participants were taught three different coordination relations and were then trained to emit two (time-based) self-discrimination responses. That is, if they did not make a response within a certain time frame then choosing a stimulus from the first coordination relation was reinforced. If they made at least one response within a given time frame choosing a stimulus from the second coordination relation was reinforced. The authors found that the self-discrimination functions established during training for one stimulus transferred to the other stimuli in those derived rela-tions (see also Dymond & Barnes, 1995; 1996). In other words, the authors found that the self-discriminations made by humans were of a fundamentally different kind to those seen in the nonhuman literature. Their work suggests that humans do not simply discriminate that they are behaving like many other organisms but rather rela-tionally frame with regard to their own behavior (i.e., they are "verbally" self-aware). This study, in addition to others, indicates that there is an important functional difference between AARR and non-AARR-based self-knowledge. Organisms with the ability to AARR can frame one aspect of their own behavior with another, in much the same way that a stimulus can be related to another stimulus or event. In other words, not only can humans relate A as being "better/worse than" B, A as coming "before/after" B, and so on, but they can also frame their own behavior in this very same way (e.g., *"My colleagues are all better than me," "I'm the worst friend ever,"* or *"I really should have finished studying before taking a break"*).

RFT therefore extends beyond earlier behavioral accounts in two important ways: it (a) functionally defines what it means to verbally self-discriminate and (b) provides a detailed account of the learning history necessary to establish such a repertoire (e.g., Y. Barnes-Holmes et al., 2001; McHugh & Stewart, 2012; Stewart, 2013). From this perspective, it is the learned ability to respond in line with deictic frames which provides the foundation for verbal self-discrimination. As we saw in chapter 9, deictic frames are comprised of temporal (NOW–THEN), spatial (HERE–THERE), and interpersonal (I–YOU) relations and their development is somewhat unique. Whereas coordination, distinction, and comparative relations emerge based on what people learn about stimuli that are physically similar, dissimilar, or quantitatively different along some dimension, deictics are not abstracted from a nonarbitrary or physical referent. Rather they emerge based on the invariance of the speaker's perspective across time and context. In their early interactions with the socio-verbal community, children learn to ask and answer questions like *"What are you doing here?,," "What am I doing now?,," "What will you do there?"* with regard to a variety of stimuli, situations, and settings. It is the constant division between the speaker (I–YOU) who is always HERE and NOW and the to-be-related stimuli which are THERE and THEN that provides the environmental consistency upon which deictic relations are abstracted and arbitrarily applied (for a more detailed treatment see Barnes-Holmes, Barnes-Holmes, & Cullinan, 2001; McHugh, Barnes-Holmes, & Barnes-Holmes, 2009).

Perspective-taking. RFT proposes that these deictic frames constitute the functional "seed" from which human self (discrimination) and perspective-taking skills grow and flourish. Perspective-taking refers to inferences about our own and other people's desires and beliefs, as well as the use of these inferences to interpret and predict behavior (Baron-Cohen, Lombardo, Tager-Flusberg, & Cohen, 2013; McHugh & Stewart, 2012). Typically developing children show early signs of perspective-taking in infancy, and, by around five years, demonstrate evidence that they understand another person's actions and motivations (Baron-Cohen et al., 2013). In contrast, children with autism spectrum disorders (ASD) show severe deficits in their ability to understand and predict events from the perspective of another (e.g., Baron-Cohen, 2000). Although many researchers have approached perspective-taking at the mental level of analysis (often in terms of "Theory of Mind" or ToM; see Doherty, 2012), others argue that this ability can be understood functionally as an instance of deictic framing. In other words, the abstraction of an individual's perspective of the world, and that of others, requires a combination of a sufficiently well-developed relational repertoire and an extensive history of multiple exemplars that take advantage of that repertoire (McHugh, Stewart, & Hooper, 2012).

Empirical support for this account has been obtained on three separate fronts. First, developmental studies with typically developing and developmentally delayed children suggest that deictic frames are prerequisites for successful perspective-taking. Much of this work has shown that deictic frames tend to be fairly well established in the behavior of children above (but not below) five years of age, the same age at which children demonstrate reasonably reliable perspective-taking skills in the ToM literature (McHugh, Barnes-Holmes, & Barnes-Holmes, 2004; McHugh, Barnes-Holmes, Barnes-Holmes, & Stewart, 2006; McHugh, Barnes-Holmes, Barnes-Holmes, Stewart, & Dymond, 2007). Second, a number of studies have assessed the deictic framing abilities of different populations and sought to remediate deficits where present. For instance, several authors have found that children with autism spectrum disorder (ASD) – a population who regularly show deficits in perspective-taking abilities – also show deficits in deictic framing (e.g., Rehfeldt, Dillen, Ziomek, & Kowalchuk, 2007) and that training in the latter produces improvements in the former (e.g., Weil, Hayes, & Capurro, 2011; see also Gould, Tarbox, O'Hora, Noone, & Bergstrom, 2011; Heagle & Rehfeldt, 2006). Third, there is a small but growing body of research on the relationship between deictic frames and the self, with some studies focusing on the therapeutic implications of this relationship, and others on the role of perspective-taking in clinical (schizophrenia) and subclinical (social anhedonia) populations. For example, individuals with known perspective-taking difficulties, such as those diagnosed with social anhedonia (Villatte, Monestès, McHugh, Freixa i Baqué, & Loas, 2008), or schizophrenia (Villatte, Monestès, McHugh, Freixa i Baqué, & Loas, 2010) also perform poorly on deictic framing tasks that involve interpersonal relations. This also seems to be true for those suffering from social anxiety disorder (Janssen et al., 2014). It may well be that perspective-taking deficits in these areas can be remediated by providing a history of learning in line with RFT's suggestions (for preliminary evidence in this regard see O'Neill & Weil, 2014).[7]

Summary. In short, RFT connects with, but extends beyond, traditional behavior-analytic accounts of self. It agrees with the Skinnerian view that self-discrimination is an important class of behavior that is functionally different for organisms with and without verbal abilities. What is innovative about RFT then is not the general direction it takes but the specifics it offers. It articulates that verbal self-discrimination involves the learned ability to deictically frame with regard to one's own behavior and outlines the history of learning necessary to produce such performances. At the same time, it also connects with cognitive and developmental approaches to the self which highlight the importance of the subjective "I" (e.g., James, 1891), the gradual development of perspective-taking skills in childhood (e.g., Baron-Cohen et al., 2013) and the importance of social contingencies in shaping self-awareness or a "reflexive consciousness" (Baumeister, 2010). Once again it extends beyond these approaches by highlighting that the subjective "I" emerges in line with the development of perspective-taking, the latter of which is based on the ability to respond in accordance with temporal, spatial, and interpersonal (deictic) relations. Indeed, RFT proposes that once deictic frames become part of an individual's behavioral repertoire they become an inherent property of most events for that person. Once deictics are in place, people can relationally frame their thoughts, feelings, actions, sensations, memories, and ideas in different ways. For example, they can relate events that took place in the past or will take place in the future (THERE and THEN) from the perspective of an "I" that is HERE and NOW. They can also frame events in the present (HERE and NOW) with an "I" that is also HERE and NOW. And, they can recognize that they always relate events from the perspective of an "I" that is located HERE and NOW about events that occur THERE and THEN.

Thus research stemming from RFT not only mirrors that seen within the psychological literature on self and perspective-taking, but the inductive, behavioral foundations of this approach lead to new conceptual and empirical insights as well as methods for establishing and remediating these abilities where previously weak or absent. This account highlights the environmental regularities and history of learning that give rise the sense of self. It draws attention to the important role that relational framing and (social) reinforcement play in the discrimination of self from the environment, self from others, and self from psychological content or context. In doing so, it provides the necessary information to remediate "self-related problems, whether in respect of the delayed development of self and perspective-taking in autistic or norma-tive populations … or of self-related psychotherapeutic problems as treated by clini-cians using Acceptance Commitment Therapy" (Stewart, 2013, p. 281).

Future directions. While the future is notoriously difficult to predict, we believe that a number of questions and issues about deictics will shape RFT research over much of the coming years. First, if deficits in deictic framing are evident in developmentally delayed (ASD), subclinical (social anhedonia) and clinical populations (schizophrenia) then the next logical step is to examine whether interventions that directly target the former lead to corresponding improvements in the latter. Once again, this will require new methodologies which can not only assess an individual's ability to deictically frame at increasing levels of complexity but also target stimuli and events that partic-ipate in deictic frames during the individual's day-to-day life (e.g., relations such as "*I think you are going to hurt me*" or "*You are always looking at me even when I'm not watching*"). Second, the majority of existing RFT work has tended to focus on the role that deictic frames play in perspective-taking, self, deception, and false belief. Future work could expand this analysis even further by clarifying their role in metaphorical reasoning (Foody et al., 2014), self-rules (see chapter 12 in this volume), delayed gratification, social stereotyping, and prejudice as well as persuasion and rhetoric (Roche et al., 2002). It could also attempt to explain why stimuli that are deictically framed are often remembered more accurately (Greenwald & Banaji, 1989) and evaluated more positively (Nuttin, 1987) or examine how the use of these frames differs when verbal communities emphasize independence (western societies) or interdependence (Asian societies) (Markus & Kitayama, 1991). Third, the "three selves" that have been discussed in the ACT/RFT literature (Hayes, 1995; Hayes et al., 2001) represent middle-level concepts that lack the precision, scope, and depth of more technical terms found in RFT. While recognizing their pragmatic utility in the clinical context it is important to realize that because the "three selves" have not been wrought out of the fires of experimental research, it will be difficult if not impossible to submit them to experimental (functional) analyses like those conducted with concepts like entailment and derived transformation of function (see Foody, Barnes-Holmes, & Barnes-Holmes, 2012). Finally, deictic frames may provide a useful means to distinguish the elaborate sense of "self" displayed by humans and the more limited forms of self-discriminative behavior seen elsewhere in the animal kingdom.

Implicit Cognition

A substantial body of evidence indicates that people often behave in two qualitatively different and potentially conflicting ways (for reviews see Banaji & Heiphetz, 2010; Nosek, Hawkins, & Frazier, 2011; Payne & Gawronski, 2010). On the one hand, and consistent with our intuitive beliefs about behavior, we can respond to stimuli in the environment in a nonautomatic fashion. These "explicit" responses are argued to be controlled, "intentional, made with awareness and require cognitive resources" (Nosek, 2007, p.65). On the other hand, our history of interacting with the social, verbal, and physical environment can also give rise to automatic or "implicit" responses that are emitted quickly without our awareness, intention, and/or control. What is interesting about these "automatic" behaviors is that, although they unfold in the blink of an eye, they often predict the way people will subsequently act, from their voting intentions in upcoming elections (Friese, Smith, Plischke, Bluemke, & Nosek, 2012), the foods and brand products they will approach and consume (Gregg & Klymowsky, 2013), their likelihood of attempting suicide in the following six months (Nock et al., 2010), or breaking up with their romantic partner (Lee, Rogge, & Reis, 2010). Likewise, automatic behaviors also predict the quality and quantity of interactions with members of other racial (McConnell & Leibold, 2001) or social groups (Agerström & Rooth, 2011) in ways that self-report questionnaires often fail to capture.

Whereas "nonautomatic" behaviors are typically captured via direct measurement procedures like questionnaires, interviews, and focus groups, their automatic counterparts are registered using indirect procedures, the most popular of which include semantic and evaluative priming (Fazio, Jackson, Dunton, & Williams, 1995; Wittenbrink, Judd, & Park, 1997), the Affective Misattribution Procedure (AMP; Payne, Cheng, Govorun, & Stewart, 2005) as well as the Implicit Association Test (IAT; Greenwald, McGhee, & Schwartz, 1998) and its second-generation variants. Indirect procedures have been adopted by researchers from nearly every corner of psychological science and have had a powerful impact on empirical and theoretical output due to their practical value in predicting human behavior.

Mental level of analysis. Unsurprisingly, the study of implicit cognition has been dominated by researchers operating at the mental level of analysis (for a discussion see Hughes, Barnes-Holmes, & De Houwer, 2011; Hughes, Barnes-Holmes, & Vahey, 2012). In line with their scientific goals, cognitive and social psychologists have attempted to explain why automatic responding corresponds, conflicts, and predicts nonautomatic behavior by appealing to some set of mediating mental mechanisms. Although there are nontrivial differences across mental models of implicit cognition, the assumption that associations (Fazio, 2007), propositions (De Houwer, 2014), dual-process models involving reflective-impulsive systems (Strack & Deutsch, 2004), associations *and* propositions (Gawronski & Bodenhausen, 2011), or multiple interactive memory systems (Amodio & Ratner, 2011) mediate between environment and behavior is foundational. In other words, mental theories are primarily concerned with how mental constructs are formed, activated, and changed as well as their influence on automatic and controlled behavior.

Functional level of analysis. Unsurprisingly, RFT researchers have approached this topic with a different set of scientific goals in mind. These researchers have sought to identify the environmental and historical regularities that give rise to different classes of behaviors, such as those captured by direct and indirect procedures. This analysis has been formalized in an RFT-inspired account known as the Relational Elaboration and Coherence (REC) model (see Barnes-Holmes, Barnes-Holmes, Stewart, & Boles, 2010; Barnes-Holmes, Murphy, Barnes-Holmes, & Stewart, 2010; Cullen, Barnes-Holmes, Barnes-Holmes, & Stewart, 2009; Hughes et al., 2012). At the core of this model reside two simple ideas: (a) that explicit and implicit cognition represent instances of the learned and contextually controlled ability to frame events relationally and that (b) these relational responses can vary in their complexity and history of derivation. Relational complexity refers to the fact that stimuli can be related to one another in a vast number of ways, from simple mutually entailed relations between single stimuli to combinatorial relations involving multiple stimuli, to the relating of relations to other relations as well as the complex relating of entire relational networks to other networks. The REC model draws attention to this fact and arranges relational

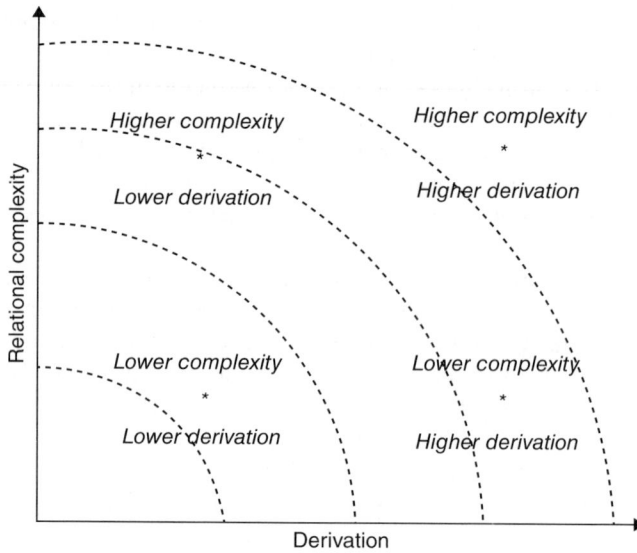

Figure 10.2 Relational responding carved into four different categories as a function of the complexity and level of derivation that characterize the response.

responding along a "complexity" continuum from high to low. At the same time, relations not only vary in their complexity but also in the degree to which they have been previously derived. Derivation refers to the finding that once a set of stimulus relations have been directly trained (e.g., A–B and B–C), a number of novel and untrained relations tend to emerge (e.g., A–C and C–B). The REC model defines the first time a person derives the relation between A and C as a "high derivation" response given that the history of deriving that particular response is minimal. As a person encounters an ever-increasing number of opportunities to derive, their responding may increasingly be defined as involving "lower" levels of derivation. The REC model draws attention to this fact and arranges relational responding along a "derivation" continuum from high to low (see Figure 10.2).[8]

Arranging relational responses along these interrelated continua affords a number of useful advantages. First, it highlights that "automatic" and "nonautomatic" thoughts, feelings, and actions are instances of the same overarching class of behavior (AARR) that varies in *degree* rather than in *kind*. From a REC perspective, when researchers use terms such as "implicit cognition" or "automatic responding" they are referring to relational responses that are typically characterized by lower levels of complexity and derivation. Likewise, terms such as "explicit cognition" or "nonautomatic respond-ing" typically refer to responses that are characterized by higher levels of complexity and derivation. In other words, the REC model equips functionally orientated researchers with a nomenclature that is not imported from either the lay community or the mental level of analysis. Instead it employs terms that are directly rooted in a bottom-up functional theory that coherently connects basic concepts to complex behavioral phenomena (i.e., it is philosophically and conceptually consistent with CBS and RFT). Adopting this approach lowers the likelihood that the functional and mental levels of analysis will be conflated and provides insight into the possible functional origins, properties, and conditions necessary to observe these classes of behavior.

Second, the idea that relational responses vary in their complexity and history of derivation is consistent with the general trend of evidence in the RFT literature. We now know that relational responses, like all behaviors, unfold across time, and that (all things being equal) more complex responses take additional time and are emitted with lower accuracy relative to their less complex counterparts. As the number and type of relations increase the speed and accuracy of responding decreases relative to relations that are at lower levels of complexity (e.g., Barnes-Holmes et al., 2005). At the same time, the extent to which a response has been derived in the past will also influence its probability of being emitted quickly (Roche, Linehan, Ward, Dymond, & Rehfeldt, 2004) and accurately in the future (Healy, Barnes-Holmes, & Smeets, 2000). Thus it appears that the complexity of a relational response, as well as the degree to which it has been derived in the past, influences the probability that it will be emitted with speed and accuracy in the future.

Third, given that relational responses vary in their complexity and derivation, and that lower complexity/derivation responses are emitted with greater speed and accuracy than their high complexity/derivation counterparts, it follows that different experimental procedures will be more or less sensitive to certain types of responses depending on how they are designed. Consider, for example, indirect tasks like the IAT or priming. Broadly speaking, these measures compare the speed with which people relate stimuli from two different classes with a common response key in ways that are either consistent (*spiders–bad*) or inconsistent (*spiders–good*) with the individual's prior learning history. In the language of RFT, these tasks (a) establish a coordination relation between two stimulus classes based on a shared response function and then (b) compare the speed with which these coordination-based responses are emitted when people have to respond in history consistent versus inconsistent ways (O'Toole, Barnes-Holmes, & Smyth, 2007). The key point here is that, by arranging the measurement context to primarily target coordination relations, the IAT and priming tasks are restricted in the complexity of the relational responses that they can capture. In other words, when viewed through the lens of the IAT and priming measures, implicit cognition seems to involve low complexity/derivation *coordination* relations between stimuli (e.g., *black people–same–good; white–same–bad*), which, at the mental level of analysis, has been interpreted as evidence for the automatic activation of mental associations in memory (Hughes et al., 2011).

Critically, however, the REC model argues that the behaviors targeted by indirect procedures are relational in nature. Given a sufficient history of learning, and a measurement context capable of capturing those relations, the behavioral effects obtained on indirect procedures should reflect other relational responses above and beyond coordination. In principle, low complexity/derivation responses can involve any relationship between stimuli, such as opposition, hierarchy, comparative, or deictic relations. Although the speed and accuracy of these responses will presumably vary in accordance with the levels of complexity and derivation of the targeted relation, there is no a priori reason why any type of relational response should not be emitted quickly and accurately. One implication of viewing implicit cognition in this way is that an indirect procedure capable of targeting stimulus relations at differing levels of complexity is not only possible but quickly becomes necessary. RFT researchers have offered the Implicit Relational Assessment Procedure (IRAP) as one such task (e.g., Barnes-Holmes, Barnes-Holmes et al., 2010).

Simply put, the IRAP was designed to target pre-existing relational response biases by placing an individual's learning history into competition with a response contingency deemed inconsistent with that history of responding. To illustrate, consider the work of Nicholson and Barnes-Holmes (2012) who examined low complexity/ derivation responding towards disgusting stimuli. Participants completed two separate IRAPs: one targeting so-called "disgust propensity" when confronted with revolting items (e.g., "I'm disgusted") and a second assessing so-called "disgust sensitivity" to the same stimuli (e.g., "I need to look away"). In either case, the IRAP presented a label stimulus (e.g., "I am disgusted") at the top of the computer screen, a target stimulus (e.g., picture of a disgusting image) in the middle of the screen, and two relational response options ("true" and "false") at the bottom of the screen. During half of the trials participants were required to respond as if pleasant images were positive and disgusting images were negative. On the other half of the trials they are required to produce the opposite response pattern (pleasant images–negative and disgusting images–positive). The difference in time taken to respond in one way versus the other – defined as the IRAP effect – indicated the strength or probability of pre-existing relational response biases. In the Nicholson and Barnes-Holmes study, the authors found that performance on the two IRAPs predicted entirely different outcomes on self-report and behavioral choice tasks. In other words, different patterns of (rapidly emitted) relational responding towards the same target stimuli predicted how people would act towards other stimuli at a future point in time (see also Remue, De Houwer, Barnes-Holmes, Vanderhasselt, & De Raedt, 2013).

Like the IAT and priming measures, the IRAP can target simple (coordination) relations between stimuli that have been derived many times in the past, and in such cases, the latter tends to produce similar outcomes to the former (e.g., Barnes-Holmes, Murtagh, Barnes-Holmes, & Stewart, 2010). However, and consistent with the REC model's predictions, a rapidly expanding IRAP literature suggests that the measure can also capture more complex relational responses which are, nevertheless, highly derived and emitted in the order of milliseconds. Not only are these latter responses emitted quickly and accurately but they often predict self-reported and real-world behaviors with greater sophistication than responses towards relations at lower levels of complexity (Roddy, Stewart, & Barnes-Holmes, 2010; 2011). In other words, when viewed through the lens of the IRAP, implicit cognition reflects relational responding that is certainly at low levels of derivation but not necessarily restricted to coordination relations. Rather relational responses which unfold in the blink of an eye can also vary in their respective complexity (e.g., *"I'm a worthless person," "I want to be successful"*), which, at the mental level of analysis, fits more readily with the idea of automatically activated propositions in memory (De Houwer, 2014). These more complex responses can predict a person's sexual orientation (Timmins, Barnes-Holmes, & Cullen, forthcoming), their likelihood of staying in a drug rehabilitation program (Carpenter, Martinez, Vadhan, Barnes-Holmes, & Nunes, 2012), of interacting with feared stimuli in the environment (Nicholson & Barnes-Holmes, 2012), or professionally burning out when working with developmentally delayed children (Kelly & Barnes-Holmes, 2013). They typically converge with those obtained from self-report tasks when people are not motivated to self-present or modify their behavior to concord with social expectations (e.g., Vahey, Barnes-Holmes, Barnes-Holmes, & Stewart, 2009). They also diverge from self-report data in "psychologically sensitive" domains, especially where racial, religious, and social groups are concerned (for a recent review of the IRAP literature see Hughes & Barnes-Holmes, 2013).[9]

Summary. Functional and mental models of implicit cognition are similar insofar as they both agree that thoughts, feelings, and actions can unfold quickly, in ways that sometimes lack self-discrimination (awareness), and which take place in the presence of other demanding tasks (efficient) or competing verbal contingencies (intentional). They also agree that these "automatic" responses can come to exert a powerful influence over our more elaborate and carefully considered behaviors. However, the former deviates from the latter by defining implicit and explicit cognition *functionally* as instances of AARR which vary in their respective levels of complexity and derivation. Researchers at these two levels also differ in their assumptions about the origins and properties of, as well as relationship between, explicit and implicit cognition. The REC model draws upon three conceptual tools (relational coherence, complexity, and derivation) as well as a methodological one (the IRAP) in order to account for thinking, both fast and slow. Unlike the notion of mental associations or propositions, these concepts simply refer to properties of the same behavioral process (AARR) that become more or less prevalent in different (measurement) contexts.

Future directions. Although the REC model is consistent with findings in the RFT literature, and those pointing to the impact of relational information on implicit measures in cognitive science (see De Houwer, 2014), a number of questions still need to be addressed. First, a detailed experimental analysis of relational complexity and derivation, as well as their interaction, is clearly needed. This also applies to relational coherence and self-discrimination ("awareness"), both as topics in and of themselves as well as their interaction with the above two factors. Second, while a small number of studies have provided experimental evidence for the development of BIRRs (e.g., Hughes & Barnes-Holmes, 2011; O'Reilly et al., 2013; O'Toole, Barnes-Holmes, & Smyth, 2007) a systematic exploration of the learning histories and current contextual variables critical to establishing, maintaining, and changing such behaviors is clearly needed. So too is an analysis of how levels of complexity and derivation impact upon an individual's behavior across the lifespan. While pragmatic considerations can interfere with the collection of data in infants, we argue that a developmental understanding of implicit cognition is certainly worth the effort (Banaji & Heiphetz, 2010; see also Rabelo, Bortoloti, & Souza, 2014). Third, we have only begun to scratch the surface when it comes to the role that complexity and derivation play in clinical, social, health, and forensic domains. Future work could determine whether the world of implicit cognition, as viewed through the lens of procedures such as the IRAP, allows us to better understand, predict, and influence real-world behaviors such as close relationships, judgment and decision-making, job-hiring situations, consumer behaviors as well as law, public policy, and organizational practices. Finally, and like all definitions, the parsing of relational responses based on complexity and derivation is a matter of convention, not fixed or absolute but rather flexible to further modification in line with empirical findings. It may well be that other properties of AARR allow us to develop a more sophisticated functional treatment of implicit cognition than that offered here. Although the REC model requires in-depth empirical scrutiny, we believe that it provides RFT researchers with an opportunity to participate fully in the study of implicit cognition alongside our contemporaries in social and cognitive psychology.

Intelligence

The study of individual differences is populated with a wide spectrum of contrasting definitions and theories about the origins and properties of "intelligence" (for a detailed treatment see Sternberg & Kaufman, 2011). For some, intelligence involves "language and the capacity to develop and transmit culture, to think, to reason, test hypotheses, and understand rules" (Mackintosh, 2011, p. 1). For others, it represents the ability to adapt to the physical, social, and verbal environment

> in which one finds oneself. If that environment is suboptimal, it involves the ability to shape the environment to make it more suitable for one's skills and desires; and if that environment still does not work, it involves the ability to select a different environment, to the extent that one is able. (Sternberg, 2014a, p. 176)

Theories of intelligence sometimes decompose this phenomenon into composite elements such as problem-solving abilities, verbal intelligence, and social competence (Sternberg, 1985) or define it in terms of a psychometrically identified general intelligence factor known as "g" (Jensen, 1998). Still others advocate for a multiplicity of intelligences (Gardner, 2006). These various ways of conceptualizing and studying intelligence are themselves guided by different metaphorical ways of viewing the mind, from geographic (psychometric methods) and computational perspectives (information-processing methods), to biological (physiological methods) and anthropological (cultural and cross-cultural) (see Sternberg & Kaufman, 2011). While some authors have attempted to identify the mental mechanics of intelligence others have looked to the brain, nervous system (Deary, 2000), genetics (Plomin, 2012), and their interaction for answers. What is clear is that intelligence is operationalized and valued in different ways in different cultures, such that characteristics which lead to successful adaptation in one culture may not do so in another (Sternberg, 2004). Finally, the steady rise in intelligence test scores over the past century (Flynn, 2007) and their sensitivity to educational and programmed interventions has led researchers to question the view of intelligence as an invariant trait that is static across the lifetime of the individual. Instead, growing consensus suggests that it can be systematically modified (see Sternberg, 2014a; 2014b), with researchers differing in how much of an increase they think is actually possible.

Intelligence at the functional level. Switching to the functional level of analysis requires that we conceptualize and approach the study of intelligence in a fundamentally different light. Intelligence is no longer considered a mental mechanism that individuals "possess" and which mediates their actions but is simply a descriptive term for a measurable quality of some class or group of behaviors that tend to occur in a given context (e.g., analogical reasoning, spatial orientation, and mathematical skills) (see Williams, Myerson, & Hale, 2008). Viewing intelligence as behavior causes researchers to shift their attention away from questions about the structure or qualities of some mental mechanism or psychometric construct and towards the functional determinants of that behavior. Stated more precisely, functionally orientated researchers are interested in the types of behavior (and contexts in which they occur) that cause psychologists and society to use terms such as intelligence as well as the current and historical regularities of which intelligent behavior is a function. Thus understanding "intelligence" at the functional level means being able to specify the environment–behavior relations that establish, maintain, and sensitize that subclass of behaviors commonly referred to as "intelligent." Addressing these and related questions has enormous practical utility insofar as it brings researchers one step closer to designing technologies that can enhance the fluency, sensitivity, and flexibility of intellectual behavior in developmentally delayed and normally developing populations.

RFT and intelligence. This is precisely the approach that RFT researchers have taken over the past decade (see Barnes-Holmes, Barnes-Holmes, & Cullinan, 2001; Cassidy, Roche, & O'Hora, 2010; O'Toole, Barnes-Holmes, Murphy, O'Connor, & Barnes-Holmes, 2009; Roche, Cassidy, & Stewart, 2013; Stewart, Roche, O'Hora, & Tarbox, 2013). The core idea underlying much of this work is a simple but bold one: that AARR represents the basic functional "building block" of those cognitive and linguistic skills (e.g., deductive and inductive reasoning, communication, etc.) that underpin intelligent behavior. Stated more precisely, intellectual performances involve the ability to elaborate entire networks of derived stimulus relations *fluently* and *flexibly*, to bring those relational responses under increasingly subtle forms of contextual control, to transform stimulus functions through entire networks, and to abstract features of the natural environment that will support and sustain relational responding.

Evidence in support of this claim has emerged on two separate fronts. We now know that the fluency and flexibility with which people derive at increasing levels of complexity predicts their performance on intelligence tests. O'Hora, Pelaez, Barnes-Holmes, and Amesty (2005) found that performance on a complex relational task involving temporal, coordination, and distinction relating predicted outcomes on the Wechsler Adult Intelligence Scale (WAIS-III). Specifically, participants who successfully completed a learning task designed to establish arbitrary relational cues, and who could then use those cues to form derived stimulus relations showed evidence of superior outcomes on the vocabulary and arithmetic subscales of the WAIS-III relative to their counterparts who failed that same task. In a follow-up study, O'Hora and colleagues (2008) found that performance on a temporal relating task was predictive of participant's full scale, verbal, and performance IQ. Similar to before, participants who passed a task designed to establish arbitrary stimuli as relational cues, and who could use those cues to frame events temporally showed evidence of superior outcomes on the verbal comprehension and perceptual organization factors of the WAIS-III relative to their counterparts who failed to do so. O'Toole and Barnes-Holmes (2009) employed an IRAP to test the fluency (speed and accuracy) with which participants could frame events temporally, in coordination and distinction with one another, in ways that were either consistent or inconsistent with their prior learning history (e.g., "*spring comes before summer*" vs. "*marriage comes before engagement*"). Results indicated that fluency in reversing previously established relations correlated with IQ as measured by the Kaufman Brief Intelligence Test (K-BIT). People who produced higher IQ scores on the K-BIT were also "relationally flexible" insofar as they were faster to respond in history-consistent and inconsistent ways on the IRAP. Their "relationally rigid" counterparts who experienced greater difficulty in reversing previously established relations scored lower on that same test. Finally, Gore, Barnes-Holmes, and Murphy (2010) exposed a number of adults with varying levels of intellectual disability to standard measures of language and IQ, as well as to an adaptation of a deictic framing protocol (McHugh et al., 2004). They found that the degree to which participants could deictically frame at increasing levels of complexity correlated with verbal ability, full scale IQ, and performance IQ on the WASI-III. Taken together, these studies suggest that the fluency and flexibility of relational responding represent important predictors of intelligent (linguistic and cognitive) behavior.

While the above findings are certainly consistent with the idea that relational framing constitutes the core functional process underlying intellectual behaviors, a more robust test of this assumption requires that the fluency and flexibility of relational responding be directly targeted and corresponding changes in intellectual performance observed. In other words, if intelligent behavior is an instance of AARR, and if AARR is itself a type of generalized operant behavior, then promoting relational flexibility (and undermining rigidity) should enhance behaviors that are generally deemed as "intelligent."

As we saw in chapter 8, MET interventions can be used to establish or improve a variety of relational frames where previously absent or weak in adults and children. Thus one possibility would be to expose participants to an intelligence test before and after MET designed to enhance relational framing skills so that corresponding changes in intellectual performance could be ascertained. This is the very strategy that Cassidy et al. (2011) adopted in their recent study. They recruited a group of educationally typical and subtypical children and then exposed them to a simple conditional discrimination task which trained and tested coordination responding towards the same set of stimuli. Thereafter half of the participants received "advanced" MET that established relational fluency in coordination, comparative, and opposition relating while the other half were exposed to the same training and testing as before. IQ tests were administered (a) at baseline, (b) following the conditional discrimination phase (after three months) and (c) after MET was completed (after two years). The authors found that training fluency in establishing and responding to multiple stimulus relations produced corresponding improvements in full and subscale IQ. Whereas fluency in coordination relating across multiple exemplars proved to be relatively beneficial, training relational fluency at higher levels of complexity led to the largest improvements in post-test IQ scores. Interestingly, follow-up testing indicated that these rises in IQ scores were still present almost four years later, suggesting that relational training and testing "successfully targeted skills that were of enduring importance in the ongoing intellectual and educational activities of the children" (Roche et al., 2013, p. 290). Although these initial findings require intensive and systematic replication, they provide the first step towards a functional analysis of the relationship between AARR and intellectual behavior. They also hint at the power of MET as a procedure for improving the flexibility and fluency of relational framing.

Summary. Attempting to kick-start intellectual development and boost educational achievement in typically developing and educationally deficient populations is an ambitious goal to say the least. Yet research at the functional level may provide the theoretical and methodological tools to make this goal a reality. RFT contributes to the study of intelligence by providing a functional definition of this phenomenon, which in turn leads to clear, testable predictions about its origins and properties. The key idea here is that AARR represents the fundamental "building block" of intelligence and that *fluent* and *flexible* relational framing underpins the skills and abilities needed to succeed in educational contexts. RFT also suggests that by directly targeting relational framing, and building fluency and flexibility in those repertoires, intellectual performance and educational attainment may be enhanced.

Future directions. Taking a step back, it should be evident that this line of research is very much in its infancy and that many conceptual and empirical challenges will require attention in the road ahead. Foremost amongst these concerns our understanding of AARR itself: limited work has been conducted on several types of framing (spatial, temporal, logical, and hierarchical) while little or no work has been carried out on others (conditionality). Nor do we know how relational frames interact with, and support each other, throughout intellectual development. Although early indications point to the importance of establishing fluency across a variety of frames and exemplars (Cassidy et al., 2010), we do not know which frames or combination of frames are more or less important for different intellectual skills and abilities. At the same time, existing procedures for training fluent and flexible framing will need to be refined and the moderating impact of biological (diet, sleep, genetics), social (family structure, social skills), and psychological (motivation, self-discipline) factors examined before these protocols are rolled out to educational and applied contexts. Existing work has almost exclusively focused on a handful of frames (e.g., coordination, temporal, and comparison) and their relationship to performance on standardized intelligence tests. Future interventions will need to determine the optimum order, sequence, and content of training needed to promote intellectual abilities across a variety of populations (children, teenagers, adults) and examine whether training in additional frames (hierarchical, deictic, and conditional) leads to even greater gains than those seen so far.

When carrying out this work researchers should also incorporate a wider range of outcomes measures. In nearly every study to date accuracy has been used as the main dependent measure of relational responding. Yet the acquisition *rate* at which contextual cues and stimulus relations are established or modified and the *speed* with which history-consistent responses are reversed may refine our understanding of intellectual behavior to a greater degree than accuracy-based measures alone. Thus alternative properties of relational responding will need to be considered and new measures for capturing such performances devised. For instance, RFT-inspired protocols such as the Training and Assessment of Relational Precursors and Abilities (TARPA) and PEAK relational training system (Dixon et al., 2014), seem to provide systematic means to assess and train the key skills implicated in flexible relational responding (see Moran, Stewart, McElwee, & Ming, 2014). Early work also suggests that the IRAP can assess the flexibility of relational responding at various levels of complexity (O'Toole & Barnes-Holmes, 2009). Researchers could draw upon the IRAP in order to identify instances of relational rigidity that could benefit from flexibility training (via the TARPA or PEAK) or assess the impact of other MET procedures designed to enhance relational framing skills. If relational flexibility is indeed a core feature of human intelligence, then it follows that rigidity, the antithesis of flexibility, is likely to be detrimental to intelligence. Finally, the majority of research to date has correlated relational performances with standardized measures of intelligence. Future work could examine whether more sophisticated framing abilities lead to other outcomes above and beyond improved intelligence scores, such as scholastic achievement, career success, or improved health and longevity. Addressing these and related issues will provide stronger evidence that an RFT approach to intellectual development makes a genuine difference in the lives of others.

Section 4: Conclusion

In their original book-length treatment of RFT back in 2001, Hayes and colleagues suggested that while the theory certainly seemed to be a generative one, we would not know if it was truly progressive and pragmatically useful until it increased our ability to predict and influence human language and cognition with precision, scope, and depth. Even a cursory glance through the current chapter (and those elsewhere in this handbook) will serve to reinforce how RFT met this challenge head on and delivered on several important fronts. Evidence indicates that we have identified the environmental regularities and history of learning necessary to predict and influence "cognitive" phenomena such as self (discrimination) and perspective-taking, intelligence, as well as thinking fast and slow. This approach has equipped researchers with variables that have fed the engines of application in order to change the world in a positive and intentional way. For instance, with a better understanding of deictic framing came technologies that enabled us to establish or enhance perspective-taking skills in developmentally delayed and (sub)clinical populations where previously weak or absent. With an appreciation for different properties of relational framing came procedures designed to capture events which unfolded in the blink of an eye, and to use those responses for predicting clinical, social, and health-related behaviors. Information about the fluency and flexibility of relational framing also pointed to possible strategies for cultivating and enhancing human potential. Two points are worth noting before we bring this chapter to a close. First, we only managed to capture a thin slice of the conceptual and empirical forces currently shaping the RFT literature. Ongoing work has also implicated AARR in a host of other complex human behaviors, from the development of false memories (Guinther & Dougher, 2010; 2014), and maintenance of auditory hallucinations (Monestès et al., 2014), to the search for meaning and sense making (Quinones & Hayes, 2014), problem-solving (Stewart et al., 2013), motivation (Ju & Hayes, 2008), and emotion (Barnes-Holmes & Hughes, 2013). Refining our functional understanding of these and related domains may provide input for a range of applications that change the world in other positive and useful ways. Second, while we have made progress over the past decade, there is still much work that needs to be done. For instance, the contribution of AARR to (a) the stability and change of behavior within and between individuals across time and context (personality; Harrington, Fink, & Dougher, 2001), (b) how an individual's thoughts, feelings and actions vary as a function of the social context (group cohesion, stereotyping, prejudice; Roche et al., 2002), (c) financial or organizational decision-making (behavioral economics; Quinones, Hayes, & Hayes, 2000) and (d) the ability for others to modify our behavior via persuasion or rhetoric has yet to be subjected to systematic empirical scrutiny. The same goes for topics such as pragmatic verbal analysis (or "thinking"), problem-solving, emotional and moral development, close relationships, and many other aspects of human psychological life. Delving into the RFT literature reveals a deep, rich vein of theoretical assumptions about these and related areas that – in many cases – have yet to be empirically mined. Transforming these ideas into generative, progressive, and pragmatically useful programs of research will require equal parts ingenuity and methodological innovation.

Notes

1   Although the current chapter separates language from cognition this is done purely in the service of communication. Indeed, it is important to recognize that the concepts of language and cognition are used to identify two broad domains in psychology but this

should not be taken to indicate that RFT aims to distinguish functionally between the two. As a bottom-up functional-contextual account, the primary purpose of RFT is to provide an analytic-abstractive theory of the key behavioural processes involved in these broadly defined domains.

2   The reason for this is simple. If a researcher's analytic goal involves predicting the origins and properties of language, then universal grammars, connectionist models, mental schemata, or any other statistical, mental or nonmental variable (e.g., brain, genetics) can be used, so long as they are reliably related to that phenomenon. Yet if that same researcher wants to achieve both *prediction-and-influence* over verbal behavior, then appeals to such explanations are ultimately insufficient. In order to exert influence over behavior the researcher must successfully manipulate events external to that behavior, and only contextual variables located in the environment can be directly manipulated (see Hayes & Brownstein, 1986). Consequently, from a CBS perspective, the scientific analysis of language is not complete until the causal variables external to verbal behavior have been identified – not because of some dogmatic adherence to a physical monism that excludes the nonphysical, mental world, but rather as a pragmatic means of achieving its scientific goals (for more on CBS see Hayes, Barnes-Holmes, & Wilson, 2012).

3   The concept of a relational network (and the relating of relational networks) also provides a way to approach the organization of larger language units in everyday terms, such as sentences, paragraphs, chapters, stories, trilogies, and so on. From an RFT perspective, human "language does not consist of isolated instances of utterances involving arbitrary applicability, mutual and combinatorial entailment, and transformation of stimulus function. Instead, each topographical unit (e.g., sentences, paragraphs, or chapters) contains multiple nested entailed relations and multiple possible functions, all of which differentially affect behavior" (Drossel, Waltz, & Hayes, 2007, p. 17).

4   The well-documented "language explosion" between the ages of two and three "seems like an obvious and salient example of the elaboration of the relational network. This typically occurs around the time that children have acquired the ability to frame in accordance with a few simple relations, allowing them to derive multiple novel relations amongst an expanding set of named objects and events" (Stewart & Roche, 2013, p. 66).

5   Although rules may be seen as involving relatively complex relational networks, relational networks are not always necessarily rules. For example, metaphors, analogies, stories, and jokes also appear to involve relational networks, but strictly speaking may not necessarily function as rules.

6   The above account is a gross oversimplification of research at the mental level of analysis. For a more detailed and carefully considered treatment see Brysbaert & Rastle, 2009; Eysenck & Keane, 2013; Miller, 2003; also see Chiesa, 1994; 1998; De Houwer, 2011).

7   It is worth noting that perspective taking and ToM are not explicitly connected with the self in the wider psychological literature. It is only in the context of the bottom-up explanation provided by RFT that the development of perspective-taking is seen as critical to the construction of self (see Stewart, 2013).

8   The descriptive terms *brief and immediate relational responding* (BIRRs) versus *extended and elaborated relational responding* (EERRs) have been used to distinguish between the types of responses that were typically targeted by indirect and direct procedures, respectively. However, the terms BIRRs and EERRs are descriptive, whereas the concepts of derivation and complexity point to variables that may be involved in producing these two broadly defined patterns of behavior.

9   The REC model appeals to a third property of derived relational responding (i.e., relational coherence) in order to explain why BIRRs can either converge or diverge from EERRs in different contexts (for a detailed treatment of coherence see Barnes-Holmes, Murphy et al., 2010; Cullen, et al., 2009; Hughes & Barnes-Holmes, 2013; Hughes et al., 2012).

References

Agerström, J., & Rooth, D. (2011). The role of automatic obesity stereotypes in real hiring discrimination. *Journal of Applied Psychology, 96*, 790–805.

Altmann, G. T. M. (2001). The mechanics of language: Psycholinguistics in review. *The British Journal of Psychology, 92*, 129–170.

Amodio, D. M., & Ratner, K. G. (2011). A memory systems model of implicit social cognition. *Current Directions in Psychological Science, 20*, 143–148.

Bach, P., & Hayes, S. C. (2002). The use of acceptance and commitment therapy to prevent the rehospitalization of psychotic patients: A randomized controlled trial. *Journal of Consulting and Clinical Psychology, 70*, 1129–1139.

Banaji, M. R., & Heiphetz, L. (2010). Attitudes. In S. T. Fiske, D. T. Gilbert, & G. Lindzey (Eds.), *Handbook of social psychology* (pp. 348–388). New York, NY: Wiley.

Bargh, J. A., & Ferguson, M. J. (2000). Beyond behaviorism: On the automaticity of higher mental processes. *Psychological Bulletin, 126*, 925–945.

Barnes, D., Hegarty, N., & Smeets, P. (1997). Relating equivalence relations to equivalence relations: A relational framing model of complex human functioning. *The Analysis of Verbal Behavior, 14*, 1–27.

Barnes, D., McCullagh, P., & Keenan, M. (1990). Equivalence class formation in non-hearing impaired children and hearing impaired children. *The Analysis of Verbal Behavior, 8*, 1–11.

Barnes-Holmes, D., Barnes-Holmes, Y., & Cullinan, V. (2000). Relational frame theory and Skinner's *Verbal Behavior*: A possible synthesis. *The Behavior Analyst, 23*, 69–84.

Barnes-Holmes, D., Barnes-Holmes, Y., Stewart, I., & Boles, S. (2010). A sketch of the Implicit Relational Assessment Procedure (IRAP) and the Relational Elaboration and Coherence (REC) model. *The Psychological Record, 60*, 527–542.

Barnes-Holmes, D., Hayes, S. C., & Dymond, S. (2001). Self and self-directed rules. In S. C. Hayes, D. Barnes-Holmes, and B. Roche (Eds.), *Relational frame theory: A post-Skinnerian account of human language and cognition* (pp. 119–140). New York, NY: Kluwer Academic/Plenum.

Barnes-Holmes, D., & Hughes, S. (2013). A functional approach to the study of human emotion: The centrality of relational/propositional processes. In D. Hermans, B. Rimé, & B. Mesquita (Eds.), *Changing emotions*. New York, NY: Psychology Press.

Barnes-Holmes, D., Murphy, A., Barnes-Holmes, Y., & Stewart, I. (2010). The Implicit Relational Assessment Procedure (IRAP): Exploring the impact of private versus public contexts and the response latency criterion on pro-white and anti-black stereotyping among white Irish individuals. *The Psychological Record, 60*, 57–66

Barnes-Holmes, D., Murtagh, L., Barnes-Holmes, Y., & Stewart, I. (2010). Using the Implicit Association Test and the Implicit Relational Assessment Procedure to measure attitudes towards meat and vegetables in vegetarians and meat-eaters. *The Psychological Record, 60*, 287–306.

Barnes-Holmes, D., Staunton, C., Whelan, R., Barnes-Holmes, Y., Commins, S., Walsh, D., ... Dymond, S. (2005). Derived stimulus relations, semantic priming, and event-related potentials: Testing a behavioral theory of semantic networks. *Journal of the Experimental Analysis of Behavior, 84*, 417–430.

Barnes-Holmes, Y., Barnes-Holmes, D., & Cullinan, V. (2001). Education. In S. C. Hayes, D. Barnes-Holmes, & B. Roche, (Eds.) *Relational frame theory: A post-Skinnerian account of human language and cognition*. New York, NY: Plenum.

Barnes-Holmes, Y., Barnes-Holmes, D., Smeets, P. M., Strand, P., & Friman, P. (2004). Establishing relational responding in accordance with more-than and less-than as generalized operant behavior in young children. *International Journal of Psychology and Psychological Therapy, 4*, 531–558.

Barnett, S. M., & Ceci, S. J. (2002). When and where do we apply what we learn? A taxonomy for far transfer. *Psychological Bulletin, 128*, 612–637.

Baron-Cohen S. (2000). Theory of mind and autism: A 15-year review. In S. Baron-Cohen, D. Cohen, and H. Tager-Flusberg (Eds.), *Understanding other minds: Perspectives from autism and developmental cognitive neuroscience* (pp. 3–20). Oxford, England: Oxford University Press.

Baron-Cohen, S., Lombardo, M., Tager-Flusberg, H., & Cohen, D. J. (2013). *Understanding other minds: Perspectives from developmental cognitive neuroscience* (3rd ed.). New York, NY: Oxford University Press.

Baumeister, R. F. (2008). Free will in scientific psychology. *Perspectives on Psychological Science, 3*, 14–19.

Baumeister, R. F. (2010). The self. In R. Baumeister and E. J. Finkel (Eds.), *Advanced social psychology: The state of science* (pp. 139–175). Oxford, England: Oxford University Press.

Berens, N. M., & Hayes, S. C. (2007). Arbitrarily applicable comparative relations: Experimental evidence for relational operants. *Journal of Applied Behavior Analysis, 40*, 45–71.

Berwick, R., Friederici, A. D., Chomsky, N., & Bolhuis, J. J. (2013). Evolution, brain, and the nature of language. *Trends in Cognitive Sciences, 17*, 89–98.

Brysbaert, M., & Rastle, K. (2009). *Historical and conceptual issues in psychology.* London, England: Pearson Education.

Carpenter, K. M., Martinez, D., Vadhan, N. L., Barnes-Holmes, D., & Nunes, E. V. (2012). Performance based measures of attentional bias and relational responding are associated with behavioural treatment outcome for cocaine dependence. *The American Journal of Drug and Alcohol Abuse, 38*, 146–154.

Carpentier, F., Smeets, P. M., & Barnes-Holmes, D. (2002). Matching functionally-same relations: Implications for equivalence–equivalence as a model for analogical reasoning. *The Psychological Record, 52*, 351–312.

Carpentier, F., Smeets, P. M., & Barnes-Holmes, D. (2003). Equivalence–equivalence as a model of analogy: Further analyses. *The Psychological Record, 53*, 349–372.

Carpentier, F., Smeets, P. M., Barnes-Holmes, D., & Stewart, I. (2004). Matching derived functionally-same relations: Equivalence–equivalence and classical analogies. *The Psychological Record, 54*, 255–273.

Cassidy, S., Roche, B., & Hayes, S. C. (2011). A relational frame training intervention to raise intelligence quotients: A pilot study. *The Psychological Record, 61*, 173–198.

Cassidy, S., Roche, B., & O'Hora, D. (2010). Relational frame theory and human intelligence. *European Journal of Behavior Analysis, 11*, 37–51.

Chiesa, M. (1994). *Radical behaviorism: The philosophy and the science.* Boston, MA: Author's Cooperative.

Chiesa, M. (1998). Beyond mechanism and dualism: Rethinking the scientific foundations of psychology. *British Journal of Psychology, 89*, 353–370.

Chomsky, N. (1959). A review of B. F. Skinner's *Verbal behavior. Language, 35*, 26–58.

Chomsky, N. (2011). Language and other cognitive systems. What is special about language? *Language Learning and Development, 7*, 263–278.

Christiansen, M. H., & Chater, N. (2008). Language as shaped by the brain. *Behavioral and Brain Sciences, 31*, 489–509.

Christiansen, M. H., & Kirby, S. (2003). Language evolution: Consensus and controversies. *Trends in Cognitive Science, 7*, 300–307.

Cullen, C., Barnes-Holmes, D., Barnes-Holmes, Y., & Stewart, I. (2009). The Implicit Relational Assessment Procedure (IRAP) and the malleability of ageist attitudes. *The Psychological Record, 59*, 591–620.

Cullinan, V., & Vitale, A. (2008). The contribution of relational frame theory to the development of interventions for impairments of language and cognition. *Journal of Speech-Language Pathology and Applied Behavior Analysis, 4*, 132–145.

Deary, I. J. (2000). *Looking down on human intelligence: From psychometrics to the brain.* Oxford, England: Oxford University Press.

Deci, E. L., & Ryan, R. M. (1985). *Intrinsic motivation and self-determination in human behavior.* New York, NY: Plenum.

De Houwer, J. (2011). Why the cognitive approach in psychology would profit from a functional approach and vice versa. *Perspectives on Psychological Science, 6,* 202–209.

De Houwer, J. (2014). A propositional model of implicit evaluation. *Social and Personality Psychology Compass, 8,* 342–353.

Dixon, M. R., Carman, J., Tyler, P. A., Whiting, S. W., Enoch, M. R., & Daar, J. H. (2014). PEAK relational training system for children with autism and developmental disabilities: Correlations with Peabody picture vocabulary test and assessment reliability. *Journal of Developmental and Physical Disabilities,* 1–12.

Dixon, M. R., Hayes, L., & Aban, I. (2000). Examining the roles of rule following, reinforcement and pre-experimental histories in risk-taking behavior. *The Psychological Record, 50,* 687–704.

Doherty, M. (2012). Theory of Mind. In L. McHugh & I. Stewart (Eds.), *The self and perspective taking* (pp. 91–107). Oakland, CA: Context Press.

Doll, B. B., Jacobs, W. J., Sanfey, A. G., & Frank, M. J. (2009). Instructional control of reinforcement learning: A behavioral and neuro-computational investigation. *Brain Research, 1299,* 74–94.

Drossel, C., Waltz, T. J., & Hayes, S. C (2007). An introduction to principles of behavior. In D. Woods & J. Kantor (Eds.), *Understanding behavior disorders: A contemporary behavior analytic perspective* (pp. 21–46). Reno, NV: Context Press.

Dymond, S., & Barnes, D. (1994). A transfer of self-discrimination response functions through equivalence relations. *Journal of the Experimental Analysis of Behavior, 62,* 251–267.

Dymond, S., & Barnes, D. (1995). A transformation of self-discrimination response functions in accordance with the arbitrarily applicable relations of sameness, more-than, and less-than. *Journal of the Experimental Analysis of Behavior, 64,* 163–184.

Dymond, S., & Barnes, D. (1996). A transformation of self-discrimination response functions in accordance with the arbitrarily applicable relations of sameness and opposition. *The Psychological Record, 46,* 271–300.

Dymond, S., & Roche, B. (Eds.). (2013). *Advances in relational frame theory & contextual behavioral science: Research & application.* Oakland, CA: New Harbinger.

Dymond, S., Schlund, M. W., Roche, B., De Houwer, J., Freegard, G. P. (2012). Safe from harm: Learned, instructed, and symbolic generalization pathways of human threat-avoidance. *PLoS ONE, 7.*

Eysenck, M., & Keane, M. T. (2013). *Cognitive Psychology 6e.* New York, NY: Psychology Press.

Fazio, R. H. (2007). Attitudes as object-evaluation associations of varying strength. *Social Cognition, 25,* 603–637.

Fazio, R. H., Jackson, J. R., Dunton, B. C., & Williams, C. J. (1995). Variability in automatic activation as an unobtrusive measure of racial attitudes: A bona fide pipeline? *Journal of Personality and Social Psychology, 69,* 1013–1027.

Flynn, J. R. (2007). *What is intelligence? Beyond the Flynn effect.* New York, NY: Cambridge University Press.

Foody, M., Barnes-Holmes, Y., & Barnes-Holmes, D. (2012). The role of self in acceptance and commitment therapy (ACT). In L. McHugh and I. Stewart (Eds.), *The self and perspective taking: Research and applications.* Oakland, CA: New Harbinger.

Foody, M., Barnes-Holmes, Y., Barnes-Holmes, D., Törneke, N., Luciano, C., Stewart, I. & McEnteggart, C. (2014). RFT for clinical use: The example of metaphor. *Journal of Contextual Behavioral Science, 3,* 305–313.

Friese, M., Smith, C. T., Plischke, T., Bluemke, M., & Nosek, B. A. (2012). Do implicit attitudes predict actual voting behavior particularly for undecided voters? *PLoS One, 7,* e44130.

Gardner, H. (2006). *Multiple intelligences* (2nd ed.). New York, NY: Basic Books.

Gawronski, B., & Bodenhausen, G. V. (2011). The associative-propositional evaluation model: Theory, evidence, and open questions. *Advances in Experimental Social Psychology, 44*, 59–127.

Gore, N. J., Barnes-Holmes, Y., & Murphy, G. (2010). The relationship between intellectual functioning and relational perspective-taking. *International Journal of Psychology and Psychological Therapy, 10*, 1–17.

Gorham, M., Barnes-Holmes, Y., Barnes-Holmes, D., & Berens, N. (2009). Derived comparative and transitive relations in young children with and without autism. *The Psychological Record, 59*, 221–246.

Gould, E., Tarbox, J., O'Hora, D., Noone, A., & Bergstrom, R. (2011). Teaching children with autism a basic component skill of perspective-taking. *Behavioral Interventions, 26*, 50–66.

Greenwald, A. G., & Banaji, M. R. (1989). The self as a memory system: Powerful, but ordinary. *Journal of Personality and Social Psychology, 57*, 41–54.

Greenwald, A. G., & Farnham, S. D. (2000). Using the implicit association test to measure self-esteem and self-concept. *Journal of Personality and Social Psychology, 79*, 1022–1038.

Greenwald, A. G., McGhee, D. E., & Schwartz, J. K. L. (1998). Measuring individual differences in implicit cognition: The implicit association test. *Journal of Personality and Social Psychology, 74*, 1464–1480.

Greer, R. D., & Longano, J. (2010). A rose by naming: How we may learn to do it. *The Analysis of Verbal Behavior, 26*, 73–106.

Gregg, A. P., & Klymowsky, J. (2013). The implicit association test in market research: Potentials and pitfalls. *Psychology & Marketing, 30*, 588–601.

Guinther, P. M., & Dougher, M. J. (2010). Semantic false memories in the form of derived relational intrusions following training. *Journal of the Experimental Analysis of Behavior, 93*, 329–347.

Guinther, P. M., & Dougher, M. J. (2014). Partial contextual control of semantic false memories in the form of derived relational intrusions following training. *The Psychological Record, 64*, 457–473.

Harley, T. A. (2013). *The psychology of language, fourth edition: From data to theory*. New York, NY: Psychology Press.

Harrington, J. A., Fink, B. C., & Dougher, M. J. (2001). Into the lion's den: Incorporating personality and evolutionary psychology to expand clinical behaviour analysis. *International Journal of Psychology and Psychological Therapy, 1*, 175–189.

Hayes, S. C. (1995). Knowing selves. *The Behavior Therapist, 18*, 94–96.

Hayes, S. C. (2012). Variation and selection in rules and rule-governance: The perspective of behavioral psychotherapy. *Social Evolution Forum*, April 6. Retrieved from http://social evolutionforum.com/2012/04/06/steven-c-hayes-variation-and-selection-in-rules-and-rule-governance-the-perspective-of-behavioral-psychotherapy

Hayes, S. C., Barnes-Holmes, D., & Roche, B. (Eds.). (2001). *Relational frame theory: A post-Skinnerian account of human language and cognition*. New York, NY: Plenum.

Hayes, S. C., Barnes-Holmes, D., & Wilson, K. G. (2012). Contextual behavioral science: Creating a science more adequate to the challenge of the human condition. *Journal of Contextual Behavioral Science, 1*, 1–16.

Hayes, S. C., & Brownstein, A. J. (1986). Mentalism, behavior–behavior relations, and a behavior-analytic view of the purposes of science. *The Behavior Analyst, 9*, 175–190.

Hayes, S. C., Brownstein, A. J., Zettle, R. D., Rosenfarb, I., & Korn, Z. (1986). Rule-governed behavior and sensitivity to changing consequences of responding. *Journal of the Experimental Analysis of Behavior, 45*, 237–256.

Hayes, S. C., Strosahl, K., & Wilson, K. G. (1999). *Acceptance and commitment therapy: An experiential approach to behavior change*. New York, NY: Guilford.

Heagle, A. I., & Rehfeldt, R. A. (2006). Teaching perspective-taking skills to typically developing children through derived relational responding. *Journal of Early and Intensive Behavior Intervention, 3,* 1–34.

Healy, O., Barnes-Holmes, D., & Smeets, P. M. (2000). Derived relational responding as generalized operant behavior. *Journal of the Experimental Analysis of Behavior, 74,* 207–227.

Holyoak, K. J. (2012). Analogy and relational reasoning. In K. J. Holyoak & R. G. Morrison (Eds.), *The Oxford handbook of thinking and reasoning* (pp. 234–259). New York, NY: Oxford University Press.

Holyoak, K. J., & Thagard, P. (1995). *Mental leaps: Analogy in creative thought.* Cambridge, MA: MIT Press/Bradford Books.

Horne, P. J., & Lowe, C. F. (1996). On the origins of naming and other symbolic behavior. *Journal of the Experimental Analysis of Behavior, 65,* 185–241.

Hughes, S., & Barnes-Holmes, D. (2011). On the formation and persistence of implicit attitudes: New evidence from the Implicit Relational Assessment Procedure (IRAP). *The Psychological Record, 61,* 391–410.

Hughes, S., & Barnes-Holmes, D. (2013). A functional approach to the study of implicit cognition: The Implicit Relational Assessment Procedure (IRAP) and the Relational Elaboration and Coherence (REC) model. In S. Dymond & B. Roche (Eds.), *Advances in relational frame theory & contextual behavioral science: Research & application.* Oakland, CA: New Harbinger.

Hughes, S., & Barnes-Holmes, D. (2014). Associative concept learning, stimulus equivalence, and relational frame theory: Working out the similarities and differences between human and non-human behavior. *Journal of Experimental Behavior Analysis, 101,* 156–160.

Hughes, S., Barnes-Holmes, D., & De Houwer, J. (2011). The dominance of associative theorizing in implicit attitude research: Propositional and behavioral alternatives. *The Psychological Record, 61,* 465–496.

Hughes, S., Barnes-Holmes, D., & Vahey, N. (2012). Holding on to our functional roots when exploring new intellectual islands: A voyage through implicit cognition research. *Journal of Contexual Behavioral Science, 1,* 17–38.

James, W. (1891). *Principles of psychology* (Vol. 1). New York, NY: Henry Holt.

Janssen, G., De Mey, H., Hendriks, A., Koppers, A., Kaarsemaker, M., Witteman, C., & Egger, J. (2014). Assessing deictic relational responding in individuals with social anxiety disorder: Evidence of perspective-taking difficulties. *The Psychological Record, 64,* 21–29.

Jensen, A. R. (1998). *The g factor.* Westport, CT: Praeger.

Ju, W. C., & Hayes, S. C. (2008). Verbal establishing stimuli: Testing the motivative effect of stimuli in a derived relation with consequences. *The Psychological Record, 58,* 339–363.

Kelly, A., & Barnes-Holmes, D. (2013). Implicit attitudes towards children with autism versus normally developing children as predictors of professional burnout and psychopathology. *Research in Developmental Disabilities, 34,* 17–28.

Kuncel, N. R., Hezlett, S. A., & Ones, D. S. (2004). Academic performance, career potential, creativity, and job performance: Can one construct predict them all? *Journal of Personality and Social Psychology, 86,* 148–161.

Laird, J. D. (2007). *Feelings: The perception of self.* New York, NY: Oxford University Press.

Lattal, K. A. (2012). Self in behavior analysis. In L. McHugh & I. Stewart (Eds.), *The self and perspective taking.* Oakland, CA: New Harbinger.

Lee, S., Rogge, R. D., & Reis, H. T. (2010). Assessing the seeds of relationship decay: Using implicit evaluations to detect the early stages of disillusionment. *Psychological Science, 21,* 857–864.

Lionello-DeNolf, K. M. (2009). The search for symmetry: 25 years in review. *Learning & Behavior, 37,* 188–203.

Lipkens, G., & Hayes, S. C. (2009). Producing and recognizing analogical relations. *Journal of the Experimental Analysis of Behavior, 91,* 105–126.

Lipkens, G., Hayes, S. C., & Hayes, L. J. (1993). Longitudinal study of derived stimulus relations in an infant. *Journal of Experimental Child Psychology, 56,* 201–239.

Luciano, C., Gómez-Becerra, I., & Rodríguez-Valverde, M. (2007). The role of multiple-exemplar training and naming in establishing derived equivalence in an infant. *Journal of Experimental Analysis of Behavior, 87,* 349–365.

Luo, Q., Perry, C., Peng, D., Jin, Z., Xu, D., Ding, G., & Xu, S. (2003). The neural substrate of analogical reasoning: An fMRI study. *Cognitive Brain Research, 17,* 527–534.

Luoma, J. B., Kohlenberg, B. S., Hayes, S. C., Bunting, K., & Rye, A. K. (2008). Reducing self-stigma in substance abuse through acceptance and commitment therapy: Model, manual development, and pilot outcomes. *Addiction Research & Theory, 16,* 149–165.

Mackintosh, N. (2011). *IQ and human intelligence.* Oxford, England: Oxford University Press.

Markus, H. R., & Kitayama, S. (1991). Culture and the self: Implications for cognition, emotion, and motivation. *Psychological Review, 98,* 224–253.

Mayer, R. E. (1999). Problem solving. In M. A. Runco & S. R. Pritzker (Eds.), *Encyclopedia of creativity,* Vol. 2. (pp. 437–447). New York, NY: Academic Press.

McAuliffe, D., Hughes, S., & Barnes-Holmes, D. (2014). The dark-side of rule governed behavior: An experimental analysis of problematic rule-following in an adolescent population with depressive symptomatology. *Behavior Modification, 38,* 587–613.

McConnell, A. R., & Leibold, J. M. (2001). Relations among the implicit association test, discriminatory behavior, and explicit measures of racial attitudes. *Journal of Experimental Social Psychology, 37,* 435–442.

McCurry, S., & Hayes, S. C. (1992). Clinical and experimental perspectives on metaphorical talk. *Clinical Psychology Review, 12,* 763–785.

McHugh, L., Barnes-Holmes, Y., & Barnes-Holmes, D. (2004). Perspective-taking as relational responding: A developmental profile. *The Psychological Record, 54,* 115–144.

McHugh, L., Barnes-Holmes, Y., & Barnes-Holmes, D. (2009). Perspective-taking. In R. A. Rehfeldt & Y. Barnes-Holmes (Eds.), *Derived relational responding: Applications for learners with autism and other developmental disabilities.* Oakland, CA: New Harbinger.

McHugh, L., Barnes-Holmes, Y., Barnes-Holmes, D., & Stewart, I. (2006). Understanding false belief as generalized operant behavior. *The Psychological Record, 56,* 341–364.

McHugh, L., Barnes-Holmes, Y., Barnes-Holmes, D., Stewart, I., & Dymond, S. (2007). Deictic relational complexity and the development of deception. *The Psychological Record, 57,* 517–531.

McHugh, L., & Reed, P. (2008). Using relational frame theory to build grammar in children with autistic spectrum conditions. *The Journal of Speech-Language Pathology and Applied Behavior Analysis, 3,* 60–77.

McHugh, L., & Stewart, I. (2012). *The self and perspective taking: Contributions and applications from modern behavioral science.* Oakland, CA: New Harbinger.

McHugh, L., Stewart, I., & Hooper, N. (2012). A contemporary functional analytic account of perspective taking. In L. McHugh & I. Stewart (Eds.), *The self and perspective taking* (pp. 55–71). Oakland, CA: Context Press.

McMullen, J., Barnes-Holmes, D., Barnes-Holmes, Y., Stewart, I., Luciano, M. C., & Cochrane, A. (2008). Acceptance versus distraction: Brief instructions, metaphors and exercises in increasing tolerance for self-delivered electric shocks. *Behaviour Research and Therapy, 46,* 122–129.

Miller, G. A. (2003). The cognitive revolution: A historical perspective. *Trends in Cognitive Sciences, 7,* 141–144.

Monestès, J. L., Villatte, M., Stewart, I., & Loas, G. (2014). Rule-based insensitivity and delusion maintenance in schizophrenia. *The Psychological Record, 64,* 329–338.

Moran, L., Stewart, I., McElwee, J., & Ming, S. (2014). Relational ability and language performance in children with autism spectrum disorders and typically developing children: A further test of the TARPA protocol. *The Psychological Record, 64,* 233–251.

Murphy, C., & Barnes-Holmes, D. (2010a). Establishing five derived mands in three adolescent boys with autism. *Journal of Applied Behavior Analysis, 43,* 537–541.

Murphy, C., & Barnes–Holmes, D. (2010b). Establishing complex derived manding with children with and without a diagnosis of autism. *The Psychological Record, 60,* 489–504.

Neisser, U. (1967). *Cognitive psychology.* Englewood Cliffs, NJ: Prentice Hall.

Nicholson, E., & Barnes-Holmes, D. (2012). Developing an implicit measure of disgust propensity and disgust sensitivity: Examining the role of implicit disgust-propensity and sensitivity in OCD. *Journal of Behavior Therapy and Experimental Psychiatry, 43*(3), 922–930.

Nock, M. K., Park, J. L., Finn, C. T., Deliberto, T. L., Dour, H. J., & Banaji, M. R. (2010). Measuring the "suicidal mind": Implicit cognition predicts suicidal behavior. *Psychological Science, 21,* 511–517.

Nosek, B. A. (2007). Implicit–explicit relations. *Current Directions in Psychological Science, 16,* 65–69.

Nosek, B. A., Hawkins, C. B., & Frazier, R. S. (2011). Implicit social cognition: From measures to mechanisms. *Trends in Cognitive Sciences, 15,* 152–159.

Nuttin, J. M. (1987). Affective consequences of mere ownership: The name letter effect in twelve European languages. *European Journal of Social Psychology, 17,* 381–402.

O'Hora, D., & Barnes-Holmes, D. (2004). Instructional control: Developing a relational frame analysis. *International Journal of Psychology and Psychological Therapy, 4,* 263–284.

O'Hora, D., Barnes-Holmes, D., Roche, B., & Smeets, P. M. (2004). Derived relational networks and control by novel instructions: A possible model of generative verbal responding. *The Psychological Record, 54,* 437–460.

O'Hora, D., Barnes-Holmes, D., & Stewart, I. (2014). Antecedent and consequential control of derived instruction following. *Journal of the Experimental Analysis of Behavior, 102,* 66–85.

O'Hora, D., & Maglieri, K. A. (2006). Goal statements and goal-directed behavior: A relational frame account of goal setting in organizations. *Journal of Organizational Behavior Management, 26,* 131–170.

O'Hora, D., Pelaez, M., Barnes-Holmes, D., & Amesty, L. (2005). Derived relational responding and human language: Evidence from the WAIS-III. *The Psychological Record, 55,* 155–174.

O'Hora, D., Pelaez, M., Barnes-Holmes, D., Rae, G., Robinson, K., & Chaudhary, T. (2008). Temporal relations and intelligence: Correlating relational performance with performance on the WAIS-III. *The Psychological Record, 58,* 569–584.

O'Neill, J., & Weil. T. M. (2014). Training deictic relational responding in people diagnosed with schizophrenia. *The Psychological Record, 64,* 301–310.

O'Reilly, A., Roche, B., Gavin, A., & Ruiz, M. R. (2013). A function acquisition speed test for equivalence relations. *The Psychological Record, 63,* 707–724.

Orsillo, S. M., & Batten, S. V. (2005). Acceptance and commitment therapy in the treatment of posttraumatic stress disorder. *Behavior Modification, 29,* 95–129.

O'Toole, C., & Barnes-Holmes, D. (2009). Three chronometric indices of relational responding as predictors of performance on a brief intelligence test: The importance of relational flexibility. *The Psychological Record, 59,* 119–132.

O'Toole, C., Barnes-Holmes, D., & Smyth, S. (2007). A derived transfer of functions and the implicit association test. *Journal of the Experimental Analysis of Behavior, 88,* 263–283.

O'Toole, C., Barnes-Holmes, D., Murphy, C., O'Connor, J., & Barnes-Holmes, Y. (2009). Relational flexibility and human intelligence: Extending the remit of Skinner's *Verbal behavior. International Journal of Psychology and Psychological Therapy, 9,* 1–17.

Payne, B. K., Cheng, S. M., Govorun, O., & Stewart, B. D. (2005). An inkblot for attitudes: Affect misattribution as implicit measurement. *Journal of Personality and Social Psychology, 89,* 277–293.

Payne, B. K., & Gawronski, B. (2010). A history of implicit social cognition: Where is it coming from? Where is it now? Where is it going? In B. Gawronski, & B. K. Payne (Eds.), *Handbook of implicit social cognition: Measurement, theory, and applications* (pp. 1–15). New York, NY: Guilford.

Pérez, V., García, A., & Gomez, J. (2011). Facilitation of the equivalence–equivalence responding: Generalization of relational responses. *International Journal of Psychological Research, 4,* 20–29.

Persicke, A., Tarbox, J., Ranick, J., & St. Clair, M. (2012). Establishing metaphorical reasoning in children with autism. *Research in Autism Spectrum Disorders, 6,* 913–920.

Perugini, M., Costantini, G., Hughes, S., & De Houwer, J. (2015). A Functional Perspective on Personality. *International Journal of Psychology.* doi:10.1002/ijop.12175

Pinker, S. (2006). Block that metaphor. *New Republic* (October 19).

Pinker, S. & Jackendoff, R. (2005). What's special about the human language faculty? *Cognition, 95,* 201–236.

Plomin, R. (2012). Genetics: How intelligence changes with age. *Nature, 482,* 165–166.

Quinones, J. L., & Hayes, S. C. (2014). Relational coherence in ambiguous and unambiguous relational networks. *Journal of the Experimental Analysis of Behavior, 101,* 76–93.

Quiñones, R., Hayes, L. J., & Hayes, S. C. (2000). On the benefits of collaboration: Consumer psychology, behavioral economics and relational frame theory. *Managerial and Decision Economics, 21,* 159–165.

Rabelo, L.Z., Bortoloti, R., & Souza, D.H. (2014). Dolls are for girls and not for boys: Evaluating the appropriateness of the Implicit Relational Assessment Procedure for school-age children. *The Psychological Record, 64,* 71–77.

Rehfeldt, R. A., & Barnes-Holmes, Y. (2009). *Derived relational responding: Applications for learners with autism and other developmental disabilities.* Oakland, CA: New Harbinger.

Rehfeldt, R., Dillen, J. E., Ziomek, M. M., & Kowalchuk, R. K. (2007). Assessing relational learning deficits in perspective-taking in children with high functioning autism spectrum disorder. *The Psychological Record, 57,* 23–47.

Remue, J., De Houwer, J., Barnes-Holmes, D., Vanderhasselt, M.-A., & De Raedt, R. (2013). Self-esteem revisited: Performance on the Implicit Relational Assessment Procedure as a measure of self- versus ideal self-related cognitions in dysphoria. *Cognition & Emotion, 27,* 1441–1449.

Reynolds, G. S., & Catania, A. C. (1962). Temporal discrimination in pigeons. *Science, 135,* 314–315.

Roche, B., Barnes-Holmes, Y., Barnes-Holmes, D., Stewart, I., & O'Hora, D. (2002). Relational frame theory: A new paradigm for the analysis of social behavior. *The Behavior Analyst, 25,* 75 –91.

Roche, B., Cassidy, S., & Stewart, I. (2013). Nurturing genius: Realizing a foundational aim of Psychology. In T. Kashdan & J. Ciarrochi (Eds.), *Cultivating well-being: Treatment innovations in positive psychology, acceptance and commitment therapy, and beyond.* Oakland, CA: New Harbinger.

Roche, B., Linehan, C., Ward, T., Dymond, S., & Rehfeldt, R. (2004). The unfolding of the relational operant: A real-time analysis using electroencephalography and reaction time measures. *International Journal of Psychology and Psychological Therapy, 4,* 587–603.

Roddy, S., Stewart, I., & Barnes-Holmes, D. (2010). Anti-fat, pro-slim, or both? Using two reaction time based measures to assess implicit attitudes to the slim and overweight. *Journal of Health Psychology, 15,* 416–425.

Roddy, S., Stewart, I., & Barnes-Holmes, D. (2011). Facial reactions reveal that slim is good but fat is not bad: Implicit and explicit measures of body size bias. *European Journal of Social Psychology, 41*, 488–494.

Rosales, R., & Rehfeldt, R. A. (2007). Contriving transitive conditioned establishing operations to establish derived manding skills in adults with severe developmental disabilities. *Journal of Applied Behavior Analysis, 40*, 105–121.

Ruiz, F. J., & Luciano, C. (2011). Cross-domain analogies as relating derived relations among two separate relational networks. *Journal of the Experimental Analysis of Behavior, 95*, 369–385.

Ruiz, F. J., & Luciano, C. (2012). Relating relations as a functional-analytic model of analogy and metaphor. *Acta comport, 20*, 5–31.

Sedikides, C., & Gregg, A. P. (2008). Self-enhancement: Food for thought. *Perspectives on Psychological Science, 3*, 102–116.

Shimoff, E., Catania, A. C., & Matthews, B. A. (1981). Uninstructed human responding: Sensitivity of low-rate performance to schedule contingencies. *Journal of the Experimental Analysis of Behavior, 36*, 207–220.

Shimp, C. P. (1983). The local organisation of behavior: Dissociations between a pigeon's behavior and self-reports of that behavior. *Journal of Experimental Analysis of Behavior, 39*, 61–68.

Sidman, M. (1994). *Equivalence relations and behavior: A research story*. Boston, MA: Authors Cooperative.

Skinner, B. F. (1957). *Verbal behavior*. Englewood Cliffs, NJ: Prentice Hall.

Skinner, B. F. (1974). *About behaviorism*. New York, NY: Knopf.

Sternberg, R. J. (1977). Component processes in analogical reasoning. *Psychological Review, 84*, 353–378.

Sternberg, R. J. (1985). *Beyond IQ*. New York, NY: Cambridge University Press.

Sternberg, R. J. (2004). Culture and intelligence. *American Psychologist, 59*, 325–338.

Sternberg, R. J. (2014a). Teaching about the nature of intelligence. *Intelligence, 42*, 176–179.

Sternberg, R. J. (2014b). Intelligence as trait – and state? *Journal of Intelligence, 2*, 4–5.

Sternberg, R. J., & Kaufman, S. B. (Eds.). (2011). *The Cambridge handbook of intelligence*. Cambridge, England: Cambridge University Press.

Sternberg, R. J., & Rifkin, B. (1979). The development of analogical reasoning processes. *Journal of Experimental Child Psychology, 27*, 195–232.

Stewart, I. (2013). A recent behaviour analytic approach to the self. *European Journal of Behavior Analysis, 14*, 271–283.

Stewart, I., & Barnes-Holmes, D. (2001). Understanding metaphor: A relational frame perspective. *The Behavior Analyst, 24*, 191–199.

Stewart, I., Barnes-Holmes, D., Hayes, S. C. & Lipkens, R. (2001). Relations among relations: Analogies, metaphors and stories. In S. C. Hayes, D. Barnes-Holmes, & B. Roche (Eds.), *Relational frame theory: A post-Skinnerian approach to language and cognition*. New York, NY: Plenum.

Stewart, I., Barnes-Holmes, D., & Roche, B. (2004). A functional-analytic model of analogy using the relational evaluation procedure. *The Psychological Record, 54*, 531–552.

Stewart, I., Barnes-Holmes, D., Roche, B., & Smeets, P. M. (2002). A functional-analytic model of analogy: A relational frame analysis. *Journal of the Experimental Analysis of Behavior, 78*, 375–396.

Stewart, I., Barnes-Holmes, D., & Weil, T. (2009). Training analogical reasoning as relational responding. In R. A. Rehfeldt & Y. Barnes-Holmes (Eds.), *Derived relational responding: Applications for learners with autism and other developmental disabilities*. Oakland, CA: New Harbinger.

Stewart, I., Barrett, K., McHugh, L., Barnes-Holmes, D., & O'Hora, D. (2013). Multiple contextual control over non-arbitrary relational responding and a preliminary model of pragmatic verbal analysis. *Journal of the Experimental Analysis of Behavior, 100*, 174–186.

Stewart, I., McElwee, J., & Ming, S. (2013). Language generativity, response generalization, and derived relational responding. *The Analysis of Verbal Behavior, 29*, 137–155.

Stewart, I. & Roche, B. (2013). Relational frame theory: An overview. In S. Dymond & B. Roche (Eds.), *Advances in relational frame theory: Research & application*. Oakland, CA: New Harbinger.

Stewart, I., Roche, B. T., O'Hora, D., & Tarbox, J. (2013). Education, intellectual development, and relational frame theory. In S. Dymond & B. T. Roche (Eds.), *Advances in relational frame theory & contextual behavioral science: Research & application*. Oakland, CA: New Harbinger.

Strack, F., & Deutsch, R. (2004). Reflective and impulsive determinants of social behavior. *Personality and Social Psychology Review, 8*, 220–247.

Tarbox, J., Tarbox, R., & O'Hora, D. (2009). Non-relational and relational instructional control. In R. A. Rehfeldt & Y. Barnes-Holmes (Eds.), *Derived relational responding: Applications for children with autism and other developmental disorders*. Oakland, CA: New Harbinger.

Tarbox, J., Zuckerman, C. K., Bishop, M. R., Olive, M. L., & O'Hora, D. P. (2011). Rule-governed behavior: Teaching a preliminary repertoire of rule-following to children with autism. *The Analysis of Verbal Behavior, 27*, 125–139.

Thibodeau, P. H., & Boroditsky, L. (2011). Metaphors we think with: The role of metaphor in reasoning. *PLoS One, 6*(2) e16782.

Timmins, L., Barnes-Holmes, D., & Cullen, C. (forthcoming). *The Implicit Relational Assessment Procedure as a measure of sexual orientation*. Manuscript submitted for publication.

Törneke, N. (2010). *Learning RFT: An introduction to relational frame theory and its clinical applications*. Oakland, CA: New Harbinger.

Törneke, N., Luciano, C., & Valdivia Salas, S. (2008). Rule-governed behavior and psychological problems. *International Journal of Psychology and Psychological Therapy, 8*, 141–156.

Traxler, M. J. (2012). *Introduction to psycholinguistics: Understanding language science*. Oxford, England: Wiley-Blackwell.

Twohig, M. P., Hayes, S. C., & Masuda, A. (2006). Increasing willingness to experience obsessions: Acceptance and commitment therapy as a treatment for obsessive compulsive disorder. *Behavior Therapy, 37*, 3–13.

Vahey, N. A., Barnes-Holmes, D., Barnes-Holmes, Y., & Stewart, I. (2009). A first test of the Implicit Relational Assessment Procedure (IRAP) as a measure of self-esteem: Irish prisoner groups and university students. *The Psychological Record, 59*, 371–388.

Valdivia, S., Luciano, C., & Molina, F. J. (2006). Verbal regulation of motivational states. *The Psychological Record, 56*, 577–595.

Villatte, M., Monestès, J. L., McHugh, L., Freixa i Baqué, E., & Loas, G. (2008). Assessing deictic relational responding in social anhedonia: A functional approach to the development of Theory of Mind impairments. *International Journal of Behavioral Consultation and Therapy, 4*, 360–373.

Villatte, M., Monestès, J. L., McHugh, L., Freixa i Baqué, E., & Loas, G. (2010). Assessing perspective taking in schizophrenia using relational frame theory. *The Psychological Record, 60*, 413–424.

Walsh, S., Horgan, J., May, R., Dymond, S., & Whelan, R. (2014). Facilitating relational framing in children and individuals with developmental delay using the relational completion procedure. *Journal of the Experimental Analysis of Behavior, 101*, 51–60.

Weil, T. M., Hayes, S. C., & Capurro, P. (2011). Establishing a deictic relational repertoire in young children. *The Psychological Record, 61*, 371–390.

Whelan, R., Cullinan, V., & O'Donovan, A. (2005). Derived same and opposite relations produce association and mediated priming. = Mismas Relaciones derivadas y Opuestas Producen la Asociación y la Preparación Mediada. *International Journal of Psychology & Psychological Therapy, 5*, 247–264.

Williams, B. A., Myerson, J., & Hale, S. (2008). Individual differences, intelligence, and behavior analysis. *Journal of the Experimental Analysis of Behavior, 90*, 219–231.

Wittenbrink, B., Judd, C. M., & Park, B. (1997). Evidence for racial prejudice at the implicit level and its relationship to questionnaire measures. *Journal of Personality and Social Psychology, 72*, 262–274.

Zentall, T. R., Wasserman, E. A., & Urcuioli, P. J. (2014). Associative concept learning in animals. *Journal of the Experimental Analysis of Behavior, 101*, 130–151.

Zimmerman, B. J. (2000). Attaining self-regulation: A social cognitive perspective. In M. Boekaerts, P. R. Pintrich, & M. Zeidner (Eds.), *Handbook of self-regulation* (pp. 13–39). San Diego, CA: Academic Press.

11

Relational Frame Theory
Implications for Education and Developmental Disabilities
Yvonne Barnes-Holmes, Deirdre Kavanagh, and Carol Murphy

There is now a substantive knowledge base in support of the basic concepts of relational frame theory (RFT) that provides good reason to begin to explore applications of the theory in educational and clinical contexts (Dymond & Roche, 2013; Hayes, Barnes-Holmes, & Roche, 2001). The application of behavioral concepts in educational settings has been dominated by the use of applied behavior analysis (ABA) with individuals with intellectual disabilities. And this is for good reason, as ABA has been undeniably effective and beneficial in this regard (Peters-Scheffer, Didden, Korzilius, & Sturmey, 2011).

But how does a field, such as behavioral psychology, know when it is doing the best it can? Often that is agreed only when the majority of individuals exposed to interventions show considerable educational or clinical gains (e.g., via randomized controlled trials, RCTs). It is perhaps surprising, therefore, that there are few RCTs examining the impact of ABA. Nonetheless, where these are available, the data suggest, for example, that adaptive and cognitive behavior are increased to the extent that original diagnoses of autism are reduced (e.g., Dawson et al., 2010).

If, in this context, we ask about whether behavioral psychology could yet produce better educational outcomes with individuals with intellectual disabilities, the current authors think the answer is "yes." Not, in our view, because the interventions currently in use aren't excellent, but because we think, as basic behavioral researchers, that the application of behavior analytic principles has yet to fully embrace relational frame theory (RFT). And we believe that doing so could potentially enhance educational outcomes emanating from behavioral psychology.

The current chapter is divided into three sections. Section 1 provides an overview of the general learning prerequisite skills for derived relational responding. These include establishing: preferences; on-task behavior (e.g., sitting and attending to task-based stimuli); generalized imitation; attending to others; simple and complex discriminations; and joint attention and social referencing. Each subsection also provides examples of how these skills may be established. Section 2 provides an overview of

The Wiley Handbook of Contextual Behavioral Science, First Edition. Edited by Robert D. Zettle, Steven C. Hayes, Dermot Barnes-Holmes, and Anthony Biglan.
© 2016 John Wiley & Sons, Ltd. Published 2016 by John Wiley & Sons, Ltd.

Skinner's verbal operants and explores how these speak to RFT's account, particularly with regard to the distinction between nonverbal and verbal behavior. This section goes on to summarize the core concepts of RFT, explaining how derived relational responding lies at the heart of the theory's approach to language. Subsections here include summaries of the different relational frames identified thus far and of some of the evidence supporting these concepts, as well as consideration of the optimal training sequence for establishing or facilitating the various frames. Section 3 explores what appear to be among the most complex types of relational responding proposed by RFT, namely the perspective-taking relations and analogical reasoning, again summarizing evidence in support of each area. Taken together, the chapter aims to provide an overview of where RFT concepts and supporting evidence are currently at in terms of applicability to education, especially in the context of the challenges presented by developmental disabilities.

Section 1: Prerequisite Skills for Derived Relational Responding

In this section, we provide a summary of the prerequisite skills that comprise some of the essential foundations for the subsequent emergence or acquisition of verbal behavior (see also Horne & Lowe, 1996). These general learning prerequisites include establishing: preferences (related to positive reinforcement procedures); on-task behavior (e.g., sitting and attending to task-based stimuli); generalized imitation; attending to others; simple and complex discriminations; and joint attention and social referencing. Each subsection also provides examples or suggestions for how these skills may be established.

The broad aims of behavioral intervention programs that include facilitating the derivation of stimulus relations are usually to teach learners complex verbal, social, and emotional repertoires (Lovaas, 2003). At this early point, it seems important to explain what we mean by "derivation" in this context (there will be more on this later). The term "derived" refers to stimulus relations that emerge and are not taught directly when language-able humans learn. For example, if a learner is taught that stimulus "A" is the same as stimulus "B," the individual will derive a bidirectional relation in terms of "B same as A." With an appropriate learning history and multiple-exemplar training, a young child taught to orient toward her mother on hearing the word "Mummy" (i.e., a word–person relation of coordination) may subsequently say "Mummy" when her mother is present (i.e., derived person–word coordination relation). Derived relational responding is thought to be essential, and fundamental, to the acquisition of advanced verbal repertoires and emergent or novel verbal responding. The following sources may be of benefit to readers of the current chapter. For RFT's theoretical account, see Hayes et al. (2001). For practical applications of RFT, see Rehfeldt and Barnes-Holmes (2009). And, for a recently developed behavioral teaching program that integrates traditional concepts of verbal behavior and derived stimulus relations, see Dixon, Belisle, Whiting, and Rowsey (2014).

Although verbal behavior is a *primary* learning target in ABA, many ABA programs do not *begin* with verbal behavior, preferring instead to establish basic nonverbal repertoires, thought to be prerequisites of verbal skills. This type of learning sequence tries to ensure that the nonverbal and preverbal bases of verbal behavior are established for the learner before language is targeted directly. The short subsections below summarize each of these important prerequisite skills for verbal behavior and derived stimulus relations.

Establishing Preference Assessments

An individual's choice of reinforcers may be highly idiosyncratic, especially for learners with developmental disabilities, but effective reinforcement is considered crucial for all forms of behavioral teaching. Although reinforcement involves more than stimulus preferences (Logan & Gast, 2001), stimulus preference assessment (SPA) procedures are often used to identify potential reinforcers, especially with individuals with developmental disabilities (Hagopian, Long, & Rush, 2004). For instance, the gold standard SPA is the paired stimulus (PS) method, also known as forced choice (Fisher et al., 1992). The instructor begins with an array of 10 items. She presents only two items from the array on each trial and requires the learner to select only one item per trial. These preferred items are then presented in pairs simultaneously across trials in order to establish a hierarchy in which each of the preferred items may be ranked in terms of selection percentages. Although this method boasts much supporting evidence with individuals with developmental disabilities (e.g., Hagopian et al., 2004), it is only rarely used because of the length of time it takes to complete (e.g., 10 items require a minimum of 20 trials). While alternative *shorter* SPA procedures are available, such as the multiple stimulus without replacement (MSWO) method (e.g., Carr, Nicholson, & Higbee, 2000), these appear less effective in identifying potential reinforcers. For example, an instructor only knows which items are preferred in terms of high versus low preference, but it has not been established that the high preference items actually function as reinforcers or that the low preference items do not (Rush, Mortenson, & Birch, 2010). Whether reinforcement *occurs* or not (i.e., behavior changes) will ultimately identify reinforcers. However, preference assessments can provide the instructor with a useful initial guide.

Establishing On-Task Behavior

Establishing on-task behavior often commences with shaping gross motor topographies (e.g., sitting) to eliminate competing disruptive behaviors (Lovaas, 2003) and is primarily concerned with teaching learners generalized attending (e.g., looking, listening, staying in-seat). Establishing attending repertoires in learners with developmental disabilities is notoriously difficult because of the variability in the stimuli that need to be attended to across tasks (Tarbox, Ghezzi, & Wilson, 2006). Nonetheless, attending to task-based stimuli (including the instructor) is essential for the student to learn to correspond her own behavior with what is seen and what is heard (e.g., to look at an object when an instructor says "Look at this," see Keohane, Pereira-Delgado, & Greer, 2009). This type of teaching often begins with establishing visual tracking procedures that involve conjugate reinforcement. That is, the instructor establishes attention to a target visual stimulus by pairing unconditioned or conditioned reinforcers with direct stimulus observation (Keohane, Greer, & Ackerman, 2006). Where verbal behavior in spoken form is the instructor's ultimate goal, aural tracking skills will be necessary to coordinate a spoken verbal stimulus and the correct speaker. Where verbal behavior in written form is the ultimate goal, visual tracking skills will be necessary to coordinate a spoken verbal stimulus and the correct printed stimulus.

Establishing Generalized Imitation

Imitation is pivotal to behavioral interventions and observational learning (Leaf & McEachin, 1999), in part because learners with developmental disabilities (especially autism) often do not readily imitate the behavior of others (Ledford & Wolery, 2011). The term "*generalized* imitation" refers to the ability to imitate a model's behavior regardless of the topography of the behavior, and imitating novel behavior is important in learning (Lovaas, 2003; Malott, 2008). The two most common means of establishing generalized imitation in learners with developmental disabilities include simultaneous stimulus prompting (Wolery, Holcombe, Billings, & Vassilaros, 1993) and shaping procedures that use differential reinforcement for successively improved approximations of that target response (Maurice, Green, & Luce, 1996). Ironically, the most common problem with efforts to establish generalized imitation is failure to *generalize* responding, wherein the imitative response is restricted to one or two explicitly taught topographies (e.g., Erjavec, Lovett, & Horne, 2009; Horne & Erjavec, 2007). Where this occurs, mirror procedures are used to enable a student to observe herself while imitating (Pereira-Delgado, Greer, & Speckman-Collins, 2006), and also to enhance correspondence between what the instructor says and what the child does.

Establishing Attending to Others

The two crucial skills on which attending to others is based are listening to others' voices (i.e., orienting appropriately when speech is heard) and eye-to-eye contact (i.e., orienting eye-gaze toward a speaker). Teaching attending to voices usually begins with conditioning procedures to establish the sound of the human voice (speaker) as conditioned reinforcement (Greer, Pistoljevic, Cahill, & Du, 2011; Peláez-Nogueras, Gewirtz, & Markham, 1996). Once this is established (or during these procedures), appropriate eye-to-eye contact is also taught. Eye-gaze repertoires have long been considered pivotal in behavioral intervention programs (e.g., Greer & Ross, 2007), but there is now recognition that this skill is established more effectively when integrated with various forms of attending to others. Specifically, integrated attendance involving appropriate eye-gaze toward a speaker is preferable to earlier procedures teaching eye-to-eye contact separately and maintaining eye-gaze for longer and longer time intervals in a manner that is unusual in the social community (Carbone, O'Brien, Sweeney-Kerwin, & Albert, 2011). In addition to conditioning procedures, positive reinforcement may be useful in establishing attendance skills for learners with developmental disabilities (Greer & Ross, 2007).

Establishing Simple and Conditional Discriminations

There are a number of types of discriminations that are important to the acquisition of educational skills (Stubbings & Martin, 1995). These vary considerably in terms of complexity, and the more complex discriminations are considered to be pivotal prerequisites for verbal behavior and related social skills.

Positioned at the lower end of a continuum of complexity are simple discriminations that occur within a standard three-term contingency. This type of discrimination is referred to as "simple" because the discriminative function of a given stimulus is not dependent upon any other stimulus. Typical examples of simple discriminations from educational interventions include simple intraverbals, expressive labels, vocal imitation, and nonvocal imitation (Tarbox, Dixon, Sturmey, & Matson, 2014). It is important to distinguish between simple and conditional discriminations. Indeed, simple discriminations are often taught using shaping procedures, because if the target behavior (e.g., selecting a red card) was established by presenting a cue, prompt, or instruction (e.g., saying "match"), that would not be a simple discrimination, it would instead be a conditional discrimination (because selecting red also depended upon the presence of "match").

Conditional discriminations occur within a four-term contingency and involve responding to a discriminative stimulus given a conditional stimulus (Axe, 2008). That is, the presence of a sample (conditional) stimulus alters the function of a discriminative stimulus. Matching-to-sample (MTS) is the prototypical format in which conditional discriminations are taught. Reflexivity (identity matching) is the simplest type of conditional discrimination and usually front-ends all intervention programs that aspire to establishing complex conditional discrimination repertoires. For example, a learner might be presented with a red card as a sample and an identical red card as a comparison, and reinforcement is provided for selecting the comparison only when the word "same" is present. Although the two stimuli are physically identical, this is still a conditional discrimination because reinforcement is differentially provided for selecting the red comparison in the presence of the red sample and the word "match," but not when the red sample is absent.

A more complex type of conditional discrimination occurs when physical stimuli are replaced with spoken words. For example, a learner might be presented with the spoken word "ball" followed by an actual ball and reinforcement is provided for touching the ball upon hearing the word "ball." Again, this is a conditional discrimination because reinforcement is differentially provided for touching the ball only in the presence of the spoken word "ball," and not when the spoken word is not emitted. Although the word in this case refers directly to the object, this is not identity matching because the stimuli are not identical.

Teaching conditional discriminations can be made more complex by presenting multiple comparison stimuli from which a learner is required to select only one. For example, in the presence of a blue circle as a sample with comparisons that include a blue circle, a red circle, and a black circle, reinforcement is provided for selecting the correct comparison (blue circle) from the array of three. In simple terms, what the learner is being taught to do is to ignore all comparisons except the blue circle (e.g., Grow, Carr, Kodak, Jostad, & Kisamore, 2011).

Conditional discriminations often involve *nonarbitrary* relational responding, because the target response is based, in part, on the formal or physical properties of the stimuli (Hayes et al., 2001). For instance, the shared color (e.g., blue) of the sample and comparison stimuli often controls a matching response. But conditional discriminations may also involve *arbitrary* relational responding, in which the target response is *not* based on the nonarbitrary properties of the stimuli, and these constitute more complex conditional discriminations (Stewart & McElwee, 2009). For example, when the sample stimulus is the spoken word "blue," and comparisons include black, red, and blue cards, selecting the blue comparison is based on an arbitrary coordination (same-as) relation. Specifically, the word "blue" has been socially designated by the verbal community to signify the color blue. This is an arbitrary relation in that there is nothing physically similar between the word and the color. This type of arbitrary relation is what is typically being referred to in RFT when defining arbitrarily applicable relational responding as fundamental to language and cognition.

Establishing Joint Attention and Social Referencing

Joint attention and social referencing are essential features of human social interactions, and both need to be established even before simple discriminations can be taught.

Joint attention appears to emerge before, or alongside, social referencing (Slaughter & McConnell, 2003), and various behavioral teaching programs require that joint attention is already well established as a prerequisite skill. For example, if a learner is unable to attend to an instructor, it will be very difficult for the instructor to even orient that learner to a teaching trial that requires any sort of discrimination. In simple terms, joint attention involves following an instructor's eye-gaze or finger-pointing to coordinate attending to a stimulus, in such a way that the learner and the instructor have some element of shared experience.

There is evidence to indicate that joint attention can be established effectively when it is found to be deficient or absent in an individual. For example, MacDonald et al. (2006) investigated joint attention in students with autism and found that after one year of participation in a comprehensive treatment program, all of the individuals demonstrated gaze shifts, gestures, and vocalizations at levels commensurate with typically developing peers. Similarly, McClannahan and Krantz (2006) demonstrated that these effects generalize to novel stimuli.

While the boundaries between joint attention and social referencing are somewhat subtle, social referencing refers specifically to checking another person's expression and responding to a stimulus on the basis of that expression (Peláez-Nogueras & Gewirtz, 1997). For example, if a child discriminates a fearful expression on his mother's face as he reaches toward a dog, he may be less likely to touch the dog. Social referencing is clearly essential to emotional and social bonding because it allows learners to discriminate the subtle relationships among contexts, expressions of others, and predicting the potential reinforcement of stimuli or events. Gewirtz and Peláez-Nogueras (1992) described various ways in which the emotional aspects of social referencing can be effectively established even in very young children.

Perspective-taking is one of the most crucial aspects of behavior in which joint attention and social referencing play a central role (Moll & Meltzoff, 2011), for example, in conversation, cooperative play, empathy, compassion, deception, and storytelling. If a learner cannot discriminate the perspective of others, this individual will be unable to interpret how another person might feel in a given context. Foundational perspective-taking can be taught using an RFT approach (see below).

Summary

Five general prerequisites appear to be pivotal to the emergence of verbal behavior, including on-task behavior; attending to others; generalized imitation; simple and conditional discriminations; and integrated attending (joint attention and social referencing). It is not surprising, therefore, that these target skills feature strongly in early behavioral intervention programs. Fortunately, the body of evidence to indicate that this array of skills can be readily established even in children with developmental delay or disability is both sizeable and compelling (e.g., Greer et al., 2011; McClannahan & Krantz, 2006; Pereira-Delgado et al., 2006).

In the following section, we explore in detail the key features of verbal behavior itself as verbal operants using Skinner's account and as derived relational responding, from the perspective of relational frame theory.

Section 2: Language and Derived Relational Responding

Establishing Skinner's Verbal Operants

Most ABA language programs are Skinnerian in their conceptual roots. And, a large body of evidence supports the educational utility of Skinner's (1957) functional account of verbal behavior, especially with individuals with autism and other developmental disorders (Greer & Ross, 2008; Sundberg & Michael, 2001). In short, Skinner proposed that verbal behavior is learned (in much the same way as other behavior) via behavioral principles (such as modeling and positive reinforcement) with the exception that there must be a "listener" with a history of reinforcement within a verbal community. Skinner defined several distinct verbal operants, namely mands, tacts, echoics, intraverbals, and autoclitics, each of which is summarized below.

A *mand* is synonymous with a request because it specifies to the listener the response or stimulus that will function as a reinforcer. For example, the mand "I want candy" specifies candy as the reinforcer. Manding, therefore, provides the speaker with some level of control over the physical and social environment. However, motivating operations (MOs) are also needed to provide the motivational context for the mand to occur in the first place (Laraway, Snycerski, Michael, & Poling, 2003). Mands are typically the first type of verbal operant targeted in traditional ABA programs, and these simply attempt to teach the learner to request an item in the presence of a relevant MO, without a prompt (Sundberg, Loeb, Hale, & Eigenheer, 2002). This usually requires the instructor to either capture naturally occurring MOs and/to or contrive MOs (Albert, Carbone, Murray, Hagerty, & Sweeney-Kerwin, 2012; Gutierrez et al., 2007; Shafer, 1994). An example of a contrived MO would involve arranging conditions of mild water deprivation for a child learning to mand for "water." The child is more likely to mand for water in MO conditions of water deprivation than if she/he has had copious amounts to drink, as satiation effects reduce motivation. A large body of evidence supports the utility of mand training in providing a learner with indirect control over the environment (see Sautter & LeBlanc, 2006 for a review).

A *tact* is similar to (but not synonymous with) a label emitted in the presence of a stimulus and the response is controlled by generalized social reinforcement (Skinner, 1957). For example, saying "tree" upon seeing a tree in the presence of others may result in a parent saying "That's right, it's a tree." Tacting is not reinforced by access to the tacted stimulus. For example, the tact "my tummy aches" is under the control of an internal stimulus, but evokes external social comforting. Naturally, although very simple in most respects, tacting is essential to social interactions, and is thus a foundation in verbal intervention programs (Leaf & McEachin, 1999; Lovaas, 2003; Sundberg & Partington, 1998). A large body of evidence supports the utility of establishing tacts (Horne, Lowe, & Randle, 2004; Sautter & LeBlanc, 2006).

Echoics are verbal behavior under the control of a verbal stimulus with full point-to-point correspondence between the verbal stimulus and the echoic response (commonly known as vocal imitation). Reinforcement, however, does not involve access to the stated stimulus – that would be a mand. For example, in teaching the echoic "puppy," the instructor says "puppy," the learner repeats the word "puppy," and the instructor delivers positive reinforcement. A large body of evidence supports the utility of training echoics (Sautter & LeBlanc, 2006). However, perhaps more importantly, echoic responding is often used to facilitate the establishment of other verbal operants, because vocal imitation provides an effective prompting procedure (Tarbox, Madrid, Aguilar, Jacobo, & Schiff, 2009). Furthermore, combining concurrent echoic training with mand or tact training has been shown to increase unprompted manding and tacting via the transfer of stimulus control (Finkel & Williams, 2001; Kodak & Clements, 2009; Valentino, Shillingsburg, & Call, 2012; Vedora & Meunier, 2009).

Intraverbals are verbal behavior under the control of other verbal stimuli. But (unlike echoics) there is no point-to-point correspondence with the verbal stimulus that evoked the intraverbal (Michael, Palmer, & Sundberg, 2011). For example, a learner may say "I'm going home now," to which another learner may respond "See you later," and the two responses are dissimilar in terms of verbal topography. Intraverbals are maintained by social reinforcement and may have primary antecedents that involve extremely complex verbal stimulus control. For example, the statement "I'd like to know what, in your opinion, are the defining features of a scientific method of research?" is a complex antecedent intraverbal that may result in an equally complex intraverbal response (see Axe, 2008; Sundberg & Sundberg, 2011). Indeed, conversations consist largely of intraverbal behavior. It is perhaps surprising, therefore, that there is much less research on intraverbals, relative to Skinner's other verbal operants (Sautter & LeBlanc, 2006). Indeed, much of the research on teaching intraverbals has focused primarily on teaching students to answer questions. For example, Finkel and Williams (2001) compared the effectiveness of textual versus echoic prompts when attempting to teach a six-year-old boy with autism to answer questions with sentences. The results suggested that textual prompts were more effective than echoic prompts in teaching intraverbals (see also Vedora & Meunier, 2009).

Autoclitics are verbal operants that depend upon the emission of other verbal behavior (Skinner, 1957). For example, if a speaker begins an interaction with the phrase "under the table," this autoclitic will affect the behavior of the listener by referencing some property of the speaker's behavior. Once again, although autoclitics (at least from Skinner's perspective) are central to verbal behavior, the research base suggesting how this operant should be trained is limited, relative to the other verbal operants (see Sautter & LeBlanc, 2006 for a review). Luke, Greer, Singer-Dudek, and Keohane (2011) described the utility of multiple exemplar instruction (MEI) for establishing autoclitic frames for spatial relations with novel tacts and mands.

ABA programs commonly target Skinner's verbal operants according to an assessment of the learner's baseline outcomes on the Verbal Behavior Milestones Assessment and Placement Program (VB-MAPP; Sundberg, 2008) or the Assessment of Basic Language and Learning Skills (ABLLS; Partington & Sundberg, 1998).

The same assessment measures are then used throughout training to track the learner's progress on the range of target verbal operants. In general, ABA advocates argue that the well-established success of ABA, particularly as a program of language remediation, attests to the accuracy and utility of Skinner's verbal operants, as measured using these tools (e.g., Sundberg & Michael, 2001).

Verbal versus Nonverbal Operants

While there is clearly good supporting evidence for the utility of Skinner's verbal operants in educational applications, not all behavioral researchers are convinced that Skinner adequately distinguished between verbal and *nonverbal* operants (e.g., Barnes-Holmes, Barnes-Holmes, & Cullinan, 2000). A key criticism in this regard is that Skinner's analysis cannot distinguish between verbal operants that are explicitly taught and those that are not but are instead emergent or derived, and that only those not explicitly taught warrant definition as "verbal." For illustrative purposes, consider manding. Murphy and Barnes-Holmes (2009) demonstrated derived manding in children with autism when manding with appropriate cards for specific tokens emerged untaught. Imagine a learner who is taught to mand for a teddy bear by pointing to the teddy (i.e., direct reinforcement of access to the teddy for the specific topographical mand). According to Murphy and Barnes-Holmes, this may be described as a nonverbal mand because the manding was directly reinforced.

Now imagine that the child learns to mand for the teddy by saying "teddy" (i.e., direct reinforcement of access to the teddy for the specific topographical mand). This might also be described as a nonverbal mand, because the child has simply learned to use a specific vocal topography to produce that reinforcer. In simple terms, the child in this case may not understand that the word "teddy" is coordinated with the object teddy in the verbal community. However, according to Skinner, the latter response is verbal. But according to RFT, this response is nonverbal.

Now consider that the child is taught that "teddy" refers to the object teddy (e.g., hear "teddy" and orient to the teddy), and subsequently mands for the teddy using the word "teddy," *without being directly taught to do so*. In this case, according to RFT, the mand is verbal because the word "teddy" participates in a relation of coordination with the object teddy. Hence, the word now has a symbolic quality and the mand is derived on the basis of that coordination relation. Furthermore, if the child now learns that "teddy" is a bear (i.e., bears and teddies are coordinated) she or he may subsequently mand for teddy using the word "bear," again without being explicitly taught this response. This would also be a derived and verbal mand, because "bear" participates in a coordination relation with other stimuli, and is not an empty or incidental vocal topography that has been taught as a mand by means of direct reinforcement. A number of researchers have described procedures for generating derived manding with individuals with autism and other developmental disorders (Murphy & Barnes-Holmes, 2009; Rosales & Rehfeldt, 2007). Similarly, Halvey and Rehfeldt (2005) used conditional discrimination instructions to establish derived tacting in adults with severe intellectual disabilities. And Pérez-González, García-Asenjo, Williams, and Carnerero (2007) used MEI to establish derived intraverbal antonyms with children with pervasive developmental disorders.

The debate around whether or not Skinner's verbal operants are more accurately defined as verbal or nonverbal (depending upon whether they have been directly reinforced or are derived) is of scientific importance, but it may also have implications for educational applications. For example, if training programs focused on derivation as generalized operant behavior, perhaps fewer individual topographies would need to be directly taught. In the subsections below, we review generalized verbal operants as defined by RFT.

Relational Frame Theory

It is important to emphasize that in an applied context (amongst others), RFT is not greatly at odds with traditional (Skinnerian) ABA programs. However, RFT places its most significant emphasis on the concept of derivation (Barnes-Holmes, Hayes, Barnes-Holmes, & Roche, 2002), as a defining feature of verbal behavior, with less of a focus on topographical responses. Indeed, numerous RFT researchers have argued that ABA programs *do* establish arbitrarily applicable relational responding, even though it is not targeted *directly*. Overall, the potential difference between the two schools of thought may have more to do with degree and sequencing, than teaching content. It is not surprising, therefore, that a working synthesis between Skinner's and RFT's accounts of verbal behavior has been suggested (Barncs-Holmes et al., 2000). Specifically, this type of synthesis involves combining the application of Skinner's behavioral principles, such as positive reinforcement, prompting, fading, and certain aspects of verbal behavior, with an RFT emphasis on derived relational responding (Berens & Hayes, 2007; Halvey & Rehfeldt, 2005; Murphy & Barnes-Holmes, 2009; Rosales & Rehfeldt, 2007).

In the subsections below, we summarize the core concepts of RFT and their utility in educational contexts. To begin, however, there are a number of fairly simple tenets that are fundamental to RFT and which should make understanding the following material somewhat easier. These are as follows: (1) For RFT, most of the behavior verbally sophisticated individuals engage in is verbal. (2) While these individuals are clearly capable of nonverbal behavior, their behavior is dominated by a verbal context. (3) While both animals and humans engage readily in nonarbitrary relational responding, verbal behavior comprises derived relational responding with an arbitrary or nonphysical basis. (4) While nonhumans may, in principle, be capable of this type of arbitrarily applicable relational responding, there is little robust evidence that they (or preverbal infants) show this type of behavior readily. (5) Nonarbitrary (i.e., nonverbal) relational responding is an essential prerequisite to verbal relational responding, but, once the latter develops, very little of the former occurs.

Arbitrary versus nonarbitrary stimulus relations. Relational frame theory distinguishes fundamentally between nonarbitrary relational responding and arbitrarily applicable relational responding (AARR). The latter is unlike the relational behavior demonstrated so readily and with such complexity in nonhumans (e.g., birds discriminating different trees based on relative greenness), because responding is not based on formal stimulus properties (Barnes-Holmes et al., 2002).

Derivation. As described previously, derivation occurs when a verbal response emerges without being directly reinforced, due to transfer or transformation of function effects. Consider a child taught to ask for a seat using the word "seat," and who subsequently learns that "seat," "chair," and "stool" are all similar (i.e., all participate in a relation of coordination). The child may then mand to sit using the word "chair" even though this response has not been previously reinforced. This is a derived mand.

Contextual cues. For RFT, relational responding is verbal when it is under the control of contextual cues *beyond* formal stimulus properties. For example, the word "is" most often functions as a contextual cue to control responding on the basis of the relation of coordination. For example, "this is an apple" or "that is a table" both often function as cues for word–object coordination relations, and this emerges across many exemplars, such that novel relational responding between two stimuli can emerge even though it was never explicitly taught. The learning process requires that specific words or phrases (such as "same as," "contrary to," "part of," "more than") become contextual cues for the specific relation (or C_{rel}) that is to be applied. It is important to note that the cues may be considered to have an arbitrary basis in the sense that the terms have no physical similarity to the relations indicated. Nevertheless, the social community has assigned different terms to particular relations, and the terms must consistently apply only to those relations; that is, they are not arbitrarily applied on an ongoing basis (e.g., "window" always refers to a window in English).

Multiple stimulus relations. What distinguishes RFT from other accounts of derived relational responding, such as stimulus equivalence (Sidman, 1971), is its focus on *multiple* stimulus relations. The various patterns or "relational frames" identified thus far include coordination, opposition, distinction, comparison, hierarchy, and perspective-taking (see Hayes et al., 2001). All relational frames are thought to involve generalized verbal operant responses that comprise the properties of mutual entailment, combinatorial entailment, and the transfer or transformation of stimulus function. What distinguishes one relational frame from another is the nature of the derived response and the specific transformation of functions in accordance with this.

Multiple-exemplar training (MET). According to RFT, MET is a critical component in the learning history that gives rise to the target generalized relational skill. Exemplars facilitate the learner abstracting the appropriate relation based on contextual cues, as unrelated to response topographies. For example, cues for coordination relations include "banana *is* a fruit," "fabric *means* cloth," and "education *goes with* school." In these examples, the topographies are unalike, but coordination relations are indicated in all cases. Similarly, cues for comparative relations include, for example, "a dollar *is more than* a quarter" and "her love for animals *is greater than* her love for people." Cues for distinction relations include, for example, "kindness *is not the same as* love" and "health *is not just* the absence of disease." And cues for opposition relations include, for example, "hot *is the other extreme of* cold" and "*at the other end of the continuum*." The following subsections review research that has demonstrated these types of differentiations in derived relational responding.

Establishing the relational frame of coordination. The frame of coordination is the most basic relational activity that infants learn in natural language and the one upon which subsequent relational frames appear to be built (Lipkins, Hayes, & Hayes, 1993). Luciano, Gomez-Becerra, and Rodríguez-Valverde (2007) demonstrated combinatorial entailment within coordination relations in a 19-month-old infant, the earliest age at which this type of derivation has been empirically demonstrated. Coordination is likely to be the first relation to be taught in educational or learning programs. For illustrative purposes, consider experimental trials presented by O'Connor, Rafferty, Barnes-Holmes, and Barnes-Holmes (2009) who successfully employed MET to establish coordination relations in children with autism. The target coordination relations involved written words ("A" stimuli), objects that relate to the words ("B" stimuli), and pictures of the objects ("C" stimuli). Participants were taught to relate the A stimuli to the B stimuli (word–object relations) and the B stimuli to C stimuli (object–picture relations). Tests for combinatorial entailment (A–C and C–A relations) showed that participants derived word–picture and picture–word relations without explicit teaching (see also Carr, Wilkinson, Blackman, & McIlvane, 2000). Interestingly, the study by O'Connor et al. (2009) also suggested a relationship between verbal ability and exemplar training requirements, such that participants with lower verbal ability required more exposures to explicit training of the target combinatorially entailed coordination relations before these performances emerged with novel stimuli (i.e., more training exemplars were necessary prior to the target performances being derived).

Luciano, Rodríguez, Manas, and Ruiz (2009) demonstrated the establishment of contextual control for coordination with nonarbitrary relations (i.e., same-as relations with identical stimuli), prior to teaching arbitrary coordination relations. And Barnes-Holmes, Barnes-Holmes, Smeets, and Luciano (2004) demonstrated the derived transfer of happy and sad mood functions through coordination relations in adults.

Establishing the relational frame of opposition. Behaving in accordance with the frame of opposition (e.g., big is opposite to small; day is opposite to night) requires the abstraction of a particular dimension along which stimuli can be differentiated at bipolar extremes. In the example of "big versus small" size is the relevant dimension, while in "day versus night" light levels and time are the relevant dimensions. According to RFT, opposition relations likely emerge after coordination relations, because opposition relations *involve* coordination relations. For example, if A is opposite to B and B is opposite to C, A and C are most likely the same. Barnes-Holmes, Barnes-Holmes, Smeets, Strand, and Friman (2004) successfully employed MET to establish opposition relations in typically developing children. In short, learners were required to select the most valuable coin/s from four possible options after being instructed that: "Coin A buys many; and A is opposite to B, and B is opposite to C, and C is the opposite to D." After extensive MET, the children demonstrated opposite responding on novel 10-coin randomized sequences. Explicit training and increasingly complex testing (e.g., where the coins were presented randomly) continued until participants were responding correctly to trials with 10-coin sequences.

Luciano, Rodríguez et al. (2009) demonstrated the establishment of contextual control for opposition with nonarbitrary relations, prior to arbitrary opposition relations (i.e., the latter involved socially designated opposite relations, rather than physical opposites, such as big vs. small). This usually involves training the student to match very different stimuli under the control of "pick the opposite of." Dunne, Foody, Barnes-Holmes, Barnes-Holmes, and Murphy (2014) who published the first study of opposition relations in children with autism reported that yes/no responding was essential prior to establishing nonarbitrary opposition relations. The researchers then taught nonarbitrary opposition relations by presenting objects such as a big ball and a small ball, and asking the learner "Show me the big/small one" followed by "Show me the opposite of big/small." These nonarbitrary opposition relations were established across a range of stimulus dimensions (e.g., long vs. short; wet vs. dry) and with novel stimuli, under the contextual cue "opposite of."

Dunne et al. (2014) also reported the establishment of arbitrary opposition relations and the same 10 dimensions targeted in the nonarbitrary trials (i.e., now using identical stimuli). To promote flexibility in relational responding, Luciano,

Rodríguez et al. (2009) suggested that training should alter the contextual cues for opposition and coordination relations, once both have been firmly established.

Dymond, Roche, Forsyth, Whelan, and Rhoden (2007) have also demonstrated the derived transfer of avoidance functions in accordance with taught opposite relations. And Whelan and Barnes-Holmes (2004) have demonstrated the transfer of a punishing function through taught opposition relations.

Establishing the relational frame of distinction. The relational frame of distinction involves responding to differences among stimuli, along a particular dimension, by applying the relational cue "is different from" (Dixon & Zlomke, 2005; Roche & Barnes, 1996; Steele & Hayes, 1991). Dunne et al. (2014) established contextual control for distinction with nonarbitrary relations in two children with autism. That is, given two identical pictures and a third different picture, participants were asked: "Show me the picture that is different." These nonarbitrary relations were taught across a range of stimulus dimensions (e.g., color, length, texture, and shape), using novel stimuli. Dunne et al. (2014) also established contextual control for distinction with arbitrary relations. That is, given two identical boxes, participants were instructed "Box A is the same as Box B" and asked "Are they different?" The results demonstrated that one of the children required extensive training on combinatorially entailed distinction relations.

Establishing the relational frame of comparison. Comparative relations involve responding to one event in terms of quantitative or qualitative relations along a specified dimension with another event. Luciano, Rodríguez, et al. (2009) describe ways in which contextual control for comparison with nonarbitrary relations can be established (e.g., more–less, heavier–lighter, etc.). And Barnes-Holmes, Barnes-Holmes, Smeets, Strand et al. (2004) successfully employed MET to establish arbitrary comparative (more-than and less-than) relations (e.g., "Coin A buys less than coin B, so which coin would you take to buy as many sweets as possible"?) These outcomes were replicated by Berens and Hayes (2007). Only two studies have established comparison relations in children with autism (Dunne et al., 2014; Gorham, Barnes-Holmes, Barnes-Holmes, & Berens, 2009). The results demonstrated that these children required extensive explicit training on the target arbitrary comparison relations.

Vitale, Barnes-Holmes, Barnes-Holmes, and Campbell (2008) investigated adult performances on different types of comparative relations, including unspecified relations (e.g., if A > B and C > B, then one cannot determine the relationship between A and C). The results indicated that accuracy on unspecified relations was significantly lower than on specified relations, especially when mixed comparative relations were presented (e.g., more–less, rather than more–more). The study also demonstrated that a combination of feedback and presenting trials in nonarbitrary form generated the largest improvements in the weak baseline performances.

Vitale, Campbell, Barnes-Holmes, and Barnes-Holmes (2012) replicated various aspects of the original Vitale et al. (2008) study, but used real word tasks (e.g., involving color names and spoken nonsense syllables). The results were largely consistent with the original study in that the weakest performances were recorded on the unspecified mixed comparative relations, but these were readily rectified with feedback and nonarbitrary trials.

Establishing the relational frame of hierarchy. Responding in accordance with hierarchical relations is usually under the control of contextual cues such as "contains," "is an attribute of/member of/part of," or "belongs to." Hierarchical relations also comprise other relations because members of a hierarchical class can be organized in many ways. Hence, learners probably require strong existing capabilities in the other relational frames before hierarchy can be established.

There appear to be only two studies to date that have been conducted on hierarchical relations with adults (Gil, Luciano, & Ruíz, 2008; Griffee & Dougher, 2002). Dunne (2011) established hierarchal relations in two participants with autism, beginning with nonarbitrary relations and involving sweets versus musical instruments. Assessment of these relations commenced with distinction relations to ensure that the two types of items were distinct (e.g., "Are toys different to items you find in the kitchen?") Establishing arbitrary hierarchical relations involved subdividing the two categories into two further categories (e.g., sweet vs. nonsweet foods and wind instruments vs. others) and introducing pictures pertaining to the various items. For example, the researcher held up one a picture of a marshmallow and asked "Where would you put the marshmallow?" and "Is the marshmallow more like sweet food or nonsweet food?" One participant passed all aspects of testing, while the second required training before doing so.

Sequencing of relations. The sequence in which the core relational frames above were described does not reflect empirical evidence to indicate that this is the natural sequence in which they emerge, although, for example, it makes intuitive and developmental sense that coordination relations develop first and emerge before the more complex hierarchical relations. However, several RFT authors and recent studies have explored the potential sequence in which these frames appear to unfold. Consider the following comments. First, coordination relations probably emerge initially, because they pertain most directly to mutual and combinatorial entailment (e.g., if A=B and B=C, then B=A, C=B, A=C, and C=A). Second, distinction relations may emerge thereafter because a learner cannot comprehend or derive the relation "different-from" if "same-as" relations are not intact (Rehfeldt & Barnes-Holmes, 2009). In other words, the concept of difference cannot arise without the concept of sameness. Third, opposition relations may emerge then because one would find it difficult to know that two stimuli were opposite without first determining that they were different (i.e., opposition is perhaps an extreme type of distinction) and coordination relations may be derived from opposition relations (e.g. if A is opposite to B and B is opposite to C, then A and C are the same). Fourth, comparison relations may follow thereafter because a learner would have to first comprehend the variations of distinction and opposition to appreciate several ways in which two stimuli might be different, while at the same time being similar along a specific dimension. For example, the statement "apples are redder than peaches" may contain many complex relations such as comparison (more/less red), difference (apples not same as peaches), and opposition (not extremely different/opposite). Fifth, hierarchical relations probably appear thereafter because they are more complex in that they involve containment, which can occur at many levels (e.g., atoms are contained in material objects, material objects are contained in the Earth, Earth is contained in the Universe).

A small number of studies have explored the putative emergent sequence in developmental terms in search of the optimal sequence for educational purposes (e.g., Cassidy, 2008; Dixon et al., 2014). For example, Dunne et al. (2014) established the following sequence of relations: coordination, opposition, distinction, and comparison, in a group of children with autism. All 10 children were successful in demonstrating coordination relations; four children subsequently demonstrated opposition relations; and two children demonstrated distinction, comparison, and hierarchical relations, in that order. The results also indicated that the number of teaching trials decreased steadily across the five frames for several children, thus implying that the earlier relational frames facilitated learning the subsequent more complex frames. More recently, Kent (2014) directly compared two training sequences. Training Sequence A consisted of teaching coordination, distinction, comparison, opposition, and hierarchical relations, while Training Sequence B switched the order of the comparison and opposition relations (coordination, distinction, opposition, comparison, and hierarchy). The results indicated that participants who completed Training Sequence A demonstrated significantly better performances in the emergence of comparison relations than did participants who completed Training Sequence B. This finding suggests that establishing opposition relations may facilitate the emergence of comparison relations.

Section 3: Higher Order Cognition and Complex Relational Responding

In the final section we review two additional RFT concepts, namely, the deictic or perspective-taking relations and the relating of relations, which looks like a functional account of analogical reasoning. While both of these concepts do not differ functionally from those described above, they do permit RFT to address highly complex features of verbal behavior.

Perspective-Taking as Relational Responding

According to RFT, perspective-taking comprises complex repertoires of derived relational responding that encompass our understanding of person, place, and time. Specifically, RFT proposes the three perspective-taking or deictic frames of: I versus you (also called interpersonal relations), here versus there (spatial relations), and now versus then (temporal relations). Although a considerable body of RFT evidence supports the functional distinctiveness of these three types of relations, it appears that these interact with each other in distinct ways as part of normal verbal behavior. Specifically, "I" is always responded to from "here" and "now," such that one's perspective comprises I–HERE–NOW.

I–YOU relations. The interpersonal relations appear to be the first of the deictic relations to emerge, and also form the basis of the spatial and temporal relations that follow. Empirical evidence also suggests that these emerge in simple form prior to the ability to reverse them in what looks like a relatively high level of relational complexity. Consider the following simple I–YOU trial from the original deictic protocol developed by Barnes-Holmes (2001) in which the researcher said "I have a red brick and you have a green brick. Which brick do I have?" and "Which brick do you have?" It is important to remember that these trials, although categorized as "simple," are still verbal because no actual props are employed. What simple I–YOU trials do is to ascertain whether the words "I" and "you" control the appropriate perspective. For example, when the researcher says "I," the learner must interpret this as "you" from the learner's perspective, and similarly when the researcher says "you," the learner must interpret this as "I" from the learner's perspective.

Barnes-Holmes (2001) studied these relations in two typically developing children and reported that both the four-year-old and the seven-year-old could derive simple I–YOU relations. McHugh, Barnes-Holmes, O'Hora, and Barnes-Holmes (2004) studied groups of participants that ranged in age from early childhood to adulthood (i.e., 3–30 years old), and reported that all five groups showed high levels of accuracy on simple I–YOU relations. Similarly, Weil, Hayes, and Capurro (2011) reported strong performances for typically developing children aged 4–5 years, as did Heagle and Rehfeldt (2006) with typically developing children aged 6–11 years (see also Davlin, Rehfeldt, & Lovett, 2011; Rehfeldt, Dillen, Ziomek, & Kowalchuk, 2007). In the latter study, Rehfeldt et al. reported similar performances with children with autism aged 6–13 as did Gore, Barnes-Holmes, and Murphy (2010) with adults with mild to moderate intellectual disabilities, and McGuinness (2005) with participants with Asperger's syndrome aged 8–11.

Several studies have shown that learners capable of demonstrating simple I–YOU relations may be *unable* to show I–YOU reversals. Consider the following trial from Barnes-Holmes (2001) in which the learner is instructed as follows: "I have a red brick and you have a green brick. *If I was you and you were me.* Which brick would I have?" and "Which brick would you have?" These trials ascertain whether the statement "If I was you and you were me" will facilitate reversal of the original "I" and "you" perspectives as controlled by the words "I" and "you." For example, rather than the learner now responding to "I" as from her own perspective, she must now switch and respond from "you" and, similarly, rather than the learner responding to "you" as from an alternative perspective, she must now switch and respond from "you" as her own perspective. This type of reversal appears to involve greater relational flexibility than a simple I–YOU trial because it asks the learner to temporarily take the perspective of another in a specific context.

Although the four-year-old in the study by Barnes-Holmes (2001) could derive simple I–YOU relations, he failed to show I–YOU reversals, while the seven-year-old produced perfect performances on these relations also. Similarly, McHugh et al. (2004) reported significantly more errors on I–YOU reversals versus simple I–YOU trials for all five age groups. Similar effects have also been recorded by Weil et al. (2011), Heagle and Rehfeldt (2006), Gore et al. (2010), and McGuinness (2005). Interestingly, Davlin et al. (2011) reported that one of their three typically developing participants produced higher accuracies on reversed than on simple I–YOU relations.

HERE–THERE relations. The spatial relations have been studied in a similar manner to the interpersonal relations, but are almost impossible to investigate without reference to the interpersonal relations. That is, HERE–THERE relations appear to contain I–YOU relations (i.e., there can be no here without I). Consider the following trial from Barnes-Holmes (2001): "I am standing here at the yellow door, and you are standing there at the brown door. Where are you standing? Where am I standing?" This trial attempts to determine the perspectives controlled by the words "I," "you," "here," and "there," and it is almost impossible to decipher whether it is the interpersonal relations, the spatial relations, or both, that control responding.

Once again, Barnes-Holmes (2001) reported that both the four-year-old and the seven-year-old could derive simple HERE–THERE relations. McHugh et al. (2004) reported that all five groups showed high levels of accuracy on simple HERE–THERE relations. Similar effects have also been recorded by Gore et al. (2010), and McGuinness (2005). Furthermore, Weil et al. (2011) reported that all three participants responded with more errors on HERE–THERE relations than on I–YOU relations.

Although the spatial relations incorporate the interpersonal relations, Barnes-Holmes (2001) created a trial that attempted to reverse one of these relations while holding the other simple (albeit not something done in everyday language). Consider the following trial that contains a simple HERE–THERE relation, but a reversed I–YOU relation: "I am standing at the yellow door, and you are standing at the brown door. If I were you and you were me, where would you be standing? Where would I be standing?" This trial attempts to ascertain whether the reversal of the I–YOU relation controls responding, in which case the perspectives should be switched. Now consider a similar trial but in this case the I–YOU relation remains simple, while the HERE–THERE relation is reversed: "I am standing at the yellow door, and you are standing at the brown door. *If here was there and there was here*, where would you be standing? Where would I be standing?" This trial attempts to ascertain whether the reversal of the HERE–THERE relation controls responding, in which case the perspectives should again be switched. While responding correctly is the same across both types of trial, any switching of perspectives relative to completely simple trials suggests that the reversal controlled responding.

Although the four-year-old in the study by Barnes-Holmes (2001) could derive simple HERE–THERE relations, he failed to show HERE–THERE reversals, while the seven-year-old produced perfect performances on both. Similar to I–YOU relations, McHugh et al. (2004) reported significantly more errors on HERE–THERE reversals versus simple HERE–THERE trials for all groups of participants. Those researchers also compared performances on HERE–THERE reversals versus I–YOU reversals, and reported significantly more errors on HERE–THERE. Similar effects have also been reported by Gore et al. (2010), McGuinness (2005), and Weil et al. (2011).

NOW–THEN relations. Similar to the spatial relations, the temporal NOW–THEN relations must always be combined with the interpersonal relations in order to have meaning (i.e., it is always from one's perspective that one discriminates time). However, Barnes-Holmes (2001) demonstrated that the temporal relations, when presented in the original protocol, must be delivered in a somewhat different format, if the researcher does not wish to make trials longer by providing additional information. Consider the trial: "Yesterday I was reading; today you are watching television." If you were then asked "What was I doing then? What are you doing now?" you would be able to answer. But if you were asked, "What am I doing now?" and "What are you doing then?," you could not answer because these relations cannot be derived from the information provided (i.e., I–NOW and YOU–THEN remain unspecified). As a result, Barnes-Holmes constructed NOW–THEN trials in which *either* I or YOU were presented, but not both.

McHugh et al. (2004) reported significantly more errors on NOW–THEN simple relations than on HERE–THERE simple relations, indicating that responding in accordance with the NOW–THEN frame produced the most difficulty for all participants. Similarly, Weil et al. (2011) reported that performances on simple NOW–THEN relations were weaker than on the other simple relations, as did Gore et al. (2010) and McHugh et al. (2004). Interestingly, McGuinness (2005) reported nearly perfect scores on simple NOW–THEN relations that were similar to those reported for simple I–YOU and simple HERE–THERE relations.

Similar to the two other deictic relations, the temporal NOW–THEN relations can also be reversed (e.g., "Yesterday I was reading, today I am watching TV. *If NOW was THEN and THEN was NOW*, what would I be doing now? What would I be doing then?) However, because of the need to isolate only one perspective (I or YOU), responding correctly can only be on the basis of the reversed temporal relation. That is, there is no switch in perspectives across people, just a switch in the reversed NOW–THEN relation.

McHugh et al. (2004) reported significantly more errors on simple NOW–THEN compared to reversed NOW–THEN relations, and more errors on reversed NOW–THEN versus reversed I–YOU relations. But, interestingly, those researchers reported no difference between reversed NOW–THEN and reversed HERE–THERE relations.

Double reversed relations. Just as any of the three deictic relations can be reversed while an adjoining relation remains simple (e.g., a simple I–YOU with a reversed HERE–THERE relation), Barnes-Holmes (2001) also constructed two types of trials in which two deictic relations can be reversed simultaneously. Consider the following trial referred to as a double reversed I–YOU/HERE–THERE relation: "I am standing here at the yellow door, and you are standing there at the brown door. If I was you and you were me, and if here was there and there was here, where would you be standing? Where would I be standing?" This trial attempts to reverse perspectives as controlled by *both* the interpersonal and spatial relations, and as a result a correct response is designated by no reversal. That is, if you switch perspective through the I–YOU reversal, you must then *switch back to the original perspective* through then reversing the HERE–THERE relation. As a result, responding in a reversed way would suggest that only one reversal controlled responding (although it would be impossible to know which), while responding in a nonreversed way (as if it was a simple trial) would suggest that responding had been controlled by both reversals. Barnes-Holmes reported that the seven-year-old participant produced greater errors on double reversed I–YOU/HERE–THERE relations compared to all other relations including other reversals. Similar findings were reported by McGuinness (2005).

Just as double reversals can be created by simultaneously reversing I–YOU and HERE–THERE relations, Barnes-Holmes (2001) also constructed double reversals by combining reversals on HERE–THERE and NOW–THEN relations. Note that given the focus on only I or YOU in the temporal relations, there is no way of creating a double reversal with I–YOU and NOW–THEN relations. Consider the following trial referred to as a double reversed HERE–THERE–NOW–THEN relation: "Yesterday I was sitting there on the blue chair, today I am sitting here on the black chair. If HERE was THERE and THERE was HERE, and if NOW was THEN and THEN was NOW: Where would I be sitting now? Where would I be sitting then?"

This trial attempts to reverse one's temporal perspective as controlled by *both* the spatial and temporal relations, and as a result a correct response is designated by no reversal. That is, if you switch your temporal perspective through the NOW–THEN reversal, you must then *switch back to the original temporal perspective* through then reversing the HERE–THERE relation. As a result, responding in a reversed way would suggest that only one reversal controlled responding (although it would be impossible to know which), while responding in a nonreversed way (as if it was a simple trial) would suggest that responding had been controlled by both reversals. McHugh et al. (2004) reported a high level of errors for double reversed HERE–THERE/

NOW–THEN relations. Interestingly, there were no significant differences in double reversed HERE–THERE/NOW–THEN compared to double reversed I–YOU/ HERE–THEN relations.

Generalizing deictic responding to natural language. Several of the studies of the deictic relations cited above have attempted to explore the extent to which performances or training on the deictic protocol generalize to natural language. Heagle and Rehfeldt (2006) presented the perspective-taking protocol to three typically developing children and tested for generalization to real-world conversation (e.g., consider the generalized simple I–YOU trial: "I have a hamburger and you have grilled cheese"). Only one child required explicit training at all three levels of relational complexity, while the remaining participants required training on the reversal and double reversals only. Following explicit training, these skills generalized to real-world conversation. Similarly, Davlin et al. (2011) presented a modified perspective-taking protocol to three typically developing children in which the YOU was replaced with the perspective of a story character (e.g., "You are reading books with me. Cinderella is doing chores. What are you doing? What is Cinderella doing?"). Following substantive training on the protocol, all three children demonstrated the target generalized performances.

In summary, basic RFT research on the deictic relations has stimulated a considerable body of empirical investigation. While there are clearly unresolved issues regarding what precisely controls responding, the evidence does support both the functional distinctiveness of the three types of deictic relations and of the three levels of relational complexity. Some studies also highlight the educational utility of establishing these relations and the possibility that these effects may generalize to natural language.

The relationship between deictic relations and emotions. In very preliminary unpublished research, Barnes-Holmes (2001) investigated the possible transfer of emotional functions through the deictic relations with the two young children described above. In short, this research suggested that once the deictic relations are operational, emotional functions can transform through them with little or no explicit training. For example, if I am happy and you are sad, and if I was you and you were me, you would be happy and I would be sad. And even more complex examples can be illustrated involving other types of relations between I and you. For example, if I feel happy and I see myself as more emotional than you (i.e., a comparative relation), I would derive that you feel less happy. Hence, competence and flexibility in the deictic and other types of relations (e.g., comparison) would be necessary for emotions to be transformed accordingly.

However, from an intervention or remediation perspective, Valdivia-Salas, Luciano, Gutiérrez-Martinez, and Visdómine (2009) argued that several other basic skills must be established before this type of sophisticated relational and emotional responding can be demonstrated. First, a learner must be able to discriminate whether events, including emotional experiences, have aversive or reinforcing functions, and must be able to tact these in a way that is interpreted appropriately by the listener. According to Skinner (1945), labeling your own emotions is part of tacting private experiences more broadly, and is established by the verbal community via public correlates (e.g., correlating an accident with pain). Second, competent perspective-taking requires a learner to discriminate and/or predict and tact the emotions of others. And third, a learner must learn to respond appropriately.

Luciano, Cabello, Molina, Gomez, and Ortega (2003) explored these skills by presenting 42 adults with a series of cards depicting the character Alfredo in different contexts (working, stressed, and with flowers). Each of these roles was signified by a specific contextual cue that coordinated that role with a particular thought and with a subsequent action (e.g., when Alfredo is stressed he sweats). As a result of multiple exemplar training, the majority of participants correctly predicted Alfredo's thoughts and actions in novel situations, and had thus learned to abstract the relevant cue that indicated the presence of specific thoughts and actions.

The relationship between deictic relations and self-rules. Self-rules are an essential feature of the relationship between public and private events, as one learns to act in accordance with one's environment now and in the future. For RFT, public and private events merge into coherent relational networks in which the deictic relations play a central role. Consider a learner who can demonstrate all of the perspective-taking and related skills described above. In this case, this individual will also be able to adopt the perspective of "I–HERE–NOW" as the locus of all her private experiences and can, from this, discriminate the causes and consequences (immediate, delayed, and probabilistic) of her behavior and the behavior of others. In short, this individual will know how to direct her own behavior and what controls it.

According to Luciano, Valdivia-Salas, Gutiérrez, Ruíz, and Páez (2009), this type of self-directed behavior is often controlled by hierarchical relations between the self and private events. Consider the following intervention for sleep disturbance reported by those researchers with a six-year-old. The child reports the following: "When I close my eyes at night I am afraid I will die, so I need to have the light on." This fear results from seeing a dead person with closed eyes on TV. The instructor altered the coordination relation between sleep and death by demonstrating that death involves much more than having one's eyes closed. For example, the child was asked to close her eyes for 30 seconds and then notice that she has not actually died.

In summary, the deictic relations appear to exert a very strong influence over our behavior and the way in which we control it. In addition, these relations also allow us to account for the complex relationship between the self and emotion and between emotion and behavior. Although much more research is need in each of these areas, it is certainly the case that these RFT concepts have added much to previous behavioral accounts of these complex verbal phenomena.

Training Analogical Reasoning as Relational Responding

No summary of RFT, from a developmental or educational perspective, would be complete without at least some recognition of the potential utility of RFT's basic account of analogical reasoning, not least because this type of behavior is so central to complex language and cognition.

Barnes, Hegarty, and Smeets (1997) provided the first RFT model of analogical reasoning as the derivation of equivalence (coordination) relations between equivalence relations, which they labelled as equivalence–equivalence responding. Consider the classic analogy: apples are to oranges as dogs are to sheep. In RFT terms, apples and oranges participate in a relation of coordination on the basis that both are fruits, while dogs and sheep also participate in a relation of coordination, but they do so on the basis that both are domestic animals. In this example, a correct analogical response involves the derivation of these two equivalence relations and the derivation of a further equivalence relation between the two equivalence relations (in other words, apples are equivalent to oranges just as dogs are equivalent to sheep, because each are members of the same respective class).

When presenting classic analogies of this type to children, Barnes et al. (1997) demonstrated that both 9 and 12-year-olds readily demonstrated the target equivalence–equivalence relations (i.e., they could perform the analogies). And similar outcomes have also been reported by Carpentier, Smeets, and Barnes-Holmes (2002) with adults and nine-year-olds. However, Carpentier, Smeets, and Barnes-Holmes (2003) showed that five-year-old children failed to solve the target analogies without explicit training. Indeed, Stewart, Barnes-Holmes, and Weil (2009) described an RFT-based protocol that targets equivalence responding and related composite skills that are necessary in order to establish the basis of analogical abilities. The protocol consists of 10 phases that progress with increasing complexity from training simple A–B relations to testing equivalence–equivalence relations. Although there is no published supporting evidence at present, this protocol may prove beneficial for training analogical reasoning on populations where these complex verbal skills are found to be deficient.

Conclusions

The body of basic research supporting the core concepts surrounding derived relational responding, and particularly as proposed by RFT, is large and compelling. And the related body of evidence investigating and supporting the applicability of these concepts to educational settings is also growing. But there is a great deal more basic and applied research to be done. In bringing behavioral psychology's basic account of verbal behavior into the twenty-first century, RFT offers the promise of enhancing the already proven track record that traditional ABA has in remedial education and particularly with individuals with developmental disabilities. But still, outcomes are far from perfect, and undoubtedly many more learners could have their lives enhanced by thorough teaching programs that will allow them, where possible, to reach their full potential in complex verbal behavior. The concepts and interventions discussed in the current chapter give us hope that the science of behavioral psychology and its educational application will continue to make progress on this important front.

References

Albert, K. M., Carbone, V. J., Murray, D. D., Hagerty, M., & Sweeney-Kerwin, E. J. (2012). Increasing the mand repertoire of children with autism through the use of an interrupted chain procedure. *Behavior Analysis in Practice, 5,* 65–76.

Axe, J. B. (2008). Conditional discrimination in the intraverbal relation: A review and recommendations for future research. *The Analysis of Verbal Behavior, 24,* 159–174.

Barnes, D., Hegarty, N., & Smeets, P. (1997). Relating equivalence relations to equivalence relations: A relational framing model of complex human functioning. *The Analysis of Verbal Behavior, 14,* 57–83.

Barnes-Holmes, D., Barnes-Holmes, Y., & Cullinan, V. (2000). Relational frame theory and Skinner's *Verbal Behavior*: A possible synthesis. *The Behavior Analyst, 23,* 69–84.

Barnes-Holmes, Y. (2001). *Analysing relational frames: Studying language and cognition in young children.* Unpublished doctoral thesis, National University of Ireland, Maynooth, Ireland.

Barnes-Holmes, Y., Barnes-Holmes, D., Smeets, P. M., & Luciano, C. (2004).The derived transfer of mood functions through equivalence relations. *The Psychological Record, 54,* 95–113.

Barnes-Holmes, Y., Barnes-Holmes, D., Smeets, P. M., Strand, P., & Friman, P. (2004). Establishing relational responding in accordance with more-than and less-than as generalized operant behaviour in young children. *International Journal of Psychology and Psychological Therapy, 4,* 531–558.

Barnes-Holmes, Y., Hayes, S. C., Barnes-Holmes, D., & Roche, B. (2002). Relational frame theory: A post-Skinnerian account of human language and cognition. *Advances in Child Development and Behavior, 28,* 101–138.

Berens, N. M., & Hayes, S. C. (2007). Arbitrarily applicable comparative relations: Experimental evidence for a relational operant. *Journal of Applied Behavior Analysis, 40,* 45–71.

Carbone, V. J., O'Brien, L., Sweeney-Kerwin, E. J., & Albert, K. M. (2011). Teaching eye contact to children with autism: A conceptual analysis and single case study. *Education and Treatment of Children, 36,* 139–159.

Carpentier, F., Smeets, P., & Barnes-Holmes, D. (2002). Matching functionally same relations: Implications for equivalence–equivalence as a model for analogical reasoning. *The Psychological Record, 52,* 351–370.

Carpentier, F., Smeets, P., & Barnes-Holmes, D. (2003). Equivalence–equivalence as a model of analogy: Further analyses. *The Psychological Record, 53,* 349–371.

Carr, D., Wilkinson, K. M., Blackman, D., & McIlvane, W. J. (2000). Equivalence classes in individuals with minimal verbal repertoires. *Journal of the Experimental Analysis of Behavior, 74,* 101–115.

Carr, J. E., Nicholson, A. C., & Higbee, T. S. (2000). Evaluation of a brief multiple-stimulus preference assessment in a naturalistic context. *Journal of Applied Behavior Analysis, 33,* 353–357.

Cassidy, S. (2008). *Relational frame theory and human intelligence: A conceptual and empirical analysis.* Unpublished doctoral thesis, National University of Ireland, Maynooth.

Davlin, N. L., Rehfeldt, R. A., & Lovett, S. (2011). A relational frame theory approach to understanding perspective-taking using children's stories in typically developing children. *European Journal of Behavior Analysis, 12,* 403–430.

Dawson, G., Rogers, S., Munson, J., Smith, M., Winter, J., & Greensom, J. (2010). Randomized, controlled trial of an intervention for toddlers with autism: The early start Denver model. *Pediatrics, 125,* 17–23.

Dixon, M. R., Belisle, J., Whiting, S. W., & Rowsey, K. E. (2014). Normative sample of the PEAK relational training system: Direct training module and subsequent comparisons to individuals with autism. *Research in Autism Spectrum Disorders, 8,* 1597–1606.

Dixon, M. R., & Zlomke, K. M. (2005). Using the precursor to the relational evaluation procedure (PREP) to establish the relational frames of sameness, opposition and distinction. *Revista Latinoamericana de Psicologia, 37,* 305–316.

Dunne, S. (2011). *Investigating perspective-taking skills in young children with a diagnosis of autistic spectrum disorder.* Unpublished master's thesis, National University of Ireland, Maynooth.

Dunne, S., Foody, M., Barnes-Holmes, Y., Barnes-Holmes, D., & Murphy, C. (2014). Facilitating repertoires of coordination, opposition, distinction, and comparison in young children with autism. *Behavioral Development Bulletin, 19,* 37–47.

Dymond, S., & Roche, B. (Eds.). (2013). *Advances in relational frame theory: Research and application.* Oakland, CA: New Harbinger.

Dymond, S., Roche, B., Forsyth, J. P., Whelan, R., & Rhoden, J. (2007). Transformation of avoidance response functions in accordance with the relational frames of same and opposite. *Journal of the Experimental Analysis of Behavior, 88*, 249–262.

Erjavec, M., Lovett, V., & Horne, P. (2009). Do infants show generalized imitation of gestures II: The effects of skills training and multiple exemplar matching training. *Journal of Experimental Analysis of Behavior, 91*, 355–376.

Finkel, A. S., & Williams, R. L. (2001). A comparison of textual and echoic prompts on the acquisition of intraverbal behavior in a six-year-old boy with autism. *The Analysis of Verbal Behavior, 18*, 61–70.

Fisher, W., Piazza, C., Bowman, L., Hagopian, L., Owens, J., & Slevin, I. (1992). A comparison of two approaches for identifying reinforcers for persons with severe and profound disabilities. *Journal of Applied Behavior Analysis, 25*, 491–498.

Gewirtz, J. L., & Peláez-Nogueras, M. (1992). Infant social referencing as a learned process. In S. Feinman (Ed.), *Social referencing and the social construction of reality in infancy* (pp. 151–173). New York, NY: Plenum.

Gil, E., Luciano, M. C., & Ruíz, F. (2008). *Transformation of functions via the relational context of hierarchy.* Unpublished master's thesis, University of Almería, Spain.

Gore, N. J., Barnes-Holmes, Y., & Murphy, G. (2010). The relationship between intellectual functioning and relational perspective-taking. *International Journal of Psychology and Psychological Therapy, 10*, 1–17.

Gorham, M., Barnes-Holmes, Y., Barnes-Holmes, D., & Berens, N. (2009). Derived comparative and transitive relations in young children with and without autism. *The Psychological Record, 59*, 221–246.

Greer, R. D., Pistoljevic, N., Cahill, C., & Du, L. (2011). Effects of conditioning voices as reinforcers for listener responses on rate of learning, awareness, and preferences for listening to stories in preschoolers with autism. *The Analysis of Verbal Behavior, 27*, 103–124.

Greer, R. D., & Ross, D. E. (2007). *Verbal behavior analysis.* New York, NY: Pearson Education.

Greer, R. D., & Ross, D. E. (2008). *Verbal behavior analysis: Inducing and expanding new verbal capabilities in children with language delays.* New York, NY: Allyn & Bacon.

Griffee, K., & Dougher, M. J. (2002). Contextual control of stimulus generalization and stimulus equivalence in hierarchical categorization. *Journal of the Experimental Analysis of Behavior, 78*, 433–447.

Grow, L. L., Carr, J. E., Kodak, T. M., Jostad, C. M., & Kisamore, A. N. (2011). A comparison of methods for teaching receptive labeling to children with autism spectrum disorders. *Journal of Applied Behavior Analysis, 44*, 475–498.

Gutierrez, A., Jr., Vollmer, T. R., Dozier, C. L., Borrero, J. C., Rapp, J. T., Bourret, J. C., & Gadaire, D. (2007). Manipulating establishing operations to verify and establish stimulus control during mand training. *Journal of Applied Behavior Analysis, 40*, 645–658.

Hagopian, L. P., Long, E. S., & Rush, K. S. (2004). Preference assessment procedures for individuals with developmental disabilities. *Behavior Modification, 28*, 668–677.

Halvey, C., & Rehfeldt, R. A. (2005). Expanding vocal requesting repertoires via relational responding in adults with severe developmental disabilities. *The Analysis of Verbal Behavior, 21*, 13–25.

Hayes, S. C., Barnes-Holmes, D., & Roche, B. (2001). *Relational frame theory: A post-Skinnerian account of human language and cognition.* New York, NY: Kluwer/Plenum.

Heagle, A. I., & Rehfeldt, R. A. (2006). Teaching perspective-taking skills to typically developing children through derived relational responding. *Journal of Early and Intensive Behavior Intervention, 3*, 1–34.

Horne, P. J., & Erjavec, M. (2007). Do infants show generalized imitation of gestures? *Journal of the Experimental Analysis of Behavior, 87*, 63–87.

Horne, P. J., & Lowe, C. F. (1996). On the origins of naming and other symbolic behavior, *Journal of Experimental Analysis of Behavior, 65*, 185–241.

Horne, P. J., Lowe, C. F., & Randle, V. R. L. (2004). Naming and categorization in young children: II: Listener behavior training. *Journal of the Experimental Analysis of Behavior, 81*, 267–288.

Kent, G. (2014). *Exploring the sequence of establishing derived relational responding in children with global developmental delay.* Unpublished doctoral thesis, National University of Ireland, Maynooth, Ireland.

Keohane, D. D., Greer, R. D., & Ackerman, S. A. (2006). *The effects of conditioning visual tracking on the acquisition of instructional objectives by prelisteners and prespeakers.* Paper presented at the 32nd annual convention of the Association for Applied Behavior Analysis International, Atlanta, GA.

Keohane, D. D., Pereira-Delgado, J. A., & Greer, D. (2009). Observing responses: Foundations of higher-order verbal operants. In R. A. Rehfeldt & Y. Barnes-Holmes (Eds.), *Derived relational responding applications for learners with autism and other developmental disabilities: A progressive guide to change* (pp. 41–62). Oakland, CA: New Harbinger.

Kodak, T., & Clements, A. (2009). Acquisition of mands and tacts with concurrent echoic training. *Journal of Applied Behavior Analysis, 42*, 839–843.

Laraway, S., Snycerski, S., Michael, J., & Poling, A. (2003). Motivating operations and some terms to describe them: Some further refinements. *Journal of Applied Behavior Analysis, 36*, 407–414.

Leaf, R., & McEachin, J. (1999). *A work in progress: Behavior management strategies and a curriculum for intensive behavioral treatment of autism.* New York, NY: DRL Books.

Ledford, R., & Wolery, M. (2011). Teaching imitation to young children with disabilities: A review of the literature. *Topics in Early Childhood Special Education, 30*, 245–255.

Lipkins, G., Hayes, S. C., & Hayes, L. J. (1993). Longitudinal study of derived stimulus relations in an infant. *Journal of the Experimental Analysis of Behavior, 56*, 201–239.

Logan, K. R., & Gast, D. L. (2001). Conducting preference assessments and reinforcer testing for individuals with profound multiple disabilities: Issues and procedures. *Exceptionality, 9*, 123–134

Lovaas, O. I. (2003). *Teaching individuals with developmental delays: Basic intervention techniques.* Austin, TX: Pro-Ed.

Luciano, M. C., Cabello, F., Molina, F., Gomez, I., & Ortega, J. (2003). *Enhancing perspective-taking in the context of thinking.* Paper presented at the 29th annual convention of the Association for Behavior Analysis, San Francisco, CA.

Luciano, M. C., Gomez-Becerra, I., & Rodríguez-Valverde, M. (2007). The role of multiple-exemplar training and naming in establishing derived equivalence in an infant. *Journal of the Experimental Analysis of Behavior, 87*, 349–365.

Luciano, M. C., Rodríguez, M., Manas, I., & Ruiz, F. (2009). Acquiring the earliest relational operants: Coordination, distinction, opposition, comparison, and hierarchy. In R. A. Rehfeldt & Y. Barnes-Holmes (Eds.), *Derived relational responding: Applications for learners with autism and other developmental disabilities: A progressive guide to change* (pp. 149–172). Oakland, CA: New Harbinger.

Luciano, M. C., Valdivia-Salas, S., Gutiérrez, O., Ruíz, F., & Páez, M. (2009). ACT-based brief protocols in children and adolescents. *International Journal of Psychology and Psychological Therapy, 9*, 237–257.

Luke, N., Greer, D. R., Singer-Dudek, J., & Keohane, D. (2011). The emergence of autoclitic frames in atypically and typically developing children as a function of multiple exemplar instruction. *The Analysis of Verbal Behavior, 27*, 141–156.

Malott, R. W. (2008). *Principles of behavior* (6th ed.). Upper Saddle River, NJ: Pearson.

MacDonald, R., Anderson, J., Dube, W. V., Geckeler, A., Green, G., & Holcomb, W. (2006). Behavioral assessment of joint attention: A methodological report. *Developmental Disabilities, 27*, 138–150.

Maurice, C., Green, G., & Luce, S. C. (1996). *Behavioral intervention for young children with autism: A manual for parents and professionals.* Austin, TX: PRO-ED.

McClannahan, L. E., & Krantz, P. J. (2006). *Teaching conversation to children with autism: Scripts and script fading.* Bethesda, MD: Woodbone House.

McGuinness, R. (2005). *Using protocols of relational responding to analyse perspective-taking and related repertoires in children with Asperger's syndrome.* Unpublished master's thesis, National University of Ireland, Maynooth.

McHugh, L., Barnes-Holmes, Y., O'Hora, D., & Barnes-Holmes, D. (2004). Perspective taking: A relational frame analysis. *Experimental Analysis of Human Behavior Bulletin, 22*, 4–10.

Michael, J., Palmer, D. C., & Sundberg, M. L. (2011). The multiple control of verbal behavior. *The Analysis of Verbal Behavior, 27*, 3–22.

Moll, H., & Meltzoff, A. N. (2011). Perspective-taking and its foundation in joint attention. In N. Eilan, H. Lerman, & J. Roessler (Eds.), *Perception, causation, and objectivity. Issues in philosophy and psychology.* Oxford, England: Oxford University Press.

Murphy, C., & Barnes-Holmes, D. (2009). Derived more/less relational mands with four children diagnosed with autism: Synthesizing Skinner's *Verbal behavior* with relational frame theory II. *Journal of Applied Behavior Analysis, 38*, 445–462.

O'Connor, J., Rafferty, A., Barnes-Holmes, D., & Barnes-Holmes, Y. (2009). The role of verbal behaviour, stimulus nameability, and familiarity on the equivalence performances of autistic and normally developing children. *The Psychological Record, 59*, 53–74.

Partington, J. W., & Sundberg, M. L. (1998). *The assessment of basic language and learning skills.* Pleasant Hills, CA: Behavior Analysts.

Peláez-Nogueras, M., & Gewirtz, J. (1997). The context of stimulus control in behavior analysis. In D. M. Baer & E. M. Pinkston (Eds.), *Environment and behavior.* Boulder, CO: Westview.

Peláez-Nogueras, M., Gewirtz, J., & Markham, M. (1996). Infant vocalizations are conditioned both by maternal imitation and motherese speech. *Infant Behavior and Development, 19*, 670.

Pereira-Delgado, J., Greer, R. D., & Speckman-Collins, J. (2006). *The effects of using a mirror to induce generalized imitation.* Paper presented as part of a symposium at the 32nd annual convention of the Association for Applied Behavior Analysis International, Atlanta, GA.

Pérez-González, L. A., García-Asenjo, L., Williams, G., & Carnerero, J. J. (2007). Emergence of intraverbal antonyms in children with pervasive developmental disorder. *Journal of Applied Behavior Analysis, 40*, 697–701.

Peters-Scheffer, N., Didden, R., Korzilius, H., & Sturmey, P. (2011). A meta-analytic study on the effectiveness of comprehensive ABA-based early intervention programs for children with autism spectrum disorders. *Research in Autism Spectrum Disorders, 5*, 60–69.

Rehfeldt, R. A., & Barnes-Holmes, Y. (Eds.). (2009). *Derived relational responding applications for learners with autism and other developmental disabilities: A progressive guide to change.* Oakland, CA: New Harbinger.

Rehfeldt, R. A., Dillen, J. E., Ziomek, M. M., & Kowalchuk, R. E. (2007). Assessing relational learning deficits in perspective-taking in children with high functioning autism spectrum disorder. *The Psychological Record, 57*, 23–47.

Roche, B., & Barnes, D. (1996). Arbitrarily applicable relational responding and human sexual categorization: A critical test of the derived difference relation. *The Psychological Record, 46*, 451–475

Rosales, R., & Rehfeldt, R. A. (2007). Contriving transitive conditioned establishing operations to establish derived manding skills in adults with severe developmental disabilities. *Journal of Applied Behavior Analysis, 40*, 105–121.

Rush, K. S., Mortenson, B. P., & Birch, S. E. (2010). Evaluation of preference assessment procedures for use with infants and toddlers. *International Journal of Behavioral Consultation and Therapy, 6*, 2–16.

Sautter, R. A., & LeBlanc, L. A. (2006). Empirical applications of Skinner's analysis of verbal behavior with humans. *The Analysis of Verbal Behavior, 22*, 35–48.

Shafer, E. (1994). A review of interventions to teach a mand repertoire. *The Analysis of Verbal Behavior, 12*, 53–66.

Sidman, M. (1971). Reading and auditory-visual equivalences. *Journal of Speech and Hearing Research, 14*, 5–13.

Skinner, B. F. (1945). The operational analysis of psychological terms. *Psychological Review, 52*, 270–277.

Skinner, B. F. (1957). *Verbal behavior.* New York, NY: Appleton-Century-Crofts.

Slaughter, V., & McConnell, D. (2003). Emergence of joint attention: Relationships between gaze following, social referencing, imitation, and naming in infancy. *The Journal of Genetic Psychology, 164*, 54–71.

Steele, D. L., & Hayes, S. C. (1991). Stimulus equivalence and arbitrarily applicable relational responding. *Journal of the Experimental Analysis of Behavior, 56*, 519–555.

Stewart, I., Barnes-Holmes, D., & Weil, T. (2009). Training analogical reasoning as relational responding. In R. A. Rehfeldt, & Y. Barnes-Holmes (Eds.), *Derived relational responding applications for learners with autism and other developmental disabilities: A progressive guide to change* (pp. 257–279). Oakland, CA: New Harbinger.

Stewart, I., & McElwee, J. (2009). Relational responding and conditional discrimination procedures: An apparent inconsistency and clarification. *The Behavior Analyst, 32*, 309–317.

Stubbings, V., & Martin, G. L. (1995). The ABLA test for predicting performance of developmentally disabled persons on prevocational disabilities training tasks. *International Journal of Practical Approaches to Disability, 19*, 12–17.

Sundberg, M. L. (2008) *Verbal behavior milestones assessment and placement program: The VB-MAPP.* Concord, CA: AVB Press

Sundberg, M. L., Loeb, M., Hale, L., & Eigenheer, P. (2002). Contriving establishing operations to teach mands for information. *The Analysis of Verbal Behavior, 18*, 15–29.

Sundberg, M. L., & Michael, J. (2001). The benefits of Skinner's analysis of verbal behavior for children with autism. *Behavior Modification, 25*, 692–724.

Sundberg, M. L., & Partington, J. W. (1998). *Teaching language to children with autism or other developmental disabilities.* Pleasant Hill, CA: Behavior Analysts.

Sundberg, M. L., & Sundberg, C. A. (2011). Intraverbal behavior and verbal conditional discriminations in typically developing children and children with autism. *The Analysis of Verbal Behavior, 27*, 23–43.

Tarbox, J., Dixon, D. R., Sturmey, P., & Matson, J. L. (Eds.). (2014). *Handbook of early intervention for autism spectrum disorders: Research, policy, and practice.* New York, NY: Springer.

Tarbox, R. S. F., Ghezzi, P. M., & Wilson, G. (2006). The effects of token reinforcement on attending in a young child with autism. *Behavioral Interventions, 21*, 155–164.

Tarbox, J., Madrid, W., Aguilar, B., Jacobo, W., & Schiff, A. (2009). Use of chaining to increase complexity of echoics in children with autism. *Journal of Applied Behavior Analysis, 42*, 901–906.

Valdivia-Salas, S., Luciano, C., Gutiérrez-Martinez, O., & Visdómine, C. (2009). Establishing empathy. In R. A. Rehfeldt & Y. Barnes-Holmes (Eds.), *Derived relational responding applications for learners with autism and other developmental disabilities: A progressive guide to change* (pp. 301–311). Oakland, CA: New Harbinger.

Valentino, A. L., Shillingsburg, M. A., & Call, N. A. (2012). Comparing the effects of echoic prompts and echoic prompt plus modelled prompts on intraverbal behavior. *Journal of Applied Behavior Analysis. 45*, 431–435.

Vedora, J., & Meunier, L. (2009). Teaching intraverbal behavior to children with autism: A comparison of textual and echoic prompt. *The Analysis of Verbal Behavior, 25*, 79–86.

Vitale, A., Barnes-Holmes, Y., Barnes-Holmes, D., & Campbell, C. (2008). Facilitating responding in accordance with the relational frame of comparison: Systematic empirical analyses. *The Psychological Record, 58,* 365–390.

Vitale, A., Campbell, C., Barnes-Holmes, Y., & Barnes-Holmes, D. (2012). Facilitating responding in accordance with the relational frame of comparison II: Methodological analyses, *The Psychological Record, 62,* 663–676.

Weil, T. M., Hayes, S. C., & Capurro, P. (2011). Establishing a deictic relational repertoire in young children. *The Psychological Record, 61,* 371–390.

Whelan, R., & Barnes-Holmes, D. (2004). The transformation of consequential functions in accordance with the relational frames of same and opposite. *Journal of the Experimental Analysis of Behavior, 82,* 77–195.

Wolery, M., Holcombe, A., Billings, S. S., & Vassilaros, M. A. (1993). Effects of simultaneous prompting and instructive feedback. *Early Education and Development, 4,* 20–31.

12

RFT for Clinical Practice

Three Core Strategies in Understanding and Treating Human Suffering

Niklas Törneke, Carmen Luciano, Yvonne Barnes-Holmes, and Frank W. Bond

Relational frame theory (RFT) is a comprehensive account of verbal behavior (Hayes, Barnes-Holmes, & Roche, 2001). Because psychotherapy almost always relies on verbal behavior, all kinds of psychological interventions could potentially be analyzed from this perspective. In this chapter, we do not attempt such an extensive analysis, but focus instead on what we think are two core and integrated areas that can be used to help people change in psychological treatment. The strategies we suggest are based on RFT and relate specifically to the complex human abilities of: (a) following instructions or rules, and (b) interacting with our own behavior. According to RFT, these two core areas not only suggest potentially useful perspectives on how we might do effective therapy, but they also provide an understanding of what, to some extent, brings individuals into psychological therapy in the first place.

Following Instructions

In traditional behavior analytic language, the behavioral repertoire of following instructions is called rule-governed behavior (O'Hora & Barnes-Holmes, 2004; Skinner, 1966). From an RFT perspective, this phenomena could perhaps more broadly be described as complex relational regulation. Once a human learns to relate stimuli or events under the influence of arbitrary contextual cues, words (spoken aloud or silently to yourself) can have stimulus functions for all kinds of action, depending on the specific learning history of the individual. A word or combination of words that specifies a particular behavior and its consequences has traditionally been called a rule or instruction. Consider the following simple example: "Turn left after the first traffic light, continue for half a kilometre and you will find yourself at the football stadium." Or, to give an example closer to psychological treatment: "It is important that you control your feeling of anxiety so that you won't have a nervous breakdown." In both these cases, the instructions specify what to do and for what

The Wiley Handbook of Contextual Behavioral Science, First Edition. Edited by Robert D. Zettle, Steven C. Hayes, Dermot Barnes-Holmes, and Anthony Biglan.
© 2016 John Wiley & Sons, Ltd. Published 2016 by John Wiley & Sons, Ltd.

consequence. When humans interact with verbal stimuli like these (instructions or rules) they are said to act with a purpose, where the purpose relates to experiencing the specified consequence. However, there is more to rule-governed behavior than understanding a rule and acting in accordance with it. Specifically, the rule-follower must have an appropriate learning history and present contingencies must also support rule following in that context (Barnes-Holmes, O'Hora et al., 2001; Hayes & Hayes, 1989).

Even if the behavior of following instructions is often done by acting in ways similar to previous behaviors and for consequences experienced earlier, additional and more novel actions are possible. Once a repertoire of following rules is available and given appropriate contextual cues, humans can act with a purpose, doing things never done before and for consequences never yet contacted. This means, for example, that a rule like "I need to stop thinking about him or I will end up in a psychiatric hospital" can readily emerge as a new rule, specifying what to avoid in a specific new context. With the emergence of new rules, and possibly new behaviors, comes the opportunity for both flexible and inflexible response classes. As argued elsewhere, the latter appear to be associated with "psychological traps" (Luciano, Valdivia-Salas, & Ruiz, 2012; Törneke, Luciano, & Valdivia Salas, 2008). We will return to this issue later.

Interacting with Your Own Behavior

Many organisms can respond to their own behavior, such that a given response can have stimulus functions for subsequent responding by the same organism. However, this ability is radically advanced or extended once humans learn relational framing (Barnes-Holmes, Hayes, & Dymond, 2001). That is, under the influence of arbitrary contextual cues, we can relate one aspect of our own behavior to another, in the same way that we can relate any other stimulus or event to another. In other words, just as external events can become "better than," "should not have been," or "more later," so can our own behavior. For example, I might advise myself that my health will be better later if I eat less now.

Early in the development of relational framing, relations of coordination are established between "I," "me," my own name, and my own behavior. Similarly, relations of opposition are established between "I" and "you," "others," other names, and so on. In turn, this helps to distinguish my behavior from the behavior of others. At one level, therefore, children learn to discriminate themselves as objects among other objects and learn to relate these objects to one another in a whole host of ways. For example, in a given context "I" can be good, bad, small, girl, boy, strong, nice, tired, funny, looking like mother, and so forth. Across thousands of interactions with the wider verbal community throughout the early years of development, complex relational networks (or stories) about "me" are established and take form.

The perspective from which each one of us comes to view the world, at least in a verbal sense, remains relatively constant across time. In other words, although our individual behaviors across contexts may differ considerably, we typically talk about viewing the world, and all that happens in it, from the perspective of "I" or "me." Thus a learning history unfolds in which I come to distinguish myself from my own behavior (including actions, feelings, thoughts, memories, etc.). Thus, for a verbally competent human, there is an experiential distinction between "what I do" on the one hand and the experience of being a (verbal) observer on the other hand; a "from-ness," if you like, of human experience. This learning is heavily influenced by others in the social context who frequently ask questions such as "Who did that?," "What did you feel?," "Where were you when that happened?," and so on, and reinforce responding that is "correct" in the sense that it is in accordance with social convention in that context. A more technical way of describing this complex behavior is to say that we learn to place our own behavior in a hierarchical relational frame with a deictic[1] "I." In other words, everything I do, see, think, and feel is experienced as being parts of me or who I am (see Luciano, Valdivia-Salas, Cabello-Luque, & Hernendez, 2009). This relationship between me, as a constant verbal "I-ness," and my behaviors is an essential feature of complex human action and allows me, for example, to direct my behavior across time and in accordance with what I want, expect, and seek to achieve, perhaps many years into the future. One might argue that this complex relational ability is integral in allowing us to make choices to follow particular courses of action, such as saving for a pension or paying off a mortgage, or having children. This also seems to accord with what Skinner (1974) was referring to in the following: "A person who has been 'made aware of himself' by the questions he has been asked is in a better position to predict and control his own behavior" (p. 35).

The Joint Venture of Complex Relational Regulation and Interacting with Your Own Behavior

As repertoires of relational framing emerge and flourish, we formulate all kinds of stories about ourselves in relation to the external and social world and these are controlled by contextual cues provided by that world. In early childhood, these stories are often spoken aloud in what is called "self-talk," but with age they typically become increasingly complex and unspoken. As well as constituting complex relational networks involving practically all types of derived relations, "stories about self" commonly function to regulate our own behavior; that is, they function as rules.

The abilities to follow instructions on the one hand and to discriminate "me" on the other, join together in the uniquely human behavior of self-instruction. We constantly tell ourselves what to do, how to act, what to aim for, and what to avoid. Almost incessantly, we also evaluate our own actions and then use these evaluations to instruct subsequent behavior. While much of this self-instruction and the behavior that goes with it is so automatic that it "occurs without thinking," a great deal is more elaborate and engaged with a higher degree of discrimination. Either way, this type of verbal behavior, like all other behavior, is under contextual control. Hence, even subtle forms of remembering, feeling, and thinking are acts in context. The complex ability to discriminate your own behavior and abstract a rule based upon this, which can, in turn, be used to instruct future behavior, has clear personal, social, and cultural benefits (e.g., social cohesion and collaboration regarding long-term goals and values). This ability can also, however, be counterproductive and reduce essential behavioral flexibility.

The Blessing and the Curse

As noted above, self-rules can specify behavior not yet performed and consequences not yet contacted, hence constituting rules for future behavior. A key advantage afforded by this type of verbal behavior is that it enables us to act in the present for unknown and remote future potential consequences. As a result, these "verbally contacted consequences" in the present may be actually contacted experientially in the future. For example, if we follow a rule like "if I eat less and exercise more I will lose weight" and we actually lose weight, the consequence that was at first verbally contacted is now an actual, experienced consequence of our behavior.

It is easy to see how self-rules such as these can be a blessing and, when applied to our physical health, for example, they may even keep us alive. Even more abstractly, we can act for world peace, a healthy environment for our grandchildren, going to heaven, or being reborn with a better karma. Unlike the health example, we may never in fact actually contact the consequences specified in the rules we follow in these situations. But again, this type of rule-following will possibly have significant other benefits for ourselves, for other individuals, and for the culture at large.

On the other hand, there is a downside to following rules that specify consequences which we will never contact directly. Several factors influence this possibility. First, as self-rules are always very much intertwined with historically established social rules, they are ultimately at "social whim." Indeed, even our direct historical experiences are observed through the lens of the social context that teaches us how to make sense of, and talk about, these experiences. There are a myriad of social rules regarding how we experience our experiences (e.g., "never criticize family members" or "it is bad to feel unhappy"). Second, empirical evidence has shown that rule-following tends to continue even when the consequences specified by the rule have ceased to occur or, indeed, have never occurred (Hayes, Brownstein, Zettle, Rosenfarb, & Korn, 1986; Matthews, Shimoff, Catania, & Sagvolden, 1977). And, third, there is evidence that extensive social reinforcement for rule following in general facilitates excessive rule following even when the consequences of doing so are aversive (Hayes, Wilson, Gifford, Follette, & Strosahl, 1996). Both of these latter factors can be described as having the common characteristic of insensitivity to direct contingencies. A classic therapeutic (indeed, ubiquitously human) example of this is called experiential avoidance. This involves following rules about the control of private events (e.g., feelings, thoughts, memories, bodily sensations, etc.) as a prerequisite to living your life well, when the control of all such events is practically always impossible and the consequences of doing so tend to increase psychological suffering.

Importantly, for effective human functioning a rule can be present without being followed. We are all aware of suggesting different plans of action (rules) to ourselves, either as a spontaneous thought ("I should stop doing this") or as a more deliberate and elaborated version ("I really should go to Morocco with Elisabeth this coming summer to have a real vacation") without necessarily acting on that rule. We suggest that early childhood training of the distinction between "I" and "my own behavior" plays an important role in this regard. Specifically, we would argue that responding to our own behavior as participating in a frame of hierarchy with the deictic I is of central importance to the way in which we follow self-rules. Furthermore, we propose that the following of self-rules when I am in a hierarchical relation with my own behavior, is likely to be relatively effective and beneficial (Luciano et al., 2009). Take the example of thinking, "I need to control this feeling," given an emotionally aversive experience. What we are suggesting is that being able to "hold these thoughts at a distance of observation" rather than automatically acting "on" them is a critically important psychological skill. This ability appears to correspond with what is often called psychological or behavioral flexibility (Bond et al., 2011; Kashdan & Rottenberg, 2010). In the next section, we will discuss the view that deficits in these relational repertoires correspond to psychological rigidity and form a central process of psychological suffering in general and of clinical problems in particular, and that training these very repertoires is a key task in psychological treatment.

A Simple Model of Psychotherapy, Informed by RFT

The line of argument so far in this chapter leads to the position that psychological treatment should be aimed at building and training psychological flexibility, which is a repertoire that may be considered a higher-order operant class and, thus, formed and possibly maintained, by multiple-exemplar training. We define psychological flexibility in the following way:

> Psychological flexibility is the ability to notice and react to your thoughts, feelings, and other behavior in order to give you the opportunity to take action toward important ends. This involves responding to your own responding as participating in a frame of hierarchy with the deictic "I." This is typically accompanied by a substantial reduction in the behavioral control functions of the response in question, thereby allowing for additional relational responding that specifies appetitive augmental functions, and further behavior that is coordinated with that relational responding.

We will now describe how such work can be conducted in accordance with this definition. For didactic purposes, we will divide this work into three key therapeutic strategies. These are not sequential because all three are a recurrent focus of treatment; hence each will be revisited as needed, and typically many times.

1 Help the client discriminate the relationship between current functional classes of responding and the problematic consequences produced by that responding. According to the current analysis, we expect the problematic functional class to be responding in coordination with certain self-instructions or rules.
2 Help the client discriminate his or her own responses by framing them as participating in a frame of hierarchy with the deictic I and train this repertoire as an alternative functional class.
3 Help the client develop this alternative repertoire in a way that will specify appetitive augmental functions for further behavior.

Before continuing it may be useful, for illustrative purposes, to consider the following example of psychological flexibility versus inflexibility. William is a young student in the middle of his studies. After studying for several months in preparation for a test, he has just found out that he failed it. This is the first time he has not passed a major test in the course of his university study. He is sad and angry. He has a lot of thoughts about the mistakes he made during the test and why he made them; he also has many questions about what will happen to him now. This thinking suggests to him that much more work is needed in the future and, for example, that he may now have to miss a special trip he had been planning. He also has thoughts about his parents' reactions to the fact that he failed the test. For example, he thinks: "I am a failure! How could I make such stupid mistakes? Why did I not prepare in a better way? I might not be suitable for this kind of career!" Some of these thoughts will likely be accompanied by strong affective reactions.

From the perspective we outlined above, we would argue that the way William interacts with these thoughts (his way of responding to them) plays a critical role in how he behaves next. On the one hand, if he responds to them by framing them in hierarchy with the deictic I, he will notice them as responses that he is having. On the other hand, having them need not control his further behavior. Such a response would facilitate psychological flexibility, because it increases the probability that other, helpful responses also will occur (such as "What should I do now, given my overall aims?") and that actions coordinated with such responses are more likely to follow. If, on the other hand, William responds in coordination with his thoughts and feelings, these responses will likely increase the probability of social withdrawal (being a "failure") or ruminating on the situation (because the content of the rumination has to be solved). If this is the case, thoughts and feelings will thus have obtained control functions for behavior that may be avoidant and problematic. For example, William may decide to give up his studies based on this single failed test.

While the example above is taken from a nonclinical situation, we would suggest that the same process lies at the core of clinical problems and the difference is more quantitative than qualitative. Consider Peter, who is a middle-aged man who recently became a father. A week before his daughter was born a neighbor used pesticide in his front garden, close to the side of Peter's house. Peter has always been keen to follow ecologically sound habits, but now gets totally obsessed with thoughts about the potential risk to his newborn daughter. He has thoughts like, "What if some pesticide was brought into our house by the wind and is concealed in our furniture?" He also has thoughts about the spread of the pesticide through his own clothes and the potential for his daughter to become contaminated by these. While Peter, who is well educated, is aware of the improbability of anything like this happening, he feels he cannot help but to act on these thoughts and in doing so he fulfils diagnostic criteria for obsessive compulsive disorder. As another example, consider Lisa. She has constant thoughts about parts of her own body being fat and about the need to lose weight to be acceptable. Acting in coordination with such thinking by engaging in a strict diet and periodically self-induced vomiting, she now fulfils the criteria for an eating disorder.

We suggest that both Peter and Lisa suffer, in certain contexts, from deficits in the behavioral repertoire of framing their own private/subtle responses in a hierarchical relation with their verbal "I-ness." Thus, they exhibit psychological rigidity as we have defined it above. As a result of repeated episodes of acting in coordination with one's own private responses or reactions, problematic forms of rule-following become established. It is not an isolated episode of such responding that constitutes the problem; instead, the problem results from many such instances across life or in specific, important moments. The task in psychological treatment is to set up a context that increases the probability of hierarchical framing of private responses from the perspective of "I" (deictic I), thus facilitating psychological flexibility. We would add that treatment usually requires repeated training of flexibility in different contexts (commonly referred to as multiple-exemplar training).

Helping Clients Discriminate the Relationship between Current Functional Classes of Behavior and Problematic Consequences

Discrimination of your own behavior is key to changing your behavior (Skinner, 1974). So in helping clients to change, we will need to help them discriminate what they do, when they do it, what normally follows their actions, and what was the purpose of their behavior. Many people who search out psychological treatment are aware that they need to change something they are doing. They are also typically aware that things are not going the way they want them to, otherwise they would not be seeking help. Nonetheless, clients are often out of contact with the relationship between the consequences they experience as aversive and their own behavior that contributes to those consequences. We have argued that a problematic behavioral repertoire involves responding in coordination with certain verbal rules, rather than in hierarchy with those rules, from the perspective of "I." But, of course, clients will first need to discriminate what they do as part of this coordination and to recognize that it is not working for them.

So the first step in therapy is to help clients identify which of their own behaviors generate problematic consequences. From an RFT perspective, this involves if–then or causal framing, connecting specific behaviors to specific consequences. This process of identification will also facilitate the formation of coordination relations among topographically distinct behaviors, such that all are seen as functionally equivalent, because they all facilitate aversive consequences. In effect, this constitutes discrimination of the client's problematic functional class of behavior. For illustrative purposes, we will consider how this can be done in a dialogue with Peter, from our example above.

Therapist: What would be a typically difficult situation for you?

Peter: It could be almost any situation at home, really …

Therapist: Such as … ?

Peter: This morning, for example, I noticed that my wife, when about to breast-feed our daughter, first put aside some of my clothes lying on the bed. Just seeing her touch those clothes made all these horrible thoughts and images turn up for me. It's incredible!

Therapist: And that would be typical? In many different situations?

Peter: Yes, almost all the time. I just see all these horrible things that can happen to my daughter.

Therapist: Like a warning?

Peter: Yes.

Therapist: So when you get these warnings about all the horrible things that could happen to your daughter, what do you do?

Peter: Well, it depends on the situation. Today I asked my wife to wash her hands so as not to contaminate our daughter. I do all kinds of things to protect her. Wash clothes, avoid going into certain places in the garden, keep the windows closed, ask my wife to do the same things, etc., etc. I know it is weird, but I just can't stop it.

Therapist: Would it be correct to say that when you get these warnings, you follow along?

Peter: Yes, sure, yes.

Therapist: And where does that take you?

Peter: Well, I get a bit less tense I guess. It feels like I am protecting my daughter. I could not stand anything happening to her! That would be horrible!

Therapist: So, some relief in the moment. And in the end, where does that take you?

Peter: Nowhere, really. But what can I do? If she comes into contact with this pesticide, who knows what that could do to her in the long run? All these reports about pesticides and cancer ...

Therapist: Hmm, so you just got a warning, here and now? Did I get that right?

Peter: Yeah, I guess ...

Therapist: And then you would typically do what?

Peter: Try to do something about it, of course. Or find out what to do.

Therapist: A warning about horrible things and then you follow along ... ?

Peter: Yes.

Therapist: And that takes you where? How is the situation in your family, with your wife and daughter?

Peter: It is not good. I don't really dare to do anything with my daughter and with my wife ... Well, we just end up in fruitless discussions. It all takes me nowhere ...

Therapist: And what about the warnings, all the scary thoughts? Do they decrease over time as you "follow along"?

Peter: No, not really. I just feel more and more tense, more and more afraid ...

At this point, let us simplify what we think the therapist is doing here as a series of steps:

1   Coordinating Peter's private events with "warnings about horrible things."
2   Identifying what Peter does in the presence of these private events.
3   Providing a label for these behaviors as "following along" and thus coordinating these behaviors together.
4   Grouping these actions that follow into causal relations (e.g., given a warning, then follow along).
5   Grouping the behaviors of following along into causal relations with their consequences ("when I follow along, it never works out well") and thus discriminating a problematic, functional class of behavior.

As any reader familiar with behavior analysis will notice, this is an example of what is called a functional analysis or assessment. Behavior, its consequences and its antecedents are specified, in order to teach the client to make these kinds of discriminations. Naturally, this one example will probably not be enough. As different examples are asked for, and given by Peter, the therapist should return to the question of whether this example fits with previous ones in terms of "an anxious warning, following along, getting nowhere."

Two further comments on the above example seem important. First, the therapist should look for and use examples of the problematic behavioral class as it appears in session, as in the example above when she asks if Peter just got a warning. This provides an opportunity for both the therapist and client to discriminate relevant aspects of the behavioral sequence "alive" and in the moment.

The second comment is about using metaphors as part of the dialogue. In the dialogue above the metaphors are not particularly vivid. Nevertheless, the therapist labeling Peter's behavior of acting on his thinking about danger as "following along" and labeling the content of his thinking as "a warning" is using metaphorical talk. Similar metaphors may have involved the therapist talking about Peter's experience of danger as "an alarm signal" and about his subsequent behavior as "acting like the emergency response team."

There are several reasons why using metaphors, such as these, may be helpful.

- The client is unlikely to remember all of the individual behaviors identified by the therapist, but will have little difficulty in remembering the single label of "following along."
- Metaphors are short and straightforward, and yet contain a surprising amount of information. For example, just labelling all of the target behaviors as "following along" means that it is not even necessary for the therapist to say that this is just the same response over and over.
- Metaphors are often a better alternative to formal instructions. Psychological treatment often includes instructions of different kinds, especially in the cognitive-behavioral tradition. As argued previously, however, excessively rigid instruction or rule following is often a central part of psychological problems. RFT would predict that using metaphorical talk may be useful in helping clients, even when metaphors technically function as rules or instructions. This is so because metaphors, by their very nature, are not as exact as more literal language. So if Peter, in the example above, is told: "Notice the warning signs but don't act on them, just pass by!" that is different from giving him more formal instructions about what to do. In following metaphorical instructions you cannot just "do as it says." You will have to be more observant as to direct contingencies and that might decrease the probability that you will get entangled in verbal traps. In other words, the use of metaphors in therapy may serve to transform the functions of excessively rigid rule-following without providing yet another formal rule for the client to follow. Or to put it more informally, metaphors may help a client to see some aspect of their own behavior as the problem without the therapist providing a formal rule or instruction to that effect.
- Using a metaphor to label a person's behavior may help to place the behavior in question "out in front" of the client as if it was an external object (e.g., an actual warning sign). Hence, the metaphor allows Peter to discriminate his own behavior as "out there" (hence distinct from "here"), whereas it was previously coordinated with his perspective (here). This may facilitate Peter's framing of his own behavior in hierarchy with "I" (i.e., part of and yet also distinct from me). In this respect, the therapist is already moving toward what we suggest is the second therapeutic strategy to be used, which is *"helping the client to frame his own responses in hierarchy with the deictic I."*

Helping Clients Frame Their Own Responses in Hierarchy with the Deictic I and Training this Repertoire as an Alternative Functional Class

Language-able humans spend virtually every day immersed in a socio-verbal world that teaches them to relate phenomena (stimuli of all kinds) under the control of arbitrary contextual cues. Some of this responding is relatively extended and elaborated, whereas some is brief and immediate (Hughes, Barnes-Holmes, & Vahey, 2012). The latter case describes verbal responding that is often highly trained or practiced and thus can take place without an individual readily discriminating that a particular instance of responding involves responding to one's own behavior. Thus a person may respond to something as "dangerous" or "impossible to do," without discriminating "the danger" and "the impossibility" as being a result of the individual's own responding. In our view, helping clients to frame their own verbal responding in hierarchy with the deictic I may serve to transform or reduce the behavioral control functions of that verbal responding, and thus increase the probability that alternative responses will be emitted (Foody, Barnes-Holmes, Barnes-Holmes, & Luciano, 2013; Luciano et al., 2011).

For illustrative purposes, consider Roger, who is suffering from dysthymia, having been moderately depressed on and off for many years. He describes himself as not being capable of establishing a permanent intimate relationship with a partner and also of having a hard time keeping up with his work as a teacher. When exploring current life situations that Roger sees as examples of his problems, he describes himself as feeling deeply insecure in any situation in which a certain level of intimacy is reached with a potential partner. He refers to this experience as a cause of why he has not dated for several years. He adds that the same insecurity is experienced at work when he senses that others are critical of what he does. As a result, he works hard to avoid making mistakes and avoids taking on extra tasks that might increase the risk of being scrutinized by his colleagues. This creates tension for him, however, because he also believes that he has the capacity to contribute more and would therein enjoy work even more than at present. In relaying this insecurity, Roger also speaks of growing up as a lonely child, with little support from his parents. His mother died when he was six and his father gave more attention to Roger's younger sister. In Roger's own words, he did not get what a young boy needs and ponders the extent to which this history has left him lacking in self-confidence to interact with other people in a "normal" way.

Let us consider how we might address Roger's problems in terms of what we said above about increasing psychological flexibility. Two areas of focus seem essential. One is Roger's "story" of how being a lonely child affects his situation today. We use the term story here to refer to an elaborated and somewhat extended verbal response (or relational network), but would emphasize that the story may indeed correspond with Roger's actual history. That is, it might very well be an accurate account of what happened. Furthermore, it may be the case that the causal relation, which Roger perceives as connecting this part of his history with his current problems, may also be true in the sense that these experiences have indeed played a central historical role in creating his current difficulties. The point we want to make, and which we suggest should be used in dialogue with Roger, is much more basic. Specifically, telling the story about his painful experiences as a child and all it includes is a verbal response of Roger's right now, and this response has certain functions regardless of whether or not its content corresponds to what actually happened in his history. And in the effort to increase his psychological flexibility, we suggest focus should be on how this responding influences other parts of Roger's behavior in his present context. The central point in the context of treatment is not "is this account accurate?" but rather "when Roger contacts this story, what does he do?"

The other response Roger is describing as part of his problem is more brief and immediate. It is the rather quick and overwhelming feeling of insecurity that he experiences. In commonsense terms, his response might be seen as largely emotional, but, from the perspective of RFT, it is still verbal, in the sense that it has "meaning" based on a history of arbitrarily applicable relational responding. In other words, it tells Roger something and can thus have functions for further action based on Roger's history of what to do when experiencing such private events in the past.

As we have repeatedly suggested, psychological problems appear to involve behavior in which one's own verbal responses participate in frames of coordination with the deictic I, in a way that leads to problematic consequences. This appears to hold for both elaborated and brief responding. The therapeutic strategy we are now discussing involves attempting to establish a greater degree of hierarchical framing between specific problematic responses that function as self-rules and the deictic I. We will now consider how this might be achieved with the example of Roger.

In the following transcript, Roger describes a situation at work in which he was asked to undertake a task, but reports feeling anxious and insecure in a way that he says is typical.

Therapist: As you recall this, can you get a sense of how that felt, right now, as you are describing it?

Roger: Yes, a bit I guess. It feels heavy, here (moving his right hand to his chest). Not so bad now, but a bit.

Therapist: Would it be okay to allow that to stay for a while, so that we can look at it, a bit closer?

Roger: Uhh, it feels bad … I've had enough of that already …

Therapist: Yeah, I get that. But would you be willing to try staying with it for some time if that could be of help to you?

Roger: Okay, I'll give it a go …

Therapist: Is it there, in your chest?

Roger: Yeah …

Therapist: Would you say you sense this only in your chest or in other parts of your body as well?

Roger: Well, mostly there but also in my neck, actually.

Therapist: What about other parts? Nothing in your legs?

Roger: When you ask, some of it in my thighs also. I did not notice that at first. But it's mostly in my chest.

Therapist: The heaviness … If it had a color, what color would that be?

Roger: Dark brown.

Therapist: Now I'm going to ask you to do something with that dark brown heaviness. It might sound a bit weird, but see if you can try it out. I would like you to gather all this dark brown heaviness together with your hands and sort of hold it out in front of you, or maybe put in on your lap. Can you see yourself doing that?

Roger: Well that's kind of tricky ...

Therapist: Yeah, I know, just use your imagination ... Can you see it out there?

Roger: Yes, I guess, in a way ...

Therapist: If you look at it, besides being dark brown, what else does it look like?

At the start of this dialogue Roger describes an experience of feeling insecure and anxious. Given this experience he follows a self-rule of avoidance imbedded in his emotional reaction, a rule telling him to back off from a suggested task. This action can be described as responding in coordination with the rule, which appears to be a well-established response for Roger. The key focus in the dialogue that followed was to interact with Roger so that he would frame these responses of insecurity, anxiety and the embedded rule of avoidance, in hierarchy with his deictic I. As a result, the self-rule and the feelings connected with it may be experienced by Roger as simply an example of how he sometimes reacts to his social world. Talking about his private experiences as an object to be observed is intended to make this point. Another way of formulating a question to Roger with the same intention on the part of the therapist would be "If that feeling or sensation were a thing, what kind of thing would it be?" Metaphorically, his own reaction is put "out there", and the framing of the experience "from the perspective of himself" is made more probable.

Framing your own responses in hierarchy with your deictic I includes both discrimination of what is observed (in the case of Roger, a sense of insecurity and the embedded rule of avoidance) and discrimination of the one observing (deictic I). This latter part could be focused on at some point in the illustrated exercise above by prompting Roger to observe the dark brown heaviness *and to observe who is observing* (Foody et al., 2013; Luciano et al., 2011). In general, encouraging clients to engage in the verbal repertoire of "observing the observer" constitutes a type of multiple-exemplar training in hierarchical framing between their own behavior and the deictic I. The following brief dialogue serves as one relevant example.

Roger: It just feels awful, it tears me up.

Therapist: So there is this tearing awfulness ... And right now, who is watching that?

Roger: Well, it is me ...

Therapist: So there is the awfulness and it is you who is able to watch it?

Roger: Yes, it is somehow weird but I can see that.

Introducing other metaphors in the ordinary conversation, outside of specific therapeutic exercises such as the one described above, can also function as a type of multiple-exemplar training in hierarchical framing; for example, referring to Roger's experience of insecurity as a road-sign telling him to take a certain direction.

The same general approach to establishing the desired hierarchical framing could also be applied when working on Roger's more elaborated verbal responses: his recollection of his historical background. Assuming that the functional assessment conducted with Roger indicates that this verbal response is part of a problematic behavioral sequence, as in rumination, a metaphor can be used to set up a context that increases the probability of Roger framing this verbal response from the perspective of, and in hierarchy with, "himself."

Therapist: If this story of your background and the different effects it has had on your life were a book, what would be the title?

Roger: Hmm … I don't know. Something about the fact that so much has happened to me during which I did not get a fair chance.

Therapist: Yeah, "The boy that did not get a fair chance." How does that sound?

Roger: Sad, but yes, it fits. It's always with me.

Therapist: It is always with you. And who is the one reading the book?

Roger: It's me, yeah.

Therapist: And right now, here, can you sense the sadness that comes with "The boy that did not get a fair chance"?

Roger: Yes, I sense it in my whole body, especially here (makes a move with his left hand over his neck and looks down).

Therapist: Can you focus on that sense over your shoulders, just watching the sadness there? Let me know when you get it.

Roger: I am. It is hard to feel that, it is heavy.

Therapist: See if you can just watch it … (silence …) Can you move your attention to some other part of your body where you can sense that sadness?

Roger: Yes, in my throat.

Therapist: Just watch the sensation and then tell me what it looks like.

Roger: It is like a small ball …

Therapist: Can you notice yourself watching that small ball?

Roger: Yes, I am.

Therapist: So who is it, noticing the ball in the throat and the heaviness over the shoulders?

Roger: It is me doing that.

Therapist: And now, can you go back, noticing again the title of the book and all the sadness with it and see what you typically do when feeling this sadness?

Roger: I don't like it. I sort of give up, I guess. Run off, in a way … You know …

Therapist: I have a thought here, let me tell you what it is and see what you think. I would suggest that the most important problem is not the book. It is a sad, painful book, definitely. "The boy that did not get a fair chance." And, here is my point, what if the most important problem is not the book but what you do when being reminded of the story, when feeling this sadness?

Roger: What do you mean?

Therapist: That the book, or the story in it, easily becomes a script, telling you to act in accordance with this sad story. I think this is a very common thing in life; our past ends up being a script we follow, one way or another. Like you just said: when experiencing this you easily give up, you easily "run off" …

At this point the reader might see that at the same time as the therapist is working to help Roger frame his elaborated verbal response from the perspective of, and in hierarchy with "I," she is back working on the principle we described first; that of helping Roger discriminate his problematic behavior. This illustrates the fact that the three presented principles do not unfold strictly one after the other, in a linear sequence, but recur throughout treatment, each one being revisited many times. In the dialogue above, the next step might be to help Roger discriminate once again what he typically does "following the book" and then start a dialogue about what behavior would constitute "stepping outside the story." And that would bring us to the third principle we have suggested, *helping the client to specify appetitive augmental functions for further behavior.*

Before we examine this third principle, it seems important to emphasize the role of experiential exercises, such as the one described above, because they constitute a type of multiple-exemplar training, which may be employed throughout therapy. The rationale for experiential exercises is simple: training clients to discriminate specific features of their own behavior. In effect, clients need to learn to discriminate two broad functional classes of behavior, one problematic functional class that currently dominates their repertoires, and a more helpful one that would constitute an alternative. These may be described as psychological rigidity and psychological flexibility, respectively.

The relevant discrimination training is often best done "live," as the behavior in question takes place. The important point is to give a client direct experiences, in session, of the two central classes of behavior. These experiences can then function as exemplars or analogues that help clients bring the experience of treatment into their lives "in the real world." Early in therapy there is often a focus on illustrating current, problematic behavior, and its connection to consequences (principle one above); subsequently, the focus is more on the alternative functional class, psychological flexibility. The two classes are often evoked as a natural part of the interactions that occur in session. Indeed, therapists are advised to watch out for potential opportunities and to use every relevant example. A more active strategy on the part of the therapist is to deliberately evoke the two relevant functional classes in session through the use of experiential exercises.

Indeed, experiential exercises and metaphorical talk often go together. An exercise that seems to help the client to make the relevant discriminations in session can be used in metaphorical talk. For example, following the exercise described earlier when Roger "held his heaviness in his hand," another concrete situation might be discussed where he reports insecurity and self-doubting thoughts concerning approaching a potential partner. Here, the therapist might ask, "Can you simply hold those thoughts and feelings in your hand, just watching them and do what is important for you, in your life?"

As pointed to earlier, we have divided the clinical work into three strategies or principles, for didactic reasons. This last question from the therapist about holding scary private thoughts and feelings "in your hand" illustrates our second principle of hierarchical framing with the deictic I, but also ends with presenting possible augmenting functions by referring to "doing what is important in your life." In doing so, we have arrived at our third principle.

Helping Clients Develop This Alternative Repertoire in a Way That Will Specify Appetitive Augmental Functions for Further Behavior

The problematic behaviors targeted in therapy are by definition well established and acting differently is no easy task, as anyone trying to change old habits would know. This is the reason why motivational factors are so important. Technically, in behavior analysis, motivational variables have often been described using concepts such as establishing and/or motivational operations (Michael, 1993). At the most basic level, an example would be using moderate levels of food deprivation in studies with nonhumans to increase the likelihood that the animals will engage in relatively high levels of operant responding that produces access to food. Or, more informally, we would expect a hungry animal to be more motivated to work for food than an animal that was not hungry. According to RFT, rules/instructions about what is important can function in a similar, albeit much more complex way for verbally able humans. Rules that have this function of increasing (or decreasing) the impact of certain consequences are called augmentals (Barnes-Holmes, O'Hora, et. al., 2001). The third therapeutic strategy we are suggesting here involves helping the client contact overarching, verbally constructed, desirable consequences (or appetitive augmental functions) and link them to new behavior (Luciano et al., 2012; Plumb, Stewart, Dahl, & Lundgren, 2009; Törneke et al., 2008). In more ordinary and less technical language, the point is to clarify what really matters to the client and, by linking this to alternative behavior, using it to motivate change. Let us now consider how this can be done in a dialogue with Roger.

At a point where the therapist concludes that Roger increasingly frames his own story ("the book") in hierarchy with the deictic I, the following would be a typical example of the third therapeutic strategy.

Therapist: So, if we assume that you, now, could do something outside of this story, what would be important to do?

Roger: What do you mean, I am not sure what you are getting at … ?

Therapist: You have described how the book, "The boy who did not get a fair chance," has a lot of impact on what you do in life. It sort of prescribes what you are supposed to do, right?

Roger: Yeah, I can see that. Often it sort of comes by itself; it's so hard to do something outside of that. The book is always with me.

Therapist: Right. So, if you could actually take steps outside of this story, even as it is present, what would those steps be about? If you where free to choose, if it was up to you? What would be important enough for you to go for?

Roger: Okay, I see what you are asking … Well, at work it would be for accomplishing something more, for showing both myself and others that I can contribute. That I belong in the game, or something. Being a teacher is doing something for and together with others, my students, my colleagues. I want to be more a part of that. Then with finding a partner, I don't know … That seems further away …

Therapist: Yeah, and still I wonder … just imagining that you would even take steps in that direction, not saying that you have to, but just exploring what would be there that really matters to you?

Roger: Just having a partner, I guess …

Therapist: Is that really so? I mean, I am pretty sure you do not want a partner who abuses you or treats you badly. So, I would guess it is about something more, something further than just a partner. Or am I mistaken here?

Roger: No, of course, you are right. It would be about being together, belonging together. Interacting in some positive way.

Therapist: So that sounds a bit like what you are saying about work, actually, about belonging, contributing … ?

Roger: Yes, exactly! Belonging in the game, as I said …

At this point Roger seems to contact "what he wants to be about," what matters to him, something that would make it worthwhile to try out new behavior. In other words, the therapist has brought him into contact with appetitive augmental functions (in this case "belonging in the game"). Other ways to help Roger contact such functions would be to ask for specific experiences he might have had earlier in life that included at least a glimpse of what matters to him. Once the client formulates something of overarching importance this can then be used in discussing further behavior, behavior that would actually increase the probability of accessing or creating more of what really matters to the client.

Let us return to an earlier client, Peter, and see how focusing on the same strategy with him might work. For Peter, possible augmental functions that could be targeted may include what kind of father Peter wants to be for his daughter in the long run. Or, what kind of partner he wants to be to his wife. The following provides an example of what working with this third strategy might look like, in helping Peter to connect such augmental functions to further behavior that differs fundamentally from the problematic response of just "following along."

Therapist: So, what would be acting in accordance with the partner you want to be, even in the presence of these "warnings"? Rather than just "following along?"

Peter: Well, not checking everything out all the time, letting go of some of the things I do when acting on these warnings.

Therapist: Like … ?

Peter: Like avoiding the backyard, washing her clothes over and over, controlling my wife and what she does, the way I do now.

Therapist: And if you would stop this "following along" with the warnings that turn up, what would you do that would be in accordance with the partner you want to be?

Peter: I would spend more time partaking in the care of my daughter, I guess. And also take care of some other things that need to be done at home and which have been sort of left behind lately, because of my preoccupation with this pesticide thing.

Therapist: Okay, what could you do along those lines until our next appointment?

Peter: I could take care of my daughter for short periods of time during the evening, both to be with her and to give my wife some time for herself. She really needs some rest.

Therapist: So that would be like the father you want to be and actually also the partner you want to be?

Peter: Yes, exactly.

Therapist: Could you just imagine yourself sitting at home, having your daughter on your lap? Maybe you can close your eyes, if that helps you to see it more clearly. Tell me when you can see it.

Peter: I can see that, sitting in my favourite chair in our living room … But it is really scary. What if the chair is contaminated? I have been sitting there with unwashed clothes. I feel really anxious!

Therapist: A warning right? Where do you feel that feeling now?

Peter: In my chest, as I told you earlier.

Therapist: I want you to notice that anxious feeling in your chest and the thoughts of contamination that turn up. And, at the same time, to watch your daughter on your lap. See if you can contact her as the father you want to be.

Peter: Yes, I am doing that. She moves her head and looks at me … She is so sweet!
Therapist: How does it feel to interact with her in that way?
Peter: Fantastic! I am so proud!
Therapist: Okay. Let yourself experience that. And see if you can also watch yourself sitting there, watching your sweet daughter and having that feeling of being proud. (silence …) And the anxiety?
Peter: It is still there, I guess. Less, and still there. But my daughter is so much more important!
Therapist: What if something like this could actually take place? What would you say?

As any reader familiar with behavior therapy would recognize, the therapist is moving here into homework assignments, similar to what is sometimes referred to as exposure treatment, using our third therapeutic strategy to motivate Peter to change his behavior in such a way that it brings him into contact with appetitive augmental functions (in this case "being a better father and spouse").

Concluding Remarks

The strategies or principles of psychological treatment we have suggested in this chapter are not entirely new or necessarily distinct from other models of treatment. First of all, any reader familiar with acceptance and commitment therapy (ACT; Hayes, Strosahl, & Wilson, 1999) will of course recognize the obvious similarity to it. This should come as no surprise because RFT and ACT codeveloped. In fact, our account specifically relies on earlier attempts to describe ACT from an explicit RFT perspective (Foody & Barnes-Holmes, 2012; Luciano, Rodríguez, & Gutiérrez, 2004; Luciano et al., 2012; Törneke, 2010). At the same time, our account of psychological flexibility does not map exactly onto the more common account used in ACT. The latter posits six psychological processes that form the "hexaflex" (Hayes & Strosahl, 2004) from which psychological flexibility emerges: (a) defusion, (b) acceptance, (c) contact with the present moment, (d) self-as-context, (e) values, and (f) committed action.

The reason for these differing accounts centers around the differing goals of RFT and ACT. Although the latter is very much influenced by the former, RFT is an empirically based theory that aims to provide a functional-analytic account of human language and cognition that will yield readily to experimental analyses. As such, its analysis of processes, such as psychological flexibility, needs to be scientifically testable in a laboratory and be consistent with basic RFT constructs, such as hierarchical and deictic relational framing. In contrast, ACT is a psychotherapy that clinicians have to learn and teach. So even though the "hexaflex" can be used to teach ACT and thus guide people to act in a manner that conforms to our definition of psychological flex-ibility, we do not find it as helpful as a basic scientific account. In our view, this is more than a pedantic point, for if we fail to construct a theoretically and empirically based definition of psychological flexibility, that yields to an experimental analysis, we risk failing to enhance and develop interventions, such as ACT. In our view, in order to refine an intervention, we need to understand and work with basic psychological processes, such as the ones we describe in this chapter. See chapter 18 in this volume for a somewhat related and more extensive discussion of the relationship between RFT and ACT.

Our discussion of psychological flexibility will also be familiar to many readers of a general behavioral orientation, and probably also to readers from other schools of psychotherapy. Indeed, it was never our intention to provide an entirely new model of therapy. Rather, we sought to describe the central principles or strategies involved in treating psychological problems, focusing on what we believe is their core process (psychological rigidity), and working to increase its opposite, psychological flexibility. In the current chapter, we have used RFT as the conceptual basis for achieving our objective. As we see it, one of the main advantages of doing this is that we thereby establish, and hopefully maintain, a close relationship between basic (experimental) research and clinical application. And even though the clinical model that grows out of this relationship may include strategies and techniques similar to other models of psychotherapy, we are hopeful that the approach we offer here will serve to focus on the most important or effective features of the psychotherapeutic process in a unique way.

Note

1   Deictic is a linguistic term pointing to the time, place, or situation from which someone is acting. Framing events from a perspective is thus called deictic framing.

References

Barnes-Holmes, D., Hayes, S. C., & Dymond, S. (2001). Self and self-directed rules. In S. C. Hayes, D. Barnes-Holmes, & B. Roche (Eds.), *Relational frame theory: A post-Skinnerian account of human language and cognition* (pp. 119–140). New York, NY: Plenum.

Barnes-Holmes, D., O'Hora, D., Roche, B., Hayes, S. C., Bissett, R. T., & Lyddy, F. (2001). Understanding and verbal regulation. In S. C. Hayes, D. Barnes-Holmes, & B. Roche (Eds.), *Relational frame theory: A post-Skinnerian account of human language and cognition* (pp. 103–118). New York, NY: Plenum.

Bond, F. W., Hayes, S. C., Baer, R. A., Carpenter, K. C., Guenole, N., Orcutt, H. K., … Zettle, R. D. (2011). Preliminary psychometric properties of the Acceptance and Action Questionnaire – II: A revised measure of psychological flexibility and acceptance. *Behavior Therapy, 42*, 676–688.

Foody, M., & Barnes-Holmes, Y. (2012). The role of self in acceptance and commitment therapy. In L. McHugh & I. Stewart (Eds.), *The self and perspective taking: Contributions and applications from modern behavioral science* (pp. 125–142). Oakland, CA: New Harbinger.

Foody, M., Barnes-Holmes, Y., Barnes-Holmes, D., & Luciano, C. (2013). An empirical investigation of hierarchical versus distinction relations in a self-based ACT exercise. *International Journal of Psychology and Psychological Therapy, 13*, 373–385.

Hayes, S. C., Barnes-Holmes, D., & Roche, B. (Eds.). (2001). *Relational frame theory: A post-Skinnerian account of human language and cognition.* New York, NY: Plenum.

Hayes, S. C., Brownstein, A. J., Zettle, R. D., Rosenfarb, I., & Korn, Z. (1986). Rule-governed behavior and sensitivity to changing consequences of responding. *Journal of the Experimental Analysis of Behavior, 45*, 237–256.

Hayes, S. C., & Hayes, L. J. (1989). The verbal action of the listener as a basis for rule-governance. In S. C. Hayes (Ed.), *Rule-governed behavior: Cognition, contingencies and instructional control* (pp. 153–190). New York, NY: Plenum.

Hayes, S. C., & Strosahl, K. (2004). *A practical guide to acceptance and commitment therapy.* New York, NY: Springer.

Hayes, S. C., Strosahl, K., & Wilson, K. G. (1999). *Acceptance and commitment therapy: An experiental approach to behavioral change.* New York, NY: Guilford.

Hayes, S. C., Wilson, K. G., Gifford, E. V., Follette, V. M., & Strosahl, K. (1996). Experiential avoidance and behavioral disorders: A functional dimensional approach to diagnosis and treatment. *Journal of Consulting and Clinical Psychology, 64,* 1152–1168.

Hughes, S., Barnes-Holmes, D., & Vahey, N. (2012). Holding on to our functional roots when exploring new intellectual islands: A voyage through implicit cognition research. *Journal of Contexual Behavioral Science, 1,* 17–38.

Kashdan, T. B., & Rottenberg, J. (2010). Psychological flexibility as a fundamental aspect of health. *Clinical Psychological Review, 30,* 467–480.

Luciano, C., Rodríguez, M., & Gutiérrez, O. (2004). A proposal for synthesizing verbal contexts in experiential avoidance disorder and acceptance and commitment therapy. *International Journal of Psychology and Psychological Therapy, 4,* 377–394.

Luciano, C., Ruiz, F. J., Vizcaíno-Torres, R. M., Sánchez-Martín, V., Gutiérrez-Martinez, O., & Lopes-López, J. C. (2011). A relational frame analysis of defusion interactions in acceptance and commitment therapy. A preliminary and quasi-experimental study with at-risk adolescents. *International Journal of Psychology and Psychological Therapy, 11,* 165–182.

Luciano, C., Valdivia-Salas, S., Cabello-Luque, F., & Hernendez, M. (2009). Developing self-directed rules. In R. A. Rehfeldt & Y. Barnes-Holmes (Eds.), *Derived relational responding: Applications for learners with autism and other developmental disabilities* (pp. 335–352). Oakland, CA: New Harbinger.

Luciano, C., Valdivia-Salas, S., & Ruiz, F. (2012). The self as the context for rule-governed behavior. In L. McHugh & I. Stewart, I (Eds.), *The self and perspective taking: Contributions and applications from modern behavioral science* (pp. 143–159.) Oakland, CA: New Harbinger.

Matthews, B.A., Shimoff, E., Catania, C., & Sagvolden, T. (1977). Uninstructed human responding: Sensitivity to ratio and interval contingencies. *Journal of Experimental Analysis of Behavior, 27,* 453–467.

Michael, J. (1993). Establishing operations. *The Behavior Analyst, 16,* 191–206.

O'Hora, D., & Barnes-Holmes, D. (2004) Instructional control: Developing a relational frame analysis. *International Journal of Psychology and Psychological Therapy, 11,* 263–284.

Plumb, J. C., Stewart, I., Dahl, J., & Lundgren, T. (2009). In search of meaning: Values in modern clinical behavior analysis. *The Behavior Analyst, 32,* 85–10.

Skinner, B. F. (1966). An operant analysis of problem solving. In B. Kleinmuntz (Ed.), *Problem solving: Research, method, and theory* (pp. 133–171). New York, NY: Wiley.

Skinner, B. F. (1974). *About behaviorism.* New York, NY: Knopf.

Törneke, N. (2010). *Learning RFT: An introduction to relational frame theory and its clinical applications.* Oakland, CA: New Harbinger.

Törneke, N., Luciano, C., & Valdivia-Salas, S. (2008). Rule-governed behavior and psychological problems. *International Journal of Psychology and Psychological Therapy, 8,* 141–156.

Part III

Contextual Approaches to Clinical Interventions and Assessment

Robert D. Zettle

13

Contextual Approaches to Clinical Interventions and Assessment
An Introduction to Part III
Robert D. Zettle

Because of its pragmatic focus, contextual behavioral science is fundamentally concerned with new and more effective ways of instigating behavior change and ultimately can be legitimately judged against this benchmark. Intentional, value-directed efforts to change human behavior can span multiple levels of complexity, ranging from the discrete actions of single individuals to the practices of entire communities (Wilson, Hayes, Biglan, & Embry, 2014). The collection of chapters in this third part of the handbook primarily focuses on contextually based efforts to influence the behavior of single individuals, while the next and concluding part is concerned with intentional behavior change occurring within larger social systems, such as families, groups, organizations, communities, and even entire cultures.

This division is admittedly somewhat arbitrary and roughly mirrors one that has historically been made between clinical and community psychology (Albee, 1998). We are primarily doing so out of convenience as well as recognition that some readers may be more interested in clinical applications of contextual behavioral science, while others are more intrigued, for example, with its potential for primary prevention and extension to larger social systems, among issues addressed in the next part. It is certainly not our view that the principles of intentional behavior change themselves vary appreciably in moving across multiple levels of analysis, especially when a consistent paradigmatic approach is taken in doing so. Indeed, to the extent that individuals are nested within groups, which are in turn situated within communities, such a perspective is the sine qua non of contextual behavioral science. Contextual behavioral science accordingly may not only promote consilience across various scientific disciplines such as biology, psychology, and anthropology, but also facilitate an integration between more clinical versus community-focused approaches to behavior change within psychology itself.

The overriding purpose of this chapter is to provide an overview of the key issues, challenges, and concerns involving contextual approaches to psychotherapy and clinical assessment that the remaining five chapters within this part will be addressing. Before doing so, it may be useful to place this part's focus on clinical behavior analysis

The Wiley Handbook of Contextual Behavioral Science, First Edition. Edited by Robert D. Zettle, Steven C. Hayes, Dermot Barnes-Holmes, and Anthony Biglan.
© 2016 John Wiley & Sons, Ltd. Published 2016 by John Wiley & Sons, Ltd.

(Kohlenberg, Tsai, & Dougher, 1993) and related contextualistic approaches to intentional behavioral change with verbally skilled populations, such as acceptance and commitment therapy (ACT; Hayes, Strosahl, & Wilson, 2012), within a wider historical and clinical context.

Historical Overview

Applied Behavior Analysis

If defined fairly broadly, a strong case can be made that applied behavior analysis (Baer, Wolf, & Risley, 1968) constituted the first systematic contextual approach to psychotherapy. It emerged in the 1960s based on the extension of basic behavioral principles, such as consequential and discriminative stimulus control, originally identified and investigated in the operant conditioning laboratory (Ferster & Skinner, 1957; Skinner, 1938) as a strategy for intentionally changing socially relevant behavior. Skinner's (1974) radical behaviorism was certainly not the only contextualistic approach represented within psychology at the time applied behavior analysis was being developed (Hayes, 1993). Kantor's (1959; 1969) interbehaviorism is another noteworthy example, but Skinner's approach was the only one that embraced a pragmatic truth criterion, and, not coincidentally, directly led to a technology of behavioral change.

When approached in more sophisticated ways, this resulting behavioral change technology took the form of applied behavior analysis in which ideographic functional assessments were initially conducted to identify environmental and contextual variables that exerted stimulus and consequential control over the to-be-changed target behaviors. It then remained to be demonstrated if manipulation of such controlling variables resulted in the desired behavioral change. Unfortunately, when approached in less contextually sensitive and sophisticated ways, applied behavior analysis by the end of the 1970s had become transformed into "behavior modification" in which the role of functional assessment became overshadowed by use of powerful consequences to influence behavior (Hayes, Rincover, & Solnick, 1980).

For understandable reasons, this shift from a more contextualized to technical approach to behavior change was largely driven by the practical exigencies of meeting the urgent clinical needs of populations, such as students with developmental disabilities, displaying very severe and challenging behavioral problems. To the extent that it's possible to push around a lot of behavior – including that of a self-injurious nature – through the contingent management of sufficiently powerful reinforcers (e.g., edibles on a food deprivation schedule) and punishers such as electric shock, a contextual analysis becomes unnecessary. Efforts became less contextualized, analytic, and individualized, and more linked with developing an all-powerful, one-size-fits-all behavior change technology. Not surprisingly, before long overreliance on the use of aversive control became the target of serious ethical questions (e.g., Guess, Helmstetter, Turnbull, & Knowlton, 1987; Shapiro, 1974) as well as countercontrol efforts in the form of lawsuits and the eventual passage of legislation, such as the Individuals with Disabilities Education Act (1997) in the United States, to protect the rights of those with recognized disabilities.

These restrictions on the use of aversive contingencies resulted in a return to a more contextualistic approach in managing challenging behaviors, especially by those with developmental disabilities, characterized by a renewed emphasis on antecedent behavioral control (Carr, 1994; Hanley, Iwata, & McCord, 2003; Luiselli & Cameron, 1998) and the development of both more precise as well as user-friendly methods and strategies for identifying the consequential functions of challenging behaviors on a case-by-case basis. Of particular note, was the work of Carr (1977) in initially proposing different functions that self-injurious behavior might serve and subsequent contributions of Iwata and his colleagues (Iwata, Dorsey, Slifer, Bauman, & Richman, 1982) in developing an analogue methodology for conducting functional analyses, and that of O'Neill and his associates (O'Neill, Horner, Albin, Story, & Sprague, 1990) in publishing a handbook on how to conduct such analyses as well as other forms of functional assessment.

In retrospect, it now seems fairly clear that the re-emergence of functional assessment procedures within applied behavior analysis allowed it to re-establish its contextual focus, but at the cost of moving it even further away from work with verbally competent clinical populations (Friman, 2006; Hayes, 2001). What diminishing focus language and verbal behavior still received within applied behavior analysis (Northrup, Vollmer, & Serrett, 1993) was largely guided by Skinner's (1957) book on *Verbal Behavior* and increasingly restricted to teaching tacting (e.g., Arntzen & Almas, 2002) and manding (e.g., Hall & Sundberg, 1987) to children with developmental disabilities. That the practical extension of what Skinner (1978) himself regarded as his most important work became limited in this narrow way was particularly unfortunate, especially given his early recognition of the critically important role that language likely plays in the prediction and control of human behavior as evidenced by the following passage: "I may say that the only differences I expect to see revealed between the behavior of rat and man (aside from enormous differences in complexity) lie in the field of verbal behavior" (Skinner, 1938, p. 442).

Cognitive Behavior Therapy

Applied behavior analysis with its emphasis on operant principles, along with psychotherapeutic approaches, such as systematic desensitization (Wolpe, 1958), based on respondent principles dominated the first generation of behavior therapy. However, the failure of behavior analysts to develop a pragmatic approach to verbal psychotherapy left a vacuum that by the mid-1970s began to be filled by what can now be referred to as the "second wave" of cognitive behavior therapy (CBT) (Hayes, 2004b). Despite some procedural and minor conceptual differences, these applications (e.g., Beck, 1976; Mahoney, 1974; Meichenbaum, 1977) shared the common feature of being noncontextualistic in nature. With their emphasis on cognitive restructuring, coping self-statements, and self-instructional training, all were implicitly, if not explicitly, both mentalistic and mechanistic in nature (Hayes & Brownstein, 1986). "Cognitive control" was not construed as a matter of ascertaining how one behavior (thinking) might participate in a controlling relationship with another (overt action), but as one of identifying the differing layers of cognitive variables and processes (ranging from automatic thoughts to schemata) that cause emotional and behavioral disorders (Zettle, 1990).

To the extent that Beck and his fellow cognitive and cognitive behavioral practitioners and theorists contributed to the development of contextual behavioral science, it was indirect by instigating a reaction against it. On the plus side, their work appropriately called attention to the influence of language and cognitive processes in human suffering and its alleviation. At the same time, however, their answer to the "cognitive challenge" of explicating the role that thinking plays in controlling other types of human behavior further underscored the need to develop a more pragmatic response to it. In short, the apparent inadequacies of such mentalistic and elemental realistic accounts, if nothing else, further underscored the need to develop a contextualistic alternative that, if necessary, extended beyond existing behavioral analyses of verbal (Skinner, 1957) and rule-governed behavior (Skinner, 1969; Zettle & Hayes, 1982).

Ferster's Contributions to Clinical Behavior Analysis

Skinner did not begin his professional life as a clinician nor did he ever become one. It is thus entirely understandable why his conceptual work on verbal behavior and rule-governance offered relatively little practical assistance to clinicians in meeting the challenges of conducting psychotherapy with verbally skilled clients. Fortunately, one of Skinner's collaborators, Charles Ferster, turned his attention to psychotherapy at about the same time that the "cognitive revolution" in behavior therapy was emerging. Regrettably, he did not develop any novel approach to psychotherapy, but contributed to the development of clinical behavioral analysis through his contextualistic interpretation of existing psychotherapeutic techniques and related clinical phenomena (Kohlenberg, Bolling, Kanter, & Parker, 2002).

Due to space limitations, I will only offer a brief summary here of Ferster's work. Among his contributions was the recommendation that therapists rely upon natural rather than arbitrary reinforcers in shaping the behavior of clients (Ferster, 1967; 1972a) and the recognition that clinically-relevant verbal, as well as other client behaviors, were likely to occur within the context of the therapeutic relationship (Ferster, 1972b; 1979a; 1979b), thereby providing the opportunity for insight (Zettle, 1980) and other verbally established forms of behavioral control to be instigated by the therapist. More important than Ferster's individual publications were the foundational contributions he made in the aggregate to several broadly defined, contextualistic clinical approaches, especially functional analytic psychotherapy (FAP; Kohlenberg & Tsai, 1991; Tsai, Kohlenberg, Kanter, Holman, & Loudon, 2012) and behavioral activation (Jacobson, Martell, & Dimidjian, 2001; Lewinsohn, 1975). To the extent that both FAP and behavioral activation can be usefully integrated with acceptance and commitment therapy (Callaghan, Gregg, Marx, Kohlenberg, & Gifford, 2004; Kanter, Baruch, & Gaynor, 2006), he also indirectly contributed to the development of ACT as well.

The Development of ACT

Because I have provided a narrative of the history and development of ACT elsewhere (Zettle, 2005), I will only provide a brief overview of it here. Some of the foundational work that lead to the emergence of ACT, and somewhat more indirectly to that of relational frame theory (RFT; Hayes, Barnes-Holmes, & Roche, 2001) as well, began in the early 1980s by extending a Skinnerian perspective on verbal control and rule-governance to traditional clinical phenomena and approaches that were part of the second generation of CBT, such as the use of coping statements (Zettle &

Hayes, 1983) and cognitive therapy (Zettle & Hayes, 1982). From this viewpoint, the component of cognitive therapy (Beck, Rush, Shaw, & Emery, 1979) that seemed most sensible was not cognitive restructuring, but "distancing," or the ability of clients to "step back" enough from their own thoughts to respond to them as mere thoughts, rather than as facts. Restated in more behavior analytic terms, observing one's own verbal behavior from the perspective of a listener can be seen as contributing to more widely recognized processes, such as mindfulness and defusion, that are targeted by ACT in increasing psychological flexibility.

What is now known as ACT was developed by largely elaborating on distancing in sensible behavior analytic ways. It was, thus, not mere happenstance that, for roughly the first decade of its existence, ACT was known as "comprehensive distancing." Consequently, perhaps most simply put, I like to think of ACT as what Beck would have created had he been a behavior analyst, or alternatively, what Skinner would have developed had he been a clinician. Expanding and revising the conceptualizations of verbal behavior, rule-governance, and related matters in ways that went beyond limitations inherent in their treatment by Skinner proved useful in developing distancing à la cognitive therapy into a separate contextualistic approach to therapeutic change (Hayes, 1987). For example, linking the functions of a "verbal stimulus" to its participation in relational frames (Hayes & Brownstein, 1985) and redefining rule-governance as control by a verbal antecedent (Zettle & Hayes, 1982) not only pointed to new therapeutic strategies within ACT of weakening the pernicious effects of language, while strengthening its beneficial ones, but also contributed to the development of RFT.

The Chapters in Part III

Contextualistic approaches to psychotherapy in the aggregate at least in part constitute what has come to be regarded as the "third wave" of CBT (Hayes, Villatte, Levin, & Hildebrandt, 2011). If defined fairly broadly, this third generation of CBT includes, but is not necessarily limited to, dialectical behavior therapy (DBT; Linehan, 1993), integrative couples therapy (Jacobson & Christensen, 1996), and even mindfulness-based cognitive therapy (MBCT; Segal, Williams, & Teasdale, 2002), in addition to behavioral activation, FAP, and ACT. Of necessity, because the territory encompassed by these approaches is fairly vast, our coverage of it in this part will be somewhat selective, with the remainder of this chapter serving as a "roadmap" as we embark upon our journey through it. While existing bodies of research will be summarized where appropriate, a series of focused literature reviews would be outdated by the time they would appear in print, given the accelerated rate, for example, of publications investigating ACT. Instead, the remaining chapters within this part will focus more on conceptual, methodological, and strategic challenges that clinical behavior analysis must meet for further advancements in the development and enhancement of related contextualistic approaches to clinical practice and assessment, in general, and of ACT more specifically, to be realized.

Perhaps in part because of its transdiagnostic focus, the contextualistic approach that has been most thoroughly investigated and that enjoys the broadest empirical support is ACT. Earlier meta-analyses were consistent in documenting significant, but moderate, effect sizes for ACT (Hayes, Luoma, Bond, Masuda, & Lillis, 2006; Ost,

2008) that did not differ from established treatments (Powers, Zum Vorde Sive Vording, & Emmelkamp, 2009). However, the most recent meta-analysis reporting mean effect sizes that significantly favor ACT over more traditional forms of CBT (Ruiz, 2012) and, as of this writing, the recognition by the Society of Clinical Psychology (http://www.psychologicaltreatments.org) of strong research support for ACT in the treatment of chronic pain and modest research support in the treatment of depression, mixed anxiety, obsessive-compulsive disorder, and psychotic symptoms more firmly establishes its empirical status. While the five chapters in this part for this reason will largely be focused on ACT, they also address broader issues and concerns that are relevant to contextualistic approaches to CBT and clinical assessment more generally.

The degree to which contextual behavioral science helps advance the impact of related psychotherapeutic approaches is, in turn, likely to be linked to how the domain of such interventions is itself defined. Chapter 14, by James Herbert, Evan M. Forman, and Peter Hitchcock, addresses this issue by providing further elaboration and discussion of a number of the core features of contextual approaches to CBT that have been proposed elsewhere (e.g., Hayes et al., 2011), but only briefly touched upon here. Specifically, they explicate the common defining features that contextual interventions share with each other and that also distinguish them in the aggregate from among the more than 500 other "brands" of psychotherapy (Eisner, 2000) currently available in the mental health marketplace.

Despite their shared and distinguishing characteristics, various contextual approaches, as Herbert et al. point out, nonetheless differ from each other in several important ways, depending on whether they are viewed primarily through a philosophical or technical lens. All contextual approaches are not "created equal" and some meaningful distinctions that can be drawn among them may be useful in furthering our knowledge of how to most efficaciously advance a progressive applied science and influence meaningful individual behavioral change.

Ultimately perhaps the most useful, as well as challenging, way of distinguishing contextual CBTs from other psychotherapeutic approaches is by identifying what particular therapist actions are instrumental in influencing specific client behaviors that are, in turn, linked to improvement both inside and outside of therapy. Such a strategy also provides an alternative means of potentially distinguishing between differing contextual approaches. It is possible, for example, that therapists within two approaches that are described as quite similar (e.g., ACT and DBT) may, nonetheless, behave in functionally different ways. Conversely, effective practitioners of seemingly discrepant contextualistic approaches (e.g., behavioral activation and MBCT) may display in-session behaviors that influence similar client responses despite their topographical differences.

Chapter 15, by Matthieu Villatte, focuses on some of the challenges in evaluating in-session therapist and client behavioral interactions that still need to be resolved for matters of this sort to be addressed empirically. As he astutely points out, one of the more formidable challenges is that which comes from having to functionally define and identify key client behaviors on a case-by-case basis. Another is the related challenge of identifying and tracking specific therapist verbal and nonverbal behaviors that are instrumental in moving both the in-session and extratherapeutic behavior of clients in ways consistent with the overall goals of psychotherapy from a contextualistic perspective. Following protocols and manuals that specify the form or topography that practitioner behaviors are to take may improve treatment integrity, but at the possible cost of decreasing the psychological flexibility of therapists, and thereby compromising the efficacy of the interventions (e.g., Plumb & Vilardaga, 2010). Human behavior in general appears to be more adaptable in the face of rapidly changing circumstances, such as those often encountered in the therapy office, when it is contingency-shaped rather than rule-governed (Catania, Matthews, & Shimoff, 1982; Hayes, Brownstein, Haas, & Greenway, 1986; Hayes, Brownstein, Zettle, Rosenfarb, & Korn, 1986; Hayes, Zettle, & Rosenfarb, 1989; Shimoff, Catania, & Matthews, 1981), and there is no reason to suspect that the behavior of psychotherapists is an exception.

The type of assessment needed to identify the key functional interactions between clients and therapists within contextual CBTs will likely entail a moment-by-moment microanalysis of the behaviors of each culled from psychotherapy transcripts and video recordings of sessions. Certainly until such endeavors prove successful, and in all likelihood even afterwards, they are apt to be seen by practitioners as of limited practical value in guiding how they select and use psychological measurements. Stated somewhat differently, knowing what particular therapist actions increase the occurrence of clinically relevant client behaviors is likely to be of little help to practitioners in choosing which questionnaires from a menu of self-report measures to administer in making treatment-related choices and decisions. As a consequence, the current gap that exists between science and practice in clinical psychology (Baker, McFall, & Shoham, 2008; Frazier, Formoso, Birman, & Atkins, 2008; McQuaid & Spirito, 2012) is unlikely to be narrowed.

The third chapter in this part of the handbook, by Joseph Ciarrochi and his collaborators, discusses the promise that a contextualistic perspective toward clinical assessment may offer in bridging this science–practice gap within a wide array of psychotherapeutic approaches that include, but are not limited to contextual CBTs. As they emphasize, a contextualistic approach to clinical assessment views psychological measures, such as questionnaires and self-report inventories, as tools that are most appropriately evaluated by the degree to which they serve their intended purpose. Clinical assessment that is being used to determine if therapeutic goals have been attained and to track process variables related to such outcomes is usefully evaluated by psychometric standards (American Educational Research Association, 1999). However, assessment that is conducted to select therapeutic goals and options and subsequently guide treatment implementation is more usefully judged by its treatment utility (Nelson, 2003), or its pragmatic value in contributing to better treatment outcomes. Unfortunately, as Ciarrochi et al. document, very few assessment techniques, procedures, and practices related to conducting psychotherapy in general and contextual CBTs, in particular, have been evaluated for their treatment utility.

The development of psychometrically sound process measures is necessary, but not sufficient, for practitioners to have the means of guiding and making adjustments to the services they offer. For example, if defusion is found to mediate reductions in depression (Zettle, Rains, & Hayes, 2011), the repeated administration of a reliable measure of this process can provide useful feedback to therapists on whether their efforts are having the intended effect. However, the practical use of process measures in this manner is contingent on knowing what variables to assess. A key aspect of contextual behavioral science is its reticulated network of research and practice (Hayes, Barnes-Holmes, & Wilson, 2012), in which applications and interventions at a macro-level, as well as "bottom-up" activities at more basic and microlevels, are integrated with each other in mutually informative ways. Consistent with this model, knowledge about what process variables therapists should be tracking and targeting may come not only from clinical trials, but also from laboratory-based studies and analogues.

The penultimate chapter in this part, by Michael Levin and Matthieu Villatte, summarizes the potential contributions that experimental analogue research, laboratory-based studies of therapeutic components (Levin, Hildebrandt, Lillis, & Hayes, 2012), experimental psychopathology investigations, and related "bottom-up" activities can offer within contextual behavioral science's reticulated network of research methods and activities. The chapter reviews exemplary studies within clinical behavior analysis, RFT, and contextual CBT that highlight how these methods help bridge basic research, applied theory, and interventions by contributing to our understanding of pathological processes, treatment components, processes of change, and contextual or moderating factors using highly controlled experimental designs. Accordingly, such basic research strategies and methods may also play a useful role in narrowing the science–practice gap in clinical psychology.

As noted by Herbert et al. in the opening chapter in this part, an argument could be made on philosophical grounds that ACT is the only "true" contextual CBT. It is after all, the one approach that has been explicitly linked to functional contextualism and a related account of human language and cognition provided by RFT. ACT in particular is commonly presented as the application of a model of six interrelated, middle-level processes that contribute to psychological flexibility (i.e., the "hexaflex"; Hayes, 2004a): (a) acceptance, (b) defusion, (c) mindfulness, (d) self-as-context, (e) values, and (f) committed action (e.g., Hayes et al., 2006). The hexaflex model, in turn, is typically depicted as derived from RFT (Hayes et al., 2006).

However, legitimate concerns have been raised recently about the degree to which ACT and RFT may have drifted apart (Barnes-Holmes & Foody, 2012) over the past decade since book-level presentations of both first appeared (Hayes et al., 2001; Hayes, Strosahl, & Wilson, 1999). The concluding chapter by Yvonne Barnes-Holmes and her associates elaborates on this development and functions as a type of counterweight to the other chapters within this part in arguing that the current purported reticulated relationship between ACT and RFT may be somewhat more dialectical in nature. As indicated by the title of their chapter, Barnes-Holmes et al. in particular make the case that the functionality of middle-level terms and processes with the hexaflex model of ACT is suspect and that they are not readily accountable by RFT. By extension, the utility of laboratory-based studies and applied process research in ACT guided by the model are also called into question.

The concluding part of this handbook will in part examine how psychological flexibility may not only be useful to individuals, but also to organizations, in living their values. As a consequence, divergent viewpoints, opinions, and ways of framing events may be especially useful to an organization such as the Association for Contextual Behavioral Science in realizing its stated mission of developing "a coherent and progressive science of human action that is more adequate to the challenges of the human condition."

Summary and Conclusions

Science in general is a cumulative and self-correcting process and contextual behavioral science is no exception. Despite some of the notable achievements and progress that have already been made in extending a contextualistic approach to psychotherapy, much more work obviously remains to be done. We can do better, but, in order to do so, it seems useful to acknowledge at the front-end that some of our current theories, models, and formulations are "wrong." Unfortunately, at this point we don't know where these errors lie. However, if the challenges identified by the chapters within this part are embraced, those areas in which we are wrong will hopefully become more obvious. If as a result, our ability to minimize the suffering of individuals is advanced in some small way, the work of myself and the other contributors to this part of the handbook can be judged as having been worthwhile.

References

Albee, G. W. (1998). Fifty years of clinical psychology: Selling our soul to the devil. *Applied and Preventive Psychology, 7,* 189–194.

American Educational Research Association. (1999). *Standards for educational and psychological testing.* Washington, DC: Author.

Arntzen, E., & Almas, I. K. (2002). Effects of mand-tact versus tact-only training on the acquisition of tacts. *Journal of Applied Behavior Analysis, 35,* 419–422.

Baer, D. M., Wolf, M. M., & Risley, T. R. (1968). Some current dimensions of applied behavior analysis. *Journal of Applied Behavior Analysis, 1,* 91–97.

Baker, T. B., McFall, R. M., & Shoham, V. (2008). Current status and future prospects of clinical psychology toward a scientifically principled approach to mental and behavioral health care. *Psychological Science in the Public Interest, 9,* 67–103.

Barnes-Holmes, Y., & Foody, M. (2012, July). What does the future hold for mid-level processes in ACT? In S. Hughes (Chair), *Back to the future II: Current directions and perspectives in RFT, ACT, and CBS.* Symposium conducted at the meeting of the Association for Contextual Behavioral Science, Washington, DC.

Beck, A. T. (1976). *Cognitive therapy and the emotional disorders.* New York, NY: International Universities Press.

Beck, A. T., Rush, A. J., Shaw, B. F., & Emery, G. (1979). *Cognitive therapy of depression.* New York, NY: Guilford.

Callaghan, G. M., Gregg, J. A., Marx, B. P., Kohlenberg, B. S., & Gifford, E. (2004). FACT: The utility of an integration of functional analytic psychotherapy and acceptance and commitment therapy to alleviate human suffering. *Psychotherapy: Theory, Research, Practice, Training, 41,* 195–207.

Carr, E. G. (1977). The motivation of self-injurious behavior: A review of some hypotheses. *Psychological Bulletin, 84,* 800–816.

Carr, E. G. (1994). Emerging themes in the functional analysis of problem behavior. *Journal of Applied Behavior Analysis, 27,* 393–399.

Catania, A, C., Matthews, B. A., & Shimoff, E. (1982). Instructed versus shaped human behavior: Interactions with nonverbal responding. *Journal of the Experimental Analysis of Behavior, 38,* 233–248.

Eisner, D. A. (2000). *The death of psychotherapy: From Freud to alien abductions.* Westport, CT: Praeger.

Ferster, C. B. (1967). Arbitrary and natural reinforcement. *Psychological Record, 22,* 1–16.

Ferster, C. B. (1972a). Clinical reinforcement. *Seminars in Psychiatry, 4,* 101–111.

Ferster, C. B. (1972b). An experimental analysis of clinical phenomena. *Psychological Record, 22,* 1–16.

Ferster, C. B. (1979a). A laboratory model of psychotherapy: The boundary between clinical practice and experimental psychology. In P. O. Sjoden, S. Bates, & W. S. Dockens, III (Eds.), *Trends in behavior therapy* (pp. 23–38). New York, NY: Academic Press.

Ferster, C. B. (1979b). Psychotherapy from the standpoint of a behaviorist. In J. D. Keehn (Ed.), *Psychopathology in animals: Research and clinical implications* (pp. 279–303). New York, NY: Academic Press.

Ferster, C. B., & Skinner, B. F. (1957). *Schedules of reinforcement.* New York, NY: Appleton- Century-Crofts.

Frazier, S. L., Formoso, S., Birman, D., & Atkins, M. S. (2008). Closing the research to practice gap: Redefining feasibility. *Clinical Psychology: Science and Practice, 15,* 125–129.

Friman, P. C. (2006). The future of behavior analysis is under the dome. *Association for Behavior Analysis International Newsletter, 29,* 4–5.

Guess, D., Helmstetter, E., Turnbull, H. R. III, & Knowlton, S. (1987). The use of aversive procedures with persons who are disabled: An historical review and critical analysis. In P. Campbell (Ed.), *The association for persons with severe handicaps monograph series, 2.* Seattle, WA: The Association for Persons with Severe Handicaps.

Hall, G., & Sundberg, M. L. (1987). Teaching mands by manipulating conditioned establishing operations. *The Analysis of Verbal Behavior, 5,* 41–53.

Hanley, G. P., Iwata, B. A., & McCord, B. E. (2003). Functional analysis of problem behavior: A review. *Journal of Applied Behavior Analysis, 36,* 147–185.

Hayes, S. C. (1987). A contextual approach to therapeutic change. In N. S. Jacobson (Ed.), *Psychotherapists in clinical practice: Cognitive and behavioral perspectives* (pp. 327– 387). New York, NY: Plenum.

Hayes, S. C. (1993). Analytic goals and the varieties of scientific contextualism. In S. C. Hayes, L. J. Hayes, H. W. Reese, & T. R. Sarbin (Eds.), *Varieties of scientific contextualism* (pp. 11–27). Reno, NV: Context Press.

Hayes, S. C. (2001). The greatest dangers facing behavior analysis today. *The Behavior Analyst Today, 2,* 61–63.

Hayes, S. C. (2004a). Acceptance and commitment therapy and the new behavior therapies: Mindfulness, acceptance and relationship. In S. C. Hayes, V. M. Follette, & M. Linehan (Eds.), *Mindfulness and acceptance: Expanding the cognitive behavioral tradition* (pp. 1–29). New York, NY: Guilford.

Hayes, S. C. (2004b). Acceptance and commitment therapy, relational frame theory, and the third wave of behavioral and cognitive therapies. *Behavior Therapy, 35,* 639–665.

Hayes, S. C., Barnes-Holmes, D., & Roche, B. (2001). *Relational frame theory: A post-Skinnerian account of human language and cognition.* New York, NY: Plenum.

Hayes, S. C., Barnes-Homes, D., & Wilson, K. G. (2012). Contextual behavioral science: Creating a science more adequate to the challenge of the human condition. *Journal of Contextual Behavioral Science, 1,* 1–16.

Hayes, S. C., & Brownstein, A. J. (1985, May). *Verbal behavior, equivalence classes, and rules: New definitions, data, and directions.* Invited address presented at the meeting of the Association for Behavior Analysis, Columbus, OH.

Hayes, S. C., & Brownstein, A. J. (1986). Mentalism, behavior–behavior relations, and a behavior analytic view of the purposes of science. *The Behavior Analyst, 9,* 175–190.

Hayes, S. C., Brownstein, A, J., Haas, J. R., & Greenway, D. E. (1986). Instructions, multiple schedules, and extinction: Distinguishing rule-governed behavior from schedule controlled behavior. *Journal of the Experimental Analysis of Behavior, 46,* 137–147.

Hayes, S. C., Brownstein, A. J., Zettle, R. D., Rosenfarb, I. , & Korn, Z. (1986). Rule-governed behavior and sensitivity to changing consequences of responding. *Journal of the Experimental Analysis of Behavior, 45,* 237–256.

Hayes, S. C., Luoma, J. B., Bond, F. W., Masuda, A., & Lillis, J. (2006). Acceptance and commitment therapy: Model, processes, and outcome. *Behaviour Research and Therapy, 44,* 1–25.

Hayes, S. C., Rincover, A., & Solnick, J. V. (1980). The technical drift of applied behavior analysis. *Journal of Applied Behavior Analysis, 13,* 275–285.

Hayes, S. C., Strosahl, K. D., & Wilson, K. G. (1999). *Acceptance and commitment therapy: An experiential approach to behavior change.* New York, NY: Guilford.

Hayes, S. C., Strosahl. K. D., & Wilson, K. G. (2012). *Acceptance and commitment therapy: The process and practice of mindful change* (2nd ed.). New York, NY: Guilford.

Hayes, S. C., Villatte, M., Levin, M., & Hildebrandt, M. (2011). Open, aware, and active: Contextual approaches as an emerging trend in the behavioral and cognitive therapies. *Annual Review of Clinical Psychology, 7,* 141–168.

Hayes, S. C., Zettle, R. D., & Rosenfarb, I. (1989). Rule following. In S. C. Hayes (Ed.), *Rule-governed behavior: Cognition, contingencies, and instructional control* (pp. 191–220). New York, NY: Guilford.

Individuals with Disabilities Education Act, 20 U.S.C. § 1400 (1997).

Iwata, B. A., Dorsey, M. F., Slifer, K. J., Bauman, K. E., & Richman, G. S. (1982). Toward a functional analysis of self-injury. *Analysis and Intervention in Developmental Disabilities, 2,* 3–20.

Jacobson, N. S., & Christensen, A. (1996). *Integrative couple therapy: Promoting acceptance and change.* New York, NY: Norton.

Jacobson, N. S., Martell, C. R., & Dimidjian, S. (2001). Behavioral activation treatment for depression: Returning to contextual roots. *Clinical Psychology: Science and Practice, 8,* 255–270.

Kanter, J. W., Baruch, D. E., & Gaynor, S. T. (2006). Acceptance and commitment therapy and behavioral activation for the treatment of depression: Description and comparison. *The Behavior Analyst, 29,* 161–185.

Kantor, J. R. (1959). *Interbehavioral psychology.* Chicago, IL: Principia Press.

Kantor, J. R. (1969). *The scientific evolution of psychology* (*Vol. 1*). Chicago, IL: Principia Press.

Kohlenberg, R. J., Bolling, M. Y., Kanter, J. W., & Parker, C. R. (2002). Clinical behavior analysis: Where it went wrong, how it was made good again, and why its future is so bright. *The Behavior Analyst Today, 3,* 248–253.

Kohlenberg, R. J., & Tsai, M. (1991). *Functional analytic psychotherapy: A guide for creating intense and curative therapeutic relationships.* New York, NY: Plenum.

Kohlenberg, R. J., Tsai, M., & Dougher, M. J. (1993). The dimensions of clinical behavior analysis. *The Behavior Analyst, 16,* 271–282.

Levin, M. E., Hildebrandt, M. J., Lillis, J., & Hayes, S. C. (2012). The impact of treatment components suggested by the psychological flexibility model: A meta-analysis of laboratory-based component studies. *Behavior Therapy, 43,* 741–756.

Lewinsohn, P. M. (1975). The behavioral study and treatment of depression. In M. Hersen, R. M. Eisler, & P. M. Miller (Eds.), *Progress in behavior modification* (Vol. 1, pp. 19–65). New York, NY: Academic Press.

Linehan, M. M. (1993). *Cognitive-behavioral treatment of borderline personality disorder.* New York, NY: Guilford.

Luiselli, J. K., & Cameron, M. J. (1998). *Antecedent control: Innovative approaches to behavioral support.* Baltimore, MD: Paul H. Brookes.

Mahoney, M. J. (1974). *Cognition and behavior modification.* Cambridge, MA: Ballinger.

McQuaid, E. L., & Spirito, A. (2012). Integrating research into clinical internship training: Bridging the science/practice gap in pediatric psychology. *Journal of Pediatric Psychology, 37,* 149–157.

Meichenbaum, D. H. (1977). *Cognitive-behavior modification: An integrative approach.* New York, NY: Plenum.

Nelson, R. O. (2003). Treatment utility of psychological assessment. *Psychological Assessment, 4,* 521–531.

Northup, J., Vollmer, T. R., & Serrett, K. (1993). Publication trends in 25 years of the *Journal of Applied Behavior Analysis. Journal of Applied Behavior Analysis, 26,* 527–537.

O'Neill, R. E., Horner, R. H., Albin, R. W., Story, K., & Sprague, J. R. (1990). *Functional analysis of problem behavior: A practical assessment guide.* Sycamore, IL: Sycamore Publishing.

Ost, L. G. (2008). Efficacy of the third wave of behavioral therapies: A systematic review and meta-analysis. *Behaviour Research and Therapy, 46*, 296–321.

Plumb, J. C., & Vilardaga, R. (2010). Assessing treatment integrity in acceptance and commitment therapy: Strategies and suggestions. *International Journal of Behavioral Consultation and Therapy, 6*, 263–295.

Powers, M. B., Zum Vorde Sive Vording, M. B., & Emmelkamp, P. M. G. (2009). Acceptance and commitment therapy: A meta-analytic review. *Psychotherapy and Psychosomatics, 78*, 73–80.

Ruiz, F. J. (2012). Acceptance and commitment therapy versus traditional cognitive behavioral therapy: A systematic review and meta-analysis of current empirical evidence. *International Journal of Psychology and Psychological Therapy, 12*, 333–357.

Segal, Z. V., Williams, J. M. G., & Teasdale, J. D. (2002). *Mindfulness-based cognitive therapy for depression: A new approach to preventing relapse.* New York, NY: Guilford.

Shapiro, M. H. (1974). Legislating the control of behavior control: Autonomy and the coercive use of organic therapies. *Southern California Law Review, 47*, 237–238.

Shimoff, E., Catania, A. C., & Matthews, B. A. (1981). Uninstructed human responding: Sensitivity of low-rate performance to schedule contingencies. *Journal of the Experimental Analysis of Behavior, 36*, 207–220.

Skinner, B. F. (1938). *The behavior of organisms.* New York, NY: Appleton-Century-Crofts.

Skinner, B. F. (1957). *Verbal behavior.* New York, NY: Appleton-Century-Crofts.

Skinner, B. F. (1969). *Contingencies of reinforcement: A theoretical analysis.* New York, NY: Appleton-Century Crofts.

Skinner, B. F. (1974). *About behaviorism.* New York, NY: Knopf.

Skinner, B. F. (1978). *Reflections on behaviorism and society.* Englewood Cliffs, NJ: Prentice Hall.

Tsai, M., Kohlenberg, R. J., Kanter, J. W., Holman, G. I., & Loudon, M. P. (2012). *Functional analytic psychotherapy: Distinctive features.* New York, NY: Routledge.

Wilson, D. S., Hayes, S. C., Biglan, A., & Embry, D. D. (2014). Evolving the future: Toward a science of intentional change. *Behavioral and Brain Sciences, 37*, 395–416.

Wolpe, J. (1958). *Psychotherapy by reciprocal inhibition.* Stanford, CA: Stanford University Press.

Zettle, R. D. (1980, November). Insight: Rules and revelations. In S. C Hayes (Chair), *The baby and the bathwater: Radical behavioral interpretations of traditional clinical phenomena.* Symposium conducted at the meeting of the Association for Advancement of Behavior Therapy, New York.

Zettle, R. D. (1990). Rule-governed behavior: A radical behavioral answer to the cognitive challenge. *The Psychological Record, 40*, 41–49.

Zettle, R. D. (2005). The evolution of a contextual approach to therapy: From comprehensive distancing to ACT. *International Journal of Behavioral Consultation and Therapy, 1*, 77–89.

Zettle, R. D., & Hayes, S. C. (1982). Rule-governed behavior: A potential theoretical framework for cognitive-behavioral therapy. In P. C. Kendall (Ed.), *Advances in cognitive-behavioral research and therapy* (pp. 73–118). New York, NY: Academic Press.

Zettle, R. D., & Hayes, S. C. (1983). Effect of social context on the impact of coping self-statements. *Psychological Reports, 52*, 391–401.

Zettle, R. D., Rains, J. C., & Hayes, S. C. (2011). Processes of change in acceptance and commitment therapy for depression: A mediation reanalysis of Zettle and Rains. *Behavior Modification, 35*, 265–283.

14

Contextual Approaches to Psychotherapy
Defining, Distinguishing, and Common Features

James D. Herbert, Evan M. Forman, and Peter Hitchcock

There can be little doubt that the past 15 years have witnessed significant developments in the field of applied psychology broadly known as cognitive behavior therapy (CBT). In particular, treatment models that emphasize mindful awareness and psychological acceptance of distressing subjective experiences have exploded in popularity. These treatment innovations have been accompanied by theoretical developments and a rapidly growing body of quantitative research. Scholars have extended these applications beyond the treatment of psychopathology to a range of other areas, including topics such as reducing workplace stress, racial prejudice, and stigma.

Metaphors for the Emergence of Contextual CBTs

In the eyes of some clinicians and clinical scientists, these changes are nothing short of revolutionary. To others, they represent mere elaborations on preexisting themes. How these new approaches are situated with respect to earlier models of CBT is reflected in the metaphors used to describe them.

Hayes's Generational Metaphor

In a widely cited analysis, Hayes (2004) described three "waves" or generations of CBT. The first generation represents the birth of the field in the 1950s and 1960s, and was characterized by the application of basic behavioral principles in the service of behavior change. The second generation, beginning in the 1970s, emphasized problematic cognitions as the key to treatment. This focus arose from the perception that

The Wiley Handbook of Contextual Behavioral Science, First Edition. Edited by Robert D. Zettle, Steven C. Hayes, Dermot Barnes-Holmes, and Anthony Biglan.
© 2016 John Wiley & Sons, Ltd. Published 2016 by John Wiley & Sons, Ltd.

earlier theories and technologies did not sufficiently appreciate the role of language and cognition in the etiology and treatment of psychopathology, especially among verbally competent adults. The first generation's tight connections linking basic theory and research on the one hand with applied work on the other were de-emphasized in favor of innovations derived from the clinical consultation room. The emphasis was on identifying and modifying the irrational or distorted thoughts and beliefs that were thought to cause emotional distress. In contrast, the third generation, which came to fruition beginning around the turn of the millennium, de-emphasized changing the content of cognition in favor of changing one's relationship with thoughts and other subjective experiences. Mindful awareness and psychological acceptance of distressing thoughts and feelings are fostered in order to facilitate behavior change. Hayes's developmental metaphor reflects a historical perspective, with each generation incorporating some aspects of the preceding one while replacing other key features.

Martell's Stream Metaphor

In contrast, while also describing these same developments, Martell (2008) prefers the metaphor of a stream, which gradually picks up stones as it grows ever stronger and more powerful as it flows downhill. Each new development builds on those that preceded it, adding strength to the overall field. This metaphor suggests a highly progressive program. From this perspective, theoretical and technical inconsistencies and differences between various models of CBT are viewed as minimal, and the emphasis is on a high progressive process of cumulative growth.

Hofmann's Branching Tree Metaphor

Yet another metaphor is offered by Hofmann (2008), who describes CBT as a branching tree, with new developments deriving from older ones. In contrast to the stream metaphor, the branching tree metaphor emphasizes that approaches become increasingly distinct as they develop, despite common roots. Of course, the tree metaphor assumes that all modern forms of CBT are derived from a single, common history (the trunk of the tree), whereas the reality may be messier. Acceptance and commitment therapy (ACT; Hayes, Strosahl, & Wilson, 2012), for example, has roots not only in CBT, but also in applied behavior analysis and existential psychotherapies, whereas more traditional forms of CBT such as cognitive therapy (CT) were far less influenced by these approaches. Moreover, the tree metaphor begs the question of how the branches are arranged with respect to one another. Depending on whether one emphasizes the underlying philosophy, or theory, or clinical technique, different models of CBT will be grouped closer together or farther apart.

The point is not that one of these metaphors is necessarily more correct than another. They are all merely heuristic devices, and their ultimate utility will have to await the retrospective analysis of historians. Rather, the important point is that despite the widespread consensus that there has been a distinct shift toward theories, principles, and technologies emphasizing mindfulness and acceptance, consensus has not been reached on how these approaches are best understood with respect to one another, both historically and currently.

Contextual CBT: Distinguishing Characteristics

The situation becomes even more complex when we consider what is meant by "contextual" CBTs. A growing number of scholars, particularly those working within the field known as contextual behavioral science (CBS), use this term to describe these novel mindfulness and acceptance-oriented models of CBT (Hayes, Levin, Plumb, Villatte, & Pistorello, 2013). However, precisely what makes any given CBT program contextual, and the boundaries separating contextual from noncontextual models, remains unclear. As the leading proponent of CBS, Hayes has addressed this issue, but has been somewhat inconsistent in his analyses. At times he describes contextual CBT narrowly, in such a way that only ACT would seem to qualify (Hayes, Barnes-Holmes, & Wilson, 2012). At other times, he casts a wider net, including most or even all of the novel mindfulness and acceptance-based models under a broad "contextual" umbrella.

For example, Hayes, Villatte, Levin, and Hildebrandt (2011), building on an analysis by Hayes (2004), recently proposed five characteristics that distinguish contextual CBTs. First, these approaches use general principles to target the function – rather than the specific content or form – of thoughts and other subjective experiences, as illustrated by the following passage:

> These new methods target the context and function of psychological events such as thoughts, sensations, or emotions, rather than primarily targeting the content, validity, intensity, or frequency of such events, and they do so in a way that is focused on principles of change and not merely on new techniques. (pp. 157–158)

Second, contextual CBTs are transdiagnostic rather than focused on specific clinical syndromes. Third, contextual approaches are self-consciously reflective in that the basic principles apply equally to the clinician as well as the target client, group, or institution. Fourth, these approaches build on other strands of CBT, incorporating useful principles and methods rather than seeking to replace them. Finally, contextual approaches are thought to apply to larger, more complex facets of the human condition beyond psychopathology, including topics such as spirituality, meaning, and the sense of self.

There is no doubt that these five features describe ACT and its associated theory. Less clear, however, is how well they describe the other acceptance-based models of CBT that have also gained traction over the past couple of decades, and that are frequently included under the "contextual" label. Although there is no consensus around a single, comprehensive list of acceptance-based CBTs, reviews of these approaches have generally included the following models: ACT (Hayes, Strosahl, et al., 2012), dialectical behavior therapy (DBT; Linehan, 1993; Linehan, Armstrong, Suarez, Allmon, & Heard, 1991), functional analytic psychotherapy (FAP; Kohlenberg & Tsai, 1991), behavioral activation (Kanter et al., 2010), integrative behavioral couples therapy (IBCT; Christensen et al., 2004; Jacobson, Christensen, Prince, Cordova, & Eldridge, 2000), mindfulness-based cognitive therapy (MBCT; Teasdale et al., 2000), mindfulness-based stress reduction (MBSR; Kabat-Zinn, 2009), and metacognitive therapy (Wells, 2008; 2011). We now explore how well these five criteria describe these various models, as well as how well they demarcate these models from more traditional forms of CBT.

Emphasis of Function over Form, and a Focus on Mindful Awareness and Psychological Acceptance of Subjective Experience

The most obvious characteristic shared by the various acceptance-based models of CBTs is their emphasis on the function of distressing subjective experiences rather than on the specific content of these experiences, and the corresponding emphasis on nonjudgmental awareness and acceptance of one's experience in the service of behavior change. Each of the approaches listed above shares this emphasis, to varying degrees. Moreover, traditional forms of CBT such as CT do not emphasize these principles nearly as much. This is not to say that acceptance-based approaches never address the content of experience. For example, although the point is sometimes misunderstood, there is nothing in the ACT model that prohibits examining the content of a thought in relation to events in the world, provided that doing so is really a matter of gathering useful data that facilitates behavior consistent with one's goals and values. Likewise, one can find references to psychological acceptance in the traditional CT literature. For example, although most lists of common cognitive distortions (Burns, 1980) focus on the truth or accuracy of cognitions, Persons (1989) added the category of "maladaptive thoughts" to describe those that may be true, but are nevertheless unhelpful to focus on. As early as 1985, A. T. Beck, Emery, and Greenberg suggested working with obsessive or anxious automatic thoughts by using the acronym AWARE: [A]ccepting anxiety, [W]atching anxiety without judgment, [A]cting with anxiety as if one were not anxious, [R]epeating the first three steps, and [E]xpecting the best. Burns (1989) describes a cost-benefit analysis of beliefs, in which one explores the pros and cons of beliefs with the goal of making "an enlightened decision to develop a healthier value system" (p. 296). J. S. Beck (2011) likewise encourages clients to "examine the advantages and disadvantages of continuing to hold a given belief" (pp. 211–212). This is not to suggest that cognitive therapists emphasize psychological acceptance nearly to the degree as do the novel acceptance-based psychotherapies. There is indeed a meaningful distinction between acceptance-based and traditional CBTs with respect to the focus on function versus form. Nevertheless, the demarcation is not hard and fast, but rather a matter of emphasis.

Transdiagnostic Scope

Hayes et al. (2011) propose that contextual CBTs are transdiagnostic. Again, this clearly applies to ACT, in which a core set of principles has been applied to a wide range of psychopathology, including mood and anxiety disorders (e.g., Arch et al., 2012; Forman, Herbert, Moitra, Yeomans, & Geller, 2007; Lappalainen et al., 2007; Zettle & Rains, 1989), eating disorders (e.g., Juarascio et al., 2013; Timko, Merwin, Herbert, & Zucker, 2013), psychosis (Bach & Hayes, 2002; Gaudiano & Herbert, 2006), etc., as well as to other issues such as drug-refractory epilepsy (Lundgren, Dahl, Melin, & Kies, 2006), trichotillomania (Woods, Wetterneck, & Flessner, 2006), idiopathic chronic pain (Wicksell, Melin, & Olsson, 2007), promotion of physical activity (Butryn, Forman, Hoffman, Shaw, & Jurascio, 2011), quality of life improvement among obese individuals (Lillis, Hayes, Bunting, & Masuda, 2009), and reducing shame among substance abusers (Luoma, Kohlenberg, Hayes, & Fletcher, 2012). In addition, some of the other models of acceptance-based CBT, such as FAP, are likewise broadly applicable. However, this is not the case with the majority of these models. DBT, for example, was originally developed as an intervention for women with parasuicidal behaviors (subsequently understood under the diagnostic label of borderline personality disorder), and was only later applied to other areas, most notably substance abuse.

Other models focus primarily or exclusively on a specific disorder or population. IBCT addresses distressed couples, and MBCT focuses on relapse prevention in recurrent depression. Moreover, various hybrid models have incorporated features of other CBTs within the ACT framework for specific populations, including acceptance-based behavior therapies for generalized anxiety disorder (Roemer, Orsillo, & Salters-Pedneault, 2008), social anxiety disorder (Herbert & Cardaciotto, 2005), obesity (Forman et al., 2013), and anorexia (Juarascio et al., 2013; Timko et al., 2013). Equally importantly, many traditional models of CBT are also transdiagnostic. A. T. Beck's (1976) classic *Cognitive Therapy of Emotional Disorders* focused on the full range of mood and anxiety disorders, and the principles and techniques outlined in that basic model have since been extended to such wide-ranging areas as schizophrenia (Sensky et al., 2000; Turkington, Dudley, Warman, & Beck, 2004), trichotillomania (Tolin, Franklin, Diefenbach, Anderson, & Meunier, 2007), recidivism of sexual offenders (Marques, Day, Nelson, & West, 1994), and anger (Beck & Fernandez, 1998). Likewise, behavioral strategies such as exposure, contingency management, and skills training have been applied across a range of problems. Thus, the transdiagnostic criterion neither describes all acceptance-based CBTs, nor demarcates them from traditional models.

Inclusion of the Theorist or Clinician in the Analysis

A hallmark characteristic of Skinner's (1945) radical behaviorism was his insistence that the behavior of scientists itself be incorporated in the analysis of their subject of study, using a common set of principles. Reflecting its behavioristic roots, this self-reflective theme is also seen in ACT. But what about other CBTs and other models of psychotherapy more broadly? In fact, both acceptance-based and traditional CBTs vary widely in this regard. FAP places the therapist's reactions to his or her patients as central to the analysis. Both MBSR and MBCT emphasize the importance of the therapist engaging in the same formal meditative practices that they prescribe to their patients. Although the general idea of applying principles and techniques to the clinician may be implicit in other acceptance-based CBT programs, it is not emphasized as much. Additionally, some traditional CBTs explicitly discuss the self-relevant nature of the principles. For example, J. S. Beck (2011) advises clinicians learning cognitive therapy to "start applying the tools described in this book to yourself" (p. 14). In addition, experts such as Liese and Beck (1997) have advocated using CT approaches in the supervision of cognitive therapists. And beyond CBT, traditional forms of psychotherapy such as psychoanalysis focus extensively on the therapist. We can therefore conclude that the self-conscious application of psychological principles to the theorist/clinician is neither common across all acceptance-based CBTs nor clearly demarcates them from traditional models of CBT.

Progressive Accumulation of Principles and Technology

Hayes et al. (2011) claim that contextual CBTs "emerged without an interest in tearing down previous CBT approaches so much as carrying them forward" (p. 159). It is true that all acceptance-based CBTs readily incorporate elements of earlier CBT models. This is especially true of the "bread-and-butter" behavioral principles (e.g., reinforcement, stimulus generalization) and techniques (e.g., exposure, skills training) characteristic of early behavior therapy. For example, all of these elements, and many more, were incorporated into DBT (Linehan, 1993). In addition, some acceptance-based CBTs incorporate features of non-CBT psychotherapies, such as ACT's use of experiential techniques derived from Gestalt therapy and FAP's incorporation of psychodynamic themes. However, it is also the case that these approaches have directly challenged some key ideas of traditional CBTs, such as the emphasis on clinical syndromes, the focus on specific cognitive content as determinative of these syndromes, the causal primacy of cognition, and the necessity or wisdom of correcting distorted or irrational thoughts (Forman & Herbert, 2009; Hayes, Barnes-Holmes et al., 2012; Hayes et al., 2011; Herbert & Forman, 2013). Thus, in the spirit of technical eclecticism, acceptance-based approaches freely incorporate useful techniques derived from other approaches. However, rather than building on them, many of their theoretical principles represent a direct challenge to traditional CBTs.

Moreover, the incorporation of earlier principles and techniques is not unique to acceptance-based approaches. Cognitive therapists, for example, have also incorporated earlier behavioral techniques into their treatment repertoire. For example, J. S. Beck's (2011) manual for learning CT encourages therapists to differentially reinforce positive attributes of their clients, and dedicates an entire chapter to behavioral activation. Similarly, Leahy's (1996) historical overview of the development of CT discusses how behavioral theories have been incorporated into CT, and devotes a significant portion of its intervention section to behavioral interventions. Therefore, the criterion of the cumulative incorporation of earlier theoretical principles and techniques is neither completely accurate with respect to acceptance-based CBTs, nor clearly differentiates these approaches from earlier CBTs.

Application to Larger Issues

The final criterion proposed to distinguish contextual CBTs is the application of basic principles to larger issues of the human condition beyond psychopathology, issues such as spirituality, meaning-making, overcoming stigma and racism, and broad societal changes (Hayes, Barnes-Holmes et al., 2012). There is no doubt that CBS and the ACT model have led the way in addressing topics beyond the traditional CBT focus on psychopathology. However, this tends to be far less true of most of the other acceptance-based CBTs, which retain the traditional focus on the conceptualization and treatment of clinical problems and disorders. It is true that these approaches often emphasize overall well-being and quality of life instead of – or in addition to – clinical symptoms per se. However, even this focus is typically framed within the context of addressing clinically significant problems of one sort or another. Similarly, traditional CBTs likewise emphasize the amelioration of psychopathology, although they have sometimes ventured into unfamiliar territory. For example, traditional CBTs have occasionally been integrated with religious-oriented interventions with a focus on improving spiritual well-being (Hawkins, Tan, & Turk, 1999; Propst, Ostrom, Watkins, Dean, & Mashburn, 1992). Additionally, a recent study comparing CBT to ACT found that, contrary to the authors' initial hypothesis, CBT improved quality of life to a greater extent than did ACT (Arch et al., 2012). Thus, the focus on larger issues of the human condition clearly characterizes ACT, but is less characteristic of other acceptance-based CBTs, and does not clearly distinguish these approaches as a group from traditional CBTs.

In summary, a group of CBT models have emerged over the past two decades that share a theoretical focus on the function of subjective experiences over their specific form, and an applied emphasis on fostering mindful awareness and psychological acceptance rather than changing the specific content of cognitions. These two closely related features distinguish these models from earlier, more traditional forms of CBT such as CT, although this is a matter of degree than of kind. Other features that have been proposed to distinguish contextual psychotherapies are in fact neither common to all such models, nor distinguish them from more traditional forms of CBT.

Approaches to Defining Contextual CBT

This leaves us with two approaches to defining "contextual CBT."

Philosophically Based Approach

One approach is to begin with a particular set of assumptions articulated in a philosophy of science and associated theories, and then unpack their implications. This is the approach taken by CBS. Functional contextualism (FC; Hayes, 1993; discussed further below and in chapter 4 in this volume) is a philosophy of psychological science that delineates specific ontological and epistemological assumptions. This philosophy then sets the stage for the development and evaluation of theories and technologies consistent with these assumptions. Relational frame theory (RFT; Barnes-Holmes, Barnes-Holmes, McHugh, & Hayes, 2004; Hayes, Barnes-Holmes, & Roche, 2001; Törneke, 2010) is an example of one such theory, and ACT is an example of one such technology.[1] Given that ACT was explicitly developed in coordination with FC, it is not surprising that its ties with the philosophy have been more clearly articulated than have other approaches.

So if one defines "contextual CBT" to mean "following explicitly from FC," then ACT is effectively the only current model that would likely meet this definition. This does not mean that other forms of acceptance-based CBT are inconsistent with FC. Rather, these approaches were developed without an explicit awareness of and focus on functional contextualistic assumptions, and any links to FC are therefore implicit and weaker than the case with ACT.

Technologically Based Approach

The alternative approach is to define contextual CBTs as those models of CBT, broadly defined, that have emerged more or less contemporaneously and that share a theoretical emphasis on the function of subjective experiences over their specific form, frequency, or intensity, and that highlight mindful awareness and psychological acceptance of distressing experiences as key technological tools. This approach clearly casts a wider net, and includes a number of related models, including those noted above.

Neither of these approaches to defining contextual CBTs is necessarily more "correct" than the other. Keeping with the contextualistic emphasis of function over form, the question becomes what purpose either classification serves. Classification systems can serve *taxonomic* functions by grouping like entities together and demarcating them from others that fall outside the group (even if the boundaries are not hard and fast). But the principles that define a taxon may also serve *normative* functions by guiding future development.

For the taxonomic purpose of describing existing CBT models as contextualistic, we acknowledge that a broader, more inclusive perspective has served as a useful starting point at this relatively early stage of the field's development. As we have seen, the emphasis on function over content and on psychological acceptance over cognitive change is sufficiently distinctive to demarcate a meaningful group of novel CBT models from their more traditional counterparts.

However, it is far from clear that such a classification is foundational to – or even especially helpful for – future progress. That is, it may not be that conceptualizing contextual CBTs in this way represents the best normative system. For one thing, new theories and technologies will undoubtedly emerge to challenge this classification scheme. The field will continue to evolve, and no single approach has a monopoly on "truth" or utility. Other classification systems may eventually make more sense. Additionally, such a broad net risks glossing over important theoretical differences between approaches whose similarities may actually be rather superficial.

An alternative approach is to articulate one's basic philosophy of science, then to develop closely linked theories and technologies that are consistent with the basic assumptions of that philosophy. In the present context, this would also entail an analysis of how contextualistic sensibilities are hypothesized to be more fruitful than alternative approaches. This is precisely the strategy envisioned by CBS.

Philosophical Issues and CBT

Historically, CBT as a field has not preoccupied itself with the intricacies of philosophy. Rather than developing in concert with clearly articulated philosophical assumptions, early behavior therapy was instead born in large part as a pragmatic reaction to the perceived failure of psychoanalytic/psychodynamic approaches to deliberate behavioral change. This is not to say that philosophical assumptions have been irrelevant. In fact, they have been implicit – even inevitable – since the earliest days of the field. For example, CBT has always emphasized empiricism, not in the philosophical sense of conclusions derived from sensory experience, but rather in the sense of basing conclusions as much as possible on quantitative data collection and analysis. This basic characteristic reflects an implicit epistemological assumption, specifically, that quantification will reduce biases to yield more reliable data, and will translate into more effective technologies. This illustrates how scientific and technological work necessarily involves philosophical assumptions. In the case of traditional models of CBT these assumptions have been mostly implicit.

The problem with implicit assumptions is that they can lead to lack of clarity and confusion about such matters as what constitutes probative evidence for a good theory or an effective clinical technique. Articulating one's basic assumptions forces the scholar to consider such issues and their implications. Philosophical clarity can also be helpful in illuminating when disputes between alternative programs are resolvable by data, or when they reflect differences in basic assumptions that are not amenable to direct test. For example, a consequence of FC's functionalism is that ACT places less emphasis on symptom reduction and more on psychosocial functioning and overall well-being. In a study of ACT for psychosis (Bach & Hayes, 2002), patients reported an *increase* in the frequency of hallucinations at post-treatment. But they also reported a significant drop in how distressing the hallucinations were, and they demonstrated a reduction in the rate of rehospitalization over a four-month follow-up period. To the ACT researchers, this represented a highly positive outcome. In contrast, some critics pointed to the lack of decrease in the frequency of hallucinations – and to the fact that they actually increased – as evidence of a poor outcome. This difference reflects fundamental differences in what types of data are considered most important, which is ultimately a philosophical issue.

Philosophical assumptions also shape how theoretical terms and issues are conceptualized, and here too lack of clarity can lead to confusion. For example, we recall a symposium at a professional CBT conference a few years ago in which ACT researchers presented data suggesting that cognitive "defusion" (experiencing one's thoughts from a psychological distance) was more central to changes in client symptoms and well-being than were changes in the content of thoughts. They argued that the results were inconsistent with the common cognitive model of psychopathology, which emphasizes changes in cognitive content. A cognitive therapist on the panel, however, insisted that the results were perfectly consistent with the cognitive model in that they simply revealed that changes in higher-order cognitions had taken place. The ensuing argument was not especially productive, because neither side appreciated the degree to which the fundamental dispute was theoretical in nature. For the cognitive therapist, any meaningful therapeutic change must by definition be driven by a change in cognition of some form or another. The ACT researcher did not share this assumption of the necessary causal primacy of cognition, nor even such a broad definition of cognition itself. Hence, both sides viewed the data as completely supporting their respective positions, and were genuinely puzzled by the other's resistance to appreciate what seemed so obvious in the data. Given that the fundamental difference was theoretical, and given that these theoretical differences were themselves rooted in different philosophical perspectives, no amount of data would have made a difference.[2]

Contextual Behavioral Science

Of the various models of CBT – both traditional and contextual – ACT has delved most deeply into philosophical waters. As noted above, the developers of ACT articulated a philosophy known as functional contextualism (Hayes, 1993; Hayes et al., 2013). Although a detailed analysis of FC is beyond the scope of this chapter, for the present purposes two interrelated aspects are noteworthy. First, FC de-emphasizes questions of ontology, and second, FC posits a highly functional epistemology. These basic assumptions set the "ground rules" for the scientific and technological program of which ACT is a part, and influence specific ACT theory and techniques.

Ontology is a branch of metaphysics that refers to the nature of being or reality, including what entities actually exist and how they are grouped with respect to one another. Elemental realist perspectives on ontology assume that certain entities exist and others do not, that the divisions between entities are fixed in nature, and that these demarcations are largely independent of human observations (Hayes et al., 2011).

The goal of science from an elemental perspective is to map this underlying reality, essentially carving nature at its joints, and success is judged by how well the maps correspond to the underlying truth (reality). Epistemology refers to the nature of knowledge, and more specifically in the present context to the rules governing when a knowledge claim is considered true or valid. Closely related to its perspective on ontology, elemental realism judges assertions as valid when experimental findings support hypotheses derived from theoretical maps of the world. Truth is defined as the degree of correspondence between theoretical statements and the physical world (Newman, 2002; O'Connor, 1975).

These philosophical perspectives are reflected in traditional forms of CBT such as CT. Theoretical deductions are subjected to empirical test. Clinically, problematic thoughts are tested against reality to determine their truth, under the assumption that unbiased observation of the world allows one to arrive at the truth and that doing so will lead to more successful outcomes for the patient (Lilienfeld, 2010). As noted by A. T. Beck (1976),

> Concepts such as distancing, reality testing, authenticating observations, and validating conclusions are related to epistemology. Distancing involves being able to make the distinction between "I believe" (an opinion that is subject to validation) and "I know" (an 'irrefutable' fact). The ability to make this distinction is of critical importance in modifying those sectors of the patient's reactions that are subject to distortion. (p. 243)

These basic assumptions tend to be implicit, because traditional CBT scholars have rarely discussed such matters explicitly. In contrast, FC de-emphasizes ontological questions in favor of a strongly functional epistemology. That is, the goal is not to discover how the world "really" is. Rather, the goal is to determine how well any given concept or analysis works in a given context. This approach requires that the goal of the analysis be specified a priori. Once specified, one can use the tools of science to determine how well a concept or analysis works with respect to that goal. There is no assumption that reality is demarcated in a fixed, invariant way.[3] Rather, the validity of a concept is contextually determined, and may change depending on the purpose at hand. In this sense, all knowledge is necessarily local, and truth claims are limited in nature.

Hayes, Strosahl, et al. (2012, pp. 33–34) present a useful analogy to illustrate the point. Imagine two representations of a skyscraper: the architect's blueprints, and a street artist's painting. Which is the more valid rendering of the building? The elemental realist would almost certainly choose the blueprint. After all, it is a far more detailed and precise map of the reality that is the building. The functional contextualist, however, would view the question as unanswerable until the goals were specified. If one's purpose is to solve a plumbing or electrical problem within the building, then the architect's rendering would undoubtedly be much more useful (and in that limited sense more "true"). But if the purpose is to assist a tourist in locating the building among other similar structures from street level, the artist's painting would likely be more useful.

This attention to philosophical assumptions is a hallmark of the scientific program known as CBS (Hayes, Barnes-Holmes et al., 2012). This program seeks to be clear about philosophical assumptions, and to tie those assumptions to basic theoretical work with broad applicability, which is in turn tied to clinical models and ultimately to applied technologies. The program seeks integration and coordination across these various domains.

It should be noted that CBS is not an inevitable result of the marriage of psychological philosophy, theory, and technology. One could imagine any number of such programs within CBT, or psychology more broadly for that matter. However, CBS is currently the project that best exemplifies such integration, and therefore serves as a useful model of a progressive psychology.

Future Directions

Ultimately the extent to which philosophical considerations – and particularly the careful linking of philosophy, theory, and technology – will result in greater progress than an approach that ignores or even eschews such issues remains to be seen. It is possible that a preoccupation with the philosophy of psychology could be counter-productive. For example, articulation of clear epistemological "ground rules" for what counts as acceptable evidence could conceivably stifle innovation. We believe it is more likely, however, that explicit attention to philosophical and theoretical issues will lead to accelerated progress, especially as gauged by the progress of applied psychological technology (Herbert, Gaudiano, & Forman, 2013). Indeed, an inter-organizational task force led by the Association for Behavioral and Cognitive Therapies and made up of the key CBT societies recently called for an increased focus on theory and even the philosophy of psychology in doctoral training in CBT (Klepac et al., 2012).

The motivations for attempting to define contextual CBTs can be grouped into two broad categories: scientific and political. Scientific goals include developing better theories, principles, and technologies. But given that science is a social enterprise, the ability to make progress depends in part on being noticed. Efforts to gain traction in the larger scientific and professional communities sometimes lead to overstating the uniqueness of new developments relative to the status quo on the one hand, and to glossing over important underlying differences among superficially similar approaches on the other. As we have seen, the differences between the new acceptance-based models of CBT as a group relative to their more traditional predecessors are more a matter of emphasis than of kind. At the same time, grouping all of these newer models under the broad rubric of "contextual" glosses over deeper philosophical and theoretical differences. Acceptance-based models of CBT have now achieved widespread recognition. Going forward, care should be taken to avoid overstating their distinctiveness with respect to earlier approaches. At the same time, grouping all such approaches under the "contextual" label may not be the best way forward. (In fact, a motivation to include many treatment approaches within the contextual tent may have led to a definition of "contextual" that is overly broad and thus in danger of diluting its essence.) Classifications based on shared basic philosophical assumptions and theoretical sensibilities may be more fruitful scientifically.

There is also the question of the extent to which the contextual label, as used here, can be usefully applied to models of psychotherapy that fall outside the broad CBT family. For example, emotion-focused therapy (Greenberg, 2004) and compassion-focused therapy (Gilbert, 2009) both emphasize psychological acceptance, although neither is generally considered a form of CBT. Consideration of such approaches brings us full circle to the question of how best to understand the term "contextual." Broad definitions based on an emphasis of function over form and the theme of psychological acceptance would need to make room for approaches such as these. On the other hand, they would likely fall outside of definitions based on a more narrow emphasis on contextualistic behavioral philosophy.

CBS represents a useful model for what a project that seeks to integrate philosophy, theory, and technology might look like. Indeed, we are unaware of any other contemporary programs, and certainly none within CBT, that focus on this integration to the extent that occurs within CBS. It is nevertheless noteworthy that FC as a philosophy of psychology, like the radical behaviorism that preceded it, was articulated by psychologists with an interest in the philosophy of psychological science, rather than by professional philosophers. It might be fruitful for psychologists to collaborate with professional philosophers of science on further developments of this and other philosophical programs (e.g., Herbert & Padovani, 2015).

Regardless of the degree to which one stresses philosophy, there is a need for CBT theorists and clinicians to subject theories and techniques to "risky" predictions (Lakatos, 1978). An important mark of a progressive science is the ability to make predictions, especially nonobvious ones, which are subsequently confirmed by controlled empirical observations. In contrast, a preoccupation with retrofitting empirical findings into an existing theory marks a program in retreat. As noted by Hayes et al. (2013), "all scientific theories are ultimately shown to be incorrect ... A progressive scientific field builds on useful ideas, continuously weeding out those that are not" (p. 180).

Notes

1   It is important to note that although RFT and ACT are consistent with FC, they are not inevitable products of the philosophy. That is, if one begins with FC, one might create a number of alternative theories and/or technologies. FC, RFT, and ACT are currently linked together as part of the integrated scientific program known as CBS, and each has likely benefited from these associations. However, the three foci are not inextricably and inevitably linked together.

2   This is not to say that data are irrelevant to selecting between alternative philosophies in the long-term. Certain assumptions may lead to more fruitful science over time and will ultimately prevail over less productive assumptions. But no single study, no matter how well conceived and executed, can directly resolve philosophical differences.

3   There are differing perspectives regarding what sorts of ontological statements, if any, can be meaningful within FC. Hayes (1997, p. 43) discusses the "one world," implying the existence of a world independent of human observation, albeit a world that does not come predivided into constituent parts. Wilson (2001) goes a step further, arguing that any statements of the existence of a world beyond human sensation is superfluous. In contrast, Herbert and Padovani (2015) argue that the very fact that some analyses work better than others with respect to a given goal logically requires that the world have some form of "texture" independent of human existence. Despite these differences, there is a consensus that strong ontological claims are avoided in FC in favor of a contextual focus on what works with respect to a specified goal.

References

Arch, J. J., Eifert, G. H., Davies, C., Vilardaga, J. C. P., Rose, R. D., & Craske, M. G. (2012). Randomized clinical trial of cognitive behavioral therapy (CBT) versus acceptance and commitment therapy (ACT) for mixed anxiety disorders. *Journal of Consulting and Clinical Psychology, 80,* 750–765.

Bach, P., & Hayes, S.C. (2002). The use of acceptance and commitment therapy to prevent the rehospitalization of psychotic patients: A randomized controlled trial. *Journal of Consulting and Clinical Psychology, 70,* 1129–1139.

Barnes-Holmes, Y., Barnes-Holmes, D., McHugh, L., & Hayes, S. C. (2004). Relational frame theory: Some implications for understanding and treating human psychopathology. *International Journal of Psychology and Psychological Theory, 4,* 161–181.

Beck, A. T. (1976). *Cognitive therapy and the emotional disorders.* New York, NY: Penguin.

Beck, A. T., Emery, G., & Greenberg, R. L. (1985). *Anxiety disorders and phobias: A cognitive approach.* New York, NY: Basic Books.

Beck, J. S. (2011). *Cognitive behavior therapy: Basics and beyond* (2nd ed.). New York, NY: Guilford.

Beck, R., & Fernandez, E. (1998). Cognitive-behavioral therapy in the treatment of anger: A meta-analysis. *Cognitive Therapy and Research, 22,* 63–74.

Burns, D. D. (1980). *Feeling good: The new mood therapy.* New York, NY: William Morrow.

Burns, D. D. (1989). *The feeling good handbook: Using the new mood therapy in everyday life.* New York, NY: William Morrow.

Butryn, M. L., Forman, E., Hoffman, K., Shaw, J., & Juarascio, A. (2011). A pilot study of acceptance and commitment therapy for promotion of physical activity. *Journal of Physical Activity & Health, 8,* 516–522.

Christensen, A., Atkins, D. C., Berns, S., Wheeler, J., Baucom, D. H., & Simpson, L. E. (2004). Traditional versus integrative behavioral couple therapy for significantly and chronically distressed married couples. *Journal of Consulting and Clinical Psychology, 72,* 176–191.

Forman, E. M., Butryn, M. L., Juarascio, A. S., Bradley, L. E., Lowe, M. R., Herbert, J. D., & Shaw, J. A. (2013). The Mind Your Health Project: A randomized controlled trial of an innovative behavioral treatment for obesity. *Obesity, 21,* 1119–1126.

Forman, E. M., & Herbert, J. D. (2009). New directions in cognitive behavior therapy: Acceptance-based therapies. In W. O'Donohue & J. E. Fisher (Eds.), *General principles and empirically supported techniques of cognitive behavior therapy* (pp. 102–114). Hoboken, NJ: Wiley.

Forman, E. M., Herbert, J. D., Moitra, E., Yeomans, P. D., & Geller, P. A. (2007). A randomized controlled effectiveness trial of acceptance and commitment therapy and cognitive therapy for anxiety and depression. *Behavior Modification, 31,* 772–799.

Gaudiano, B. A., & Herbert, J. D. (2006). Acute treatment of inpatients with psychotic symptoms using acceptance and commitment therapy: Pilot results. *Behaviour Research and Therapy, 44,* 415–437.

Gilbert, P. (2009). Introducing compassion focused therapy. *Advances in Psychiatric Treatment, 15,* 199–208.

Greenberg, L. S. (2004). Emotion-focused therapy. *Clinical Psychology and Psychotherapy, 11,* 3–16.

Hawkins, R. S., Tan, S. Y., & Turk, A. A. (1999). Secular versus Christian inpatient cognitive-behavioral therapy programs: Impact on depression and spiritual well-being. *Journal of Psychology and Theology, 27,* 309–318.

Hayes, S. C. (1993). Analytic goals and varieties of scientific contextualism. In S. C. Hayes, L. J. Hayes, H. W. Reese, & T. R. Sarbin (Eds.), *Varieties of scientific contextualism* (pp. 11–27). Reno, NV: Context Press.

Hayes, S. (1997). Behavioral epistemology includes nonverbal knowing. In L. J. Hayes & P. M. Ghezzi (Eds.), *Investigations in behavioral epistemology* (pp. 35–43). Reno, NV: Context Press.

Hayes, S. C. (2004). Acceptance and commitment therapy, relational frame theory, and the third wave of behavioral and cognitive therapies. *Behavior Therapy, 35,* 639–665.

Hayes, S. C., Barnes-Holmes, D., & Roche, B. (2001). *Relational frame theory: A post-Skinnerian account of human language and cognition.* New York, NY: Kluwer/Plenum.

Hayes, S. C., Barnes-Holmes, D., & Wilson, K. G. (2012). Contextual behavioral science: Creating a science more adequate to the challenge of the human condition. *Journal of Contextual Behavioral Science, 1,* 1–16.

Hayes, S. C., Levin, M. E., Plumb, J. C., Villatte, J. L., & Pistorello, J. (2013). Acceptance and commitment therapy and contextual behavioral science: Examining the progress of a distinctive model of behavioral and cognitive therapy. *Behavior Therapy, 44,* 180–198.

Hayes, S. C., Strosahl, K. D., & Wilson, K. G. (2012). *Acceptance and commitment therapy: The process and practice of mindful change* (2nd ed.). New York, NY: Guilford.

Hayes, S. C., Villatte, M., Levin, M., & Hildebrandt, M. (2011). Open, aware, and active: contextual approaches as an emerging trend in the behavioral and cognitive therapies. *Annual Review of Clinical Psychology, 7,* 141–168.

Herbert, J. D., & Cardaciotto, L. (2005). A mindfulness and acceptance-based perspective on social anxiety disorder. In S. Orsillo & L. Roemer (Eds.), *Acceptance and mindfulness-based approaches to anxiety: Conceptualization and treatment* (pp. 189–212). Norwell, MA: Kluwer/Plenum.

Herbert, J. D., & Forman, E. M. (2013). Caution: The differences between CT and ACT may be larger (and smaller) than they appear. *Behavior Therapy, 44,* 218–223.

Herbert, J. D., Gaudiano, B. A., & Forman, E. B. (2013). The importance of theory in cognitive behavior therapy: A perspective of contextual behavioral science. *Behavior Therapy, 44,* 580–591.

Herbert, J. D., & Padovani, F. (2015). Contextualism, psychological science, and the question of ontology. *Journal of Contextual Behavioral Science.*

Hofmann, S. G. (2008). Common misconceptions about cognitive mediation of treatment change: A commentary to Longmore and Worrell (2007). *Clinical Psychology Review, 28,* 67–70.

Jacobson, N. S., Christensen, A., Prince, S. E., Cordova, J., & Eldridge, K. (2000). Integrative behavioral couple therapy: An acceptance-based, promising new treatment for couple discord. *Journal of Consulting and Clinical Psychology, 68,* 351–355.

Juarascio, A., Shaw, J., Forman, E. M., Timko, C. A., Herbert, J. D., Butryn, M. L., & Lowe, M. (2013). Acceptance and commitment therapy for eating disorders: Clinical applications of a group treatment. *Journal of Contextual Behavioral Science, 2*(3), 85–94.

Kabat-Zinn, J. (2009). *Full catastrophe living: Using the wisdom of your body and mind to face stress, pain, and illness.* New York, NY: Delta.

Kanter, J. W., Manos, R. C., Bowe, W. M., Baruch, D. E., Busch, A. M., & Rusch, L. C. (2010). What is behavioral activation? A review of the empirical literature. *Clinical Psychology Review, 30,* 608–620.

Klepac, R. K., Ronan, G. F., Andrasik, F., Arnold, K., Belar, C., Berry, S., … Strauman, T. J. (2012). Guidelines for cognitive behavioral training within doctoral psychology programs in the United States of America: Report of the Inter-Organizational Task Force on Cognitive and Behavioral Psychology Doctoral Education. *Behavior Therapy, 43,* 687–697.

Kohlenberg, R. J., & Tsai, M. (1991). *Functional analytic psychotherapy.* New York, NY: Springer.

Lakatos, I. (1978). *The methodology of scientific research programmes: Philosophical papers Volume 1.* Cambridge, England: Cambridge University Press.

Lappalainen, R., Lehtonen, T., Skarp, E., Taubert, E., Ojanen, M., & Hayes, S. C. (2007). The impact of CBT and ACT models using psychology trainee therapists: A preliminary controlled effectiveness trial. *Behavior Modification, 31,* 488–511.

Leahy, R. L. (1996). *Cognitive therapy: Basic principles and applications.* New York, NY: Jason Aronson.

Liese, B. S., & Beck, J. S. (1997). Cognitive therapy supervision. In C. E. Watkins, Jr. (Ed.), *Handbook of psychotherapy supervision* (pp. 114–133). New York, NY: Wiley.

Lilienfeld, S. O. (2010). Can psychology become a science? *Personality and Individual Differences, 49,* 281–288.

Lillis, J., Hayes, S. C., Bunting, K., & Masuda, A. (2009). Teaching acceptance and mindfulness to improve the lives of the obese: A preliminary test of a theoretical model. *Annals of Behavioral Medicine, 37,* 58–69.

Linehan, M. (1993). *Skills training manual for treating borderline personality disorder.* New York, NY: Guilford.

Linehan, M. M., Armstrong, H. E., Suarez, A., Allmon, D., & Heard, H. L. (1991). Cognitive-behavioral treatment of chronically parasuicidal borderline patients. *Archives of General Psychiatry, 48,* 1060–1064.

Lundgren, T., Dahl, J., Melin, L., & Kies, B. (2006). Evaluation of acceptance and commitment therapy for drug refractory epilepsy: A randomized controlled trial in South Africa – a pilot study. *Epilepsia, 47,* 2173–2179.

Luoma, J. B., Kohlenberg, B. S., Hayes, S. C., & Fletcher, L. (2012). Slow and steady wins the race: A randomized clinical trial of acceptance and commitment therapy targeting shame in substance use disorders. *Journal of Consulting and Clinical Psychology, 80,* 43–53.

Martell, C. R. (2008, July). *Twenty years of behavior therapy: Trends and counter-trends.* Address given at the annual convention of the British Association of Behavioural and Cognitive Psychotherapies, Edinburgh, Scotland.

Marques, J. K., Day, D. M., Nelson, C., & West, M. A. (1994). Effects of cognitive-behavioral treatment on sex offender recidivism preliminary results of a longitudinal study. *Criminal Justice and Behavior, 21,* 28–54.

Newman, A. (2002). *The correspondence theory of truth: An essay on the metaphysics of predication.* Cambridge, England: Cambridge University Press.

O'Connor, D. J. (1975). *The correspondence theory of truth.* London, England: Hutchinson.

Persons, J. B. (1989). *Cognitive therapy in practice: A case formulation approach.* New York, NY: Norton.

Propst, L. R., Ostrom, R., Watkins, P., Dean, T., & Mashburn, D. (1992). Comparative efficacy of religious and nonreligious cognitive-behavioral therapy for the treatment of clinical depression in religious individuals. *Journal of Consulting and Clinical Psychology, 60,* 94–103.

Roemer, L., Orsillo, S. M., & Salters-Pedneault, K. (2008). Efficacy of an acceptance-based behavior therapy for generalized anxiety disorder: Evaluation in a randomized controlled trial. *Journal of Consulting and Clinical Psychology, 76,* 1083–1089.

Sensky, T., Turkington, D., Kingdon, D., Scott, J. L., Scott, J., Siddle, R., ... Barnes, T. R. (2000). A randomized controlled trial of cognitive-behavioral therapy for persistent symptoms in schizophrenia resistant to medication. *Archives of General Psychiatry, 57,* 165–172.

Skinner, B. F. (1945). The operational analysis of psychological terms. *Psychological Review, 52,* 270–276.

Teasdale, J. D., Segal, Z. V., Williams, J. M. G., Ridgeway, V. A., Soulsby, J. M., & Lau, M. A. (2000). Prevention of relapse/recurrence in major depression by mindfulness-based cognitive therapy. *Journal of Consulting and Clinical Psychology, 68,* 615–623.

Timko, C. A., Merwin, R. M., Herbert, J. D., & Zucker, N. (2013, Winter). Acceptance-based separated family treatment for adolescent anorexia nervosa. *The Renfrew Perspective,* 1–5.

Tolin, D. F., Franklin, M. E., Diefenbach, G. J., Anderson, E., & Meunier, S. A. (2007). Pediatric trichotillomania: Descriptive psychopathology and an open trial of cognitive behavioral therapy. *Cognitive Behaviour Therapy, 36,* 129–144.

Törneke, N. (2010). *Learning RFT: An introduction to relational frame theory and its clinical application.* Oakland, CA: New Harbinger.

Turkington, D., Dudley, R., Warman, D. M., & Beck, A. T. (2004). Cognitive-behavioral therapy for schizophrenia: A review. *Journal of Psychiatric Practice, 10,* 5–16.

Wells, A. (2008). *Metacognitive therapy: A practical guide.* New York, NY: Guilford.

Wells, A. (2011). *Metacognitive therapy for anxiety and depression.* New York, NY: Guilford.

Wicksell, R. K., Melin, L., & Olsson, G. L. (2007). Exposure and acceptance in the rehabilitation of adolescents with idiopathic chronic pain – a pilot study. *European Journal of Pain, 11,* 267–274.

Wilson, K. G. (2001). Some notes on theoretical constructs: Types and validation from a contextual behavioral perspective. *International Journal of Psychology and Psychological Therapy, 1,* 205–215.

Woods, D. W., Wetterneck, C. T., & Flessner, C. A. (2006). A controlled evaluation of acceptance and commitment therapy plus habit reversal for trichotillomania. *Behaviour Research and Therapy, 44,* 639–656.

Zettle, R. D., & Rains, J. C. (1989). Group cognitive and contextual therapies in treatment of depression. *Journal of Clinical Psychology, 45,* 438–445.

15

Evaluating In-Session Therapist and Client Behaviors from a Contextual Behavioral Science Perspective

Matthieu Villatte

The aim of this chapter is to show how the principles of contextual behavioral science (CBS; Hayes, Barnes-Holmes, & Wilson, 2012) can be applied in understanding how interchanges between therapists and their clients eventuate in behavioral change both inside and outside of the clinical setting. Within this larger endeavor, three main areas will be covered: (a) the targets of assessment in therapy, (b) the strategies to measure psychological problems in session, and (c) the strategies to measure changes in client and therapist in-session behaviors.

Targets of In-Session Assessment

What is a Psychological Problem from a CBS Perspective?

Contextual approaches to psychotherapy frame behavioral problems in ways that often challenge more traditional views on psychopathology. Instead of looking at psychological suffering through categories of disorders as in the medical model (e.g., American Psychiatric Association, 2013; World Health Organization, 1992), therapists from a CBS perspective consider what people do, how it affects their well-being, and what contextual features contribute to the initiation and maintenance of these behaviors (Hayes, Villatte, Levin, & Hildebrandt, 2011). Categories can also be used in such an approach, but they are entirely defined by the context, and thus no fixed topographical description of psychological problems is possible within this framework.

A concrete example will illustrate this approach. Consider a person who checks the news on his smartphone more than 100 times per hour. Most people would probably consider this behavior excessive, but, out of context, it is actually impossible to tell if it is. This person might be a journalist in the midst of a major event, and checking the news so frequently might be a part of doing his job. On the other hand, this person

The Wiley Handbook of Contextual Behavioral Science, First Edition. Edited by Robert D. Zettle, Steven C. Hayes, Dermot Barnes-Holmes, and Anthony Biglan.
© 2016 John Wiley & Sons, Ltd. Published 2016 by John Wiley & Sons, Ltd.

might be checking the news to alleviate the fear that a war has been declared against his country, while nothing in the current international context indicates that this is likely to happen at the moment. The same behavior in two different contexts leads to a very different analysis of the psychological health and functioning of the person displaying it.

Taking the context into account is not foreign to categorical medical classifications, but CBS therapists go beyond the mere recognition that the meaning of a behavior varies across contexts. They seek to identify how the context *influences* the production of a behavior. The observation of the occurrence of a behavior is thus not as important as the functional relationship it shares with contextual variables. In our example above, what is important from a CBS perspective is that checking the news allows for a consequence to occur. In the first case, the journalist is better informed and can write an article that includes as much currently available information as possible. In the second case, the person feels briefly less anxious as soon as he learns that no war has been declared yet. The consequences occurring as a result of checking the news can be seen as changes in the context, which increase the likelihood that checking the news will occur again. In other words, the context influences (and not only predicts) the occurrence of this behavior.

From a CBS perspective, three main categories of psychological problems can occur, all defined by a different relationship between a behavior and its context. Avoidance and escape correspond to behaviors people do to discount or remove aversive events. When doing so doesn't work, or actually increases contact with the aversive event and impairs overall well-being, avoidance and escape is problematic. Examples of ineffective or costly avoidance and escape are numerous in psychological suffering. A person might temporarily reduce anxiety triggered by obsessive thoughts through engaging in compulsive behaviors, avoid going out to discount fear of public places, or drink alcohol to be less bothered by traumatic memories. In each case, the behavior likely impairs quality of life.

Approach corresponds to behaviors people do to contact desirable events. When doing so doesn't work or impairs overall well-being, then approach is also problematic. Examples of problematic approach behavior are also frequent in psychopathology. People might use a drug because it triggers satisfying feelings and sensations, start fights to get more attention from their partner, or lie about themselves to be appreciated by others. If these behaviors are not effective at contacting the expected outcomes, or lead to greater suffering in the long run, they might become targets of change in psychotherapeutic work. Often, approach and avoidance overlap or are two sides of the same coin. For example, using drugs might be done both for escaping painful emotions and for contacting pleasant sensations. Procrastination also often involves both the avoidance of anxiety triggered by doing a task and approach toward competing sources of satisfaction.

The last main category of behavior problems is defined by a lack of actions contributing to well-being. Although behavior deficits can result from problematic approach and avoidance (the person doesn't do what would be effective because she is doing what is not effective instead), they can also be caused by a lack of contact with satisfying qualities of the given behavior. For example, people may have lost interest in their job and as a result they stop going to work, then stop going out and seeing friends, and finally don't even get out of bed anymore.

In these three functional categories of psychological problems, contextual variables influence the occurrence of the behavior and determine whether it might be a relevant target of clinical intervention. Given the contextual nature of behavior problems, identifying to what extent they correspond to avoidance, approach, and deficits is already a step toward identifying what needs to be done to improve these problems. However, more specific contextual variables need to be identified in order to achieve behavior change. We will come back to this point after we review the overarching goals and means of psychotherapy from a CBS perspective.

What Are the Goals and Means of Psychotherapy Based on CBS?

Because psychological problems are defined by excessive behaviors that are ineffective and/or deficits in effective behaviors, the natural aim of psychotherapy is the modification of client behavior. CBS therapists[1] need to resolve two main issues in order to achieve this apparently simple goal. The first pertains to identifying goals that are relevant to each client. The second issue pertains to activating actual change toward these goals.

Just as problematic behaviors are defined in context, identifying effective behaviors also requires considering contextual variables. An action beneficial to one client in a given context might not be useful in another context or to another client. Thus, for each clinical case, CBS therapists need to determine *with* their clients what directions need to be taken to improve well-being. What criterion can they use to identify what is effective? The answer to this question echoes the underlying philosophical foundations of CBS (see chapters 3 and 4 in this volume): What is selected is what works for a given purpose. Because each client might have different purposes, the overarching goal of therapy is to help clients learn to identify, choose, and actually engage in behaviors that serve their purposes (regardless of which purpose is pursued, as long as it promotes sustainable well-being).

The overarching goals of therapy based on CBS can be formulated as functional coherence and flexible sensitivity to the context (Villatte, Villatte, & Hayes, in press). The former refers to the capacity of making choices and conceptualizing life experiences in ways that serve sustainable well-being, and the latter to the capacity of responding to the context in ways that match these choices. Consider the following example of a client who is afraid of flying and thus doesn't travel afar even though she would like to visit her family living in another country. Based on what the client cares about in this context (being with her family), choosing not to take planes can be seen as a failure of functional coherence. Her decision makes sense at some level (it is logical to avoid flying because it is probably the surest way to avoid dying in a plane crash), but it doesn't make sense with regard to what she cares about in the context of connecting with her family. A functionally coherent choice in this case might be to fly to go see her family, while acknowledging the risk of dying in a plane crash and normalizing the painful emotions that this thought triggers.

In order to reach functional coherence, one needs to be in contact with relevant information and evaluate this information in terms of its effectiveness. The client in the example above may currently be avoiding traveling by plane because she is mostly contacting the fear of dying in a plane crash, and not enough of the desire to see her family. She is sensitive to a part of the context, and less sensitive to other parts.

To come to the conclusion that flying is a more useful decision, she thus needs to be more aware of what she cares about.

Once the functionally coherent decision is made, the client may still struggle to actually engage in this new behavior. When the time comes to get on the plane, the impact of the fear of dying likely increases, while the impact of the desire to see her family decreases. Sensitivity to elements of the context needs to support functional choices or else effective actions are not performed. Thus, flexible sensitivity to the context consists of responding to the desire of contacting her family and not responding to the fear of dying. Note that in another context, a reverse sensitivity to these elements of the context might be more functionally coherent. If the plane was not safe, it might be better not to take it to avoid dying in a crash, rather than attempting to satisfy the desire to see her family.

What can CBS therapists do to help clients reach functional coherence and flexible sensitivity to the context? Here again, the answer lies in the context. This is because contextual variables are the elements of the equation that can be reached to indirectly change behaviors. In contingency management interventions (e.g., Liberman, Teigen, Patterson, & Baker, 1973; Petry, 2000; Sallows & Graupner, 2005), therapists can arrange the context so that variables that sustain effective behaviors are added and others that maintain problematic behaviors are removed (e.g., giving and maintaining attention to children when they are behaving well or behaving in a neutral way and removing attention temporarily when undesired behaviors occur). These types of contextually based interventions are generally effective, but they require concrete access to the situations in which problematic behaviors occur.

In many cases, however, the relevant aspects of the context are not directly reachable or they can't be removed or replaced. This is generally the case in psychotherapy for at least two reasons. First, most relevant contextual variables within the lives of clients lie outside the therapy room. Second, while CBS therapeutic approaches acknowledge the controlling role that language may play in problematic behavior, and in that sense venture into the "heads" of clients, they are careful not to stay there and not to do so with the goal of replacing one way of thinking with another. Rather, thinking and other cognitive activities of clients are themselves viewed as more behavior situated within a broader contextual chain that may be linked to problematic behavior. Thus, from a contextualistic perspective, the clinician rarely intervenes directly in the environment of clients outside the therapy room,[2] and never inside their heads, especially insofar as the relational and derived nature of language makes it almost impossible to remove or replace psychological experiences influencing client behavior (see chapter 12 in this volume).

If therapists must alter the context to change behaviors, but can't access or concretely change relevant features of the context, they can instead change the symbolic impact of these variables by using language. The CBS approach to language and cognition proposed by relational frame theory (RFT; Hayes, Barnes-Holmes, & Roche, 2001; see chapter 10 in this volume) provides the tools to alter the way clients respond to contextual variables even if these variables are intrinsically unchanged. Consider again the example of the client who refuses to take planes, despite wanting to see her family. Therapists using CBS and RFT principles would, for example, help the client assess the effectiveness of her behavior with regard to what she cares about. They might ask questions such as "When you decide not to fly, what impact does it have on your relationship with your family?", use exercises leading the client to contact the desired consequences of traveling afar by imagination (e.g., "Picture in your mind the arrival at the airport, and your family welcoming you at the terminal"), or present a metaphor drawing a parallel with the cost of avoiding anxiety. In each case, therapists use language (i.e., their "arbitrarily applicable relational responding") to change the function of avoiding the client's fear of dying in a plane crash on the one hand, and of seeing her family on the other hand. Asking questions that attract the client's attention to the consequence of avoiding flying increases sensitivity to the ineffectiveness of this behavior, and thus increases the perceived incoherence of this choice at a functional level.

In a nutshell, this is what CBS therapists do. They alter contextual variables, directly when they can, but most often symbolically in psychotherapy, to change the function (i.e., the impact or meaning) of these variables and as a result, increase clients' flexible sensitivity to the context and functional coherence. Those overarching means and goals are what guide the CBS therapist and thus what need to be measured in session on both sides of the therapeutic relationship.

The Challenges of Measuring In-Session Behavior

The advantages of a CBS approach to psychotherapy don't come without certain difficulties. On the one hand, interventions can be specifically designed for each client and each contextual feature. On the other hand, the assessment of client behavioral problems and therapist skills can't be defined out of context, which makes the assessment of treatment effectiveness and adherence more difficult than in approaches using protocols topographically defined.

Consider the example of a client who experiences social anxiety and avoids social interactions. If effective change is defined by a decrease of anxiety, it is theoretically possible to set a threshold under which anxiety is considered tolerable, perhaps by comparing the client's level of anxiety to what average people experience in similar contexts. However, because CBS-based therapies don't define psychological problems through emotional levels, but through the discrepancy between responses and meaningful life directions, reduction of anxiety is not sufficient or necessary to declare the success of an intervention.

Consider now an example of CBS-based intervention to treat this client's problem. In a typical move from acceptance and commitment therapy (ACT; Hayes, Strosahl, & Wilson, 1999; 2012), the therapist might say to the client:

> So you are having the thought that you can't engage in a conversation because people will judge you. What do you feel in your body just as you are about to speak with another person? Can you stay in touch with this sensation for a moment, without defense, just as a way to fully experience this fear of others' judgment?

In this short turn of speech, the therapist attempts to alter the context around the fear of judgment (by reframing it as a thought), and evokes an alternative response by creating a context of exploration and compassion. The intention of the therapist is that these symbolic alterations of the context will lead to a transformation of function of the fear of judgment, and eventually to a more effective response based on flexible sensitivity to the context and functional coherence (e.g., engaging in enjoyable conversations and social interactions even if fear of judgment is present).

Now consider the same therapist's turn of speech with a client similarly reporting fear of judgment and avoidance of social interactions if reporting this experience in session is driven by the desire to receive attention from the therapist. In this case, altering the context around fear of judgment will have little effect. The client's problem is elsewhere, perhaps in his or her difficulties to build relationships based on authenticity. A CBS-based intervention can't be defined out of context.

The success of measuring client behavioral changes and therapist skills in session thus requires a constant inclusion of the context. The therapist attempts to alter the context and observes whether the function of the relevant variables are transformed as a result, which should be reflected by a different response from the client. For example, a therapist might ask clients who express no interest in any activity, "If you could do anything you want just now, what would you be doing?" as a way to reconnect them to sources of life meaning. A client response of "I would be riding my bike" would be quite different than "I don't know," and perhaps even be a first step toward identifying genuine values. If the client responded "I don't know," the intervention has likely not worked, unless the change of function occurs in a delayed fashion, as when clients begin a new session saying "I have been thinking of what you said last time ..." Even in this case, the marker of change is a new response indicating greater flexible sensitivity to the context and functional coherence. In the example above, the client identifying that he would be riding his bike might be a sign of greater sensitivity to available satisfying activities. This type of verbal response is key to assessment in psychotherapy because it can be observed in session. Most of the time, therapists will have to trust their client's verbal reports or self-monitoring diaries of what they actually do in their lives outside, except if functionally similar behaviors occur in the therapy room, as we will see later in this chapter.

Thus, verbal reports constitute the core matter of observation in therapy, but observation must be conducted within a functional contextual framework to provide information on the relevance and success of a CBS-based intervention. In the next two sections, we will review more concrete means therapists can use to ensure that assessment of clients' problems and improvement is conducted in accordance with CBS principles.

Assessing Function and Context through Verbal Reports

Because context and function are the pillars of CBS, therapists using this approach need methods of assessment that focus on the functional relationships between relevant behaviors and contextual variables. As explained earlier, these relationships are potentially different for each client and each situation. Therefore, therapists need overarching strategies that guide their assessment in a functional contextualistic way, regardless of the specific experience being reported or directly observed. Such overarching guidelines can be found in the assessment of behaviors (avoidance-escape, approach, and deficits) and their sources of influence (antecedents, consequences, and rules). This process is described particularly explicitly in dialectical behavior therapy (i.e., "chain analysis"; Linehan, 1993). For example, clients who report difficulties doing complex tasks at work might be influenced by anxiety of not doing their job well (immediate antecedent), short-term relief of postponing the task (immediate consequence), the belief that they are not competent, and that they therefore should decline complex tasks (rule). Unfortunately, the long-term or delayed consequence of this chain may be failure to advance in a job or career, or even termination of employment. Once the relationship between behaviors and contextual variables has been identified, the therapist has a baseline against which future behaviors can be compared. A new response to a similar variable indicates change, and moreover effective change, if this new response allows clients to improve their overall functioning and well-being. In this example, client acceptance of complex tasks even in the presence of anxiety, thoughts that they are not competent, and temptation to find relief by declining such assignments, would reflect effective change.

This approach is grounded in the principles of functional analysis, which is not surprising given the behavioral roots of CBS. However, doing psychotherapy primarily through verbal interactions requires therapists to adapt their methods of assessment. Relevant behaviors, contextual variables, and new responses are generally not directly observed, but reported. Fortunately, therapists can use these reports as long as they conduct verbal interactions in a functional contextual fashion, and recognize that the verbal behavior of clients is also contextually determined by historical and current situational factors, including the actions of the therapist. In practice, therapists encourage clients to report what they are doing and what they are not doing outside of therapy as well as the antecedents, consequences, and rules surrounding clinically relevant behavior.

Strategies to evoke descriptions of behaviors include questions about what the client does in a variety of situations, at different times, and in various interpersonal contexts. For example, a therapist might ask "What does a usual day look like for you?," "What do you enjoy doing?," "What would you like to do more?," and "What would you like to do less?" As simple as these questions are, they constitute important tools to orient clients to what is in their control and what they will be able to change. Often, clients spontaneously report experiences over which they have little or no control at all, even with the help of a therapist. For example, a client might say "I came to see you because I worry all the time and I want to feel more confident." Although successful therapeutic work often indirectly decreases anxiety and increases confidence, CBS therapists prefer targeting behaviors that clients can choose to do or not do. Thus, a response from a CBS therapist to the statement above might be "What do you do and not do when you worry? What impact does it have in your life?" Such questions help identify responses to the previously reported experiences and give some first indications of what clients care about in life.

Antecedent sources of influences can be explored by orienting client reports to what they experience before engaging in a problematic behavior (or before they miss an opportunity to do something effective). The therapist asks questions such as "In what situations do you ____? What do you notice just before you ____? Who is generally present with you when you ____? How do you feel before you ____? (blanks filled with relevant behaviors)". Consequential sources of influence can be explored by orienting client reports to what happens after relevant behaviors. The therapist asks questions such as "What happens when you ____? What do you notice as a result of ____? How do people react when you ____?" Rules can be explored by orienting client reports to what they think before they engage in relevant behaviors or to how they justify their behaviors. The therapist asks questions such as "What comes to your mind before you ____? Why do you think you ____? Do you have a particular intention when you ____?"

Because rules can be followed for different reasons, it is useful to distinguish between tracking (i.e., following the rule is reinforced by the consequence described by the rule) and pliance (i.e., following the rule is socially reinforced based on a correspondence between the behavior of the rule-follower and the behavior described by the rule, regardless of the correspondence between the experienced consequence and the consequence described by the rule) (see Hayes, 1989; Törneke, Luciano, & Valdivia Salas, 2008;).[3] The latter is often involved in the persistence of problematic behavior because rule-followers can lose contact with the effectiveness of their actions very quickly in these conditions. The therapist can identify pliance by asking questions that virtually remove social approval such as "If nobody knew what you are doing, would you still do it?," "If people's reaction to your behavior was different, do you think you would still ____?," and "If the consequence of doing that was different than what you expect, would you still consider that it is the right thing to do?"

As suggested earlier, some problematic behaviors are contingency-shaped and can be successfully modified by directly manipulating situational variables, as is commonly done in applied behavior analysis. Problematic behaviors, however, may present an even greater clinical challenge when they arise from following rules that are inapplicable or inaccurate. In particular, rules describing short-term consequences, but neglecting to mention more important long-term effects, or rules describing the behaviors of others or actions that can't be performed, are useful to notice. The therapist can ask questions such as "It seems like you get what you want in the moment when you do that. How about in the long run?," "So, you are saying that if your partner was more kind to you, you'd be happier. What would you need to do so that she is more kind?," and "So, you are saying that if you could go back in time, you would make a different choice and be happier now. What do you think the next step is for you?"

It is important that assessment is not done in a unilateral way, or else function and context may end up defined from the perspective of the therapist alone. In other words, although therapists guide the assessment process, they are not the only ones to observe and analyze client behavior. To ensure that the assessed information actually leads to a functional understanding of the problem at hand, clients must be fully included. Ultimately, they are the only one who can tell if a behavior is problematic, unless their judgment is severely impaired (e.g., in acute psychotic episodes), or if causing harm to others doesn't impact their perceived well-being (e.g., in psychopathy). Given the private nature of many salient human experiences and reactions (thoughts, emotions, sensations), only clients can directly observe the functional relationship between these variables and their problematic behaviors.

An example will illustrate the potential risk of assessing psychological matters without a clear involvement of the client in the process. Imagine that a client reports to her therapist that she doesn't want to have sexual intercourse in a romantic relationship. She doesn't enjoy sex and doesn't see that as a problem, but given that her relationship to sex is incompatible with her boyfriend's interest in it, they have decided to break up. If the therapist, who experiences satisfaction in sexual intercourse in her own life, approaches the functional relationship between the absence of sexual interest and the breakup from her own point of view exclusively, there is a risk that she will see that as a problem regardless of what the client actually experiences. She might for example see the breakup as problematic avoidance of sexual intimacy. This might then lead to a biased exploration of sources of influence, as she looks for what is maintaining avoidance regardless of whether avoidance is involved in this situation. Even if avoidance was actually involved, not all avoidant behavior is dysfunctional, and only the client could tell if it is a problem that needs intervention. Of course, noticing that avoidance is involved and evaluating whether it is a problem or not requires awareness skills that therapy often aims to increase, but this doesn't mean that the therapist can a priori assume what the client is experiencing.

Strategies to conduct a collaborative assessment include reflective listening and validation of clients' psychological experiences; reformulations that state functional relationships without taking away opportunities for clients to observe on their own; sharing of observations with distance and openness to contradicting feedback; and encouragement to observe and describe without arbitrarily praising reports that match the therapist's own observations and analysis (even subtlety through smiles or increased attention). Including clients in the assessment process is also a step toward behavior change insofar as flexible sensitivity to the context and functional coherence naturally require awareness of one's own behaviors and sources of influence on these behaviors.

Assessing Function and Context through What Happens in Session

The therapy room is a sort of experimental lab. Although the context created by a warm and caring therapeutic relationship is nothing like the impersonal atmosphere of a scientific study, a therapy session is an opportunity for the client and the therapist to observe processes and test hypotheses together. In the previous section, we reviewed ways to use verbal reports to assess behaviors and contextual variables happening outside the session. Through verbal interactions and other symbolic moves (e.g., gestures, postures, music, pictures), the therapist can also create a context that allows for relevant behaviors to be observed in the here and now – an approach at the core of functional analytic psychotherapy (FAP; Kohlenberg & Tsai, 1991) as well as being historically central to other models of treatment (e.g., psychoanalysis).

A first general method is the use of antecedents that are able to trigger a problematic or effective behavior in session. For example, with a client who struggles with accepting help from others, the therapist might offer problem-solving advice. If the client usually withdraws, feels ashamed, and then quickly gets angry, it would be useful to observe signs of a similar sequence in therapy. The client might, for example, stop looking at the therapist, blush, and then frown. The evocation of a relevant behavior is useful in addition to the report of occurrences outside the therapy room because the therapist can observe the event with the client more directly and also instigate alternative ways of responding. The client and therapist can establish a common understanding of the client's experience, avoid misinterpretations of it, and conduct a more fine-grained analysis of the behavioral sequence together. If necessary, formal exercises can also be used for evoking problematic or effective behaviors. Many experiential therapies use exercises in which a specific thought is contacted (e.g., a painful memory or a hypothetical future episode of the client's life) so as to observe the client's reactions in this context (e.g., emotional avoidance, identification of values, etc.). As clients engage in the relevant behavior, the therapist helps them notice this occurrence and checks if it actually belongs to the same functional category (e.g., "I notice you stopped looking at me. Is that similar to your withdrawal when you are offered help by others in your life?").

Another method, derived from the approach described above, is to evoke relevant behaviors by bringing external or imaginary situations to the here and now through metaphors and perspective-taking. There is a long tradition of using metaphors in therapy (McCurry & Hayes, 1992) but, in CBS-based psychotherapy, their application aims in particular to help clients observe concrete features of a situation and functional relationships between relevant behaviors and the context (Stewart, Barnes-Holmes, Hayes, & Lipkens, 2001; Villatte, Villatte, & Monestès, 2014). For example, a typical ACT metaphor consists of drawing a parallel between driving a bus with passengers shouting in the back and living one's life with difficult psychological experiences (Hayes et al., 1999, pp. 157–158). The goal of using this metaphor is to help clients notice what consequences result from attempting to control their experiences. If the metaphor is presented in a brief and didactic manner, there will be limited opportunity for the client and the therapist to actually observe relevant behaviors. In contrast, presenting the metaphor as a role-play, perhaps even with other people acting as the passengers as is it often possible in group therapy or workshops, allows for engaging in the behavior rather than just reporting on it. When it is not possible to physicalize the metaphor, the therapist can use techniques to make the metaphor more experientially-based and the relevant behavior more likely to occur (Villatte et al., 2014; in press). For example, the therapist can use the present tense, draw the client's attention to concrete features of the situation included in the metaphor, and mix the vocabulary from both situations (e.g., "You are driving your life and your thoughts are shouting in the back, can you hear them now? What do you feel like doing in this moment?").

Perspective-taking techniques also allow for contacting distant or hypothetical situations without leaving the therapy room (see McHugh & Stewart, 2012 for a book-length CBS-approach to perspective-taking). The therapist can orient the client's attention to a variety of situations, times, or interpersonal interactions and bring them into the here and now through perspective shifts. For example, the therapist might say "Imagine that I am your sister now, and I'm telling you that I am sorry. How does that make you feel? What do you want to tell me?" Other perspective-shifting questions might include "If you were 10 years from now, and nothing had changed, what would you tell yourself?" and "If we were in your office right now, what would I see you do?" Variations of these techniques are numerous, and they are used in many different psychotherapy approaches for varied purposes (e.g.. in cognitive therapy: Alford & Beck, 1998, and Gestalt therapy: Perls, 1969). In CBS-based therapy, the explicit goal is to alter the symbolic context so that relevant behaviors may occur in the therapy room and interventions be applied more directly.

Clinically relevant behaviors can also happen spontaneously in therapy. Because different behavioral topographies can have the same function, therapists must be ready to notice occurrences of relevant behaviors that sometimes look very different than what clients experience in their lives. For example, a client who goes out late every night to avoid being alone at home and as a result is unable to function well in his professional life might have a hard time ending a session. He might begin a new topic of conversation when the therapist is wrapping up, or he might ask for advancing their next session. Here also, it is useful for the assessment process – at the beginning of therapy and as the therapeutic work progresses – that therapists share observations with their clients and verify if they are instances of problematic behavior.

An Example of an Assessment Protocol Based on CBS: Creative Hopelessness

Some CBS psychotherapies organize the different methods of assessment in session through verbal reports or direct observations into a sort of protocol guiding the therapist through the steps of identifying relevant behaviors and their sources of influence. An example of such a protocol is that which engenders *creative hopelessness* in ACT by exploring strategies used by clients to control unwanted psychological experiences (Hayes et al., 1999). It can also be applied to address attempts to reach inaccessible, unsafe, or costly sources of positive reinforcement as can be the case for example in addictions, eating disorders, or procrastination.

After collaboratively identifying sources of suffering in the life of clients (e.g., anxiety, obsessive thoughts, traumatic memories, interpersonal conflicts, etc.), the therapist initiates the exploration of contexts in which the difficulties are experienced (e.g., "In what situations do you experience this feeling?"). Then, the therapist enquires about client responses to psychological events and the consequences of doing so (e.g., "What do you do when you experience this feeling? What happens as a result?"). The experiential dimension of this protocol resides in that the therapist doesn't provide answers to these questions, but encourages clients to notice the potentially relevant features of the situation for themselves. Clients are also encouraged to draw functional conclusions at a pace that respects the progression of their own reasoning.

Often, reporting difficulties experienced outside the therapy room brings difficult emotions into the session. Beginning to realize that past and current strategies are not effective is often a source of confusion, and sometimes of distress for clients. They may begin to envision alternative approaches to their difficulties, but also contact the painful realization that considerable energy and time have been spent, sometimes for years, in ineffective actions. The related pain and resistance to change that often shows up during this process are rich opportunities to observe and intervene in session. The therapist might, for example, ask "What do you feel, as you notice that what you have tried to do to fix this problem has not worked so far?," "Do you have urges to do something about this feeling?," and "What do you think will happen if you do that now?" The process of observation and description of experiences and functional relationships among these experiences is thus brought from the content of verbal reports to the current situation.

Numerous metaphors and exercises are employed in instigating creative hopelessness with the purpose of assessing the effectiveness of client behavior and increasing their awareness of the behavioral sequence. For example, the man in the hole metaphor (Hayes et al., 1999, pp. 101–104; 2012, pp. 192–196) invites clients to imagine falling into a hole and attempting to escape it while the only tool available is a shovel. As clients notice that continued digging will only take them deeper into the hole, the therapist helps them consider if what they've been doing in life might be similar. Associated exercises may consist of asking clients to engage in a preferred experiential control strategy with less emotional material, to observe the result in-session (e.g., trying not to think of a white bear for a few minutes to notice the counter productivity of thought suppression; see Wegner, 1989).

Assessing Changes in Client and Therapist In-Session Behaviors

Assessing Client Behavioral Change

In the previous section we focused on the assessment of client problematic behaviors and sources of influence maintaining these behaviors. The therapist and the client also need to recognize when effective change is happening so that interventions can be evaluated and new useful behaviors strengthened. Although effective change depends on idiographic parameters (i.e., a behavior is evaluated with regard to its function in the context of clients' lives), there are overarching methods to recognize when clients begin to respond in ways that support their well-being. We mentioned earlier that flexible sensitivity to the context and functional coherence are the two overarching skills that clinical interventions based on CBS aim to develop in clients. These skills need to be specified further to facilitate in-session observations. This is possible if more specific categories of behaviors that support these overarching sets of competences are defined.

Flexible sensitivity to the context and functional coherence require (a) awareness based on function and context (clients must be able to notice their experiences, what they do, and what happens as a result); (b) effective "sense-making" (clients must be able to draw conclusions and make decisions that support their well-being); (c) response flexibility (clients must be able to engage in different responses if the context demands it); (d) a flexible sense of self (clients must be able to conceptualize their experiences as normal and distinct from the perspective they have on these experiences); (e) a sense of meaning based on positive, intrinsic, overarching, and inexhaustible reinforcement (clients must be able to identify overarching goals and qualities of actions in their lives); and (f) augmenting of the reinforcing qualities of meaningful actions (clients must be able to connect their actions to what they care about even when they are not immediately satisfying or are difficult to perform).

These subsets of skills are more specific than the overarching goals of clinical interventions, but it is possible to go even further in order to provide more guidance to assessment of change in session. As mentioned earlier in this chapter, what happens in the therapy room is essentially verbal. Clients report about their experiences outside the session, and communicate about what is happening in the here and now. Language is not only a means to communicate; it is also a relevant behavior in its own right that takes part in the development of psychopathology *and* in the resolution of psychological problems. For this reason, the way clients speak is an important indicator of clinically relevant change.

While RFT was early linked to the development of clinical tools (Hayes et al., 1999), it is only recently that its *direct* use in therapy has been more explicitly and systematically formulated (Villatte et al., in press; see also Luciano, Rodríguez Valverde, & Gutiérrez Martínez, 2004; Törneke, 2010 for examples of earlier explorations in this area). At the core of this formulation, therapy transcripts are analyzed through types of relational framing at a broad level. For example, a client statement of "When I come home, I need to drink a lot of alcohol in order to feel less anxious," can be analyzed as a frame of condition linking coming home, feeling anxious, drinking, and feeling less anxious. These conditional relations indicate that the client feels anxious in certain situations and that drinking decreases anxiety. Furthermore, this way of relating experiences indicates that from the client's perspective, drinking is necessary. Because drinking such amounts of alcohol is likely problematic, at least for the client's health, it is reasonable to conclude that the client currently lacks flexible sensitivity to the context (i.e., he responds to the relief of anxiety rather than to the damage to his health) and functional coherence (i.e., he believes that it is what he needs to do).

From an RFT perspective, a sign of effective change observable in session in the example above would be reflected by a new way of relating experiences. In particular, the client would include his health in the relational network through a relation of condition (e.g., "If I keep drinking this way, I will gravely damage my health"). Deictic framing (perspective-taking) would also be expected as a sign of awareness of the process (e.g., "I can see better what I am doing now") and hierarchal framing as a sign of functional coherence (e.g., "I don't want to damage my heath further. It is too important. I want to put my health above my need to feel better"). Naturally, not drinking excessive amounts of alcohol anymore when contacting anxiety is key to effective change in this situation. Increased response flexibility, however, will also be reflected by the client's way of relating his experiences, in particular through coordination framing taking over opposition framing between painful psychological experiences and effective behavior (e.g., from "I want to live a healthy life, *but* I feel anxious" to "I want to live a healthy life *and* I feel anxious"). This method can be applied to the different areas of intervention listed earlier, while taking into account the specifics of the targeted domain (e.g., hierarchical framing in meaning and motivation, deictic and hierarchical framing in the flexible sense of self, and so on).

Approaching client changes with behavioral principles is not incompatible with assessment based on middle-level terms (e.g., values, self-as-context, committed action in ACT), but they allow for more precision. A sufficiently trained therapist is able to read the clinical situation, recognize changes in processes at the levels of both basic principles and middle-level terms, and can go back and forth between these two levels depending on what is most practical in a given situation.

Assessing Therapists' Skills and Behavior

Assessing therapists' skills from a CBS perspective entails similar difficulties to those in assessing client behavioral change. What the therapist does also needs to be viewed through a functional contextualistic lens. For this reason, defining what a therapeutic intervention should look like is a challenge for clinical researchers and trainers (Plumb & Vilardaga, 2010). To date, attempts to describe CBS therapists' skills have consisted of listing overarching rules or processes consistent with the overall model and broad enough to include a variety of topographies (e.g., Kohlenberg & Tsai, 1994; Luoma, Hayes, & Walser, 2007; Twohig et al., 2010). These strategies are useful because they give therapists and assessors of treatment adherence a general direction, but in some cases, they have paradoxically led to a narrowing of the range of techniques that CBS therapists can use. For example, "self-as-process" in ACT is often defined as the awareness of ongoing psychological experiences that therapists ought to train through observation in the present moment (e.g., Foody, Barnes-Holmes, & Barnes-Holmes, 2012). For example, clients might be invited to observe the flow of their sensations and thoughts moment by moment, and to notice how they change over-time. Yet, it is possible to develop a sense of self-as-process detached from specific and rigid definitions and experiences by observing a variety of contexts and noticing how these experiences and definitions change (Villatte et al., in press). For instance, clients rigidly attached to the self-definition "I am socially anxious" might be invited to recall what emotions and sensations they feel in the presence of different people, and how they see themselves across these situations, in order to notice that experiences and definitions linked to social interactions are more various than what they were originally noticing.

Another example is the proscription of strategies to ostensibly change client's thoughts or to encourage rational thinking in ACT (Twohig et al., 2010, see Plumb & Vilardaga,

2010 for the full treatment adherence manual). While, from an RFT perspective, it makes sense to generally recommend that therapists avoid attempts to eliminate or replace client thoughts (Hooper, Saunders, & McHugh, 2010), it is possible to develop alternative thoughts that exert a new and more useful influence on the client behavior (Villatte et al., in press). As long as the therapist's strategy relies on adding and strengthening new ways of thinking without removing thoughts already present in the client's repertoire (i.e., increasing the flexibility of arbitrarily applicable relational responding), the intervention is consistent with RFT and CBS. Interestingly, this approach has always been at the core of ACT (e.g., defusion techniques encourage the client to reformulate thoughts with "I have the thought that" or with "and" instead of "but"; Luoma et al., 2007), but attempts to discriminate ACT therapists' skills from more traditional forms of CBT may have given the impression that ACT excluded these types of interventions. Rational thinking can also be useful and has arguably always been part of ACT (e.g., in values and committed action) if what is meant by "rational" is "functionally coherent."

The recent efforts to include RFT principles more directly in clinical practice might constitute a new path allowing for greater precision in the definition of CBS therapists' skills without losing the benefit of the functional contextual framework. Therapists' interventions might be defined with the types of framing they use during their interactions with clients in session. For example, values can be defined as positive overarching goals and qualities of actions situated at the top of a hierarchical network that includes specific goals and actions at its base (Villatte et al., in press). With this definition in mind, therapists can use a variety of framings to help clients build the hierarchical network. They can explore values by connecting actions to overarching goals through hierarchical framing questions ("What would doing this action be part of?") or identify actions consistent with values ("What are the things you could do that would be part of this value?"). They can help clients build broad patterns of actions using distinction and coordination framing ("If you could not do this action, what else could you do that would have a similar function?").

Such a principles-based approach doesn't completely avoid the difficulties that middle-level terms entail insofar as identifying a type of framing is also subject to interpretation. However, combined with the overarching goals and means of CBS therapy described earlier in the current chapter, it is arguably a more precise way of defining what therapists do, and it may help prevent the rigid interpretation of middle-level terms over time. Although further research is needed to support the utility of using RFT principles in the definition of CBS therapists' skills, recent studies in the area of the self are promising in this regard (Foody, Barnes-Holmes, Barnes-Holmes, & Luciano, 2013; Luciano et al., 2011).

Conclusion

The CBS approach to assessment in therapy is to some extent very intuitive and similar to other approaches of psychopathology and clinical interventions. Problems are measured with regard to their impact on quality of life, and with attention to the features of the context in which these problems occur. However, assessment based on CBS requires a further step in that client behaviors and contextual variables need to be related in a functional way so that the information gathered in session leads to interventions that change relevant behaviors. The benefit of such an approach is to allow therapists to adapt their interventions to each client while staying in contact with universal principles of psychology and evidence-based strategies. The challenge in assessing function and context is that no psychological problem or effective change can be described topographically. For this reason, therapists need to apply overarching strategies firmly grounded in the functional contextual philosophy underlying CBS, and gather and interpret information using experiential techniques.

Notes

1   Throughout this chapter, I use the term CBS therapy (or CBS therapists) to refer to all psychotherapeutic practices based on, or compatible with, contextual behavioral science. As discussed in chapter 14, this definition would clearly include, but not necessarily be limited to, acceptance and commitment therapy (ACT), although several instances of therapist behaviors discussed throughout this chapter exemplify how ACT is typically conducted.
2   Even when the intervention consists of changing the clients' environment outside the therapy room (e.g., creating a more peaceful place for working or sleeping, setting an alarm to cue certain behaviors), it still requires clients to make these changes themselves.
3   Augmenting has also been recognized as yet a third functional class of rule-governed behavior included in tracking or pliance. Interested readers are encouraged to consult Hayes et al. (2001) for an extensive coverage of it.

References

Alford, B. A., & Beck, A. T. (1998). *The integrative power of cognitive therapy.* New York, NY: Guilford.

American Psychiatric Association. (2013). *Diagnostic and statistical manual of mental disorders* (5th ed.). Arlington, VA: American Psychiatric Publishing.

Foody, M., Barnes-Holmes, Y., & Barnes-Holmes, D. (2012). The role of self in acceptance and commitment therapy (ACT). In L. McHugh & I. Stewart (Eds.), *The self and perspective taking: Research and applications* (pp. 126–142). Oakland, CA: New Harbinger.

Foody, M., Barnes-Holmes, Y., Barnes-Holmes, D., & Luciano, C. (2013). An empirical investigation of hierarchical versus distinction relations in a self-based ACT exercise. *International Journal of Psychology and Psychological Therapy, 13*, 373–388.

Hayes, S. C. (Ed.). (1989). *Rule-governed behavior: Cognition, contingencies, and instructional control.* New York, NY: Plenum.

Hayes, S. C., Barnes-Holmes, D., & Roche, B. (Eds.). (2001). *Relational frame theory: A post-Skinnerian account of human language and cognition.* New York, NY: Plenum.

Hayes, S. C., Barnes-Holmes, D., & Wilson, K. G. (2012). Contextual behavioral science: Creating a science more adequate to the challenge of the human condition. *Journal of Contextual Behavioral Science, 1*, 1–16.

Hayes, S. C., Strosahl, K., & Wilson, K. G. (1999). *Acceptance and commitment therapy: An experiential approach to behavior change.* New York, NY: Guilford.

Hayes, S. C., Strosahl, K., & Wilson, K. G. (2012). *Acceptance and commitment therapy: The process and practice of mindful change* (2nd ed.). New York, NY: Guilford.

Hayes, S. C., Villatte, M., Levin, M., & Hildebrandt, M. (2011). Open, aware, and active: Contextual approaches as an emerging trend in the behavioral and cognitive therapies. *Annual Review of Clinical Psychology, 7*, 141–168.

Hooper, N., Saunders, S., & McHugh, L. (2010). The derived generalization of thought suppression. *Learning and Behavior, 38*, 160–168.

Kohlenberg, R. J., & Tsai, M. (1991). *Functional analytic psychotherapy*. New York, NY: Plenum.

Kohlenberg, R. J., & Tsai, M. (1994). Functional analytic psychotherapy: A behavioral approach to treatment and integration. *Journal of Psychotherapy Integration, 4*, 175–201.

Liberman, R. P., Teigen J., Patterson, R., & Baker, V. (1973). Modification of delusional speech in paranoid schizophrenics. *Journal of Applied Behavior Analysis, 6*, 57–70.

Linehan, M. M. (1993). *Cognitive-behavioral treatment of borderline personality disorder*. New York, NY: Guilford.

Luciano, M. C., Rodríguez Valverde, M., & Gutiérrez Martínez, O. (2004). A proposal for synthesizing verbal contexts in experiential avoidance disorder and acceptance and commitment therapy. *International Journal of Psychology and Psychological Therapy, 4*, 377–394.

Luciano, C., Ruiz, F. J., Vizcaíno Torres, R. M., Sanchez-Martin, V., Gutierrez-Martinez, O., & Lopez-Lopez, J. C. (2011). A relational frame analysis of defusion interactions in acceptance and commitment therapy. A preliminary and quasi-experimental study with at-risk adolescents. *International Journal of Psychology and Psychological Therapy, 11*, 165–182.

Luoma, J., Hayes, S. C., & Walser, R. (2007). *Learning ACT*. Oakland, CA: New Harbinger.

McCurry, S., & Hayes, S. C. (1992). Clinical and experimental perspectives on metaphorical talk. *Clinical Psychology Review, 12*, 763–785.

McHugh, L., & Stewart, I. (2012). *The self and perspective taking: Contributions and applications from modern behavioral science*. Oakland, CA: New Harbinger.

Perls, F. (1969). *Gestalt therapy verbatim*. Lafayette, CA: Real People Press.

Petry, N. M. (2000). A comprehensive guide for the application of contingency management procedures in standard clinic settings. *Drug Alcohol Dependence, 58*, 9–25.

Plumb, J. C., & Vilardaga, R. (2010). Assessing treatment integrity in acceptance and commitment therapy: Strategies and suggestions. *International Journal of Behavioral Consultation and Therapy, 6*, 263–295.

Sallows, G. O., & Graupner, T. D., (2005). Intensive behavioral treatment for children with autism: Four-year outcome and predictor. *American Journal of Mental Retardation, 110*, 417–438.

Stewart, I., Barnes-Holmes, D., Hayes, S. C., & Lipkens, R. (2001). Relations among relations: Analogies, metaphors and stories. In S. C. Hayes, D. Barnes-Holmes, & B. Roche (Eds.), *Relational frame theory: A post-Skinnerian approach to language and cognition*. New York, NY: Plenum.

Törneke, N. (2010). *Learning RFT: An introduction to relational frame theory and its clinical applications*. Oakland, CA: New Harbinger.

Törneke, N., Luciano, C., & Valdivia Salas, S. (2008). Rule-governed behavior and psychological problems. *International Journal of Psychology and Psychological Therapy, 8*, 141–156.

Twohig, M. P., Hayes, S. C., Plumb, J. C., Pruitt, L. D., Collins, A. B., Hazlett-Stevens, H., & Woidneck, M. R. (2010). A randomized clinical trial of acceptance and commitment therapy vs. progressive relaxation training for obsessive-compulsive disorder. *Journal of Consulting and Clinical Psychology, 78*, 705–716.

Villatte, M., Villatte, J. L., & Hayes, S. C. (2015). *Mastering the clinical conversation: language as intervention*. New York, NY: Guilford.

Villatte, M., Villatte, J. L., & Monestès, J. L. (2014). Bypassing the traps of language with experiential practice. In J. Stoddard & N. Afari (Eds.), *The big book of ACT metaphors: The complete guide to ACT metaphors and experiential exercises.* Oakland, CA: New Harbinger.

Wegner, D. M. (1989). *White bears and other unwanted thoughts: Suppression, obsession, and the psychology of mental control.* London, England: Guilford.

World Health Organization. (1992). *ICD-10 classifications of mental and behavioural disorders: Clinical descriptions and diagnostic guidelines.* Geneva: Author.

16

Measures That Make a Difference

A Functional Contextualistic Approach to Optimizing Psychological Measurement in Clinical Research and Practice

Joseph Ciarrochi, Robert D. Zettle,
Robert Brockman, James Duguid, Philip Parker,
Baljinder Sahdra, and Todd B. Kashdan

The basic researcher and the practitioner seem perpetually at odds. The basic researcher spends years building a beautiful model of the world. The practitioner takes one look at the model and says, "How will that help me to improve the lives of the clients I will work with this week?" The basic researcher often seems stumped for a legitimate answer.

This chapter seeks to help bridge the gap between basic theory and practice, between obscure psychometric concepts and the concrete needs of the therapist sitting in the room with a client. The chapter comprises five sections. Because some of the gap we seek to bridge may be attributable to differing philosophical approaches to psychological measurement, Section 1 will examine some fundamental differences in how researchers and practitioners typically think about and use clinical assessment. Section 2 focuses on the different ways that a particular measure can be useful to a practitioner, and on various research designs that can be used to assess the utility of clinical assessment. Section 3 then takes a closer look at classic psychometric theory and how it can aid the practical goals of measuring therapeutic change. It will also examine longitudinal research as a means to understanding processes of change and as a complement to the treatment utility designs reviewed in Section 2. Section 4 will seek to organize the bewildering number of clinical process and outcome measures into a simple behavioral framework. Finally, Section 5 will discuss promising new directions in contextual behavioral measurement.

Section 1: Philosophical Approaches to Psychological Assessment

The quality of a psychological measure is typically judged by the degree to which it meets the psychometric standards of reliability and validity (American Educational Research Association, 1999). Broadly speaking, reliability is concerned with the degree

The Wiley Handbook of Contextual Behavioral Science, First Edition. Edited by Robert D. Zettle,
Steven C. Hayes, Dermot Barnes-Holmes, and Anthony Biglan.
© 2016 John Wiley & Sons, Ltd. Published 2016 by John Wiley & Sons, Ltd.

to which a measure yields consistent assessment data, and is a necessary, but insufficient, condition in determining a measure's validity, or how well it assesses what it purports to (Anastasi & Urbina, 1997). Often overlooked is that psychometric theory is at least implicitly, if not explicitly, based on an elemental realistic perspective of the psychological world that in our view can be antithetical to functional contextualism (Nelson & Hayes, 1986).

Elemental Realism

Elemental realism assumes that one can know the true nature of reality, and objectively discover the elements of which it is composed. Elemental realists view the human psyche as a complex machine, and their purpose is to accurately identify the parts and understand what they do. A key question for elemental realists is "What psychological characteristics are we made up of, how do those characteristics interrelate and influence each other, and how do they link to behavior?" Success is defined by how well a construct is able to predict and help establish meaningful, reliable causal patterns.

The elemental realist assumes that building a good working model of the universe will lead to an ability to change how it works. This is not necessarily true. Consider the example of self-esteem. Research has shown that high self-esteem is likely to precede the development of positive social support networks (Marshall, Parker, Ciarrochi, & Heaven, 2014). Does this suggest that the temporal relationship between self-esteem and the development of social support is causal in nature? Even if it is interpreted in this manner, what is the optimum way to increase self-esteem? Do we seek to undermine negative self-concepts via cognitive disputation? Or is it better to accomplish the same goal via the process of defusion as practiced in acceptance and commitment therapy (Hayes, Strosahl, & Wilson, 2012)? Knowing that self-esteem predicts social support does not tell us how we might best change self-esteem.

Functional Contextualism

In contrast to elemental realism, functional contextualism assumes we can never know the true nature of reality or the elements that comprise it. Thus, measures are not assumed to reflect hidden "things." Rather, measures are "behavioral samples" in a particular context. "Context" means whatever comes before the behavior (antecedents) and whatever follows it (consequences). For example, responses on an extraversion scale are not assumed to be caused by an underlying trait. Rather they are viewed as verbal behavior that, like all behavior, is influenced by the context in which it occurs. For example, the same item might be answered differently on an anonymous personality inventory administered during an online research project than when used for employee selection.

Functional contextualists do not view measurement development as its ultimate goal. They view measurement as a tool that can help them improve the human condition. The functional contextualist *will* divide measures into parts and factors, but purely for pragmatic purposes (i.e., does the division help us achieve our goals?). The functional contextualist would make no assumption that this "division" uncovers or reveals something of the "true nature" of character or personality; it is nothing more or less than a useful strategy for achieving a specific goal in a particular context.

The goal of functional analysis is to find ways to predict-and-influence behavior. Prediction in itself is not enough. Typical research in this tradition focuses on manipulating antecedents and consequences and observing how behavior changes as a result. A particular activity is "successful" if it helps to achieve stated goals.

Truth and Error

The distinction between the two philosophical approaches to psychological assessment is illustrated clearly in the notion of measurement error. According to classic psychometric theory, a score on a measure is comprised of a "true score" plus measurement error (Nunnally, 1967). This formulation follows a clear correspondence-based truth criterion. Differing "true scores" hypothetically exist for respondents and their obtained or observed scores on an inventory would exactly *correspond* to these true scores were it not for error in measurement. By contrast, from a contextualistic perspective, interindividual variability in psychological assessment data is not attributed to differences in true scores and intraindividual variability across settings and time is not assumed to result from measurement error. Scores on a psychological inventory are a measure of behavior and "error" has no place in a contextual approach to understanding behavior (Hayes, Nelson, & Jarrett, 1986). Instead, behavior that varies across individuals, as well as across time and place within individuals, is something to be explained by an analysis of contextual factors that include differing learning histories and current situational variables (e.g., the behavior of the assessor, demand characteristics, recent life events, etc.).

One way to minimize this seeming conflict between elemental realism and contextualism is to use terms other than "true score" and "error" in framing variability in assessment data. Rather, we can talk about sources or types of behavioral variability. Each item in a scale can be seen as being associated with "common variance" plus "unique" or unexplained variance (Kline, 2010). Common variance is what the item shares with every other item on the scale. For example, in an assertiveness scale, the common variance of an item can be thought of as the extent that the item refers to assertive behavior and not to some other type of behavior. In contrast, unique variance is assumed, from the elemental realist perspective, to consist of both random error and specific variance. The functional contextualist would not assume random error, but could assume specific variance, which refers to the variability in the scale that is due to a type of behavior that is different from the "common" behavior measured by the scale items. For example, a measure of assertiveness may contain the following item: "I often fail to assert myself and I ruminate about my failure." Let's assume that this item reflects two "behaviors," assertion and rumination. If this item was part of an assertiveness scale, then the rumination component would contribute to what might be termed "error," but it is clearly more usefully conceptualized as "unexplained variance." Almost all modern measures reflect variance related to the intended target of the measure (common variance) and variance due to specific factors (unique variance) (Marsh et al., 2009).

There is an important reason for the functional contextualist to be interested in ideas like "common variance" and "unique variance." They suggest that a scale that is assumed to be unidimensional may actually be multidimensional, or indicative of multiple kinds of behavior. Interventions that influence behavior associated with "common variance" may not be the same as those that impact behavior associated with "unique variance." Using the example from above, we may want to use different types of intervention to increase adaptive assertiveness and to reduce unhelpful rumination. If a client's response to scale items reflects both of these kinds of behaviors, we practitioners want to be made aware of this, so we don't merely average scores and assume we are talking about one kind of behavior, assertiveness, rather than two (i.e., both assertiveness and rumination).

Conceptual Flexibility

When people are unaware of philosophical assumptions, they often engage in unnecessary dispute. For example, the elemental realistic scientist may accuse the functional contextualistic therapist of not creating a model where different internal, psychological parts are hypothesized to influence each other. The therapist, in turn, accuses the basic researcher of focusing on obscure theoretical models and failing to provide guidance to practitioners. This is a dispute that can never be won, because worldviews are based on assumptions, not evidence. Acknowledging one's philosophical worldview simply means owning up to one's improvable assumptions.

The philosophical gap that sometimes divides basic researchers and mental health professionals is narrowed if both parties temporarily shift perspectives. The elemental realistic who carefully constructs and tests an information-processing model of anxiety, also seeks to identify interventions that reduce anxiety. The functional contextualistic therapist who wants to alleviate client suffering right now, also has an interest in understanding how different processes interrelate to contribute to psychological pain. The larger philosophical dispute can thus be ended by saying that nobody *is* an elemental realist or a functional contextualist. These are just philosophical glasses we sometimes wear, perhaps without even knowing it.

We have reservations about the exclusive use of reliability and validity in evaluating the quality of psychological assessment, but recognize that an outright rejection of psychometric standards would reflect an inflexible and dogmatic stance that is itself inconsistent with functional contextualism. In fact, we will argue in this chapter that the relevance of psychometric standards in selecting clinically appropriate measures is contextually dependent and depends on purpose. Sometimes it may be useful to rely primarily on psychometric standards, and sometimes it may be useful to ignore these standards in favor of others.

In our view, all measures, both within as well as outside of psychology, are simply tools whose usefulness and related critical attributes vary depending on the context in which, and the purpose for which, they are being used. Often the most useful measures may be those that are the most psychometrically sound. However, neither reliability nor validity, as we will argue, may be necessary for a given psychological measure to demonstrate treatment utility.

Section 2: Treatment Utility of Clinical Assessment

Treatment utility refers to "the degree to which assessment is shown to contribute to beneficial treatment outcome" (Hayes, Nelson, & Jarrett, 1987, p. 963), where "assessment" can be broadly defined. Although designs in treatment utility research can be either correlational or experimental in nature, here we selectively emphasize those that evaluate the impact of manipulating assessment practices on treatment outcome. Interested readers are encouraged to consult Hayes et al. (1986, 1987) and Nelson-Gray (2003) for more comprehensive discussions of treatment utility research designs.

While reliability and validity are indispensable psychometric standards, treatment utility is in our view the sine qua non of a functional contextualistic approach to evaluating, selecting, and utilizing clinically relevant measures. Asking whether certain assessment practices enhance desired outcomes is not unique to psychotherapy. Recent developments within medical research and practice provide clear illustrations of treatment validity that might be generalized to psychological research. We thus present treatment utility examples from both medical and psychological domains.

Manipulated Assessment Design

Mammograms are performed to identify cancerous tumors that would otherwise go undetected. If such tumors can be identified early and successfully treated, survival rates should improve. However, a recent Canadian experiment utilizing what is commonly known as a manipulated assessment design (Nelson-Gray, 2003) found no evidence for the treatment utility of mammography among women aged 40–59 (Miller et al., 2014). The mortality rates from breast cancer among women from this age range who were randomly assigned to receive routine annual mammography screenings were no better than those for women in the control condition. It is important to note that these findings do not call into question the reliability and validity of mammograms, nor do they suggest that mammography is ineffective in reducing deaths from breast cancer among women of younger or older ages. Further research is obviously necessary to determine if age functions as a moderating variable, such that mammograms display treatment utility with one age range of women, but not others.

Somewhat similar to the use of mammography, it is common clinical practice for mental health professionals to screen for psychiatric conditions such as psychotic disorders, substance abuse, and/or suicidality by administering assessment batteries to all new clients. While doing so certainly has the appearance of "good clinical practice," we are aware of no empirical support for such screenings. For example, for all we know, clinics that at intake administer the Millon Clinical Multiaxial Inventory-III (MCMI-III; Millon, 2006) and/or the Minnesota Multiphasic Personality Inventory-2 (MMPI-2; Butcher, Dahlstrom, Graham, Tellegen, & Kaemmer, 1989) provide treatment that is no more efficacious than facilities that routinely do not. Note that our skepticism here is not about the psychometric properties of the MCMI-III or the MMPI-2, but centers around their treatment utility; that is, does their use lead to better treatment outcomes? Those who argue for the use of psychiatric screenings have the burden of providing evidence that such practices are efficacious. Otherwise, both clients and therapists are wasting considerable time, expense, and effort.

Manipulated Use of Assessment Design

Continuing with our medical example, if it is determined that treatment for breast cancer is advisable, the oncologist is then faced with a treatment selection question. That is, which treatment choice or combination of options (e.g., radiation, chemotherapy, mastectomy, etc.) is likely to be most effective for each given patient? Recent oncological research increasingly suggests that genomic testing of tumors may make it possible to personalize cancer treatment by matching differing therapeutic options to differing types of tumors (Andre et al., 2014). Evaluating the benefit of assessment on treatment selection has been referred to as a manipulated use of assessment design (Nelson-Gray, 2003). However, we prefer the more descriptive term "manipulated match" for this design, as it highlights the independent variable.

Practicing clinicians face difficult practical questions. How does one intervene with clients that have specific presenting problems, such as certain personality disorders, for which there are no empirically supported treatments like those recognized by Division 12 of the American Psychological Association (aka Society of Clinical Psychology)? Another question arises, similar to that presented to the oncologist, when the practitioner has the "luxury" of selecting among several empirically supported therapeutic options for a presenting problem. Are certain kinds of interventions a more optimal "match" for particular types of clients? For example, is there any psychological assessment that can guide practitioners in most effectively matching cognitive therapy, interpersonal therapy, behavioral activation, and acceptance and commitment therapy to their different clients? Are some clients better candidates for one of these therapies than the rest, whereas others would respond optimally to another choice, and, if so, what are the psychological variables that distinguish one subgroup from another?

A similar question can be asked concerning the ingredients of therapy. Are there some components of an intervention that should be highlighted with some clients, but not others? For example, values clarification might be ideally suited to those who have unclear direction in their lives, whereas emotional awareness training may suit those who are alexithymic, or have trouble identifying and describing feelings.

Treatment Determination and Guidance

Specific questions about treatment determination and treatment guidance are centrally related to the broader issue of treatment utility. Before further discussion, it may be useful to first clarify what we mean by each of these terms. "Treatment determination" refers to the process of ascertaining what types of presenting problems and issues are to be addressed in therapy. Once a determination has been made to target a particular concern, "treatment guidance" refers to the role of assessment in adjusting treatment of it on a client-by-client basis.

Treatment determination. Oftentimes, one or more presenting problems may be readily apparent based on a client's stated reason for seeking treatment, the referral source, the context surrounding the initiation of therapy, and so on. Nonetheless, administering an intake assessment battery seems reasonable given high rates of psychiatric comorbidity (Regier et al., 1990; Sartorius, Ustun, Lecruiber, & Wittchen, 1996) and evidence that half of clients keep secrets from their therapists (Farber, Berano, & Capobianco, 2004). The costs of such assessment would presumably be outweighed by the benefits of detecting salient issues and concerns (e.g., dangerousness to self or others, possible substance abuse, sexual matters, etc.) that might complicate treatment of the more obvious presenting problems. In effect, an intake assessment can help make a determination that unidentified psychological issues warrant treatment in their own right. The relative benefits of psychiatric screenings would ostensibly be even greater with clients who have vague and ambiguous presenting problems.

Despite the reasonableness of the above arguments, we are unaware of any treatment utility research that has examined the cost-benefit ratio of using screening batteries. In order to do so, a manipulated assessment experiment could be conducted in which half of the clients at an outpatient mental health clinic are randomly assigned to complete a comprehensive assessment battery. The treatment utility of the assessment could be determined by comparing client responsiveness to therapy. If those clients who were administered the screening battery improve more than their control group counterparts, its treatment utility is empirically supported.

It is important to note that screening batteries are just one example of what might be evaluated by a manipulated assessment design. Recall that this design asks whether the inclusion of some form of assessment for identifying focal problems and issues in therapy results in improved treatment outcomes. The independent variable in such experiments could be as broad as an extensive psychiatric screening or as narrow as the administration of a brief questionnaire (e.g., the Hopelessness Scale of Beck, Weissman, Lester, & Trexler, 1974).

Treatment guidance. Treatment determination is seldom an issue in providing psychological services to those with pervasive developmental disorders. This is particularly the case, for example, in targeting self-stimulatory and/or self-injurious behaviors displayed by autistic children. While the need for intervention and its goals are thus readily apparent (e.g., to significantly reduce, if not eliminate head banging), how to most efficaciously guide treatment is not. For this reason, we will use clinical work with children displaying developmental disorders to illustrate the utility of assessment in guiding individualized treatment programs.

Functional analysis represents the oldest and most quintessential contextualistic approach to assessing behavior (Ferster, 1965). Treatment determination is met by identifying a target behavior in need of modification, followed by the systematic manipulation of antecedent and consequential events that are suspected of functioning as its controlling variables (Iwata, Dorsey, Slifer, Bauman, & Richman, 1982). For example, hand biting occasioned by the presentation of a nonpreferred task might serve an avoidant function. To evaluate this possibility, changes in the frequency of the target behavior could be documented in response to the systematic introduction and withdrawal of the task. The findings of such mini-experiments are then used to guide the development of treatment plans, such as teaching the child a more appropriate way of requesting a break. A complete functional analysis would also "test" for other controlling variables, such as receipt of attention, sensory reinforcement (i.e., hand biting is maintained by its sensory consequences), and tangible reinforcement (e.g., the child stops biting his hand when offered a favorite toy). Insofar as the same topographical behavior (e.g., hand biting) can serve different functions for different children, and different topographical behaviors (e.g., head banging and hand biting) can serve the same function (e.g., attention-getting) both within and across children, functional analyses must be conducted on a case-by-case basis. The data from the functional analysis thereby guide a "customized" treatment program for each child, even among those displaying the same target behavior.

Direct observations of target behaviors in which correlated antecedent and consequential events are systematically tracked (but not experimentally manipulated as during a functional analysis), and detailed interviewing of caretakers and teachers of the autistic child about their observations, provide two less costly and more efficient strategies for identifying controlling variables (O'Neill, Horner, Albin, Story, & Sprague, 1990). Unlike the use of screening batteries with psychiatric outpatients, there have been some efforts to evaluate the utility of functional analyses in designing and guiding treatment programs for autistic children and others with pervasive development disorders. The treatment utility of functional analyses appears to be moderated by the severity of behavioral problems being assessed. While programs to modify severe target behaviors based on functional analyses have been shown to be more efficacious than those guided by other means (Nelson-Gray, 2003), such as behavioral observations and assessment interviews, the same pattern does not seem to hold in providing services with children displaying milder developmental disabilities and behavioral problems. For example, English and Anderson (2006) reported that interventions based on descriptive obser-vations of target behaviors as detailed by O'Neill et al. (1990) for three children with developmental delays were more effective than those derived from functional analyses. The children displayed mild intellectual disabilities and appeared to be less severely impaired than participants in other projects investigating the treatment utility of functional analyses (e.g., Repp, Felce, & Barton, 1988).

The evidence base for the treatment utility of functional analyses is sobering. After all, if the one assessment strategy that is widely recognized as the "poster child" for contextualized approaches to psychological assessment has limited treatment utility, how likely is it that the use of other forms of assessment enhance treatment outcome? Our response is that this is an empirical question that can only be addressed by more manipulated assessment experiments and not by generalizing what is known to date about the treatment utility of functional analyses to other measures. To underscore our point, consider the possible treatment utility of projective techniques.

The reliability and validity of projective techniques, when used in unstructured ways, has long been recognized as being weak (Eysenck, 1959; Jensen, 1965). This has led some to argue that projective techniques should not be regarded and evaluated as psychological tests, but as clinical tools (Anastasi & Urbina, 1997). This point of view is similar to, but less expansive than our own that all forms of psychological assessment, including standardized tests, are usefully seen as tools; and also echoes that articulated by proponents of projective techniques. For example, defenders of the Rorschach typically have claimed that its clinical utility outweighs its poor psychometric properties (Meyer, 1999). While some have argued that there is sufficient empirical support for the clinical utility of the Rorschach (Viglione, 1999), others have pointed out that there is an absence of research that has addressed this matter, particularly when applying a strong definition of "clinical utility" that is indistinguishable from treatment utility (Hunsley & Bailey, 1999).

Our "take-home message" at this point is that the treatment utility of the Rorshach, despite claims to the contrary, remains unknown. But with relatively few exceptions (e.g., functional analyses) and in the absence of systematic treatment utility research, the same must be regrettably said both now and in the future about clinical assessment more broadly. With regard to the Rorschach, a manipulated assessment experiment could be conducted where practitioners who routinely use the Rorschach only admin-ister it to a randomly selected subset of their clients. Do those clients who are admin-istered the test show better therapeutic outcomes than the control group clients? If they do, preliminary support would be provided for the treatment utility of the Rorschach, although follow-up experimental research would be necessary to fully understand the effect. Several explanations are plausible, including a placebo, self-fulfilling prophecy type effect related to clinicians' belief that having a Rorschach protocol enables them to be more effective therapists. Would they be just as effective if given bogus protocols? Another possibility is that having access to a completed protocol is not the critical variable; rather the critical variable is the testing itself, during which therapists pick up on more subtle client behavioral cues. Before moving on, we again would remind our readers that the same questions and issues raised about projective techniques also apply to other therapeutic approaches and related forms of assessment. For example, does the use of the Valued Life Questionnaire (VLQ; Wilson, Sandoz, Kitchens, & Roberts, 2010) in guiding committed action homework assignments within acceptance and commitment therapy (ACT; Hayes, Strosahl, & Wilson, 2012) improve treatment outcomes?

Treatment Selection

The term "treatment selection" refers to the process of choosing a preferred therapeutic option from an array of two or more alternatives. It is preceded by treatment determination (e.g., deciding to treat depression) and can provide a therapeutic context within which relevant issues of treatment guidance can also emerge (e.g., use of the VLQ to guide behavioral activation as the treatment selected to treat depression). Treatment selection can be made on the basis of conceptual reasons (e.g., a new approach is consistent with an agency or therapist's theoretical orientation), practical considerations (e.g., the therapist is more familiar with one approach than other options that enjoy the same level of empirical support), or relevant research.

The type of research that we believe is most likely to increase the utility of assessment used for the purpose of treatment selection is that investigating moderating variables, or characteristics that influence the direction or magnitude of the relationships between the independent variable of psychological interventions and the dependent variable of therapeutic outcomes (Kazdin, 2007). Sometimes moderating variables are demographic in nature (e.g. gender, age, racial/ethnic status), such as suggested earlier in our discussion of genomic testing of cancerous tumors, and are of limited psychological relevance except to those who study gender and age-related differences. Other times, as indicated by our overview of the treatment utility of functional analyses, moderating variables (e.g., severity of behavioral problems) are of both psychological and pragmatic importance. Unfortunately, the assessment of moderating psychological variables can be considerably more challenging than evaluating those that are demographic in nature. Not only must the relevant variables themselves first be identified, but ways of assessing them that maximize treatment utility must also either be chosen or developed.

A correlational treatment utility design known as "post hoc identification of dimensions" (Hayes et al., 1986) is one method that can be used to identify psychologically relevant moderating variables associated with therapeutic responsivity. For example, Masuda et al. (2007) and Zettle (2003) reported that those who initially scored high on psychological inflexibility benefited most from ACT, in terms of reduced stigmatizing attitudes and mathematics anxiety, respectively. By contrast, *low* inflexibility was associated with improvement in the mental health of call center employees participating in a work reorganization intervention designed to enhance job control (Bond, Flaxman, & Bunce, 2008). More recently, Forman and colleagues (2013) found that susceptibility to eating cues, depression, and emotional eating positively moderated responsivity to an acceptance-based behavioral treatment for obesity.

Unfortunately, the above findings may be of limited practical utility for at least two reasons. First, while the findings may point to a psychological profile of those who might be preferred candidates for a specific treatment, such as ACT, they don't necessarily directly point to comparably efficacious options for those who are not. To approach this objective, post hoc analyses are preferable within studies in which the therapeutic benefits of two or more interventions have been shown to be essentially equivalent. For example, within a large research program for treatment of depression (Sotsky et al., 1991), low social dysfunction predicted superior response to interpersonal therapy (Klerman, Weissman, Rounsaville, & Chevron, 1984), while low cognitive dysfunction was associated with greater responsivity to cognitive therapy (Beck, Rush, Shaw, & Emery, 1979). Second, while such findings suggest that treatment of depression might be optimized by assessing both the social and cognitive functioning of clients and matching them to therapeutic options on that basis, a manipulated match design would be necessary to empirically evaluate this possibility.

Previous research by one of us (RDZ) provides an illustration of how correlational and experimental treatment utility designs can be combined in the manner described to address the question of whether outcomes can be enhanced by matching client moderating variables to therapeutic options. An initial study found that group and individual cognitive therapy of depression were equally efficacious (Zettle, Hafflich, & Reynolds, 1992). A post hoc analysis, however, indicated that pretreatment scores on the Sociotropy-Autonomy Scale (SAS; Bieling, Beck, & Brown, 2000) were differentially associated with treatment outcome. Specifically, depressed participants high in sociotropy, reflective of relying on social relationships for gratification and support, responded better to group than individual therapy, while their counterparts high in autonomy, or a tendency to derive gratification from personal accomplishments, showed an opposite pattern. Based on these findings, a subsequent manipulated match experiment was conducted in which depressed participants were either matched or mismatched to group versus individual cognitive therapy based on their pretreatment SAS scores (Zettle & Herring, 1995). As expected, a higher proportion of matched participants displayed marked improvement at follow-up, thereby providing empirical support for the treatment utility of the SAS in matching depressed clients to the format of cognitive therapy.

Similar to the previously cited example of genomic testing of cancer cells, knowledge of psychologically relevant variables that moderate psychotherapeutic outcomes may also enable mental health professionals to offer a "personalized approach" with their clients. By assessing such moderating variables, treatment options may be selected that are better matched to individual clients.

Section 3: Treatment Outcome and Process

Psychometrics is one of those areas that appears irrelevant to a practitioner. And it often is. Yet, if you are a practitioner, you are stuck with psychometrics, because if you want to get better at improving people's lives, you need to be able to answer two measurement questions, one concerning outcome and the other involving process.

First, how would we know if we were creating positive outcomes and improving someone's life? What does that even mean? Is "improvement" measured in reductions in anxiety, depression, and self-harm? Does it mean increases in positive indices, such as vitality and resilience? Does it mean activation of value-congruent behavior, regardless of the emotional consequences? Second, how do we know what process, in particular, leads to improvement? That is, what are we doing with our clients that actually produces change? If we cannot measure outcomes and intervention processes hypothesized to lead to those outcomes, it becomes difficult if not impossible for practitioners to become better at their craft.

Outcome Measure Selection

As suggested earlier, psychometric considerations are important in selecting an appropriate measure for assessing treatment outcome.

Reliability. Psychological measures are typically evaluated for their internal as well as temporal consistency. There are several ways of evaluating whether therapeutic change can be considered clinically significant. Test–retest reliability is of particular importance if the reliable change index (RCI) of Jacobson and Truax (1991) is used to do so. Any pre- to post-treatment improvement in an outcome measure should exceed what would be expected by chance given its test–retest reliability. Measures that display higher levels of test–retest reliability accordingly require less of an absolute change for such improvement to be regarded as clinically significant. In selecting an outcome measure, it is important that test–retest reliability is assessed over a span of time comparable to the length of many treatment protocols (e.g., 12 weekly sessions) in order for that reliability estimate to be of most use to the practitioner.

Validity. A significant RCI suggests that the degree of therapeutic change is meaningful and unlikely to be an artifact of the temporal instability of the particular measure used to assess it. However, such a finding does not address the question of what exactly has changed as a result of the intervention. Discriminant validity (Campbell & Fiske, 1959) may be of particular importance in helping the practitioner identify specific ingredients of change.

Recall our earlier discussion of common versus unique variance in an assertiveness inventory containing items that assess both assertiveness and rumination. The inventory might fail to demonstrate sufficiently discriminant validity by being correlated too highly with a questionnaire such as the Ruminative Response Scale (Nolen-Hoeksema, Morrow, & Fredrickson, 1993). Such a finding should be of concern to both the basic researcher and the clinician. For the basic researcher, the construct validity of the assertiveness inventory comes into question. For the practitioner, the concern is more practical. If the goal of therapy was to increase assertiveness, does reliable change in the assertiveness inventory mean that this goal was attained or does this apparent improvement instead reflect reduced rumination? One strategy to minimize this issue is to develop measures that are unidimensional and are sensitive to change in the therapeutic target. Another strategy is to administer multiple outcome measures, with some being specific to the goal of therapy and others being of less relevance to that objective. For example, an ACT intervention for depression might assess for reductions in both depression and anxiety.

Process Measure Selection

Let's now take a more detailed look at how traditional psychometrics can aid the practical goal of understanding what process or mechanism might account for therapeutic change. If changes in a process measure, such as a defusion inventory, can be shown to mediate therapeutic improvement (e.g., lessened depression) by reliably preceding it, repeated administration of it provides useful feedback to practitioners. Reductions in defusion suggest that the therapy is having its intended effect, even if similar reductions in depression are not yet apparent, and that it is advisable to "stay the course."

Intervention packages such as ACT and CBT include many possible "ingredients." Process research can help the practitioner hone in on which of these ingredients is most essential to positive outcomes. For example, ACT has shown that positive change occurs by promoting psychological flexibility and not experiential control (Dalrymple & Herbert, 2007). ACT also has been show to target different processes than CBT (see Ciarrochi, Bilich, & Godsel, 2010, for a review). CBT appears to promote self-confidence and not psychological flexibility, whereas the reverse is true for ACT (Lappalainen et al., 2007). Research on mindfulness-based cognitive therapy suggests that promoting self-compassion may be the key to therapeutic change (Kuyken et al., 2010).

Given the potential utility of process measures, it is worth taking a closer look at the psychometrics used to develop them. Figure 16.1 illustrates a traditional psychometric measurement model involving three possible process variables: (a) psychological flexibility, (b) mindfulness, and (c) optimism. Items 1 through 6 are observed indicators, or more simply items from the flexibility and mindfulness scales. According to psychometric theory, these indicators are assumed to be caused by underlying, correlated latent constructs, indicated by circles. Thus, psychological flexibility influences how people respond to items 1 through 3 and mindfulness influences items 4 through 6. In the below figure, items 3 and 5 are unintentionally linked to a third latent variable, optimism. This kind of crossloading is common (Marsh et al., 2009). Given that there

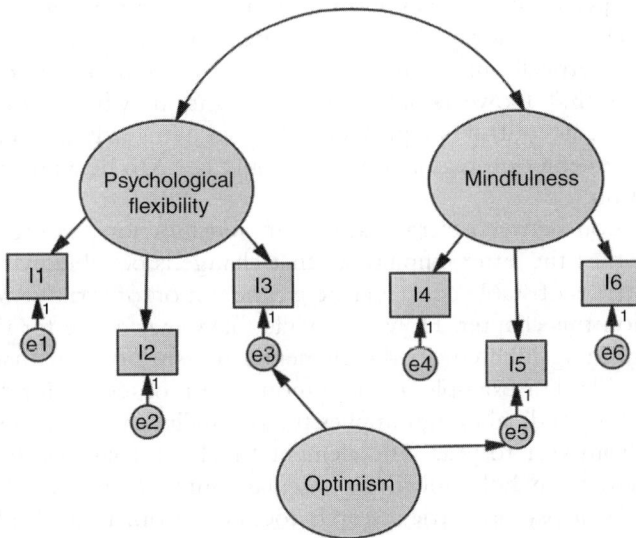

Figure 16.1   Hypothetical psychometric measurement model.

are thousands of constructs, it is unlikely any test item a human can create will be an indicator of one and only one process variable. For example, the first item from the measure of psychological flexibility – "I am in control of my life" – is likely to reflect both flexibility and self-efficacy.

The quality of a measurement model from a psychometric perspective can be assessed via fit indices (Hooper, Coughlan, & Mullen, 2008). For example, imagine that optimism was not represented in the Figure 16.1 model. Then, the constraint would be that items 1 through 3 are caused only by psychological flexibility, and items 4 through 6 are caused only by mindfulness. This model is likely to fit poorly, because the correlation between the unique variance in item 3 (E3) and item 5 (E5) is constrained to be 0. There are many other constraints in Figure 16.1 that might be incorrect, such as the constraint that E1 does not correlate with E4. In general, the more parameters that are incorrectly constrained to be 0, the worse the model fit.

Measurement model evaluation allows us to assess the extent that items and factors (psychological flexibility and mindfulness) overlap. It allows the practitioner to ask questions like, "If the therapy I provide targets psychological flexibility, am I also likely to increase mindfulness?" If someone claims that an intervention such as ACT works by increasing psychological flexibility, then the measurement model in Figure 16.1 would suggest that an alternative interpretation needs to be explored. Perhaps the intervention works by increasing optimism. Thus, a clear measurement model, when combined with intervention outcomes, can guide the practitioner toward what is and is not being changed in a client.

When we look at assessment through the lens of functional contextualism we often respond negatively to the typical measurement model in Figure 16.1, because it seems to imply that there are latent, unchanging things that underpin responses. We assume that the responses to items on an inventory are just behavior under the influence of context, and therefore often can be altered, sometimes even rapidly, by changing controlling variables. For example, it may be possible for an intervention like ACT to alter the very structure of the measure. Imagine an inventory that has two items: (a) "I am able to persist at my goals, even when I feel distressed" and (b) "I am able to control my feelings." Prior to therapy, these items are likely to be positively correlated and psychometrically might be said to reflect an underlying construct called "emotion regulation." However, after the intervention, when people have been taught that emotional control is a problem, the two items may no longer correlate. Thus, the two-item emotion regulation scale would cease to be a reliable estimate of emotion regulation.

One basic tension between elemental realism and functional contextualism often comes down to this: the latter emphasizes that change is possible, while the former often speaks in terms of stable constructs, e.g., the notion of "true scores" discussed in the first section this chapter. However, while many may argue for the stability of traits, there is nothing inherent in the elemental realism position that implies that change is impossible. For example, the common notion of testing for "measurement invariance" in a longitudinal design implies the possibility that measures may change their structure from year to year. The elemental realist recognizes that a particular measurement model may hold only in a particular context (time and place).

In summary, classic psychometric research does not automatically lead to treatment utility, but there is no reason why it can't support treatment utility. Practitioners need to be able to assess outcomes and processes of change in order to be able to identify what is and is not working. If a measure does not meet traditional psychometric standards, or the measurement model is mis-specified, then the practitioner is unlikely to get precise, useful information from the measure. For example, if a measure of mindfulness lacks predictive validity, it is unlikely that changing responses to that measure will cause positive outcomes. If two therapies claim to be distinct, but the measures of their core process variables and purported mechanisms of change lack discriminant validity, then researchers within each therapy type will have a great deal of trouble showing distinctiveness. Finally, if a measure is heterogeneous and reflects many constructs, then it will be hard to interpret the meaning of scores, and if an intervention changes those scores, it will be hard to know exactly what changed. There is nothing so practical as reliable and valid measures in determining how and if a desired therapeutic goal has been realized.

Identifying processes of change in longitudinal research. For a process measure to mediate treatment outcome, three conditions need to be met. First, the measure must be correlated with the outcome. Second, measures of suspected processes must be shown to temporally precede, or be antecedent to the outcome. Third, one must rule out the possibility that a third variable accounts for the relationship between the process measure and the outcome.

It is commonly thought that experiments are always the best method for satisfying all three of these conditions. Random assignment supposedly solves the third variable problem, by distributing the unmeasured third variable equally between conditions. In Section 1 of this chapter, we provided examples of strong experimental designs for evaluating treatment utility. However, experimental designs get somewhat more difficult when it comes to analyzing complex questions, and experiments don't always have the perfect answer (Bullock, Green, & Ha, 2010). Let's say that you show that an ACT intervention improves psychological flexibility, and psychological flexibility mediates the relationship between intervention and some positive outcomes such as emotional well-being. If we assume randomization worked perfectly, then it is reasonable to conclude that the intervention caused changes in the mediator and outcome. However, to have strong support for mediation, we must also show that the intervention affected only psychological flexibility and no other mediator (Bullock et al., 2010). In the above example, there could be an unmeasured mediator that explains the link between psychological flexibility and emotional well-being. For example, perhaps the intervention increased clients' sense of hope. If changes in hope correlate with changes in flexibility, then it may be hope is promoting outcome, rather than psychological flexibility.

We, therefore, do not see experiments as the only tool for addressing causal questions. Rather, we propose that longitudinal designs can complement the experimental designs. Because longitudinal research does not manipulate variables, it is always subject to the criticism that a third variable could explain the link between the hypothesized antecedent and consequent variable. Controlling for confounds can reduce, but never completely eliminate, the third variable problem.

However, longitudinal designs have at least two strengths. First, one can examine a wide range of therapeutic process variables in a single study. For example, one could look at the effects of self-compassion, self-esteem, mindfulness, hope, and psychological flexibility on the positive transition from high school to adult life. It would be difficult for an experimental paradigm to simultaneously manipulate each of these five explanatory variables. The longitudinal design is excellent at narrowing down the possible list of process variables that are relevant to any outcome. Those variables that uniquely predict positive change are identified as candidates for further intervention research.

A second strength of a longitudinal design is that it can be used to detect heterogeneity in effects between participants. One difficulty with much experimental mediational research is that it assumes that links between intervention, mediator, and outcome are the same for all participants. If there is heterogeneity in links, then conclusions based on the average subject response can be misleading (McNulty & Fincham, 2011). Longitudinal designs with many repeated measures can be used to identify heterogeneity by estimating the positive effects of the mediator (say increased psychological flexibility) on the outcome within subject. Then we can set about identifying the contextual factors that predict benefit or lack of benefit for different types of clients, and we can potentially use this information to guide experimental, treatment utility research.

It is also possible to combine experimental and longitudinal designs by utilizing interventions that repeatedly manipulate the mediator and the outcome (Bullock et al., 2010). For example, one could repeatedly manipulate daily mindfulness and examine daily positive affect. This approach would allow one to assess the effect of mindfulness interventions within subject, and thus identify those who fail to respond to the intervention and identify the contextual factors that predict such failure. Like all designs, this design has its assumptions, including assumptions that within-person effects don't change and that the effect of the mediator on the outcome has worn off before the next manipulation is administered (Bullock et al., 2010).

Ecological momentary assessment. Ecological momentary assessment (EMA) refers to a cluster of longitudinal data collection approaches that include experience sampling methods (ESM), ambulatory assessment, and diary methods. In an EMA study, data are collected from individuals in real world environments as they go about their daily life, resulting in greater *ecological* validity than other methodological approaches (Shiffman, Stone, & Hufford, 2008). The assessments are *momentary*, focusing either on the current state of an individual's experience, or very recent states, thus minimizing the impact of retrospective biases. There are several strengths of EMA for the contextual behavioral scientist.

Assessing variability of behavior. One index of flexible responding is variability. Does the client use the same response in every situation (inflexible) or do responses vary from situation to situation? EMA allows one to assess not just the mean of responses, but also the variability of response, a statistic that is impossible to calculate in a one-off trait measure (Kashdan, Ferssizidis, Collins, & Muraven, 2010).

Linking changes in context to changes in outcomes. EMA can be used to measure antecedent events in people's lives, their behavioral reactions to those events (e.g., coping strategies), and the consequences of those behavioral reactions (e.g., levels of stress, mental health, affect, value-consistent behavior, etc.). See Delespaul and van Os (2002) for an illustration. For example, EMA can be used to record the extent that people experience daily positive and negative social interactions, their coping response (e.g., reappraisal, mindfulness, suppression), and the consequence of those responses on their mental health. In many ways, this data collection mimics the data collected on the traditional thought record that is used by many therapeutic traditions as a means of assessing and building awareness of *in the moment* chains of experience.

EMA as a clinical intervention. A small but growing literature focuses on extending EMA methods to clinical intervention research. This literature can be broken down into examining the use of EMA for the purposes of *assessment* versus its use as an *intervention*. Using EMA as an assessment tool with clients engaged in psychotherapy can be useful for many of the same reasons that single-case methodologies are popular among clinicians. Such assessment methods can have the impact of increasing client motivation through consistent monitoring, and can be based on behaviors and experiences (processes) that are derived from a client's clinical formulation (Shiffman et al., 2008). EMA data allow for the analyses of the therapy process as it occurs, revealing possible opportunities for intervention, or for "taking stock" at given points so as to aid clinical decision-making regarding the progress of therapy (Cohen et al., 2008).

The use of the EMA methodology as an *intervention* strategy has the potential to bring the therapy room more closely into the client's life. Recently, Heron and Smyth (2010) systematically reviewed 27 EMA intervention studies (EMIs) that had provided treatment for such problems as smoking cessation, weight loss, anxiety disorders, diabetes self-management, eating disorder symptoms, and general health behaviors (e.g., exercise). The review found evidence that EMI can be effectively implemented across a range of clinical problems and health conditions, and that the method has high acceptability among clients. Of note, trials of cognitive behavioral therapy (CBT) with and without supplementary EMI for anxiety disorders and weight loss have found that in general, clients in CBT+EMI groups are able to achieve the same levels of treatment efficacy as standalone CBT with approximately half of the face-to-face sessions, and that EMI augmentation improved the overall efficacy of the face-to-face interventions.

Section 4: Mapping Interventions to Measures: A Field Guide

Self-report measures are the most widely used means of evaluating interventions. They are also the most regularly criticized (Haeffel & Howard, 2010). Many view them as inherently biased and less valid than behavioral or biological measures. We shall argue here, though, that the case is not so simple. Self-reports can be considered behavioral samples, just like those obtained from observing behavior or measuring blood pressure. As such, they are neither inherently superior nor inferior to other behavioral methods. It is clear that self-reports can be valid measures of moods, attributions, plans, attitudes, and beliefs, and can be as good or even better predictors of behavior than behavioral measures (Haeffel & Howard, 2010). We are not saying that all self-report measures are created equally, only that they cannot be treated as inherently worse than other types of measures. Each method of measurement is likely to have its strengths and weaknesses.

The biggest challenge in discussing measures is that there are so many of them, and we don't always know how they relate to each other or how they relate to particular interventions. Gross's (1998; 2002) process model of emotional regulation provides one organizing framework. According to this model, emotion can be regulated at several stages. Antecedent-focused regulation involves strategies that occur before emotional responses become fully activated, and includes altering the situation (situation selection or modification) and altering responses to the situation (attentional deployment and cognitive change, or reappraisal). Response-focused strategies refer to what the person does once the emotion is underway, such as hiding expressive behavior, suppressing emotions, and using drugs or exercise to alter the physiological components of emotion.

Gross's model has one major limitation from a contextual behavioral science (CBS) perspective. It puts emotion regulation at the center of the measurement universe, whereas a CBS proponent would put behavior at the center. The Gross perspective emphasizes the idea that emotions are the key therapeutic challenge and the central question is how are emotions moderated, downregulated, hidden, and managed? In contrast, a contextualist approach views behavioral activation as the key therapeutic challenge, and the central question is, how do we help people to behave flexibly in a way that increases their sense of meaning, purpose, and vitality? The regulation of emotion, as defined by Gross, may be a subset of factors that influence value-consistent action, but would not include everything of relevance.

As an alternative to the Gross emotion regulation model, we present the choice point model of behavioral regulation (Ciarrochi, Bailey, & Harris, 2014). This model makes use of some of the Gross distinctions, but puts valued behavior as the primary outcome. The model is illustrated in Figure 16.2, along with hypothesized measures that map to each process type in the model (see Appendix for measure references).

A choice point is a moment in time when it is possible to choose between values-consistent and values-inconsistent behavior. This model begins with an understanding of the situation (bottom of model), which describes when, where, and in what circumstances the client finds it challenging to engage in values-based behavior. Some examples might be a divorce, a problem at work, a medical diagnosis, death of a loved one, an upcoming exam or speech, a past regrettable action, a "temptation," and so on. Problem-solving therapy and stimulus control (e.g., removing the temptation) are ways of modifying or improving the situation (Nezu & Nezu, 2001).

Not every situation can be modified, and so, when faced with a challenging situation, we often experience difficult thoughts and feelings, such as sadness, anxiety, hopelessness, and self-criticism, as illustrated in the lower left corner of Figure 16.2. These are the typical clinical outcomes assessed in randomized control trials. We make a distinction between verbal behavior that is relatively "explicit," slow and elaborated, and is generally measured with self-report measures, and verbal behavior that is relatively "implicit," quick and immediate, and measured using reaction time tasks (Barnes-Holmes, Barnes-Holmes, Stewart, & Boles, 2010). The elaborated verbal responses are presumably more susceptible to social desirable responding than the brief responses.

The lower right corner panel of Figure 16.2 illustrates our responses to the situation and to the inner experience, and these responses can be roughly mapped to different therapy types. Traditional cognitive behavior therapy emphasizes the direct modification of the form or frequency of inner experiences, through interventions such as cognitive reappraisal, reframing, and practicing positive coping statements (Beck, 1995; Ciarrochi & Bailey, 2008). Mindfulness-based therapies such as ACT de-emphasize the direct modifying of inner experience, and instead focus on helping clients respond flexibly to inner experience and the situation (Hayes, Strosahl, & Wilson, 2012). Thus, people learn to have difficult thoughts and feelings, as they are, without modification,

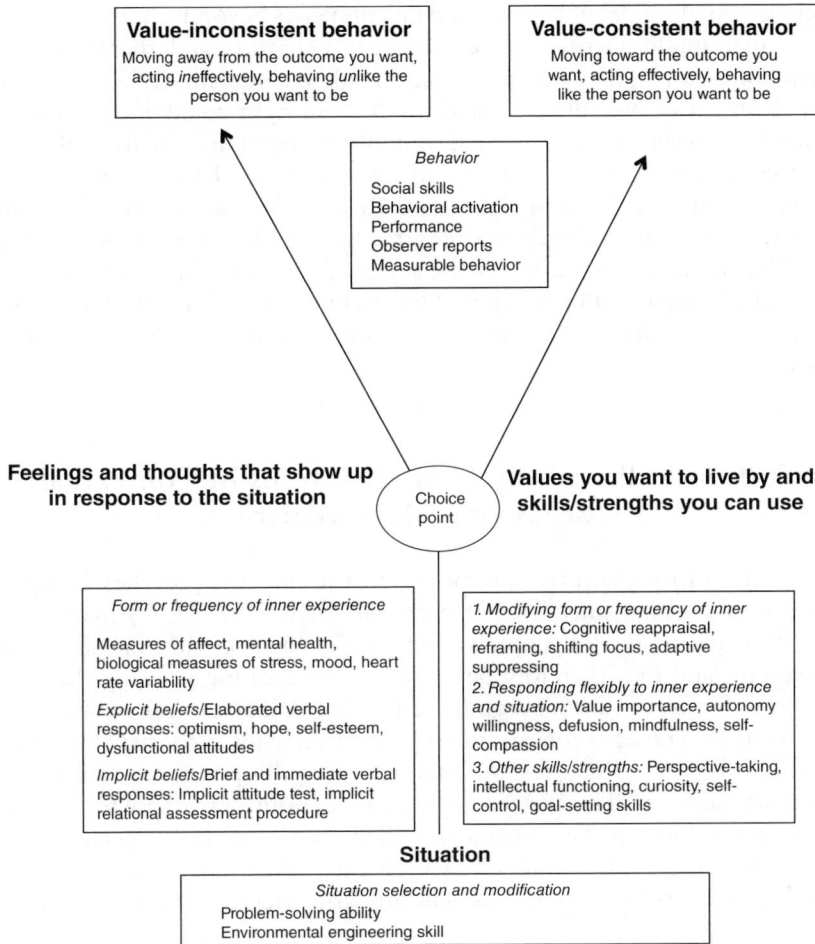

Figure 16.2 Choice point model and points of measurement and intervention.

and to choose value-consistent action. Finally, a host of interventions, such as those found in positive psychology, seek to promote a wide range of skills and strengths, such as self-control, perspective-taking, and goal-setting (Kashdan & Ciarrochi, 2013). It is important to note that most therapies probably target all three of the value/skill/ strength components in the bottom right panel of Figure 16.2. They differ perhaps only in emphasis.

Note that the choice point model makes no a priori assumption as to whether a particular strategy or skill is inherently good or bad. Thus, suppression, in some contexts may support value-consistent behavior, whereas other times it may promote value-inconsistent behavior. Each skill and strength on the right side of the model is tied to the situation in which it is used and the consequences of using it (value-consistent versus value-inconsistent). For example, if suppressing was a toxic strategy for a particular client in a particular context, it would not be listed under the skills/strengths side of the choice point. For more examples on using the choice point model in interventions, please see Ciarrochi et al. (2014).

This choice point model of behavioral regulation goes beyond emotions to capturing any factor that might increase value-consistent behaviors and therefore might be measured. For example, the bottom left panel could include unhelpful beliefs and rules ("I must never eat carbohydrates"), and the bottom right could encompass a skill to undermine the power of that rule (e.g., mindfully stepping back from the rule and noticing that it doesn't force you to act in a certain way.) There are many skills that could appear within the bottom right panel that do not have to do with regulating feelings, such as empathy, character strengths, transcendent sense of self, intellectual skills, etc. The model is not intended to be a map of physical structures in the brain, but rather a practical map of different types of intervention and intervention measurement. Please see the Appendix for measures that appear to map to each part of the choice point model.

Section 5: Promising New Directions in Contextual Behavioral Measurement

This final section focuses on two promising measurement approaches for contextual behavioral science. First, measures of heart rate variability (HRV) may provide an objective, biological index of people's ability to flexibly respond to positive and negative situations, and may therefore be an important tool for assessing the biological consequences of interventions. Second, the Implicit Relational Assessment Procedure (IRAP) provides an observation measure of verbal behavior, a construct that is central to all cognitive behavior therapies, but that has, up to this point, been largely assessed via self-report measures. The IRAP may be a useful, nonreactive tool for assessing the effect of interventions on client attitudes, beliefs, and other verbal behavior. Because other chapters within this handbook (see chapters 9 and 10) discuss the IRAP in greater detail, our coverage of it here will primarily focus on its possible use within clinical assessment.

Heart Rate Variability (HRV)

HRV is a measure of beat-to-beat temporal changes in heart rate. HRV reflects the output of the central autonomic network that comprises the prefrontal cortex, cingulate cortex, insula, amygdala, and brainstem regions (Kemp & Quintana, 2013). Heart rate variability can be low because of excessive activity of the sympathetic system, underactivity of the parasympathetic system, or both. Low HRV, then, can be understood as reduced differentiation between contexts that elicit parasympathetic activity (i.e., positive) and those that elicit sympathetic activity (negative). For example, imagine a workaholic on a beach, stressing about a deadline, insensitive to all the peace, calm, and beauty around him. Consistent with this interpretation of HRV, Ruiz-Padial, Sollers, Vila, and Thayer (2003) found that those with highest HRV showed the most differentiated emotion-modulated start effects, with little startle response to pleasant pictures, more response for neutral pictures, and the greatest response to negative pictures. In general, HRV has been linked to low self-regulatory strength, reduced motivation to engage in social situations, and lower psychological flexibility in the face of stressors (Appelhans & Luecken, 2006;

Kemp & Quintana, 2013; Segerstrom & Nes, 2007). In the long run, lower HRV leads to reduced immune function, inflammation, cardiovascular disease, and mortality (Kemp & Quintana, 2013).

We believe measuring HRV has several strengths within contextual behavioral intervention approaches. First, it appears to be a biological measure of sensitivity to positive, neutral, and negative contexts. CBS interventions such as ACT are intended to increase responsiveness to environmental feedback, and so HRV would seem to be an excellent way of assessing this outcome. Second, HRV does not rely on self-report and is therefore relatively objective and difficult to fake. Third, HRV links broadly to both physical and psychological health. Thus, if a practitioner seeks to improve both physical and psychological functioning, HRV may offer a simple index of improvement.

Implicit Relational Assessment Procedure

Relational frame theory (RFT) emphasizes the importance of learning and applying relational frames in human language and cognition (Hayes, Barnes-Holmes, & Roche, 2001). The Implicit Relational Assessment Procedure (IRAP) provides a method for directly observing and recording verbal behavior, and variables that influence that behavior (Barnes-Holmes, Barnes-Holmes, et al., 2010; Hayes, Barnes-Holmes, & Wilson, 2012). A number of studies have demonstrated the utility of the IRAP in domains such as food preferences (Barnes-Holmes, Murtagh, Barnes Holmes, & Stewart, 2010), depression (Hussey & Barnes-Holmes, 2012), self-esteem (Timko, England, Herbert, & Forman, 2010), eating disorders (Parling, Cernvall, Stewart, Barnes-Holmes, & Ghaderi, 2012), and formation of new attitudes (Hughes & Barnes-Holmes, 2011). The IRAP also appears to be very difficult to fake, which offers a potential advantage of this method over questionnaires, interviews, and implicit cognition measures (McKenna, Barnes-Holmes, Barnes-Holmes, & Stewart, 2007).

The Implicit Association Test (IAT) offers an alternative to the IRAP (Greenwald, McGhee, & Schwartz, 1998), but it does have a major limitation from a behavioral perspective. It infers attitudes by taking the difference between negative responses (e.g., "Thin people are bad") and positive response ("Thin people are good"). From a CBS perspective, these are two different behaviors, not two items reflecting a single hidden construct called "attitude." If one uses the IAT and finds no evidence for a negative attitude, this does not indicate the absence of positive and negative responses. A null result in the IAT could mean that people either have no verbal reactions to thin people or they could have anti-thin and pro-thin reactions. In the latter case, the two responses would counteract each other and amount to no bias in the IAT. In contrast, the IRAP would be able to detect both responses. For example, Roddy, Stewart, and Barnes-Holmes (2010) found that the overall IRAP score correlated significantly with the IAT, suggesting pro-slim/anti-fat attitudes. However, the IRAP included four trial types that showed that the participants demonstrated a so-called "pro-slim" response, but there was no "anti-fat" response.

Concerning the potential link between the IRAP and therapy, the IRAP has been used to predict treatment outcome for cocaine dependence (Carpenter, Martinez, Vadhan, Barnes-Holmes, & Nunes, 2012) and increases in weight, body dissatisfaction, and disordered eating over a span of 7.8 months (Juarascio et al., 2011). Cullen, Barnes-Holmes, and Barnes-Holmes (2009) found that presenting pictures of admired old people influenced how participants responded on the IRAP. The images reduced the pro-young IRAP effect, and reversed the anti-old IRAP effect, that was maintained when retested 24 hours later. Also, Hooper, Villatte, Neofotistou, and McHugh (2010) found that a mindfulness induction influenced performance on an experiential avoidance IRAP; the mindfulness group experienced lower levels of experiential avoidance after the induction when compared to a thought suppression group. Hence, the IRAP offers CBS researchers a way to objectively measure verbal behavior and examine the influence of context on that behavior.

Summary and Conclusions

With the recent passing of Gordon Paul, we are reminded of the challenging question he posed to clinical researchers and practitioners now nearly a half century ago: "What treatment, by whom, is most effective for this individual, with that specific problem, under which set of circumstances, and how does it come about?" (Paul, 1969, p. 44). This chapter sought to provide answers to most parts of this question (except that dealing with "by whom" or ideal therapist characteristics).

Our discussion of treatment determination and guidance addressed the question, "*What treatment* with what *specific problem* is likely to be the most effective?" Our discussion of moderating variables addressed the question of "What is likely to be *most effective for a particular individual.*" None of these questions, of course, can be adequately answered without the administration of reliable and valid outcome measures. In addition, if we do have sound outcome measures and demonstrate positive outcomes, we then also must have psychometrically sound process measures to address the question, "*How does it come about?*"

Considerable progress has been made over the past five decades in providing empirically based answers to Paul's question. This is the good news. The bad news is that addressing the question is an ongoing process and there is still much more critical work to be done by both clinical researchers and practitioners. There are, for example, still remarkably few treatment utility studies, and we don't know the extent that measures improve treatment outcomes. Our belief is that contextual behavioral science can make a significant contribution in improving the utility of clinical assessment. Our hope is that this chapter may make at least a small contribution to this larger process.

Appendix: Process and Example Measures

Situation Selection and Modification

D'Zurilla, T., Nezu, A., & Maydeu-Olivares, A. (2004). Social problem solving: Theory and assessment. In E. Change, T. D'Zurilla, & L. Sannna (Eds.), *Social problem solving: Theory, research, and training* (pp. 11–27). Washington, DC: American Psychological Association.

Form and Frequency of Inner Experience

Mental Health and Well-Being

Diener, E., Emmons, R. A., Larsen, R J., & Griffin, S. (1985). The Satisfaction with Life Scale. *Journal of Personality Assessment, 49*, 71–75.

Goldberg, D. (1978). *Manual of the General Health Questionnaire.* Windsor, England: National Foundation for Education Research.

Keyes, C. (2006). Mental health in adolescence: Is America's youth flourishing. *The American Journal of Orthopsychiatry, 76*, 395–402.

Lovibond, S., & Lovibond, P. (1995). *Manual for the Depression Anxiety Stress Scales.* Sydney, Australia: Psychology Foundation of Australia.

Implict Beliefs/Brief and Immediate Verbal Responses

Barnes-Holmes, D., Murtagh, L., Barnes Holmes, Y., & Stewart, I. (2010). Using the Implicit Association Test and the Implicit Relational Assessment Procedure to measure attitudes towards meat and vegetables in vegetarians and meat-eaters. *The Psychological Record, 60*, 287–306.

Bosson, J. K., Swann, W. B., & Pennebaker, J. W. (2000). Stalking the perfect measure of implicit self-esteem: The blind men and the elephant revisited? *Journal of Personality and Social Psychology, 79*, 631–43.

Explicit Beliefs/Elaborated Verbal Responses

Brown, G. P., Hammen, C. L., Craske, M. G., & Wickens, T. D. (1995). Dimensions of dysfunctional attitudes as vulnerabilities to depressive symptoms. *Journal of Abnormal Psychology, 104*, 431–435.

Rosenberg, M. (1965). *Society and the adolescent self-image.* Princeton, NJ: Princeton University Press.

Snyder, C. R., Harris, C., Anderson, J. R., Holleran, S. A., Irving, L. M., Sigmon, S. T., ... Harney, P. (1991). The will and the ways: Development and validation of an individual-differences measure of hope. *Journal of Personality and Social Psychology, 60*, 570–585.

Efforts to Modify Form or Frequency of Inner Experience

Carver, C. S., Scheier, M. F., & Weintraub, J. K. (1989). Assessing coping strategies: A theoretically based approach. *Journal of Personality and Social Psychology, 56*, 267–283.

Gratz, K. L., & Roemer, L. (2008). Multidimensional assessment of emotion regulation and dysregulation: Development, factor structure, and initial validation of the difficulties in Emotion Regulation Scale. *Journal of Psychopathology and Behavioral Assessment, 26*, 41–54.

Gross, J. J., & John, O. P. (2003). Individual differences in two emotion regulationprocesses: Implications for affect, relationships, and well-being. *Journal of Personality and Social Psychology, 85*, 348–362.

Responding Flexibly to Inner Experience

Baer, R. A., Smith, G. S., Hopkins, J., Krietemeyer, J., & Toney, L. (2006). Using self-report assessment methods to explore facets of mindfulness. *Assessment, 13*, 27–45.

Bond, F. W., Hayes, S. C., Baer, R. A., Carpenter, K. M., Guenole, N., Orcutt, H. K., ... Zettle, R. D. (2011). Preliminary psychometric properties of the Acceptance and Action Questionnaire – II: A revised measure of psychological flexibility and experiential avoidance. *Behavior Therapy, 42*, 676–688.

Forman, E., Herbert, J., Juarascio, A., Yeomans, P., Zebell, J., Goetter, E., & Moitra, E. (2012). The Drexel Defusion Scale: A new measure of experiential distancing. *Journal of Contextual Behavioral Science, 1*, 55–65.

Neff, K. D. (2003). The development and validation of a scale to measure self- compassion. *Self and Identity, 2*, 223–250.

Values and Personal Strivings

Sheldon, K. M., & Kasser, T.. (2001). Goals, congruence, and positive well-being: New empirical support for humanistic theories. *Journal of Humanistic Psychology, 41*, 30–50.

Veage, S., Ciarrochi, J., & Heaven, P. C. L. (2011). Importance, pressure, and success: Dimensions of values and their links to personality. *Personality and Individual Differences, 50*, 1180–1185.

Wilson, K. G., Sandoz, E. K., Kitchens, J., & Roberts, M. E. (2010). The Valued Living Questionnaire: Defining and measuring valued action within a behavioral framework. *The Psychological Record, 60*, 249–272.

Other Skills/Strengths

Davis, M. (1983). Measuring individual differences in empathy: Evidence for a multidimensional approach. *Journal of Personality and Social Psychology, 44*, 113–126.

Peterson, C., & Seligman, M. E. P. (2004). *Character strengths and virtues: A handbook and classification*. New York, NY and Washington, DC: Oxford University Press and American Psychological Association.

Observable Behavior

Manos, R. C., Kanter, J. W., & Busch, A. M. (2010). A critical review of assessment strategies to measure the behavioral activation model of depression. *Clinical Psychology Review, 30*, 547–561.

Smither, J. W., London, M., & Reilly, R. R. (2005). Does performance improve following multisource feedback? A theoretical model, meta-analysis, and review of empirical findings. *Personnel Psychology, 58*, 33–66.

Note: Many of the measures mentioned in the values section assess value-consistent activity.

References

American Educational Research Association (1999). *Standards for educational and psychological testing*. Washington, DC: Author.

Anastasi, A, & Urbina, S. (1997). *Psychological testing* (7th ed.). Upper Saddle, NJ: Pearson.

Andre, F., Bachelot, T., Commo, F., Campone, M., Arnedos, M., Dieras, V., … Bonnefoi, H. (2014). Comparative genomic hybridisation array and DNA sequencing to direct treatment of metatastic breast cancer: A multicentre, prospective trial (SAFIRO1/UNICANCER). *Lancet Oncology, 15*, 267–274.

Appelhans, B. M., & Luecken, L. J. (2006). Heart rate variability as an index of regulated emotional responding. *Review of General Psychology, 10*, 229–240.

Barnes-Holmes, D., Barnes-Holmes, Y., Stewart, I., & Boles, S. (2010). A sketch of the implicit relational assessment procedure (IRAP) and the relational elaboration and coherence model (REC). *The Psychological Record, 60*, 527–542.

Barnes-Holmes, D., Murtagh, L., Barnes-Holmes, Y., & Stewart, I. (2010). Using the Implicit Association Test and the Implicit Relational Assessment Procedure to measure attitudes towards meat and vegetables in vegetarians and meat-eaters. *The Psychological Record, 60*, 287–306.

Beck, J. S. (1995). *Cognitive therapy: Basics and beyond*. New York, NY: Guilford.

Beck, A. T., Rush, A. J., Shaw, B. F., & Emery, G. (1979). *Cognitive therapy of depression.* New York, NY: Guilford.

Beck, A. T., Weissman, A., Lester, D., & Trexler, L. (1974). Measurement of pessimism: The Hopelessness Scale. *Journal of Consulting and Clinical Psychology, 42,* 861–865.

Bieling, P. J., Beck, A. T., & Brown, G. K. (2000). The Sociotropy–Autonomy Scale: Structure and implications. *Cognitive Therapy and Research, 24,* 763–780.

Bond, F. W., Flaxman, P. E., & Bunce, D. (2008). The influence of psychological flexibility on work redesign: Mediated moderation of a work reorganization intervention. *Journal of Applied Psychology, 93,* 645–634.

Bullock, J., Green, D., & Ha, S. (2010). Yes, but what's the mechanism? (Don't expect an easy answer). *Journal of Personality and Social Psychology, 98,* 550–558.

Butcher, J. N., Dahlstrom, W. G., Graham, J. R., Tellegen, A., & Kaemmer, B. (1989). *Minnesota Multiphasic Personality Inventory-2 (MMPI-2): Manual for administration and scoring.* Minneapolis, MN: University of Minnesota Press.

Campbell, D. T., & Fiske, D. W. (1959). Convergent and discriminant validation by the multitrait-multimethod matrix. *Psychological Bulletin, 56,* 81–105.

Carpenter, K. M., Martinez, D., Vadhan, N., Barnes-Holmes, D., & Nunes, E. V. (2012). Measures of attentional bias and relational responding are associated with behavioral treatment outcome for cocaine dependence. *The American Journal of Drug and Alcohol Abuse, 38,* 146–154.

Ciarrochi, J., & Bailey, A. (2008). *A CBT-practicioner's guide to ACT: How to bridge the gap between cognitive behavioral therapy and acceptance and commitment therapy.* Oakland, CA: New Harbinger.

Ciarrochi, J., Bailey, A., & Harris, R. (2014). *The weight escape.* Sydney, Australia: Penguin.

Ciarrochi, J. Bilich, L., & Godsel, C. (2010). Psychological flexibility as a mechanism of change in acceptance and commitment therapy. In R. Baer (Ed.), *Assessing mindfulness and acceptance: Illuminating the processes of change* (pp. 51–76). Oakland, CA: New Harbinger.

Cohen, L. H., Gunthert, K., Butler, A., Parrish, B., Wenze, S., & Beck, J. (2008). Negative affective spillover from daily events predicts early response to cognitive therapy for depression. *Journal of Consulting and Clinical Psychology, 76,* 955.

Cullen, C., Barnes-Holmes, D., & Barnes-Holmes, Y. (2009). The implicit relational assessment procedure (IRAP) and the malleability of ageist attitudes. *The Psychological Record, 59,* 591–620.

Dalrymple, K. L., & Herbert, J. D. (2007). Acceptance and commitment therapy for generalized social anxiety disorder: A pilot study. *Behavior Modification, 31,* 543–568.

Delespaul, P., & van Os, J. (2002). Determinants of occurrence and recovery from hallucinations in daily life. *Social Psychiatry and Psychiatric Epidemiology, 37,* 97–104.

English, C. L., & Anderson, C. M. (2006). Evaluation of the treatment utility of the analog functional analysis and the structured descriptive assessment. *Journal of Positive Behavior Interventions, 8,* 212–229.

Eysenck, H. J. (1959). Review of the Rorschach Inkblot Test. In O. K. Buros (Ed.), *The fifth mental measurements yearbook* (pp. 276–278). Highland Park, NJ: Gryphon Press.

Farber, B. A., Berano, K. C., & Capobianco, J. A. (2004). Clients' perceptions of the process and consequences of self-disclosure in psychotherapy. *Journal of Counseling Psychology, 51,* 340–346.

Ferster, C. (1965). Classification of behavior pathology. In L. Krasner & L. P. Ullman (Eds.), *Research in behavior modification* (pp. 6–26). New York, NY: Holt, Rinehart & Winston.

Forman, E. M., Butryn, M. L., Juarascio, A. S., Bradley, L. E., Lowe, M. R., Herbert, J. D., & Shaw, J. A. (2013). The Mind Your Health Project: A randomized controlled trial of an innovative behavioral treatment for obesity. *Obesity, 21,* 1119–1126.

Greenwald, A., McGhee, D., & Schwartz, J. (1998). Measuring individual differences in implicit cognition: The Implicit Association Test. *Journal of Personality and Social Psychology, 74*, 1464–1480.

Gross, J. (1998). The emerging field of emotion regulation: An integrative review. *Review of General Psychology, 2*, 271–299.

Gross, J. (2002). Emotion regulation: Affective, cognitive and social consequences. *Psychophysiology, 39*, 281–291.

Haeffel, G., & Howard, G. (2010). Self-report: Psychology's four-letter word. *American Journal of Psychology, 123*, 181–188.

Hayes, S. C., Barnes-Holmes, D., & Roche, B. (Eds.). (2001). *Relational frame theory: A post-Skinnerian account of human language and cognition.* New York: Kluwer/ Plenum.

Hayes, S. C., Barnes-Holmes, D., & Wilson, K. G. (2012). Contextual behavioral science: Creating a science more adequate to the challenge of the human condition. *Journal of Contextual Behavioral Science 1*, 1–16.

Hayes, S. C., Nelson, R. O., & Jarrett, R. B. (1986). Evaluating the quality of behavioral assessment. In R. O. Nelson & S. C. Hayes (Eds.), *Conceptual foundations of behavioral assessment* (pp. 461–503). New York, NY; Guilford.

Hayes, S. C., Nelson, R. O., & Jarrett, R. B. (1987). The treatment utility of assessment: A functional approach to evaluating assessment quality. *American Psychologist, 42*, 963–974.

Hayes, S. C., Strosahl, K., & Wilson, K. G. (2012). *Acceptance and commitment therapy: The process and practice of mindful change* (2nd ed.). New York, NY: Guilford.

Heron, K. E., & Smyth, J. M. (2010). Ecological momentary interventions: Incorporating mobile technology into psychosocial and health behaviour treatments. *British Journal of Health Psychology, 15*, 1–39.

Hooper, D., Coughlan, J., & Mullen, M. (2008). Structural equation modeling guidelines for determining model fit. *Electronic Journal of Business Research Methods, 6*, 53–60.

Hooper, N., Villatte, M., Neofotistou, E., & McHugh, L. (2010). The effects of mindfulness versus thought suppression on implicit and explicit measures of experiential avoidance. *The International Journal of Behavioral Consultation and Therapy, 6*, 233–243.

Hughes, S., & Barnes-Holmes, D. (2011). On the formation and persistence of implicit attitudes: New evidence from the Implicit Relational Assessment Procedure. *The Psychological Record, 61*, 391–410.

Hunsley, J., & Bailey, J. M. (1999). The clinical utility of the Rorschach: Unfulfilled promises and an uncertain future. *Psychological Assessment, 11*, 266–277.

Hussey, I., & Barnes-Holmes, D. (2012). The implicit relational assessment procedure as a measure of implicit depression and the role of psychological flexibility. *Cognitive and Behavioral Practice, 19*, 573–582.

Iwata, B. A., Dorsey, M. F., Slifer, K. J., Bauman, K. E., & Richman, G. S. (1982). Toward a functional analysis of self-injury. *Analysis and Intervention in Developmental Disabilities, 2*, 3–20.

Jacobson, N. S., & Truax, P. (1991). Clinical significance: A statistical approach to defining meaningful change in psychotherapy research. *Journal of Consulting and Clinical Psychology, 59*, 12–19.

Jensen, A. R. (1965). Review of the Rorschach Inkblot Test. In O. K. Buros (Ed.), *The sixth mental measurements yearbook* (pp. 501–509). Highland Park, NJ: Gryphon Press.

Juarascio, A., Forman, E., Timko, C. A., Herbert, J., Butryn, M., & Lowe, M. (2011). Implicit internalization of the thin ideal as a predictor of increases in weight, body dissatisfaction and disordered eating. *Eating Behaviors 12*, 207–213.

Kashdan, T. B., & Ciarrochi, J. (Eds.). (2013). *Mindfulness, acceptance, and positive psychology: The seven foundations of well-being.* Oakland, CA: New Harbinger.

Kashdan, T. B., Ferssizidis, P., Collins, R. L., & Muraven, M. (2010). Emotion differentiation as resilience against excessive alcohol use: An ecological momentary assessment in underage social drinkers. *Psychological Science, 21,* 1341–1347.

Kazdin, A. E. (2007). Mediators and mechanisms of change in psychotherapy research. *Annual Review of Clinical Psychology, 3,* 1–27.

Kemp, A., & Quintana, D. (2013). The relationship between mental and physical health: Insights from the study of heart rate variability. *International Journal of Psychophysiology, 89,* 288–296.

Klerman, G. L., Weissman, M. M., Rounsaville, B. J., & Chevron, E. S. (1984). *Interpersonal therapy of depression.* New York, NY: Basic Books.

Kline, R. (2010). *Principles and practice of structural equation modelling* (3rd ed.). New York, NY: Guilford.

Kuyken, W., Watkins, E., Holden, E., White, K., Taylor, R., Byford, S., ... Dalgleish, T. (2010). How does mindfulness-based cognitive therapy work? *Behavior Research and Therapy, 48,* 1105–1112.

Lappalainen, R., Lehtonen, T., Skarp, E., Taubert, E., Ojanen, M., & Hayes, S. C. (2007). The impact of CBT and ACT models using psychology trainee therapists. *Behavior Modification, 31,* 488–511.

Marsh, H., Muthen, B., Asparouhove, T., Ludtke, O., Robitzsch, A., Morin, A., & Trautwein, U. (2009). Exploratory structural equation modeling, integrating CFA and EFA: Applications to students' evaluations of university teaching. *Structural Equation Modeling, 16,* 439–476.

Marshall, S., Parker, P., Ciarrochi, J., & Heaven, P. (2014). Is self-esteem a cause or consequence of social support? A 4-year longitudinal study. *Child Development, 85,* 1275–1291.

Masuda, A., Hayes, S. C., Fletcher, L. B., Seignourel, P. J., Bunting, K., Herbst, S. A., ... Lillis, J. (2007). Impact of acceptance and commitment therapy versus education on stigma toward people with psychological disorders. *Behaviour Research and Therapy, 45,* 2764–2722.

McKenna, I., Barnes-Holmes, D., Barnes-Holmes, Y., & Stewart, I. (2007). Testing the fake-ability of the Implicit Relational Assessment Procedure (IRAP): The first study. *International Journal of Psychology and Psychological Testing, 7,* 253–268.

McNulty, J., & Fincham, F. (2011). Beyond positive psychology? Toward a contextual view of psychological processes and well-being. *American Psychologist, 67,* 101–110.

Meyer, G. J. (1999). Introduction to the special series on the utility of the Rorschach for clinical assessment. *Psychological Assessment, 11,* 235–239.

Miller, A. B., Wall, C., Baines, C. J., Sun, P., To, T., & Narod, S. A. (2014). Twenty-five year follow-up for breast cancer incidence and mortality of the Canadian National Breast Screening Study: Randomised screening trial. *British Medical Journal, 348,* g366.

Millon, T. (2006). *Millon Clinical Multiaxial Inventory-III manual.* Minneapolis, MN: NCS Pearson.

Nelson, R. O., & Hayes, S. C. (1986). The nature of behavioral assessment. In R.O. Nelson & S. C. Hayes (Eds.), *Conceptual foundations of behavioral assessment* (pp. 3–41). New York, NY: Guilford.

Nelson-Gray, R. (2003). Treatment utility of psychological assessment. *Psychological Assessment, 15,* 521–531.

Nezu, A. M., & Nezu, C. M. (2001). Problem solving therapy. *Journal of Psychotherapy Integration, 11,* 187–205.

Nolen-Hoeksema, S., Morrow, J., & Fredrickson, B. L. (1993). Response styles and the duration of depressed mood. *Journal of Abnormal Psychology, 102,* 20–28.

Nunnally, J. (1967). *Psychometric therory.* New York, NY: McGraw-Hill.

O'Neill, R. E., Horner, R. H., Albin, R. W., Story, K., Sprague, J. R. (1990). *Functional analysis of problem behavior: A practical assessment guide.* Sycamore, IL: Sycamore Publishing.

Parling, T., Cernvall, M., Stewart, I., Barnes-Holmes, D., & Ghaderi, A. (2012). Using the Implicit Relational Assessment Procedure to compare implicit pro-thin/anti-fat attitudes of patients with anorexia nervosa and nonclinical controls. *Eating Disorders 20*, 127–143.

Paul, G. L. (1969). Behavior modification research: Design and tactics. In C. M. Franks (Ed.), *Behavior therapy: Appraisal and status* (pp. 29–62). New York, NY: McGraw-Hill.

Regier, D. A., Farmer, M. E., Rae, D. S., Locke, B. Z., Keith, S. J., Judd. L. L., & Goodwin, F. K. (1990). Comorbidity of mental disorders with alcohol and other drug abuse: Results from the Epidemiologic Catchment Area (ECA) Study. *Journal of the American Medical Association, 264*, 2511–2518.

Repp, A. C., Felce, D., & Barton, L. E. (1988). Basing the treatment of stereotypic and self-injurious behaviors on hypotheses of their causes. *Journal of Applied Behavior Analysis, 21*, 281–289.

Roddy, S., Stewart, I., & Barnes-Holmes, D. (2010). Anti-fat, pro-slim, or both: Using two reaction-time based measures to assess implicit attitudes to the slim and overweight. *Journal of Health Psychology, 15*, 416–425.

Ruiz-Padial, E., Sollers, J., Vila, J., & Thayer, J. (2003). The rhythm of the heart in the blink of an eye: Emotion-modulated startle magnitude covaries with heart rate variability. *Psychophysiology, 40*, 306–313.

Sartorius, N., Ustun, T. B, Lecruiber, Y., & Wittchen, H-U. (1996). Depression comorbid with anxiety: Results from the WHO study on "Psychological disorders in primary health care." *The British Journal of Psychiatry, 168*, 38–43.

Segerstrom, S. C., & Nes, L. S. (2007). Heart rate variability reflects self-regulatory strength, effort, and fatigue. *Psychological Science, 18*, 275–281.

Shiffman, S., Stone, A., & Hufford, M. (2008). Ecological momentary assessment. *Annual Review of Clinical Psychology, 4*, 1–32.

Sotsky, S. S., Glass, D. R., Shea, T., Pilknois, P. A., Collins, J. F., Elkin, I., … Oliveri, M, E. (1991). Patient predictors of response to psychotherapy and pharmacotherapy: Findings in the NIMH Treatment of Depression Collaborative Research Program. *The American Journal of Psychiatry, 148*, 997–1008.

Timko, C. A., England, E. L., Herbert, J. D., & Forman, E. (2010). The Implicit Relational Assessment Procedure as a measure of self-esteem. *The Psychological Record, 60*, 679–698.

Viglione, D. J. (1999). A review of recent research addressing the utility of the Rorschach. *Psychological Assessment, 11*, 251–265.

Wilson, K. G., Sandoz, E. K., Kitchens, J., & Roberts, M. (2010). The Valued Living Questionnaire: Defining and measuring valued action within a behavioral framework. *The Psychological Record, 60*, 249–272.

Zettle, R. D. (2003). Acceptance and commitment therapy (ACT) vs. systematic desensitization in treatment of mathematics anxiety. *The Psychological Record, 53*, 197–215.

Zettle, R. D., Haflich, J. L., & Reynolds, R. A. (1992). Responsivity to cognitive therapy as a function of treatment format and client personality dimensions. *Journal of Clinical Psychology, 48*, 787–797.

Zettle, R. D., & Herring, E. L. (1995). Treatment utility of the sociotropy/autonomy distinction: Implications for cognitive therapy. *Journal of Clinical Psychology, 51*, 280–288.

17

The Role of Experimental Psychopathology and Laboratory-Based Intervention Studies in Contextual Behavioral Science

Michael E. Levin and Matthieu Villatte

One of the defining features of contextual behavioral science (CBS) is its emphasis on a reticulated approach that integrates different levels of analysis and research methods in a coherent way (Hayes, Barnes-Holmes, & Wilson, 2012 and chapter 3 in this volume). Bridging analytic levels ranging from basic research, to applied, middle-level theoretical models, to specific treatment technologies, is essential for progressive treatment development and testing, as the other chapters in this book highlight. Yet, the gap between basic principles, applied theory, and treatment can also be substantial and presents methodological challenges for research.

Within the psychosocial treatment literature, mediational analyses and additive/dismantling designs are often used to test theory. Mediational analysis examines whether the differential impact of an intervention on a putative process of change accounts for treatment effects. For example, a mediational analysis might test whether acceptance and commitment therapy (ACT; Hayes, Strosahl, & Wilson, 2012) reduces cognitive fusion more than cognitive therapy, whether changes in fusion predict changes in depression, and whether these reductions in fusion statistically account for the differential impact of ACT on depression (Zettle, Rains, & Hayes, 2011).

Alternatively, additive and dismantling designs can test whether the systematic inclusion/exclusion of treatment components impacts efficacy. For instance, a study might compare just the behavioral activation component of cognitive therapy to cognitive therapy excluding methods treating core schemas and to the full cognitive therapeutic package (Jacobson et al., 1996). These designs can help determine whether treatment produces effects through measures of putative processes and whether identified active and inactive treatment components are consistent with the theoretical model.

However, mediational analyses and dismantling designs alone are not sufficient for wading through the challenges of bridging basic research, applied theory, and applied technologies. These methods are typically conducted within treatment outcome research in which a variety of methodological factors reduce sensitivity to testing more

The Wiley Handbook of Contextual Behavioral Science, First Edition. Edited by Robert D. Zettle, Steven C. Hayes, Dermot Barnes-Holmes, and Anthony Biglan.
© 2016 John Wiley & Sons, Ltd. Published 2016 by John Wiley & Sons, Ltd.

precise manipulations (i.e., multiple treatment sessions, treatment is not perfectly identical across participants, etc.), measurement typically relies on self-report questionnaires, and iterative testing is limited due to the substantial resources required to conduct studies. The focus of these methods is also more on testing the relationship of interventions to middle-level theoretical models, rather than basic principles. These methods are unlikely to answer questions such as whether direct instructions to practice acceptance are sufficient or if experiential exercises are needed to produce behavior change, whether new learning through exposure transfers to novel stimuli through derived stimulus relations, how each treatment component functions in isolation and combination with each other, or how values clarification might alter the stimulus functions of an aversive task.

Methods are needed that focus more on internal validity in which the effects of precise, sometimes subtle, experimental manipulations can be compared on sensitive measures assessing specific phenomena of interest. This is critical to understanding the detailed aspects of and interconnections between basic and applied research. In many cases this can best be done through laboratory-based studies, which provide highly controlled contexts and opportunities for precise measurement as well as a setting in which comparison conditions and contextual manipulations, which may not be feasible or ethical in outcome research, can be used. Similarly, laboratory-based methods are needed in understanding psychopathology and exploring the relationship of basic principles to more applied models of pathology.

For reasons such as these, laboratory-based studies have long been a core aspect of psychological research. This chapter will focus on how these methodologies may be best used from a CBS perspective to help bridge basic research, applied theory, and interventions. Given the scope of these methods and the focus of this section of the handbook, we will specifically focus on the domains directly relevant to psychopathology and therapeutic interventions.

Bridging Basic Research and Applied Theories of Psychopathology and Intervention

Laboratory-based studies provide the foundation for basic research, and thus are key in connecting basic principles to applied, middle-level theory. Bridging such research involves examining middle-level theoretical concepts of psychopathology and intervention from a basic approach to test whether these concepts are consistent with the basic account and whether extensions of the basic account can further inform the middle-level theory.

To illustrate how these methods can help bridge levels of analysis, this section will focus on research conducted in the field of relational frame theory (RFT; Hayes, Barnes-Holmes, & Roche 2001). Because RFT has been extensively discussed elsewhere in this volume (see chapters 9 and 10), we will only present key concepts of the theory here. The core idea of RFT is to conceptualize language and cognition as the behavior of building, understanding, and responding to symbolic relations among events, which provides a behavioral framework from which to study the implications of cognition for psychological problems and interventions.

Testing Extensions of Basic Principles to Theories of Psychopathology

Research is needed to elaborate on and test theoretical suppositions about how basic principles might contribute to psychopathology. One method for exploring this is to model pathological processes using basic principles.

For example, a major component of RFT is that relations among events are mutually and combinatorially entailed. In simple terms, this means that if we learn that A=B, we can derive that B=A (mutual entailment) and if we learn that B=C, we can derive that A=C (combinatorial entailment) without being explicitly taught to do so. Furthermore, the functions of stimuli can change due to their relationship to other stimuli, which is termed transformation of stimulus functions (i.e., if A is associated with a shock and A=B, then B may acquire a similar aversive function in some contexts). This feature of RFT has been theorized to account for the development of avoidant behaviors that have not been shaped by direct consequences (e.g., avoiding intimacy despite never having experienced negative consequences from being intimate) and that generalizes beyond formal properties of the context (i.e., an adult who was beaten when he was a child may avoid verbal expressions of affection from others).

The symbolic acquisition and generalization of avoidance has been tested in a number of laboratory studies conducted by RFT researchers. In a typical protocol (see Dymond & Roche, 2009 for a review), a participant learns to relate different stimuli as equivalent (A=B=C). An aversive function is then attributed to one of the stimuli by classical conditioning (e.g., a slight electric shock is delivered every time A is presented on a computer screen that the participant can avoid by pressing the space bar). As a result, the participant avoids the stimulus A, and all the stimuli that are in the same equivalence class, even though they do not share similar formal properties.

Theoretically, stimuli that have acquired aversive functions through symbolic generalization can also produce greater effects than the original source of pain. For example, a child bitten by a big dog might be even more afraid of a small dog if he is told that "this one is even more dangerous." While the small dog's physical appearance would trigger a smaller reaction if only formal generalization was involved, language processes allow for a transformation independent from intrinsic characteristics. A small dog can be scarier than a big dog. In an illustrative study, Dougher, Hamilton, Fink, and Harrington (2007) tested the role of language in this process by establishing a relational network in which stimuli are not equivalent, but connected through relations of comparison (A<B<C). The stimulus B was then paired with an electric shock and skin conductance was measured as each stimulus was presented on a computer screen. Results showed that the participants' reaction was greater for C and lower for A than for B, which suggests that stimuli can acquire an aversive function to a different degree than the original source of pain through relational learning, independently of their formal characteristics.

In addition to testing analogues for pathological processes, laboratory-based studies can compare the performance of individuals with or without identified disorders on procedures tightly linked to basic principles. For instance, research has explored the role of relational responding repertoires in autism and psychosis. More specifically, deficits in perspective taking, a core component of these psychological disorders often studied under the rubric of theory of mind impairments, have been approached through a type of relational responding called deictics (McHugh, Barnes-Holmes, & Barnes-Holmes, 2004). Instead of relating events as equivalent or bigger/smaller as in the previous examples cited, deictic relational responding consists of relating events based on spatial, temporal, and interpersonal perspectives. For example, a person can say to a friend on the phone "I am home right now. I will pick you up at your place in 10 minutes." In more generic terms emphasizing the implications of deictics, this statement could be translated as follows "I am here now, and I will be there then where you are now."

This conceptualization of perspective taking in terms of relational responding led Rehfeldt and colleagues (2007) to study deictic performance of children with autistic spectrum disorders using a protocol created by McHugh et al. (2004). In this protocol, participants respond to questions testing their capacity to take simple, reversed, and double reversed perspectives along the I–YOU, HERE–THERE, and NOW–THEN dimensions. For example, a simple perspective question was formulated such as "I have a red brick and you have a green brick. Which brick do you have?"; a reversed perspective was formulated such as "I have a red brick and you have a green brick. If I were you and you were me, which brick would you have?"; a double reversed perspective was formulated such as "I am sitting here on the black chair and you are sitting there on the blue chair. If you were me and I were you and if here was there and there was here, where would you be sitting?" Results showed deficits in increased levels of complexity consistent with the literature on theory of mind impairments in autism, suggesting the importance of deictic relational responding repertoires in this problem. Subsequent research similarly showed that mental state attribution in psychosis and social anhedonia were similarly correlated with deficits in deictic relational responding using this assessment protocol (e.g., Villatte, Monestès, McHugh, Freixa i Baqué, & Loas, 2008; 2010).

Laboratory-based studies such as these can help link basic principles and more middle-level pathological processes such as experiential avoidance and deficits in perspective taking. If aspects of middle-level theoretical constructs are invalidated by findings with basic principles, it suggests the applied theory needs to be revised, while positive results support the connection of these applied concepts to basic processes. Furthering our understanding of how basic principles extend into pathological processes can help guide identifying new middle-level concepts and novel intervention strategies. For example, identifying the role of deficits in deictic relational responding in psychopathology suggests that validated methods for improving deictic repertoires (e.g., O'Neill & Weil, 2014) could be incorporated into treatments.

Developing Laboratory-Based Assessments to Test Extensions of Basic Principles

The laboratory provides a controlled setting in which assessment procedures can be developed that help connect applied models of psychopathology and intervention to basic principles. For example, the Implicit Relational Assessment Procedure (IRAP, see Hughes, Barnes-Holmes, & Vahey, 2012 as well as chapter 10 of this volume) was developed to assess key aspects of relational responding. The principle of the IRAP is to measure brief and immediate relational responses (BIRRs) rather than more extended and elaborated relational responses (EERRs). In simple terms, the IRAP allows for measuring what people think (what derived relational responses they produce) within a short time frame.

The IRAP has been used in a number of studies to test how patterns of BIRRs predict psychopathology and response to treatment. For example, stronger BIRRs toward positive effects of cocaine use prior to substance abuse treatment were associated with poorer outcomes (Carpenter, Martinez, Vadhan, Barnes-Holmes, & Nunes, 2012); the IRAP was able to detect a decrease in experiential avoidance resulting from a mindfulness intervention not detected by means of a self-report questionnaire (Hooper, Villatte, Neofotistou, & McHugh, 2010); BIRRs related to spider fear predicted overt avoidance behavior with a live spider (Nicholson & Barnes-Holmes, 2012); and BIRRs reflecting increased negative future thinking predicted clinical depression (Kosnes, Whelan, O'Donovan, & McHugh, 2013).

Studies such as these highlight how well-validated laboratory methods can be developed to help connect basic and applied theory. In the case of the IRAP, research demonstrates how BIRRs might alter the functions of stimuli such as appetitive motivation for cocaine use or avoidance of spiders. It is important to note that although this method was developed and validated in the laboratory, once validated it could similarly be used in applied treatment research, further helping to bridge levels of analysis.

Testing Extensions of Basic Principles to Theoretical Models of Intervention

The connection between basic principles and applied theoretical models for interventions is critical for progressive treatment development (Hayes, Barnes-Holmes, & Wilson, 2012; chapter 18 in this volume). This connection can help ensure that middle-level concepts are oriented to manipulable variables that are broadly applicable and yet relatively precise in what they refer to. Laboratory-based research provides an ideal method for testing and building these connections. Such studies might include testing analogues that model the effects of an intervention using basic principles or examining how precise manipulations of basic principles within an intervention might alter its impact. The results of these studies can both test extensions of basic principles, identifying limiting factors and areas for revision of the basic model, as well as clarifying ways to connect and revise middle-level theory and intervention technologies.

For example, research has begun to use RFT to understand and enhance exposure in laboratory studies. Roche, Kanter, Brown, Dymond, and Fogarty (2008) compared two extinction strategies – either direct or derived – following a phase of derived relational acquisition of avoidance similar to that presented above in this chapter (see Dymond & Roche, 2009). After learning to relate A=B=C and to avoid A, extinction was either established with the presentation of A (direct extinction) or C (derived extinction). The results showed that the derived extinction procedure was more effective than the direct extinction procedure at extinguishing avoidance, which suggest that targeting stimuli symbolically related to direct sources of fear might be more effective than using the direct sources of fear.

Another set of exemplary studies examined how certain types of relational responding operate within components of ACT. One study explored the role of deictic and hierarchical relational responding in defusion (Luciano et al., 2011). Adolescents with impulsivity and emotional problems were either exposed to a protocol emphasizing conditional and deictic relations or to one emphasizing hierarchical relations in addition to conditional and deictic relations. According to the authors, the first protocol promoted a sense of self distinct from psychological experiences, while the second protocol promoted an additional sense of self as the container of psychological experiences and greater awareness of values. The results of these interventions showed that only the protocol including hierarchical relational responding produced significant improvement at four-month follow-up, which confirms, at the level of basic principles, the benefit of adding values and self-as-context interventions to defusion techniques. In a further exploration of the role of hierarchical relational responding in ACT interventions, a second study showed that distress was significantly reduced by a protocol emphasizing a sense of self as a container (hierarchical deictic framing) rather than only being distinct from psychological experiences (distinction deictic framing) (Foody, Barnes-Holmes, Barnes-Holmes, & Luciano, 2013).

Overall, laboratory-based methods are an ideal setting for developing and testing the connection of basic principles to applied, middle-level theory and intervention. Extensions of basic principles to the modeling and understanding of psychopathology can be tested, preparations that capture key aspects of basic processes can be explored, and innovative designs can examine how basic principles relate to interventions and middle-level theory.

Evaluating Treatment Components and Technologies

In addition to bridging basic and applied theory, laboratory-based intervention studies can be used to examine the connections between middle-level theory and intervention technologies. Laboratory-based studies can test the isolated and combined effects of theoretically specified components of a larger treatment or specific technologies (i.e., writing about personally relevant values, urge surfing, etc.) in relation to theoretically distinct interventions (i.e., thought suppression, cognitive reappraisal, etc.), with laboratory-based process measures or clinical analogues (i.e., distress tolerance, mood induction, etc.), and in contexts or formats that may moderate their impact (i.e., degree of social demand). In the sections that follow, we discuss some of the important ways laboratory-based intervention research adds to a program of research seeking to bridge treatment, middle-level theory, and basic principles.

Testing the Isolated and Combined Impact of Treatment Components and Technologies

A key aspect of testing a treatment model is to examine whether treatment components function as theorized in isolation and in combination with other components, including those theorized to be necessary to produce meaningful outcomes. Although additive and dismantling studies are essential for testing clinical efficacy of components, they are also costly, often delayed until late in treatment development, and difficult to conduct in an iterative fashion with a range of components. Laboratory-based methods provide a cost-effective method to test components iteratively throughout treatment development. However, in contrast to additive/dismantling designs, laboratory-based studies do not test the clinical efficacy of components per se as they typically involve brief interventions, using nontreatment-seeking samples, assessing effects on processes of change and analogue measures, and with highly controlled designs focused on internal rather than external validity.

Rather, laboratory-based studies can test whether isolated and combined treatment components are psychologically active in ways that are consistent with a theoretical model (i.e., have a meaningful impact on relevant behavior and processes of change). These studies provide important information on treatment effects with multimethod assessments such as clinical analogues and unique laboratory-based process measures. Treatment components can also be compared to carefully matched comparison conditions that can test alternative explanations for findings (e.g., mood induction, social demand). Components found to be inert from such laboratory-based research inform revisions to the theory and treatment package, while positive findings provide further support for the existing approach. However, even though a component has an active effect in the lab does not prove the component has an additive benefit in actual treatment, which would require subsequent additive/dismantling research within clinical trials. Yet, laboratory-based research can help guide these investigations, reducing the number of additive/dismantling studies needed, focusing on core issues for theory and treatment, and providing earlier and iterative testing throughout development.

Responses to distressing laboratory-based tasks (i.e., reactivity, persistence, etc.) are one of the most frequently used preparations, in part because of their utility as an analogue to clinically-relevant behavior. For example, Levitt, Brown, Orsillo, and Barlow (2004) compared acceptance, thought suppression, and an inactive (i.e., inert) control condition on reactions to a CO_2 exposure procedure among participants with panic disorder. Results indicated acceptance led to greater willingness to participate in a second exposure session and less anxiety during exposure relative to the other two conditions. Studies such as these, particularly those involving a clinically relevant task, can provide useful information regarding the psychologically active effects of a component with regards to both putative processes of change as well as its potential impact on important clinically relevant behaviors (i.e., willingness to do exposure). Other examples of clinical analogues used to test treatment components include a behavioral approach test for spider phobia (e.g., Wagener & Zettle, 2012), persistence in a painful task such as a cold pressor (e.g., Branstetter, Cushing, & Douleh, 2009), response to mood (e.g., Grisham, Flower, Williams, & Moulds, 2011) and intrusive thought induction procedures (e.g., Marcks & Woods, 2007), and resisting eating candies from a container carried throughout the day (e.g., Forman et al., 2007). Such measures often provide a face valid and direct assessment of clinically relevant behaviors, which, among other benefits, helps address the overreliance on self-report measures in clinical trials.

Iterative research with well-designed control conditions can provide further information regarding the aspects of an intervention that are necessary to have an active effect. For example, a series of studies tested the "milk, milk, milk" cognitive defusion strategy, involving repeating a word over and over to reduce its literal functions (Masuda, Feinstein, Wendell, & Sheehan, 2010; Masuda, Hayes, Sackett, & Twohig, 2004; Masuda et al., 2009; Watson, Burley, & Purdon, 2010). An initial time series study found that the defusion exercise produced stronger effects on believability and distress with negative self-relevant thoughts relative to both inactive (i.e., inert) and thought control conditions, although when the defusion rationale was presented without repeating a negative thought, it had no effect (Masuda et al., 2004). A follow-up study explored whether the length of the word repetition task affected results, finding stronger effects on believability when words were repeated for 20–30 seconds, but that the maximum benefits on distress were achieved after only 3–10 seconds (Masuda et al., 2009). Another study randomized participants to the full defusion exercise, a limited defusion intervention without repetition of the target word, a full distraction intervention, a limited distraction intervention, and an inactive control condition. The study found that the full defusion exercise had a greater impact on believability and distress from negative self-relevant words relative to all of the other conditions, including the limited defusion intervention in which the target word was not repeated (Masuda et al., 2010). Results were similar among the subgroup of participants with elevated depressive symptoms.

Another research group compared the full "milk, milk, milk" defusion exercise to a brief imaginal exposure intervention among students with elevated contamination fears across two experiments (Watson et al., 2010). Both studies found that defusion had a greater immediate impact on negative reactions to contamination thoughts relative to imaginal exposure and an inactive control condition, but, in study 2, only imaginal exposure had a significant impact on self-reported behavioral avoidance. This research highlights how a series of studies can test important aspects of a specific technique to identify sources of active intervention effects including necessary and sufficient parameters (i.e., length of repetition, repetition with neutral vs. target words, etc.), differences with theoretically distinct interventions (i.e., distraction, imaginal exposure, etc.), and generalizability of effects with clinically relevant samples.

If two components are found to be psychologically active, it does not yet answer the question of whether combining components has an additive benefit, or even possibly a negative effect. Laboratory-based studies can address important theoretical and practical concerns regarding the interaction between treatment components. Despite the need for such research, there have been few such studies with regards to acceptance, mindfulness, and values-based components (Levin, Hildebrandt, Lillis, & Hayes, 2012). One illustrative example tested the benefit of combining a values and acceptance component relative to acceptance alone on performance in a cold pressor task (Branstetter et al., 2009). The study found that, although the acceptance alone condition produced greater persistence in the cold pressor task relative to an inactive control condition, participants in the combined values and acceptance intervention had significantly higher persistence than both conditions. Studies such as these can provide key tests for theory specifying how treatment components interact and the treatment packages they inform.

Assessing the Impact of Components on Theoretical Processes of Change

In addition to testing *if* treatment components work, laboratory-based studies can explore *how* treatment components work. These studies provide opportunities to use process measures that may be difficult to assess in clinical trials, such as behavioral observation, responses to laboratory preparation, and physiological measures, and to more precisely test the direct relation of experimental manipulations to their effects.

For example, there has been increasing interest in examining the role of implicit cognition in treatment, but these measures are rarely integrated into outcome studies due to issues such as assessment burden and logistics of incorporating a laboratory-based assessment. These measures also have reliability issues at the individual client level, which reduces sensitivity to intervention effects (Levin, Hayes, & Waltz, 2010). Laboratory-based studies provide a useful setting in which incorporating such assessments is more feasible and extraneous sources of variance can be reduced through highly controlled environmental and experimental manipulations to increase measurement sensitivity. An exemplary study explored whether mindfulness might "decouple" the relationship between automatic approach tendencies toward alcohol and subsequent heavy drinking (Ostafin, Bauer, & Myxter, 2012). Students completed an implicit measure of approach versus avoidance tendencies toward alcohol versus water, followed by a series of audio-recorded mindfulness sessions or inactive control sessions. A subsequent session assessed recent heavy drinking over the past week. Researchers found an interaction between tendencies toward alcohol and condition such that implicit approach was only related to heavy drinking in the inactive control condition, suggesting that mindfulness "decoupled" the relationship between implicit motivations and alcohol use. Research such as this with laboratory-based measures provides important information regarding possible processes by which an intervention has its effects.

Another study that exemplifies the use of laboratory-based measures to test processes of change examined the impact of loving kindness meditation on affective responding to others, relative to a neutral imagery condition (Hutcherson, Seppala, & Gross, 2008). Before and after the intervention, participants rated a series of pictures including of themselves, someone they were close to, and three pictures of strangers, on variables including how positive, connected, and similar they felt to the person, as well as an affective priming task to assess implicit positive and negative evaluations. Results varied on the implicit and explicit measures and by type of picture, but overall suggested loving kindness produced greater positivity toward strangers and oneself relative to the neutral imagery control condition.

Assessing a variety of domains in relation to a laboratory preparation can be helpful in gaining a better understanding of how an intervention functions. An illustrative study compared thought suppression and acceptance using an intrusive thought induction in which participants stated they hoped a specific loved one died in a car accident and then imagined the scene (Marcks & Woods, 2007). After the induction, participants monitored the frequency of accident-related thoughts in two five-minute monitoring periods and rated their reactions at the end of each period. Variables included frequency of accident-related thoughts during monitoring periods and subsequent ratings of anxiety, negative appraisals, and willingness to re-experience the intrusive thoughts. Interestingly, the study also explored the relationship of suppression effort (i.e., the degree to which participants tried to suppress thoughts) to these variables. Results indicated that although the acceptance group reported more intrusions during the first period following intervention, they also reported greater willingness to re-experience these thoughts and a greater decrease in thoughts in the second thought monitoring period. In addition, greater self-reported efforts to suppress thoughts in the thought suppression condition were related to greater anxiety, thought frequency, guilt, perceived moral wrongness, feelings of responsibility, likelihood ratings of an accident occurring, and urges to neutralize thoughts. Preparations and analyses such as these can provide a more detailed understanding of how such strategies function and in some cases be associated with iatrogenic effects.

In some cases, mediational analyses can test how an experimental manipulation impacts proximal outcomes. For instance, a self-affirmation study examined the effects of writing about personally relevant values (vs. writing about values that are not important to oneself) on positive emotions and acceptance of a message about the health effects of smoking (Crocker, Niiya, & Mischkowski, 2008). Researchers found that writing about relevant values increased acceptance of the health message and positive emotions, particularly love, relative to the other condition. Furthermore, increases in love and feeling connected to others fully mediated the intervention effects on health message acceptance, but increases in other positive, self-directed emotions did not. Mediational analyses such as these in the context of highly con-trolled manipulations can provide useful insights into how interventions work, including specific technologies such as writing about important values.

These studies highlight the types of theoretical questions regarding how interven-tions work that can uniquely be addressed by laboratory-based studies. Laboratory-based measures such as examining responses to a thought intrusion preparation (Marcks & Woods, 2007) or generalization of both implicit and explicit positivity toward strangers (Hutcherson et al., 2008) can be difficult to implement in treatment outcome studies. These studies also test a more direct connection between specific experimental manipulations, such as a values writing technique, (Crocker et al., 2008) and treatment effects.

Comparing Interventions That Target Disparate and Opposing Therapeutic Processes

Laboratory-based studies provide a unique opportunity to compare treatment com-ponents to experimental manipulations designed to target disparate and opposing processes. Such research can answer important theoretical questions regarding whether components and techniques are distinct at the level of putative processes of change. In some cases, such research can be difficult if not impossible to conduct within clinical trials due to the degree of precision required for the experimental con-ditions and potential ethical concerns when using maladaptive coping strategies (i.e., thought suppression).

In some cases, two interventions might have expected active effects, but through theoretically distinct processes. A common comparison has been between acceptance and mindfulness approaches and traditional cognitive behavior therapy (CBT) inter-ventions focused on strategies to control thoughts and feelings. In such cases, mea-sures may be selected that are theoretically more primary for one or the other intervention (i.e., acceptance more likely having an effect on approach behavior and decreased avoidance; control-based strategies on level of distress). For example, a spider phobia study compared acceptance- and control-based (i.e., cognitive restruc-turing and relaxation) approaches to one providing accurate information about spi-ders (Wagener & Zettle, 2011). Consistent with theoretical predictions, there were no differences among the three conditions on subjective distress in a spider-approach task, but only acceptance led to significant improvements in approach behavior and a willingness to participate in the task relative to the informational condition. The assessment of multiple domains served to highlight potential common and differential processes for distinct interventions, such as the expected distinct impact on approach behavior and willingness with acceptance-based interventions.

Researchers may compare interventions that overlap to a considerable degree, but are also distinct in theoretically critical ways. An illustrative study explored whether mindful breathing has a unique effect on decentering (i.e., noticing thoughts as just thoughts) or if it is more generally impacted by other eyes-closed exercises, such as progressive muscle relaxation and loving kindness meditation (Feldman, Greeson, & Senville, 2010). Following the intervention, participants were asked to indicate frequency of repetitive thoughts during the exercise (i.e., worry, rumination, problem-solving, and self-criticism) as well as negative reactions to these thoughts. The mindful breathing participants reported a higher frequency of thoughts relative to the other two conditions, but no difference in reactions to repetitive thoughts. A moderation result indicated a decentering effect for mindful breathing specifically in that the correlation between frequency of repetitive thoughts and negative reactions to these thoughts was weakest in the mindful breathing condition. Designs such as these can provide important information regarding the specificity of intervention effects on processes of change and the characteristics of these interventions that may account for these effects.

Comparison conditions may also be used to control for specific alternative hypotheses for intervention effects. For example, a study on counteracting ego depletion effects compared a values-writing exercise designed to target self-affirmation (writing about why one's top rated values are important to oneself) to a control exercise (writing about why one's lowest rated values are important to others) and a positive mood induction (Schmeichel & Vohs, 2009). The results indicated that ego depletion in an effortful task led to decreased puzzle-solving persistence for those in the positive mood induction and control exercise, but not in the self-affirmation condition. This suggests that the impact of writing about one's values on persistence after ego depletion is not likely due to other features of the writing task (i.e., writing about unimportant values) or the impact of values writing on positive mood. Laboratory-based methods provide a unique opportunity to test these more specific questions with well-matched comparison conditions.

In some cases, researchers induce pathological processes to explore distinctions between problematic and effective coping strategies. For instance, a study compared two strategies that involve reflecting on a negative experience, though with distinct goals (i.e., rumination vs. reappraisal) (Grisham et al., 2011). Participants were instructed to recall a recent sad event and then received instructions to reflect on the memory again using rumination or reappraisal. Results indicated significant improvements in both negative and positive mood in the reappraisal condition relative to rumination. Research such as this can help model differences between typical problematic ways that clients cope with problems relative to more effective strategies.

Studies might also explore theoretical claims concerning moderating variables and for whom particular coping strategies are more or less effective. For example, a study compared the effects of an acceptance- and control-based approach as well as a nonintervention control group on coping with food cravings (Forman et al., 2007). The study found an interaction effect. Among those with low susceptibility to food, the acceptance condition performed equivalently to, or in some cases worse than, the other conditions on cravings. However, among those with high susceptibility to food, the acceptance condition was most effective. This is consistent with theoretical predictions in which acceptance may be more effective in contexts in which avoidance is not easily achieved (such as high availability and susceptibility of food cues).

Testing Contextual Factors Related to How Interventions Function

Laboratory-based studies provide the opportunity to experimentally control and manipulate contextual factors in ways that may not be feasible in clinical trials. Such research can answer important theoretical and practical questions regarding interactions with contextual variables and how best to implement interventions.

Theories often provide guidelines about how an intervention might best be implemented. For example, ACT emphasizes experiential learning over direct instruction, in part because such interventions seek to undermine overly rigid rule- governed behavior (Hayes, Strosahl, & Wilson, 2012). To explore this, a study using a self-administered shock paradigm compared brief instruction-only versions of an acceptance and a distraction intervention to versions that included experiential exercises and metaphors as well as a no-instruction control condition (McMullen et al., 2008). Only the full acceptance-based intervention led to increases in tolerance (i.e., number of shocks), while the instruction-only acceptance condition was relatively inert. Research such as this can test theoretical claims regarding how processes can be effectively targeted.

In some cases, potential contextual variables that may serve a moderating function may be experimentally tested in the lab to explore how they affect an intervention. For instance, a study compared an acceptance-based intervention to a control-based approach on work performance under either a high or low job control context (i.e., whether they could select their sequence and schedule of tasks to be completed) (Kishita & Shimada, 2011). The study found that the job control condition interacted with intervention effects such that those in the acceptance condition with high job control made the fewest errors in the work task. In addition, the job control condition only predicted participants' perceived job control in the acceptance condition, suggesting this intervention specifically increased awareness of one's level of control. Moderators such as job control may be difficult to experimentally manipulate in the context of a clinical trial and studies such as this can provide important tests regarding how such contextual factors influence treatment.

In some cases, contextual features may be manipulated to test alternative hypotheses for why an intervention produces its effect. For example, research has examined whether the effects of techniques such as coping self-statements can be accounted for by social processes rather than other putative mechanisms (i.e., self-instruction or self-efficacy). One study had participants select coping self-statements related to a cold pressor task from a bag supposedly at random (in actuality they all included the same type of statements) and manipulated whether the statements were public (i.e., after reading the statement they gave it to the experimenter to read) or private (i.e., the statement was not shared with anyone) (Hayes & Wolf, 1984). Results indicated a significant difference between the public self-statement group and a control condition, but not with the private self-statement group, suggesting the effects of self-statements were due more to social processes such as setting a social standard for expected behavior.

Overall, these studies highlight the variety of methodological features available in laboratory-based studies, which can be used to examine the connections between applied theory and treatment components/technologies. Of note, many of these features are unique to laboratory-based studies and would be difficult to conduct in outcome research (i.e., iterative research on isolated and combined component effects, testing effects on laboratory-based measures, inclusion of well-controlled and precise comparison conditions, manipulating contextual factors that moderate treatment, and so on).

Limitations of Laboratory-Based Studies

As for any method, there are a number of limitations with laboratory-based studies that impact the questions they can examine and the conclusions that can be drawn from findings. An awareness of these limitations can help avoid misapplications of their use and promote a better understanding of their role within the CBS scientific strategy. As there has been more research on laboratory-based intervention studies than research bridging basic and applied theory, this review will focus particularly on limitations in the former.

Due to their focus on internal validity, laboratory-based methods can have limited generalizability. As previously mentioned, laboratory-based intervention studies typically do not provide direct evidence regarding clinical efficacy. Findings with convenience samples, such as college students, need to be replicated with treatment-seeking samples and specific functional diagnostic groups to test generalizability. Similarly, results from isolated components, often with very brief interventions, tested in laboratory-based studies may not necessarily generalize to entire treatment packages. Follow-up clinical trials, clinical component studies, and additive/dismantling designs are needed to further test the clinical efficacy and impact of components within treatment. Nevertheless, laboratory-based intervention studies have an important role in examining the effects of isolated and combined components, which can provide critical information for further treatment development and testing. Recognizing this role can reduce an excessive focus on studying the effectiveness of techniques tested in the lab, focusing on the more specific theoretical questions these designs can best answer.

A common issue in laboratory-based component studies is limitations in comparison conditions. Some studies only test components relative to a negative coping strategy comparison condition (i.e., rumination, thought suppression, etc.), which although helpful for distinguishing these processes, generally does not allow interpretation of one condition independently (i.e., was it that acceptance had a positive effect, rumination had a negative effect, or some combination of the two?). Failing to recognize this issue can lead to faulty conclusions regarding the harmful or positive effects of particular strategies. The use of inert control conditions can help address this issue, but in some cases such conditions do not adequately control for important factors. For instance, a common comparison condition involves having subjects learn about a completely unrelated topic (i.e., reading a research methods book), but such conditions are thus unable to control for common intervention factors likely to produce a positive effect (i.e., expectancies/placebo, demand characteristics, mood induction, and so on). Careful design of studies can overcome this issue and there are valuable examples in the literature of highly controlled comparison conditions used to test alternative explanations for observed intervention effects (e.g., Kehoe, Barnes-Holmes, Barnes-Holmes, Cochrane, & Stewart, 2007).

Laboratory-based interventions are typically very brief. This raises questions regarding whether a purported treatment component was effectively targeted by an experimental manipulation and whether results are likely to generalize to a treatment context. The use of brief rationales without additional exercises or metaphors to target psychological flexibility components has been found to be relatively inert in past studies (Levin et al., 2012). Brief interventions may not provide adequate training to learn a skill or may not be sufficient to overcome default ways of responding to stressors. For example, a study comparing suppression to observation of experiences during a CO_2 exposure found in coding the manipulation check that almost every participant reported focusing on trying to think differently to change how they felt during the task, a strategy that was not provided in either condition (Feldner, Zvolensky, Eifert, & Spira, 2003). This can particularly be an issue with inert control conditions. For example, the study by Marcks and Woods (2007) discussed earlier included a monitor-only condition with no coping strategy instructions. Participants within this condition reported spontaneous use of suppression strategies similar to that of the thought suppression condition and thus were excluded from analyses. Without adequate checks, researchers cannot determine whether experimental manipulations were sufficient nor the impact of strategies actually used by participants in control conditions on study results.

In addition to testing what participants did, there is a challenge of finding a shared theoretical language in describing what treatment components were targeted in a laboratory-based study. Within the contextual psychotherapeutic literature, many of the component interventions are referred to as "acceptance-based," which may be misinterpreted as specifically targeting the acceptance component of the psychological flexibility model. However, when viewed from the model of psychological flexibility on which ACT is based (Hayes, Luoma, Bond, Masuda, & Lillis, 2006), many of these interventions ostensibly target a variety of acceptance, mindfulness and values-based processes. This can lead to confusion regarding the empirical support for specific treatment components and failures to identify important gaps in components that have been tested in isolation and combination. For instance, a recent meta-analysis that coded intervention scripts for components targeted found only three eligible studies that specifically targeted acceptance alone (Levin et al., 2012).

Laboratory-based intervention studies require fewer resources to conduct, which is an important benefit in conducting iterative theory and treatment testing, but the ready availability for conducting such studies may also lead to lower quality designs. A clear set of criteria for coding the methodological rigor of such studies has yet to be agreed upon by the scientific community, although a list of standards has been proposed (Barnes-Holmes & Hayes, 2003). This list includes several key points, which are not always addressed in studies, such as adequate power for planned comparisons, balanced intervention conditions except on the target of manipulation, use of manipulation checks, automated procedures when possible, and strategies to examine effects when multiple components are combined (Barnes-Holmes & Hayes, 2003).

Summary

Throughout this chapter we have highlighted exemplary studies illustrating how laboratory-based methods can be integrated into a CBS approach as well as limitations in these methods that should be considered. We will briefly summarize these points with a list of recommendations for future laboratory-based research from a CBS perspective:

Laboratory-Based Studies Bridging Basic Principles and Middle-Level Theory

- Continue to conduct basic research modeling pathological processes such as generalization of avoidance, cognitive fusion, and perspective-taking deficits.
- Develop more laboratory-based methods like the IRAP and deictic framing measures to assess key facets of basic principles (i.e., sensitivity to changing contingencies, motivative augmentals, etc.).
- Conduct more research testing the connection of basic principles to middle-level theoretical constructs (i.e., testing basic analogues to cognitive defusion and values interventions, testing the role of specific relational framing repertoires in ACT components, etc.).

Laboratory-Based Intervention Studies

- Conduct more theoretically targeted tests of isolated and combined treatment components (rather than combining acceptance, mindfulness, and values processes in each intervention under umbrella terms such as "acceptance-" or "mindfulness-based").
- Consider alternative explanations for study findings and include contextual manipulations and control conditions to test for these explanations.
- Include detailed and valid manipulation checks.
- Use multimethod assessments and assess multiple domains within clinical analogues and other preparations.
- Develop and test a broader array of laboratory-based measures besides distress tolerance and mood induction procedures (i.e., behavioral variability, perspective-taking, delayed discounting, decoupling relationship of thoughts, feelings, and urges to overt behavior, and so on).
- When comparing two distinct, active interventions, consider key theoretical questions rather than testing comparative efficacy.
- Conduct more research on contextual factors that influence intervention effects.

This list is not designed to be comprehensive, but to orient to some of the key themes in exemplary laboratory-based research being conducted within the CBS tradition. These methods provide a cost-effective means of testing important theoretical questions that bridge levels of analysis within a carefully controlled experimental context, which is often not feasible in outcome research. In order to make best use of these methods, it is important to maintain a focus on theory testing and bridging levels of analysis from basic to more applied theory. Approached in this way, laboratory-based methods are an integral part of a CBS approach to treatment development.

References

Barnes-Holmes, D., & Hayes, S. C. (2003). How to do ACT laboratory-based component studies. Retrieved from http://contextualpsychology.org/how_to_do_act_laboratory_based_component_studies

Branstetter, A. D., Cushing, C., & Douleh, T. (2009). Personal values and pain tolerance: Does a values intervention add to acceptance? *Journal of Pain, 10*, 887–892.

Carpenter, K. M., Martinez, D., Vadhan, N. L., Barnes-Holmes, D., & Nunes, V. E. (2012). Performance based measures of attentional bias and relational responding are associated with behavioral treatment outcome for cocaine dependence. *The American Journal of Drug and Alcohol Abuse, 38*, 146–154.

Crocker, J., Niiya, Y., & Mischkowski, D. (2008). Why does writing about important values reduce defensiveness? Self-affirmation and the role of positive other-directed feelings. *Psychological Science, 19*, 740–747.

Dougher, M. J., Hamilton, D., Fink, B., & Harrington, J. (2007). Transformation of the discriminative and eliciting functions of generalized relational stimuli. *Journal of the Experimental Analysis of Behavior, 88*, 179–197.

Dymond, S., & Roche, B. (2009). A contemporary behavior analysis of anxiety and avoidance. *The Behavior Analyst, 32*, 7–28.

Feldman, G., Greeson, J., & Senville, J. (2010). Differential effects of mindful breathing, progressive muscle relaxation, and loving-kindness meditation on decentering and negative reactions to repetitive thoughts. *Behaviour Research and Therapy, 48*, 1002–1011.

Feldner, M. T., Zvolensky, M. J., Eifert, G. H., & Spira, A. P. (2003). Emotional avoidance: An experimental test of individual differences and response suppression during biological challenge. *Behaviour Research and Therapy, 41*, 403–411.

Foody, M., Barnes-Holmes, Y, Barnes-Holmes, D., & Luciano C. (2013). An empirical investigation of hierarchical versus distinction relations in a self-based ACT exercise. *International Journal of Psychology and Psychological Therapy, 13*, 373–388.

Forman, E. M., Hoffman, K. L., McGrath, K. B., Herbert, J. D., Brandsma, L. L., & Lowe, M. R. (2007). A comparison of acceptance- and control-based strategies for coping with food cravings: An analog study. *Behaviour Research and Therapy, 45*, 2372–2386.

Grisham, J. R., Flower, K. N., Williams, A. D., & Moulds, M. L. (2011). Reappraisal and rumination during recall of a sad memory. *Cognitive Therapy and Research, 35*, 276–283.

Hayes, S. C., Barnes-Holmes, D., & Roche, B. (2001). *Relational frame theory: A post-Skinnerian account of human language and cognition.* New York, NY: Plenum.

Hayes, S. C., Barnes-Holmes, D., & Wilson, K. G. (2012). Contextual behavioral science: Creating a science more adequate to the challenge of the human condition. *Journal of Contextual Behavioral Science, 1*, 1–16.

Hayes, S. C., Luoma, J. B., Bond, F. W., Masuda, A., & Lillis, L. (2006). Acceptance and commitment therapy: Model, processes, and outcomes. *Behaviour Research and Therapy, 44*, 1–25.

Hayes, S. C., Strosahl, K. D., & Wilson, K. G. (2012). *Acceptance and commitment therapy: The process and practice of mindful change* (2nd ed.). New York, NY: Guilford.

Hayes, S. C., & Wolf, M. R. (1984). Cues, consequences and therapeutic talk: Effects of social context and coping statements on pain. *Behaviour Research and Therapy, 22*, 385–392.

Hooper, N., Villatte, M., Neofotistou, E., & McHugh, L. (2010). The effects of mindfulness versus thought suppression on implicit and explicit measures of experiential avoidance. *International Journal of Behavior Consultation and Therapy, 6*, 233–244.

Hughes, S., Barnes-Holmes, D., & Vahey, N. (2012). Holding on to our functional roots when exploring new intellectual islands: A voyage through implicit cognition research. *Journal of Contextual Behavioral Science, 1*, 17–38.

Hutcherson, C. A., Seppala, E. M., & Gross, J. J. (2008). Loving-kindness meditation increases social connectedness. *Emotion, 8*, 720–724.

Jacobson, N. S., Dobson, K. S., Truax, P. A., Addis, M. E., Koerner, K., Gollan, J. K., ... Prince, S. E. (1996). A component analysis of cognitive-behavioral treatment for depression. *Journal of Consulting and Clinical Psychology, 64*, 295–304.

Kehoe, A., Barnes-Holmes, Y., Barnes-Holmes, D., Cochrane, A., & Stewart, I. (2007). Breaking the pain barrier: Understanding and treating human suffering. *The Irish Psychologist, 33*, 288–297.

Kishita, N., & Shimada, H. (2011). Effects of acceptance-based coping on task performance and subjective stress. *Journal of Behavior Therapy and Experimental Psychiatry, 42*, 6–12.

Kosnes, L., Whelan, R., O'Donovan, A., & McHugh, L. A. (2013). Implicit measurement of positive and negative future thinking as a predictor of depressive symptoms and hopelessness. *Conscious and Cognition, 22*, 898–912.

Levin, M. E., Hayes, S. C., & Waltz, T. (2010). Creating an implicit measure of cognition more suited to applied research: A test of the Mixed Trial–Implicit Relational Assessment Procedure (MT-IRAP). *International Journal of Behavioral Consultation and Therapy, 6*, 245–262.

Levin, M. E., Hildebrandt, M., Lillis, J., & Hayes, S. C. (2012). The impact of treatment components suggested by the psychological flexibility model: A meta-analysis of laboratory-based component studies. *Behavior Therapy, 43*, 741–756.

Levitt, J. T., Brown, T. A., Orsillo, S. M., & Barlow, D. H. (2004). The effects of acceptance versus suppression of emotion on subjective and psychophysiological response to carbon dioxide challenge in patients with panic disorder. *Behavior Therapy, 35*, 747–766.

Luciano, C., Ruiz, F. J., Vizcaíno Torres, R. M., Sanchez-Martin, V., Gutierrez-Martinez, O., & Lopez-Lopez, J. C. (2011). A relational frame analysis of defusion interactions in acceptance and commitment therapy. A preliminary and quasi-experimental study with at-risk adolescents. *International Journal of Psychology & Psychological Therapy, 11*, 165–182.

Marcks, B. A., & Woods, D. W. (2007). Role of thought-related beliefs and coping strategies in the escalation of intrusive thoughts: An analog to obsessive-compulsive disorder. *Behaviour Research and Therapy, 45*, 2640–2651.

Masuda, A., Feinstein, A. B., Wendell, J. W., & Sheehan, S. T. (2010). Cognitive defusion versus thought distraction: A clinical rationale, training, and experiential exercise in altering psychological impacts of negative self-referential thoughts. *Behavior Modification, 34*, 520–538.

Masuda, A., Hayes, S. C., Sackett, C. F., & Twohig, M. P. (2004). Cognitive defusion and self-relevant negative thoughts: Examining the impact of a ninety year old technique. *Behaviour Research and Therapy, 42*, 477–485.

Masuda, A., Hayes, S. C., Twohig, M. P., Drossel, C., Lillis, J., & Washio, Y. (2009). A parametric study of cognitive defusion and the believability and discomfort of negative self-relevant thoughts. *Behavior Modification, 33*, 250–262.

McHugh, L., Barnes-Holmes, Y., & Barnes-Holmes, D. (2004). Perspective-taking as relational responding: A developmental profile. *The Psychological Record, 54*, 115–144.

McMullen, J., Barnes-Holmes, D., Barnes-Holmes, Y., Stewart, I., Luciano, C., & Cochrane, A. (2008). Acceptance versus distraction: Brief instructions, metaphors, and exercises in increasing tolerance for self-delivered electric shocks. *Behaviour Research and Therapy, 46*, 122–129.

Nicholson, E., & Barnes-Holmes, D. (2012). The Implicit Relational Assessment Procedure (IRAP) as a measure of spider fear. *The Psychological Record, 62*, 263–277.

O'Neill, J., & Weil, T. M. (2014). Training deictic relational responding in people diagnosed with schizophrenia. *The Psychological Record, 64*, 301–310.

Ostafin, B. D., Bauer, C., & Myxter, P. (2012). Mindfulness decouples the relation between automatic alcohol motivation and heavy drinking. *Journal of Social and Clinical Psychology, 31*, 729–745.

Rehfeldt, R., Dillen, J. E., Ziomek, M. M., & Kowalchuk, R. K. (2007). Assessing relational learning deficits in perspective-taking in children with high functioning autism spectrum disorder. *The Psychological Record, 57,* 23–47.

Roche, B., Kanter, J. W., Brown, K. R., Dymond, S., & Fogarty, C. C. (2008). A comparison of "direct" versus "derived" extinction of avoidance. *The Psychological Record, 58,* 443–464.

Schmeichel, B. J., & Vohs, K. (2009). Self-affirmation and self-control: Affirming core values counteracts ego depletion. *Journal of Personality and Social Psychology, 96,* 770–782.

Villatte, M., Monestès, J. L., McHugh, L., Freixa i Baqué, E., & Loas, G. (2008). Assessing deictic relational responding in social anhedonia: A functional approach to the development of theory of mind impairments. *International Journal of Behavioral Consultation and Therapy, 4,* 360–373.

Villatte, M., Monestès, J. L., McHugh, L., Freixa i Baqué, E., & Loas, G. (2010). Assessing perspective taking in schizophrenia using relational frame theory. *The Psychological Record, 60,* 413–424.

Wagener, A. L., & Zettle, R. D. (2011). Targeting fear of spiders with control-, acceptance-, and information-based approaches. *The Psychological Record, 61,* 77–92.

Watson, C., Burley, M. C., & Purdon, C. (2010). Verbal repetition in the reappraisal of contamination-related thoughts. *Behavioural and Cognitive Psychotherapy, 38,* 337–353.

Zettle, R. D., Rains, J. C., & Hayes, S. C. (2011). Processes of change in acceptance and commitment therapy and cognitive therapy for depression: A mediation reanalysis of Zettle and Rains. *Behavior Modification, 35,* 265–283.

18

Scientific Ambition

The Relationship between Relational Frame Theory and Middle-Level Terms in Acceptance and Commitment Therapy

Yvonne Barnes-Holmes, Ian Hussey,
Ciara McEnteggart, Dermot Barnes-Holmes,
and Mairéad Foody

Most natural sciences aspire to a unified theory, such as Einstein's (1945) "unified field theory" that would specify how all space and time behave under changes in the parameters of the total field. According to Wilson (2012), a unified theory requires the unity of knowledge as derived from different, but fundamentally consistent, theorizing. The mere presence of Einstein's grand ambition functions as a constant source of encouragement and guidance for physicists toward this aim. This guidance is recognizable through progress to date in terms of the natural sciences' strong adherence to parsimonious theorizing, and well-defined, testable, and coherent units of analysis.

By contrast, a unified theory of psychology seems a long way off. Wilson (2012) referred to the "archipelago" of human-related disciplines, each speaking different languages with minimal connections across islands. While it may be the case that some sections of the discipline of psychology lack ambition regarding a unified theory, it is certainly clear that any progress in this regard, even when desired, is marred in part by failure to establish consensus on overarching conceptual units of analysis that would allow us to predicate and test theories. For example, we have nothing equivalent to time, distance, or genetic inheritance. Perhaps the rarity or absence of a unified theory in psychology legitimately derives from the diversity or complexity of our subject matter. However, this seems unlikely given the extensive conceptual, and often methodological, overlap across different domains of psychology. Furthermore, Darwin's grand theory of all life on this planet certainly aimed to tackle diversity and complexity head on with a high degree of scientific parsimony.

The Wiley Handbook of Contextual Behavioral Science, First Edition. Edited by Robert D. Zettle, Steven C. Hayes, Dermot Barnes-Holmes, and Anthony Biglan.
© 2016 John Wiley & Sons, Ltd. Published 2016 by John Wiley & Sons, Ltd.

Contextual Behavioral Science: Progress to Date

Behavioral psychology, especially of the traditional Skinnerian variety, did not lack scientific or societal ambition. On the former, Skinner (1953) first sought a unified theory of nonhuman animal behavior, followed by a similar approach to human behavior that more specifically included an attempt to account for the complexity of language (1957). On societal ambition, Skinner went even beyond the limits of psychology in *Walden Two* (1948) and *Beyond Freedom and Dignity* (1971). Emerging directly from Skinner's legacy, the current approach described as contextual behavioral science (CBS) is equally lofty in its ambitions on both scientific and societal fronts to help create "a behavioral science more adequate to the challenge of the human condition" (Hayes, Barnes-Holmes, & Wilson, 2012, p. 5). While we are indeed proud of these ambitious aims, it is important to recognize that natural sciences often have extremely high aspirations as standard (e.g., Dawkins, 1986; Hawking, 1988).

In the sections that follow, we begin to explore how much success we have had in CBS toward these aims. As part of these reflections, we ask questions about our scientific model, its assumptions, and how these feed our perceptions of progress. This exercise seems consistent with a recommendation by Vilardaga, Hayes, Levin, and Muto (2009) that "When there are changes in the scientific practices of a field, it is periodically necessary to identify and describe a systematic position and the philosophical orientation and assumptions on which it stands" (p. 105).

The current chapter is divided into two broad sections: (1) a scientific analysis of acceptance and commitment therapy's (ACT; Hayes, Strosahl, & Wilson, 1999) middle-level terms, especially those comprising the hexaflex; and (2) an exploration of CBS's reticulating model between these clinical middle-level terms and the basic scientific concepts of relational frame theory (RFT; Hayes, Barnes-Holmes, & Roche, 2001). Within the former section, we conclude that:

1 Middle-level terms are problematic in certain contexts and these problems are not solved by simply describing the terms as "functional."
2 The suggested functionality of ACT's middle-level terms is problematic because the terms themselves do not appear to adhere to the philosophical truth criterion of precision-and-influence that guides functional contextualism.

In Section 2, we articulate a number of concerns we have with CBS's reticulating model. These concerns broadly center around how reticulation works and we make the following conclusions:

1 Reticulation between basic and applied/therapeutic work is asymmetrical.
2 RFT may readily reticulate, albeit in an asymmetrical way, with "middle-level terms" derived from perhaps *any* philosophical or therapeutic tradition.

We would like to acknowledge from the beginning that we recognize our own bias toward a basic scientific perspective, especially our ambition toward identifying empirically testable functional processes. While, on balance, we are no less committed to the critically important ambition of alleviating human suffering, it is our firm belief that a unified theory of psychology can only be achieved if basic functional processes lie at the very heart of its analysis. We are not the first to have adopted this view (Blackledge,

Moran, & Ellis, 2009; Hayes & Plumb, 2007; Luciano, Valdivia-Salas, & Ruiz, 2012) and see it as fundamentally important in driving our ambition forward.

Section 1: A Scientific Analysis of ACT's Middle-Level Terms

In the current section, we open with a brief summary of the middle-level terms that comprise the ACT hexaflex, as well as mention of a number of additional middle-level terms commonly used by ACT practitioners and researchers. To commence, we would like to discuss what we mean by the term "middle-level." A middle-level term is a theoretically specific, nontechnical term that has not been generated within basic scientific research. In other words, middle-level terms are not "high-level" (e.g., attention) because they cohere directly with a specific theoretical account. However, they are not "low-level" or "basic" terms either (e.g., reinforcement) because they have not been generated directly from experimental data. In other words, describing something as a middle-level term is a way of placing it on a continuum between the analytic units of the basic science (of psychology) and folk psychological terms (e.g., emotion, memory, stress, etc.) within a given domain.

The ACT Hexaflex

The ACT hexaflex model pivots on the concept of psychological flexibility into which six primary middle-level terms feed: (a) being in the present moment, (b) acceptance, (c) cognitive/emotional defusion, (d) self-as-context, (e) values, and (f) committed action (Hayes, Villatte, Levin, & Hildebrandt, 2011). According to ACT theory, this represents psychological well-being. The inverse model of psychological *inflexibility* that accounts for human suffering comprises the same six, but antagonistic concepts: (a) lack of contact with the present moment, (b) avoidance, (c) fusion, (d) self-as-concept, (e) lack of influence of values, and (f) absence of committed action in the service of values. Furthermore, ACT practitioners and researchers employ additional concepts to describe or explain psychological suffering and/or its mechanisms of change. These range from middle-level theoretically specific terms, such as self-as-process, to high-level, nontheory-specific terms, such as rigid attention, mindfulness, and meditation (e.g., see Blackledge & Barnes-Holmes, 2009; Blackledge & Drake, 2013; Hayes et al., 2011).

Hexaflex middle-level terms as "processes". The last 30 years have seen a proliferation in the number of middle-level terms used in clinical psychology (e.g., distraction, endurance, hypervigilance, reactivity, rumination, etc.). These represent well-intended attempts to specify key psychological variables that can be manipulated in the therapeutic context. The contemporary question for clinical psychology is no longer only whether treatment is effective, but what makes it so. Answering this "why" question has proven much more challenging than answering the "what" questions usually addressed by outcome research (Barlow, Sauer-Zavala, Carl, Bullis, & Ellard, 2014; Kazdin & Nock, 2003). ACT's answer to the clinical process question is the hexaflex, based on the assumption that its middle-level terms in single or in tandem represent functional behavioral processes (Hayes, Strosahl, & Wilson, 2012).

The relationship between hexaflex middle-level terms and psychological flexibility. We think it is important to draw attention to the perceived wisdom that the six middle-level terms of the hexaflex in combination, or in total, represent or comprise psychological flexibility. An immediate source of confusion that may emerge is the lack of clarity surrounding the terms psychological *flexibility* (Hayes, Strosahl, & Wilson, 2012), behavioral *flexibility* (Blackledge & Drake, 2013), and relational *flexibility* (O'Toole & Barnes-Holmes, 2009), all used by CBS researchers. Anecdotally, the current authors have noted that the term "flexibility" is often used (e.g., on the ACT and RFT listserves) without specifying which of the three types of flexibility is being referred to. This confusion is compounded by the fact that published works by CBS researchers have used the term flexibility in different ways. For instance, in one study employing the implicit relational assessment procedure or IRAP (as a measure of IQ), the concept of *relational* flexibility appears in the title (O'Toole & Barnes-Holmes, 2009). But, in another IRAP study on depression (Hussey & Barnes-Holmes, 2012), a relative change in an IRAP score is used as a measure of *psychological* flexibility as assessed by the Acceptance and Action Questionnaire-II (Bond et al., 2011). It currently remains unclear to what extent any of these terms denote functionally similar or functionally distinct processes.

Clinical utility of ACT's middle-level terms. Theoretically specific middle-level terms are largely the stock and trade of therapeutic models in general because they have broad and meaningful appeal. Classic examples include "exposure" and "cognitive restructuring," and the hexaflex components are similarly characteristic of this type of term. While the merits of an individual concept may be debated (e.g., Hayes & Plumb, 2007; Hermans, Craske, Mineka, & Lovibond, 2006; Luciano et al., 2012), this category of terms has undeniable utility as "shortcuts" for practitioners (Vilardaga et al., 2009). Indeed, we strongly agree that the middle-level terms in the hexaflex are of exceptional clinical value, not only as orienting exercises for clinicians without behavioral training, but also for all clinicians trying to ensure that they deliver ACT in a manner that is likely to achieve its therapeutic goals.

Scientific utility of ACT's middle-level terms. According to Hayes, Barnes-Holmes, and Wilson (2012), "any disconnect between science and practice slows down practice and undermines the usefulness of science" (p. 13). However, the connection between these two pillars has troubled both scientists and practitioners within psychology (e.g., Baker, McFall, & Shoham, 2008; Hayes & Berens, 2004; Melchert, 2013; Nock, 2007). Practically all would agree that such a connection is essential, but there are many interpretations of the nature and extent of integration. For behavior therapy, Franks and Wilson (1974) adopted the rather strict requirement of adherence to "operationally defined learning theory," as well as "conformity to well established experimental paradigms" (p. 7). Although strict, this would appear to be a reasonable demand of a therapy that is embedded in a behavior analytic tradition. However, Hayes, Barnes-Holmes, and Wilson (2012) have argued that it is not possible for ACT's middle-level terms to meet this demand. In their own words, they noted the limits of these terms as follows: "none of these are technical terms; none of them have the same degree of precision, scope, and depth of classical behavioral principles such as 'reinforcement,' nor of technical RFT concepts such as 'the transformation of stimulus functions" (p. 7). In the following paragraphs, we consider why this is the case, and what constitutes a technical term from a CBS perspective.

Meeting the philosophical truth criterion. In a contextual behavioral analysis, the truth criterion is prediction-and-influence with precision, scope, and depth (Hayes, Barnes-Holmes, & Wilson, 2012). A focus on precision ensures that the number of analytic concepts is limited; scope ensures that the concepts have relatively broad appeal; and depth ensures that they cohere across relevant scientific domains. *All* of these elements must be satisfied if an analytic concept is to meet the truth criterion in any contextual behavioral analysis. If a concept does *not* meet the truth criterion, it cannot be used as a "technical" term, even if it has clinical utility. Clinical utility should not therefore be conflated with scientific utility.

It is important to note at this point that from a strictly behavioral perspective, a term is not functional *in an ontological sense* (see Barnes-Holmes, 2000). For example, reinforcement is not a "real" thing. That is, it does not exist literally, but is an abstraction that has pragmatic utility based upon a substantive body of empirical evidence. This utility emerges gradually within a scientific community as its utility becomes more widely demonstrated through verifiable experience, rather than through either "truth by agreement" or "truth by democracy." Only a limited range of terms have been deemed pragmatically useful (i.e., functional) within the behavioral tradition, including reinforcement, punishment, and stimulus generalization. For example, reinforcement constitutes a functional unit of analysis in the sense that the term denotes a causal relationship between a class of responses (e.g., lever pressing) and a class of consequences. The term causal is used here to indicate that there is an increase in the class of responses only when they produce or lead to an increase in the class of consequences. More generally, according to Vilardaga et al. (2009), functionality is defined as being "based on sets of functional analyses based on behavioral principles based on behavioral observations" (pp. 115–116). In what follows, we will argue that none of these specifications is the case for ACT's middle-level terms.

The Functionality of ACT's Middle-Level Terms

The procedure–process–outcome problem. In order to articulate the concerns we have about the suggested functionality of ACT's middle-level terms, we would like to introduce the reader to a classic problem in cognitive psychology, commonly known as the conflation of procedure, process, and outcome (De Houwer & Moors, 2010), which leads to circular reasoning. Consider the circularity in the following example. An ACT practitioner might say that a new client is highly fused with her psychological content (e.g., "I'm stupid"), hence defusion techniques will be needed to defuse her, and thus reduce her level of fusion. In other words, a defusion procedure will be used to create an outcome of defusion through the process of defusion. If the procedure "worked" (e.g., the client reported a decrease in the believability of her thoughts, which the therapist interpreted as defusion), then the clinician might say that the defusion procedure had, through the process of defusion, produced the desired outcome of defusion.

The process–procedure–outcome distinction helps highlight the circularity in talking about defusion in this way. Indeed, the key problem with all middle-level terms (and ill-defined mentalistic terms generally), is that it is frequently difficult to determine which of these is being targeted in any given (scientific) narrative. For example, there are defusion procedures, or at least a set of techniques collectively known by clinicians as such, and these are arranged together in the service of a common therapeutic aim. And there may even be a process of defusion that defusion procedures are designed to activate. And there are likely to be defusion outcomes, or at least defusion effects. Hence, used in an ACT context, defusion is used in multiple ways to refer to three different phenomena. How these three elements can be separated out and discriminated accurately remains unclear. Admittedly, separating outcome from technique might be relatively straightforward, but isolating defusion as a functional process appears more problematic. As we will argue below, mediation analyses and analogue studies alone will never serve this purpose.

Blackledge and Drake (2013) summarized the two main types of analyses typically used to investigate the "functionality" of the ACT hexaflex: (a) mediation analyses, and (b) analogue studies. We will argue, however, that these forms of analyses do not necessarily provide empirical evidence that ACT's middle-level concepts capture functional processes. Furthermore, we would argue that these types of analyses do not "prove" that the so-called processes (functional or otherwise) are being manipulated in the context of therapy.

Mediation analyses. Various statistical techniques are often used to identify the variables that mediate outcomes, where mediation refers to whether change on one measure (e.g., scores on a questionnaire that putatively assesses defusion) explains change on another measure (e.g., reduced scores on an inventory that ostensibly evaluates depression). These techniques are typically performed in situations where it is difficult to conduct functional analyses (see Kazdin & Nock, 2003 for a broader discussion). Paradoxically, the questionnaires that putatively assess these mediating constructs are often referred to as "process" measures. At this point, we think it is important to distinguish between the concept of a "process" measure used in the psychometric and/or clinical research sense and the types of functional processes with which the current chapter is concerned. In short, we would argue that, in spite of its name, a psychometric "process" measure does not necessarily capture a functional process. In fact, psychometric instruments serve at best as nothing more than proxies of psychological processes (functional or otherwise). To put it bluntly, filling out a questionnaire or completing a diary that aims to measure fusion, for example, simply captures a self-report about fusion. But it does not necessarily capture the psychological process of fusion itself. Instead, it captures the behavior of filling out a questionnaire or completing a diary.

A lot of clinical research, including that which occurs within CBS, relies on the use of proxy measures. An example is measuring suicidal ideation using a self-report questionnaire. Consistent with our earlier argument pertaining to questionnaires, the tool is not measuring the behavior of ideating, but the respondent's report on ideating, and even this is done only in the specific context of the questionnaire. We would call this measurement a proxy. Proxies have utility because some level of reliability and validity can be ascertained psychometrically. That is, the proxy behavior (i.e., responses on a suicidal ideation questionnaire such the Scale for Suicide Ideation; Beck, Kovacs, & Weissman, 1979) can be shown to be relatively consistent, both within the measure itself and across time (i.e., reliability). Furthermore, this proxy behavior can also be shown to be predictive of the behavior of interest, and not predictive of behaviors that are not of interest (i.e., convergent and divergent validity). However, even if a measure were shown to have all of the above (i.e., sound psychometric properties), it would remain a measure of proxy behavior rather than a direct observation of the behavior of interest. For example, reports of suicidal ideation may have utility, but they do not provide direct access to ideating as it is occurring. Proxies, by definition, remain forever proxies.

As is standard practice in clinical psychological science, mediation analyses employ proxy measures and these are also used extensively within ACT's randomized controlled trials (RCTs), especially to substantiate the claim that outcomes are mediated by psychological flexibility and the hexaflex processes that purportedly comprise it. However, the reliance upon mediation analyses raises questions about the functional distinctiveness of ACT's middle-level terms. Specifically, questions arise around the boundary conditions that must be met in order to distinguish one middle-level term from another. In other words, without knowing where one term ends and another begins, how can we know that there are *six* "processes" rather than seven, or five, and so on? Even aside from the relationships *across* middle-level terms, a question also arises about the relationship between these terms and the concept of psychological flexibility. That is, even if we were to find through mediation analyses that the six hexaflex terms (and other relevant middle-level terms) could be reduced to a single mediating variable, such as "psychological flexibility," such results would not render "psychological flexibility" a functional process. Indeed according to Nock (2007), the use of mediation analyses within clinical psychology is generally problematic because it does not provide *direct* evidence for the isolation of a psychological process. Specifically, Nock argued that "while statistical mediation is necessary to support the operation of a mechanism of change, it does not provide sufficient evidence for such a relation. Indeed, just as correlation does not equal causation, mediation does not equal mechanism" (Nock, 2007, p. 5; see also De Houwer, Gawronski, & Barnes-Holmes, 2013). Analogously, just as Nock argues that mediational analyses do not provide direct evidence of a cognitive mechanism, we would argue that such analyses cannot provide direct evidence of a functional process.

Analogue studies. It is often suggested that analogue studies complement mediation analyses. In particular, analogue studies have been used in ACT research to scrutinize middle-level terms (e.g., hexaflex components, such as defusion) in highly controlled experimental settings (see chapter 17 in this volume, for example). Typically, these studies investigate outcome effects (using proxy measures) following stress induction procedures in nonclinical populations (e.g., Foody, Barnes-Holmes, & Barnes-Holmes, 2012). However, even under optimal experimental conditions (see Dymond, Roche, & Bennett, 2013; and Kazdin & Nock, 2003 for a broader discussion), analogue studies, almost by definition, must remain silent with regard to whether or not ACT's middle-level terms refer to functional processes. This is not to argue that analogue studies are without value, but simply to underscore that they do not, in our view, move the field forward in terms of identifying basic scientific (functional) processes (e.g., Gutiérrez-Martínez, Luciano-Soriano, Rodríguez-Valverde, & Fink, 2004; Kehoe, Barnes-Holmes, Barnes-Holmes, Cochrane, & Stewart, 2007; Keogh, Barnes-Holmes, & Barnes-Holmes, 2008; McMullen et al., 2008).

To fully appreciate the foregoing point, consider the number of errors underlying the logic of analogue studies as the basis for identifying functional processes. An analogue study usually selects a specific component from a larger treatment package (e.g., such as those tested in RCTs) with the goal of creating a procedure that can be studied in a controlled environment. Although this seems perfectly logical, the very first step of selecting the component constitutes the first error. This selection is based upon a presumed correspondence between the designated component (selected as a "good candidate") and a target "functional" process. For example, we might select a word repetition task as a good example of *defusion-the-procedure* in order to target *defusion-the-process*. The error thus involves conflating procedure with process. In making the first error, we also make a second in assuming that there "is" such a functional process (i.e., defusion). The third error is in assuming that the procedure in question will provide *direct evidence* of any functional process (i.e., does not rely on proxy measures). The fourth error lies in assuming that the relationship between *that* procedure and *that* outcome demonstrates the specific process one attempted to target in the first place (rather than some other process).

Even if the foregoing errors are fully recognized, it may still be tempting to seek convergent evidence of the target process by seeking similar evidence from another (defusion) task (e.g., the floating leaf exercise). This constitutes the fifth and final error: that is, assuming that having two "defusion" procedures that yield a similar outcome will provide better evidence for defusion-the-process. This simply involves repeating the first error noted above. Indeed, no number of nonfunctionally defined procedures that lead to similar outcomes will provide direct evidence for defusion-the-process. In short, while analogue studies can answer the "what" questions (e.g., what procedures produce what outcomes), they cannot answer the "why" questions (e.g., why do those procedures produce those outcomes), insofar as the "why" question is about processes rather than about procedures or outcomes.

Summarizing and Illustrating the Dilemma as We See It

At this point, we would like to summarize our points from the paragraphs above:

1 ACT's middle-level terms most frequently refer to outcomes or procedures, and not functional processes.
2 Attempts to provide evidence that middle-level terms refer to functional processes involve mediation analyses and analogue studies, neither of which has provided direct evidence of functional processes.

In the paragraph below, we offer a metaphor that we hope captures at least some of the points above regarding our concerns with middle-level terms, such as those in the hexaflex. The reader should note that the original rocket metaphor was created by Blackledge et al. (2009) for a broader purpose, and the current metaphor is an adaptation of same for a more specific purpose.

A team of researchers built a rocket – a metal tube that used controlled explosions to hurl itself into space. The team became well respected in the field of building rockets. They knew all about rocket construction and its details, and even had a coherent philosophy of rocket building to which all of their construction adhered. Most importantly, they knew the rockets could indeed fly: many of their rockets made it into orbit.

A second team of researchers had the same aim of building rockets that could go to space. They too had a coherent philosophy on good rocket building, to which they adhered. However, they had very different ideas about how to build and test rockets.

In short, everyone agreed that building rockets was important, but the two teams could not agree on what specifically made a good rocket, although both teams thought it had something to do with "speed." The first team theorized that the concept of speed was influential to rockets successfully reaching space. They articulated this theory and generated testable hypotheses. For example, a more powerful engine would result in a higher speed, and a rocket must fly faster than a specific minimum speed to be successful.They tested these and related hypotheses across repeated trials involving many different speeds. They concluded from these tests that speed must be manipulated carefully in order for the rocket to successfully reach space. More importantly, they arrived at a basic scientific principle: "speed = distance divided by time," and from this they were able to work out the minimum speed necessary for a rocket to escape the Earth's atmosphere.

The other team of researchers also speculated that the concept of speed played a role in rocket travel, but they had a very different approach to its measurement. They employed crowds of spectators to collect data from the ground during the launch of all their test rockets. They asked each spectator questions such as "How fast was the rocket, from 1/Not speedy to 10/Very speedy?" Based on the responses of large samples of spectators, across many rocket trials, and using excellent statistical analyses, the researchers confirmed their view that speed had a role to play in rocket travel, but were unable to work out how much speed was needed for a rocket to escape the Earth's atmosphere. As a result the second team built many rockets that made it into space, but many that did not.

If you wanted to develop a therapy to solve a complex psychological problem, which of the two models would you adopt? The strategy adopted by the first team would require great patience and time, and many clients might suffer in the interim. However, you would persevere in abstract testing of the critical concept of X, in the knowledge that X was not only essential to your therapy, but that it was the key process to be manipulated in order for you to create change and, more importantly, to understand how change occurs. Ironically, while many of these tests would not even involve participants with the same complex psychological problem, the large body of data would allow you to understand the critical concept of X within therapy and how to manipulate it precisely. In the wider context, your understanding of X could also be generalized to develop other applications of X in other areas of psychology.

The strategy adopted by the second team would require much less patience and time, and as a result fewer clients would suffer in the interim because you could conduct your treatment as soon as possible. However, although you have developed a broad knowledge of the concept X, your limited experimental testing would not afford precise understanding nor manipulation of X. As such, it would become apparent as more and more clients were treated that your treatment is less effective than initially thought, because the limitations in your knowledge of X do not permit you adequate flexibility when novel scenarios emerge.

In a nutshell, we believe that ACT's middle-level terms are an example of the second strategy. They are undoubtedly useful in therapeutic change and they may even reflect the core functional processes that are essential to changing human psychology. This achievement is supported by considerable evidence of psychological change and both mediational analyses and analogue studies of how this change might have happened. However, it is important to note that researchers from a variety of therapeutic traditions have expressed growing dissatisfaction with this general approach (Barlow et al., 2014; Nock, 2007). We too believe that this strategy will not be enough in the long run because it cannot provide *direct* evidence of the *core* process(es) at work.

We strongly believe that while theorizing in ACT has been of enormous clinical benefit to date, its scientific potential is limited. Many more sufferers of the human condition may indeed access treatment in the interim. However, there may be even more that cannot be helped in the future because the core processes have not been isolated, and therefore cannot be targeted appropriately. As basic research scientists, we are no less dedicated, metaphorically, to the flying of rockets, even though we may not pilot them ourselves. We believe that building and flying rockets is an incredibly complex scientific endeavor that will not be served adequately without understanding the core processes; without testing these rigorously and directly; and without understanding the precise manipulation of these processes in the construction of each individual rocket.

Section 2: CBS: Toward a Unified Theory

In this section, we open with the need for clarity around how the CBS community can harness each of its elements to progress the science toward a unified theory. We consider whether the recently proposed "reticulating model" (Hayes, Long, Levin, & Follette, 2013) can facilitate this agenda. Specifically, we address the question of how successfully we can close the gap between RFT and ACT. We finish by considering future directions for basic research in the service of a unified theory for CBS.

The Pursuit of a Unified Theory

Given that a primary ambition of CBS lies in the construction of a unified theory of human suffering and its treatment, its ultimate goal must be toward a unified theory of psychology by uniting multiple levels of analysis under a single theoretical umbrella. Toward this latter aim, the field can only progress with constructive discussions about how its different elements can, and should, interact with one another. However, it is important to emphasize that our own view is that these discussions should be open and respectful to avoid any sense of prescription about how any elements of the field should conduct their business. For us, it is more a matter of the community clarifying pragmatic avenues through which coherent progress can be made.

Discussions about unification are not unique to CBS, but can be seen within many areas of psychology. For example, De Houwer et al. (2013) have recently discussed how different levels of scientific analysis within cognitive psychology can effectively communicate with one another (see also Marr, 1982). Many similar debates have taken place within various therapeutic traditions, although it is well known that progress has been limited (e.g., Barlow et al., 2014; Blackledge et al., 2009; Egan, Wade, & Shafran, 2011).

For CBS, the key question concerns how basic researchers and clinicians can exchange information in a meaningful and progressive way. The methods of doing this are often reduced to what are loosely referred to as "top-down" versus "bottom-up" models (Hayes & Plumb, 2007). Some of the problems inherent in the top-down approach are reflected in our discussion of middle-level terms in Section 1. In contrast, a bottom-up approach seeks to first identify basic processes before using them to build a conceptual analysis. Again, we noted some of the problems associated with an exclusively bottom-up approach in the previous section. In our view, however, the contrast between top-down and bottom-up models is often overly simplistic and potentially unhelpful. Indeed, Hayes et al. (2013) appear to have more accurately characterized the relationship as one of "reticulation" motivated by mutual interest in the service of fostering a productive relationship between basic research and applied therapeutic interests.

Most psychologists would agree, in principle, with the potential benefits of a productive relationship between basic research and therapy. However, this does not suggest that everyone's work must be directly in the service of this relationship. For example, basic researchers often conduct studies that seem irrelevant to clinicians, and clinicians do effective therapy that is of no interest to basic researchers. These individual endeavors of the scientist and the practitioner should be treated with the utmost respect, and should not be shoehorned into a broader organizational or philosophical agenda. After all, the point of a unified theory is to enhance the field as a whole, not to be pursued as an end in itself. As Hayes et al. (2013) have argued, "only a very small number of researchers need to be willing to pursue both sides of the issue (basic and applied) to allow an overall team to cooperate" (p. 876).

In the paragraphs below, we discuss whether the reticulating model of treatment development[1] suggested by Hayes et al. (2013; see also Hayes, Barnes-Holmes, & Wilson, 2012) will serve CBS's prosecution of a unified theory of psychology. First, we summarize the reticulating model. Second, we elaborate the mechanisms of reticulation implied by the model, as we see them. For example, what forms of information pass between basic scientists and clinicians, and does comparable information pass in each direction? Third, after outlining our concerns with the model, we conclude that it does not offer a fair reflection of the current relationship between basic research and practice in CBS and, more importantly, that this relationship may not appropriately facilitate the pursuit of a unified theory.

A Reticulating Model in CBS

According to Hayes, Barnes-Holmes, and Wilson (2012), the working model that captures CBS currently is "a reticulated (that is, web-like) model of scientific and practical development, in which theoretical and technological progress occurs at multiple levels but in an interconnected way" (p. 6). The current chapter focuses on the relationships among what Hayes et al. refer to as philosophical assumptions, analyses, and theory (see Figure 18.1, adapted from Hayes et al., 2013).

In Figure 18.1, for CBS, we assume that "basic theory" refers to basic behavior analytic concepts such as reinforcement and punishment, and the technical terms found in RFT. "Applied theory," we assume, refers for example to ACT's hexaflex model of psychological flexibility (Hayes, Strosahl, & Wilson, 2012). Mutual interest-based analyses of "middle-level terms" might therefore include analogue studies and mediation analyses of defusion, acceptance, etc. "Basic analysis" might refer to, for example, the study of derived relational responding as a model of semantic relations in natural language (e.g., Dymond & Barnes, 1995).[2] In summary, for a unified theory of CBS, the bridge to be crossed is specifically, but not exclusively, between RFT and ACT.

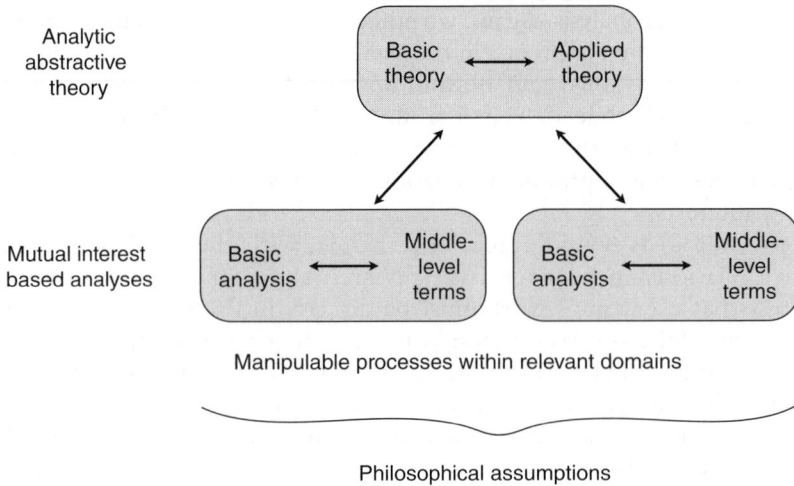

Figure 18.1 The contextual behavioral science model of treatment development. From Hayes et al., 2013, p. 872.

Reticulation is Asymmetrical

Hayes and colleagues' (2013; see also Hayes, Barnes- Holmes, & Wilson, 2012) reticulating model appears to assume a transfer of information between basic science and applied theory in a bidirectional, symmetrical manner. Put simply, these authors suggest that ACT can inform RFT as much, and in the same manner, as RFT can inform ACT. The implication is that they are equally and mutually beneficial. In other words, Hayes et al. (2013) suggest that the "traffic" that goes from ACT to RFT contains functional middle-level terms that have clinical and psychological precision and utility. As such, they tell us something important about psychology and particularly about the human condition, and therefore warrant empirical analysis. In return, the traffic that goes from RFT to ACT comprises empirical support for ACT's middle-level terms through a language of relational translation (e.g., an RFT "interpretation" of a given defusion procedure). For Hayes et al. (2013), this is a special relationship built upon supposed functionality and shared philosophical roots.

For us, the traffic that goes from ACT to RFT is an orienting exercise that highlights phenomena, domains, and classes of behavior, such as "fusion," "literality," or "psychological flexibility." In return, the expansion of RFT's remit is guided by the consideration of how its established functional processes might be at work in these areas. For example, we might ask "Is relational flexibility as measured on an IRAP akin to the type of psychological flexibility that is described in ACT?" In short, the traffic that goes in each direction between RFT and ACT is not symmetrical. We will elaborate on this below.

Before continuing with our traffic metaphor in the context of exploring reticulation, we would like to use the current paragraph to express our concerns about the RFT translations of ACT middle-level terms that are increasingly prevalent in the CBS literature. In short, an RFT *interpretation* does not equate to an RFT *analysis*. For example, Blackledge and Barnes-Holmes (2009) defined defusion as "well established verbal stimulus transformations being disrupted via the displacement of contextual conditions that control relational responding in general" (p. 49). Although this description appears to be consistent with the language of RFT, one could question the extent to which it could direct clear functional (experimental) analyses of relational responding. In this respect, RFT interpretations that remain nothing but interpretations have little more to offer than relying exclusively on middle-level terms. Let us put it another way, a functional-sounding interpretation is not a functional analysis (see Hayes & Brownstein, 1986). We consider this to be an important point as behavioral psychology has already witnessed the problems caused by conflating the two (e.g., Skinner, 1957).

Is Asymmetrical Reticulation the Same as "Bottom-Up"?

Historically, the science of behavior analysis has advocated a bottom-up approach (e.g., Skinner, 1938) and some have argued that CBS continue in this tradition (e.g., Hayes & Plumb, 2007; Vilardaga et al., 2009). However, other authors within CBS have pointed to a number of generic limitations in adopting a bottom-up approach (Hayes, Barnes-Holmes, & Wilson, 2012). These are as follows:

1   Scientific progress is slow.
2   Basic scientists may not be interested in investigating concepts of primary interest to clinicians.
3   Even if basic researchers and clinicians have shared interests in the same concepts, the complexity of the scientific analysis may limit its direct translation to clinical practice.

In short, Hayes, Barnes-Holmes, and Wilson (2012) argued that the key dilemma facing the relationship between basic science and therapy is more practical than theoretical. With these limitations in mind, the authors proposed the reticulating model of scientific progress for CBS.

Given the difficulties inherent in trying to reticulate a basic science approach (e.g., RFT) with a therapeutic model that espouses nonfunctional middle-level terms (e.g., ACT), we would argue that this dilemma is, on the contrary, more theoretical than practical. First and foremost, science is not guided by the proximal demands of therapeutic work. Second, if we are pursuing a unified theory, we will only know that we are succeeding when we can observe expansion of the basic science. While the process involves asymmetrical reticulation with middle-level terms, it cannot rely solely on hijacking functionally precise terms and using them to construct interpretations of therapeutically-important phenomena. Rather, scientific progress is defined by the expansion of the basic account. As such, in our view, progress is not entirely *driven* from the bottom-up, but is *accomplished through it*.

The End of the Special Relationship?

For us, the relationship between RFT and ACT is not necessarily a special one. We have already made useful developments in RFT by drawing on middle-level terms from other domains of psychology as an orienting exercise. Examples include associations versus propositions (Hughes & Barnes-Holmes, 2011; Smyth,

Barnes-Holmes, & Barnes-Holmes, 2008), Theory of Mind (McHugh, Barnes-Holmes, & Barnes-Holmes, 2004), and implicit cognition (Hughes, Barnes-Holmes, & Vahey, 2012). Once we assume the position that ACT's middle-level terms are not necessarily functional – and are therefore comparable in value to orienting terms from any other area of the discipline – we must also accept that a basic science can reticulate with any middle-level terms insofar as they are heuristic or orienting. Similarly, CBS's basic researchers (i.e., relational frame theorists) might be oriented by *any* therapeutic model, such as cognitive therapy, cognitive behavioral therapy, or mindfulness-based cognitive therapy (see Hussey & Barnes-Holmes, 2012; Nicholson & Barnes-Holmes, 2012; Remue, De Houwer, Barnes-Holmes, Vanderhasselt, & De Raedt, 2013 for examples).

It is of course plausible, given that RFT and ACT have shared philosophical roots, that ACT may require less expansion, modification, and/or discard in order to be aligned more closely with RFT than a therapy with philosophically disparate roots (see Barlow et al., 2014 for a broader treatment of the modification of therapy in light of basic research findings). Critically, however, conceptualizing this greater alignment as a move toward integrating ACT with RFT ignores the potential for wider consolidation of psychotherapeutic strategies. Put simply, the point of a unified theory is to bring closer together basic science and its applications *more generally*. Furthermore, we would argue that this type of relationship between a basic science and the full breadth of its professional domain is precisely the type of web-like model that has been proposed for CBS (Hayes, Barnes-Holmes, & Wilson, 2012).

How to Advance the Basic Account toward a Unified Theory

We would like to be clear that we are not opposed to the eloquent model of reticulation that Hayes, Barnes-Holmes, and Wilson (2012; see also Hayes et al., 2013) have proposed for CBS. Indeed, depending upon how one defines reticulation, we would agree that this is preferable to a "purely" bottom-up approach and clearly more desirable to a "top-down" strategy. Admittedly also, we do not yet have an RFT model of human suffering. Nonetheless, we feel it essential to remain exact and coherent in the concepts we use for both science and practice. Indeed, the field of behavioral psychology is predicated on this. While the call for unification through basic science is not unique (e.g., Blanton & Jaccard, 2006; Hayes & Berens, 2004; Kazdin & Nock, 2003; Lindsley, Skinner, & Solomon, 1953; see also Baker et al., 2008; Henriques, 2013; Melchert, 2013), we believe that the core conceptual units and their properties proposed by RFT, and those that may yet be forthcoming, have something unique to offer the understanding of the human condition and how psychological suffering might be alleviated.

Throughout the current chapter, we have argued strongly for the advancement of basic science. At this point in time, the evidence for RFT's key conceptual unit of relational responding seems robust (e.g., Dymond & Barnes, 1995; 1996; Healy, Barnes-Holmes, & Smeets, 2000; McHugh et al., 2004; Stewart, Barnes-Holmes, & Roche, 2004; Whelan, Barnes-Holmes, & Dymond, 2006). In our view, it is now time to go beyond demonstration research on individual frames and the transformation of functions. Specifically, we think an important direction for future research will be to conduct experimental functional analyses of the role that RFT's verbal units, and their various properties, play in human suffering and its alleviation.

Concluding Comments

We would like to close the chapter by drawing attention to our overriding sense that CBS is a living tradition. We would be disappointed if anything in this chapter served to restrict or constrain the scientific or therapeutic interests of the community or its individual members. It takes courage and creativity to expand science or therapy and/ or to take them in a new direction, but doing so is probably essential for achieving progress. For us, progress also involves clearly articulating one's own view and aspirations, and discussing these openly as they relate to the views and aspirations of others. Sometimes these exchanges can be disheartening, but they are nonetheless honest and productive. If the community of CBS is to move further in the direction of its ambition toward a unified theory this seems a humble place to start.

Acknowledgment

The authors would like to thank Dr. Miles Thompson for his insightful and constructive comments on an earlier version of this chapter.

Notes

1   We focus here on a reticulating model of treatment development specifically, rather than basic science and its application more generally for two related reasons. First, Section 2 is concerned specifically with the relation between RFT and ACT as the basic science of CBS and a psychotherapeutic application, respectively. Second, the reticulating model proposed by Hayes et al. (2013) pertained specifically to psychotherapeutic development.

2   In making a clear distinction between basic and applied analyses, it is important to note that we are at risk of oversimplifying the nature of research conducted within CBS. For example, studies have employed the IRAP as a measure of fluency in relational responding (which is clearly a basic science focus) and sought to determine if this fluency correlates with measures of middle-level terms such as the AAQ (e.g., Hussey & Barnes-Holmes, 2012). One could argue that such research lies somewhere between the two extremes of basic and applied.

References

Baker, T. B., McFall, R. M., & Shoham, V. (2008). Current status and future prospects of clinical psychology: Toward a scientifically principled approach to mental and behavioral health care. *Psychological Science in the Public Interest, 9*, 68–103.

Barlow, D. H., Sauer-Zavala, S., Carl, J. R., Bullis, J. R., & Ellard, K. K. (2014). The nature, diagnosis, and treatment of neuroticism: Back to the future. *Clinical Psychological Science, 2*, 344–365.

Barnes-Holmes, D. (2000). Behavioral pragmatism: No place for reality and truth. *The Behavior Analyst, 23*, 191–202.

Beck, A. T., Kovacs, M., & Weissman, A. (1979). Assessment of suicidal intention: The Scale for Suicide Ideation. *Journal of Consulting and Clinical Psychology, 47*, 343–352.

Blackledge, J. T., & Barnes-Holmes, D. (2009). Core processes in acceptance and commitment therapy. In J. T. Blackledge, J. Ciarrochi, & F. P. Deane (Eds.), *Acceptance and commitment therapy: Contemporary research and practice* (pp. 41–58). Sydney, Australia: Australian Academic Press.

Blackledge, J. T., & Drake, C. E. (2013). Acceptance and commitment therapy: Empirical and theoretical considerations. In S. Dymond & B. Roche (Eds.), *Advances in relational frame theory and contextual behavioral science: Research and application* (pp. 219–252). Oakland, CA: New Harbinger.

Blackledge, J. T., Moran, D. J., & Ellis, A. E. (2009). Bridging the divide: Linking basic science to applied psychotherapeutic interventions – A relational frame theory account of cognitive disputation in rational emotive behavior therapy. *Journal of Rational-Emotive & Cognitive-Behavior Therapy, 27*, 232–248.

Blanton, H., & Jaccard, J. (2006). Arbitrary metrics in psychology. *American Psychologist, 61*, 27–41.

Bond, F. W., Hayes, S. C., Waltz, R., Baer, R. A., Carpenter, K. S., Guenole, N., ... Zettle, R. D. (2011). Preliminary psychometric properties of the Acceptance and Action Questionnaire-II: A revised measure of psychological inflexibility and experiential avoidance. *Behavior Therapy, 42*, 676–688.

Dawkins, R. (1986). *The blind watchmaker*. New York, NY: Norton.

De Houwer, J., Gawronski, B., & Barnes-Holmes, D. (2013). A functional-cognitive framework for attitude research. *European Review of Social Psychology, 24*, 252–287.

De Houwer, J., & Moors, A. (2010). Implicit measures: Similarities and differences. In B. Gawronski & B. K. Payne (Eds.), *Handbook of implicit social cognition: Measurement, theory, and applications* (pp. 176–193). New York, NY: Guilford.

Dymond, S., & Barnes, D. (1995). A transformation of self-discrimination response functions in accordance with the arbitrarily applicable relations of sameness, more-than, and less-than. *Journal of the Experimental Analysis of Behavior, 64*, 163–184.

Dymond, S., & Barnes, D. (1996). A transformation of self-discrimination response functions in accordance with the arbitrarily applicable relations of sameness and opposition. *The Psychological Record, 46*, 271–300.

Dymond, S., Roche, B., & Bennett, M. (2013). Relational frame theory and experimental psychopathology. In S. Dymond & B. Roche (Eds.), *Advances in relational frame theory and contextual behavioral science: Research and application* (pp. 199–218). Oakland, CA: New Harbinger.

Egan, S. J., Wade, T. D., & Shafran, R. (2011). Perfectionism as a transdiagnostic process: A clinical review. *Clinical Psychology Review, 31*, 203–212.

Einstein, A. (1945). A generalization of the relativistic theory of gravitation. *Annals of Mathematics, 46*, 578–584.

Franks, C. M., & Wilson, G. T. (1974). *Annual review of behavior therapy: Theory and practice.* New York, NY: Brunner/Mazel.

Foody, M., Barnes-Holmes, Y., & Barnes-Holmes, D. (2012). Empirical investigation of the single-sentence paradigm as a method of stress induction. *International Journal of Psychology and Psychological Therapy 12*, 127–138.

Gutiérrez-Martínez, O., Luciano-Soriano, C., Rodríguez-Valverde, M., & Fink, B. C. (2004). Comparison between an acceptance-based and a cognitive-control-based protocol for coping with pain. *Behavior Therapy, 35*, 767–783.

Hawking, S. (1988). *A brief history of time*. New York, NY: Bantam Books.

Hayes, S. C., Barnes-Holmes, D., & Roche, B. (Eds.). (2001). *Relational frame theory: A post-Skinnerian account of human language and cognition*. New York, NY: Plenum.

Hayes, S. C., Barnes-Holmes, D., & Wilson, K. G. (2012). Contextual behavioral science: Creating a science more adequate to the challenge of the human condition. *Journal of Contextual Behavioral Science, 1*, 1–16.

Hayes, S. C., & Berens, N. M. (2004). Why relational frame theory alters the relationship between basic and applied behavioral psychology. *International Journal of Psychology and Psychological Therapy, 4,* 341–335.

Hayes, S. C., & Brownstein, A. J. (1986). Mentalism, behavior-behavior relations, and a behavior-analytic view of the purposes of science. *The Behavior Analyst, 9,* 175–190.

Hayes, S. C., Long, D. M., Levin, M. E., & Follette, W. C. (2013). Treatment development: Can we find a better way? *Clinical Psychology Review, 33,* 870–882.

Hayes, S. C., & Plumb, J. C. (2007). Mindfulness from the bottom up: Providing an inductive framework for understanding mindfulness processes and their application to human suffering. *Psychological Inquiry: An International Journal for the Advancement of Psychological Theory, 18,* 242–248.

Hayes, S. C., Strosahl, K., & Wilson, K. G. (1999). *Acceptance and commitment therapy: An experiential approach to behavior change.* New York, NY: Guilford.

Hayes, S. C., Strosahl, K.D., & Wilson, K. G. (2012). *Acceptance and commitment therapy: The process and practice of mindful change* (2nd ed.). New York, NY: Guilford.

Hayes, S. C., Villatte, M., Levin, M., & Hildebrandt, M. (2011). Open, aware, and active: Contextual approaches as an emerging trend in the behavioral and cognitive therapies. *Annual Review of Clinical Psychology, 7,* 141–168.

Healy, O., Barnes-Holmes., D., & Smeets, P. (2000). Derived relational responding as generalized operant behavior. *Journal of the Experimental Analysis of Behavior, 74,* 207–227.

Henriques, G. (2013). Evolving from methodological to conceptual unification. *Review of General Psychology, 17,* 168–173.

Hermans, D., Craske, M. G., Mineka, S., & Lovibond, P. F. (2006). Extinction in human fear conditioning. *Biological Psychiatry, 60,* 361–368.

Hughes, S., & Barnes-Holmes, D. (2011). The dominance of associative theorizing in implicit attitude research: Propositional and behavioral alternatives. *The Psychological Record, 61,* 465–496.

Hughes, S., Barnes-Holmes, D., & Vahey, N. (2012). Holding on to our functional roots when exploring new intellectual islands: A voyage through implicit cognition. *Journal of Contextual Behavioral Science, 1,* 17–38.

Hussey, I., & Barnes-Holmes, D. (2012). The Implicit Relational Assessment Procedure as a measure of implicit depression and the role of psychological flexibility. *Cognitive and Behavioral Practice, 19,* 573–582.

Kazdin, A. E., & Nock, M. K. (2003). Delineating mechanisms of change in child and adolescent therapy: Methodological issues and research recommendations. *Journal of Child Psychology and Psychiatry, 44,* 1116–1129.

Kehoe, A., Barnes-Holmes, Y., Barnes-Holmes, D., Cochrane, A., & Stewart, I. (2007) Breaking the pain barrier: Understanding and treating human suffering. *The Irish Psychologist, 33,* 288–297.

Keogh, C., Barnes-Holmes, Y., & Barnes-Holmes, D. (2008). Fused or defused? Getting to grips with what your mind is telling you. *The Irish Psychologist, 35,* 1–8.

Lindsley, O., Skinner, B.F., Solomon, H.C. (1953). *Studies in behavior therapy: Status report. I.* Waltham, MA: Metropolitan State Hospital.

Luciano, C., Valdivia-Salas, S., & Ruiz, F. (2012). The self as the context for rule-governed behavior. In L. McHugh & I. Stewart (Eds.), *The self and perspective taking: Contributions and applications from modern behavioral science* (pp. 143–160). Oakland, CA: New Harbinger.

Marr, D. (1982). *Vision.* San Francisco, CA: Freeman.

McHugh, L., Barnes-Holmes, Y., & Barnes-Holmes, D. (2004). Perspective-taking as relational responding: A developmental profile. *The Psychological Record, 54,* 115–144.

McMullen, J., Barnes-Holmes, D., Barnes-Holmes, Y., Stewart, I., Luciano, C., & Cochrane, A. (2008). Acceptance versus distraction: Brief instructions, metaphors and exercises in increasing tolerance for self-delivered electric shocks. *Behaviour Research and Therapy,* *46*, 122–129.

Melchert, T. P. (2013). Beyond theoretical orientations: The emergence of a unified scientific framework in professional psychology. *Professional Psychology: Research and Practice, 44*, 11–19.

Nicholson, E., & Barnes-Holmes, D. (2012). Developing an implicit measure of disgust propensity and disgust sensitivity: Examining the role of implicit disgust propensity and sensitivity in obsessive-compulsive tendencies. *Journal of Behavior Therapy and Experimental Psychiatry, 43*, 922–930.

Nock, M. K. (2007). Conceptual and design essentials for evaluating mechanisms of clinical change. *Alcoholism: Clinical and Experimental Research, 31*, 4S–12S.

O'Toole, C., & Barnes-Holmes, D. (2009). Three chronometric indices of relational responding as predictors of performances on a brief intelligence test: The importance of relational flexibility. *The Psychological Record, 59*, 119–132.

Remue, J., De Houwer, J., Barnes-Holmes, D., Vanderhasselt, M. A., & De Raedt, R. (2013). Self-esteem revisited: Performance on the implicit relational assessment procedure as a measure of self- versus ideal self-related cognitions in dysphoria. *Cognition & Emotion, 27*, 1441–1449.

Skinner, B. F. (1938). *The behavior of organisms.* New York, NY: Appleton-Century-Crofts.

Skinner, B. F. (1948). *Walden two.* New York, NY: Macmillan.

Skinner, B. F. (1953). *Science and human behavior.* New York, NY: Free Press.

Skinner, B. F. (1957). *Verbal behavior.* Englewood Cliffs, NJ: Prentice Hall.

Skinner, B. F. (1971). *Beyond freedom and dignity.* New York, NY: Knopf.

Smyth, S., Barnes-Holmes, D., & Barnes-Holmes, Y. (2008). Acquired equivalence in human discrimination learning: The role of propositional knowledge. *Journal of Experimental Psychology: Animal Behavior Processes, 34*, 167–177.

Stewart, I., Barnes-Holmes, D., & Roche, B. (2004). A functional-analytic model of analogy using the relational evaluation procedure. *The Psychological Record, 54*, 531–552.

Vilardaga, R., Hayes, S. C., Levin, M. E., & Muto, T. (2009). Creating a strategy for progress: A contextual behavioral science approach. *The Behavior Analyst, 32*, 105–133.

Whelan, R., Barnes-Holmes, D., & Dymond, S. (2006). The transformation of consequential functions in accordance with the relational frames of more-than and less-than. *Journal of the Experimental Analysis of Behavior, 86*, 317–335.

Wilson, D. S. (2012). Making contextual behavioral science part of the united ivory archipelago. *Journal of Contextual Behavioral Science, 1*, 39–42.

Part IV

Extending the CBS Tradition
Anthony Biglan

19

A Functional Contextualist Approach to Cultural Evolution
An Introduction to Part IV
Anthony Biglan

As many other scientists do, contextual behavioral scientists aspire to make broad and significant contributions to the improvement of human well-being. Thus far, the strength of the movement has been its laser-like focus on identifying variables that predict and influence behavior. Most of the work has focused on basic questions about human verbal and cognitive processes or research on clinical interventions. However, if the movement is ultimately to achieve its broader aspirations, it must influence many other areas of the human endeavor and must work effectively with other human sciences.

In this regard, it may be useful to consider the experiences of some of our forebears. Behavior analysts have often had a rocky relationship with the rest of the behavioral science community. A common complaint has been that other areas pay no attention to behavior analytic theory and findings (e.g., Poling, 2010). At the same time, behavior analysts have often rejected or ignored the research of those who were not behavior analysts. One reason for the rejection was of course that other scientists were not pursuing the prediction and influence of behavior. However, the tendency of behavior analysts to isolate themselves from nonbehavior analytic approaches got in the way of the field using the principles of behavior analysis to transform society in all of the ways that are needed. In short, it seems that isolation has not helped to advance the ultimate goals of behavior analysis. Perhaps a more flexible approach that holds tight to the goal of improving human welfare through the prediction and influence of behavior, but is open to any practice that seems likely to advance that goal, can be more productive.

In this chapter, we suggest a framework that could organize how we move from current knowledge to widespread improvements in human well-being. Then we discuss how the spread of psychological flexibility could contribute to these improvements and what is known about the environments needed to ensure that people thrive. Finally, we propose a research and practice agenda that goes beyond the clinic and we introduce this section's chapters, which are intended to further this agenda.

The Wiley Handbook of Contextual Behavioral Science, First Edition. Edited by Robert D. Zettle, Steven C. Hayes, Dermot Barnes-Holmes, and Anthony Biglan.
© 2016 John Wiley & Sons, Ltd. Published 2016 by John Wiley & Sons, Ltd.

The Public Health Perspective

The public health perspective can organize what contextual behavioral science needs to do to contribute to widespread improvements in human well-being. Once a disease, behavior, or environmental condition has been shown to affect well-being, we become concerned about its incidence and prevalence in the population. This leads to the development of a surveillance system for monitoring incidence and prevalence. Research on the factors that affect incidence and prevalence contribute to the evolution of more effective ways to affect incidence and prevalence. Public health approaches tend to be quite pragmatic, implementing whatever programs, policies, or practices can be shown to affect the incidence and prevalence of the problem.

Public health practices evolved out of the often desperate efforts to control infectious disease. Beginning in 1348 with the bubonic plague, which killed as many as 40% of the people in Europe (Kelly, 2005), societies have evolved methods to identify epidemics, track their course, and control their spread. For centuries after this sentinel event, people found themselves trying to cope with outbreaks of plague, cholera, and other diseases. By Galileo's time (1564–1642), Italian cities had developed systems for monitoring the outbreak and spread of epidemics and controlling their spread largely through quarantine (Sobel, 1999). When John Snow proved that contaminated water caused the London cholera outbreak in 1854 (Johnson, 2006), the value of searching for causes of problems became clearer.

The public health framework can apply to any aspect of human well-being. The tobacco control movement involves targeting and tracking the prevalence of smoking and the incidence of young people beginning to smoke. A large and growing body of epidemiological evidence shows that smoking is highly harmful to health and delineates the major influences on youth taking up smoking. When this evidence was effectively publicized through Surgeon General Reports and other media, support for tobacco control mounted and efforts to reduce smoking expanded. When evidence emerged that as many as 50,000 nonsmoking Americans die each year from exposure to other people's smoke, clean indoor air policies began to be adopted by communities and whole states. Through advocacy, policy changes, and the dissemination of effective cessation and prevention programs, a dramatic change in US culture has occurred. Forty years ago, people smoked in most meetings; today it is largely unthinkable.

The tobacco control movement illustrates another aspect of public health: Once a risk factor for a disease is identified, changing the incidence and prevalence of the risk factor itself becomes a public health goal. Thus, we have gone from a concern about the incidence of cancer and heart disease to a focus on reducing the incidence and prevalence of smoking, to efforts to reduce the number of teens who are exposed to cigarette marketing (National Cancer Institute, 2008).

The generic features of the public health framework can be applied to any aspect of the cultural evolution. Indeed changes in a culture can themselves be measured in terms of the incidence and prevalence of behaviors and the practices of groups and organizations (Biglan, 1995). A key question, then, is whether we can articulate and target a set of conditions that, if effectively modified, would result in widespread improvements in human well-being.

Nurturing Environments: Conditions that Appear to Be Fundamental to Human Well-being

Enough evidence about the development of psychological, behavioral, and physical health has amassed that we can specify the basic conditions that seem necessary for human well-being. Because we are striving to organize a public health movement that improves all aspects of well-being, it seems useful to encapsulate the key conditions under one heading. We have proposed the term *nurturing environments* (Biglan, Flay, Embry, & Sandler, 2012). These environments have four features.

Minimizing Toxic Conditions

Humans evolved in circumstances that varied in degree of threat. At times, food was abundant and threats were minimal. At other times, not so much. For this reason, we have an evolved capacity to express different genes depending on circumstances. Evidence is mounting that during pregnancy, stressful maternal experiences, including social threats and nutritional shortages, result in epigenetic processes that can permanently "wire" offspring to become hypervigilant to threat and quick to be aggressive (Gatzke-Kopp, 2011; Kaiser & Sachser, 2005). In former times, such an orientation apparently increased the chances that a group would survive. However, in the current world, threatening circumstances generally heighten tendencies that lead to myriad problem behaviors including aggression, depression, drug abuse, and early childbearing (Biglan, Brennan, Foster, & Holder, 2004; Dishion, Ha, & Véronneau, 2012).

The impact of socially threatening conditions is substantial and wide-ranging. Sapolsky (1994) provides a compendium of the influence of stress on diverse human problems. A threat stimulates the hypothalamic-pituitary-adrenal (HPA) axis to release a cascade of hormones, which culminate in high levels of cortisol. The process elevates blood pressure and pulse and energizes the organism to fight or take flight. The removal of the threatening stimulus reverses the process; the hormones are reabsorbed and the organism calms. Chronic exposure to threatening stimuli can reset the HPA system, which can result in a host of deleterious effects, including hypertension, diabetes, gastrointestinal disorders, stunting of growth, cardiovascular disease, ulcers, immune system suppression, erectile dysfunction, and problems in learning and memory.

In an analysis compatible with ACT/RFT research, Sapolsky argues that, unlike humans, zebras do not get ulcers, because, for them, once the environmental threat goes away, the HPA system returns to normal. Humans, however, are capable of verbally keeping the threat present, thus exposing themselves to chronic stress.

Coercive social processes. Understanding the social processes that shape and maintain human conflict are vital to reducing these toxic social conditions that cause so much harm to human well-being. Patterson and his colleagues (e.g., Patterson, Reid, & Dishion, 1992) conducted a series of direct observation studies of family interactions that delineated a coercive process that underlies conflict. They found that in families with an aggressive child, family members had higher levels of aversive interactions in which family members would tease, criticize, bully, and attack each other. Moment-to-moment analysis of their interaction patterns revealed a negative reinforcement process in which family members' aversive behavior was maintained by its intermittent effect of getting others in the family to desist from their own aversive behavior

(Patterson, Dishion, & Bank, 1984). Aggressive children became quite skilled in using aggression to get others to "back off."

Longitudinal studies of these children showed that this process began a trajectory in which aggressive children failed in school due to their lack of cooperation with teachers and faced social rejection from peers due to their aggression. These experiences led aggressive children to form friendships with other rejected peers (Dishion & Dodge, 2005) and these deviant peer groups became training grounds for the development of multiple problem behaviors (Patterson, DeBaryshe, & Ramsey, 1989).

Subsequent studies have shown that coercive social processes are also involved in marital conflict and depression. Studies of marital conflict show that spouses are responding to each other's slights, criticisms, complaint, and put-downs with their own nasty reactions. What keeps it going is that each person occasionally escalates their angry behavior and it temporarily puts a stop to their partner's unpleasant behavior. Direct observation studies of the interactions of depressed mothers and their families showed that the depressive behavior of the mother resulted in other family members ceasing their critical behavior toward the mother (Biglan et al., 1985; Hops et al., 1987).

Interventions that reduce coercive interactions. Some of the strongest evidence of the importance of minimizing socially toxic conditions comes from experimental evaluations of family and school interventions that reduce conflict and coercion. Each of the empirically supported parenting interventions that has been developed over the past 25 years involves helping parents replace impatient, angry, and coercive methods of dealing with their children with more patient, attentive, and positively reinforcing styles (Biglan, 2003; Biglan et al., 2012). The evidence is especially compelling from studies showing that the effect of these interventions are mediated by reductions in coercive parenting practices (Patterson, Forgatch, & DeGarmo, 2010; Zhou, Sandler, Millsap, Wolchik, & Dawson-McClure, 2008).

Similarly, effective school-wide interventions focusing on social behavior replace punitive discipline with promotion and reinforcement of prosocial behavior (Beets et al., 2008; Bradshaw, Mitchell, & Leaf, 2010; Durlak et al., 2007; Flannery et al., 2003; Horner et al., 2009; Snyder et al., 2010).

Biological toxins. Biologically toxic conditions create additional medical and behavioral problems. One such condition is a low level of omega 3 in the diet, which epidemiological and experimental studies have shown to affect aggression, obesity, and cognitive development (e.g., Hooper et al., 2006; Lin & Su, 2007). Another is airborne lead, which is associated with rates of aggression in US counties (Haynes et al., 2011).

Model, Promote, and Richly Reinforce Prosocial Behavior

An extensive repertoire of cooperative, prosocial behavior is beneficial to the individual and those around them (Wilson, O'Brien, & Sesma, 2009) and families, schools, and neighborhoods need to nurture these behaviors and the values that underpin them (Biglan et al., 2012; Wilson, 2011).

If you look inside every one of the family or school interventions that has been shown to prevent problem development, you will see that a key component is the modeling and reinforcement of prosocial behavior (Biglan, 2003). For example, behavioral parenting skills programs teach parents to interact attentively with their children, often letting the child take the lead in the interaction (Webster-Stratton, 2000). They encourage parents to praise children's desirable behavior (e.g., Dishion & Stormshak, 2007) and to use stickers, points, and privileges as rewards for desirable behavior (Forgatch & DeGarmo, 1999).

Effective school-wide programs that support prosocial development teach specific cooperative behaviors and set up systems to recognize and reward such behavior (e.g., Embry, Flannery, Vazsonyi, Powell, & Atha, 1996; Flay & Allred, 2003; Horner et al., 2009).

Limiting Influences and Opportunities that Promote Problem Behavior

Environments that nurture positive social development and prevent problem development must limit influences and opportunities for young people to experiment with problem behavior. Jean Richardson and her colleagues found that young people who were at home after school without adult supervision were more likely to use drugs and engage in other problem behavior (Richardson et al., 1989). Family interventions for adolescents that prevent problem development invariably encourage parents to monitor what their child is doing and set limits on opportunities to hang out with deviant peers (Dishion & McMahon, 1998). School-wide programs to support positive behavior have systems to track disruptive behavior in all the settings of the school and to intervene and prevent problems in "hot spots" where problem levels are rising (Sugai & Horner, 2002).

Some problem behaviors result from marketing's influence. Cigarette marketing has a well-established influence on young people's initiation of smoking (National Cancer Institute, 2008). Evidence also indicates that marketing influences youth alcohol use (Grube, 2004) and the consumption of unhealthful food (Nestle, 2002).

The Promotion of Psychological Flexibility

The concept of psychological flexibility is well known to the contextual behavioral science community, but will be new to many of the people who helped to delineate the importance of the first three sets of nurturing conditions. It is defined as "the ability to contact the present moment more fully as a conscious human being and to change, or persist in, behavior when doing so serves valued ends" (Biglan, Hayes, & Pistorello, 2008).

The evidence for the importance of psychological flexibility is of three types. The first includes studies showing that people who lack psychological flexibility are more likely to have psychological problems such as depression, anxiety, substance abuse, and risky sexual behavior (Hayes, Strosahl, & Wilson, 2012). Second, numerous studies show that, as people become more psychologically flexible, they become better able to change a wide variety of behaviors including smoking (Gifford et al., 2004; 2011), depression (Zettle & Hayes, 2002), drug abuse (Hayes et al., 2004), weight control (Lillis, Hayes, Bunting, & Masuda, 2009), physical activity (Butryn, Forman, Hoffman, Shaw, & Juarascio, 2011), epilepsy (Lundgren, Dahl, Yardi, & Melin, 2008), coping with pain (Wicksell, Melin, Lekander, & Olsson, 2009), and coping with psychotic symptoms (Bach & Hayes, 2002; Gaudiano & Herbert, 2006). Together these first two types of evidence suggest that people will do better with encouragement to be psychologically flexible.

Third, evidence indicates that increasing psychological flexibility is associated with less prejudice toward others (Lillis & Hayes, 2007; Lillis et al., 2009; Masuda et al., 2007) and greater empathy and compassion (Vilardaga, Estévez, Levin, & Hayes, 2012). Although the evidence remains limited, this evidence suggests that promoting psychological flexibility in individuals will benefit others. It may contribute to improving the other facets of nurturing environments. That is, people with greater empathy toward others may be less likely to attack others and more likely to behave in prosocial ways, thereby reducing the level of toxic social conditions around them and modeling caring, prosocial behavior.

In sum, there appear to be reciprocal relationships among psychological flexibility, toxic social conditions, and prosocial behavior. To reduce the prevalence of socially toxic conditions and increase prosociality, we should promote psychological flexibility. And, although evidence is less clear, it may also be that to promote psychological flexibility, we must minimize socially toxic conditions and promote prosociality.

The Relevant Environments

The evidence reviewed thus far comes from research on family and school environments. These are the most important environments for child and adolescent development and the most efficient way to lower the prevalence of problems in the population may be to concentrate on ensuring that young people develop successfully. However, other environments also affect well-being. In particular, workplaces can provide social and material support for people, but they can also be a source of great stress (Flaxman & Bond, 2010). Similarly, neighborhoods vary in the degree to which they provide social support to residents and the degree to which they promote prosocial or problematic behavior (Sampson, Morenoff, & Gannon-Rowley, 2002; Sampson & Raudenbush, 2004; Szapocznik et al., 2006).

An Agenda for Going beyond the Clinic

If the preceding is a roughly accurate account of the conditions that affect human well-being, then achieving the aspirations of the ACBS community to improve human well-being can be operationally defined: *We need to increase the prevalence of nurturing environments.* In part, this is a matter of increasing the prevalence of psychological flexibility, which will increase individual well-being and likely reduce stress for others. However, public health research shows that much can be done in addition to directly treating individuals. We may be able to prevent the development of psychological inflexibility and the problems associated with it through preventive interventions that alter the conditions that lead to these problems. In addition to intervening with people who already have problems, we can decrease the prevalence of socially and biologically toxic conditions, promote prosocial behavior, and limit opportunities for problem behavior – all of which will contribute to preventing problem development, including the development of experiential avoidance.

The Tobacco Control Movement as a Model

The tobacco control movement is a model for how to achieve widespread societal change. Fifty years ago, the majority of men and a large proportion of women in the United States smoked; smoking was commonplace in nearly every home, meeting, and public space. Most people considered smoking to be sophisticated, even glamorous. Think of any conference you have been to in recent years ... 40 years ago, cigarette smoke would have filled the room.

Yet despite the tobacco companies' expenditure of hundreds of millions of dollars to prevent any reduction in smoking, the smoking culture has dwindled dramatically. The change resulted from four types of activity. First, "creative epidemiology" expanded research that documented the harm of smoking, and found effective ways of communicating these harms to the general public. Thanks to Surgeon General reports, National Cancer Institute monographs, and media campaigns, an increasing proportion of the population came to see smoking as a dangerous habit. This led many people to stop smoking and generated support for policies that increasingly restricted smoking and practices that promoted smoking. Every policy change further strengthened the norms against smoking, motivated more smokers to quit, and increased support for research and efforts to reduce smoking (Biglan & Taylor, 2000).

Second, the tobacco control movement developed a surveillance system to track the prevalence of smoking, the incidence of young people taking up smoking, the practices of tobacco companies that promoted smoking, and the efforts of government and nonprofit organizations to curtail smoking. Data on increases and decreases in smoking and influences on smoking have guided the movement to put more resources into efforts that seemed to be working and abandon or modify those that were not.

Third, as evidence of the harm of smoking increased and spread through the population, organizations formed to combat smoking. This network of organizations further spread the word, obtained a growing amount of money to support anti-tobacco efforts, and advocated for policies that further influenced smoking and the environmental conditions and practices that supported it.

Fourth, the movement took a flexible and pragmatic approach to reducing the prevalence of smoking. It implemented and evaluated programs, policies, and practices that seemed likely to affect smoking or influences on smoking, expanding those that were working and dropping those that were not. Similar to the current situation with clinical interventions to affect psychological flexibility, efforts began with behaviorally based programs provided to individuals (Lichtenstein & Rodrigues, 1977; Schmahl, Lichtenstein, & Harris, 1972). However, once it became clear that few people who wanted to quit would sign up for a formal program (Lichtenstein & Glasgow, 1977), efforts shifted to media campaigns to motivate quitting (Flay & Sobel, 1983), policies to restrict smoking (Bauer, Hyland, Li, Steger, & Cummings, 2005), taxation that had been shown to prevent young people from taking up smoking (Grossman & Chaloupka, 1997), and helplines to support quit attempts (Lichtenstein, Zhu, & Tedeschi, 2010). What drove this flexibility was the understanding that the ultimate goal should be not just convincing individual smokers to quit but reducing the prevalence of smoking. By that measure, the movement has been quite successful: between 1965 and 2005, the prevalence of adult smoking in the United States declined from more than 50% for men and 35% for women to less than 30% for men and 25% for women (Centers for Disease Control and Prevention, 2007). In California, where the movement has been most active, the rate of adult smoking has declined to 11.9% (California Department of Public Health, 2011). The movement provides a model for how we might increase the prevalence of nurturing environments. We have sketched such a movement elsewhere (Biglan, 2015; Biglan & Embry, 2013).

Extending the Reach of Contextual Behavioral Science

Evolving societies that ensure the long-term well-being of the human population requires addressing all major influences on well-being. Each chapter in this section discusses the application of the CBS framework to an influence on well-being. The chapters emphasize the unique contributions the ACBS movement can make. But, in an effort to avoid the mistakes the behavior analysis movement made, they incorporate the extant evidence from other approaches on how environments can be made more nurturing, integrate it within a CBS perspective, and highlight the ways that CBS can enhance and is enhancing progress.

Chapter 20 (Backen Jones, Whittingham, Coyne, & Lightcap) focuses on families. Families are the crucibles that produce each new generation. Depending on the quality of our families, the next generation will consist of prosocial and productive members or will be a population with a high density of crime, drug abuse, depression, conflict, and ill health. Enormous progress has been made on how families can learn to reduce coercive processes and nurture prosocial behavior (Biglan, 2015). This chapter provides a brief overview of the evidence on behavioral approaches to family interventions and integrates that work with recent work from the CBS perspective.

Schools are the second vital component of a society that ensures well-being. Chapter 21 (Szabo & Dixon) focuses on the impact of schools on the development of prosocial behavior. (Part 2 of the handbook covers the growing body of work on the CBS approach to cognitive and academic development.) This chapter presents a CBS conceptualization of schools' influences on positive social development. It describes existing evidence-based approaches to creating nurturing schools, delineates the ways in which a CBS framework can strengthen these efforts, and examines the problem of how to increase the prevalence of schools that adopt and effectively implement schoolwide approaches to nurturing student and staff well-being.

The third major institution of society that affects well-being is the workplace. Chapter 22 (Bond, Lloyd, Flaxman, & Archer) describes considerable recent research on how workplaces can increase psychological flexibility. The chapter also provides a framework for the thinking about the flexibility of organizations.

From a different angle, chapter 23 (Levin, Lillis, & Biglan) approaches the problem of evolving more effective societies. In a more speculative vein, the chapter focuses on two important problems and considers what public health campaigns to affect the prevalence of these problems might look like. Given the growing evidence from CBS research on the importance of psychological flexibility, the first section of the chapter considers what a comprehensive effort to increase the prevalence of psychological flexibility might look like. The second section reviews recent research on prejudice and stigma and suggests ways in which this evidence might guide efforts to reduce prejudice, stigma, and intergroup conflict in communities.

The revolutionary progress in our understanding of human behavior over the past 50 years is derived largely from the analysis of the selection of behavior by its consequences (Biglan, 2003). The way in which the practices of groups and organizations evolve has received much less attention (Biglan & Glenn, 2013). Yet our ability to predict and influence the selection of group and organization practices is vital to achieving societies in which most people are healthy, productive, and caring. Examples range from the need to influence corporations not to market harmful products (Biglan, 2011) to the need to strengthen the ability of advocacy organizations to support effective public policies (Biglan & Cody, 2013). Chapter 24 (Biglan, Lee, & Cody) provides a functional contextualist framework for understanding the evolution of organizational practices within capitalist systems. It explains how this analysis fits into a multilevel account of evolution and, in particular, how behavioral and symbolic selection affects and is affected by the selection of group practices.

All of the growing progress on how to build more nurturing societies will be like ashes in our mouths if we do not reverse the trajectory of global warming. The rate of warming is distinctly higher than what climate scientists predicted 20 years ago (Hansen, Sato, & Ruedy, 2012). Credible estimates state that we will experience very serious harm to human well-being in the next 100 years unless we virtually eliminate carbon emission (Akuginow & Haines-Stiles, 2011). Yet just as with many other areas of human endeavor, behavioral science has had a limited role in addressing this problem. It would be a sad irony if the progress made in the behavioral sciences brought us to the verge of truly achieving the kind of healthy, caring societies that humans have ever longed for, but in failing to alter the cultural practices that are producing global warming, we end up swamping all of our progress. Chapter 25 (Alavosius, Newsome, Houmanfar, & Biglan) therefore presents a CBS perspective on how to address this critical problem.

References

Akuginow, E. (Producer), & Haines-Stiles, G. (Director). (2011). *EARTH: The Operators' Manual* [Motion picture]. United States: Passport to Knowledge/Geoff Haines-Stiles Productions.

Bach, P., & Hayes, S. C. (2002). The use of acceptance and commitment therapy to prevent the rehospitalization of psychotic patients: A randomized controlled trial. *Journal of Consulting and Clinical Psychology, 70*, 1129–1139.

Bauer, J. E., Hyland, A., Li, Q., Steger, C., & Cummings, K. M. (2005). A longitudinal assessment of the impact of smoke-free worksite policies on tobacco use. *American Journal of Public Health, 95*, 1024–1029.

Beets, M. W., Flay, B. R., Vuchinich, S., Acock, A. C., Li, K. K., & Allred, C. (2008). School climate and teachers' beliefs and attitudes associated with implementation of the positive action program: A diffusion of innovations model. *Prevention Science, 9*, 264–275.

Biglan, A. (1995). *Changing cultural practices: A contextualist framework for intervention research*. Reno, NV: Context Press.

Biglan, A. (2003). Selection by consequences: One unifying principle for a transdisciplinary science of prevention. *Prevention Science, 4*, 213–232.

Biglan, A. (2011). Corporate externalities: a challenge to the further success of prevention science. *Prevention Science, 12*, 1–11.

Biglan, A. (2015). *The nurture effect: How the science of human behavior can improve our lives and our world*. Oakland, CA: New Harbinger.

Biglan, A., Brennan, P. A., Foster, S. L., & Holder, H. D. (2004). *Helping adolescents at risk: Prevention of multiple problem behaviors*. New York, NY: Guilford.

Biglan, A., & Cody, C. (2013). Integrating the human sciences to evolve effective policies. *Journal of Economic Behavior & Organization, 90*, S152–S162.

Biglan, A., & Embry, D. D. (2013). A framework for intentional cultural change. *Journal of Contextual Behavioral Science, 2*, 95–104.

Biglan, A., Flay, B. R., Embry, D. D., & Sandler, I. (2012). Nurturing environments and the next generation of prevention research and practice. *American Psychologist, 67*, 257–271.

Biglan, A., & Glenn, S. S. (2013). Toward prosocial behavior and environments: Behavioral and cultural contingencies in a public health framework. In G. J. Madden, W. V. Dube, T. Hackenberg, G. P. Hanley, & K. A. Lattal (Eds.), *APA handbook of behavior analysis, Volume 2: Translating principles into practice* (pp. 255–275). Washington, DC: American Psychological Association.

Biglan, A., Hayes, S. C., & Pistorello, J. (2008). Acceptance and commitment: Implications for prevention science. *Prevention Science, 9*, 139–152.

Biglan, A., Hops, H., Sherman, L., Friedman, L. S., Arthur, J., & Osteen, V. (1985). Problem-solving interactions of depressed women and their husbands. *Behavior Therapy, 16*, 431–451.

Biglan, A., & Taylor, T. K. (2000). Why have we been more successful in reducing tobacco use than violent crime? *American Journal of Community Psychology, 28*, 269–302.

Bradshaw, C. P., Mitchell, M. M., & Leaf, P. J. (2010). Examining the effects of schoolwide positive behavioral interventions and supports on student outcomes: Results from a randomized controlled effectiveness trial in elementary schools. *Journal of Positive Behavior Interventions, 12*, 133–148.

Butryn, M. L., Forman, E., Hoffman, K., Shaw, J., & Juarascio, A. (2011). A pilot study of acceptance and commitment therapy for promotion of physical activity. *Journal of Physical Activity & Health, 8*, 516–522.

California Department of Public Health (2011). *California adult smoking rate reaches historic low*. Retrieved from http://www.cdph.ca.gov/Pages/NR11-031.aspx

Centers for Disease Control & Prevention. (2007). Cigarette smoking among adults – United States, 2006. *Morbidity & Mortality Weekly Report, 56*, 1157–1161. Retrieved from http://www.cdc.gov/mmwr/preview/mmwrhtml/mm5644a2.htm

Dishion, T. J., & Dodge, K. A. (2005). Peer contagion in interventions for children and adolescents: Moving towards an understanding of the ecology and dynamics of change. *Journal of Abnormal Child Psychology, 33*, 395–400.

Dishion, T. J., Ha, T., & Véronneau, M.-H. (2012). An ecological analysis of the effects of deviant peer clustering on sexual promiscuity, problem behavior, and childbearing from early adolescence to adulthood: An enhancement of the life history framework. Special section: Beyond mental health: an evolutionary analysis of development under risky and supportive environmental conditions. *Developmental Psychology, 48*, 703–717.

Dishion, T. J., & McMahon, R. J. (1998). Parental monitoring and the prevention of child and adolescent problem behavior: A conceptual and empirical formulation. *Clinical Child and Family Psychology Review, 1*, 61–75.

Dishion, T. J. & Stormshak, E. (2007). *Intervening in children's lives: An ecological, family-centered approach to mental health care*. Washington, DC: APA Books.

Durlak, J. A., Taylor, R. D., Kawashima, K., Pachan, M. K., DuPre, E. P., Celio, C. I., … Weissberg, R. P. (2007). Effects of positive youth development programs on school, family, and community systems. *American Journal of Community Psychology, 39*, 269–286.

Embry, D. D., Flannery, D. J., Vazsonyi, A. T., Powell, K. E., & Atha, H. (1996). PeaceBuilders: A theoretically driven, school-based model for early violence prevention. *American Journal of Preventive Medicine, 22*, 91–100.

Flannery, D. J., Vazsonyi, A. T., Liau, A. K., Guo, S., Powell, K. E., Atha, H., … Embry, D. D. (2003). Initial behavior outcomes for the PeaceBuilders universal school-based violence prevention program. *Developmental Psychology, 39*, 292–308.

Flaxman, P. E., & Bond, F. W. (2010). A randomised worksite comparison of acceptance and commitment therapy and stress inoculation training. *Behaviour Research and Therapy, 48*, 816–820.

Flay, B. R., & Allred, C. G. (2003). Long-term effects of the Positive Action program. *American Journal of Health Behavior, 27*, S6–S21.

Flay, B. R., & Sobel, J. L. (1983). The role of mass media in preventing adolescent substance abuse. In T. J. Glynn, C. G. Leukefeld, & J. P. Ludford (Eds.), National Institute of Drug Abuse, *Preventing adolescent drug abuse: intervention strategies*, NIDA Research Monograph 47 (pp. 5–35). Washington, DC: US Department of Health and Human Services.

Forgatch, M. S., & DeGarmo, D. S. (1999). Parenting through change: An effective prevention program for single mothers. *Journal of Consulting and Clinical Psychology, 67*, 711–724.

Gatzke-Kopp, L. M. (2011). The canary in the coalmine: The sensitivity of mesolimbic dopamine to environmental adversity during development. *Neuroscience & Biobehavioral Reviews, 35*, 794–803.

Gaudiano, B. A., & Herbert, J. D. (2006). Acute treatment of inpatients with psychotic symptoms using acceptance and commitment therapy: Pilot results. *Behaviour Research and Therapy, 44*, 415–437.

Gifford, E. V., Kohlenberg, B. S., Hayes, S. C., Antonuccio, D. O., Piasecki, M. M., Rasmussen-Hall, M. L., & Palm, K. M. (2004). Acceptance-based treatment for smoking cessation. *Behavior Therapy, 35*, 689–705.

Gifford, E. V., Kohlenberg, B. S., Hayes, S. C., Pierson, H. M., Piasecki, M. P., Antonuccio, D. O., & Palm, K. M. (2011). Does acceptance and relationship focused behavior therapy contribute to bupropion outcomes? A randomized controlled trial of functional analytic psychotherapy and acceptance and commitment therapy for smoking cessation. *Behavior Therapy, 42*, 700–715.

Grossman, M., & Chaloupka, F. J. (1997). Cigarette taxes. The straw to break the camel's back. *Public Health Reports, 112*, 290–297.

Grube, J. W. (2004). Alcohol in the media: Drinking portrayals, alcohol advertising, and alcohol consumption among youth. In National Research Council and Institute of Medicine, *Reducing underage drinking: a collective responsibility* (pp. 597–624). Committee on Developing a Strategy to Reduce and Prevent Underage Drinking, Board on Children, Youth, and Families, Division of Behavioral and Social Sciences and Education. Washington, DC: The National Academies Press.

Hansen, J., Sato, M., & Ruedy, R. (2012). Perception of climate change. *Proceedings of the National Academy of Sciences, 109*, E2415–E2423.

Hayes, S. C., Strosahl, K. D., & Wilson, K. G. (2012). *Acceptance and commitment therapy: The process and practice of mindful change* (2nd ed.). New York, NY: Guilford.

Hayes, S. C., Wilson, K. G., Gifford, E. V., Bissett, R., Piasecki, M., Batten, S. V., … Gregg, J. (2004). A preliminary trial of twelve-step facilitation and acceptance and commitment therapy with polysubstance-abusing methadone-maintained opiate addicts. *Behavior Therapy, 35*, 667–688.

Haynes, E. N., Chen, A., Ryan, P., Succop, P., Wright, J., & Dietrich, K. N. (2011). Exposure to airborne metals and particulate matter and risk for youth adjudicated for criminal activity. *Environmental Research, 111*, 1243–1248.

Hooper, L., Thompson, R. L., Harrison, R. A., Summerbell, C. D., Ness, A. R., Moore, H. J., … Smith, G. D. (2006). Risks and benefits of omega 3 fats for mortality, cardiovascular disease, and cancer: systematic review. *British Medical Journal, 332*, 752–760.

Hops, H., Biglan, A., Sherman, L., Arthur, J., Friedman, L., & Osteen, V. (1987). Home observations of family interactions of depressed women. *Journal of Consulting and Clinical Psychology, 55,* 341–346.

Horner, R. H., Sugai, G., Smolkowski, K., Eber, L., Nakasato, J., Todd, A. W., & Esperanza. J. (2009). A randomized, wait-list controlled effectiveness trial assessing school-wide positive behavior support in elementary schools. *Journal of Positive Behavior Interventions, 11,* 133–144.

Johnson, S. (2006). *The ghost map.* New York, NY: Riverhead Books.

Kaiser, S., & Sachser, N. (2005). The effects of prenatal social stress on behaviour: Mechanisms and function. *Neuroscience & Biobehavioral Reviews, 29,* 283–294.

Kelly, J. (2005). *The great mortality: An intimate history of the Black Death, the most devastating plague of all time.* New York, NY: Harper International.

Lichtenstein, E., & Glasgow, R. E. (1977). Rapid smoking: Side effects and safeguards. *Journal of Consulting and Clinical Psychology, 45,* 815–821.

Lichtenstein, E., & Rodrigues, M. R. P. (1977). Long-term effects of rapid smoking treatment for dependent cigarette smokers. *Addictive Behaviors, 2,* 109–112.

Lichtenstein, E., Zhu, S. H., & Tedeschi, G. J. (2010). Smoking cessation quitlines: An under-recognized intervention success story. *American Psychologist, 65,* 252–261.

Lillis, J., & Hayes, S. C. (2007). Applying acceptance, mindfulness, and values to the reduction of prejudice: A pilot study. *Behavior Modification, 31,* 389–411.

Lillis, J., Hayes, S. C., Bunting, K., & Masuda, A. (2009). Teaching acceptance and mindfulness to improve the lives of the obese: A preliminary test of a theoretical model. *Annals of Behavioral Medicine, 37,* 58–69.

Lin, P. Y., & Su, K. P. (2007). A meta-analytic review of double-blind, placebo-controlled trials of antidepressant efficacy of omega-3 fatty acids. *Journal of Clinical Psychiatry, 68,* 1056–1061.

Lundgren, T., Dahl, J., Yardi, N., & Melin, L. (2008). Acceptance and commitment therapy and yoga for drug-refractory epilepsy: A randomized controlled trial. *Epilepsy & Behavior, 13,* 102–108.

Masuda, A., Hayes, S. C., Fletcher, L. B., Seignourel, P. J., Bunting, K., Herbst, S. A., ... Lillis, J. (2007). Impact of acceptance and commitment therapy versus education on stigma toward people with psychological disorders. *Behaviour Research and Therapy, 45,* 2764–2772.

National Cancer Institute. (2008). *The role of the media in promoting and reducing tobacco use.* Tobacco control monograph no. 19, NIH publication no. 07-6242. Bethesda, MD: Author. Retrieved from http://cancercontrol.cancer.gov/tcrb/monographs/19/

Nestle, M. (2002). *Food politics: How the food industry influences nutrition and health.* California studies in food and culture. Berkeley, CA: University of California Press.

Patterson, G. R., DeBaryshe, B. D., & Ramsey, E. (1989). A developmental perspective on antisocial behavior. *American Psychologist, 44,* 329–335.

Patterson, G. R., Dishion, T. J., & Bank, L. (1984). Family interaction: A process model of deviancy training. *Aggressive Behavior, 10,* 253–267.

Patterson, G. R., Forgatch, M. S., & DeGarmo, D. S. (2010). Cascading effects following intervention. *Development and Psychopathology, 22,* 949–970.

Patterson, G. R., Reid, J. B., & Dishion, T. J. (1992). *Antisocial boys: A social interactional approach* (Vol. 4). Eugene, OR: Castalia.

Poling, A. (2010). Looking to the future: Will behavior analysis survive and prosper? *The Behavior Analyst, 33,* 7–17.

Richardson, J. L., Dwyer, K., McGuigan, K., Hansen, W. B., Dent, C., Johnson, C. A., ... Flay, B. (1989). Substance use among eighth-grade students who take care of themselves after school. *Pediatrics, 84,* 556–566.

Sampson, R. J., Morenoff, J. D., & Gannon-Rowley, T. (2002). Assessing "neighborhood effects": Social processes and new directions in research. *Annual Review of Sociology, 28,* 443–478.

Sampson, R. J., & Raudenbush, S. W. (2004). Seeing disorder: Neighborhood stigma and the social construction of "broken windows." *Social Psychology Quarterly, 67,* 319–342.

Sapolsky, R. M. (1994). *Why zebras don't get ulcers.* New York, NY: Freeman.

Schmahl, D. P., Lichtenstein, E., & Harris, D. E. (1972). Successful treatment of habitual smokers with warm, smoky air and rapid smoking. *Journal of Consulting and Clinical Psychology, 38,* 105–111.

Snyder, F. J., Flay, B. R., Vuchinich, S., Acock, A., Washburn, I. J., Beets, M. W., & Li, K.-K. (2010). Impact of the Positive Action program on school-level indicators of academic achievement, absenteeism, and disciplinary outcomes: A matched-pair, cluster randomized, controlled trial. *Journal of Research on Educational Effectiveness, 3,* 26–55.

Sobel, D. (1999). *Galileo's daughter: A historical memoir of science, faith, and love.* London, England: Fourth Estate.

Sugai, G., & Horner, R. (2002). The evolution of discipline practices: School-wide positive behavior supports. *Child & Family Behavior Therapy, 24,* 23–50.

Szapocznik, J., Lombard, J., Martinez, F., Mason, C. A., Gorman-Smith, D., Plater-Zyberk, E., ... Spokane, A. (2006). The impact of the built environment on children's school conduct grades: The role of diversity of use in a Hispanic neighborhood. *American Journal of Community Psychology, 38,* 299–310.

Vilardaga, R., Estévez, A., Levin, M. E., & Hayes, S. C. (2012). Deictic relational responding, empathy, and experiential avoidance as predictors of social anhedonia: further contributions from relational frame theory. *Psychological Record, 62,* 409–432.

Webster-Stratton, C. (2000). *The incredible years training series.* Washington, DC: US Department of Justice, Office of Justice Programs, Office of Juvenile Justice and Delinquency Prevention.

Wicksell, R. K., Melin, L., Lekander, M., & Olsson, G. L. (2009). Evaluating the effectiveness of exposure and acceptance strategies to improve functioning and quality of life in long-standing pediatric pain - a randomized controlled trial. *Pain, 141,* 248–257.

Wilson, D. S. (2011). *The neighborhood project: Using evolution to improve my city, one block at a time.* New York, NY: Little, Brown.

Wilson, D. S., O'Brien, D. T., & Sesma, A. (2009). Human prosociality from an evolutionary perspective: Variation and correlations at a city-wide scale. *Evolution and Human Behavior, 30,* 190–200.

Zettle, R. D., & Hayes, S. C. (2002). Brief ACT treatment of depression. In F. W. Bond & W. Dryden (Eds.), *Handbook of brief cognitive behavior therapy* (pp. 35–54). New York, NY: Wiley.

Zhou, Q., Sandler, I. N., Millsap, R. E., Wolchik, S. A., & Dawson-McClure, S. R. (2008). Mother–child relationship quality and effective discipline as mediators of the 6-year effects of the New Beginnings Program for children from divorced families. *Journal of Consulting and Clinical Psychology, 76,* 579–594.

20

A Contextual Behavioral Science Approach to Parenting Intervention and Research

Laura Backen Jones, Koa Whittingham, Lisa Coyne, and April Lightcap

Professionals working with parents commonly observe that parents from all backgrounds, cultures, and occupations want the best for their children. Parents are children's earliest and arguably most important influence. An extensive literature spanning decades underlines parents' important role. Studies of parenting interventions provide a rich source of information about parental attitudes and practices and the family contexts that foster children's healthy development. Yet, despite the good intentions of many parents, the growth in scientific knowledge around parenting, and efforts to disseminate this knowledge to the population, many parents struggle to be effective and to provide their children with an optimal context for development.

Of course, parents do not raise their children in a vacuum. Multiple contextual influences are in play. Parents may contend with limited support, poverty, barriers to education and resources, stress, and a host of other factors that may affect parenting. Individual factors, such as parent attitudes, lack of understanding of children's development and needs, substance abuse, and mental health issues such as depression are significant influences. As Biglan asserts in the introduction to this section, our efforts to learn about how best to support our most precious resource – children – would benefit by a consideration of any practice that might move us toward this goal.

The Prevention of Psychological and Behavioral Problems

Beginning over 50 years ago, work by Patterson and contemporaries defined an approach based on principles of operant conditioning, stimulating a growing recognition that, to change child behavior, we first must change parenting behavior (Patterson, 1986; Patterson, Forgatch, & DeGarmo, 2010; Patterson, Reid, & Dishion, 1992; Vuchinich, Bank, & Patterson, 1992). This pioneering work led to the development and evaluation of a number of programs, generally known as Behavioral Parent Training (BPT), that target parenting behavior in order to change disruptive child behavior.

The Wiley Handbook of Contextual Behavioral Science, First Edition. Edited by Robert D. Zettle, Steven C. Hayes, Dermot Barnes-Holmes, and Anthony Biglan.
© 2016 John Wiley & Sons, Ltd. Published 2016 by John Wiley & Sons, Ltd.

Rigorous studies of BPT have provided a wealth of information about family processes and specific parenting behaviors that foster disruptive behavior. Through this research, effective methods for reducing child disruptive behavior have been developed and utilized successfully in a variety of settings (Forehand, Jones & Parent, 2013; Michelson, Davenport, Dretzke, Barlow & Day, 2013). Numerous studies in Europe and the United States have found BPT to significantly reduce coercive processes in families, increase positively reinforcing interactions, and reduce children's aggressive social behavior; these intervention gains have maintained for as long as nine years after treatment (Patterson et al., 2010).

Coercion in the Context of Childrearing

A notable contribution from BPT has been to increase our understanding of the direct conditioning processes that lead to cycles of coercion between parents and children. Within the context of operant conditioning, coercion is a process of mutual reinforcement between caregiver and child, governed by direct environmental contingencies that affect the frequency, duration, magnitude, and latency of future behavior. In a typical coercive parent–child exchange, the parent makes a command or request, and the child responds aversively in an attempt to escape the parental demand. If the child is "successful," and the parent backs down, that cessation reinforces the child's aversive responding. At the same time, the child's cessation of the aversive behavior reinforces the mother's backing down. Over countless interactions, these exchanges set up a pattern of coercion in the family that contributes to a host of adverse developmental outcomes, including aggression, academic failure, and peer rejection. As children extend into the larger world, they bring this coercive pattern into their interactions with peers, in school settings, and into adulthood (Patterson, 1982; Patterson, DeBaryshe, & Ramsey, 1989; Patterson & Narrett, 1990).

The Contribution of Parents to Coercive Processes

It is worth taking a moment here to highlight the contribution of parents to this process. As Patterson (2002) noted, coercion emerges from mutual parent–child exchanges. In incidents of coercive exchanges between children and parents, parents play a pivotal role. Given their comparative levels of experience and maturity, the onus is on the parent to step out of the cycle and take steps toward positive change. At the same time, in the context of aggression and oppositional behavior, parents' own ineffective responses in the context of their heightened negative emotion, such as backing down in the face of a child's aversive behavior, can actually fuel increased levels of conflict (Smith et al., 2014). How parents fail to employ effective practices, even when they "know better," makes sense when we consider the effects of stress on human behavior. A normal and natural response to stress is to respond defensively. A typical household exchange – such as parent's thwarted expectations for child behavior – can trigger the same physiological and psychological defensive response on the part of the parent as a physical threat. A response that fosters the release of a cascade of hormones, rise in blood pressure, acceleration of the heart rate, and, quite literally, tunnel vision (Rogers, Alderman, &

Landers, 2003). At the level of neuroscience, the amygdala, a group of nuclei located in the medial temporal lobe of the brain, plays an important role in regulating the effects of stress on our processing of events (Dębiec & LeDoux, 2009). Stress-activated hormones and neurotransmitters facilitate a process by which we identify strongly with new events and, through interactions with other brain regions, bias our recall of past events.

Parenting is Stressful

Even under the best of conditions, the tasks and responsibilities associated with parenting can be stressful. Evidence points to an increase in distress among new parents, with 42% of mothers and 26% of fathers reporting symptoms of clinical depression (Dave, Petersen, Sherr, & Nazareth, 2010). In a recent APA survey of stress (American Psychological Association, 2010), one-third of US parents reported extreme stress levels, and the majority indicated that their stress levels exceeded their definition of healthy. Forty-six percent said they lost patience or yelled at their spouse, partner, or children when stressed over the last month. Stressed parents experience heightened negative affect and are more likely to engage in harsh and reactive parenting (Pinderhughes, Dodge, Bates, Pettit, & Zelli, 2000). Parents with high stress levels are less responsive and affectionate and engage in fewer positive interactions than parents who are not stressed (Crnic, Gaze, & Hoffman, 2005; Deater-Deckard, 2005; McKelvey, Fitzgerald, Schiffman, & Von Eye, 2002).

Conditions that can elicit stress within families have led to diminished effectiveness of BPT interventions. Studies indicate that these positive BPT outcomes can be undermined by individual parent factors, such as psychological distress, adverse childrearing practices, and stress and contextual factors such as conflicted family relations and economic strain (Kazdin, 2005).

Contextual Behavioral Science Can Build on Good Science

BPT grew out of the application of contingency analysis to family interactions, with a focus on setting up immediate contingencies to influence child behavior. The impact of this approach in helping us identify methods of effective parental influence on child behavior cannot be overstated. Yet this approach has not done as much to further our understanding of cognitive and language processes involved in family relations. How do problematic parent–child interactions develop over time, and become so fraught with meanings for both parents and children? While traditional behavioral accounts certainly explain a great deal of this process, they fail to adequately describe – in such a way as to enhance our ability to influence – why certain behaviors and situations become so powerfully aversive, and why their absence is so reinforcing. Contextual behavioral science can build on the impressive body of knowledge about conditions that nurture children's development by providing an empirically based theory of the role of language in family interactions, including the development of specific methods for reducing the impact of cognitive/verbal processes that undermine parenting, and the stress that those processes produce.

Processes that contribute to ineffective parenting behaviors emerge from a parent's learning history, with respondent and operant processes playing a key role (Murrell, Wilson, LaBorde, Drake, & Rogers, 2008). Parents, and all humans, have the capacity to stay physiologically activated long after the perceived threat has passed. While animals have a "reset" response once the threat has subsided, humans have the capacity to keep threats verbally and psychologically present. Language permits us to predict and plan for future events and to learn from the past, but it also allows us to imagine all sorts of unpleasant futures and ruminate on past pain and disappointment. With language, we tend to over identify with the experience and memories of these stressful events (Roozendaal, McEwen, & Chattarji, 2009). We can create our own conditions for chronic stress and suffering – and we have the capacity to inflict our stress and suffering on others.

Relational Frame Theory

Relational Frame Theory (RFT; Hayes, Barnes-Holmes, & Roche, 2001) provides an account of how relational capacities associated with language enable us to be in the presence of painful or stressful stimuli psychologically, even when the stimuli are not physically present. From an RFT perspective, the development of language and cognition is underpinned by learned generalized patterns of relational responding, or *arbitrarily applicable relational responding* (AARR).

Humans are able to derive all sorts of relations among different objects: they may be equivalent, they may be opposite, or one may take precedence over another. Our social environment shapes the process of "relating," or defining things via their relations to other things that can result from our contact with real-world contingencies or from relations we derive arbitrarily. The process of relating becomes more complex with development. Over time, children learn a multitude of relational frames, such as distinction (we run outside, *not* in the house), spatial (my toy box is *under* the bed), temporal (*after* toys are picked up, we will go to the park), and hierarchical (a terrier *is a type of* dog). For example, in the United States, coins hold a certain monetary value that is socially constructed. We can teach a young child that a quarter is worth more than a dime and a dime is worth more than a nickel. From this information, the child is able to derive new, more complex relations, such as a quarter is worth more than a nickel, and a nickel is worth less than a quarter. A child is capable of deriving these relations in spite of the fact that the worth of these coins does not correspond to their physical properties with respect to size.

Three primary properties underpin these phenomena. *Mutual entailment* refers to the ability to derive a reciprocal relationship between two stimuli based on knowledge of only one relation (e.g., a quarter is worth more than a dime so a dime is worth less than a quarter). *Combinatorial entailment* involves deriving relations between two stimuli on the basis of each of their relations to a third stimulus (e.g., if a quarter is worth more than a dime and a dime is worth more than a nickel, then a quarter must be worth more than a nickel). *Transformation of stimulus functions* occurs when a person derives a function of one stimulus based on functions of another stimulus in accordance with the derived relation between the two, without additional training (Dymond & Rehfeldt, 2000). In this situation, we give the child a previously learned contextual cue ("more than") to control a specific pattern of generalized relational responding. With continued exposure to these socio-verbal interactions, the child abstracts these contextual cues and then arbitrarily applies them in new situations. These arbitrarily established relations then effectively transform stimulus functions (Törneke, Luciano, & Valdivia-Salas, 2008). For example, a child may come to desire a piece of paper that she previously had no interest in, when she learns that the paper is a ticket that will get her into an amusement park.

The Power of Rule-Governed Behavior

The processes described above support *rule-governed behavior*. Three kinds of rule-governed behavior emerge from variations in an individual's learning history: pliance, tracking, and augmenting. With *pliance*, rule-governed behavior is under the control of socially mediated consequences specified in a rule, or *ply* that may not correspond to actual contingencies in the environment. For example, a parent tells a child that when toys are picked up, a story follows. After the child picks up the toys, shared story time provides reinforcement for following the rules. There are tremendous advantages to this form of behavioral control: A child learns to delay immediate gratification (discontinue playing with the toys) and indirectly contacts the appetitive consequences (shared story time). With pliance, the child might internalize that rule (pick up toys and then have story time) and follow it whether it accurately specifies consequences; however, if mom is inconsistent about storytelling after cleaning up, the child may eventually give up because no storytelling follows.

Tracking is a type of rule-governed behavior influenced by the relationship between a rule and the way the world operates (Hayes et al., 2001). When pliance is present, parents who respond consistently promote tracking by helping children see the effects of their behavior on the natural world. Finally, an *augmental* behavior influences tracking and pliance by altering the reinforcement or punitive qualities of the specified consequence. In other words, linking a relational framework to the consequence changes the function of the consequence. In the case of cleaning up toys, the parent can mitigate the effort and unpleasantness of cleaning up toys by noting how good it feels to have our chores done and time left over to snuggle up and read a story together.

How Rule-Governed Behavior Can Fuel Coercive Family Processes

Inflexible Responding

With rule-governed behavior, we learn to anticipate events before they occur and adjust our behavior in the service of future consequences, whether they are concrete or abstract. For instance, imagine that bedtime has always been a pleasant time for mother and child, with shared story time and cuddles. One night, when mom initiates the bedtime routine, her child suddenly shows strong resistance, accompanied by aversive and disruptive protests. Mom attempts to understand the child's behavior by examining the context of the situation: "When I tell my child it is time for bed, she actively opposes me." Elements in the mom's emerging bedtime "relational frame" can elicit new functions, or meanings, for her based on this new context. These derived meanings from the bedtime experience, such as "my child will actively oppose me" are verbal, and thus function as self-rules, which foster an expectation of what will take place. When expectations lead to inflexible responding, ineffective parenting can result. This can happen in a variety of ways. In an effort to control painful aspects of these private events, a parent who anticipates that "enforcing bedtime equals active opposition" might be inclined to give in to the child's protests (lax parenting behavior). If giving in effectively ends the protest, the resulting parent and child behaviors provide some short-term relief from distress; yet they become immediately reinforcing, increasing the likelihood the problem will reoccur. Moreover, the parent's tendency to give in can be stimulated even in the absence of oppositional behavior on the part of the child. Based on her pliance with the rule "bedtime equals my child will be oppositional," mom might avoid setting limits even when the child is behaving well, missing opportunities to reinforce child behavior that contributes to desired outcomes.

Learning in the Absence of Training

Another potential problem related to rule-governed behavior is that it tends to overgeneralize to other situations and prescribe behaviors that result in undesired consequences. Indirect conditioning – or learning in the absence of direct training – may be at play here, and may play a role in how coercive parent–child interactions begin, and why they seem so intractable. Imagine in the toy clean up situation above that the child protests, insisting that she watch another program on the television before cleaning up her toys. In this scenario, mom responds aversively (yelling, threatening), and the child acquiesces, picking up her toys. Mom might derive that harsh parenting behaviors will "work" to thwart her child's demands in other situations, such as bids for candy at the grocery store.

Or, perhaps the child's aversive protests for more screen time results in mom giving in. The child may derive that protesting behaviors (or their functional equivalent) will "work" in other settings, like at the candy-lined grocery checkout. If mother's command has particular psychological properties for the child – for instance, that her enforcement is contingent on the child's behavior – the child may derive that "opposition equals mom gives in" across many other functionally similar situations, even though they may be topographically distinct. Likewise, when mom's attempts to maintain limits on screen time result in protests and a corresponding increase in her own distress, mom might derive that setting and maintaining limits in other situations, such as refusing candy at the grocery checkout, will also include opposition. Mom's tendencies in these situations – whether they be responding harshly, or giving in – increase the likelihood of problematic interactions in a variety of situations that necessitate a child's compliance to an adult directive.

Shared Psychological Properties

Given the ubiquity of indirect relational conditioning, all the elements in this frame – the thoughts about the child's active opposition, the child's behavior, even the parenting behavior – may come to share similar psychological properties. No doubt, parents in this situation perceive all of these elements as aversive – and perhaps more importantly, as *only* aversive. It is also critically important to note that the meanings that both mother and child come to derive about their interactions are under contextual control: in other words, given a history of coercive interchanges, both may continue to experience *all* interactions – even those that are neutral or positive – as aversive. Or, mother might anticipate aversive behavior and act in ways that actually elicit it. This is because all elements in a particular relational frame come to have similar psychological properties – so even if a child behaves well in a particular situation, mother may simply be "waiting for the other shoe to drop," and thus, may be more likely to engage in coercive behavior herself.

Insensitivity to Direct Experience

Moreover, as described earlier, because such derived meanings are verbal and function as rules, parents' awareness of, and ability to attend to, other available cues is constrained. For example, a parent who behaves following the rule, "She always gets out of control in the supermarket," may not notice when a child is engaged in prosocial or helping behavior, such as loading the shopping cart. Thus, parents can become insensitive to reinforceable behaviors due to their assumption that their children will get "out of control." This precludes development of more sensitive and responsive limit setting, and delivery of reinforcement. In essence, parents cannot "see" the helping behaviors because they have derived that most of the child's behaviors are "bad." As you might imagine, this proves a very difficult context in which to engage in positive interactions, or "catch your child being good," as is encouraged by many parent-training programs. Finally, this process may account for parents' and children's difficulty in taking perspective, a foundational element of empathy and prosocial behavior. Consider, if a parent experiences the child's behavior through the filter of "always defiant," thus leading to an inability to notice and reinforce behaviors that do not fit with that label, it may not even occur to the parent to make an effort to see things from the child's perspective. However, empathic attunement to a child's perspective may be exactly what is necessary for sensitive parent responses (e.g., Coyne & Wilson, 2004).

The Role of Experiential Avoidance and Cognitive Fusion in Inflexible Parenting

Like most humans, parents have had little practice engaging in their direct experience except through the lens of verbal descriptions. What if this "direct experience" appears to be threatening and elicits unwanted thoughts, feelings, and physical sensations? As in the bedtime example above, it is a natural and normal human tendency to withdraw from experiences that elicit unwanted private experiences. And, time and time again, we receive immediate reinforcement when we avoid these unwanted experiences. The term for this tendency to avoid unwanted private inner experiences, even when doing so can lead to unwelcome consequences in the long term, is experiential avoidance (EA; Hayes, Strosahl, & Wilson, 2012). Across a variety of populations and situations, overuse of EA is associated with distress and impaired psychological well-being (Chawla & Ostafin, 2007). In parents, EA predicts psychological maladjustment in mothers of children who have intellectual disabilities (Lloyd & Hastings, 2008), mothers of children with cerebral palsy (Whittingham, Wee, Sanders, & Boyd, 2013) and mothers of infants born preterm (Evans, Whittingham, & Boyd, 2012; Greco et al., 2005). Further, EA is associated with harsh and coercive parenting practices and behavior problems in children (Shea & Coyne, 2011). Evans et al. (2012) also found EA to interfere with bonding and responsiveness in mothers of premature infants.

Cognitive fusion underpins EA. Cognitive fusion occurs when a person's verbal processes (derived relational networks) regulate their overt behavior in ineffective ways (Hayes, Luoma, Bond, Masuda, & Lillis, 2006). Parents engaging in EA are, by definition, less sensitive to actual environmental cues and are thus less likely to respond to these contextual cues or to change their behavior based on their own values or goals (Hayes et al., 2012). Attempts to control unwanted private experiences stimulate an increase in the intensity and frequency of the experiences, which contributes to more aversive behaviors (Hayes, 2004; Hayes, Masuda, Bissett, Luoma, & Guerrero, 2005; Hayes et al., 2012). Coyne and Wilson (2004) proposed that fusion with verbal rules, such as "My child cannot be disrespectful to 'me!'" and the private experiences associated with the thought can trigger coercive parental behaviors that actually undermine the parent's effectiveness in influencing their child's behavior.

Avoidant Behaviors Undermine Parent and Child Well-being

Basic research data from parents of children aged newborn to adolescence has demonstrated links between avoidant emotion regulatory strategies, such as EA, and both parent and child psychological well-being. For example, mothers of newborns in a neonatal intensive care unit (NICU) who reported reliance on EA were also more likely to report adjustment difficulties. Moreover, EA partially accounted for the relationship between their stress level and poor adjustment (Greco et al., 2005).

At least four studies have examined parents' emotion regulatory strategies with mothers of preschool-aged children. Independent observers rated mothers as more sensitive and responsive to their children if they were more empathic with and accepting of their children's emotions (Coyne, Low, Miller, Seifer, & Dickstein, 2006). In a study of 75 diverse, low socioeconomic status (SES) mothers of preschoolers, those reporting higher emotional suppression also reported reacting in a more punitive and minimizing way to their children's negative emotions. Additionally, mothers who reported frequent negative expressivity also reported experiencing more intense emotions, and behaving in more inhibited ways (Currie & Coyne, in preparation). One study of 145 low-income, diverse, urban mothers found that EA was associated with maternal distress, harsh and punitive parenting behaviors, and child behavior problems. Further, EA partially accounted for the relationship between parenting stress and maternal depression (Shea & Coyne, 2012).

In a similar sample ($N = 74$), mothers reporting higher levels of EA also reported more depression, feeling less control in their parenting role, and described more internalizing problems in their preschoolers (Coyne & Thompson, 2013). Parents of teenagers who reported higher levels of EA also reported greater use of inconsistent discipline, monitoring their children less effectively, and less parental involvement, which in turn predicted adolescent behavior problems (Berlin, Sato, Jastrowski, Woods, & Davies, 2006). Links between parental EA and parent distress have also been found in parents of children with autism (Birtwell & Coyne, 2014; Birtwell, Davis, & Coyne, 2012; Blackledge & Hayes, 2006) and parents raising children with anxiety disorders (Cheron, Ehrenreich, & Pincus, 2009).

Although the above are correlational studies, there is also some evidence from at least one experimental study. Murrell and colleagues have shown that distressed parents have difficulty deriving relations between negative child behaviors and positive parenting words (Murrell et al., 2008). This inflexibility in formation of stimulus classes is important because it highlights the important role of derived relational responding in the development and maintenance of impaired parenting. Specifically, parents may have difficulty responding to contingencies that contradict their previous experiences with their children. For example, parents may have difficulty using planned ignoring in response to mild disruptive behaviors, when in the past they may have engaged in punitive, or alternately, acquiescent parenting behaviors. This, in turn, may explain why parents of children who have a pattern of disruptive behavior have great difficulties learning and carrying out this technique in a consistent way, across challenging situations. In the context of all of this verbal activity (and reactivity), it is easy to see how parents fall into patterns of ineffective parenting behavior. Parents commonly derive that their behavior "doesn't work" if they set any sort of limit or place a demand and the child responds aversively. This equivalence relation is likely a key player in fueling parenting inconsistency. In the face of aversive child behavior, the process of establishing patterns of more sensitive and responsive limit setting and delivery of reinforcing behaviors can be challenging. Coercive patterns take days, months, and even years to develop and, accordingly, effectively transforming these entrenched patterns into patterns of cooperative, prosocial exchanges requires consistent parental responding over time.

Studies of the effects of these relational processes on parenting point to the need to extend our examination beyond the observable contingencies that are involved in parent–child dynamics. Parents' psychological inflexibility stems from ineffective contextual control over associative learning processes. A consideration of the influences of *indirect relational conditioning* on parents' behavior might deepen our understanding of mechanisms underlying these patterns of ineffective parenting behavior and inform interventions that have the potential to reach a broader range of parents and could stimulate lasting changes in parenting behavior to support children's well-being (Murrell et al., 2008).

Bringing Parenting Behavior under Appetitive Contextual Control

Warm, nurturing interactions serve as important buffers for the natural human response to stress (Miller et al., 2011) and this is arguably particularly important for children. A recent meta-analysis conducted by Kaminski, Valle, Filene, and Boyle (2008) examined the specific content of evidence-based parenting programs to learn about the practices and skills parents can engage in to maximize the physical, psychological and emotional well-being of children. The meta-analysis revealed that significant effects in positive child outcomes resulted from training content focused on teaching positive and emotionally responsive interactions with children. Parent training elements that predicted reductions in child externalizing behavior included (a) strategies for developing warm, positive relationships with children, parental sensitivity, nurturing, and responsiveness; (b) emotional communication; (c) active promotion of social skills; (d) appropriate and effective use of time out; and (e) modeling desired behaviors.

Whittingham (2014) suggests that the attachment concept of parental sensitivity or responsiveness can be understood, from a contextual perspective, as parenting behavior under appetitive contextual control, that is, flexible and responsive to the moment by moment needs of the child and guided by the parent's values; caregiving behaviors experienced by the parent as freely chosen, grounded in personal values, and ultimately rewarding.

In order for parental behavior to be truly nurturing or sensitive, it must be not merely be warm but also under the contextual control of the child's cues (Whittingham, 2014). Nurturing environments can ease our human tendency to react defensively under threatening conditions. And nurturing environments, early in life, may change the way we respond to threats later in life. This suggests that, if parents are able to reconnect with their values and find ways to engage in warm, nurturing interactions, even under stress, they will improve their own health and optimize the long-term health of their children.

Fostering Psychological Flexibility in Parents

Psychological flexibility refers to two interdependent processes: acceptance of experiences and value-based behavior (Fledderus, Bohlmeijer, Smit, & Westerhof, 2010). Relational frame theory (RFT) underpins acceptance and commitment therapy (ACT), which contains intervention approaches that promote psychological flexibility. Such interventions may prove ideal in assisting parents to provide a nurturing environment for their own children, even in the presence of significant painful emotional stimuli and cognitions (Coyne & Murrell, 2009; Whittingham, 2013). Promoting parents' psychological flexibility involves helping them learn to attend to the present moment more fully and directly contact and accept their inner experiences without attempting to control or suppress them. Increasing a parent's ability to maintain nonjudgmental contact with private experiences might lead to more flexible parenting behavior and increase their capacity for choosing behaviors that are more in line with what they value (Whittingham, 2013). Studies with a wide variety of populations have shown that people can learn skills that help them become more psychologically flexible and respond with behavior that is in line with their values for the situation (Fortney & Taylor, 2010). The ACT treatment model targets six subprocesses: present moment, defusion, perspective-taking, acceptance, values, and committed action. Given that evidence for these subprocesses in parenting is scarce, in the next section we describe the processes in more detail within the context of a parent–child–school situation.

Imagine that a father arrives home at the end of a stressful workday and sees his 12-year-old child fuming at the kitchen table. "What's wrong?" he asks. "I got a referral for leaving class today. My science teacher is *so stupid*." This type of interaction is a stressor and many parents, even under the best of circumstances, might react defensively to this information and respond unhelpfully. Typical parental thoughts might include "What did you do this time?" or "It's disrespectful to call your teacher stupid!" Further, such cognitions are likely to be immersed in a web of relational frames that give the cognitions weighty psychological meaning, for example, "children who disrespect teachers amount to nothing." For a parent, much may appear to be at stake, even in a simple interaction. Common feelings might include frustration and outrage. Unhelpful parenting behaviors such as using an angry, contemptuous tone or labeling the child in some negative way might occur. And, while dad might know that asking questions in an open and warm manner can be an effective way to learn more, under stress he might still respond in unhelpful ways.

Present Moment

The subprocess referred to as *present moment* is akin to mindfulness. Definitions of mindfulness vary, but a central element is nonjudgmental awareness of one's own inner process as well as nonjudgmental awareness of what is outside of us (Whittingham, 2013). As described earlier, perception of a threat activates a defensive process that can undermine warm, nurturing human interactions. Mindfulness practice engenders a stable sense of self beyond threat (Atkins, 2013), reducing the power of events to trigger rigid rule-governed behavior and thus increasing parents' capacity to stay with their uncomfortable direct experience (Duncan, Coatsworth, & Greenberg, 2009; Fledderus et al., 2010). Large-scale, rigorous studies of mindfulness and parenting have not been done, and existing studies have not attended to the mechanisms underlying change (Harnett & Dawe, 2012). However, studies of mindfulness in adults suggest that this stance decreases the likelihood that dad would over identify with his negative thoughts and feelings and react automatically to these painful private experiences (Bishop et al., 2004). With mindfulness, parents are better able to note and label internal experiences (Vago & Silbersweig, 2012), become more aware of their own contribution to patterns of interaction, and flexibly respond to meet the needs of a situation (Harnett & Dawe, 2012). In one study of mothers and adolescents, mothers who rated themselves higher in mindfulness were less intrusive and more able to effectively prevent escalation of conflicts with their adolescents (Bluth & Wahler, 2011).

Reflecting back on the child-at-table situation, dad could, instead of reacting, respond by bringing an awareness of now into the situation, thus satisfying his curiosity about his own inner experiences and those of his child. Appreciating the context instead of struggling with it, dad will use his newly enhanced ability to stay with the uncomfortable experience and respond to his son with behavior that fits with his values instead of just reacting. Present moment awareness could broaden dad's repertoire for responding and give him a sense of choice about how to respond in the situation. As he gets in touch with his own "self-as-process" in the present moment, possibilities for the situation expand. He can use his awareness of feelings of frustration to inform his next action.

Mindfulness might also help dad become more aware of his child's perspective and perhaps even recognize his shared vulnerability with the child (human condition), viewing the child as someone needing his support and compassion rather than seeing the situation as a threat. Atkins and Parker (2012) note that direct contact with the present moment enhances our capacity to attend to another's experience because we direct our attention to what is actually happening in the situation, rather than being preoccupied with our own judgments, memories, or interpretations.

Defusion and Acceptance

As noted above, cognitive fusion occurs when a person's verbal processes (derived relational networks) regulate their overt behavior in ineffective ways (Hayes et al., 2006). *Defusion* aims to undermine the language processes that foster cognitive fusion. As parents learn to make room for their unwanted private experiences, and accept them rather than trying to eliminate or control them, they are more apt to allow thoughts and feelings to come and go, rather than allowing their thoughts and feelings to sweep them away. This shifts the context of the experience (Coyne & Murrell, 2009; Whittingham, 2013). Parents can view thoughts as observed events: simply thoughts – symbols of one's experience rather than actual "reality" (Ciarrochi, Bilich, & Godsell, 2010). When dad has the thought, "children who disrespect teachers amount to nothing," he can accept the thought as an observed event rather than an actual truth. Accepting these inner experiences without judgment calms dad's stress response, reducing the likelihood that he will engage in EA and behave in ways that are counter to what he values in a situation. Defusion helps dad contact more available contingencies in the environment (tracking) rather than simply reacting to those specified by the thoughts (pliance). Dad can get in touch with what underlies his reactive "problem-solving" response and recognize this reaction as a sign that he has something important to address.

Perspective-taking

In this situation, dad might have the notion that to be a good parent, he must firmly control the situation and *make* his son behave respectfully. *Self-as-story*, or our tendency to view ourselves and others as the contents of our verbal experience, affords great benefits. A concise story about our preferences, history, goals, and values can facilitate social exchanges and allows us to predict behavior. The risks with self-as-story arise when it leads to oversimplification and/or judgments about ourselves or others. This capacity can interfere with empathy and self-compassion because it interferes with our ability to connect with direct experience (Atkins & Parker, 2012). With perspective taking, dad can see, "this is a story about me that life has given me, and I – being able to observe it – am more than my story about myself" (Törneke et al., 2010). With his reactivity low, dad would be better able to take a nonjudgmental stance toward his child and be more likely to view the situation from his son's perspective.

Again, it is unknown, but plausible and worthy of investigation, whether repeated interactions with parents who take an open, accepting stance to their children, their own private experiences, and their shared private experiences may increase the likelihood of the children developing such a stance themselves. In support of this possibility, parental acceptance of and responsiveness to child emotion has been found to promote better child emotional regulation abilities and prosocial behavior (e.g., Currie & Coyne, in preparation; Davidov & Grusec, 2006; Morris, Silk, Steinberg, Myers, & Robinson, 2007; Ramsden & Hubbard, 2002).

Values and Committed Action

What is important to a parent is a reflection of their values (Coyne & Murrell, 2009; Whittingham, 2013). Values are the directions in life we choose and these directions serve as a guide for our behavior. Committed action is the process of engaging in value-guided behavior, even in the midst of difficult thoughts, feelings, and inner experiences, and being willing to have these inner experiences in order to "do what matters." As parents choose alternative behaviors that are more in line with their values, they also encounter the reinforcing qualities of these valued actions, such as reduced conflict, increased fun, and more harmony in the parent–child relationship (Coyne & Murrell, 2009; Whittingham, 2013).

In the example above, as he he learns to become present and to make room for his inner experiences, dad might identify what is important to him in the situation. Perhaps what he values is supporting his child, being a responsive parent, or knowing his child fully – the "good" and the "bad." In the service of one of these values, dad might ask an open-ended question to learn more, such as "What happened?" Because dad is responding with curiosity rather than confronting, his son is more likely to share what really happened: that the teacher called him in front of the whole class and made fun of him for failing a test. He felt so overwhelmed with embarrassment that he fled the room. This moment presents an opportunity, once again, for dad to get in touch with his shared vulnerability with the child. A compassionate and empathic response provides his child with a sense of "being on his side" in meeting the problems of life. Dad then has the opportunity to listen and look for opportunities to help support his child in reconciling the situation. The child, in turn, is calmed and able to engage in a discussion rather than respond in a more inflexible, defensive manner.

ACT in Practice: An ACT-Based Parenting Intervention

One way to promote psychological flexibility is to utilize the strengths of rule-governed behavior while also undermining its capacity to dominate behavior. As described earlier, a rule puts the listener in contact with a relational network that transforms the functions of the stimuli that are inherent in the network; this process can be useful in stimulating effective change in parenting behavior. Jones and Lightcap have developed several possible strategies for influencing rule-governed parenting behavior. In the next section, we describe a sampling of activities from an ACT-based parenting program to illustrate how specific methods can influence parents' cognitive/verbal processes. These methods, derived from key RFT principles, aim to reduce coercion and, at the same time, increase the incidence of nurturing parenting behaviors. Modeling of psychological flexibility by the PE sets the stage for effective group process and lends credibility to the "rule stater" (PE). Interactions between peers and the PE are also a source of reinforcement. Parents can receive responses to their behavior that might differ from their interactions at home, creating a new context for their behavior and thus increasing the probability of behavioral change.

Values as Influence

Often problems with child behavior result from patterns of behavior that have developed over time, and it might take time before a change in parenting behavior leads to change in child behavior. Because the immediate consequences of engaging in the alternative parenting behavior are not always rewarding, getting parents in touch with what they value in their parenting can be helpful. This process of augmenting can be stimulated in a couple of ways. First, during a class discussion about what matters to them, parents connect with desired relational networks that might be difficult to access in the home environment where coercive patterns predominate. Second, given the inherent rigidity of pliance, a value in the form of a verbal rule can help the parent persist in committed action, regardless of the immediate nonappetitive direct contingencies. With persistence, parents eventually encounter the appetitive long-term consequences. Over time, the practice of choosing alternative behavior rooted in values becomes reinforcing and can form the foundation of a new rule type for the parent and child. As parents experience the direct contingencies of engaging in the alternative behavior, such as reduced conflict, increased fun, and harmony, they begin tracking or practicing new behaviors for their own sake rather than as the result of a "rule."

One activity that guides parents in making contact with desired consequences is an eyes-closed reflection that takes place in the first class session. During this exercise, parents consider what their family life would be like if everything were, "just the way they wanted it to be": what they would be seeing and hearing, and what they and others would be doing. This is the first step in helping parents to begin augmenting, to identify motivations for behavior change. Through this process, parents verbally construct globally valid desirable consequences that may function as antecedents for alternative behaviors in the future. At this point, parents are not necessarily making contact with their own values. Rather, they are simply making contact with desirable consequences they want to move toward.

Functional Analysis

Structured class activities are designed to stimulate parents' practice of skills both inside and outside of class. The PE sets up in-class verbal antecedents (rules) intended to govern parents' new alternative behaviors in the home setting. In practice at home, parents begin this process by following the verbal rule given in class (antecedent) to engage with their direct experience in the moment of conflict. New behaviors at home can lead to positive change that is subsequently generalized. The PE can initiate this process by listening for contingencies in the parent's self-story that might be appropriate targets for intervention, and then helping parents see the futility of their current unhelpful practices. To facilitate this, the PE guides a process in which parents learn to discriminate problematic behaviors and identify possible alternative responses. Either with the use of hypothetical scenarios, or parents' real-life examples, a particular behavior is understood and influenced by analyzing the contextual factors that precede (antecedent) and follow upon (consequence) that behavior. With this functional analysis, parents see that the behaviors they engage in do not lead them to what they want or what they value in the situation.

A class exercise designed to help parents make contact with their own individually held values utilizes the functional analysis described above. This activity is a whole group discussion that begins by generating a list of parenting behaviors parents "don't want" to engage in. These might include parenting they experienced themselves as children, what they see their neighbor doing, or maybe even practices they are currently engaging in but know they don't want to continue (e.g., yelling). As noted earlier, problem behaviors parents typically identify are behaviors that are dominated by indirect stimulus functions (fusion), or behaviors that are dominated by attempts at controlling private experiences (experiential avoidance). For example, when a parent yells at her child, she might be acting on the self-rule, "I must stop this defiant behavior." In an attempt to extinguish this perceived threat and the unwanted experiences associated with the event, parents can engage in a kind of "behavioral excess," such as yelling or talking too much, which can make a situation worse. Regardless of the long-term consequences of fused and avoidant behaviors like yelling, parents often continue to engage in them as if they are captives in a verbal trap. One method for dealing with fused and avoidant behavior is to introduce perspective-taking: one's perspective of self and/or the perspective of another.

The next phase of the whole-group discussion gives parents practice in both aspects of perspective-taking. First, parents are encouraged to list all of the things they imagine a child experiences in the wake of each of these problematic parenting behaviors. Parents in the whole group contribute, and the resulting list includes a wide range of child experiences, most of them painful and undesirable. As the discussion ensues, parents begin to see the unintended consequences of their avoidant behaviors. Parents also begin to make contact with their own childhood experiences of aversive parenting, which can kindle a sense of empathy and compassion for their children's experience. In addition, viewing this long list of "unwanted" parenting practices, and the resulting child experiences, underlines the futility of "don't want" parenting behaviors. For example, a parent's yelling at a child might actually lead to the child's defensive shutdown or an "in kind" response. If parents want cooperation from a child, they might begin to question whether yelling achieves that aim.

Finally, in the "what I want" segment of the exercise, parents learn to identify global qualities of behaviors they want. At this point, parents are not brainstorming alternative "effective" parenting behaviors. To skip right to brainstorming alternative behaviors would be to miss out on establishing augmental verbal antecedents that have the potential for lasting impact on long-term behavior change, including parents' ability to widen their behavioral repertoire. For example, if I catch myself yelling at my child, I may actually want cooperation. Making contact with "what I want" establishes a motivation for identifying and engaging in alternative parenting behaviors. To skip right to alternative parenting behaviors without first establishing motivation for those alternative behaviors could actually be repertoire narrowing. If a parent wants cooperation from her child, what does she value from her own behavior that would stimulate cooperation? Parents then are guided in identifying values associated with each of their "wants," a global quality of ongoing action that a parent can choose to act on in any given moment. Over the course of the series, this initial in-class practice of transforming "don't wants" into "wants," and then tying these "wants" to values, is followed up by several activities where parents are asked to get in touch with the aversive qualities of a problem situation they are experiencing with their child in order to identify what they value in the situation. Parents learn experientially from these activities that making contact with their unwanted internal experience is actually the key to identifying what they value most, and that by jumping to problem-solving they are less likely to make changes that are in line with their values.

These values-based exercises lay the groundwork for future sessions in which parents engage in activities using metaphors, mindfulness, and defusion that help them gain perspective, get in touch with what is important to them in their parenting, and take committed action in the form of behaviors that move them closer to what they value.

Suggestion Circle

After parents are familiar with a handful of key ACT practices, they participate in a weekly structured five-phase activity, adapted from a more widely used group activity called a "Suggestion Circle" (Clarke, 1984). With this activity, and other activities in the parenting class, a set of rules or structure sets the stage for parents' practice of key ACT processes. During the first phase, a parent volunteer describes a problem they are currently experiencing with their child. This description is followed by a period in which other parents in the group are prompted to ask a series of contextual questions: "Where does it happen?," "Who else is present?," "When do you do this?," "What happens?," etc. For example, in a recent class, a target parent (mother) described a situation in which her four-year-old daughter leaves home on her bike without parental supervision. Mother shared how she, upon finding her daughter with her bike outside of the home boundaries, was flooded with thoughts about her own inadequacy as a mother. She blew up and yelled at her daughter, telling her that she would never ride her bike again.

In the second phase, parents brainstorm alternative behaviors while the PE posts the ideas for all to see. This brainstorming phase is structured so that parents focus on generating possibilities and withhold from acting on their internal judgment of these possibilities, or engage in problem-solving. In the case of the four-year-old child riding her bike in the neighborhood without supervision, parents' ideas included that mother plan more park trips to give ample opportunities for safe bike rides, and that mother restrict access to the bike to times when she can be present. The target parent might notice she is having the thought, "I already do that," or "that won't help" but she refrains from acting on the content of those thoughts by returning her attention back to her direct experience in the classroom. Another "rule" governing the brainstorming period is that parents keep the focus on the parent who presented the problem (rather than shifting the focus to themselves); as with the urge to problem-solve, parents are encouraged to observe these tendencies, and not act on them. During this phase, parents in the class may notice the urge to share thoughts like, "I went through this with my son, and I want to tell you my personal story." Acting in pliance, parents follow the verbal rules the PE has constructed, and with guided practice in being present to their direct experience, parents can repeatedly observe their own inclination to fall automatically into behavior that their own derived stimulus functions dominate.

During the third phase, parents are encouraged to look at the brainstormed list and define the broad class of principles that emerge from the brainstorm. In doing so, parents begin tracking the consequences of observing their internal experience without acting on it: in this case, brainstorming without problem-solving resulted in the expansion of possible alternative behaviors, rather than a narrowing behavioral repertoire. Connecting alternative behaviors to the principles and strategies learned in previous sessions adds to and strengthens the relational networks formed throughout the class series, increasing the likelihood for behavior change outside of class. One example of a principle divined from the discussion of the child riding her bike away from home was for mother to "take a Parent Moment," a skill taught in class in which a parent notices and accepts thoughts and feelings (*I notice I am having the thought that I am a bad mother*) and then practices a brief mindfulness activity learned in class (take three deep breaths) before reacting.

In the fourth phase, target parents identify values for themselves and their children in the situation. As mentioned above, this process increases the likelihood they will be able to engage in alternative behaviors at home that result in long-term gains, despite any immediate nonappetitive consequences. Then, based on values they have identified, parents look over the brainstormed alternatives, picking and choosing ideas that they would like to try. Inevitably, there are ideas on the list that the target parent has already tried. From the brainstormed list, the parent begins to discriminate the behaviors that "have not worked" and see that there are many other possibilities for responding. As the parent sits before this visual array of these "already tried" experiences in the midst of a wide range of alternative behaviors, a process of defusion is stimulated, accompanied by a broadening of their behavioral repertoire.

Valuing both safety and independence for her child, the target parent might choose to place a lock on her four-year-old daughter's bike while scheduling time for her child to ride in a wide open space under parental supervision. Augmenting again occurs as the parent chooses a valued action, increasing the likelihood that the target parent will encounter the longer-term appetitive consequences of engaging in this alternative behavior, despite her immediate internal discomfort.

Finally, in the fifth phase, the target parent takes the alternative behavior(s) chosen during the activity and engages in them outside of class, in the "real world" arena. At home, the daughter might protest when she no longer has free access to her bike, and the target parent, having already practiced in class, can notice her urge to argue or give in to her child, while not acting on it. She has already had many discussions with her daughter regarding the dangers of riding her bike away from home and the discussions have not helped. She might instead express some empathy for her child's distress, "You loved being able to ride your bike whenever you wanted and you'll miss it."

Parents who are the recipients of Suggestion Circle input routinely report in class the following week about their experiences of trying the new chosen behavior(s). In this case, mother reported that, upon hearing her child's protests, she noticed an urge to argue or give in, but refrained from acting on that urge in the service of her values. When mother shared the joy she experienced watching her daughter ride in a wide open space during their scheduled time, despite the hardships encountered earlier in the week, the entire class was stimulated to make contact with the consequences of engaging in values-directed behavior.

Weekly Small Group Meetings

A structured small group check-in that takes place at the beginning of each class is another example of how in-class contingencies of reinforcement can be set up to promote practice of skills outside of class. Parents gather in small groups to discuss their experiences with the prior week's home practice activity. During the small group check-in, parents receive visual prompts to focus their discussion on key ACT processes they have learned in class: noticing thoughts, feelings, and physical sensations; defusion, acceptance, present moment awareness; and getting in touch with what is important in the situation. The structure of the prompts helps to shift the emphasis from "right" or "wrong" behavior in the situation to "what's missing." This is important. Many of us (including the PE) are tempted to skip immediately to problem-solving.

In doing so, we miss an opportunity for practice in all of the processes that underpin psychological flexibility. The value is in increasing experience and awareness of the interplay between these processes, which can widen parents' behavioral repertoire and capacity for valued action. The routine "in-class" small group discussion is removed from the home setting, thus affording parents some distance from the situation. With this distance, parents can more readily examine the contextual function of their parenting behaviors and flexibly choose behaviors that might "work," regardless of topography.

The activities described above are not an exhaustive list; rather, they are just a handful of activities we (Jones and Lightcap) have developed for parents that align with RFT and ACT principles. As with other ACT parenting interventions described below, this work is just beginning; however, preliminary evidence suggests that the program is helpful. A pilot pre-post feasibility study with parents who attended an eight-week series (N = 10) was recently conducted (Jones, Lightcap, & Lee, in preparation). Paired t-tests for parent report measures in a retrospective pre- and post-test showed significant change in the anticipated direction, including parent psychological flexibility ($t = 3.07$, $p = .01$, $d = .81$), parenting skills including proactive discipline ($t = 5.41$, $p < .0001$, $d = 1.78$), use of ACT principles ($t = 6.04$, $p < .001$, $d = 2.48$), child prosocial behavior ($t = 4.64$, $p = .001$, $d = 1.85$), and child-related parenting stress ($t = -2.09$, $p = .018$, $d = 1.18$).

Empirical Support for ACT Parenting Interventions

Research on the application of ACT interventions to parenting is still in its infancy. However, the results so far are promising. Blackledge and Hayes (2006) demonstrated, in a within-subject repeated-measures design, improvements in psychological adjustment for 20 parents of children with autism after a two-day (14-hour) group ACT workshop. Improvements were seen pre to post in depressive symptomology, psychological distress, and general psychological health. In this study, evidence suggested that psychological flexibility mediated these changes.

Further, a randomized controlled trial demonstrated the efficacy of a combined behavioral parent training and ACT intervention for families of children with acquired brain injury (Brown, Whittingham, Boyd, McKinlay, & Sofronoff, 2014; Brown, Whittingham, McKinlay, Boyd, & Sofronoff, 2013). A brief (four-hour) ACT for parents intervention merged with Stepping Stones Triple P (Positive Parenting Program), a variant of Triple P specifically developed for families of children with developmental disabilities. Fifty-nine families of children with acquired brain injuries participated; with the intervention group demonstrating improvements in child behavior and parenting style, compared with a wait-list control group. In particular, the researchers identified reductions in the intensity and number of child behavior problems, in child emotional symptoms, and in the parental dysfunctional styles of laxness and over reactivity.

A recent randomized controlled trial was the first to test additive benefits of ACT above and beyond established behavioral parent training (Whittingham, Sanders, McKinlay, & Boyd, 2013; 2014). By random allocation, 67 families of children with cerebral palsy entered one of three groups – a wait-list control group, a group that received Stepping Stones Triple P only, and a group that received Stepping Stones Triple P combined with a brief (four-hour) ACT intervention for parents. Families who received Stepping Stones Triple P alone showed decreases in the number of child behavior problems and emotional symptoms compared to the wait-list controls, consistent with the extensive literature on the benefits of behavioral parent training as noted earlier. Families who received ACT combined with Stepping Stones Triple P showed decreases in the number and intensity of child behavior problems and child hyperactivity compared to wait-list controls. They also showed reductions in the dysfunctional parenting styles of over reactivity and verbosity. Further, at six-month follow-up, families who had received the combined Stepping Stones Triple P and ACT intervention showed reductions in child hyperactivity, parental laxness, and parental verbosity compared with families who received Stepping Stones Triple P alone. This suggests that ACT has an additive benefit, above and beyond established behavioral parent training; however, further research is necessary to draw definite conclusions.

The finding that families receiving Stepping Stones Triple P showed a reduction in child emotional symptoms, while families receiving the combined ACT and Stepping Stones Triple P intervention did not is provocative. In fact, the differences between the Stepping Stones Triple P and the combined ACT and Stepping Stones Triple P groups approached significance for child emotional symptoms, with the Stepping Stones Triple P alone group showing better outcomes. It is difficult to understand how adding ACT may have decreased the intervention effect of Stepping Stones Triple P on child emotional symptoms. However, a plausible explanation emerges when we consider that parent reports measured the child emotional symptoms. It may be that ACT, with a focus on mindfulness, acceptance of emotions, and valued parenting acts, increased parental capacity to recognize child affect; this increased capacity masked intervention gains, which the parent reports measured. If ACT is able to bolster parental capacity to recognize child affect then ACT may provide the means to target parental emotional responsiveness and the parent–child relationship. This requires further investigation.

What Contextual Behavioral Science Can Bring to Parenting

Investigating coercive family interactions from the lens of RFT and ACT may help us more effectively tailor interventions for those families we are having trouble reaching – those with myriad contextual challenges, those with parents struggling with psychopathology, and those experiencing significant stress. But these are empirical questions, and while they are theoretically and conceptually compelling, we need work that is more rigorous. In terms of ACT intervention studies, while some data are beginning to emerge, this work is still nascent and varies in quality. There are a number of single-case studies, open trials with small sample sizes, and, as described above, very recently, some rigorous randomized controlled trials. Replication and the use of large samples in randomized controlled trials that compare ACT with gold standard treatments, as well as careful investigation of mediators, moderators, and mechanisms of treatment are essential. Most importantly, perhaps, there needs to be investigation regarding how ACT might add to established behavioral treatments.

The future lies in integration. Just as ACT for anxiety disorders incorporates traditional behavioral therapy techniques such as exposure therapy, ACT for parents would incorporate parenting practices known to contribute to child well-being. Again, as with ACT for anxiety disorders, true integration would involve not merely tacking ACT onto existing evidence-based parenting interventions, but, rather, rethinking parenting intervention from within the ACT model. Just as we understand and practice third-wave exposure therapy in a subtly different way than second- or first-wave exposure therapy, behavioral parenting training techniques would subtly change. Focusing on parenting practices and family contexts that underpin the early development of psychological flexibility (Whittingham, 2014) might inform such changes. Can repeated interactions with a mindful, accepting parent encourage the early development of psychological flexibility? Does compassionate parenting increase child self-compassion? What kinds of parental responses to heightened child emotion promote child experiential avoidance or acceptance? The results of Whittingham et al. (2014), the first RCT to test the additive benefits of ACT to behavioral parent training, suggest that ACT may enhance parental capacity to recognize child affect. If true, ACT may provide the means to target parental emotional responsiveness and strengthen the parent–child relationship. Research can help confirm if this is the case and to confirm benefits for the child. With such understandings, ACT may prove an ideal intervention for targeting the parent–child relationship, an aspect of parent–child outcomes that has received surprisingly little attention in the behavioral parent training literature (with the majority of the literature, instead, focusing on child behavioral outcomes).

Moving Forward

What happens moment to moment, day by day, in families has a profound influence on how children develop. The rich resource of accumulated parenting research informs a set of guiding principles that can influence the incidence and prevalence of behaviors to promote family and child well-being. However, a sole focus on identifying effective parenting behaviors is not enough. Parents do influence children via direct contingencies, but verbal behavior, particularly rule-governed behavior, is another salient influence. Traditional accounts also do not explain parent/child insensitivity to other available contingencies, nor do they explain the inflexibility of behavior, especially in families facing high stress. Contextual behavioral science permits us to expand the focus beyond parenting behaviors themselves to an examination of the processes that underpin effective parenting – to understanding how psychological flexibility may aid in effective parenting, and how psychologically flexible parents may through moment by moment interactions produce psychologically flexible children. Further, we may consider the wider cultural context that we must guide in order to ensure that effective parenting receives both support and rich positive reinforcement.

Knowledge gained about these processes will help us develop interventions that promote psychological flexibility within families with benefits that can extend to the broader society. When parents engage in practices that enhance their own psychological flexibility, they respond in ways that foster the physical, psychological, and emotional well-being of each family member, even under stressful conditions. Moreover, nurturing parenting practices foster prosocial child behavior. Within families, children can learn how to behave in ways that make a positive difference. When children engage in prosocial skills and practices, they experience being a meaningful and important part of the family and they are stimulated to behave in ways that further benefit family well-being. The process is undoubtedly reciprocal. Family members on the receiving end of nurturing practices tend to respond in kind. Cycles of prosocial exchanges not only serve to promote the overall well-being of families, they have significant implications for our cultural well-being. As in the development of coercive cycles, repeated nurturing exchanges could engender a prosocial pattern that children carry into the broader social context.

References

American Psychological Association. (2010). *Stress in America 2010*. Washington, DC: Author.

Atkins, P. W. B. (2013). Empathy, self-other differentiation and mindfulness. In K. Pavlovich & K. Krahnke (Eds.), *Organizing through empathy*. Oxford, England: Routledge.

Atkins, P., & Parker, S. (2012). Understanding individual compassion in organizations: The role of appraisals and psychological flexibility. *Academy of Management Review, 37*, 524–546.

Berlin, K.S., Sato, A. F., Jastrowski, K. E., Woods, D. W., & Davies, W. H. (2006, November). *Effects of experiential avoidance on parenting practices and adolescent outcomes*. In K. S. Berlin & A. R. Murrell (Chairs), *Extending acceptance and mindfulness research to parents, families, and adolescents: Process, empirical findings, clinical implications, and future directions*. Symposium presented to the 2006 Association for Behavioral and Cognitive Therapies, Chicago, IL.

Birtwell, K. B., & Coyne, L. W. (2014, July). *Topography of autism spectrum disorders and parent dysfunction: The mediational role of parents' experiential avoidance*. Poster presented at the Association of Contextual Behavioral Science World Conference, Minneapolis, MN.

Birtwell, K. B., Davis, E. C., & Coyne, L.W. (2012, July). *Using ACT with families of autistic children: Supporting parents and siblings*. Workshop accepted for presentation at the Association of Contextual Behavioral Science (ACBS) World Conference, Washington, DC.

Bishop, S. R., Lau, M., Shapiro, S., Carlson, L., Anderson, N., Carmody, J., Devins, G. (2004). Mindfulness: A proposed operational definition. *Clinical Psychology: Science and Practice, 11*, 230–241.

Blackledge, J. T., & Hayes S.C. (2006). Using acceptance and commitment training in the support of parents of children diagnosed with autism. *Child and Family Behavior Therapy, 28*, 1–18.

Bluth, K., & Wahler, R. G. (2011). Does effort matter in mindful parenting? *Mindfulness, 2*, 175–178.

Brown, F., Whittingham, K., Boyd R., McKinlay, L., & Sofronoff, K. (2014). Improving child and parenting outcomes following pediatric acquired brain injury: A randomised controlled trial of Stepping Stones Triple P plus acceptance and commitment therapy. *Journal of Child Psychology and Psychiatry, 55*, 1172–1183.

Brown, F., Whittingham, K., McKinlay, L., Boyd, R.N., & Sofronoff, K. (2013). Efficacy of Stepping Stones Triple P plus a stress management adjunct for parents of children with acquired brain injury: The protocol of a randomised controlled trial. *Brain Impairment, 14*, 253–269.

Chawla, N., & Ostafin, B. (2007). Experiential avoidance as a functional dimensional approach to psychopathology: An empirical review. *Journal of Clinical Psychology, 63*, 871–890.

Cheron, D. M., Ehrenreich, J. T., & Pincus, D. B. (2009). Assessment of parental experiential avoidance in a clinical sample of children with anxiety disorders. *Child Psychiatry and Human Development, 40*, 383–403.

Ciarrochi, J., Bilich, L., & Godsell, C. (2010). Psychological flexibility as a mechanism of change in acceptance and commitment therapy. In R. Baer (Ed.), *Assessing mindfulness and acceptance: illuminating the processes of change* (pp. 51–76). Oakland, CA: New Harbinger.

Clarke, J. I. (1984). *Who, me lead a group?* Seattle, WA: Parenting Press.

Coyne, L. W., Low, C. M., Miller, A. L., Seifer, R., & Dickstein, S. (2007). Mothers' empathic understanding of their toddlers: Associations with maternal depression and sensitivity. *Journal of Child and Family Studies, 16*, 483–497.

Coyne, L. W., & Murrell, A. R. (2009). *The joy of parenting: An acceptance and commitment therapy guide to effective parenting in the early years.* Oakland, CA: New Harbinger.

Coyne, L. W., Thompson, A. D. (2011). Maternal depression, locus of control, and emotion regulatory strategy as predictors of child internalizing problems. *Journal of Child and Family Studies, 20*, 873–883.

Coyne, L. W., & Wilson, K. G. (2004). The role of cognitive fusion in impaired parenting: An RFT analysis. *International Journal of Psychology and Psychological Therapy, 4*, 469–486.

Crnic, K. A., Gaze, C., & Hoffman, C. (2005). Cumulative parenting stress across the preschool period: Relations to maternal parenting and child behaviour at age 5. *Infant and Child Development, 14*, 117–132.

Currie, A. M. & Coyne, L. W. (in preparation). *Maternal avoidant emotion regulation and its role in parent- and teacher-rated emotion regulation in early childhood in a diverse, low-income sample of preschoolers.*

Dave, S., Petersen, I., Sherr, L., & Nazareth, I. (2010). Incidence of maternal and paternal depression in primary care: a cohort study using a primary care database. *Archives of Pediatrics & Adolescent Medicine, 164*, 1038–1044.

Davidov, M., & Grusec, J. E. (2006). Untangling the links of parental responsiveness to distress and warmth to child outcomes. *Child Development, 77*, 44–58.

Deater-Deckard, K. (2005). Parenting stress and children's development: Introduction to the special issue. *Infant and Child Development, 14*, 111–115.

Dębiec, J., & LeDoux, J. (2009). The amygdala and the neural pathways of fear. In P. J. Shiromani, T. M. Keane, & J. E. LeDoux (Eds.), *Post-traumatic stress disorder: Basic science and clinical practice* (pp. 23–38). Totowa, NJ: Humana Press.

Duncan, L. G., Coatsworth, J. D., & Greenberg, M. T. (2009). A model of mindful parenting: Implications for parent–child relationships and prevention research. *Clinical Child and Family Psychology Review, 12*, 255–270.

Dymond, S., & Rehfeldt, R. A. (2000). Understanding complex behavior: The transformation of stimulus functions. *The Behavior Analyst, 23*, 239–254.

Evans, T., Whittingham, K., & Boyd, R. (2012). What helps the mother of a preterm infant become securely attached, responsive, and well-adjusted? *Infant Behavior and Development, 35*, 1–11.

Fledderus, M., Bohlmeijer, E. T., Smit, F., & Westerhof, G. J. (2010). Mental health promotion as a new goal in public mental health care: A randomized controlled trial of an intervention enhancing psychological flexibility. *American Journal of Public Health, 100*, 2372–2378.

Forehand, R., Jones, D. J., & Parent, J. (2013). Behavioral parenting interventions for child disruptive behaviors and anxiety: What's different and what's the same? *Clinical Psychology Review, 33*, 133–145.

Fortney, L., & Taylor, M. (2010). Meditation in medical practice: A review of the evidence and practice. *Primary Care: Clinics in Office Practice, 37*, 81–90.

Greco, L. A., Heffner, M., Poe, S., Ritchie, S., Polak, M., & Lynch, S. K. (2005). Maternal adjustment following preterm birth: Contributions of experiential avoidance. *Behavior Therapy, 36*, 177–184.

Harnett, P. H., & Dawe, S. (2012). The contribution of mindfulness-based therapies for children and families and proposed conceptual integration. *Child and Adolescent Mental Health, 17*, 195–208.

Hayes, S. C. (2004). Acceptance and commitment therapy, relational frame theory, and the third wave of behavioral and cognitive therapies. *Behavior Therapy, 35,* 639–665.

Hayes, S. C., Barnes-Holmes, D., & Roche, B. (2001). *Relational frame theory. A post-Skinnerian account of human language and cognition.* New York: Kluwer Academic.

Hayes, S. C., Luoma, J. B., Bond, F. W., Masuda, A., & Lillis, J. (2006). Acceptance and commitment therapy: Model, processes and outcomes. *Behaviour Research and Therapy, 44,* 1–25.

Hayes, S. C., Masuda, A., Bissett, R., Luoma, J., & Guerrero, L. F. (2005). DBT, FAP, and ACT: How empirically oriented are the new behavior therapy technologies? *Behavior Therapy, 35,* 35–54.

Hayes, S. C., Strosahl, K. D., & Wilson, K. G. (2012). *Acceptance and commitment therapy: The process and practice of mindful change* (2nd ed.). New York, NY: Guilford.

Jones, L. B., Lightcap, A., & Lee, J. (in preparation). *Increasing parents' psychological flexibility and parenting skills with group-based training.*

Kaminski, J. W., Valle, L. A., Filene, J. H., & Boyle, C. L. (2008). A meta-analytic review of components associated with parent training program effectiveness. *Journal of Abnormal Child Psychology, 36,* 567–589.

Kazdin, A. E. (2005). *Parent management training: Treatment for oppositional, aggressive, and antisocial behavior in children and adolescents.* New York, NY: Oxford University Press.

Lloyd, T. J., & Hastings, R. (2009). Hope as a psychological resilience factor in mothers and fathers of children with intellectual disabilities. *Journal of Intellectual Disability Research, 53,* 957–968.

McKelvey, L. M., Fitzgerald, H. E., Schiffman, R. F., & Von Eye, A. (2002). Family stress and parent–infant interaction: The mediating role of coping. *Infant Mental Health Journal, 23,* 164–181.

Michelson, D., Davenport, C., Dretzke, J., Barlow, J., & Day, C. (2013). Do evidence-based interventions work when tested in the "real world"? A systematic review and meta-analysis of parent management training for the treatment of child disruptive behavior. *Clinical Child and Family Psychology Review, 16,* 18–34.

Miller, G. E., Lachman, M. E., Chen, E., Gruenewald, T. L., Karlamangla, A. S., & Seeman, T. E. (2011). Pathways to resilience maternal nurturance as a buffer against the effects of childhood poverty on metabolic syndrome at midlife. *Psychological Science, 22,* 1591–1599.

Morris, A. S., Silk, J. S., Steinberg, L., Myers, S. S., & Robinson, L. R. (2007). The role of the family context in the development of emotion regulation. *Social Development, 16,* 361–388.

Murrell, A. R., Wilson, K. G., LaBorde, C. T., Drake, C. E., & Rogers, L. J. (2008). Relational responding in parents. *Behavior Analyst Today, 9,* 196–214.

Patterson, G. R. (1982). *Coercive family process.* Eugene, OR: Castalia.

Patterson, G. R. (1986). Performance models for antisocial boys. *American Psychologist, 41,* 432–444.

Patterson, G. R. (2002). Future extensions of the models. In J. B. Reid, G. R. Patterson, & J. Snyder (Eds.), *Antisocial behavior in children and adolescents: A developmental analysis and model for intervention* (pp. 273–283). Washington DC: American Psychological Association.

Patterson, G. R., DeBaryshe, B. D., & Ramsey, E. (1989). A developmental perspective on antisocial behavior. *American Psychologist, 44,* 329–35.

Patterson, G. R., Forgatch, M. S., & DeGarmo, D. S. (2010). Cascading effects following intervention. *Development and Psychopathology, 22,* 949–970.

Patterson, G. R., & Narrett, C. M. (1990). The development of a reliable and valid treatment program for aggressive young children. *International Journal of Mental Health, 19,* 19–26.

Patterson, G. R., Reid, J. B., & Dishion, T. J. (1992). *Antisocial boys: A social interactional approach* (Vol. 4). Eugene, OR: Castalia.

Pinderhughes, E. E., Dodge, K. A., Bates, J. E., Pettit, G. S., & Zelli, A. (2000). Discipline responses: Influences of parents' socioeconomic status, ethnicity, beliefs about parenting, stress, and cognitive-emotional processes. *Journal of Family Psychology, 14*, 380–400.

Ramsden, S. R., & Hubbard, J. A. (2002). Family expressiveness and parental emotion coaching: Their role in children's emotion regulation and aggression. *Journal of Abnormal Child Psychology, 30*, 657–667.

Rogers, T. J., Alderman, B. L., & Landers, D. M. (2003). Effects of life-event stress and hardiness on peripheral vision in a real-life stress situation. *Behavioral Medicine, 29*, 21–26.

Roozendaal, B., McEwen, B. S., & Chattarji, S. (2009). Stress, memory and the amygdala. *Nature Reviews Neuroscience, 10*, 423–433.

Shea, S. E., & Coyne, L. W. (2011). Maternal dysphoric mood, stress, and parenting practices in mothers of Head Start preschoolers: The role of experiential avoidance. *Child & Family Behavior Therapy, 33*, 231–247.

Smith, J. D., Dishion, T. J., Shaw, D. S., Wilson, C., Winter, C., & Patterson, G. R. (2014). Coercive family process and early-onset conduct problems from age 2 to school entry. *Development and Psychopathology, 26*, 917–932.

Törneke, N., Luciano, C., & Valdivia-Salas, S. (2008). Rule governed behavior and psychological problems. *International Journal of Psychology and Psychological Therapy, 8*, 141–156.

Vago, D. R., & Silbersweig, D. A. (2012). Self-awareness, self-regulation, and self-transcendence (S-ART): A framework for understanding the neurobiological mechanisms of mindfulness. *Frontiers in Human Neuroscience, 6*, 1–30.

Vuchinich, S., Bank, L., & Patterson, G. R. (1992). Parenting, peers, and the stability of antisocial behavior in preadolescent boys. *Developmental Psychology, 28*, 510–521.

Whittingham, K. (2013). *Becoming mum*. Brisbane, Australia: Pivotal Publishing.

Whittingham, K. (2014) Parenting in context. *Journal of Contextual Behavioral Science, 3*, 212–215.

Whittingham, K., Sanders, M. R., McKinlay, L., & Boyd, R. N. (2013). Stepping Stones Triple P and acceptance and commitment therapy for parents of children with cerebral palsy: Trial protocol. *Brain Impairment, 14*, 270–280.

Whittingham, K., Sanders, M., McKinlay, L., & Boyd, R. N. (2014). Interventions to reduce behavioral problems in children with cerebral palsy: An RCT. *Pediatrics, 133*(5). Retrieved from www.pediatrics.org/cgi/doi/10.1542/peds.2013-3620

Whittingham, K., Wee, D., Sanders, M. R., & Boyd, R. (2013). Predictors of psychological adjustment, experienced parenting burden and chronic sorrow symptoms in parents of children with cerebral palsy. *Child: Care, Health and Development, 39*, 366–373.

21

Contextual Behavioral Science and Education

Thomas G. Szabo and Mark R. Dixon

Overview

Contextual behavioral science (CBS) approaches to education have the potential to produce great change and meaningful results for students, educators, and the culture at large. The principles of acceptance, mindfulness, defusion, values, flexible perspective-taking, and committed action all have direct utility when presented individually or collectively within a classroom environment. In order for CBS to have the greatest impact, the educational community must be open to large-scale implementations that involve curricular and systemic modifications to traditional educational practices. Individual student outcomes can also be impacted by direct interaction with learning experiences aimed at improving psychological flexibility. As our culture moves toward an era of evidence-based practices, CBS stands at the forefront of approaches both large-scale and individualized that offer the ability to make meaningful differences in education.

The rich history of behavioral interventions in education can be traced back to the early days of behavior analysis, and continue to ripple throughout the schoolwide communities of today. Initial attempts concentrated on identifying certain target behaviors and delivering consequences accordingly. Some interventions involved acquiring positive outcomes, while others yielded negative or aversive consequences. What seems to have been left without a complete analysis is an understanding of the psychological mechanisms that participate in the eventual emission of the challenging behaviors in the first place. Furthermore, when the issue is not problem behavior but skill deficits, and the typical desirable consequences are available for engaging in study behavior, why is it the case that a certain student fails to seek out and contact these consequences? Perhaps what has been missing in these traditional interventions was an understanding of the *why* behind *what* happened with a given child. Managing contingencies yields great results, but there seems to be a need for a more comprehensive analysis of the psychological condition of the child and how to maximize it to get the most out of the educational experience.

An emerging strand within behavior analysis, cognitive behavior therapy (CBT), and prevention science is the focus upon psychological flexibility to promote effective

The Wiley Handbook of Contextual Behavioral Science, First Edition. Edited by Robert D. Zettle, Steven C. Hayes, Dermot Barnes-Holmes, and Anthony Biglan.
© 2016 John Wiley & Sons, Ltd. Published 2016 by John Wiley & Sons, Ltd.

living, working, and relating within a variety of social contexts (Hayes, Villatte, Levin, & Hildebrandt, 2011). Psychological flexibility can be characterized as orienting to current emotions, thoughts, or bodily sensations without being dominated by them, and seeing oneself from a variety of different angles so as to take action in the service of freely chosen values. Basic research in the experimental analysis of human behavior has yielded a theory of language and cognition that extends Skinner's functional account of verbal behavior and explains the development of both flexibility and its antagonist: psychological rigidity. When behaviorally rigid, a person cannot disentangle from unwanted thoughts or emotions about the past, present, or future, believes that such content is inescapable, holds fast to a narrowly defined concept of self, and does not take action on matters of importance in life (Hayes, Barnes-Holmes, & Roche, 2001).

Two avenues within human operant research spawned efforts to improve psychological flexibility. The first involved research on rule governance. A number of studies demonstrated human schedule insensitivity on standard schedules of reinforcement after instructions were delivered that did not correspond to the programmed contingencies (e.g., Galizio, 1979; Matthews, Shimoff, Catania, & Sagvolden, 1977; Shimoff, Catania, & Matthews, 1981). One implication was that, when given a rule, humans tend to follow the rule even when it produces nonoptimal outcomes. Whereas rule insensitivity fosters narrow and rigid repertoires, a second avenue of research was demonstrating that through multiple-exemplar training, humans learn to relate events with no formal or topographical similarity and without direct reinforcement for doing so (Sidman & Tailby, 1982; Steele & Hayes, 1991). The behavior of relating as such is uniquely verbal and extends beyond relations of equivalence to distinction, opposition, hierarchy, causality, temporality, and perspective. Framing relationally is thus seen as a generalized operant repertoire that confers remarkable evolutionary advantages to verbally competent humans. We learn through normal verbal processes to generate responses to a wide variety of otherwise unrelated stimulus events and to arbitrarily apply newly formed functions to these events. Although framing makes abstract pattern recognition possible, it also leads at times to overextended rule adherence. Thus, very early lab results indicated that framing provides an explanation of rule insensitivity as well as a way toward improved functioning in verbal contexts.

Findings in the basic labs with respect to rule governance and relational framing happened concurrently with the development of contextually oriented CBTs. As a consequence, a number of contextual CBTs target the basic behavioral processes that underlie psychological flexibility. However, one in particular, acceptance and commitment therapy (ACT; Hayes, Strosahl, & Wilson, 1999; 2012), seems uniquely capable of being applied with nonclinical populations to address a range of behavior in nonclinical contexts (Hayes, Luoma, Bond, Masuda, & Lillis, 2006). This is because ACT targets behavioral processes that are common to all verbally competent organisms, with or without a context for clinical intervention. That is, ACT aims to reduce the dominance of cognitive fusion and experiential avoidance (explained below). These processes are common in all language users and occur when the functions of stimuli with no physical or shared historical context are related and transformed through verbal extension (Hayes et al., 2012). Additionally, ACT relies heavily upon the development of metaphors and exercises that are easy to understand without an overreliance on verbal explanation. In fact, the metaphors and exercises in ACT work best when they are left as experiences that are repeated and elaborated upon without verbal explication of their meaning. In this way, ACT is a particularly useful strategy for teaching very young people flexible ways to relate to their thoughts and emotions.

The focus of this chapter is to highlight critical issues in education and a variety of approaches for conceptualizing and addressing them. We will review these issues, a number of behavioral and nonbehavioral agendas for tackling them, and then highlight the particular contribution that CBS can make within these contexts. Next, we will detail an existing schoolwide ACT platform and offer ways that nonclinical workers can train psychological flexibility in the classroom. Finally, we will recommend educational programs, policies, and practices with the aim of enhancing human well-being in ever widening circles of influence.

Global Issues in Mainstream Education

Educational institutions are beset with a number of broad areas of concern to which educational reformers have tried to respond. The list that follows includes only the first and most notable of those listed in the US Department of Education School Survey on Crime and Safety (2014). This short list only begins to touch the exterior of these problems, and it is not possible to form overarching generalizations from the disparate studies listed below. However, this brief survey of prevalence rates serves as an entry point to a discussion of CBS-consistent approaches within these contexts.

Bullying

Bullying is typically defined as being exposed, repeatedly and over time, to negative actions on the part of one or more persons (Olweus, 1994). In recent years, bullying and its online counterpart, cyberbullying, have become central targets of media and community attention. Large survey studies (N > 10,000) conducted in different nations with equivalent populations report slim differences in prevalence across geographic margins. Sample prevalence figures range from 31.4% in rural India (Kshirsagar, Agarwal, & Bavdekar, 2007) to 29.9 across the rural United States (Nansel et al., 2001). However, several studies suggest differences exist in the socio-economic patterns of bullying (e.g., Spriggs, Ianotti, Nansel, & Haynie, 2007; Wang, Ianotti, & Nansel, 2009; Vaughn et al., 2010). In brief, children from less affluent families, neighborhoods, and regions appear to be at higher risk of being bullied than those from more affluent backgrounds. For example, reported prevalence is as high as 39.8% in the poorer nation of Lithuania and as low as 5.7% in the relatively wealthier nation Sweden (Schuster, 1999). The social costs associated with bullying include depression, isolation, low self-esteem, and lack of hope, according to data reported by Pranjic and Bajraktarevic (2010). Specifically, these investigators surveyed 290 secondary school students aged 13–17 across Bosnia-Herzegovina. Bullied respondents reported a significantly increased prevalence of depression (29% versus 8.8%) and suicide ideation (15.8% versus 3.5%) compared to those that did not report a history of being bullied. Such costs suggest behavior that at one time was considered age-typical can no longer be summarily dismissed, and that efforts across international borders to address bullying have not yet met the overwhelming demand for evidence-based prevention and intervention.

School Violence

In contrast to bullying, violence is usually defined in the prevalence literature as behavior by people against people liable to cause physical or psychological harm (Morrell, 2002). Hill and Drolet (1999) used logistical regression to calculate predictors and prevalence rates of school violence among high school students in the United States between 1993 and 1995. The team found that gender, race, and grade but not socioeconomic status in school predicted aggressive behavior. For youth aged 12–15 during the same years, 37% of reported violent crimes occurred on school grounds, according to the Bureau of Justice (as cited in Friday, 1996). Akpochafo (2014) reported a 15% rise in school violence in the United Kingdom from 2006 to 2010, and that no discernible differences in the rising rates were noted between socio-economic groups or between urban and suburban schools. In South Africa, sexual violence rates in the schools are notably pronounced; in a survey study of 446 males aged 12 to 22 in the greater Durban area, 66.8% reported aggressive behavior, with 17.5% reporting an act of sexual aggression that met the legal definition of rape or attempted rape (Magojo & Collings, 2003). This small sampling of studies across global borders suggest problems of great magnitude for which existing prevention and intervention mechanisms are insufficient.

Substance Use

Despite widespread school-based psychoeducation programs targeting substance use, US adolescents report rapidly increasing initiation of substance use across the middle and high school grades. In 2007, students reported a 23% increase in alcohol consumption from the 8th to the 10th grade and another 11% from the 10th to the 12th. Comparable increases in illicit drug use (16 and 11%, respectively) were also reported (Monitoring the Future, 2007). In a study sampling over 20,000 students in grades 6 through 10 across six African nations, prevalence of risky alcohol use (two or more drinks per day for at least 20 days consecutively) was 6.6% and 10.5% for illicit drug use between 2003 and 2004 (Peltzer, 2009). During the following five years, over half of those who reported early alcohol and drug use later reported depression, interpersonal violence, and risky sexual behavior. A recent report on drug use in European schools compared high school student illicit drug consumption reported by over 70,000 15- to 16-year-old students in 22 European nations (Olszewski, Matias, Monshouwer, & Kokkevi, 2010). Of note, the investigators found polydrug use reported by a third of all respondents and that cannabis and cocaine use predicted high levels of alcohol and tobacco consumption. Taken together, these studies suggest that problems among school-age children with psychoactive drugs cut across socioeconomic and geographic borders and present lasting problems for school-age children and their families.

The short list of issues recounted above is by no means exhaustive. Other global issues that beleaguer schools include soaring dropout rates and scholastic under-achievement, suspensions and expulsions, delinquent behavior, educational and social exclusion of people with disabilities, and the overuse of restraint and seclusion. Space limits preclude us from detailing prevalence rates in all these areas. Nevertheless, data reported above indicate that existing mechanisms for addressing public health issues in education are stretched beyond capacity. Needed are systemic, evidence-based strategies for influencing behavior at the levels of the individual, peer group, classroom, school, community, and region. Research on the impact of policies and practices is currently in its infancy. Behavioral data are needed to evaluate the consequences that select damaging behaviors such as those listed above. Effectiveness studies on strategic initiatives are needed to evaluate successful and efficient use of limited resources. Finally, advocacy groups should push through media and legislative channels to influence social and fiscal policy in these areas. Before expanding on these recommendations from a CBS perspective, we will detail some existing initiatives in these areas that are compatible with a CBS framework for prediction and influence of socially important human behavior.

Behavior Analysis in Education: Small Steps and Large

Since its outgrowth from the experimental analysis of behavior, applied behavior analysis (ABA) has responded to issues in educational reform. An inductive, ground-up scientific enterprise, behavior analysis sought to break down the global problems faced by schools and the communities that house schools into discrete problems with environmental determinants that can be readily identified and modified. This approach, rooted in pragmatism and the view that psychology is the science of behavior and is, as such, a sub-disciple of biology (Pierce & Cheney, 2013), has produced both piecemeal and comprehensive interventions for a variety of issues that range from academic to social and life-skill difficulties.

Early Examples of Behavior Analysis in the Schools

Depicting the full range of behavior analytic forays into school environments would be a volume-length treatment beyond the scope of this chapter. Nevertheless, it is of benefit to highlight a few strains in the literature in order to extract the relevant features to which CBS can contribute. Early examples of behavior analytic approaches within school settings include the teaching of math skills and attending behavior (Kirby & Shields, 1972), increasing voice volume to match that of peers (Jackson & Wallace, 1974), teaching conversational skills to predelinquent girls (Minkin et al., 1976), and attending school (Bizzis & Bradley-Johnson, 1981). These and a smattering of other studies in the first two decades following the inauguration of the *Journal of Applied Behavior Analysis* upheld a rigorous methodological standard that included direct and daily measurement, replicable procedures, individual and visual data analysis, programming for generalization, and social validation (Johnston & Pennypacker, 2009).

Although early efforts at demonstrating the power of behavior analysis in tackling problems faced by students and teachers in school settings followed well-documented behavior analytic strategies and tactics, the problems investigators addressed were often idiosyncratic to a minority of students: those with severe emotional issues or intellectual and developmental disabilities. During the 1990s, some investigative attention shifted from innovative school-based interventions to the improvement of behavioral assessment that could be used across large school classrooms. For example, Kern, Childs, Dunlap, Clarke, and Falk (1994) evaluated a procedure that mixed descriptive, analogue, and curricular assessment procedures for increasing on-task behavior in the classroom. Repp and Karsh (1994) showed the utility of analyzing conditional probabilities of classroom problem behavior functions. In one of the first studies to teach large groups of school personnel to use behavioral strategies, Northrup, Wacker, Berg, Kelly, Sasso, and DeRaad (1994) taught teachers and para-professionals to use functional assessment procedures.

Lessons from Organizational Behavior Management

Organizational behavior management is the application of behavioral principles derived from the experimental analysis of behavior to issues of individual and group performance and worker safety (Bucklin, Alvero, Dickinson, Austin, & Jackson, 2000). In school settings, OBM approaches have sought to extend behavior analytic strategies to improve the quality, efficiency, and scale of teacher training and management efforts. Early efforts focused on the preservice or inservice model (e.g., Filler, Hecimovic, & Blue, 1978; Haring, Neetz, Lovinger, Peck, & Semmel, 1987; Langone, Kooorland, & Oseroff, 1987) but these efforts were limited without the presence of additional contingencies. Combining antecedent with consequential strategies has yielded more robust and durable effects. Reid et al. (1985) used partic-ipatory management during inservice training. Gillat and Sulzer-Azaroff (1994) combined inservice training, feedback, and praise to improve principal performance at goal-setting, feedback, and praise toward students and teachers. Importantly, OBM researchers looked comprehensively at durable and large-scale school interventions (Gage, Fredricks, Johnson-Dorn, & Lindley-Southard, 1982; Selinske, Greer, & Lodhi, 1991). Along these lines, larger studies investigated efficiency of training and management (Selinske et al., 1991), pyramidal training (Green & Reid, 1994), social validity (Gillat & Sulzer-Azaroff, 1994), generalization of teaching skills (Fleming & Sulzer-Azaroff, 1992; Ingham & Greer, 1992). Taken as a whole, the OBM interest in education has deepened and responded to some needs within educational circles for systemic reform. However, long-term utilization and large-scale adoption beyond the immediate oversight and involvement of behavioral researchers has remained an elusive goal that is of particular interest with respect to the CBS agenda for school improvement.

Promoting Literacy: Project Follow Through

Perhaps the largest scale empirical evaluation of behavior analytic educational reform methods was a federally funded comparison of cognitive, affective, and behavioral teaching systems called Project Follow Through (PFT; Stebbins, St. Pierre, Proper, Anderson, & Cerva, 1977). PFT emerged in response to findings that low-income, minority students are usually at the 20th–28th percentiles by the end of third grade in reading and math (Moliter, Watkin, Napior, & Proper, 1977) and that this is dif-ficult to reverse using traditional educational methods in large, urban centers

(Cohen, Koehler, Datta, & Timpane, 1980). Initiated by the US Office of Education, PFT began in 1968 and continued for a decade, involving more than 20,000 children (Engelmann & Carnine, 1982).

The behavioral methods evaluated and contrasted with eight affective and cognitive methods were direct instruction (DI; Engelmann, 2007) and behavior analysis. Sites across the nation reported that significantly greater scholastic gains were found in the direct instruction and behavior analysis classrooms. These approaches involved (1) homogeneous skill grouping, (2) scripted class sessions, (3) intense, constant student interaction, and (4) teaching to mastery. Reported improvements were more rapid than in any of the other eight methods and were retained during subsequent annual evaluations (Gersten, Becker, Heiry, & White, 1984).

Several schools conducted and published independent papers on specifics of the behavioral PFT models they employed. Meyer, Gersten, and Gutkin (1983) reported results from their DI trials at a New York City elementary school located in a lower socioeconomic neighborhood plagued with poor educational outcomes, conflict over community control of the schools, and well-publicized conflict between district educational administrators and the United Federation of Teachers. Between 1968 and 1981, 12 classrooms participated, three at each grade level from kindergarten through third grade. An evaluation summary of end-of-third-grade achievement on the Metropolitan Achievement Test showed PFT students performed at or near the national median in all measures and substantially higher than any schools pooled by socioeconomic status. In a follow-up study, Meyer (1984) reported long-term effects from the first three cohorts that participated. In all cohorts, over half of the graduates finished high school as compared to just over a third of the control group students. Only 4.3% of the PFT students were held back, compared to 42% of the control group. There were also significantly fewer dropouts and more college applicants, as well as stronger reading and math scores, all in the context of a school serving children living in poverty, single-parent families surviving on government subsidies, plus newsworthy neighborhood drug and violence concerns.

Sadly, PFT results were not widely publicized, or, worse, were covered up by the US Department of Education (Lindsley, 1992; Watkins, 1988). Teachers in most schools enjoy autonomy to select educational materials and receive no training on the basis by which to make selections. Consequently, many choose on the basis of aesthetic qualities rather than effectiveness (Lindsley, 1992).

Despite these unsuitable developments, a number of profound lessons can be gleaned from the empirical research on behavior analysis, direct instruction, and its contemporary counterpart, precision teaching (PT; Lindsley, 1972, 1990) that are of interest to those seeking to reform educational practices and ameliorate problems of the sort addressed in this chapter. First, as stated above, model implementation appears to be contingent upon a number of variables that can be summarized in terms of training, buy-in, and direct contingency management related to implementation. Second, it appears educational outcomes are related to better instructional methods, not in the socioeconomic and cultural factors so often blamed for poor academic achievement. Third, tiered training in the model for administrators, teachers, and paraprofessionals is associated with stronger outcomes in urban areas with high teacher turnover. Fourth, future dissemination strategies building upon lessons learned in the efforts detailed above ought to incorporate advances in current educational practices that are being reported in the behavioral journals. For example,

Newsome, Berens, Ghezzi, Aninao, and Newsome (2014) found that children learned to respond to relational tasks involving frames of similarity and distinction when taught a "describe and classify" repertoire. Training provided in a DI and PT format on concrete and combined features, functions, and class resulted in derived hierarchical relations that, in novel probes, generalized to relations of similarity and distinction. Such advancements in the use of PT and DI to shape relational repertoires when teaching reading can easily be scaled up to the level of whole schools to promote flexible, adaptive learning. In the final section of this chapter, we will discuss ways to use these teaching methods to build prosocial repertoires in children, teachers, administrators, and stakeholders.

Educational Interventions Grounded in Behavioral Science

Good Behavior Game

A behavior analytic strategy with empirical support for reforming school and classroom procedures that dates back to the earliest days of ABA is the Good Behavior Game (GBG; Barrish, Saunders, & Wolf, 1968). In the seminal study, Barrish and colleagues reduced out-of-seat and talking-out behaviors during math and reading classes. Children were divided into two groups that competed during two set periods during the day at following classroom expectations to earn privileges. The study was soon replicated and extended by other investigators (Harris & Sherman, 1973; Medland & Stachnik, 1972) and variations of the GBG continue today to be reported in the literature (e.g., Leflot, Lier, Onghena, & Colpin, 2013; Poduska & Kurki, 2014). GBG results have been replicated in urban schools with at-risk children (Grandy, Madsen, & de Mersseman, 1973; Lannie & McCurdy, 2007), Sudanese and Belgian elementary school students (Leflot et al., 2013; Saigh & Umar, 1983), international students in US school settings (Nolan, Houlihan, Wanzek,& Jenson, 2014) regular education students (Kleinman & Saigh, 2011), children in mainstream classes with serious behavior problems (Darveaux, 1984), nonclassroom settings (Patrick, Ward, & Crouch, 1998), and very young children (Swiezy, Matson, & Box, 1992). Importantly, Johnson, Turner, and Konarski (1978) showed that GBG effects at reducing disruptive behavior are maintained months after initial training.

Probably the most striking utility of the GBG in the context of CBS and schools is the appearance of *large-scale, epidemiological, prevention-based school* adaptations. Kellam and Anthony (1998) implemented the GBG with 2,311 first and second grade students in four public elementary schools over a two-year period. Since aggression, disruptive behavior, and coercive interactions with adults had been found repeatedly to predict tobacco and illicit drug use, as well as criminal behavior (Block, Block, & Keyes, 1988; Robins, 1978; Tremblay et al., 1992) the authors asked whether interventions targeting aggressive and disruptive behavior would reduce the incidence of the initiation of smoking. Longitudinal data showed that, in two consecutive cohorts, the estimated risk of initiating tobacco use was lower than expected for boys assigned to the GBG intervention.

In a related outcome study, Kellam et al. (2014) randomly assigned first- and second-grade children in 19 Baltimore schools spread across five African American urban areas with lower socioeconomic status to either a GBG or control condition beginning in the 1985–1986 school year. The authors evaluated interrelationships among aggression, risky sexual behavior, drug abuse, and dependence disorder of the children in these two groups and found significantly reduced high-risk sexual behavior, drug abuse, and dependence disorders among those 19–21-year-old respondents that had been assigned to the GBG group 15 years earlier.

GBG is representative of a behavior-based prevention science approach to school reform that involves careful attention to epidemiological variables that include risk factors, prevalence, and outcomes. Like other prevention methodologies, GBG is part of a more global approach to reform that includes selective and targeted interventions for those with moderate and intensive support needs, respectively. Although universal strategies can be criticized for not being linked back to experimentally identified behavioral functions, they are nonetheless likely to be useful first-stage strategies that prevent the need for future intensive behavioral intervention. Kellam et al. (2014) report that, of the children exposed to GBG, 29% had drug problems 15 years later. In contrast, of those assigned to the control condition, 83% were addicted to drugs as adults. The correlation needs to be evaluated experimentally before causal statements can be made, but the size of the effect of this study alone certainly warrants such further attention from the behavioral research community.

Reducing Prejudice and Increasing Literacy: Jigsaw Classroom

The toll paid by societies around the globe for prejudice includes (1) systematic genocide committed by large, dominant groups, (2) coordinated mass murders committed by small outgroups, (3) loosely coordinated gang violence, and (4) hate crimes committed by individuals experiencing disenfranchisement (Allport, 1954). Common to all these events is a sense that shared community spaces are threatening environments in which the likelihood of harm is intolerably high. Since school environments often involve intergroup contact in shared spaces, it follows that anxiety and fear of imminent conflict preoccupies students to the detriment of learning requisite academic and social skills. Numerous studies point to low rates of literacy in schools where intergroup conflict is high (e.g., Aronson & Bridgeman, 1979; Stephan, 1985). Moreover, youth violence in regions high in intergroup conflict is a leading cause of death in both developing and developed nations (Spano, Rivera, & Bolland, 2010).

One well-researched approach to reducing prejudice in schools is intergroup contact. The contact hypothesis suggests that prejudice can be reduced when ingroup and outgroup members join together to accomplish shared objectives that lead to a recognition of common humanity (Allport, 1954). Although not all intergroup contact efforts are successful (cf., Brown, 1995), one technique has received considerable empirical support and warrants examination for its compatibility with the CBS agenda for school reform.

The "jigsaw classroom" (Aronson, Blaney, Stephan, Sikes, & Snapp, 1978) utilizes cooperative intergroup contingencies to develop academic and social competencies. Student interdependence and cooperation are selected response repertoires when students are divided into several groups tasked with teaching each other component repertoires of a larger task. Each student teaches a necessary and unique component and meets with "experts" from the other groups who are tasked with teaching coordinated component segments. Students are not evaluated based on group performance, but on their own individual learning of the material. Material needed for successful completion of the task is only available from other students. Thus, jigsaw contingencies favor cooperation and interdependence more than other cooperative learning strategies in which lesson material is always accessible to the motivated individual.

Empirical evaluations of the jigsaw technique have focused on cooperative learning for school desegregation (Aronson et al., 1978), social competency development (Moskowitz, Malvin, Schaeffer, & Schaps, 1983), cooperative learning in developing nations (Alebiosu, 2001; Chang, 2004; Huang, Huang, & Yu, 2011), and reducing prejudice (Aronson, Bridgeman, & Geffner, 1978; Walker & Crogan, 1998). Of relevance to the CBS agenda for school reform, all of these have been large-scale, epidemiological studies. These studies are important in that they demonstrate that large-scale prevention and intervention strategies that involve little teacher training can have sizable effects on relevant variables, making the jigsaw technique another candidate "behavioral vaccine" that inoculates against physical, mental, and behavioral disorders. Further implications will be discussed in the final section of this chapter.

Schoolwide Positive Behavior Support

Whereas mainstream behavior analysis efforts at school reform focus on teaching discrete social and academic skills, OBM approaches extend behavioral strategies to improve teacher training and management efforts. Above, we note efforts at large-scale schoolwide or multisite approaches that involve either preventative or responsive interventions (Gage, Fredricks, Gillat & Sulzer-Azaroff, 1994; Green & Reid, 1994; Fleming & Sulzer-Azaroff, 1992; Ingham & Greer, 1992; Johnson-Dorn, & Lindley-Southard, 1982; Selinske, Greer, & Lodhi, 1991). Also, we detailed strategies such as the GBG and the Jigsaw technique in which contextual features of the classroom environment select prosocial behavior. Each of these advancements has been useful, and yet widespread adoption and durability have remained elusive goals. In fact, until recently, large-scale and comprehensive interventions that simultaneously serve individuals and groups of students have been absent. However, over the last 20 years a multitier service delivery model has garnered noteworthy empirical support in the United States. Schoolwide Positive Behavior Support (SWPBS), first evaluated by Walker and colleagues (1996), switches the research paradigm from child-specific to macrosystem interventions in schools and communities. Utilizing functional behavioral assessment techniques at the individual level and OBM methods to increase the capacity of schools to accomplish and maintain systemic change, SWPBS incorporates support-building efforts at the level of school leadership (i.e., federal, state, municipal, district, and school administrations), data-based decision-making, and team consensus building. Schools implement three levels of service: universal support to all children, targeted support to those at risk for discipline problems or school failure, and individual support to those whose behavior responds to neither of the first two levels of care. Commonalities across a variety of SWPBS programs include team goal-setting, data analysis regarding problem behaviors and the settings in which they occur, functional assessment of individual problem behavior, incentives, a continuum of consequences, staff training, and data analysis regarding efficacy and fidelity of implementation (Anderson & Kincaid, 2005).

ACT in the Classroom

A precise account of mindfulness is challenging because a functional analysis of private events involves either inference by others, or potentially inaccurate self-reporting. That is, the behavior of interest appears to many applied workers to be inaccessible and therefore out of bounds. Additionally, antecedent and consequent maintaining variables with respect to mindfulness are not easy to specify because they may involve covert self-rules or statements that are equally inaccessible. Finally, a fair number of researchers investigating mindfulness are content to change self-report of psychological health without looking for changes in overt behavior; thus, a vast portion of the literature on mindfulness is not helpful to the behaviorally oriented scientist-practitioner. Our stance is that contextual behavior science has much to contribute to education, and that perhaps utility may trump traditional experimental measures of treatment success. Mindfulness practices can be evaluated in behavioral terms, and overt behavior changes can be directly measured in relation to changes in stimulus control. Although a number of mindfulness researchers in school settings report results that are of interest here, the current review is limited to empirically measurable findings concentrating on acceptance and action practices.

Six core processes link successful performance outcomes. *Acceptance* involves the behavior of tacting bodily sensations, thoughts, and emotions without effort to change their content or form. In contrast to noncontextual cognitive behavior therapies that aim to eliminate these events through reappraisal, the ACT approach is more akin to noticing than challenging. *Defusion* is the act of separating the content of thoughts from their meaning. The impact of defusing is that thoughts are recognized as behavior that needs no further action; when one defuses from a thought, the thought is deliteralized such that it is not taken to be true, even if it seems to be so. *Present moment awareness* involves bringing diffuse, unfocused behavior under narrowed stimulus control. When the dominant functions of past and present are replaced with those of the present context, behavior can be more sensitized to direct contingencies of reinforcement or can be brought under the distal control of indirect contingencies related to verbal products, such as statements regarding one's values. *Flexible perspective-taking* involves framing events with respect to person, place, and time. I–HERE–NOW and YOU–THERE–THEN can be merged into numerous relational networks with different functions, and each of these functions can then be transformed through arbitrarily derived relational responding to produce different psychological events from the same networks. The result is perspective that can be at once located in the present and yet complete enough to provide a sense of overview or bird's-eye view. Such a flexible sense of self is distinct from the more rigid self-concept that accompanies inability to tact behavioral alternatives regarding what it would be like to be in a different person, place, or time. *Valuing* is the act of identifying patterns of action that are reinforcing and that may lead to immediate direct reinforcement or to delayed, valuable consequences. The sixth targeted repertoire in the psychological flexibility model, *committing*, involves setting goals and taking action that moves the person behaving in a direction consistent with the verbal products of his valuing. *In short, ACT involves noticing and unhooking from powerful thoughts and emotions, engaging flexibly in the present with a flexible sense of perspective, and taking action in a valued direction.*

ACT for students

Investigations into the needs of students have focused attention upon three distinct age groups. The needs of kindergarten through age 12 children has been the focus of a handful of researchers interested in prevention of or interventions for challenging behaviors that have addressed the value of mindfulness, defusion, and overall psychological flexibility. A second area of growing empirical interest is mindfulness and psychological flexibility work for college undergraduates. Finally, a third area of research has examined how mindfulness and acceptance might have utility for training of graduate school students in psychology, nursing, and special education.

ACT interventions for primary and secondary school children. To date, there has been one single-case design investigation of the utility of mindfulness within the classroom. Wilson and Dixon (2010) used an ABA withdrawal design to evaluate changes in attending behavior that followed mindfulness exercises delivered to 12 first- and second-grade students. The authors defined attending behaviorally. Using a 10-second momentary time sampling procedure, they scored attending as engagement that included looking at or in the direction of the teacher or student who was talking, following instructions, looking (and/or completing) a worksheet, and engaging in classroom activities. Experimenters delivered five different mindfulness exercises, each after a 30-minute baseline observation condition, and following each delivery of the exercise, a subsequent 30-minute return to baseline phase was conducted. Results demonstrated that directly observed changes in behavior follow careful operational definition of the dependent variable and selection of an independent variable suited to the interests and skills of students in a particular classroom setting. The significance of this study cannot be overstated. Behavior analysis is built upon evidence that builds from the ground up. That is, preliminary evidence from tightly controlled experiments using strong designs that demonstrate functional relationships between dependent and independent variables is necessary before scaling up to large studies aimed at demonstrating efficacy and effectiveness. Although studies of this kind are in evidence with adults, Wilson and Dixon present the only peer-reviewed data with children showing this level of experimental control.

As noted earlier in the chapter, a significant societal problem that shows up in school environments is religious, racial, and ethnic prejudice. The verbal practice of evaluating categorical relations builds repertoires related to both prejudice and problem-solving (Hayes, Barnes-Holmes, & Roche, 2001). The arbitrary nature of social categorization (Kohlenberg, Hayes, & Hayes, 1991) allows for the verbal construction of in- and outgroup functions that ameliorate the difficulties attendant to noticing simultaneous similarities and differences. Instead of evoking social categorization of complexly nuanced coordinative frames, burdensome environments evoke simple frames of distinction and hierarchy that pit one group against and over the other. Given such an operant analysis, increased acceptance and decreased believability of evaluations become targets for intervention. Lillis and Hayes (2007) conducted one such investigation. Undergraduates were split into two groups; one received an educational lecture on racial prejudice and the other a class session based on ACT. Only the ACT group demonstrated increased positive behavioral intentions at post and one-week follow up. Whereas other efforts to reduce prejudice detailed earlier in this chapter focus on either decategorization (reducing harmful category distinctions; cf. Bradshaw, Mitchell, and Leaf, 2010) or recategorization (creating a single group identity for all individuals; cf. Aronson et al., 1978), ACT promises to do both through defusion and flexible perspective-taking.

Luciano, Valdivia, Gutierrex, Ruiz, and Paez Blarrina (2009) outlined three protocols with different goals but common functional components. One group of adolescents received a values and acceptance protocol aimed at increasing safer sexual behavior. A second protocol targeting acceptance and defusion was designed to increase flexibility among young chess players. The third, a protocol that targeted values, acceptance, and defusion was applied to adolescents with impulsive and anti-social behavior. Students in the first group reported fewer sexual partners and less use of drugs after the ACT intervention compared to those who received only information. In the second group, chess-playing students who received the ACT intervention displayed improved performance compared to controls. The children showing antiso-cial behaviors who received the ACT intervention all demonstrated positive clinical impact upon behavior in class and other school environments. As reported by Wilson and Dixon (2010), Luciano and colleagues demonstrated that flexible and carefully selected independent variable components in an ACT protocol make a substantial impact upon treatment outcomes with students.

In a basic science investigation, Luciano, Ruiz, Vizcaíno Torres, Sanchez Martin, Gutiérrez Martínez, and López López (2011) compared two defusion exercises typical of ACT with 15 adolescents identified with problem behavior in a local secondary school. The purpose of this study was to identify necessary and sufficient framing components to be built into defusion interactions that will be useful for children in similar settings. The function of a person's discomfort and behavior can change in the presence of a variety of different framing modalities (i.e., deictic, hierarchical, comparison, and function-regulating cues). The authors compared four framing modalities and found that students who completed defusion exercises involving only deictic framing did not improve discrimination of ongoing behavior. In contrast, those whose defusion exercises included deictic and hierarchical framing components plus behavior regulation cues showed improved perspective-taking.

Because this study represents a rare example of bridge research offering both basic science answers and preliminary evidence of a generalizable intervention, it is worthwhile to provide more detailed explication of the two conditions that Luciano and colleagues compared. Defusion I (using deictic framing cues) included guided imagery such as,

> Imagine that you have not eaten during a very long day. What sensation would you have? Would your stomach be full or empty? Now imagine that you can see that sensation of emptiness in your stomach. Can you imagine it?

Participants in the Defusion I condition would receive more imagery along these lines. Those exposed to Defusion II would receive additional cues for hierarchical, deictic, and behavior regulation framing:

> Now tell me if you can imagine yourself so big as to have room for all the thoughts that you have had today, for all the sensations, all the memories … Now, think about you as the captains of a big boat and your thoughts and feelings as the passengers … Now, can you see that you are who is having that image of yourself with your thoughts and sensations? Can you see that you are more than your thoughts and sensations? Now imagine that you are writing these thoughts into a document on your computer. Let the thought move to enter into a folder that will contain all the thoughts you may have.

We have detailed conditions evaluated by Luciano et al. (2011) explicitly to indicate the value and need for more research that extends our understanding of the basic principles that undergird ACT interventions and how these can most efficiently be utilized to achieve the strongest outcomes. If practitioners working in schools struggle to balance psychological well-being with educational priorities, effective and efficient strategies are needed. Basic researchers are well poised to provide torque to this end.

Livheim et al. (2014) conducted two pilot studies (N = 66, 32) in school settings comparing eight-session ACT workshops to individual support delivered by school healthcare workers. Participants were adolescents targeted for psychosocial distress. Self-report measures in these two studies showed reduced stress and depressive symptoms in the ACT intervention groups, suggesting that larger controlled studies in school settings are warranted. Of note, Livheim et al. targeted symptom reduction and did not report behavioral outcomes. Future studies that provide evidence of changes in overt behavior using similar workshop formats would be useful.

ACT interventions for college undergraduates. Problems related to cultural differences, language barriers, and reduced social support from diminished family contact result in remarkably high rates of distress among young people studying abroad. Psychological distress among such international students was the focus of a bibliotherapy study conducted by Muto, Hayes, and Jeffcoat (2011). Japanese college students (N = 70) at school in America were given copies of an ACT self-help book translated into Japanese. Participants who received the ACT self-help book demonstrated improved general mental health compared to wait-list controls. Wait-list participants showed desired outcomes following distribution of the workbook.

Gold standard psychotherapies have not frequently been compared to ACT with college students. To bridge this gap, Block and Wulfert (2000) compared one of the most well-established contemporary psychotherapies, cognitive behavior group therapy (CBGT; Hope & Heimberg, 1993) to ACT with 11 undergraduates with public speaking anxiety. Measures on three self-report scales showed comparable clinical improvement consistent with their conceptual and procedural approaches. That is, in each of the treatment groups, willingness to engage with feared stimuli increased, but anxiety decreased only in the CBGT group and ACT participants showed greater willingness to engage in feared situations. The very small sample size limits the degree to which statements can be made with confidence. Additionally, as is the case in many of the studies reviewed herein, self-reported clinical improvement must be viewed with caution since the students' verbal responses could have been influenced by social desirability.

A few studies that are not ACT interventions per se are useful to review in this section. Hayes (2004) described an emerging "third wave" of behavior therapies that together form the contextual wing of CBTs (Hayes et al., 2011). Although differing in philosophical and conceptual orientations, this family of treatment modalities seems to share a focus on mindfulness and acceptance. Common to a number of these contextual CBTs is an emphasis on openness to unwanted thoughts, feelings, memories, and sensations; improved flexible awareness of the present moment – including both physical surroundings and others' points of view; and heightened activation in service of valued life directions (Szabo, Long, Villatte, & Hayes, 2014).

For example, Pistorello, Fruzzetti, MacLane, Gallop, and Iverson (2012) compared dialectical behavior therapy (DBT; Linehan, 1993) to an optimized control condition in 63 college students who were suicidal at baseline and reported at least one nonsuicidal self-injurious act. Significant decreases in suicidality, depression, the number of self-injurious acts, and psychotropic medication usage was noted in the DBT group compared to the control condition, as was improved social adjustment. Collard, Avny, and Boniwell (2008) evaluated mindfulness, satisfaction with life, positive affect, and negative affect in 15 university students using a different contextual CBT, mindfulness-based cognitive therapy (MBCT; Segal, Williams, & Teasdale, 2002). Using a repeated measures design, the authors found that students' mindfulness significantly increased and negative affect significantly decreased. Positive affect remained unchanged, but life satisfaction improved, though not to the level of statistical significance. The small sample size, lack of a control group, and lack of behavioral measures limit this study's generalizability. Nevertheless, clinical gains seem to have been correlated with mindfulness practice; in fact, those students with longer practice times of mindfulness during the program reported higher levels of mindfulness at the end of the study. Taken together, these studies suggest that college students could benefit from mindfulness and acceptance practices regardless of whether they are experiencing high levels of baseline distress or not. Since these are preliminary investigations, more research is needed to further identify the variables that lead to successful treatment outcomes using these contextual CBT modalities.

ACT interventions for graduate students. Empirical efforts to help graduate students who plan to enter helping professions have focused principally on stress management. For example, clinical psychology trainees are susceptible to high levels of stress during their training (Cushway, 1992) that results in decreased personal and professional effectiveness (Schwartz-Mette, 2009). Contextual CBT researchers employing non-ACT interventions have conducted some noteworthy studies in this area. In a study with first-year medical students conducted by Saunders et al. (2007), participants demonstrated improved stress management skills and academic performance after receiving an experiential mind-body skills course.

Stafford-Brown and Pakenham (2012) evaluated clinical psychology trainee work stress, distress, life satisfaction, counseling self-efficacy, self-compassion, and therapeutic alliance using an ACT workshop with experimental and wait-list control groups (N = 56). Statistically significant outcomes were attained across all main outcome measures, which were maintained at follow-up. Importantly, meditational analyses revealed that most of these effects were mediated by ACT processes. In a related study, Pakenham and Stafford-Brown (2013) asked 56 clinical psychology students to complete questionnaires regarding their views regarding an ACT intervention focused on stress management. The authors found that most respondents were willing to recommend the training to other students. Many students also reported improved psychological flexibility.

Similar to the issues faced by clinical psychology trainees, nursing students have been shown to experience burnout and exhaustion that leads to emotional distancing and ineffectiveness. From a relational framing perspective, avoidant coping is indicative of framing fatigue in coordination with patients. Similar to the evaluative framing involved in racial and ethnic prejudice, the natural language processes involved in framing burnout and patients in coordination with work leads to equating any contact with patients with exhaustion and decreased effectiveness. Thus, emotional disengagement is common among nursing trainees as a consequence of unmanaged stress and a natural outgrowth of such avoidant coping is absenteeism, poor performance, and occupational turnover (Biglan, Hayes, & Pistorello, 2008; Maslach, Schaufeli, & Leiter, 2001).

To address these issues, Djordjevic and Frögéli (2012) conducted an RCT examining the effect of a stress management ACT workshop delivered to nursing students compared to treatment as usual. ACT participants ($n=113$) reported significant increases in work engagement, health, psychological flexibility, and mindful awareness as well as decreases in perceived stress and burnout. At three-month follow-up, results were maintained for perceived stress, burnout, work engagement, and mindful awareness.

ACT for Teachers

Another helping profession in which high stress and burnout are pervasive is teaching (Madden-Szeszko, 2000). Teachers are often supported with wellness programs that emphasize exercise and relaxation, but they are rarely provided with data-based methods to improve emotional or behavioral well-being (Couser, 2008). As a result, it is likely that teachers engage in avoidant brief, immediate relational responses with respect to behavioral health. An additional consequence could be the implicit framing of those teachers that seek such remedies as opposite from healthy or desirable. Stigmatization of teachers seeking behavioral health assistance would thus be likely, and teachers may wish to avert such outcomes.

Jeffcoat and Hayes (2012) attempted an intervention aimed at avoiding possible stigmatization for teachers (N=236). Participants read an ACT self-help book for two months, completed exercises and quizzes, and after post-testing were followed for 10 weeks. Wait-list participants were then provided the same treatment. The authors reported overall improved psychological health for participants, with significant preventative effects for depression and anxiety. Follow-up general mental health, depression, anxiety, and stress appeared to be related to the degree to which participants used the book. Additionally, the authors noted that those who experienced high levels of stress at the onset of treatment were more likely to show improvement at post-test and follow up, whereas those who were not distressed at baseline were less likely to worsen in general mental health. Because the level of need and level of perceived risk associated with seeking help is high in this population, innovative treatment delivery platforms such as this are worthy of further investigation. To date, this appears to be the only study investigating bibliotherapy for teachers and other helping professionals.

Early childhood special education teachers are equally prone to high stress, burnout, and turnover, according to Biglan, Layton, Backen Jones, Hankins, and Rusby (2011). Using a randomized wait-list control design, Biglan and colleagues provided ACT workshops to preschool special education teachers and evaluated stress, depression, burnout, and collegial support. The intervention decreased avoidant behavior, increased mindful awareness and valued living, and improved teachers' reports of self-efficacy. Anecdotally, the authors reported that teachers completing the program were more willing to implement emotion coaching and this appears to have helped them to teach children about emotions and ways to manage difficult situations.

Outcomes of Full-Scale ACT Implementation in the Educational System

To date, there has been one large-scale, epidemiological, prevention-based ACT intervention in the schools. Dixon (2013) describes a year-long ACT life-skills curriculum implemented with elementary school-aged children in a midwestern US state.

The curriculum was first introduced in a single classroom and was later adopted across the school. After program evaluation data were reviewed, the program was adopted in schools across the district. The following section details the necessary steps involved in implementing a full-scale ACT life-skills curriculum across a large educational system.

1 *The buy in.* As providers seek to install a treatment protocol in an existing school system, they need to be aware of the various complex contingencies that may affect eventual success. The ACT model, and specifically the "acceptance" component, will be somewhat counterintuitive to most school personnel. Having a child that is upset be told to "accept that you are feeling bad" instead of being soothed and told "everything will be alright," is a different mindset for most professionals in education. Furthermore, any additional treatment requires additional effort by those parties involved. It is naive to assume that school professionals will want to do ACT just because it works. They need to be sold on the fact that ACT will make their job easier. Yet more work up front to eventually get to "easy," is an adventure that many people will not be willing to take.

The initiator of the ACT application in a school should seek top administrative support prior to implementation. For example, if a teacher wishes to use ACT as the social skills curriculum in her classroom, she may need support to deviate from the existing protocol. There might be language in a student's Individual Education Plan (IEP) specifying number of minutes of time per week designated to protocol X, and if ACT is replacing X, then many meetings and approvals must occur. If the implementer is a social worker for an entire district, that individual may need authorization to change approaches, as well as transition students served from more traditional cognitive-based therapy to ACT. A behavioral specialist who recently discovered ACT might recommend to a district that certain children or classrooms use the model, yet, without administrative authority, those consultations may fall on deaf ears from staff not interested in doing more for essentially nothing.

In summary, the most successful application of ACT, whether it is for a single child or an entire school, is to have strong support from the top down. Administration will eventually hear stories of the student(s) doing better with their emotional or social challenges, but also hear stories about how odd metaphors, activities, or dialogue was used to create such change. Keeping buy-in from the top educates, protects, and ensures adherence to the ACT treatment model.

2 *The contextual landscape.* The context of a school system is a complex and dynamic interaction of many people, locations, and students. It is far from the simple client–therapist relationship that occurs in private practice settings. As a result, there are many factors to consider when undergoing an ACT installation within a school setting. The time spent doing ACT will require a deletion of some other subject or activity within the school day. The therapist will not have the luxury of simply "adding" ACT on to the child's existing schedule. Various federal, state, and district regulations dictate how much time per day should be spent in math, language, arts, science, and physical education. ACT cannot replace these subjects. Creative scheduling into "life-skills" time, personal development, health, or social work groups all serve as possibilities for fitting ACT into the school day. Another consideration is to determine if existing practices are worth the time they take up of the school day. For example, if an elementary classroom spends 45 minutes singing about the weather, the day of the week, and the calendar, one might

debate that utility for children with emotional challenges. It seems perfectly rational to assume that learning ACT skills is more important for such a child to successfully navigate his world than becoming an expert on discriminating cloud formations and placing a hat on the classroom "Weather Bear."

3 *The resistance.* Asking school personnel to work harder for no additional financial gain is a difficult battle at best. It is also unlikely that people will work harder for the long-term, delayed, and probabilistic consequences of a student's better well-being. Resistance to the ACT model by staff, the student, or both should be expected. However, careful discussion with the parties involved could lead to eventual adoption of the ACT approach. Below we consider ACT-consistent methods of addressing potential sources of resistance.

When dealing with school employees, the initiator of ACT should present the treatment in a nonthreatening and noncorrective way. Resistance will occur if one states, "What you have been doing in your classroom really doesn't work that well, and I have this ACT thing that will be much better." One must keep in mind that school employees may have spent considerable time and effort in the existing approach, and simply telling them that there is something better will not generate acceptance of ACT. Instead phrases such as the following should be used: "What you have been doing is very good, and I was wondering if you might consider looking at ACT with me. There seems to be a lot of emerging data on its utility" or "Since the student is not really getting better with X as our therapeutic approach, perhaps it might be time to try something different. I can help get you started and take the hassle out of your hands."

When interacting with students in a therapeutic context, an introduction to ACT may also be met with resistance. ACT will challenge the student to think differently, to not fight the thoughts, and to accept being in the moment as much as possible. These are radically different ways to go through a school day than what is typically preached by caregivers at home and school. The resistance we all feel to letting our minds be, focusing on all thoughts, and staying committed to values will be exaggerated dramatically in a child of any age. The implementer may hear utterances such as "I liked the way we used to talk better" or "I hate ACT, it makes me think too hard." The skilled ACT therapist will need to welcome resistance into the relationship, and stay the course through the push back common in children when new approaches are introduced into a part of the school day that may not be preferred to begin with.

4 *The implementers.* Any variety of school personnel could be identified to implement the ACT intervention. The more formal training in ACT will logically yield better results, however, with commitment to learning the approach and taking the time necessary for delivering ACT, many novice staff can make change happen. When a teacher implements an ACT program for the entire classroom, she may develop a series of group-based activities and narratives surrounding the behavioral flexibility model. In the case of group implementation, the goals may be centered more around successful classroom working than intimate individualized psychological challenges. Even so, once the students contact the various ACT metaphors and gain an understanding of psychological flexibility, the teacher may see personal connections occur between the model and the student. A careful balance must be maintained between group activity and personal disclosure. This is especially true if such disclosure could be used maliciously between students to provoke interpersonal friction.

When a social worker or school psychologist delivers ACT, it may take the form of a closer approximation to the one-to-one client–therapist relationship. In this arrangement, the student is more capable of interacting with their own personal psychological distress than when in a group. However, the limitation of the 1-1 arrangement is that the student may find himself or herself with difficulty maintaining psychological flexibility in a larger community that is not aware of how to use or foster the use of the ACT model. Instead, we recommend that when the implementers are social workers, counselors, or school psychologists, these professionals could be offered additional training in a nonclinical approach that has been called "ACTraining" (Moran, 2015). Moran suggests the use of a coaching approach, in contrast to the typical ACT therapy model, when introducing psychological flexibility skills to groups in nonclinical settings. This is especially important in addressing the issue of personal disclosure that can be used maliciously by some children when the ACT implementers are not present, such as during recess and lunchtime. Although groups that have been working with ACT for a time may develop strong personal ties and individual skills for navigating malicious behavior, beginning groups are likely to test the boundaries of acceptable behavior. The ACTraining coaching approach and exercises suggested in Dixon's *ACT for Children with Autism and Emotional Challenges* (2014) are geared to help groups discriminate issues that are useful to discuss at the group level from those best handled in one-to-one sessions. There may also be situations in which the implementer may dance between coach and therapist roles in attempting to find the most functional position to facilitate behavior change for the individual child.

Another facilitating option is taking the role of leadership mentor for the group. The mentor role is to help groups identify (1) their prosocial and cooperative values, (2) things both observable and private that get in the way of their moving toward those values, (3) the experience members and others observing the group have when physical events and emotions dominate the group's behavior, and (4) the experience members and others observing the group have when values articulated by the group itself guide the behaviors of its members. The leadership mentor or prosocial guide model is a useful variation because the emphasis is on positive behavior. It is only from a slightly defused and humorously looking "at" rather than "from" perspective that problematic psychological experiences are explored. This obviates the need for talk in a manner that is more commonly associated with psychotherapy and yet brings into focus all the aims and strategies required of the group to build behavioral flexibility.

5   *Installing ACT in various classroom types.*

   5.1   *Emotional and behavioral disorders.* Perhaps the most logical place for ACT to find a home within the educational system is within classrooms that are treating children with emotional and behavioral disabilities. Such students are placed within this type of environment due to wide range of histories, which often include challenging behaviors, drastically unstructured home environments, and mental health concerns. As such, these students are in need of a wide-reaching intervention designed to alter how much of their life is conducted. Typically these classrooms contain simplistic token systems, level systems, or other punitive approaches to managing bad behaviors that are predicted to occur from this population. What is often missing in such classrooms is a therapeutic underbelly that helps teach the preventative strategies that such children will need as they bump into the various challenges that life offers. Reactive strategies such as positive or negative points for behaviors are fine, but they really only manage, rather than teach the child how to more optimally behave in the future.

5.2 *High functioning autism.* There has been no greater success story for behavioral science than early intensive intervention for children with autism. A generation of this population now has access to services that have the true ability to alter their lives. Nonverbal children will often learn how to speak or communicate, social skills will be developed, and cognitive capacities will be grown. However, what tends to happen once this population acquires complex language and cognitive abilities is that they start to do the things we all do – worry about the future and ruminate on the past. Many of these children begin to leave the present moment and become lost in the thoughts their mind is now telling them. ACT has the potential to assist such students to manage this newly acquired mental life that grows out of verbal abilities. When ACT is incorporated into the intervention protocols for children with autism, similar gains can be expected to those persons with emotional and social disabilities.

5.3 *Typical development.* Although ACT is considered most purely as a therapeutic approach for persons with psychological distress, there is no reason to limit its application to those students who have formalized psychological conditions necessitating therapy. Even within the regular education classroom, ACT allows for the educator to guide students into making better choices during the day which are focused on things they value, and remaining present to the various work tasks at hand. The simple Accept, Commit, and Take Action phrase holds utility for any child, with or without a disability, and can serve as the theme for behavior management, social skill building, and respect for others. In a recent study by Kennedy, Whiting, and Dixon (2014), very young preschool-age children who were afraid to try novel (and healthy) foods were exposed to a brief ACT intervention emphasizing mindfulness (touch, smell, taste the food) and values (health, try new things, get social praise/stickers). Over the course of a few short weeks, the refusal of food was dramatically reduced at the overall classroom level for these children. In summary, ACT has a significant potential for many dimensions of regular education, ranging from food selections to bullying and work completion.

6   *Hands-on metaphors.* One important consideration to factor in to the ACT treatment for children in school settings is that talking will probably not be enough. Young children, and even high school students, are talked to all day by a variety of teachers and staff. Speaking to them as one might consider doing in a one-to-one therapy context with an adult, will not yield ideal outcomes. The metaphoric underpinnings of ACT allow for a wide variety of creative explorations of the model using hands on activities. In Dixon (2014) a series of 180 such activities is provided whereby students from kindergarten through high school learn aspects of ACT through art projects, writing, drawing, motor tasks, and dialogue with the implementer. For example, in Dixon's text students are asked to think of what a dragon is and the words, thoughts, and feelings associated with a dragon.

Afterwards, the child is to place the word "paper" in front of dragon and to now describe a "paper dragon." Additional discussion occurs around the idea that the additional word "paper" alters many of the prior thoughts the word dragon may have evoked. The child eventually asked to make their own paper dragon from art supplies, and to write various "dragon" thoughts on this seemingly powerless paper beast. Doing so provides the student with the opportunity to accept thoughts, distance themselves from such thoughts, and to reevaluate the "truth" those thoughts possess. Bringing the concepts to life for a child can make the metaphor take on additional psychological functions, and set the context for eventual behavior change.

Another example of bringing ACT to life for a child is reported in Dixon's text that instructs the child to "draw the real you" on a piece of paper and label it as the self which is always them. The next step is to crush up that paper and place it into a brown lunch sack. On the outside of the sack the child is then asked to "draw the you which people always see" which may be quite different than the paper on the inside. After completion, the child is instructed to show their various "selves" and eventually reveal the real self as the bag is opened and tossed aside. While the Dixon book provides an ACT implementer with a plethora of possibilities, the creative therapist, schoolteacher, or social worker will undoubtedly be capable of crafting novel hands-on metaphors as well. Figure 21.1 displays an

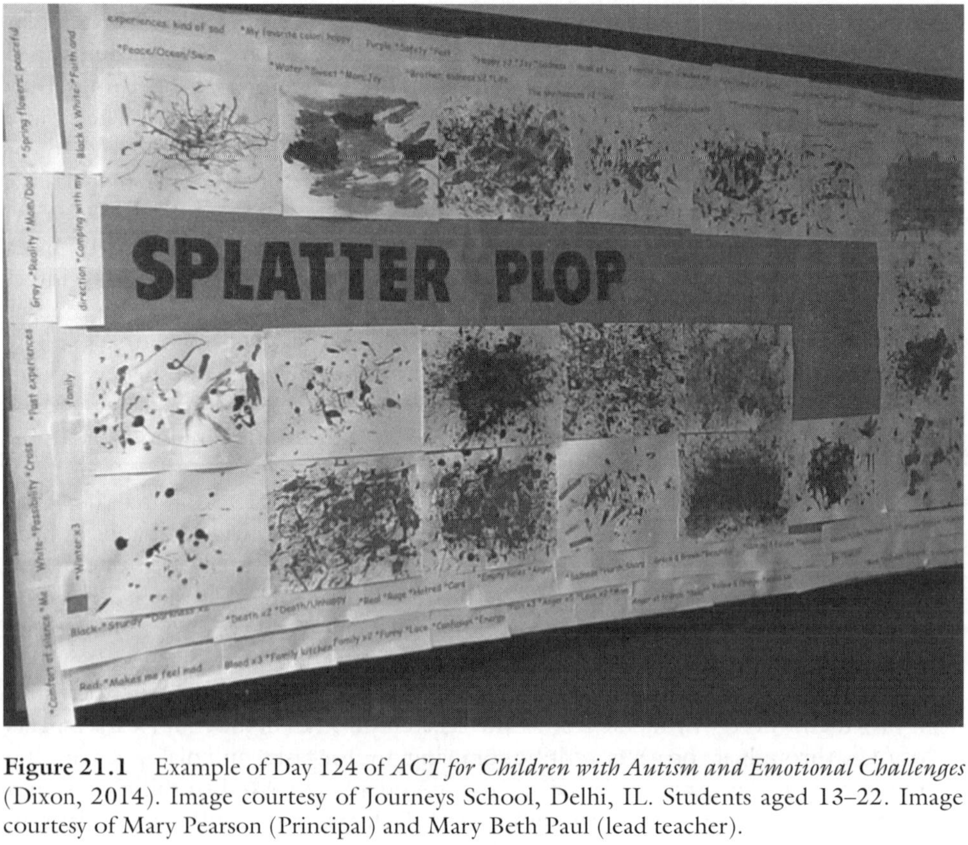

Figure 21.1   Example of Day 124 of *ACT for Children with Autism and Emotional Challenges* (Dixon, 2014). Image courtesy of Journeys School, Delhi, IL. Students aged 13–22. Image courtesy of Mary Pearson (Principal) and Mary Beth Paul (lead teacher).

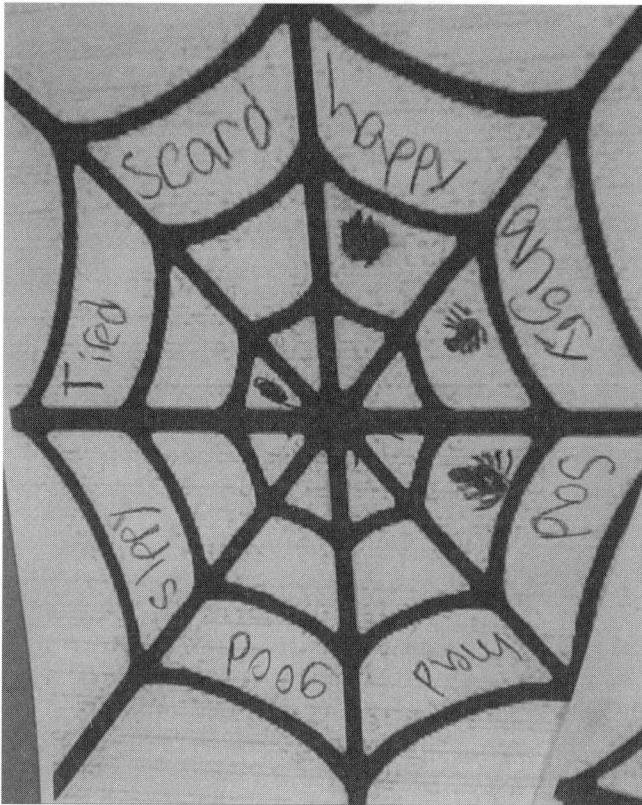

Figure 21.2 Example of Day 134 of *ACT for Children with Autism and Emotional Challenges* (Dixon, 2014). Image courtesy of Eastwood Elementary School, Woodriver, IL. Student age 10. Image courtesy of Cindy Penrod (Director of Special Education).

example of such a metaphor whereby students were asked to create abstract pictures using various colored paints. In this experience, students were asked to identify a thought or emotion and give it a color. After a variety of thoughts were assigned to colors, the students were instructed to let these colors drop on the page. The metaphor here is that the thoughts are defusing from the student, as they first become physicalized as colors of paint, and then even more so as they are placed on the paper in front of them. After this exercise, all the students' projects are collected and displayed on the hallway outside of the classroom. This process of public display adds another depth of defusion from these thoughts that occupy the person's mind.

Another example of the interactive possibilities of ACT from a talk therapy to an experiential therapy can be found in Figure 21.2. This image displays the outcome of a young child who has been instructed to label both good and bad thoughts that she has within a spider web. Discussion with the caregiver occurs along the lines of, "Getting stuck in the web is much like getting stuck in our thoughts. And just like how one part of the web may 'catch us,' so can our thoughts catch us and prevent us from moving forward in a values-driven life."

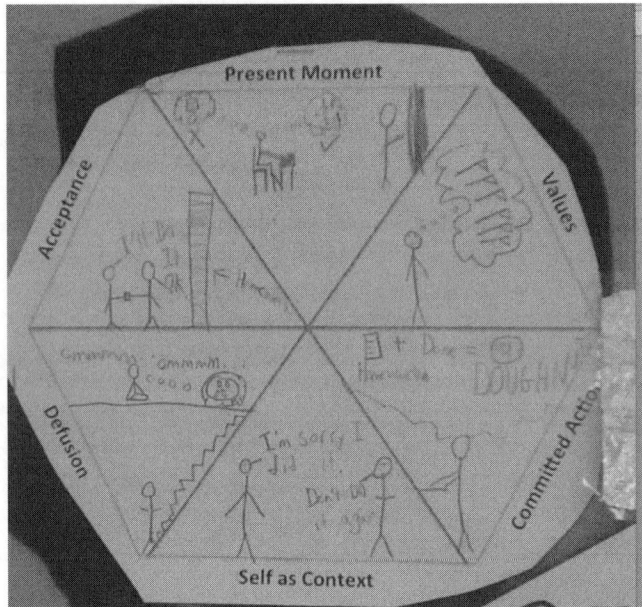

Figure 21.3 Example of a personal hexaflex from *ACT for Children with Autism and Emotional Challenges* (Dixon, 2014). Image courtesy of Eastwood Elementary School, Woodriver, IL. Student age 8.

Further dialogue includes how the spider can for some reason walk around the web without getting entangled. Questions are posed as to how the child can become more like a spider and less like a fly. These basic metaphors, coupled with the creativity of making the actual spider web, provide effective ways of teaching ACT's complex concepts to young children. Figure 21.3 also displays an example of incorporating the hexaflex components of ACT at a very young age. This image displays a "personalized hexaflex" for a young male student that illustrates what ACT means to him. This session required him to draw himself engaging in the various components of the hexaflex; once completed, he was instructed to keep this personalized hexaflex at his desk throughout the school year. As Figure 21.3 shows, this child appears to practice defusion by "walking away" from various distracting stimuli, being in the present moment by focusing on school work when at school and not thinking about computers, depicting his values by a series of flags at a finish line, realizing that if he does nonpreferred work by staying committed to action he will get tasty treats like doughnuts, and conceptualizing his real self as a person who takes responsibility and apologizes for wrongdoings. What is most impressive about this hand-drawn illustration is its complexity for an eight-year-old, as well as how ACT truly can be related down to the level of younger individuals.

While large-scale studies are still in need of validation for the ACT model in education, the initial results appear promising. In Dixon (2013), a series of outcomes were described regarding what appears to be the first ACT-school. In this report, Dixon mentions a variety of change measures that had been displayed by

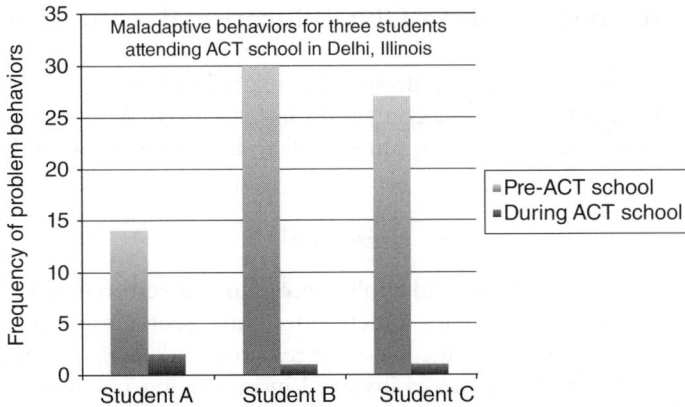

Figure 21.4 Frequency of challenging behavior across three students before and after entry into Journeys School in Delhi, Illinois. Data courtesy of Mary Pearson (Principal) and Mary Beth Paul (lead teacher).

the student body as a whole. They included an increase in attendance, improvements in grade point average, and greater psychological flexibility. To further explore how these outcomes trickle to the level of the individual student, Figure 21.4 displays data on three students who have attended the Journeys school during the past year. These data depict the frequency of challenging behaviors exhibited by the students before and after enrollment in the ACT-based program. While there are any number of additional factors which could be responsible for the drastic levels of behavioral changes, it does appear this pattern of promising results echoes for anyone who has entered this program. Student A engaged in 12 episodes of significant behavioral disruptions from bullying, physical fighting, harassment, and elopement from the classroom. Following transfer out of his home school district to Journeys, he has had two such incidents. Student B engaged in 30 such challenging behaviors with topographies ranging from skipping detention, property destruction, and noncompliance. One such incident has occurred since enrollment at the ACT school. Finally, Student C shows a similar pattern across the behaviors of verbal aggression, work refusal, and property destruction. In summary, this figure suggests that meaningful and lasting change can happen for our culture's most troubled youth when ACT becomes part of the day-to-day fabric of their education.

Additional replication sites have emerged using ACT as the therapeutic model for behaviorally and emotionally challenged students. Many such schools also embed contingencies for engaging in psychologically flexible behaviors throughout the school day. That is, in addition to students earning "good behavior points" or tokens, they also earn such reinforcers for engaging in pro-ACT behaviors such as accepting what happened, defusion from a problem situation, or engaging in values-driven activities. Furthermore, Dixon has been successful at getting ACT on student report cards as an actual course that must be completed in order to graduate. The goal is to continue to move ACT from a therapist-driven clinical intervention to a life-skill curriculum that can be implemented in a variety of educational contexts by any number of people.

Recommendations for a CBS Educational Reform Agenda

In the sections to come, we will address issues related to research and practice. Our aim is to provide (a) an overview of contributions CBS can make to school reform and (b) recommendations to the CBS community as to how to proceed in this enterprise.

Research

In any progressive science, basic and applied programs of research serve as legs up to each other. In psychological science, practitioners have problems in need of scientific support. To support the practice agenda, basic researchers develop functional accounts of necessary and sufficient processes involved in producing phenomena of interest, and applied investigators develop strategies for using the tools uncovered in the basic labs. Philosophical inquiry is also needed. Philosophical system building interprets the state of current knowledge and sets the agenda for future scientific enterprises.

We will address needed research in each of these three areas. To date, little empirical research on the use of ACT or psychological flexibility training has been published. As an organizing framework, we suggest four criteria for evaluating the evidence base as data from ACT trials emerge in the context of education. First, as in all behavioral research, operational definitions are tantamount to strong procedural integrity. Second, researchers are encouraged to build the evidence base using valid and reliable measures. Direct observation of dependent variables and manipulable independent variables are easily assessed for reliability and validity. Standardized test scores, office discipline referrals, suspensions, expulsions, emergency room visits, and other trend data are correlational, but can be collected in a time series to improve experimental control. Self-report instruments are more challenging to interpret, but can be of interest in some cases, such as when the students are clinicians in training. Third, experimental designs should be rigorous. It is possible and preferable when conducting RCTs to embed single case design elements. Additionally, investigators should consult with statisticians when designing larger studies to make certain their studies are sufficiently powered, results are interpretable, and analysis procedures are consistent with the assumptions of the test. Fourth, researchers should publish data that show strong experimental effects on socially significant targets of change. Data showing social validity, treatment and procedural integrity, functional assessment results, and long-term sustainability add to the overall strength of an investigation. Consistent with this framework, researchers in the CBS tradition are prepared to offer those interested in educational reform an evidence base that policy makers and funding sources can be confident about.

Philosophy

Functional contextualism and the public health perspective involve values (Biglan & Hinds, 2009). CBS places value upon prediction and influence of human well-being. Philosophical system building is needed to organize findings with respect to human well-being because of psychological flexibility. System building is also needed to generate agendas for future research with respect to the value of increasing and preserving human well-being.

The philosophical core of ACT and other approaches within ABA is Skinner's philosophy of radical behaviorism, which can be conceptualized as the functional wing of contextualist philosophies (Hayes, Hayes, & Reese, 1988; Pepper, 1942). In this tradition, actions situated in immediate and historical context are broken into functional segments for pragmatic purposes. A behavioral event is parsed into functional units as small as necessary to achieve scientific aims.

It is important to place our discussion of the research agenda for CBS in education inside *this* context. Given a particular set of aims with respect to educational reform, the behavioral event we set out to measure and change within a three-term contingency analysis of antecedent, behavior, and consequence may look different than it would were our aims different. In fact, the kinds of events that were once useful when behavior analysis focused on discrete actions of individual students may not meet the current set of needs on which a progressive, functional contextualistic philosophy of science shines a spotlight. Thus, philosophical system building provides the compass by which to set a course; basic and applied research methods supply the methodological rudder and keel by which to stay that course. From our perspective, such system building is ongoing and continuously in need of refinement.

It is useful to detail the kinds of situations for which this type of refinement could be beneficial. Discussing philosophy of science may seem out of place in a paper on practice in the schools. However, it is precisely because CBS is nested in functional contextualism that researchers and practitioners can articulate goals and measurement strategies that transcend traditional boundaries that define methodological behaviorism and other disciplines. Within the broader aim of pragmatic action, any behavioral goals, units of analysis, and analytic strategies can be employed – so long as they work to accomplish the goal. As an example, three very distinct goals: group action in a valued direction, reduction of office discipline referrals, and increased number of minutes attending to a lesson, could equally be of interest. These goals would each warrant unique analytic units and strategies. Although the philosophical core of functional contextualism is secure, we need to examine the nuances of success in working in the context of other disciplines with different ontological assumptions (Szabo & Tarbox, 2015). Thus, system building is an ongoing and continuous process.

Basic – RFT Basic Studies on ACT with Young Learners in Groups

Because any time given to teaching basic life skills takes time away from other subject instruction, basic research is needed to uncover the most efficient procedures by which to establish relational skills that correlate with the six psychological flexibility skills. For example, flexible perspective-taking repertoires that are shaped in many ACT exercises probably involve deictic relations for which teaching methods and tests appropriate for use with young children and learners with special needs have yet to be established. RFT researchers could help educators working with more advanced learners by focusing on the means by which to teach areas of logic that involve symbolic and deductive reasoning necessary for psychologically flexible responding. For example, relations of deduction involve mastery of IF–THEN contextual cues. A robust history of reinforcement with respect to logical and illogical arbitrary applications of these cues will speed the development of learning to take committed action with respect to valued outcomes. For example, "I value keeping my word, and

I promised I'd get this homework done by tomorrow. I am tired now. If I write for another hour tonight even though I feel tired, then I will submit the homework on time, which is in keeping with my value of being true to my word." This logic, which involves the derived transformation of stimulus functions in line with multiple stimulus relations, should be teachable to very young children using RFT-based strategies once these methods are fully developed.

Applied – Public Health Framework

Epidemiological. CBS researchers can identify key risk factors for rigid systems and practices that maintain the problems identified at the beginning of this paper. Applied CBS research is needed to fully explicate factors related to incidence, prevalence, and deleterious effects of psychological rigidity in children, teachers, and school systems. Research on factors related to prosocial behavior incidence and prevalence in school environments is equally necessary. Specifically, the prevalence of experiential avoidance and flexibility needs to be evaluated for their relationships to well-established psychological and behavioral problems. With evidence of this nature in hand, garnering support for implementing ACT in schools will be easier to obtain.

To this end, the development of a Web-based database for the CBS community working in schools to collectively repository, index, and analyze epidemiological data will aid applied workers in determining priorities for future work. An example of this is the Schoolwide Information System (SWIS; Irvin et al., 2006). SWIS has been implemented in over 25,000 schools internationally. It was developed by researchers at the University of Oregon, where faculty have analyzed and used the data to guide schools in behavioral data-based decision-making for over a decade. CBS researchers could develop an information system of this nature to collect needed data on psychological flexibility and experiential avoidance.

Prevention. A second area of applied focus is prevention. We suggest eight areas for future prevention research attention. First, to avoid fiascos such as the dismissal of Project Follow Through results, investigators should evaluate the conditions under which negative practices will thrive in the face of research. At a minimum, given scant resources, this will spotlight those situations that are not likely to benefit from protracted CBS efforts in the current climate. Second, both coercive and prosocial educational policies must be catalogued and the conditions that foster each must be well understood. Third, evidence is needed regarding the protective factors that will reduce the risk of consequences selecting unworkable educational practices. For example, zero tolerance and institutionalized coercion can be prevented once we know the strategies and tactics that can buttress schools against their adoption. Fourth, impact assessments are needed before adoption of policies that will affect existing and proposed educational programs and practices. Fifth, meta-analysis techniques and other data analysis strategies should be employed to determine the necessary and sufficient attributes of large-scale psychological flexibility programs. Sixth, CBS is poised to develop a tiered structure of research starting with single case design studies for protocol development that are followed with efficacy, effectiveness, and dissemination trials. Seventh, sustained use of the psychological flexibility model in schools will require that all members of the educational community become "fellow travelers." To this end, CBS investigators can contribute by studying the psychological flexibility training needs of administrators, teachers, aides, parents, and students. Finally, also with respect to sustainability, research is needed into the most efficient practices that will bring down costs.

Outcomes. CBS researchers should be especially interested in evaluating outcomes when schools adopt psychological flexibility training. We suggest five criteria for CBS researchers conducting outcome research to consider. First, design strategies should meet the needs identified above. Useful designs in these areas could be single case design experiments, RCTs, and longitudinal studies. Time series designs are particularly helpful in between group studies, and both RCTs and longitudinal studies are best when single case design studies are embedded (cf., Coryn, Schroter, & Hanssen, 2009). Second, outcome research should test protocols with different well-described populations in different geographical regions to test for generality. Third, data accuracy, reliability, treatment integrity, and social validity should all be assessed and documented. Fourth, if the data bear out the predictions, effectiveness should be strongest with those in the highest risk categories. Fifth, to demonstrate generality, findings should replicate across investigative teams and geographic locations. Multisite projects and separate projects conducted by unrelated research teams will build confidence in the models under development.

Practice

As with research, CBS educators can contribute a wealth of knowledge and practical wisdom. To this end, we address the need for sound planning and preparation and we end with recommendations for successful implementation of ACT and other psychological flexibility programs within school environments. However, we wish to state at the outset of this section that we are beholden to first laying the groundwork in solid research. Until peer-reviewed studies are published explicitly revealing relationships between psychological flexibility, experiential avoidance, and school outcomes, the recommendations below place the cart before the horse. Given that we are aware of studies in preparation that have this aim, we tentatively submit the following suggestions regarding planning and preparation for implementation. Moreover, we offer the recommendations that follow in light of the fact that behavior-based prevention science requires strong partnerships between scientists, research institutions, and school districts (Kellam et al., 2014). In order to establish these partnerships and to assure successful implementation, the following suggestions are in order.

Planning and Preparation

Above, we detailed a number of important points regarding setup for successful implementation of an ACT psychological flexibility curriculum in school settings. To review, we suggest six steps. First, capacity building begins with buy-in from all levels within a school. Making certain that janitors are on board and not asked to perform tasks for which they are not compensated is as important as securing pay for implementers and letters of support from administrators within and beyond the school. Second, include student leaders, average students, at-risk students, students with known difficulties, teachers, administrators, and policy-makers in leadership, management, and planning teams. Engaging a representative cross-section of the groups that will be engaged increases the probability of buy-in and support from the ground up. Such a large and diverse group is likely to be challenging to unify, but we see no better way to plan than by inviting chaos into the process. By embracing resistance rather than ignoring or fighting it, the implementer models an ACT stance of being a "fellow traveler" who gets stuck too, but has found a way to get unstuck and wants to share this new way of behaving. ACT works when there is acceptance of difficulties; docile rule-following leads to poor outcomes and low sustainability. Third, take any opportunity that presents itself to help build new programs or schools with psychological flexibility before the bricks are laid. Once things get heated between stakeholders, you are playing catch up. Better to teach the flexible ACT stance before it is really needed. Fourth, target the risk and protective factors that have been identified by researchers. Strive from the very beginning to generate an ongoing, evidence-based practice. Along these lines, use what is known about relational framing to address known and anticipated flexibility barriers during the planning stages. Fifth, in preparing budget, base projections on research and assure that adequate funds are secure before launch. Build credibility and sustainability with senior administrators by submitting fair cost-benefit analyses.

Intervention Recommendations

Ten points are useful to track with respect to implementation. First, set clear goals with specific and measurable objectives. ACT remains rooted in behavior analysis, and the hallmark of applied behavior analysis is observable, measurable changes in performance. Second, as during planning and preparation, include all stakeholders from the support staff to district level administrators in implementation teams. This provides you with information that can be used in crafting protocol refinements as well as opportunities to disseminate data on milestones met and to celebrate these achievements. Third, train presenters to use behavioral momentum strategies (cf. Mace et al., 1988) and to be reinforcing of each other's efforts. Presenters who build momentum to following their leads and who reinforce all efforts will be liked and trusted. Fourth, train presenters to use the ACT model functionally. That is, presenters should be prepared to adhere to the model but apply function-based treatment extensions and novel ACT metaphors or exercises to meet the needs of specific learners. Rote memorization of metaphors and lock-step facilitation of exercises may work, but is not likely to foster the kinds of trans-formation of stimulus function that ACT hinges on for successful implementation. Fifth, train presenters to be alert to diverse cultural perspectives within each group. Cultural sensitivity is likely to foster interest and goodwill from leaders among the learners. Sixth, train presenters to use a coaching model as opposed to a therapy model. This is especially important when implementers are clinical therapists whose training is not in teaching. ACT in the schools is best conceptualized as a life-skills curriculum, not a therapy modality. Seventh, even as a life-skills training, psychological flexibility work can bring up issues that are not appropriate to deal with in a classroom setting. Be prepared to refer and assist participants in obtaining outside assistance if they need it. It is always useful to have two trainers present, so that if things do come up, the second trainer can deal with the issues directly without stopping the group. Eighth, manualizing protocols is useful to assure sustainability. Train-the-trainer models enhance the probability of program durability. Ninth, flexibly scale the intervention to groups of differing size and need. A school that starts ACT in one classroom and later implements the same program in other regions in the school, will find a one-size-fits-all protocol will not suffice. Conduct functional assessments in each locale that the intervention will be implemented. Program components that are selected by the environment from a manual rather than selected by the manual itself are function-based and inherently more useful. Further, it is wise to incorporate other ABA contingency management strategies when these are found to aid learners. Above we detail the Jigsaw technique and the GBG as two such strategies that, within functional contexts, can be useful. Tenth, collect data. Four types of data are beneficial: data on participant outcomes, social validity, fidelity of implementation, and data reliability.

Discussion

During the last 50 years, applied behavior analysis laid foundations for systemic reform in education, and yet the needed changes have not resulted from ABA research and practice demonstrations. CBS began as a wing of behavior analysis concerned with alleviating human suffering. Psychotherapy applications such as ACT have been useful to that end, but may not suffice unless we also address toxic environmental variables that emerge in contexts such as schools, hospitals, places of worship, neighborhoods, and government agencies. In educational environments, the consequences that select unproductive practices are available for research and intervention with such methods as clinical RFT and ACT. As a life-skills curriculum, ACT is of great utility because it can be scaled to the needs of diverse groups within and between school environments.

The intractability of problems such as – but by no means limited to – school violence, substance use, and bullying suggests that a different framework for intervention is needed. We propose a public health framework for assessing and addressing school reform. CBS is poised to provide leadership in this area. Epidemiological, prevention, and outcomes research can build upon the foundations of philosophical system building, basic, and applied science to lead practice initiatives.

One goal of such efforts is to clear a path for large-scale implementations that require policy directives at the highest levels. At issue is the fact that schools are designed to bring about effective changes in the behavior of large groups of people. Behavior analysis has traditionally focused on the needs of individual learners, and we suggest this strategy continues to be of merit. However, it may be *because* of its focus on the needs of the few that behavior analysis has not ignited the changes that basic and applied science suggest will lead to successful outcomes. Hence, a focus on the needs of the many could be of benefit to all. CBS is suited to leading this effort.

At the level of the individual learner, scientific understanding of the verbal relations that participate as contextual variables influencing problem behavior has gained increasing empirical support. We are now at a stage in the development of behavior science where explaining complex behavior in applied contexts is empirically possible. We are now poised to identify the *why* behind *what happened* with a given learner in a given context and to offer that learner a new way of interacting with these variables. CBS is at the ready to lead this enterprise.

References

Akpochafo, G. O. (2014). Teachers' perception of prevalence and forms of violence in early childhood classes in Delta State of Nigeria. *Journal of Educational and Social Research, 4,* 469–474.

Alebiosu, K. A. (2001). Cooperative learning and students' affective learning outcome in Nigerian chemistry classrooms. *IFE Psychologia: An International Journal, 9,* 135–142.

Allport, G. A. (1954). *The nature of prejudice.* New York, NY: Addison-Wesley.

Anderson, C. M., & Kincaid, D. (2005). Applying behavior analysis to school violence and discipline problems: Schoolwide positive behavior support. *The Behavior Analyst, 28,* 49–63.

Aronson, E., Blaney, N., Stephan, C., Sikes, J., & Snapp, M. (1978). *The jigsaw classroom.* Beverly Hills, CA: Sage.

Aronson, E., & Bridgeman, D. (1979). Jigsaw groups and the desegregated classroom: In pursuit of common goals. *Personality and Social Psychology Bulletin, 5,* 438–446.

Aronson, E., Bridgeman, D. L., & Geffner, R. (1978). Interdependent interactions and prosocial behavior. *Journal of Research and Development in Education, 12,* 16–27.

Barrish, H. H., Saunders, M., & Wolf, M. M. (1969). Good Behavior Game: Effects of individual contingencies for group consequences on disruptive behavior in a classroom. *Journal of Applied Behavior Analysis, 2,* 119–124.

Biglan, A., Hayes, S. C., & Pistorello, J. (2008). Acceptance and commitment: Implications for prevention science. *Prevention Science, 9,* 139–152.

Biglan, A., & Hinds, E. (2009). Evolving prosocial and sustainable neighborhoods and communities. *Annual Review of Clinical Psychology, 5,* 169–196.

Biglan, A., Layton, G. l., Backen Jones, L., Hankins, M., & Rusby, J. C. (2011). The value of workshops on psychological flexibility for early childhood special education staff. *Topics in Early Childhood Special Education, 20,* 1–16.

Bizzis, J., & Bradley-Johnson, S. (1981). Increasing the school attendance of a truant adolescent. *Education and Treatment of Children, 4,* 149–155.

Block, J. A., & Wulfert, E. (2000). Acceptance or change: Treating socially anxious college students with ACT or CBGT. *The Behavior Analyst Today, 1,* 1–55.

Block, J., Block, J. H., & Keyes, S. (1988). Longitudinally foretelling drug usage in adolescence: Early childhood personality and environmental precursors. *Child Development, 59,* 336–355.

Bradshaw, C. P., Mitchell, M. M., & Leaf, P. J. (2010). Examining the effects of schoolwide positive behavioral interventions and supports on student outcomes. *Journal of Positive Behavioral Interventions, 12,* 133–148.

Brown, R. J. (1995). *Prejudice: Its social psychology.* Oxford, England: Blackwell.

Bucklin, B., Alvero, A., Dickinson, A., Austin, J., & Jackson, A. (2000). Industrial-organizational psychology and organizational behavior management: An objective comparison. *Journal of Organizational Behavior Management, 20,* 27–75.

Chang, C. K. (2004). Constructing a streaming video-based learning forum for collaborative learning. *Journal of Educational Multimedia and Hypermedia, 13,* 245–263.

Cohen, M., Koehler, V., Datta, L., & Timpane, M. (1980). *Instructionally effective schools: Research area plan.* Washington, DC: National Institute of Education.

Collard, P., Avny, N., & Boniwell, I. (2008). Teaching mindfulness based cognitive therapy (MBCT) to students: The effects on the levels of mindfulness and subjective well-being. *Counseling Psychology Quarterly, 21,* 323–336.

Coryn, C. L., Schroter, D. C., & Hanssen, C. E. (2009). Adding a time-series design element to the success case method to improve methodological rigor. *American Journal of Education, 30,* 80–92.

Couser, G. (2008). Challenges and opportunities for preventing depression in the workplace: A review of the evidence supporting workplace factors and interventions. *Journal of Occupational and Environmental Medicine, 50,* 411–427.

Cushway, D. (1992). Stress in clinical psychology trainees. *British Journal of Clinical Psychology, 31*, 169–179.

Darveaux, D. X. (1984). The Good Behavior Game plus merit: Controlling disruptive behavior and improving student motivation. *School Psychology Review, 13*, 510–514.

Dixon, M. R. (2013). Don't stop believing: Journeys school. *Behavior Analysis in Practice, 6*, 23–24.

Dixon, M. R. (2014). *ACT for children with autism and emotional challenges.* Carbondale, IL: Shawnee Scientific Press.

Djordjevic, A., & Frögéli, E. (2012). *Mind the gap: Acceptance and commitment therapy (ACT) for preventing stress-related ill-health among future nurses. A randomized controlled trial (graduate thesis).* Stockholm, Sweden: Institute for Clinical Neuroscience, Karolinska Institute.

Engelmann, S. (2007). *Teaching needy kids in our backward system.* Eugene, OR: ADI Press.

Engelmann, S., & Carnine, D. (1982). *Theory of instruction.* New York, NY: McGraw Hill.

Filler, J., Hecimovic, A., & Blue, S. (1978). An analysis of the effectiveness of a preservice workshop for educators of severely handicapped young students. *American Association for the Education of the Severely/Profoundly Handicapped Review, 3*, 173–177.

Fleming, R., & Sulzer-Azaroff, B. (1992). Reciprocal peer management: Improving staff instruction in a vocational training program. *Journal of Applied Behavior Analysis, 25*, 611–620.

Friday, J. C. (1996). Weapon-carrying in school. In A. M. Hoffman (Ed.), *Schools, violence, and society.* Westport, CO: Praeger.

Gage, M. A., Fredricks, H. D. B., Johnson-Dorn, N., & Lindley-Southard, B. (1982). Inservice training for staff of group homes and work activity centers serving developmentally disabled adults. *The Journal of the Association for Persons with Severe Handicaps, 7*, 60–70.

Galizio, M. (1979). Contingency-shaped and rule-governed behavior: Instructional control of human loss avoidance. *Journal of the Experimental Analysis of Behavior, 31*, 53–70.

Gersten, R., Becker, W. C., Heiry, T. J., & White, W. A. T. (1984). Entry IQ and yearly academic growth of children in direct instruction programs: A longitudinal study of low socio-economic children. *Educational Evaluation and Policy Analysis, 6*, 109–121.

Gillat, A., & Sulzer-Azaroff, B. (1994). Promoting principals' managerial involvement in instructional improvement. *Journal of Applied Behavior Analysis, 27*, 115–129.

Grandy, G. S., Madsen, C. H., & de Mersseman, L. M. (1973). The effects of individual and interdependent contingencies on inappropriate classroom behavior. *Psychology in the Schools, 10*, 488–493.

Green, C. W., & Reid, D. H. (1994). A comprehensive evaluation of a train-the-trainers model for training education staff to assemble adaptive switches. *Journal of Developmental and Physical Disabilities, 6*, 219–238.

Haring, T. G., Neetz, J. A., Lovinger, L., Peck, C., & Semmel, M. I. (1987). Effects of four modified incidental teaching procedures to create opportunities for communication. *The Journal of the Association for Persons with Severe Handicaps, 12*, 218–226.

Harris, V. W., & Sherman, J. A. (1973). Use and analysis of the "Good Behavior Game" to reduce disruptive classroom behavior. *Journal of Applied Behavior Analysis, 6*, 405–417.

Hayes, S. C. (2004). Acceptance and commitment therapy, relational frame theory, and the third wave of behavior therapy. *Behavior Therapy, 35*, 639–665.

Hayes, S.C., Barnes-Holmes, D., & Roche, B. (2001). *Relational frame theory: A post-Skinnerian account of human language and cognition.* New York, NY: Kluwer /Plenum.

Hayes, S. C., Hayes, L. J., & Reese, H. W. (1988). Finding the philosophical core: A review of Stephen C. Pepper's *World hypotheses: A study in evidence. Journal of the Experimental Analysis of Behavior, 50*, 97–111.

Hayes, S. C., Luoma, J. B., Bond, F. W., Masuda, A., & Lillis, J. (2006). Acceptance and commitment therapy: Model, processes, and outcomes. *Behavior Research and Therapy, 44*, 1–25.

Hayes, S. C., Strosahl, K. D., & Wilson, K. G. (1999). *Acceptance and commitment therapy: The process and practice of mindful change*. New York, NY: Guilford.

Hayes, S. C., Strosahl, K. D., & Wilson, K. G. (2012). *Acceptance and commitment therapy: The process and practice of mindful change*. New York, NY: Guilford.

Hayes, S. C., Villatte, M., Levin, M., & Hildebrandt, M. (2011). Open, aware, and active: Contextual approaches as an emerging trend in the behavioral and cognitive therapies. *Annual Review of Clinical Psychology, 7*, 141–168.

Hill, S. C., & Drolet, J. C. (1999). School-related violence among high school students in the United States, 1993–1995. *Journal of School Health, 69*, 264–272.

Hope, D. A., & Heimberg, R. G. (1993). Social phobia and social anxiety. In D. H. Barlow (Ed.), *Clinical handbook of psychological disorders* (2nd ed.). New York, NY: Guilford.

Huang, T. C., Huang, Y. M., & Yu, F. Y. (2011). Cooperative weblog learning in higher education: Its facilitating effects on social interaction, time lag, and cognitive load. *Educational Technology and Society, 14*, 95–106.

Ingham, P., & Greer, R. D. (1992). Changes in student and teacher responses in observed and generalized settings as a function of supervisor observations. *Journal of Applied Behavior Analysis, 25*, 153–164.

Irvin, L. K., Horner, R. H., Ingram, K., Todd, A. W., Sugai, G., Sampson, N. K., & Boland, J. B. (2006). Using office discipline referral data for decision making about student behavior in elementary and middle schools: An empirical evaluation of validity. *Journal of Positive Behavior Interventions, 8*, 10–23.

Jackson, D. A., & Wallace, R. F. (1974). The modification and generalization of voice loudness in a fifteen-year-old retarded girl. *Journal of Applied Behavior Analysis, 7*, 461–471.

Jeffcoat, T., & Hayes, S. C. (2012). A randomized trial of ACT bibliotherapy on the mental health of K-12 teachers and staff. *Behavior Research and Therapy, 50*, 571–579.

Johnson, M. R., Turner, P. F., & Konarski, E. A. (1978). The Good Behavior Game: A systematic replication in two unruly transitional classrooms. *Education and Treatment of Children, 1*, 25–33.

Johnston, J. M., & Pennypacker, H. S. (2009). *Strategies and tactics of behavioral research* (3rd ed.). New York, NY: Routledge.

Kellam, S. G., & Anthony, J. C. (1998). Targeting early antecedents to prevent tobacco smoking: Findings from an epidemiologically based randomized field trial. *American Journal of Public Health, 88*, 1490–1495.

Kellam, S. G., Wang, W., Mackenzie, A. C. L., Hendricks Brown, C., Ompad, D. C., Or, F., … Windham, A. (2014). The impact of the Good Behavior Game, a universal classroom-based preventative intervention in first and second grades, on high-risk sexual behaviors and drug abuse and dependence disorders into young adulthood. *Prevention Science, 15*, S6–S18.

Kennedy, A. E., Whiting, S. W., & Dixon, M. R. (2014). Improving novel food choices in preschool children using acceptance and commitment therapy. *Journal of Contextual Behavioral Science, 3*, 228–235.

Kern, L., Childs, K. E., Dunlap, G., Clarke, S., & Falk, G. D. (1994). Using assessment-based curricular intervention to improve the classroom behavior of a student with emotional and behavioral challenges. *Journal of Applied Behavior Analysis, 27*, 7–19.

Kirby, F. D., & Shields, F. (1972). Modification of arithmetic response rate and attending behavior in seventh-grade student. *Journal of Applied Behavior Analysis, 5*, 79–84.

Kleinman, K. E., & Saigh, P. A. (2011). The effects of the Good Behavior Game on the conduct of regular education New York City high school students. *Behavior Modification, 35*, 95–105.

Kohlenberg, B. S., Hayes, S. C., & Hayes, L. J. (1991). The transfer of contextual control over equivalence classes through equivalence classes: A possible model of social stereotyping. *Journal of the Experimental Analysis of Behavior, 56*, 505–518.

Kshirsagar, V. Y., Agarwal, R., & Bavdekar, S. B. (2007). Bullying in schools: Prevalence and short-term impact. *Indian Pediatrics, 44,* 25–28.

Langone, J., Koorland, M., & Oseroff, A. (1987). Producing changes in the instructional behavior of teachers of the mentally handicapped through inservice education. *Education and Treatment of Children, 10,* 146–164.

Lannie, A. L., & McCurdy, B. L. (2007). Preventing disruptive behavior in the urban classroom: Effects of the Good Behavior Game on student and teacher behavior. *Education and Treatment of Children, 30,* 85–98.

Leflot, G., van Lier, P. A. C., Onghena, P., & Colpin, H. (2013). The role of children's on-task behavior in the prevention of aggressive behavior development and peer rejection: A randomized controlled study of the Good Behavior Game in Belgian elementary classrooms. *Journal of School Psychology, 51,* 187–199.

Lillis, J., & Hayes, S. C. (2007). Applying acceptance, mindfulness, and values to the reduction of prejudice: A pilot study. *Behavior Modification, 31,* 389–411.

Lindsley, O. R. (1972). From Skinner to precision teaching. In J. B. Jordan & L. S. Robbins (Eds.), *Let's try doing something else kind of thing* (pp. 1–12). Arlington, VA: Council on Exceptional Children.

Lindsley, O. R. (1990). Precision teaching: By children for teachers. *Teaching Exceptional Children, 22,* 10–15.

Lindsley, O. R. (1992). Why aren't effective teaching tools widely adopted? *Journal of Applied Behavior Analysis, 21,* 21–26.

Linehan, M. M. (1993). *Cognitive behavioral therapy of borderline personality disorder.* New York, NY: Guilford.

Livheim, F., Hayes, L., Ghaderi, A., Magnusdottir, T., Högfeldt, A., Rowse, J., ... Tengström, A. (2014). The effectiveness of acceptance and commitment therapy for adolescent mental health: Swedish and Australian pilot outcomes. *Journal of Child and Family Studies, 24,* 1016–1030.

Luciano, C., Ruiz, F., Vizcaíno Torres, R. M., Sanchez Martin, V., Gutiérrez Martínez, O., & López López, J. C. (2011). A relational frame analysis of defusion interactions in acceptance and commitment therapy: A preliminary and quasi-experimental study with at-risk adolescents. *International Journal of Psychology and Psychological Therapy, 4,* 165–182.

Luciano, M. C., Valdivia, S., Gutiérrez, O., Ruiz, F. J., & Páez, M. (2009). Brief acceptance-based protocols applied to the work with adolescents. *International Journal of Psychology and Psychological Therapy, 9,* 237–257.

Mace, F. C., Hock, M. L., Lalli, J. S., West, B. J., Belfiore, P., Rinter, E., & Brown, D. K. (1988). Behavioral momentum in the treatment of noncompliance. *Journal of Applied Behavior Analysis, 2,* 123–141.

Madden-Szeszko, G. (2000). Variables contributing to teacher efficacy: An examination of burnout, affect, demographic variables, and general self-efficacy. *Dissertation Abstracts International Section A, 61,* 881.

Magojo, T. S., & Collings, S. J. (2003). Prevalence and attitudinal predictors of child sexual offending in a non-forensic sample of South African high school males. *Journal of Child and Adolescent Mental Health, 15,* 27–32.

Maslach, C., Schaufeli, W. B., & Leiter, M. P. (2001). Job burnout. *Annual Review of Psychology, 52,* 397–422.

Matthews, B. A., Shimoff, E., Catania, A. C., & Sagvolden, T. (1977). Uninstructed human responding: Sensitivity to ratio and interval contingencies. *Journal of the Experimental Analysis of Behavior, 27,* 453–467.

Medland, M. B., & Stachnik, T. J. (1972). Good Behavior Game: A replication and systematic analysis. *Journal of Applied Behavior Analysis, 5,* 45–51.

Meyer, L. A. (1984). Long-term academic effects of the direct instruction Project Follow Through. *The Elementary School Journal, 84,* 380–394.

Meyer, L. A., Gersten, R. M., & Gutkin, J. (1983). Direct Instruction: A Project Follow Through success story in an inner-city school. *The Elementary School Journal, 84,* 241–252.

Minkin, N., Braukmann, C. J., Minkin, B. L., Timbers, G. D., Timbers, B. J., Fixsen, D. L., ... Wolf, M. M. (1976). The social validation and training of conversational skills. *Journal of Applied Behavior Analysis, 9,* 127–139.

Moliter, J., Watkin, N., Napior, D., & Proper, E. C. (1977). *Education as experimentation: The non-follow through study.* Cambridge, MA: Abt.

Monitoring the Future. (2007). Trends in lifetime prevalence of use of various drugs for eighth, tenth, and twelfth graders. Retrieved from http://www.monitoringthefuture.org/data/07data.html

Moran, D. J. (2015). Acceptance and commitment training in the workplace. *Current Opinion in Psychology, 2,* 26–31.

Morrell, R. (2002). A calm after the storm? Beyond schooling as violence. *Educational Review, 54,* 37–46.

Moskowitz, J. M., Malvin, J. H., Schaeffer, G. A., & Schaps, E. (1983). Evaluation of a cooperative learning strategy. *American Educational Research Journal, 20,* 687–696.

Muto, T., Hayes, S. C., & Jeffcoat, T. (2011). The effectiveness of acceptance and commitment therapy bibliotherapy for enhancing the psychological health of Japanese college students living abroad. *Behavior Therapy, 42,* 323–335.

Nansel, T. R., Overpeck, N., Pilla, R. S., Ruan, W. J., Simons-Morton, B., & Scheidt, P. (2001). Bullying behaviors among US youth: Prevalence and association with psychosocial adjustment. *Journal of the American Medical Association, 285,* 2094–2100.

Newsome, K. B., Berens, K. N., Ghezzi, P. M., Aninao, T., & Newsome, W. D. (2014). Training relational language to improve reading comprehension. *European Journal of Behavior Analysis, 15,* 165–197.

Nolan, J. D., Houlihan, D., Wanzek, M., & Jensen, W. R. (2014). The Good Behavior Game: A classroom-behavior intervention across cultures. *School Psychology International, 35,* 191–205.

Northrup, J., Wacker, D. P., Berg, W. K., Kelly, L., Sasso, G., & DeRaad, A. (1994). The treatment of severe behavior problems in school settings using a technical assistance model. *Journal of Applied Behavior Analysis, 27,* 33–47.

Olszewski, D., Matias, J., Monshouwer, K., & Kokkevi, A. (2010). Polydrug use among 15-to 16-year olds: Similarities and differences in Europe. *Drugs: Education, Prevention and Policy, 17,* 287–302.

Olweus, D. (1994). Bullying at school: Basic facts and effects of a school based intervention program. *Journal of Child Psychology and Psychiatry, 35,* 1171–1190.

Pakenham, K. I., & Stafford-Brown, J. (2013). Postgraduate clinical psychology students' perceptions of an ACT stress management intervention and clinical training. *Clinical Psychologist, 17,* 56–66.

Patrick, C. A., Ward, P., & Crouch, D. W. (1998). Effects of holding students accountable for social behaviors during volleyball games in elementary physical education. *Journal of Teaching in Physical Education, 17,* 143–156.

Peltzer, K. (2009). Prevalence and correlates of substance use among school children in six African countries. *International Journal of Psychology, 44,* 378–386.

Pepper, S. C. (1942). *World hypotheses: A study in evidence.* Berkeley, CA: University of California Press.

Pierce, W. D., & Cheney, C. D. (2013). *Behavior analysis and learning* (5th ed.). New York, NY: Psychology Press.

Pistorello, J., Fruzzetti, A. E., MacLane, C., Gallop, R., & Iverson, K. M. (2012). Dialectical behavior therapy (DBT) applied to college students: A randomized clinical trial. *Journal of Consulting Clinical Psychology, 6,* 982–994.

Poduska, J. M., & Kurki, A. (2014). Guided by theory, informed by practice: Training and support for the Good Behavior Game, a classroom-based behavior management strategy. *Journal of Emotional and Behavioral Disorders, 22*, 83–94.

Pranjić, N., & Bajraktarević, A. (2010). Depression and suicide ideation among secondary school adolescents involved in school bullying. *Primary Health Care Research & Development, 11*, 349–362.

Reid, D. H., Parsons, M. B., McCarn, J. E., Green, C. W., Phillips, J. F., & Schepps, M. M. (1985). Providing a more appropriate education for severely handicapped persons: Increasing and validating functional classroom tasks. *Journal of Applied Behavior Analysis, 18*, 289–301.

Repp, A. C., & Karsh, K. G. (1994). Hypothesis-based interventions for tantrum behaviors of persons with developmental disabilities in school settings. *Journal of Applied Behavior Analysis, 27*, 21–31.

Robins, L. N. (1978). Sturdy childhood predictors of adult antisocial behavior: Replications from longitudinal studies. *Psychological Medicine, 8*, 611–622.

Saigh, P. A., & Umar, A. M. (1983). The effects of a Good Behavior Game on the disruptive behavior of Sudanese elementary school students. *Journal of Applied Behavior Analysis, 16*, 39–344.

Saunders, P. A., Tractenberg, R. E., Chaterji, R., Amri, H., Harazduk, N., Gordon, J. S., ... Haramati, A. (2007). Promoting self-awareness and reflection through an experiential mind-body skills course for first year medical students. *Medical Teacher, 29*, 778–784.

Schuster, B. (1999). Outsiders at school: The prevalence of bullying and its relation with social status. *Group Processes & Intergroup Relations, 2*, 175–190.

Schwartz-Mette, R. A. (2009). Challenges in addressing graduate student impairment in academic professional psychology programs. *Ethics and Behavior, 19*, 91–102.

Segal, Z. V., Williams, J. M. G., & Teasdale, J. D. (2002). *Mindfulness-based cognitive therapy for depression: A new approach to preventing relapse*. New York, NY: Guilford.

Selinske, J. E., Greer, R. D., & Lodhi, S. (1991). A functional analysis of the comprehensive application of behavior analysis to schooling. *Journal of Applied Behavior Analysis, 24*, 107–117.

Sidman, M. & Tailby, W. (1982). Conditional discrimination vs. matching-to-sample: An expansion of the testing paradigm. *Journal of the Experimental Analysis of Behavior, 37*, 5–22.

Shimoff, E., Catania, A. C., & Matthews, B. A. (1981). Uninstructed human responding: Sensitivity to low-rate performance to schedule contingencies. *Journal of the Experimental Analysis of Behavior, 36*, 207–220.

Spano, R., Rivera, C., & Bolland, J. M. (2010). Are chronic exposure to violence and chronic violent behavior closely related developmental processes during adolescence? *Criminal Justice and Behavior, 37*, 1160–1179.

Spriggs, A. L., Iannotti, R. J., Nansel, T. R., & Haynie, D. L. (2007). Adolescent bullying involvement and perceived family, peer and school relations: Commonalities and differences across race/ethnicity. *Journal of Adolescent Health, 41*, 283–293.

Stafford-Brown, J., & Pakenham, K. I. (2012). The effectiveness of an ACT informed intervention for managing stress and improving therapist qualities in clinical psychology trainees. *Journal of Clinical Psychology, 68*, 592–613.

Stebbins, L. B., St. Pierre, R. G., Proper, E. G. C., Anderson, R. B., & Cerva, T. R. (1977). *Education as experimentation: A planned variation model. An evaluation of follow through*. Cambridge, MA: Abt.

Steele, D. & Hayes, S.C. (1991). Stimulus equivalence and arbitrarily applicable relational responding. *Journal of the Experimental Analysis of Behavior, 56*, 519–555.

Stephan, W. (1985). Intergroup relations. In G. Lindzey and E. Aronson (Eds.), *Handbook of Social Psychology* (3rd ed., Vol. 2, pp. 599–658). New York, NY: Random House.

Swiezy, N. B., Matson, J. L., & Box, P. (1992). The Good Behavior Game: A token reinforcement system for preschoolers. *Child and Family Behavior Therapy, 14,* 21–32.

Szabo, T. G., Long, D. M., Villatte, M., & Hayes, S. C. (2014). Mindfulness in contextual cognitive-behavioral models. In K. W. Brown, J. D. Creswell, & R. M. Ryan (Eds.), *Handbook of mindfulness: Theory and research* (pp. 130–147). New York, NY: Guilford.

Szabo, T. G., & Tarbox, J. (2015). Beyond what "is" and what "is not." *Journal of Contextual Behavioral Science.* Retrieved from http://dx.doi.org/10.1016/j.jcbs.2015.05.005

Tremblay, R. E., Masse, B., Perron, D., LeBlanc, M., Schwartzman, A. E., & Ledingham, J. E. (1992). Early disruptive behavior, poor school achievement, delinquent behavior, and delinquent personality: Longitudinal analyses. *Journal of Consulting Clinical Psychology, 60,* 64–72.

United States Department of Education School Survey on Crime and Safety (2014). Retrieved from http://nces.ed.gov/surveys/ssocs/index.asp?FType=4

Vaughn, M. G., Fu, Q., Bender, K., DeLisi, M., Beaver, K. M., Perron, B. E., & Howard, M. O. (2010). Psychiatric correlates of bullying in the United States: Findings from a national sample. *Psychiatric Quarterly, 81,* 183–195.

Walker, H. M., Horner, R. H., Sugai, G., Bullis, M., Sprague, J. R., Bricker, D., … Kaufman, M. J. (1996). Integrated approaches to preventing antisocial behavior patterns among school-age children and youth. *Journal of Emotional and Behavioral Disorders, 4,* 194–209.

Walker, I., & Crogan, M. (1998). Academic performance, prejudice, and the jigsaw classroom: New pieces to the puzzle. *Journal of Community & Applied Social Psychology, 8,* 381-393.

Wang, J., Iannotti, R. J., & Nansel, T. R. (2009). School bullying among adolescents in the United States: Physical, verbal, relational, and cyber. *Journal of Adolescent Health, 45,* 368–375.

Watkins, C. L. (1988). Project Follow Through: A story of the identification and neglect of effective instruction. *Youth Policy, 10,* 7–12.

Wilson, A. N., & Dixon, M. R. (2010). A mindfulness approach to improving classroom attention. *Journal of Behavioral Health and Medicine, 1,* 137–142.

22

Psychological Flexibility and ACT at Work

Frank W. Bond, Joda Lloyd, Paul E. Flaxman, and Rob Archer

Acceptance and commitment therapy (ACT; Hayes, 1987; Hayes, Strosahl, & Wilson, 1999) is a contextual cognitive behavior therapy (CBT) that aims to improve people's mental health and behavioral effectiveness by increasing their levels of psychological flexibility. This process is the proposed mechanism of change within the ACT model and is cultivated through enhancing acceptance and mindfulness processes, in combination with commitment and behavior change processes (Hayes, Villatte, Levin, & Hildebrandt, 2011). While ACT has been shown to be an effective treatment for a number of psychological and behavioral difficulties, research has indicated that it can also promote meaningful change in nonclinical populations (Hayes, Luoma, Bond, Masuda, & Lillis, 2006). Likewise, while psychological flexibility has been found to be a primary individual determinant of these psychological and behavioral difficulties, research has indicated that it also predicts, and correlates with, a range of behaviors in nonclinical contexts (Hayes et al., 2006).

In the present chapter we focus on the application of ACT and psychological flexibility to one particular nonclinical context: the workplace. In the sections that follow we will first outline why ACT and psychological flexibility are relevant to the workplace and discuss the research evidence relating to their beneficial impacts. After this, we will summarize our most recent, evidence-based protocol for ACT at work, in order to demonstrate how we cultivate psychological flexibility in order to promote employee health and performance. Finally, we will examine how ACT and psychological flexibility, while useful for understanding and influencing outcomes at the individual employee level, may also inform the design and development of effective and healthy organizational systems.

ACT and Psychological Flexibility in the Workplace

ACT's applicability to the workplace can be traced back to its transdiagnostic approach to human difficulty. Rather than classifying problematic behaviors according to the standard clinical taxonomies (e.g., syndromes described in the Diagnostic and Statistical Manual of Mental Disorders; DSM), ACT maintains that all problematic behavior (from

The Wiley Handbook of Contextual Behavioral Science, First Edition. Edited by Robert D. Zettle, Steven C. Hayes, Dermot Barnes-Holmes, and Anthony Biglan.
© 2016 John Wiley & Sons, Ltd. Published 2016 by John Wiley & Sons, Ltd.

psychopathology to poor work performance) can largely be explained by the impact of people's difficult or challenging internal experiences on their ability to contact the present moment and pursue their personally chosen values and goals, that is, psychological inflexibility (Hayes et al., 1999). In attempting to enhance psychological flexibility, ACT positions itself as a broadly focused CBT that can be applied to any life context, including the workplace. To further appreciate ACT's applicability to the workplace, it is necessary to examine the function of psychological flexibility in this context.

ACT promotes psychological flexibility by encouraging people to focus on the present moment and, depending upon the opportunities available to them, take action toward achieving their goals and values, even when experiencing difficult or unwanted psychological events (e.g., challenging thoughts, feelings, physiological sensations, images, and memories) (Hayes et al., 2006). In the workplace, the degree to which people can do this may have a profound effect on their well-being and success in this context. For example, when carrying out one's duties at work, certain situations may provoke difficult and/or unwanted psychological events. This could be feelings of worry arising from a conflict with a colleague, or self-doubt associated with a job change. If people focus excessively on, attempt to avoid, overanalyze, or otherwise interact unhelpfully with these feelings, they may begin to feel overwhelmed and distracted. In turn, this may make it difficult for them to stay focused on the present moment and notice, or respond effectively to, goal-related opportunities in their work environments. Eventually, this may lead to a reduced capacity to take action toward their broader goals and values, culminating in diminished performance and reduced mental health.

On the other hand, if people can let go of their unhelpful efforts to control their difficult or unwanted psychological events, they may be better able to focus on the present moment, and notice and respond effectively to goal-related opportunities. Relinquishing these unhelpful efforts involves observing one's thoughts and feelings on a moment-to-moment basis and from a noncontrolling, nonelaborative, and non-judgmental perspective: this way of thinking is commonly described as mindful (Brown & Ryan, 2003; Kabat-Zinn, 1990; Linehan, 1993; Marlatt & Kristeller, 1999). By adopting a mindful perspective, people are less needlessly focused on avoiding, suppressing, or otherwise controlling unwanted or difficult internal experiences, which, in itself, facilitates better mental health (Baer, 2003; Hayes et al., 2006). In addition, when people are not expending their cognitive resources on trying to control and regulate their internal events, they have more resources with which to notice and respond effectively to goal-relevant opportunities in their environments (Bond & Bunce, 2003). Over time, such effective responses will produce flexible behavioral repertoires characteristic of enhanced performance and better mental health. This "goal-related context sensitivity" feature of psychological flexibility can produce better levels of performance, job satisfaction, engagement, mental health, and absence rates (Bond & Hayes, 2002; Bond, Lloyd, & Guenole, 2013).

Research on ACT at Work

Over the last 13 years, there has been an array of published studies that has examined the impact of ACT interventions in the workplace. This research has not only sought to demonstrate the efficacy of ACT in this context, but to broach a number of important research questions relating to its impact, for example, what is the psychological mechanism by which ACT produces its positive benefits?

In the very first study of ACT at work, Bond and Bunce (2000) compared the differential impact of ACT and a problem-focused worksite training intervention. Results indicated that, while both interventions improved employee dysphoria and their propensity to innovate, only ACT led to improvements in general mental health. An interesting feature of this study was that it demonstrated unique mechanisms of change for each intervention. Consistent with ACT theory, increases in psychological flexibility mediated all of the improvements in the ACT condition, while increases in innovative modifications to work methods and processes mediated the improvements in the problem-focused intervention.

Since this pioneering study, Bond and colleagues have replicated and extended these findings in several interesting ways. Flaxman and Bond (2010a) also found that ACT improved employee general mental health and that increases in psychological flexibility mediated these changes. However, they also found that improvements in psychological flexibility mediated the changes in outcomes following a Stress Inoculation Training (SIT; a stress-management intervention based on Beckian CBT) intervention. These findings suggest that mental health intervention strategies unrelated to ACT may also produce their benefits through improving psychological flexibility. Flaxman and Bond (2010b) also found that ACT improved employee general mental health, and that its effects were more pronounced for participants who were more distressed at the start of the study. Finally, Lloyd, Bond, and Flaxman (2013) found that ACT, once again, improved general mental health, but it also improved emotional exhaustion and depersonalization, both aspects of emotional burnout. Consistent with both ACT and emotional burnout theories (Lloyd et al., 2013), findings also indicated that psychological flexibility first mediated improvements in emotional exhaustion, which, subsequently, prevented increases in depersonalization.

Another strand of research on ACT in the workplace has focused on its efficacy in relation to the problems experienced by specific groups of clinical professionals. This work shows that ACT is effective in: reducing burnout and stigmatizing attitudes in substance misuse counselors (Hayes, Bissett et al., 2004); decreasing sickness absence and use of medical treatment resources in public health sector workers (Dahl, Wilson, & Nilsson, 2004); improving general mental health among intellectual disability (ID) services support staff (Noone & Hastings, 2009; 2010); decreasing stress and emotional burnout, as well as improving general mental health, in social workers (Brinkborg, Michanek, Hesser, & Berglund, 2011); and improving professional self-doubt, general mental health, self-efficacy beliefs, and self-compassion in clinical psychology trainees (CPTs) (Stafford-Brown & Pakenham, 2012).

A further important line of work has been that which has looked at ACT's capacity to enhance clinical professionals' adoption of empirically validated treatments. Luoma and colleagues (2007) investigated substance misuse counselors and found that a continuing education workshop on group drug counseling (GDC) in combination with ACT led to higher levels of treatment adoption and personal accomplishment than the GDC workshop alone. In another study Varra, Hayes, Roget, and Fisher (2008) also examined substance misuse counselors and found that a workshop on empirically supported treatments for substance abuse, in combination with ACT, led to significantly higher levels of referrals to pharmacotherapy than the treatments for substance abuse workshop in combination with an educational control workshop.

Finally, one study has examined ACT bibliotherapy in the workplace. Results indicated that participants exposed to an ACT self-help book showed significant improvements in psychological health, compared to those in a wait-list control condition (Jeffcoat & Hayes, 2012). In addition, for those who were not currently distressed, exposure to the ACT self-help book made them significantly less likely to become distressed over time.

Research on Psychological Flexibility in the Workplace

While psychological flexibility is often assessed as a mediator during ACT interventions, it is also possible to assess people's naturally occurring levels of the construct and treat it as a kind of individual characteristic or quality. Over the last 10 years, researchers have sought to address several interesting questions relating to how people's innate levels of psychological flexibility affect their health and behavioral effectiveness in the workplace.

In the first study examining employee psychological flexibility Bond and Bunce (2003) found that higher levels of the construct predicted, one year later, better mental health and job performance outcomes, and that these effects were maintained even when controlling for three well-established work-relevant variables: locus of control, negative affectivity, and job control. Findings also showed that psychological flexibility interacted with job control at Time 1 to impact mental health and job performance at Time 2. In other words, the beneficial effects of job control on mental health and performance were enhanced when people had higher levels of psychological flexibility. Since this initial work several studies have extended these findings in interesting ways. Donaldson-Feilder and Bond (2004) further investigated psychological flexibility's predictive capability relative to other well-established work-relevant individual characteristics. They found that while psychological flexibility and emotional intelligence both significantly correlated with better mental and physical health, when each were controlled for when the other served as a predictor, only psychological flexibility remained a significant predictor. Bond and Flaxman (2006) further investigated the ability of psychological flexibility to predict work-related outcomes longitudinally. They found that higher levels of psychological flexibility longitudinally predicted better job-related learning, in addition to better mental health and performance. Finally, Bond, Flaxman, and Bunce (2008) sought to test more explicitly the interactive relationship between psychological flexibility and job control. They found that people with higher levels of flexibility perceived that they had greater levels of job control because of a work reorganization intervention designed to improve job control, and this perception of higher levels of control allowed these people to experience greater improvements in mental health and absence levels.

A number of workplace ACT studies have examined the relationship between psychological flexibility and outcomes amongst clinical professionals. This work has shown that higher levels of psychological flexibility in rehabilitation workers correlate with: lower levels of stress, reduced emotional exhaustion, less work interference due to pain, and higher levels of general health, vitality, social functioning, emotional functioning, and emotion role functioning (McCracken & Yang, 2008); in addition, among addiction counselors, greater levels of flexibility is associated with lower levels of the three burnout components: emotional exhaustion, depersonalization, and reduced personal accomplishment (Vilardaga et al., 2011). Interestingly, Vilardaga et al. (2011) also found that the three burnout components were more strongly associated with psychological flexibility than they were with work-related characteristics that are often associated with burnout: job control, coworker support, supervisor support, salary, workload, and tenure.

The final line of work-related research that we wish to highlight concerns the measurement of psychological flexibility in the workplace. In all of the studies reviewed above, the Acceptance and Action Questionnaire (AAQ; Hayes, Strosahl et al., 2004), and its revised version, the AAQ-II (Bond et al., 2011) was used to assess psychological flexibility. These measures were designed for use in both clinical and community samples, and they assess people's general levels of psychological flexibility, effectively averaged across different contexts of their lives. (e.g., consider the AAQ-II item, "Emotions cause problems *in my life*"; our emphasis). However, ACT theory suggests that psychological flexibility can reliably fluctuate across situations, and, therefore, it may be beneficial to utilize measures of this construct that are specifically tailored to those given contexts (Bond et al., 2013). To this end, Bond et al. (2013) developed the Work-Related Acceptance and Action Questionnaire (WAAQ) to assess psychological flexibility in work contexts. Consistent with their hypotheses, they found that, in comparison with the AAQ-II, the work-specific measure correlated significantly more strongly with work-specific variables (e.g., task performance, work engagement, and job satisfaction). In contrast, the AAQ-II correlated more strongly with outcomes that are likely to be more stable across different contexts (e.g., mental health and personality variables).

Delivering ACT in the Workplace

In the previous section, we discussed research showing not only that psychological flexibility predicts a wide array of outcomes in the workplace, but that ACT interventions can improve such outcomes, because they increase psychological flexibility. In the second part of this chapter, we present an example of such an evidence- and workplace-based ACT training program. This intervention evolved from the earliest application and empirical evaluation of ACT in workplace settings (Bond & Bunce, 2000; Bond & Hayes, 2002). Some fundamental features of those earlier ACT interventions have stood the test of time – including the basic ethos of the program and the focus on helping employees cultivate an effective *combination* of mindfulness, defusion, acceptance, and valuing skills. Other aspects of our training have developed over the years, and the program content continues to evolve. This continual updating of the program is influenced by a number of factors, including (a) our personal observations of the ACT strategies that seem most effective, efficient, and engaging when delivered to workplace groups; informal feedback provided by our participants; (b) outcomes of ACT intervention studies conducted by our own and other research teams; and (c) various developments reported in the wider ACT/RFT literature.

We lack the space here to describe our training in full detail (see Flaxman, Bond, & Livheim, 2013 for a book-length account). Hence, we use the remainder of this chapter to provide a general overview of the program, and to consider the rationale behind a few of the strategies we employ in the service of increasing psychological flexibility in workplace settings. Toward the end of this section we offer some reflections on the challenge of "selling" ACT-based programs to organizational decision-makers.

Overview of an ACT-Based Training Program

Table 22.1 provides an overview of a program we recently implemented and evaluated. It is organized into a "2 + 1" mode of delivery, with the first two sessions delivered in consecutive weeks, and a third "booster" session delivered a month or so after Session 2. We scheduled three hours for each training session, but find that 2.5 hours is often sufficient. It is not essential to adopt this format. We have, for example, successfully delivered a similar ACT program over four sessions (three two-hour sessions, followed by a fourth session a few weeks later), and have also merged the initial training sessions into a single day workshop.

Although this ACT training program is delivered in work settings, we tell participants that they can apply the psychological and behavioral skills that they learn across *all* areas of their life. One advantage of this approach is that it helps to ensure employees will view the training as something "for them," rather than as an initiative being implemented with some sort of hidden agenda (e.g., a management drive to improve productivity or reduce absenteeism). Consistent with this "general life skills" view of the training program, we have given our ACT-based training a broad range of titles over the years, such as: "work and life effectiveness training," "personal resilience training," and "psychological skills training." We view all of these as accurate descriptions of what the ACT program delivers; however, some titles have been more resonant amongst different groups or at different times.

Some general features of the program structure and content deserve mention before we consider a few intervention strategies in more detail. First, the program is explicitly designed to cultivate two related skills: *mindfulness* (which includes present moment awareness, defusion, acceptance, and self-as-perspective strategies) and *values-based action* (which includes identifying one's values, and committing to moving toward them). Second, the program provides for *repeated* practice and behavioral rehearsal. For example, toward the end of every session, participants are invited to translate one personal value into three specific values-based actions that might be performed mindfully over the following week. We find this strategy helps our participants transfer learning from the sessions into their daily lives, and it usually ensures that all participants are able to get the gist of the valuing process.

Another feature of this program is that we include some "classic" mindfulness practices, borrowed from other (i.e., non-ACT) mindfulness-based interventions (the raisin exercise, mindful awareness of breath and body, awareness of routine activities, and an adaption of the three-minute breathing space). We use these well-established procedures primarily to target one of ACT's core processes (present moment awareness), and they provide the necessary foundation for subsequent experiential work that helps to promote defusion, acceptance, values-oriented practices, and self-as-context. The diagram in Figure 22.2 is commonly referred to as the hexaflex and portrays the six inter-related processes that contribute to psychological flexibility according to the model on which ACT is based. As the hexaflex shows, the trainer can leverage work on one of its six points (e.g., defusion) to strengthen other points (e.g., values-committed action), thus more effectively promoting psychological flexibility.

Table 22.1   Overview of an ACT-based workplace training program (adapted from Flaxman, Bond, & Livheim, 2013).

Session 1

Training segment	Key intervention strategies
Welcome and introductions	Mindfulness warm-up exercise
Overview of the training	Two skills organizing framework
Introduction to mindfulness	Raisin exercise; mindfulness of body and breath exercise; mindful routine activity for next week
Introduction to values-based action	Definition of valuing; compass metaphor; values card sort; translate a value into specific actions
Presentation of training rationale	Two sheets of paper technique
Discussion of home practice assignments	Three valued actions for the next week; environmental cues; public commitment

Session 2 (the following week)

Training segment	Key intervention strategies
Opening mindfulness practice	Mindfulness of body and breath exercise
Home practice review	Pairs and group discussion
Presentation of training rationale	Passengers on the bus metaphor
Untangling from thought barriers to valued action	Self-reflection on unhelpful thought content; defusion exercises – experience unhelpful thoughts in voice of cartoon and film characters; then to a familiar tune
Mindfulness of mood/emotion	Physicalizing exercise
Presentation of training rationale	Two sheets of paper technique
Defining values and values-based goal and action planning	Construction of four-week values-based goal and action plan
Discussion of home practice assignments	Three valued actions for the next week; four valued goals before next session; environmental cues; public commitment

Session 3 (one month to six weeks later)

Training segment	Key intervention strategies
Welcome back	Two skills organizing framework
Opening mindfulness practice	Mindfulness of body and breath exercise; brief three-step exercise for frequent use
Reflection on past few weeks	Pairs and group discussion; assessing values-consistency
Values questionnaire	A quick look at your values (Harris, 2009); group debrief
Presentation of program rationale	Two sheets of paper technique
Noticing and untangling from internal barriers	Physicalizing exercise; noticing the mind's commentary on a values-based goal; taking your mind for a walk; resilient "observer" perspective
Values-based goal and action planning	Three valued actions for the next week; short-, medium-, and long-term goal setting; environmental cues; public commitment
Keeping things going	Reflection on continued practice; top tips for values-based living
Final personal reflections	What impact has the training had on you? How would you like to use it from here?

In our ACT training program, we keep the duration of formal mindfulness practices (e.g., mindfulness of body and breath) to about 10 minutes, and distribute 10- and 15-minute audio recordings for participants to practice outside of the sessions. Many of the employees that attend our ACT training are unlikely to practice mindful meditations that are much longer than this. However, we tend to see good levels of engagement in more informal mindfulness practices, such as becoming mindfully aware of routine and values-based activities, and the use of frequent "mindful check-ins" throughout the day. Participants are often receptive to the message that practicing a little every day will naturally lead, over time, to an increase in one's ability to be more mindful.

A final, important feature of the program is that we have designed it to emphasize how ACT's six processes (and their associated intervention strategies) are highly interrelated and can serve to strengthen one another. For instance, the defusion and acceptance exercises we introduce in Session 2 are not used in isolation, but are, instead, presented to participants as skillful ways of relating to unhelpful thoughts, feelings, sensations, and urges that might otherwise function as "internal barriers" in the pursuit of personally valued goals and patterns of behavior. In fact, emphasizing the intimate links between acceptance and mindfulness processes and values-based action processes lies at the very heart of the training we are describing here, just as it does in other ACT interventions (Hayes, Strosahl, & Wilson, 2012). Thus, we employ a variety of techniques designed to communicate these links and, by extension, the overarching rationale for the entire program.

Techniques for Communicating the Program's Rationale

While we use a wide-range of ACT techniques in the training sessions, we believe that two techniques are particularly good at conveying the training goal of showing participants how mindfulness-based processes can facilitate values-based action processes (and vice versa); these are the *passengers on the bus* metaphor and the *two sheets of paper* technique.

Passengers on the Bus Metaphor

Passengers on the bus is a metaphor that portrays internal events (e.g., thoughts, moods, feelings, memories) as passengers on the "bus of life," and the person experiencing those private events is the driver of that bus. The trainer might use this metaphor to highlight different ways humans *respond or relate to* their passengers. For example, one response involves the driver allowing the "bossy" (and perhaps unhelpful) passengers to dictate where the bus goes. Alternatively, the driver might stop the bus, disappear into the back, and begin wrestling or arguing with less desirable passengers in a futile attempt to placate them or remove them from the bus. An important message to emphasize is that even the most unpleasant or threatening passengers cannot, *in themselves*, cause us harm – but the way the driver responds to them can interfere with the progress and direction of the bus (Dahl, Plumb, Stewart, & Lundgren, 2009).

The trainer communicates that the skills being taught on this program offer an alternative – and potentially much more effective – way of relating to our passengers, reducing the need to fight or reason with unwanted passengers, and reducing the extent to which certain passengers exert an unhelpful influence over the movement and direction of the bus. In this way, the metaphor is used as part of a more general strategy of generating a shift in people's perspective. That is, a shift *away* from viewing undesirable or unhelpful thoughts and feelings as things that must be removed, acted upon, changed, or reduced, and *toward* a view of such experiences as events that can simply be noticed for what they are and "brought along for the ride" (Hayes et al., 2012; Törneke, 2010).

We have traditionally presented this metaphor alongside a cartoon picture of monsters on a bus, which members of the ACT community created. However, it is also possible for members of the training group to physically act out the driver and passengers roles, or participants can view one of the freely available animations that help to bring the metaphor to life (for a recent example see Oliver, 2013).

Two Sheets of Paper Technique

As its name indicates, this technique requires just two pieces of paper! On one sheet, the trainer writes the word *VALUE* in large font. The other sheet states: "*UNHELPFUL*" *THOUGHT/MOOD/FEELING*. The trainer presents these sheets as representing two types of phenomena that can have a powerful influence over our behavior.

To indicate the basic purpose of the training, the trainer moves the *VALUE* sheet slightly to the fore (leaving the other sheet where it is; see Figures 22.1 a, b). While doing so, the trainer might state that a key aim of the training is "for our values to become a more prominent guide to action." Importantly, the trainer points out that, when making this move, there is no need to waste energy trying to change, avoid, reduce, or remove unhelpful thoughts, feelings, and urges. Instead, the trainer communicates that the program is designed to help us take a different (more mindful) perspective on our inner world, thereby reducing the extent to which unhelpful thoughts and feelings interfere with our ability to engage in personally valued patterns of action and pursue value-guided goals.

We conduct this two sheets demonstration in every session, usually more than once per session. The technique supports the delivery of ACT-consistent messages over the three sessions. For example, in the latter stages of Session 1 (after introducing values),

(a) (b)

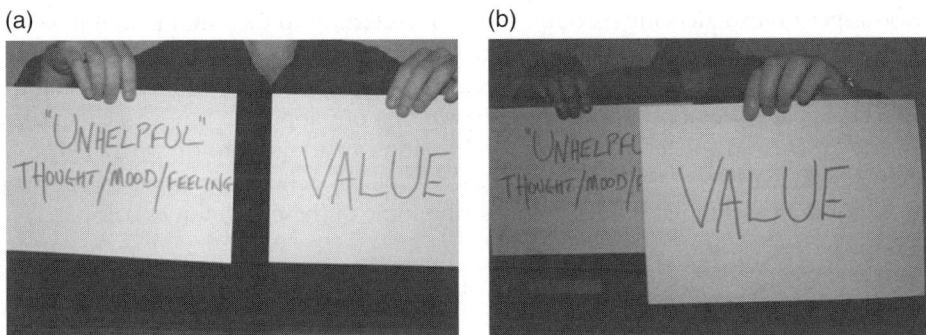

Figure 22.1 a, b   The two sheets of paper technique; used here to demonstrate the overreaching rationale of ACT-based training. (Photos from Flaxman et al., 2013 reprinted with permission).

we use the two sheets to communicate simply that an important aim of the training is to help us make our personal values a more prominent guide to action, while reducing the *influence* (but not the presence or frequency) of unhelpful thoughts, feelings, and urges.

In Session 2, we use the same technique to convey the message that valued action and unhelpful thoughts and feelings do not have to operate in opposition to one another, and that the skills we are developing enable us to take valued action even when we don't feel like it or when our minds are giving us plenty of reasons not to take action. From the perspective of RFT, this strategy is designed to place unhelpful private events and values-based action in a frame of coordination (Törneke, 2010). The underlying aim is to increase the likelihood of participants consciously and deliberately engaging in valued action outside of the sessions, while in the presence of difficult or simply unhelpful psychological content.

Finally, in Session 3, we use the same two sheets to communicate ACT's central notion of *willingness*: that we can become increasingly more effective at pursuing valued actions and goals by being open to whatever thoughts, feelings, and sensations happen to show up as we do so. As we have noted elsewhere, we have witnessed workplace participants become noticeably empowered by this possibility of behavioral willingness, particularly by the final session of training (Flaxman et al., 2013).

Cultivating Defusion and Acceptance Skills

Defusion and acceptance are closely related processes in ACT's model of psychological flexibility. Indeed, Hayes et al. (2012) suggest it is useful to think of defusion and acceptance as a natural pair of functional processes, both of which reflect an "open" response style.

Accordingly, in our workplace training, defusion and acceptance skills are organized together under the theme of "noticing and untangling from internal barriers to values-based action." We establish a simple distinction between these processes by presenting defusion exercises as offering "a skillful way of relating to thoughts," and an acceptance-oriented exercise to demonstrate "a skillful way of relating to fluctuating moods, sensations, and emotions" (Hayes et al., 2012; Zettle, 2007).

In practice, the trainer is looking for ways to promote defusion and acceptance throughout the entire program. For example, from the very outset, the trainer routinely employs language designed to highlight the distinction between the mind and the conscious person experiencing its output (e.g., by referring to the "mind" as if it were a separate entity). Similarly, acceptance-oriented instructions are embedded within most of the program's strategies. One example already mentioned involves the trainer using the two sheets of paper demonstration to emphasize that our approach is not to change the form or frequency of unhelpful thoughts and feelings. In addition to these strategies, we employ experiential exercises that are aimed more explicitly at helping participants develop these important psychological skills. We describe some of these techniques below.

Defusion Exercises

When first introducing defusion, we follow recommendations in the ACT literature by providing a brief psycho-educational dialogue that sets the scene for the subsequent exercises. The aim is to communicate that the human mind is very good at comparing, judging, evaluating, describing, criticizing, problem-solving, planning, and antici-pating all the things that could go wrong. We suggest to our participants that it is likely that the human mind evolved primarily to keep us out of serious danger, and to help us function within social groups. Thus, it is not surprising that the human mind is so good at (for example) predicting the worst, and wondering whether we are "good enough" as it compares ourselves to others. This trainer dialogue helps to normalize the mind's proclivity for negative content, and is a useful way to begin reducing entanglements with such content (see Harris, 2009; Hayes et al., 2012).

Following this introduction, we provide participants with some time to reflect on any internal dialogue they personally find self-limiting or which holds them back in some way from more effective or consistent engagement in personally valued action. Participants are asked to write down thought content on a handout designed for this purpose. This process is itself likely to serve a defusive function, as the exercise natu-rally encourages participants to step back from their thought content and to see it "out there" on the page.

As part of this same exercise, we encourage our participants to identify any particular theme (or themes) in their unhelpful mind chatter and to come up with a label or cheeky nickname that describes the mind when its output seems to be particularly unhelpful, perhaps threatening to hijack the effective pursuit of valued action. Following a suitable period of self-reflection, we invite participants to get into pairs or small groups in order to share their experiences with this exercise, and, if they choose to do so, to share their labels for their unhelpful mind chatter.

For the next technique, participants are invited to identify what they see as their most unhelpful or self-critical thought, and we ask them to experience that thought as if it were being "voiced" by a cartoon character with a distinctive or comedic voice (e.g., a member of the Simpson family), or a film or television character with an unusual voice (e.g., Arnold Schwarzenegger or C3PO or Yoda from the *Star Wars* films). We then ask them to repeat their thought, using this voice, over and over to the tune of a well-known song or nursery rhyme (e.g., "Happy birthday"). Participants are asked to do this, with their eyes closed, "in their own heads" rather than out loud. Afterwards, we ask participants to open their eyes, and to take another look at the thought written down "out there" on the page and simply to notice how they respond to it.

We have found this set of exercises offers a useful experiential introduction to the basic nature and function of defusion. Following such practices, it is common for par-ticipants to report taking previously troublesome thoughts a bit less seriously, and/or noticing thoughts losing some of their power, meaning, menace, or impact. It is also not unusual for participants to find themselves chortling at a thought that may have previously been viewed as rather unpleasant. All of these responses suggest the begin-nings of a more defused relationship to cognitive content.

Acceptance Exercise: Physicalizing a Mood/Emotion

We have come to view the physicalizing exercise as one of the most important mindfulness practices in our ACT-based training. In the version of the exercise that we use, we ask participants to think of something that is currently (or has recently been) causing them some stress or difficulty. This might be a looming work deadline or a person with whom they are having some difficulty. This should not be a massive issue, just something that is likely to bring up an unwanted mood or emotion, or to make their body react as soon as it is brought to mind.

Following a brief mindfulness practice, we invite participants to begin thinking about their stressful event or person. As they do so, participants are encouraged to become aware of how the body reacts: noticing any feelings or physical sensations unfolding somewhere in the body. They are asked to explore their bodily reactions with curiosity and interest, even if the sensation or feeling that arises is a little unpleasant. We encourage participants to explore various features of their bodily reactions, noticing whether the feeling or sensation is cool or hot, static or moving, dull or sharp, on the surface of the body or deep down inside (or both). We ask participants to draw an imaginary line around the sensation or feeling to identify "exactly whereabouts in your body it sits." We also include some acceptance-oriented instructions, such as "Practice simply noticing this feeling or sensation for what it is, without struggling with it or trying to push it away." We then ask participants to continue thinking about their stressful event or person and to imagine that the feeling or sensation is now temporarily located outside of the skin. We ask a series of questions that encourage them to imagine the feeling or sensation with physical properties: If this feeling or sensation were a physical object what would it look like? ...What color and shape would it have? ... How heavy does it look? ... What kind of surface texture does it have? ... If it could move, how fast does it look like it could move?

We then ask participants to notice any reaction they have toward this object, before "welcoming it back" inside the skin. We conclude by asking participants to notice once again – with interest and curiosity – exactly whereabouts the feeling or sensation sits within the body. The group discussion following this type of practice is a crucial part of the learning process. The trainer gathers and reflects participants' feedback on the exercise in a way that reinforces and models willingness to sit with and notice what might be a somewhat difficult inner experience.

The defusion/acceptance training segments described here can be neatly wrapped up by revisiting the ultimate purpose of cultivating such skills. Here the trainer might employ the two sheets of paper technique to reinforce that these exercises are designed to help us develop skillful ways of relating to unhelpful thoughts and feelings, so that they do not exert too much influence over our day-to-day ability to pursue our most valued actions and goals.

Cultivating Values-Based Action Skills

All three training sessions place significant emphasis on values and taking committed action toward those values. The structure of the exercises we use follows typical steps for ACT values interventions: identifying personal values; identifying values-based goals and then committing to appropriate action; noticing internal barriers; and assessing values-consistency of recent behavior (e.g., Dahl et al., 2009; Flaxman, Blackledge, & Bond, 2011; Harris, 2009). More specifically, the values-oriented presentations and exercises found in this program are designed to provide the following learning experiences:

- Help participants grasp the basic nature, function, and benefits of *valuing*.
- Help participants contact and construct personal values statements.
- Support participants as they engage in values-based goal and action planning.

- Encourage participants to take small values-guided actions outside of the sessions and to notice what happens when they do so.
- Communicate strategies for keeping values more psychologically present in daily life.

We start out in Session 1 with an introduction to ACT's concept of values. We tend to define values simply as the "personal qualities or strengths we most want to express in our actions" and "the principles that we personally choose to guide our behavior." We note the functional distinctions between values and goals; that is, values are *personally chosen* ideals to which we aspire but cannot sustain without continued action (e.g., being a loving father), while goals are discrete actions, in the service of a value, that can be achieved (e.g., attending one's child's football match). We also find it useful to highlight potential benefits of using personal values as a more prominent guide to action, particularly the increase in meaning and purpose that can be gained by becoming more aware of personal values, and by deliberately "bringing those values to life" via our actions and goals.

The values process is kick-started in the first session with a values card sort exercise that encourages participants to identify their "top five values." For this first exercise, we tend to use Ciarrochi and Bailey's (2008) Survey of Life Principles (SLP), omitting the cards that indicate power motives (e.g., "Being Wealthy") along with the cards that indicate a desire for experiential control (e.g., "Experiencing Positive Mood States"). We have found values tools such as the SLP to be extremely useful in brief ACT programs, as they offer participants an experiential sense of values as *qualities of action*, and they begin to put participants in contact with what they want their lives to be about.

As noted earlier, toward the end of every session we encourage participants to brainstorm a series of small and specific value-based actions they might perform over the next week. Participants are asked to choose three of these actions to perform mindfully outside of the sessions as part of the program's home practices. The instruction to be mindful during this learning process is particularly important. Participants are encouraged to use the home assignments to become aware of any thoughts and feelings that have the potential to function as internal barriers to valued action. Moreover, if participants are psychologically present when pursuing values, it increases the likelihood that they will come into contact with sources of behavioral reinforcement (such a renewed sense of vitality or purpose) that can lead to an expansion of values-based action over time (Dahl et al., 2009).

The Challenge of Getting ACT Principles into the Workplace

The program we have described, above, has been implemented and evaluated in a range of large public sector organizations in the United Kingdom. Often, this training has been offered to organizations free of charge, with grants provided by research funding bodies and university bursaries, and so these organizations have been happy to have this "free" training. Outside of this applied research context, however, it is important to consider how best to "sell" the benefits of ACT training to organizations. One of the authors (Rob Archer) has built a successful organizational consultancy that offers services and products that are all underpinned by the ACT approach to human functioning. Rob has learned the hard way how difficult it is to sell stand-alone ACT-based training packages to the corporate world. As an organizational practitioner working at the "coal face," Rob offers the following reflections on tailoring ACT to fit with corporate agendas and needs.

First, it is not always possible to persuade organizations to invest in what might be seen as a fairly comprehensive training package, such as the "2 + 1" model described in this chapter. We therefore need to adapt our protocols and embed them into things that organizations care about and for which they have budgets. One option is to package ACT-based offerings into smaller "bite-sized" training and coaching programs, geared toward addressing specific issues such as customer sales training, leadership development, as well as employee resilience training. The ultimate goal is to find ways to disseminate ACT principles throughout organizations, so that they are known to CEOs, human resource directors, occupational health professionals, health and safety operatives, staff at every level of the organizational hierarchy, and policy-makers. Ideally, ACT's processes would become part of "the way we do things around here"; to achieve this, we may need to aim for ACT-consistency rather than imple-menting whole protocols. Given the almost constant process of change in organiza-tions, ACT processes may also be usefully embedded within wider change initiatives, and we can inculcate psychological flexibility in terms of how we do things, rather than training people in it directly.

All of this involves meeting businesses where they are, learning to speak their language and seeking to understand their needs. For example, in many workplace contexts, ACT might be most attractive when it is presented as a performance technology, which can help people become more present and less distracted, and more engaged in what they are doing by connecting to personal values. Also, organi-zational practices often encourage a workforce to subscribe to the organization's core values and it may be possible to empower this type of process with ACT principles – for example, by first helping staff members get in touch with their own values and using the organizational values simply as the context for living these. Such initiatives require us to think carefully about how ACT is packaged and presented and to be flexible in terms of delivery.

In sum, we are only at the beginning in terms of thinking about how ACT can have an influence on organizational life. Our own experience with private and public sector companies in the United Kingdom has provided us with some insight into how ACT's processes can be part of, and indeed enhance, programs that organizational decision-makers are already familiar with and willing to invest in.

Psychological Flexibility and Organizational Behavior

The concept of psychological flexibility emphasizes the need for flexible and varied behaviors (both private and public) that promote effective action in relation to one's values. Importantly, it highlights the need to be flexible in how we relate to internal events that we find troubling (e.g., sometimes problem-solving, sometimes mindful-ness, depending upon the context and goal). Likewise, organizational theorists have long emphasized the importance of flexible organizations, and their ability to adapt across dimensions such as time, range, intention, and focus (Golden & Powell, 2000).

Very few, however, have discussed the importance of handling, or, indeed, even acknowledging, discomfort in relation to pursuing the aims of an organization.

One notable exception is Elliott Jaques, a Kleinian psychoanalyst who helped to establish the Tavistock Institute of Human Relations in London. He postulated (1955) that leaders and workers unconsciously collaborate to design organizational structures, processes, and even technology, not only to achieve the company's primary aim (e.g., manufacturing a product), but also to defend employees against unwanted thoughts and feelings (e.g., through heavily standardized – or dehumanizing – processes in social care facilities). If such defence mechanisms are not "made conscious" to leaders, they serve to produce a rigid organization that will be less effective in achieving its goals. To this day, work psychologists still use the Tavistock's T-group intervention as part of their efforts to make leaders aware of group processes that may lead to unhelpful organizational cultures (see de Board, 1978 for a comprehensive account of psychoanalysis and organizations).

As has been done with psychoanalysis, we believe that we can scale up the concept of psychological flexibility to the organizational level, thus, producing a contextual behavioral science (CBS)-informed guide to creating flexible and successful organizations (and employees). As we will show, such a model can be constructed using key principles of organizational behavior (OB). OB is a field of study that investigates the impact that individual (e.g., personality, mental health), group (leadership, teams), and organizational characteristics (e.g., structure, processes) have on organizational effectiveness (including the health of individuals) (Robbins & Judge, 2007). The applied goal of OB is, of course, to design and *influence* (or change) characteristics at these three levels, in order to maximize organizational effectiveness.

ACT's overriding goal, consistent with its philosophical roots in CBS – see Hayes (1993), is to develop science and practices that predict-*and-influence* human behavior. We can adopt this pragmatic aim and use it as a criterion by which to select constructs, strategies, and techniques from existing OB models that are focused on prediction-and-control; we can then combine those that meet that criterion to establish a new model that we can use to predict-and-influence the levers that produce organizational effectiveness. Such a pragmatic model can help OB researchers and practitioners stay laser-focused on affecting change, unencumbered by superfluous constructs that no OB practitioner could directly influence (e.g., motivation, meaningfulness of work[1]). The hexaflex (see Figure 22.2) is a graphic representation of ACT's six core psychological processes, discussed above, and, as described above, we can influence these processes through various ACT techniques, which results in flexible and effective human behavior. We maintain that if we can identify OB characteristics that correspond to each of the six hexaflex processes, then we will have specified organizational variables that we can actually influence, and the result of such influence may be a flexible and effective organization.

To this end, Bond (forthcoming) selected, from the many OB constructs, models, and strategies, the characteristics, depicted in Figure 22.3, for the organizational flexibility model (or "orgflex"). (We should note that Steven Hayes developed an organizational flexibility model, but it was not explicitly informed by the OB literature but, rather, by Ostrom's 1990 core design principles for group efficacy.) As we discuss in the following section, we believe that the six organizational characteristics that constitute the orgflex serve a related function to their (spatially) corresponding psychological process in the hexaflex (compare Figures 22.2 and 22.3); thus, "purpose and goals"

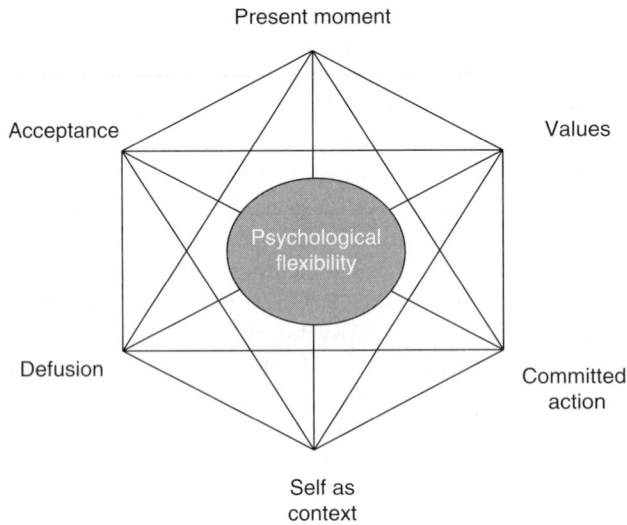

Figure 22.2 ACT's hexaflex model.

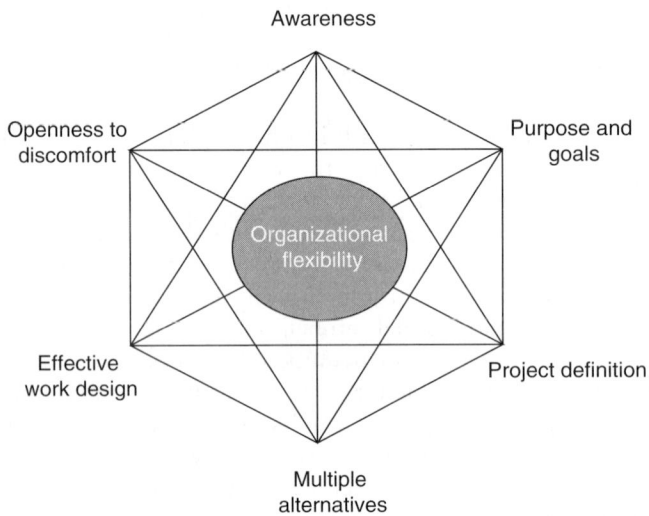

Figure 22.3 Organizational flexibility model.

is located in the orgflex in the same position as "values" are in the hexaflex, and we maintain that they serve similar functions in terms of setting a meaningful course in the life of the organization or individual, respectively. Furthermore, we hypothesize that each organizational characteristic on the orgflex can promote, to varying degrees, in individual workers, the corresponding psychological process on the hexaflex; thus, an organization that is open to discomfort (e.g., ambiguity and conflict) can model and reinforce those characteristics of acceptance in relation to workers' own psychological events.

The Six Characteristics of Organizational Flexibility

Purpose and Goals

For individuals, values, in ACT's hexaflex, refer to a direction of travel that people choose to take; they give meaning to their lives, and people need constantly to work toward them, as they can never be forever achieved, or sustained; for example, a person has to work constantly on being a loving partner: it cannot be achieved in perpetuity. Similarly, the OB literature notes the importance of the *purpose* of an organization. Like a value, it guides an organization's goals (or vision) and day-to-day actions (or mission). Marquis, Glynn, and Davis (2007) state that an organizational purpose has three characteristics: (1) it meets a need in the world that will function to make the world a better place (e.g., anything from making machines for cancer treatment to providing entertainment to people); (2) it meets a need in society (e.g., providing transport for Londoners); and, (3) as with ACT's definition of a value, it is aspirational but not sustainable (e.g., "preserve and improve human life"; Merck Corporation, n.d.).

Project Definition – Starting with the Goal, Not the Problem

In ACT, individuals commit themselves to actions that will attain their values-based goals, and an action plan will likely be drawn up that outlines how this will be achieved, psychological and external barriers that may get in the way of achieving those goals, and perhaps even a time frame in which subgoals and goals will be met. The equivalent plan for organizations is also required (and it should, ideally, be a bit more structured and formalized). In the OB literature, such a process is commonly referred to as project definition, with the term "project" referring, essentially, to any values-based goal of the organization; thus, a project (or "goal") could be a product, a new HR strategy, or whole-scale organizational change.

Project definition is a process that should result in the following: the problem definition (e.g., where are we now and where do we need to go); the specification of the project outcome; the project plan that outlines the approach to analysis, design, and completion of the plan, as well as the timeline for all of these processes; and, finally, it should clearly specify the project team, project leader, and reporting structure. This approach to project definition attempts to establish a clear framework that will help to ensure the successful and on-time delivery of an organization's goal. Importantly, and consistent with ACT, the process of project definition places considerable emphasis on identifying, at the start, the desired outcome (not all of the problems) and ensuring it is clearly linked to the organization's purpose (or one of its purpose-driven goals).

Ensuring a clear link to the organization's purpose (or related goals) can actually shape the desired outcome, or goal, and, as a result, the choice of intervention. For example, a telephone call centre asked one of the authors to reduce their absence rates. While an understandable request, there are a number of ways that this can be accomplished, and the purpose-related mission of this organization would help to determine what strategies would be used, and what they would try to accomplish. In the end, the organization determined that they wanted to provide the best customer experience in their sector. This organizational purpose led us to recommend, and the company to accept, the expansion of the role of call centre operators so that they were able to handle most customer matters from start to finish, without having to pass callers on to other people or departments. This job expansion intervention had the desired outcome of reducing absence rates (and increasing well-being and performance), but it also greatly improved their customers' experience. Normally, we would not even suggest such a complex and expensive solution to high absence rates, but knowing the purpose-driven goals of this company convinced everyone that this job expansion intervention was worth the effort.

Multiple Alternatives

One of the key, desirable functions of self-as-context (or self-as-perspective) in the hexaflex is that "it situates self-knowledge in a more expansive temporal, social, and spatial context. This flexibility increases the ability to respond to the consequences of actions that are delayed, that occur elsewhere, or that are felt primarily by others" (Hayes et al., 2012, p. 89). In the context of the orgflex, we believe that a similar perspective on team and organizational levels, which we term *multiple perspectives*, allow decision-makers to better assess the impact that their judgments and products will have on their employees, customers, and community.

The decision-making strategy of systematically identifying and exploring multiple ideas as to how best to arrive at a solution stems from the OB approach termed design thinking (e.g., Martin, 2009). It encourages an iterative approach to decision-making in which (normally) teams, consciously and systematically generate, evaluate, modify, and abandon alternative solutions to problems and products. While this defusion promoting method is often used in product development (e.g., the iPod), "playing with multiple solutions" is not widely used outside of product design departments. From anecdotal evidence, we believe a reason for this is, as one television executive wrote in an email, "It can be career limiting to look foolish by coming up with ideas that are eventually abandoned, modified out of all recognition or, worse, dismissed out of hand." This view led the executive to design his department's work processes in such a (rigid) way as to prevent taking a systematic approach to considering multiple perspectives.

Conceptualization of such unwillingness to explore curiously alternative approaches to moving toward purpose based organizational goals in order to protect one's self, and team, has long been discussed. Early organizational theorists, such as Bion (1948), noted that employees have the tendency to "nonconsciously" collude to design work structures and processes to prevent threats to people's conceptualized self. We believe that processes, such as generating multiple alternatives, can be an effective way to "design out" (or at least minimize) that avoidant tendency and, thus, set the context for a better way of seeing the consequences of different solution alternatives.

Effective Work Design

Cognitive defusion is an approach that people take toward their internal events that alters the undesirable functions of those events, without changing their form, frequency, or situational sensitivity (Hayes et al., 2011). Put another way, cognitive fusion involves changing the way that people interact with their private experiences, so, while they may still be present, they no longer have detrimental effects on them. Likewise, organizational researchers have long hypothesized that various forms of work design – that is, ways that people interact with their work tasks – can limit the impact that work demands have on people's physical and mental health. Karasek's (1979) demands-control model perhaps most explicitly makes this prediction. It maintains that highly demanding jobs will only have detrimental effects on people, such as coronary heart disease and psychological distress, if they have to approach their work without sufficient job control. In contrast, if organizations provide people with some influence over how they carry out their (even demanding) work, they will not only experience fewer and less deleterious effects, but they will also perform their work more effectively and be more motivated in carrying it out. A comprehensive review of the work control literature largely supports this hypothesis (Terry and Jimmieson, 1999; see also Bond et al., 2008).

Other well-established and empirically supported OB theories also posit beneficial effects of job control (e.g., the job characteristics model: Hackman & Lawler, 1971; the sociotechnical systems approach: e.g., Emery & Trist, 1960; and job demands-resources model: e.g., Bakker & Demerouti, 2007). Furthermore, they hypothesize that other work design characteristics can also have advantageous impacts on the health, performance, and the attitudes of workers; these include support in carrying out one's work, the opportunity to do a variety of tasks, and the ability to do a complete job, from start to finish (e.g., a team that builds a car from start to finish, or guiding a customer complaint from the time it is made to the time it is resolved). As for job control, there is longstanding and considerable research that shows the health and performance benefits of these and other work design characteristics (Humphrey, Nahrgang, & Morgeson, 2007).

Thus, the concepts of both cognitive defusion and well-designed work maintain that unwanted thoughts and demanding work, respectively, do not necessarily have to lead to detrimental consequences: they only do so when they are approached from a fused stance or in a context of poor work design. As the hexaflex shows, individuals can change the context in which they experience their internal experiences, but, as the orgflex highlights, only organizations can create the context in which people carry out (or approach) their work.

Openness to Discomfort

It will come to no one's surprise that organizations can evoke challenging, unwanted emotions in people. The hexaflex shows how it is useful to individuals to be accepting and open to those emotions; the orgflex advocates this same open stance at the organizational level, and the OB literature recommends many different structures, processes, strategies, and leadership approaches that require such openness to discomfort. Minimal critical specification, just noted, is one such design principle; others include allowing employee participation in decision-making; clearly, openly, and honestly communicating with employees in a timely manner; the project definition process, noted above; and a transformational approach to leadership, which requires a personal, open, and "lead by example" leadership style. All of these OB features require leaders, and the teams and organizations that they design, to be willing to be uncomfortable in the service of the organization's purpose and values.

Awareness

As ACT advocates the need for individuals to be in the present moment and be aware of their internal events, so the orgflex, consistent with OB practices, maintains the same advice for teams and organizations. Indeed, there is a whole field within OB that focuses on maintaining system awareness: human resources (HR). Most organizations of any size will have an HR department that will develop policies and practices that function either to understand what is happening within the organization (e.g., performance evaluation, staff surveys), or to train employees (essentially) to be aware of their actions (e.g., diversity training, career development planning).

The role of maintaining awareness does not lie only in HR, however. For organizations to have flexible and high-performing individuals, teams, and departments, consistent monitoring needs to occur at each of those levels. For example, one useful technique that leaders can use with their teams or departments is referred to as "decision tracking." This approach to maintaining awareness aims to obtain almost immediate feedback on results, in order to improve both learning and the decision-making process. Decision makers – even if they are not formal leaders – record a decision they have just made, along with the outcomes they anticipate, and they later read that document to reflect on and learn from the decision's consequences.

Conclusions: Process above Technology

In this chapter, we discussed research that demonstrated that psychological flexibility can predict mental health and behavioral effectiveness at work; we also considered findings that ACT tends to improve the health and effectiveness of employees by increasing psychological flexibility. We then described our evidence-based ACT intervention, and how it targets the six psychological processes that constitute psychological flexibility. Finally, we discussed how we could scale up those psychological flexibility processes to the organizational level, in order to create flexible and effective organizations. As one can clearly see, we have greatly emphasized the concept of psychological flexibility in this chapter. In so doing, we wished to highlight that ACT, while a demonstrably effective workplace (and clinical) intervention, is, at the end of the day, a technology used to enhance the key psychological process underlying mental health and behavioral effectiveness: psychological flexibility. Emphasizing the importance of this process (even over ACT) allows us more effectively to develop appropriate strategies for enhancing mental health and effectiveness at societal levels where ACT techniques may be impossible to implement, such as at organizational and even community levels. For example, in the organizational hexaflex, we did not try to apply ACT's individual-level concepts (i.e., the hexaflex) to the organizational level; rather, we used organizational-level strategies and techniques to target what ACT targets at the individual level: flexibility.

By emphasizing psychological flexibility, and how we can enhance it, ACT's strategy and techniques will change over time – as they have in our ACT at work intervention. Furthermore, such an emphasis provides a clear target at which researchers and practitioners can aim, when developing workplace training, structures, processes, and technologies that are designed to maximize mental health and human vitality. We look forward to seeing what people produce.

Note

1   This is not to say that we consider psychological events, such as motivation, unimportant – quite the contrary, they bring energy and vitality to our lives – it is simply that we cannot directly impact them, and our theories and models may be more useful if we treated those internal events as outcomes, or dependent variables.

References

Baer, R. A. (2003). Mindfulness training as a clinical intervention: A conceptual and empirical review. *Clinical Psychology: Science and Practice, 10*, 125–143.

Bakker, A.B., & Demerouti, E. (2007). The Job Demands-Resources model: State of the art. *Journal of Managerial Psychology, 22*, 309–328.

Bion, W. R. (1948). Experiences in groups. *Human Relations, 1*, 314–320.

Bond, F. W. (forthcoming). *How to create a flexible organisation: Scaling-up ACT's model of psychological flexibility.* Manuscript submitted for publication.

Bond, F. W., & Bunce, D. (2000). Mediators of change in emotion-focused and problem-focused worksite stress management interventions. *Journal of Occupational Health Psychology, 5*, 156–163.

Bond, F. W., & Bunce, D. (2003). The role of acceptance and job control in mental health, job satisfaction, and work performance. *Journal of Applied Psychology, 88*, 1057–1067.

Bond, F.W., & Flaxman, P. E. (2006). The ability of psychological flexibility and job control to predict learning, job performance, and mental health. *Journal of Organizational Behavior Management, 26*, 113–130.

Bond, F. W., Flaxman, P. E., & Bunce, D. (2008). The influence of psychological flexibility on work redesign: Mediated moderation of a work reorganization intervention. *Journal of Applied Psychology, 93*, 645–654.

Bond, F. W., & Hayes, S. C. (2002). ACT at work. In F. W. Bond & W. Dryden (Eds.), *Handbook of brief cognitive behavior therapy* (pp. 117–140). Chichester, England: Wiley.

Bond, F. W., Hayes, S. C., Baer, R. A., Carpenter, K. M., Guenole, N., Orcutt, H. K., ... Zettle, R. D. (2011). Preliminary psychometric properties of the Acceptance and Action Questionnaire – II: A revised measure of psychological inflexibility and experiential avoidance. *Behavior Therapy, 42*, 676–688.

Bond, F. W., Lloyd, J., & Guenole, N. (2013). The work-related acceptance and action questionnaire: Initial psychometric findings and their implications for measuring psychological flexibility in specific contexts. *Journal of Occupational and Organizational Psychology, 86*, 331–347.

Brinkborg, H., Michanek, J., Hesser, H., & Berglund, G. (2011). Acceptance and commitment therapy for the treatment of stress among social workers: A randomized controlled trial. *Behaviour Research and Therapy, 49*, 389–398.

Brown, K. W., & Ryan, R. M. (2003). The benefits of being present: Mindfulness and its role in psychological well-being. *Journal of Personality and Social Psychology, 84*, 822–848.

Ciarrochi, J., & Bailey, A. (2008). *A CBT-practitioner's guide to ACT: How to bridge the gap between cognitive behavioral therapy and acceptance and commitment therapy.* Oakland, CA: New Harbinger.

Dahl, J. C., Plumb, J. C., Stewart, I., & Lundgren, T. (2009). *The art and science of valuing in psychotherapy: Helping clients discover, explore, and commit to valued action using acceptance and commitment therapy.* Oakland, CA: New Harbinger.

Dahl, J., Wilson, K. G., & Nilsson, A. (2004). Acceptance and commitment therapy and the treatment of persons at risk for long-term disability resulting from stress and pain symptoms: A preliminary randomized trial. *Behavior Therapy, 35,* 785–802.

De Board, R. (1978). *The psychoanalysis of organisations: A psychoanalytic approach to behaviour in groups and organisations.* London, England: Tavistock.

Donaldson-Feilder, E. J., & Bond, F. W. (2004). The relative importance of psychological acceptance and emotional intelligence to workplace well-being. *British Journal of Guidance and Counselling, 32,* 187–203.

Emery, F. E., & Trist, E. L. (1960). Sociotechnical systems. In C. W. Churchman and M. Verhulst (Eds.), *Management science, models and techniques* (vol. 2, pp. 83–97). Oxford, England: Pergamon.

Flaxman, P. E., Blackledge, J. T., & Bond, F. W. (2011). *Acceptance and commitment therapy: The CBT distinctive features series.* Hove, England: Routledge.

Flaxman, P. E., & Bond, F. W. (2010a). A randomised worksite comparison of acceptance and commitment therapy and stress inoculation training. *Behaviour Research and Therapy, 48,* 816–820.

Flaxman, P. E., & Bond, F. W. (2010b). Worksite stress management training: Moderated effects and clinical significance. *Journal of Occupational Health Psychology, 15,* 347–358.

Flaxman, P. E., Bond, F. W., & Livheim, F. (2013). *The mindful and effective employee: An acceptance and commitment therapy training manual for improving well-being and performance.* Oakland, CA: New Harbinger.

Golden, W., & Powell, P. (2000). Towards a definition of flexibility: In search of the Holy Grail? *Omega, 28,* 373–384.

Hackman, J. R., & Lawler, E. E. (1971). Employee reactions to job characteristics. *Journal of Applied Psychology, 55,* 259.

Harris, R. (2009). *ACT made simple: An easy-to-read primer on acceptance and commitment therapy.* Oakland, CA: New Harbinger.

Hayes, S. C. (1987). A contextual approach to therapeutic change. In N. Jacobson (Ed.), *Psychotherapists in clinical practice: Cognitive and behavioral perspectives* (pp. 327–387). New York, NY: Guilford.

Hayes, S. C. (1993). Analytic goals and the varieties of scientific contextualism. In S. C. Hayes, L. J. Hayes, H. W. Reese, & T. R. Sarbin (Eds.), *Varieties of scientific contextualism.* Reno, NV: Context Press.

Hayes, S. C., Bissett, R., Roget, N., Padilla, M., Kohlenberg, B. S., Fisher, G., Masuda, A., Pistorello, J., Rye, A. K., Berry, K., & Niccolls, R. (2004). The impact of acceptance and commitment training and multicultural training on the stigmatizing attitudes and professional burnout of substance abuse counselors. *Behavior Therapy, 35,* 821–835.

Hayes, S. C., Luoma, J. B., Bond, F. W., Masuda, A., & Lillis, J. (2006). Acceptance and commitment therapy: Model, processes and outcomes. *Behaviour Research and Therapy, 44,* 1–25.

Hayes, S. C., Strosahl, K. D., & Wilson, K. G. (1999). *Acceptance and commitment therapy: An experiential approach to behavior change.* New York, NY: Guilford.

Hayes, S. C., Strosahl, K., & Wilson, K. G. (2012). *Acceptance and commitment therapy.* New York, NY: Guilford.

Hayes, S. C., Strosahl, K. D., Wilson, K. G., Bassett, R. T., Pastorally, J., Toarmino, D., & McCurry, S. M. (2004). Measuring experiential avoidance: A preliminary test of a working model. *The Psychological Record, 54,* 553–578.

Hayes, S. C., Villatte, M., Levin, M., & Hildebrandt, M. (2011). Open, aware, and active: Contextual approaches as an emerging trend in the behavioral and cognitive therapies. *Annual Review of Clinical Psychology, 7,* 141–168.

Humphrey, S. E., Nahrgang, J. D., & Morgeson, F. P. (2007). Integrating motivational, social, and contextual work design features: A meta-analytic summary and theoretical extension of the work design literature. *Journal of Applied Psychology, 92*, 1332.

Jaques, E. (1955). *Social systems as a defence against persecutory and depressive anxiety.* London, England: Tavistock.

Jeffcoat, T., & Hayes, S. C. (2012). A randomized trial of ACT bibliotherapy on the mental health of K-12 teachers and staff. *Behaviour Research and Therapy, 50*, 571–579.

Kabat-Zinn, J. (1990). *Full catastrophe living: Using the wisdom of your mind and body to face stress, pain, and illness.* New York, NY: Delacorte.

Karasek, Jr., R. A. (1979). Job demands, job decision latitude, and mental strain: Implications for job redesign. *Administrative Science Quarterly, 2*, 285–308.

Linehan, M. M. (1993). *Cognitive-behavioral treatment of borderline personality disorder.* New York, NY: Guilford.

Lloyd, J., Bond, F. W., & Flaxman, P. E. (2013). The value of psychological flexibility: Examining psychological mechanisms underpinning a cognitive behavioural therapy intervention for burnout. *Work and Stress, 27*, 181–199.

Luoma, J. B., Hayes, S. C., Twohig, M. P., Roget, N., Fisher, G., Padilla, M., … Kohlenberg, B. (2007). Augmenting continuing education with psychologically focused group consultation: Effects on adoption of group drug counseling. *Psychotherapy: Theory, Research, Practice, Training, 44*, 463–469.

Marlatt, G. A., & Kristeller, J. L. (1999). Mindfulness and meditation. In W. R. Miller (Ed.), *Integrating spirituality into treatment* (pp. 67–84). Washington, DC: American Psychological Association.

Marquis, C., Glynn, M. A., & Davis, G. F. (2007). Community isomorphism and corporate social action. *Academy of Management Review, 32*, 925–945.

Martin, R. L. (2009). *The design of business: Why design thinking is the next competitive advantage.* Cambridge, MA: Harvard Business Press.

McCracken, L. M., & Yang, S. Y. (2008). A contextual cognitive-behavioral analysis of rehabilitation workers' health and well-being: Influences of acceptance, mindfulness, and values-based action. *Rehabilitation Psychology, 53*, 479–485.

Merck Corporation. (n.d.) *Our values.* Retrieved from http://www.merck.ca/English/about-us/Pages/our-values.aspx

Noone, S. J., & Hastings, R. P. (2009). Building psychological resilience in support staff caring for people with intellectual disabilities: Pilot evaluation of an acceptance-based intervention. *Journal of Intellectual Disabilities, 13*, 43–53.

Noone, S. J., & Hastings, R. P. (2010). Using acceptance and mindfulness based workshops with support staff caring for adults with intellectual disabilities. *Mindfulness, 1*, 67–73.

Noone, S. J., & Hastings, R. P. (2011). Values and psychological acceptance as correlates of burnout in support staff working with adults with intellectual disabilities. *Journal of Mental Health Research in Intellectual Disabilities, 4*, 79–89.

Oliver, J. (2013). *Passengers on a bus - an acceptance & commitment therapy (ACT) metaphor.* YouTube. Retrieved from http://bit.ly/1flviKM

Ostrom, E. (1990). *Governing the commons: The evolution of institutions for collective action.* Cambridge, England: Cambridge University Press.

Robbins, S. P. & Judge, T. A. (2007). *Organizational behavior* (12th ed.). Upper Saddle River, NJ: Pearson Education.

Stafford-Brown, J., & Pakenham, K. I. (2012). The effectiveness of an ACT informed intervention for managing stress and improving therapist qualities in clinical psychology trainees. *Journal of Clinical Psychology, 68*, 592–613.

Terry, D. J., & Jimmieson, N. L. (1999). Work control and employee well-being: A decade review.

Törneke, N. (2010). *Learning RFT: An introduction to relational frame theory and its clinical application.* Oakland, CA: New Harbinger.

Varra, A. A., Hayes, S. C., Roget, N., & Fisher, G. (2008). A randomized control trial examining the effect of acceptance and commitment training on clinician willingness to use evidence-based pharmacotherapy. *Journal of Consulting and Clinical Psychology, 76,* 449–458.

Vilardaga, R., Luoma, J. B., Hayes, S. C., Pistorello, J., Levin, M. E., Hildebrandt, M. J., & Bond, F. (2011). Burnout among the addiction counseling workforce: The differential roles of mindfulness and values-based processes and work-site factors. *Journal of Substance Abuse Treatment, 40,* 323–335.

Zettle, R. D. (2007). *ACT for depression: A clinician's guide to using acceptance and commitment therapy in treating depression.* Oakland, CA: New Harbinger.

23

The Potential of Community-Wide Strategies for Promoting Psychological Flexibility

Michael E. Levin, Jason Lillis, and Anthony Biglan

Increasing the Prevalence of Psychological Flexibility in Entire Populations

Clinical and etiological work both show that psychological flexibility contributes to human well-being. Measures of flexibility and experiential avoidance (EA) indicate a correlation with a wide variety of psychological and behavioral problems (Hayes et al., 2004). Even stronger evidence comes from clinical intervention studies showing that changes in psychological flexibility mediate the impact of ACT interventions on a diverse array of psychological and behavioral problems (Hayes, Luoma, Bond, Masuda, & Lillis, 2006).

We believe there is enough evidence to justify efforts to increase the prevalence of psychological flexibility in populations and to examine the impact of such increases on population well-being. In this chapter, we briefly describe ideas for increasing the prevalence of psychological flexibility and the research that could advance this goal.

Epidemiological Research on Psychological Flexibility in Populations

Epidemiological studies are needed that assess the prevalence of psychological flexibility in the population; its distribution across genders, ethnic groups, and levels of economic well-being; and its relationship to all psychological, behavioral, and health problems. Such research would clarify the degree to which psychological flexibility is universally important and would suggest factors that may influence the occurrence of EA.

Most important will be research that delineates the conditions that make psychological flexibility less likely. Or to put it differently, what influences the development of experiential avoidance? Biglan, Hayes, and Pistorello (2008) speculated that stressful events may increase people's tendency to avoid unpleasant thoughts and feelings. Those who have never been experientially avoidant and have had few stressful events in their lives may suddenly find themselves inundated with distressing

The Wiley Handbook of Contextual Behavioral Science, First Edition. Edited by Robert D. Zettle, Steven C. Hayes, Dermot Barnes-Holmes, and Anthony Biglan.
© 2016 John Wiley & Sons, Ltd. Published 2016 by John Wiley & Sons, Ltd.

feelings due to the death of a loved one, a job loss, or a marital breakup. This may motivate them to do whatever they can to reduce their distress: some of their strategies may involve avoidance (Kashdan & Kane, 2011). This is important in that it may show that a variety of stressful conditions undermine psychological flexibility. To the extent that common stressors such as coercive social interactions (Dishion & Snyder, 2015) and poverty (Yoshikawa, Aber, & Beardslee, 2012) affect psychological flexibility, it will point to the likely value of population-wide policies and programs that can prevent the development of psychological inflexibility.

It is also important to examine whether PF is related to the most common and costly physical illnesses – cardiovascular disease and cancer. In the healthcare system, preventing and treating psychological and behavioral disorders continues to be secondary to addressing physical illness. If PF is found to be associated with cancer and cardiovascular disease, some of the most influential segments of the healthcare research and practice communities would likely begin to focus on PF. Evidence already points to stressful environments contributing to psychological and behavioral disorders and to physical illness (Galobardes, Lynch, & Smith, 2008; Wegman & Stetler, 2009). And there is evidence that PF exacerbates psychological and behavioral problems that contribute to physical illness. Examples of disorders associated with PF include depression and cigarette smoking (Hayes et al., 2006). If a direct relationship between PF and physical illness can be established it would have a powerful influence on getting resources put into affecting the prevalence of psychological flexibility in the population.

All of this evidence will be fodder for public education campaigns. Imagine a Surgeon General Report that brought together all evidence about the role of psychological flexibility in diverse problems; the factors that affect flexibility; and the programs, policies, and practices that might be widely disseminated to affect psychological flexibility. Such a report could influence the allocation of research resources, the practices of prevention and treatment specialists, and the behavior of individuals who learn of the value of flexibility from news media.

Work on the assessment of PF in the population would constitute the first step in the creation of a surveillance system to track the prevalence of flexibility in the population. Such a system would make it possible to focus communities and policy-makers on the need to increase flexibility and would enable the evaluation of any population-based interventions designed to increase flexibility.

Reducing Conditions That Make People Less Flexible

To the extent that aversive conditions impair psychological flexibility, interventions to reduce those conditions will be important. Two widely occurring conditions seem particularly likely to be associated with inflexibility. Poverty is a well-established stressor, which is associated with higher rates of most psychological, behavioral, and health problems (Galobardes et al., 2008; Yoshikawa et al., 2012). In the United States at least, the proportion of people living in poverty has increased in recent years (National Center for Law & Economic Justice [NCLEJ], 2013). Among those under age 18, more than 20% are living in poverty (NCLEJ, 2013). To the extent that poverty conditions influence people to become psychologically inflexible, efforts to increase the prevalence of PF in the population will need to target the reduction of poverty.

Interpersonal coercion is probably another important influence on PF. Coercion involves the use of aversive behavior to reduce others' aversive behavior. It is one of the most important stressors on humans (Dishion & Snyder, 2015). Coercive interpersonal processes have been shown to influence the development of aggressive social behavior and marital conflict and thereby most of the psychological and behavioral problems that develop in childhood and adolescence including depression, substance abuse, early pregnancy, and academic failure (Biglan, Brennan, Foster, & Holder, 2004; Dishion & Snyder, 2015). Coercion is also involved in marital discord (Biglan, 2015) and the relationships of depressed women and their families (Biglan, 1991; Biglan, Rothlind, Hops, & Sherman, 1989). It seems highly likely that coercive processes will emerge as related to lower levels of psychological flexibility: A cardinal feature of inflexibility is avoidance of aversive events and that avoidance is precisely the function of coercive behavior.

The importance of policies. Perhaps the majority of the current CBS community comes from a clinical background. Those of us with this background will not necessarily think about how public policy can affect well-being. However, a comprehensive and pragmatic approach to improving human well-being will use whatever tools are available, and public policy can be a very powerful influence for enhancing well-being – including increasing the prevalence of psychological flexibility.

First, a set of policies could leverage further developments. One such policy would require existing health surveillance systems, such as the Behavioral Risk Factor Surveillance System (Centers for Disease Control & Prevention, 2014) and Monitoring the Future (Johnston, O'Malley, Bachman, & Schulenberg, 2010) to assess the prevalence of PF in the population. Other policies would require that the healthcare system and schools provide effective prevention and treatment interventions that affect psychological flexibility. Numerous family and school interventions reduce stress and promote prosocial behavior (National Research Council & Institute of Medicine, 2009). However, few of these have explicitly affected psychological flexibility. As the evidence on the importance of PF emerges, the impact of these interventions on PF will undoubtedly undergo investigation. In any case, to the extent that these programs improve human well-being, the CBS community will be interested in seeing them made widely available.

A second set of policies would focus on reducing the widespread use of punishment in families, schools, workplaces, and the criminal justice system. Ample justification for such policies exists, given the evidence of the harm of punitiveness and the availability of more effective and more reinforcing strategies (Gershoff, 2010). That justification will increase to the extent that epidemiological research shows that punitive practices undermine PF.

A third set of policies would focus on reducing poverty. There is good evidence that policies such as the earned income tax credit, increases in the minimum wage, unemployment insurance, and housing subsidies improve well-being (Hacker & Pierson, 2011). The CBS community should be working to have such policies enacted on that basis alone, even though there is not yet evidence that PF will increased as a result of such policies. Finding evidence that psychological inflexibility decreases along with a reduction in poverty would provide additional motivation to reduce poverty.

Efforts to Increase Psychological Flexibility in Populations

As this volume attests, extensive evidence from clinical research and research in work organizations shows that PF can be increased and that numerous psychological and health benefits result from such efforts. The natural next step would be to develop strategies that influence PF in populations through mass media or other means of reaching a wide audience.

We have been unable to find a full-blown effort to increase PF in this way, although there are some examples of approximations. Burton, Pakenham, and Brown (2010) reported a pilot test of an intervention designed to increase psychosocial resilience among volunteering administrative staff members at the University of Queensland. The intervention consisted of 11 two-hour sessions of an ACT intervention. For the 16 participants in this intervention, they found significant improvements at post-test on measures of mastery, positive emotions, personal growth, mindfulness, acceptance, stress, self-acceptance, valued living, autonomy, and total cholesterol.

Fledderus, Bohlmeijer, Smit, and Westerhof (2010) reported the evaluation of an ACT intervention they designed to promote positive mental health. They recruited a sample of 93 adults who were reporting mild to moderate psychological distress and randomly assigned them to the ACT intervention, which was delivered to seven-person groups, or a wait-list control condition. The intervention involved eight two-hour sessions. They found that the intervention led to significantly increased emotional and psychological well-being and greater psychological flexibility at three-month follow-up. Changes in psychological flexibility during the intervention mediated the effect of the intervention on well-being.

Fledderus, Bohlmeijer, Pieterse, and Schreurs (2012) reported a randomized trial of an ACT intervention that was provided to people with mild to moderate depression and thus at risk to become more seriously depressed. They randomly assigned 376 people to one of three conditions: (a) a self-help program with extensive email support, (b) the self-help program with minimal email support, or (c) a wait-list control group. Both of the self-help conditions improved people's positive mental health and mindfulness more than was true for those in the control condition at post-test and at three-month follow-up.

These studies show that psychological flexibility is a useful goal in nonclinical settings and can benefit people who are at risk for psychological difficulties. A natural next step will be to seek methods that are even more efficient in promoting psychological flexibility among populations.

Triple P – A Model for Affecting Behavior in Populations

Triple P – the Positive Parenting Program – provides a model for how we might increase the prevalence of psychological flexibility in entire populations (Prinz, Sanders, Shapiro, Whitaker, & Lutzker, 2009). Triple P reaches all families in a community with advice and support for effective parenting. Since families vary in how much information or support they need or want, Triple P provides varying levels of support. These range from mass media, public seminars on common parenting problems, tip sheets with advice about dealing with common problems, group settings, online interventions to achieve comprehensive understanding of Triple P strategies, and clinical work with individual families with serious behavioral problems. There are also interventions for families having marital problems or multiple problems. The research strategy that developed Triple P tested individual components and refined their effectiveness over time, combined them, and evaluated their impact on populations.

A substantial body of research shows the benefits of both individual components of Triple P and the whole program (Sanders, Kirby, Tellegen, & Day, 2014).

A randomized trial of Triple P conducted in South Carolina is particularly noteworthy. Prinz et al. (2009) randomly assigned 18 counties to get or not get Triple P. The targeted population consisted of parents of young children. In the nine counties that implemented Triple P, about 600 people who would regularly encounter parents of young children (e.g., preschool teachers, healthcare providers) learned to deliver Triple P components. These counties had significantly lower levels of hospital-reported child abuse and lower levels of placement of children in foster care than did the counties not receiving Triple P.

As chapter 20 of this volume indicates, little of the behavioral parenting skills training research has included and evaluated ACT-like components. But recently, Whittingham compared a version of Stepping Stones Triple P (SSTP) that included ACT components with SSTP alone and a wait-list control. Parents of children with cerebral palsy received the interventions (Whittingham, Sofronoff, Sheffield, & Sanders, 2009). She and her colleagues found that ACT improved outcomes on a variety of child behavior measures and measures of mothers' functioning.

The organization of Triple P interventions suggest a model that ACT-oriented researchers might adopt. Research on intensive levels of ACT interventions is already well advanced. And there are a number of studies that show that brief interventions can have a significant impact on important psychological outcomes (e.g., Bach & Hayes, 2002; Bach, Hayes, & Gallop, 2012; Gregg, Callaghan, Hayes, & Glenn-Lawson, 2007). Two things seem key in achieving a full Triple P-like model: (a) efficacious media interventions, including mass media, tip sheets, and apps; and (b) demonstrations that a full-blown comprehensive intervention targeting an entire population can affect psychological flexibility and important outcomes.

Methods for Reaching Populations

The Internet. One example of an ACT intervention designed to reach a population is the work of Jonathon Bricker and his colleagues at Fred Hutchinson Cancer Research Center (Heffner, Wyszynski, Comstock, Mercer, & Bricker, 2013). They developed and tested an Internet program to assist people in quitting smoking. Although the initial test included 222 nationally recruited smokers, the intervention has the potential to reach millions of smokers. The study was a double-blind randomized controlled pilot trial that compared Web-based ACT for smoking cessation (WebQuit. org) with the National Cancer Institute (NCI)'s Smokefree.gov, a web-based smoking cessation intervention. The ACT intervention consisted of a metaphor of a car journey in which the smokers try to navigate in the direction of their values for being smoke free: their thoughts, feelings, and urges are backseat passengers who undermine efforts to quit. Former smokers then model the experiential exercises and metaphors that support acceptance, defusion, self-as context, and committed action. The study found that the 30-day quit rate was 23% for the ACT intervention, which was significantly higher than the rate for the NCI website program (10%). A larger trial with a larger sample size and longer follow-up of the intervention is underway.

Tip sheets. A brief tip sheet might seem an unlikely way to help people with their problems but at least two reasons demonstrate why this could succeed. First, an intensive, community-wide effort to promote psychological flexibility could create a context in which the recommendations of one tip sheet for dealing with the loss of a loved one might be more credible and more likely for a recipient to attempt. Second, a tip sheet that reached hundreds of people might have an impact on the population, even if it affected only a small proportion of those receiving it.

Mass media. Mass media have affected many aspects of health and behavior. Experimental evaluations have shown the benefit of media campaigns in preventing smoking (Flynn et al., 1992) and marijuana use (Palmgreen, Donohew, Lorch, Hoyle, & Stephenson, 2001), and seat belt use and drinking and driving (Snyder & Hamilton, 2002). Less well-controlled studies suggest that media campaigns likely affect many other aspects of human behavior. It would thus seem useful to develop and test media campaigns to affect psychological flexibility. One approach might be to target an important health behavior such as exercise and test messages that emphasize the core components of an ACT intervention, then compare that approach with more traditional messages that emphasize the harm of not engaging in the behavior.

Empirical Evaluation

Empirical work on population-based ACT interventions could move forward in numerous ways. Experimental tests of tip sheets and apps targeting specific problems or psychological flexibility per se would be helpful. Such tests might initially proceed with convenience samples. However, the ultimate test will be whether such interventions can affect the prevalence of psychological flexibility and important psychological and behavioral outcomes in entire populations.

Given the apparent centrality of psychological flexibility in affecting diverse problems, it is possible that a community-wide intervention to increase psychological flexibility could reduce the incidence and prevalence of multiple psychological and behavioral problems. Testing such a proposition would be challenging, however. One would need to show not only that a community-wide ACT intervention affected psychological flexibility in the population, but also that it significantly lowered the rates of multiple psychological and behavioral problems. For statistical reasons, the former outcome would be easier to detect than an impact on multiple problems. That is, increasing the psychological flexibility of people who are at risk for different problems could produce small changes in the rates of multiple problems that do not rise to the level of statistically significant effects, even though collectively the impact on problems would be substantial.

Alternatively, one might target psychological flexibility in a population selected due to its risk of a specific problem. For example, one might target psychological flexibility relevant to exercise and assess its impact on the exercise levels in the population.

A CBS Public Health Approach to Reducing Prejudice

The Paradoxical Side Effects of Social Pressure to Suppress Prejudice

At a societal level, efforts to reduce prejudice[1] have often emphasized preventing and punishing problematic behaviors including racist comments, discriminatory hiring behaviors, and unequal treatment based on belonging to stigmatized groups. This includes policy efforts such as affirmative action and "hate crime" legislation as well as social processes such as activism and establishing new social norms. From a CBS perspective, establishing contingencies and reducing opportunities for prejudiced behaviors is important, but can also have unintended psychological side effects if used without additional supports.

Research indicates that motivating individuals to reduce prejudice through social pressure and to avoid social sanctions (i.e., external motivation) can worsen the problem (for a review see Butz & Plant, 2009). External motivation to control prejudiced reactions can lead to feeling angry and threatened and result in efforts to suppress prejudice, all of which ultimately increases prejudice (e.g., Plant & Devine, 2001; Wyer, 2007). This can affect interracial interactions, with excessive external motivation leading to greater anxiety and perceived threat from interracial interactions, being overly focused on not appearing racist (rather than having a positive interaction), and exhibiting more avoidance behaviors (i.e., avoiding sensitive topics, looking away from faces), which ironically leads to being perceived as more racist (Butz & Plant, 2009).

The covert and automatic forms of prejudice now common amid changing social norms and policies reveal the costs of social pressure to suppress prejudice. Aversive racism involves the competing processes of explicitly supporting egalitarian values and being motivated not to seem prejudiced while continuing to have automatic prejudiced reactions toward stigmatized groups (Gaertner & Dovidio, 2005). Automatic prejudiced reactions, sometimes referred to as implicit stereotyping (Greenwald & Banaji, 1995), involve the immediate, spontaneous, and sometimes unconscious associations people make between stigmatized groups and negative attributes (e.g., bad, dangerous, lazy, incompetent), which may be learned through exposure to these attitudes in society and media. Although social pressure may have reduced some of the most overt forms of stigmatization, research highlights the continued prevalence of many forms of discriminatory behaviors (i.e., employment, social, helping behaviors, legal) due to these automatic prejudiced reactions, even when individuals do not want to appear prejudiced, particularly in contexts involving more covert and difficult-to-control behaviors (Gaertner & Dovidio, 2005). Thus, without additional intervention strategies to address automatic prejudiced reactions, social pressure alone may simply make prejudice more difficult to detect.

Overall, this research suggests that focusing on social pressure and contingencies to prevent discriminatory behavior have side effects that need attention. A CBS analysis highlights the importance of additional public health factors, including promoting and reinforcing positive intergroup behaviors as well as increasing psychological flexibility. In the following two sections, we will discuss the use of these practices in targeting prejudice at a public health level.

Modeling, Promoting, and Reinforcing Positive Intergroup Behaviors

One of the most effective methods for prejudice reduction is intergroup contact, which targets prejudice by increasing positive interactions with members of a stigmatized group (Pettigrew & Tropp, 2006). This promotes a set of effective alternative behaviors in conjunction with strategies to prevent discriminatory behavior. Consistent with a CBS approach, context is important, as not all forms of intergroup contact will be productive: Contexts that support equality, cooperation, approval from authority, and have group members working toward a shared goal are the most effective. Thus, emphasizing establishment of nurturing environments is key in reducing toxic conditions that highlight distinctions between ingroup and outgroup (i.e., competition and inequality).

Public health efforts may seek to promote intergroup contact in almost any setting in which individuals can interact with outgroup members in a positive context. For example, within schools, the "jigsaw classroom" technique (Aronson, Blanley, Stephan, Sikes, & Snapp, 1978) is very helpful. With this technique, each student receives only part of an assignment, and students from various social groups must work together to complete the assignment. Neighborhoods and other broader communities can work together toward common goals such as setting up community parks or planning community events. In some cases, more structured experiences are helpful. These could be camping expeditions or worksite retreats, with participants from various social groups completing various activities and team-building exercises together. Modeling positive intergroup contact is also useful: Books, TV shows, public service announcements, or other media can show people of a similar background having positive contact experiences with people from other groups. Ultimately, a public health strategy may be most effective by promoting positive intergroup contact across a variety of contexts as the examples above illustrate. Developing policies and practices to promote and reinforce effective alternative behaviors with members of other groups is key to prejudice reduction and may serve to reduce the negative side effects of more punitive strategies seeking to prevent prejudice.

Promoting Psychological Flexibility to Enhance Contact and Cope With Prejudice Reactions

Public health strategies to reduce problem behavior and increase prosocial behavior are key, but these approaches do not yet address the psychology of the individual confronted with contingencies to make these behavior changes. A CBS analysis also includes consideration of the individual's psychological and historical context, which may interact with contingencies to reduce prejudice and promote positive intergroup contact. This analysis would address issues such as finding effective motivators for behavior change, promoting empathy and effective coping with anxiety during intergroup contact, and coping with learned automatic prejudiced reactions.

Enhancing motivation for intergroup contact and prejudice reduction. Excessive social pressure to be nonprejudiced may interfere with effective intergroup contact through previously mentioned pathways including increased anxiety, perceived threat, and avoidance behaviors (Butz & Plant, 2009). Furthermore, research shows that if an intergroup contact does not seem as important and meaningful to the person, it may have little psychological impact (Van Dick et al., 2004). Values work, focused on helping people identify and connect with reinforcing, meaningful patterns of activity, could be useful in shifting the focus from suppressing prejudice and appeasing others to identifying personally meaningful reasons for engaging in intergroup interactions (i.e., internal motivation). Greater internal motivation can improve the quality of intergroup contact experiences and increase intergroup contact, even when one is anxious or expects an interaction to go badly (Butz & Plant, 2009).

Values work may also help individuals identify personally relevant motivators for avoiding prejudiced behavior. Research indicates that those who are internally motivated are more effective at inhibiting prejudiced reactions, even under conditions that typically evoke them such as when self-control resources have been depleted or when intoxicated (Butz & Plant, 2009). Furthermore, when one fails to regulate prejudice, those who are more internally motivated respond by using strategies to regulate prejudice, rather than ineffective avoidance behavior or otherwise not learning from the experience (Butz & Plant, 2009).

Values work might weave into contact efforts and anti-prejudice campaigns through a combination of de-emphasizing social pressure while modeling and eliciting clarification of personal values related to equality and intergroup relationships. For example, brief writing exercises focused on identifying personal values for contact might be helpful before an intergroup event. Schools might include brief interventions in which students reflect on possible values linked to interactions with other groups and how that might translate into action. Worksite diversity programs may include overt discussion of the negative effects of social pressure and ways to clarify personal values for prejudice reduction and intergroup contact. Public service announcements might model examples of individuals valuing aspects of prosocial behavior and intergroup contact. Community events could link contact with other groups to prosocial values. At a larger level, discussions might focus on community values and their relationships to nondiscriminatory practices.

Promoting empathy and perspective-taking. Mediation results suggest intergroup contact reduces prejudice in part by increasing empathy (Pettigrew, Christ, Wagner, & Stellmacher, 2007; Pettigrew & Tropp, 2008). Similarly, perspective-taking exercises such as imagining what a minority group member is thinking and feeling have been found to reduce prejudice and enhance interracial interactions (e.g., Todd, Bodenhausen, Richeson, & Galinsky, 2011). Theoretically, empathy and perspective-taking are largely incompatible with stereotyping and prejudice and thus may be critical components to promote in conjunction with efforts to increase intergroup contact.

The psychological flexibility model highlights a number of strategies in promoting empathy and perspective-taking, including exercises to enhance flexibility and fluency with perspective-taking, practicing Vipassana (loving kindness) meditation, seeking to enhance compassion and empathy toward others, and connecting empathic responding to personal values. In some cases, connecting with the suffering of others can arouse personal distress, which if not effectively handled can further promote prejudice and avoidance behaviors. A psychological flexibility approach may also introduce methods for how to "make room" for such responses and continue to engage in the process of perspective-taking and empathy.

Such interventions may take place before an intergroup contact event, possibly as a workshop or brief intervention. Alternatively, prompts made throughout activities, such as exercises or games that involve taking another person's perspective, can be helpful. Books and other media could describe the experiences of stigmatized individuals from their perspective and characters could even model the practice of taking another's perspective.

Coping with prejudiced reactions. A key feature of modern forms of prejudice such as aversive racism (Gartner & Dovidio, 2005) is that, despite holding egalitarian values and motivation to not be prejudiced, individuals continue to hold implicit, automatic prejudice attitudes and demonstrate prejudice behaviors in certain contexts (i.e., when behavior is difficult to control). These learned, automatic prejudiced reactions are commonplace given the continued prevalence of prejudiced information in society. Examples of automatic prejudiced reactions include spontaneous, even sometimes unconscious, associations between a social group and negative attitudes such as being untrustworthy, inferior, or bad. External pressures to suppress these reactions may worsen the problem and individuals need to learn alternative ways to cope. From a psychological flexibility perspective, interventions would focus on becoming more aware of these automatic prejudiced reactions (i.e., noting the automatic thought "black people are dangerous" when seeing an African American on the street), defusing from the content of these thoughts (i.e., noticing them as just thoughts that are learned over time and not literally true), and reorienting to chosen values in guiding intergroup interactions (rather than these psychological reactions).

In addition to automatic prejudiced thoughts, some individuals might experience anxiety, or other negative emotions, in response to potential intergroup contact. Without guidance on how to respond to these emotions, some may react with maladaptive avoidance behaviors or possibly even aggressive behaviors. Promoting acceptance of intergroup anxiety as an alternative and recognizing the harmful consequences of avoidance behaviors may improve outcomes. An intergroup contact event might include direct acknowledgment that anxiety may arise but this is natural and not something to avoid.

This set of psychological flexibility processes (i.e., awareness, defusion, and acceptance of prejudiced reactions) may be particularly challenging to implement at a public health level. Concepts such as acceptance of prejudiced reactions can be misunderstood (i.e., "it's okay to have prejudiced reactions" may be perceived as "it's okay to act prejudiced") and may stand in opposition to commonsense approaches to stigma reduction (i.e., suppression). These processes may be most effective in combination, as raising awareness of prejudice without promoting acceptance and defusion could increase prejudiced reactions. Similarly, acceptance and defusion work is most effective when individuals are actively noticing their prejudiced reactions.

This combined set of processes might be effective at a public health level through ACT workshops or structured interventions in schools, worksites, and communities (cf. Lillis & Hayes, 2007). Dialogues on these themes with leaders at various levels (i.e., within a community, organization, nationally) may be encouraged through an array of outlets such as news media and town hall meetings (i.e., acknowledging the prevalence of prejudiced thoughts while also highlighting that they are just thoughts and can be treated as such rather than needing to be suppressed or acted on; normalizing anxiety reactions to intergroup contact while emphasizing the importance of making room for these emotions and persisting in having positive intergroup interactions; discussing prosocial values related to prejudice reduction while highlighting the importance of identifying your own personal motivators). Media, including TV shows, books, and movies, might also model applying these processes with prejudice, such as showing a character struggling with a biased reaction to someone, catching the process and "stepping back" from prejudiced thoughts, and modeling having an effective interaction while making room for discomfort that may arise. Implementing a variety of strategies at different levels may be most effective in developing a more flexible relationship to prejudiced reactions.

Summary of a CBS Approach to Prejudice Reduction

This chapter outlined how a CBS approach might target a prevalent, multifaceted societal issue through a combination of strategies seeking to prevent discriminatory behaviors and promote positive intergroup contact in the context of psychological flexibility processes including personal values, perspective-taking/empathy, and awareness, acceptance, and defusion from prejudiced reactions. This highlights how, even at a public health level, a CBS approach targets contingencies to prevent and promote behaviors, consideration of the individual's history, and how one might relate to the resulting internal reactions to change behavior effectively. The available evidence does not provide clear guidance regarding how best to implement a PF-informed prejudice reduction campaign at a public health level. Given the CBS focus on theoretical processes rather than static techniques, a particularly wide range of potential strategies exists. The best path forward may be to implement a variety of approaches to determine the most effective.

Note

1   We use the term "prejudice" in this chapter to refer to the broad range of prejudiced attitudes, stigmatizing thoughts, and discriminatory behaviors directed toward socially identified groups of people or the individuals perceived as belonging to those groups.

References

Aronson, E., Blanley, N., Stephan, W., Sikes, J. & Snapp, M. (1978). *The jigsaw classroom.* Thousand Oaks, CA: Sage.

Bach, P., & Hayes, S. C. (2002). The use of acceptance and commitment therapy to prevent the rehospitalization of psychotic patients: A randomized controlled trial. *Journal of Consulting and Clinical Psychology, 70,* 1129–1139.

Bach, P., Hayes, S. C., & Gallop, R. (2012). Long-term effects of brief acceptance and commitment therapy for psychosis. *Behavior Modification, 36,* 165–181.

Biglan, A. (1991). Distressed behavior and its context. *The Behavior Analyst, 14,* 157–169.

Biglan, A. (2015). Coercion and public health. In T. J. Dishion & J. Snyder (Eds.), *The Oxford handbook of coercive dynamics in close relationships: Implications for development, psychopathology and intervention science* (chapter 27). New York, NY: Oxford University Press. DOI: 10.1093/oxfordhb/9780199324552.013.10

Biglan, A., Brennan, P. A., Foster, S. L., & Holder, H. D. (2004). *Helping adolescents at risk: Prevention of multiple problem behaviors.* New York, NY: Guilford.

Biglan, A., Hayes, S. C., & Pistorello, J. (2008). Acceptance and commitment: Implications for prevention science. *Prevention Science, 9,* 139–152.

Biglan, A., Rothlind, J., Hops, H., & Sherman, L. (1989). Impact of distressed and aggressive behavior. *Journal of Abnormal Psychology, 98,* 218–228.

Burton, N. W., Pakenham, K. I., & Brown, W. J. (2010). Feasibility and effectiveness of psychosocial resilience training: A pilot study of the READY program. *Psychology, Health, & Medicine, 15,* 266–277.

Butz, D. A., & Plant, E.A. (2009). Prejudice control and interracial relations: The role of motivation to respond without prejudice. *Journal of Personality, 77,* 1311–1342.

Centers for Disease Control & Prevention. (2014). *Behavioral Risk Factor Surveillance System.* Retrieved from http://www.cdc.gov/brfss/

Dishion, T. J., & Snyder, J. (Eds). (2015). *The Oxford handbook of coercive dynamics in close relationships: Implications for development, psychopathology and intervention science.* New York, NY: Oxford University Press.

Fledderus, M., Bohlmeijer, E. T., Pieterse, M. E., & Schreurs, K. M. G. (2012). Acceptance and commitment therapy as guided self-help for psychological distress and positive mental health: A randomized controlled trial. *Psychological Medicine, 42*, 485–495.

Fledderus, M., Bohlmeijer, E. T., Smit, F., & Westerhof, G. J. (2010). Mental health promotion as a new goal in public mental health care: A randomized controlled trial of an intervention enhancing psychological flexibility. *American Journal of Public Health, 100,* 2372–2372.

Flynn, B. S., Worden, J. K., Secker-Walker, R. H., Badger, G. J., Geller, B. M., & Costanza, M. C. (1992). Prevention of cigarette smoking through mass media intervention and school programs. *American Journal of Public Health, 82*, 827–834.

Gaertner, S. L., & Dovidio, J. F. (2005). Understanding and addressing contemporary racism: From aversive racism to the common ingroup identity model. *Journal of Social Issues, 61,* 615–639.

Galobardes, B., Lynch, J. W., & Smith, G. D. (2008). Is the association between childhood socioeconomic circumstances and cause-specific mortality established? Update of a systematic review. *Journal of Epidemiology and Community Health, 62*, 387–390.

Gershoff, E. T. (2010). More harm than good: A summary of scientific research on the intended and unintended effects of corporal punishment on children. *Law and Contemporary Problems, 73*, 31–56.

Greenwald, A. G., & Banaji, M.R. (1995). Implicit social cognition: Attitudes, self-esteem, and stereotypes. *Psychological Review, 102*, 4–27.

Gregg, J. A., Callaghan, G. M., Hayes, S. C., & Glenn-Lawson, J. L. (2007). Improving diabetes self-management through acceptance, mindfulness, and values: a randomized controlled trial. *Journal of Consulting and Clinical Psychology, 75*, 336–343.

Hacker, J. S., & Pierson, P. (2011). *Winner-take-all politics: How Washington made the rich richer – and turned its back on the middle class.* New York, NY: Simon & Schuster.

Hayes, S. C., Luoma, J. B., Bond, F. W., Masuda, A., & Lillis, J. (2006). Acceptance and commitment therapy: Model, processes and outcomes. *Behaviour Research and Therapy, 44*, 1–25.

Hayes, S. C., Strosahl, K., Wilson, K. G., Bissett, R. T., Pistorello, J., Toarmino, D., … McCurry, S. M. (2004). Measuring experiential avoidance: A preliminary test of a working model. *The Psychological Record, 54*, 553–578.

Heffner, J. L., Wyszynski, C. M., Comstock, B., Mercer, L. D., & Bricker, J. (2013). Overcoming recruitment challenges of web-based interventions for tobacco use: The case of web-based acceptance and commitment therapy for smoking cessation. *Addictive Behaviors, 38*, 2473–2476.

Johnston, L. D., O'Malley, P. M., Bachman, J. G., & Schulenberg, J. E. (2010). *Monitoring the Future: National Survey Results on Drug Use, 1975–2009.* NIH Publication No. 10-7584. Bethesda, MD: National Institute on Drug Abuse.

Kashdan, T. B., & Kane, J. Q. (2011). Post-traumatic distress and the presence of post-traumatic growth and meaning in life: Experiential avoidance as a moderator. *Personality and Individual Differences, 50*, 84–89.

Lillis, J., & Hayes, S. C. (2007). Applying acceptance, mindfulness, and values to the reduction of prejudice: A pilot study. *Behavior Modification, 31*, 389–411.

National Center for Law & Economic Justice. (2013). *Poverty in the United States: A snapshot.* Retrieved from http://www.nclej.org/poverty-in-the-us.php

National Research Council and Institute of Medicine. (2009). *Preventing mental, emotional, and behavioral disorders among young people: Progress and possibilities.* Washington, DC: National Academies Press.

Palmgreen, P., Donohew, L., Lorch, E. P., Hoyle, R. H., & Stephenson, M. T. (2001). Television campaigns and adolescent marijuana use: Tests of sensation seeking targeting. *American Journal of Public Health, 91*, 292–296.

Pettigrew, T. F., Christ, O., Wagner, U., & Stellmacher, J. (2007). Direct and indirect intergroup contact effects on prejudice: A normative interpretation. *International Journal of Intercultural Relations, 31*, 411–425.

Pettigrew, T. F., & Tropp, L. R. (2006). A meta-analytic test of intergroup contact theory. *Journal of Personality and Social Psychology, 90*, 751–783.

Pettigrew, T. F., & Tropp, L. R. (2008). How does intergroup contact reduce prejudice? Meta-analytic tests of three mediators? *European Journal of Social Psychology, 38*, 922–934.

Plant, E. A., & Devine, P. G. (2001). Responses to other-imposed pro-black pressure: Acceptance or backlash? *Journal of Experimental Social Psychology, 37*, 486–501.

Prinz, R. J., Sanders, M. R., Shapiro, C. J., Whitaker, D. J., & Lutzker, J. R. (2009). Population-based prevention of child maltreatment: The US Triple P system population trial. *Prevention Science, 10*, 1–12.

Sanders, M. R., Kirby, J. N., Tellegen, C. L., & Day, J. J. (2014). The Triple P-Positive Parenting Program: A systematic review and meta-analysis of a multi-level system of parenting support. *Clinical Psychology Review, 34*, 337–357.

Snyder, L. B., & Hamilton, M. A. (2002). A meta-analysis of US health campaign effects on behavior: Emphasize enforcement, exposure, and new information, and beware the secular trend. In R. Hornik, *Public health communication: Evidence for behavior change* (pp. 357–383). New York, NY: Erlbaum.

Todd, A. R., Bodenhausen, G. V., Richeson, J. A., & Galinsky, A. D. (2011). Perspective taking combats automatic expressions of racial bias. *Journal of Personality and Social Psychology, 100*, 1027–1042.

Van Dick, R., Wagner, U., Pettigrew, T. F., Christ, O., Wolf, C., Petzel, T., ... Jackson, J. S. (2004). The role of perceived importance in intergroup contact. *Journal of Personality and Social Psychology, 87*, 211–227.

Wegman, H. L., & Stetler, C. (2009). A meta-analytic review of the effects of childhood abuse on medical outcomes in adulthood. *Psychosomatic Medicine, 71*, 805–812.

Whittingham, K., Sofronoff, K., Sheffield, J., & Sanders, M. R. (2009). Stepping Stones Triple P: An RCT of a parenting program with parents of a child diagnosed with an autism spectrum disorder. *Journal of Abnormal Child Psychology, 37*, 469–480.

Wyer, N. A. (2007). Motivational influences on compliance with and consequences of stereotype suppression. *Journal of Experimental Social Psychology, 43*, 417–424.

Yoshikawa, H., Aber, J. L., & Beardslee, W. R. (2012). The effects of poverty on the mental, emotional, and behavioral health of children and youth: Implications for prevention. *American Psychologist, 67*, 272–284.

24

The Evolution of Capitalism
Anthony Biglan, Jean Lee, and Christine Cody

"As a functional contextualist sees it, the ultimate purpose of behavioral science is to change the world in a positive and intentional way." (Hayes, Barnes-Holmes, & Wilson, 2012, p. 2)

It might seem that a contextual analysis of capitalism is far afield from the interests of the CBS community. However, if our goal is to improve human well-being (Hayes et al., 2012), we are naturally concerned with predicting and influencing all the factors affecting it. In this chapter, we briefly review the ways that capitalism has both enhanced and detracted from well-being. We then offer an evolutionary account of capitalism and sketch its implications for evolving an economic and political system that more effectively contributes to human well-being.

The Impact of Capitalism on Human Well-Being

Economic, Technological, and Health Benefits of Capitalism

It is easy to see the benefits of capitalism. Its economic benefits are substantial. Catherine Mulbrandon estimated that the gross domestic product per capita over the past 2,000 years (Mulbrandon, 2007) went from $467 to $667 between the birth of Christ and 1800. Since then it has risen to $6,055. This dramatic increase was initially concentrated in Europe, the United States, Canada, and Japan, all of which have evolved capitalist systems. In the past 50 years, economic well-being has increased dramatically in other countries. If you search online for Hans Rosling and "200 years of global growth," you can view a fascinating depiction of this growth and its impact on longevity; it illustrates how countries such as India and China have grown economically since they adopted capitalist practices (Rosling, 2010).

Consider engineering and technology: In 1850, it took about two and a half months to travel from New York to San Francisco. Now it takes five and a half hours. Or consider telecommunications: In 1900, you could speak to someone across the country, but it was very expensive and the connection was often not good. Now you can see and speak to anyone in the world at no cost. In healthcare, we have drugs and

The Wiley Handbook of Contextual Behavioral Science, First Edition. Edited by Robert D. Zettle, Steven C. Hayes, Dermot Barnes-Holmes, and Anthony Biglan.
© 2016 John Wiley & Sons, Ltd. Published 2016 by John Wiley & Sons, Ltd.

surgical procedures that have significantly enhanced lives. These advances are due to developments in science and engineering, but they occurred first in capitalist countries, which had the financial contingencies to motivate innovation and the translation of scientific findings into marketable products.

Deleterious Consequences of Capitalism

Three of the most important and well-documented harms of the capitalist system are the marketing of harmful substances, the successful advocacy of some sectors of the capitalist system to achieve and maintain public policies that benefit some at the expense of the well-being of the rest of society, and the environmental degradation associated with the productive capacities of capitalism.

Marketing. To be profitable, companies must market their products. The public benefit of marketing practices includes making people aware of useful products and services and stimulating economic activity that contributes to prosperity. However, companies can also market harmful products. Perhaps the most extensively studied and well-documented example of this is tobacco marketing. Thanks to numerous lawsuits and considerable public health research, the harm of tobacco company marketing is well established. In *United States vs. Philip Morris USA, Inc.* (2006), the federal court held that, over a 50-year period, the companies had (a) systematically denied that cigarettes were harmful despite knowing that they caused cancer; (b) marketed to youth, while all the while denying that they did so; and (c) falsely claimed that low tar and nicotine cigarettes were safer in order to prevent smokers from quitting. Despite tobacco company denials regarding the impact of cigarette marketing on youth smoking initiation, substantial empirical evidence – including randomized trials of the impact of marketing – shows that such marketing leads directly to youth starting to smoke (National Cancer Institute, 2008). A study by Pierce, Gilpin, and Choi (1999) concluded that the marketing of Marlboro cigarettes between 1988 and 1998 would eventually lead to the deaths of 300,000 young people who became addicted as teens. Because the Joe Camel campaign was so successful during this period, they concluded that it would eventually result in the death of 520,000 people. Such marketing is thus a health hazard in the same way that raw sewage is.

Marketing of alcohol and unhealthful food is also a health hazard, although the impact of these practices is not as well established as marketing for cigarettes. Evidence indicates that a larger volume of alcohol ads reach youth than adults, despite an industry standard that limits advertising on TV and in magazines to media with an audience comprised of 30% or less of those under 18. By concentrating advertising in the venues closer to 30% than 0%, the companies reach many young people. An average teen sees about 245 alcohol ads on TV per year, while those who view the most may see as many as 780 per year (Pechmann, Biglan, Grube, & Cody, 2012).

One indication of the impact of alcohol advertising is that young people who see more alcohol ads know more about alcohol and are more familiar with the brands (Pechmann et al., 2012). Several experiments indicate that showing alcohol ads to young people makes them more interested in drinking (Grube, Madden, & Friese 1996). Some, but not all, studies show communities with more alcohol advertising have more youth who drink and more alcohol-related motor vehicle fatalities (Grube & Nygaard 2005), though it is not currently possible to draw firm conclusions about whether advertising causes these outcomes.

There is an association with low socioeconomic status, obesity, and lack of access to health foods. Studies have suggested that availability is associated with the consumption of fruits and vegetables (Krebs-Smith, Cook, Subar, Cleveland, & Friday, 1995; Pamuk, Makuk, Heck, & Reuben, 1998). A nationwide US study found that zip codes of low income had 1.3 times as many convenience stores and 25% fewer supermarket chains than middle-income zip code areas (Powell, Slater, Mirtcheva, Bao, & Chaloupka, 2007). A study of more than 10,000 adults found that those living in neighborhoods with supermarkets and grocery stores had 20% obesity rates and those living with access to only convenience or smaller grocery stores had rates of 32 to 40% (Morland, Diex Roux, & Wing, 2006). Though many studies focus on urban communities, access is also a challenge in rural communities. A study of 418 communities nationwide showed that 20% of rural US counties had residents that lived 10 miles or more from the nearest supermarket (Morton & Blanchard, 2007). It has been found that larger stores were more likely to stock a greater variety of healthful foods (Baker, Schootman, Barnidge, & Kelly, 2006; Horowitz, Colson, Hebert, & Lancaster, 2004; Hosler, Varadarajulu, Ronsani, Fredrick, & Fisher, 2006; Jetter & Cassady, 2006) at lower prices (Mantovani, Daft, Macaluso, Welsh, & Hoffman, 1997).

Poverty and economic inequality. Despite the general improvement in economic wellbeing that has accompanied capitalist development, there are also economic problems that have resulted from some recent practices of capitalism. The most obvious example is the Great Recession, which began in 2008 when stock markets around the world crashed, banks went under, and unemployment soared, resulting in home foreclosures and enormous stress and difficulty for millions of people. Below, we describe the changes in public opinion and policy-making over the last 40 years that led to increased poverty and inequality and to the economic crisis that began in 2008.

Environmental degradation. The increased productivity that has accompanied the growth of capitalism in the past 200 years has increased economic well-being on a massive scale. However, it has also contributed to degradation of the environment. There is no longer doubt that human caused climate change is occurring (National Aeronautics and Space Administration Consensus, n.d.). Yet governmental response to the problem remains limited, in part because of lobbying by industries that stand to lose if policies are enacted that curb the emission of greenhouse gases (e.g., Greenpeace, n.d.). A science that could increase our ability to curtail corporate practices that are contributing to climate change may ultimately prove to be the most important contribution that contextual behavioral scientists could make to human well-being.

An Evolutionary Account of Capitalism

It is useful to think of capitalism as an evolutionary system in which the practices of those participating in a market are selected by their economic consequences.

Ellen Meiksins Wood has written about the nature and evolution of capitalism (Wood, 2002). She argues that capitalism evolved out of a set of unique conditions in England that led to a form of agrarian capitalism. According to her account, capitalism first emerged in the agricultural system of England beginning in the sixteenth century. The unique conditions in England included the fact that peasants did not own the land they farmed. Instead, landowners owned very large parcels of land, which they rented to farmers. In other countries, feudal lords extracted wealth from peasant farmers through taxation. However, in England, the large landowners did not have the power to extract wealth in this way; only the monarchy enjoyed such power. Thus, large landowners had an incentive to rent their land to the highest bidder. In turn, this created an incentive for farmers to increase their productivity, as doing so would increase their income, which, among other things, enabled them to rent more land. It also meant that the more productive farmers pushed out the less productive ones, creating a growing population of people with no property who subsisted on wages only. Over the ensuing centuries, these trends accelerated. Wealthy landlords appropriated land that had been common property as the law increasingly favored such "enclosures." Agricultural productivity increased substantially due to the competition among farmers. The mass of landless peasants increased and London grew as these wage-seekers flooded the city.

These conditions set the stage for the evolution of industrial capitalism. The large pool of relatively poor wage-earners provided both a resource for the creation of manufacturing and a market for inexpensive mass-produced goods. The competition among these wage laborers meant that owners could produce goods at low cost and the competition among producers drove them to pay as little as possible. The high level of agricultural productivity ensured that this mass of wage laborers was not necessary to produce the food for feeding the population.

Wood contrasts these conditions with the way in which merchants had made their money throughout history. Up until this point, their wealth arose from arbitrage: "buying low in one market and selling high in another." That system did not put the same pressure on owners to increase their wealth by increasing the productivity of the producers.

From this perspective, the two critical features of capitalism were (a) the competition among owners for the most efficient production, which could mean the difference between survival or extinction in the marketplace; and (b) competition among laborers, which ensured an inexpensive labor force and made possible the production of inexpensive mass-produced goods, such as textiles and cooking utensils.

The Marxist view of this evolution is that the owners – the capitalists – were expropriating the value produced by the workers (Wood, 2002). The surplus of workers forced workers to compete for jobs by agreeing to work for wages that were well below the value that they created in the goods they produced. That value turned into profits for the owners. This is a key issue that we will come back to, because how society allocates that wealth is pivotal for human well-being.

The Evolution of Corporate Capitalism

David Sloan Wilson (Sober & Wilson, 1999; Wilson, 2007) has shown that evolution proceeds at multiple levels. Whether we are concerned with genes, single-celled organisms, individual multicelled organisms, groups of organisms, individual organizations, or groups of organizations, environmental conditions can vary such that they select the individual or the collectivity. By this view, multicelled organisms evolved when environmental conditions favored the working together of single-celled organisms.

Consider the environmental conditions that were in place as capitalism evolved. Competition among owners favored those who cooperated in business ventures. For example, in the early stages of exploration and international trade, an investor might pay to have a ship cross the Atlantic, an endeavor with substantial risk. Loss of that ship would mean the ruin of the investor. However, if a group of investors put together the capital for a fleet of ships, they could hedge their bets in such a way the loss of one ship would ruin nobody yet all would profit from the success of those ships that "made it." Over time, competition has increasingly favored organizations over individuals. The cooperation of groups of investors that constituted the early corporations frequently advantaged them in the marketplace, compared with investors acting alone. Thus, over the past 200 years, the competition at the heart of capitalism has selected corporations.

Cray (2007) reviewed the history of US corporations. During the nineteenth century, states allowed corporations to exist through a chartering system. Corporations had to meet certain public obligations. The charters placed limits on their "capitalization, debt, land holdings, and sometimes even profits" (Cray, 2007, p. 67). The charters' intent was to ensure that corporations acted in the public interest. The charters remained in place for a set number of years, which helped to ensure that the corporations remained accountable to the state.

Today, none of this is true. Virtually any group can incorporate to pursue any goal. This was illustrated when Robert Hinkley, a corporate lawyer turned activist, created a corporation in Virginia called "Licensed to Kill, Inc." The state readily registered this corporation, whose stated aim was "the manufacture and marketing of tobacco products in a way that each year kills over 400,000 Americans and 4.5 million other persons worldwide" (Cray & Drutman, 2005).

Corporations now dominate not only business but also the making of public policy. The freedom and power of corporations is the natural result of capitalism's evolution. Considering the competitive nature of the market, it behooves actors – whether individual or corporate – to do whatever it takes to maximize their profits. This of course includes improving the quality of goods and services and producing efficiently. But any other action that would increase profits will contribute to the survival of the business enterprise. Two of the most important practices that have evolved are influencing governments and marketing goods and services.

Influencing Governments

Businesses can benefit in at least two ways from influencing governments. One way is to ensure that government laws and regulations are favorable to the interests of the company. That would include preventing or reducing taxation and regulations that are costly. The other is by influencing governments to purchase the company's product.

In recent years, at least in the United States, businesses have increased their investment in influencing governments. Expenditures on lobbying in the United States rose from $1.45 billion in 1998 to $3.31 billion in 2012 (OpenSecrets, 2014).

Marketing

Over the past 200 years, companies have evolved increasingly effective methods of influencing people to buy their products and services. This too is an evolutionary process in which any company's success in wresting market share from its competitors through advertising reinforced those successful practices and encouraged competitors to adopt them or attempt to improve on them.

(The behavioral sciences played a role in these developments. After John B. Watson, the "father" of behaviorism, had to leave academia because of an extramarital affair, he went into advertising and became a vice president in the J. Walter Thompson advertising agency.) Increasingly, the skill and resources that large corporations can devote to marketing have translated into influencing public opinion to be favorable to business interests.

Influencing the Practices of Modern-Day Capitalism

From the perspective of the contextual behavioral science movement, we are concerned with predicting and influencing corporate practices. And given our explicit commitment to ensuring human well-being (chapter 19 in this volume; Biglan & Embry, 2013), we are particularly interested in pinpointing practices that are harmful – as we have done above – and identifying manipulable variables that will evolve those practices in directions that are more beneficial.

Prescientific Efforts to Influence Capitalist Practices

Like the evolutionary "arms race" that occurs in the natural world (e.g., the natural camouflage of a chameleon or pathogens increasing resistance to antibiotics), a natural and continuing struggle exists between individuals and organizations that are trying to maximize their profits and individuals and organizations that are attempting to moderate or mitigate harmful business practices (Frank, 2011). As noted above, among the practices that business evolves are methods of influencing governments to allow profitable practices. But, as harmful practices emerge, citizens and governments will seek to implement new laws and regulatory practices to prohibit or regulate harmful practices. Recognizing these as parallel evolutionary processes may help to identify ways to strengthen practices that ensure protection of the public interest.

The history of efforts in the United States to moderate the worst influences of capitalism is instructive in this regard. As the industrial revolution proceeded in the United States, the political and market power of large industrial trusts grew with it. At the same time, between 1850 and 1930, about 25 million Europeans immigrated to the United States, creating a large pool of cheap labor, which kept labor costs low for companies.

Political movements to reign in the power of corporations have waxed and waned since the late nineteenth century. In the Progressive Era in the United States, between 1890 and 1920, the congress passed numerous laws to increase corporate regulation (Kearns Goodwin, 2013). The Interstate Commerce Act created the Interstate Commerce Commission and restricted monopolistic practices of railroads. The Sherman Anti-Trust Act prohibited monopolistic control in any industry.

However, Progressive Era laws did not set limits on banking and stock market practices. The Great Depression, which began in 1929, eventually led to a Senate investigation of the banking industry. Ferdinand Pecora, the chief counsel of the Senate Committee on Banking and Currency, who led the hearings, revealed that commercial banks had moved into the sale of stock, despite laws that ostensibly prohibited them from doing so. Pecora showed that major banks, such as City Bank (now Citicorp) were aggressively marketing stocks and bonds that were of questionable value, without informing consumers – or their own stockholders – of the risks involved (Perino, 2010). The hearings led to the enactment of the Glass-Steagall Act, which prohibited banks from simultaneously engaging in both commercial lending and investment, and to the creation of the Securities and Exchange Commission, which imposed stringent requirements regarding the information to be provided to would-be purchasers of stocks and bonds (Perino, 2010).

These reforms contributed to a period of economic stability in which recessions were mild and short-lived compared with those of earlier eras (Moynihan, 1997). However, that period ended in 2008, when a very substantial recession set in. Several authors document the causes of this catastrophe (e.g., Lewis, 2010; 2011; McLean & Nocera, 2010; Smith, 2012). The repeal of Glass-Steagall allowed banks to return to the creation and marketing of stocks and bonds. They created "collateralized debt obligations" (CDOs), consisting of sets of home mortgages, which banks then sold to investors. Whereas traditionally banks held home mortgages, leaving the banks liable to lose money if the homeowner defaulted, local lenders now had a market in which they could sell these CDOs. They thus no longer had an incentive to be cautious about the creditworthiness of borrowers.

At the same time, the big banks which were creating and selling these CDOs put pressure on the three major auditing companies to give these instruments high ratings for soundness, which they did (McLean & Nocera, 2010). Here, too, understanding the contingencies involved is pivotal to understanding what happened. The auditing firms received payment from the banks to certify that CDOs were safe investments. They were competing with the other firms for this business. Their incentives were entirely on the side of their providing high ratings. No behaviorally sophisticated person would expect the firms to act other than the way they did. This is an important example of why the thoroughgoing application of the selection by consequences principles is so important.

Building a Functional Contextualist Science of Capitalism

There is no doubt that research on the evolution of corporate practices goes well beyond the areas in which contextual behavioral scientists have been working. However, there are at least two reasons why such an expansion is appropriate. The first is that achieving improvements in the well-being of entire populations will require understanding the impact of our capitalist system on these problems and an improvement in our ability to predict and influence the organizational practices that affect these problems.

Second, no other area of the human sciences is pursuing a functional contextualist analysis of the actions of corporations. The development of a science that enables the prediction – and influence – of the actions of corporations seems fundamental to achieving a society in which the deleterious effects of capitalism are minimized, while its benefits for human well-being are retained.

This is not to say that the current community of contextual behavioral scientists has all of the knowledge and skill needed to make progress in this area. But the "grand vision" of the CBS movement is that it will bring together people from all areas of the human sciences who (a) share the commitment to "change the world in a positive and intentional way," (b) have relevant expertise, and (c) become convinced that pursuing the goal of prediction-and-influence will be most likely to bring about the desired positive changes (Wilson, Hayes, Biglan, & Embry, 2014a; 2014b).

Below are suggestions for the major research activities that seem needed to advance a functional contextualist science of corporate action. The analysis has focused almost entirely on the United States. However, the basic processes influencing the practices of capitalism in the United States are applicable to other countries. Over the past 20 years, the world has seen an enormous increase in capitalist practices as most communist countries have moved to some form of capitalism.

Identify harmful corporate practices through correlational and experimental research. Above we have sketched some of the evidence regarding a number of harmful corporate practices. Further research that elaborates the evidence is necessary for at least three reasons. First, at least for the impact of alcohol and food marketing, we still lack *experimental* evidence that these practices influence youth behavior (Biglan, 2015). Until we have experimental evidence, we cannot rule out the possibility that those who encounter more ads and who drink or eat unhealthful foods do so because of some third variable. Companies engaged in the marketing will make these arguments and it will be impossible to get vital policy change without experimental evidence (Biglan, 2011; Biglan & Embry, 2013).

Second, it will be critical to have clear and convincing evidence about the harmfulness of a corporate practice in generating public support for the needed policy changes. Third, identifying deleterious corporate practices will delineate the practices whose contextual influences we need to study.

Analyze the contingencies that shape and maintain harmful and beneficial practices. As we pinpoint corporate practices that are most strongly related to human well-being, we will need to understand the context that shapes and maintains these practices. It would seem that there are two types of influences on corporate practice: economic consequences and the social system that shapes and maintains the values of corporate leaders. An adequately reticulated theory will need to integrate them.

1   *Economic consequences to corporations.* There is ample suggestive evidence of the influence of economic consequences on corporate practices (Chaloupka, 2013). However, there is little experimental evidence. Correlational studies would lay the groundwork and justification for experimental manipulation. At first glance, it might seem impossible to conduct an experimental manipulation of the economic consequences of corporate practices. However, given the multiplicity of legal jurisdictions in the United States and around the world, it is possible to implement a policy in some jurisdictions and not others and compare the outcomes. This is particularly true in the United States, where states have considerable latitude in implementing laws that affect consequences for corporations, for Australian states, and for members of the European Union.

For example, consider a policy that might have affected the marketing of cigarettes to young people. When 46 states sued the tobacco companies over the harm of cigarettes, the states discussed a policy that they ended up not adopting: they proposed that the Master Settlement Agreement (National Association of Attorneys General, 1998) then under negotiation would include a "look-back" provision so that the companies would have to pay more for every teenager who started smoking. The policy would have provided a clear, negative consequence for influencing young people to smoke. The tobacco companies did not agree to the provision and so the provision was not part of the final agreement. Incidentally, the companies continued to market to young people after adoption of the Master Settlement Agreement (Biglan, 2004).

It would be possible to implement such a policy in individual states or countries and to observe its impact on the initiation of youth smoking. In fact, this could take place in rigorous experiments.

One of the oft-praised features of the US federalist system is that it enables states to "experiment" with public policy, thus enabling the nation as a whole to benefit from useful innovations arising in individual states. For the most part, such experimentation has simply involved "natural experiments" in which one state happens to implement a policy and others observe its impact. For example, Wagenaar, Erickson, Harwood, and O'Malley (2006) evaluated the impact of coalitions to reduce underage drinking in 10 states. They compared their impact to what happened over eight years in the 40 states that did not implement coalitions. They found that states that implemented coalitions had greater changes on media coverage of the problem, state policies enacted, youth drinking behaviors, and alcohol-related car crash fatalities.

Nothing prevents additional organized experiments. An organization that wanted to reduce youth smoking could choose a small number of states that might implement such a policy. The group could identify a set of states in which such a policy had some hope of passing, choose one at random and concentrate their resources for advocacy in that state, and go on to a second, randomly chosen state only after they had succeeded in the first state. Such a strategy would test not only the effect of the policy on tobacco company practices but also the strategy for getting the policy adopted. And, it would likely be more efficient and effective than a strategy that spread the organization's resources thinly across many states.

2   *Relational networks involving values.* Human behavior is rule-governed and people run corporations. Analyzing the contingencies that influence corporate practices could identify powerful consequences, but if we also analyze the relational responding of the people running the corporations, we will better understand what it will take to influence change in corporate practices. Below are some examples of relational networks that seem likely to affect the actions of corporate leaders.

The first is the ideology of capitalism. Much discussion about free market capitalism implies well-established, unalterable verities. For example, the free market ideology promoted over the past 40 years indicates that virtually any government regulation or business taxation is harmful and that corporations' unfettered pursuit of profit is necessary in the interest of everyone in society (e.g., Friedman & Friedman, 1990). Corporate leaders who subscribe to these relational networks will naturally resist any policy proposals that would curtail their profits, regardless of any claims that the policy would benefit the greater public. (Indeed, according to this ideology, a regulatory policy that was beneficial to the society would be impossible.)

Related relational networks that could motivate corporate leaders to resist policies that threaten their profits include the ideology of materialism, and simply the competitive ideology that equates making money to a person's value as a human being. Obviously, there is no inherent reason why these ideologies would be influential in every corporation. Warren Buffett's criticism (Isidore, 2013) of a tax system that has him paying a lower rate of income tax than his secretary is an example.

More research would illuminate the relational networks that motivate opposition to publicly beneficial policies. Interventions that would modify such thinking could be of great benefit. For example, strategies that involve embedding existing relational networks within larger systems that alter the functions of existing networks could identify ways of framing the matter to help reduce resistance (Barnes-Holmes, Hayes, Barnes-Holmes, & Roche, 2002). For example, approaches such as, "We want policies that benefit not only our company, but the public at large," or "Policies should be empirically evaluated for their impact on well-being," could lower resistance to policy proposals.

Strengthening Advocacy Organizations

Ironically, effective action in influencing corporate and capitalist practices may depend more on our strengthening the effectiveness of organizations working for the needed changes than on directly influencing the practices of corporations.

To understand the ecology of public policy-making, it is instructive to study the evolution of advocacy for business over the past 40 years. In 1970, public opinion and policy-making were not as favorable to corporations as they had been in earlier eras. Concerns about the risk to business if public opinion remained so negative led a small circle of business people to create a network of organizations to advocate for business and business-friendly policies. A memo from the soon-to-be Supreme Court Justice Lewis Powell, which he wrote for the Chair of the Chamber of Commerce Education Committee, is widely credited with providing the strategic plan for this effort (Alterman, 2008; Hacker & Pierson, 2011; Lapham, 2004). The memo recommended comprehensive and coordinated efforts from the business community. It led to the creation and increased funding of a large number of think tanks and advocacy organizations, such as the Heritage Foundation and the American Enterprise Institute, which have consistently advocated free market views. It also prompted establishing scholarships in major universities (e.g., Harvard, Yale, and the University of Chicago) to nurture the careers of conservative scholars.

Hacker and Pierson (2011) and Alterman (2008) document the details and the success of these efforts. Due to these efforts, public opinion and policies affecting business have changed dramatically in the past 40 years. The income tax rates on the highest earners in the United States decreased from 91% in 1956 to 35% in 2003 (Tax Foundation, 2013). The Glass-Steagall law that put controls on banks' involvement in securities trading was slowly eroded, starting in the 1960s, and was repealed in 1999. The percentage of Americans who are union members has declined from 35% in 1954 to 12% in 2012 (Bureau of Labor Statistics, 2014), due in part to a series of policies that have curtailed the ability of unions to organize (Hacker & Pierson, 2011). Perhaps the most telling indication of the increase in power of business corporations is the Supreme Court's Citizens United decision. The court ruled that corporations had essentially the same free speech rights as individual citizens. They now can spend any amount of money they want to get candidates they favored elected.

A similar development appears needed if we are going to reverse the evolution of the past 40 years and evolve societies that constrain the harmful practices of corporate capitalism. That is, it is necessary to create a societal movement that strengthens prosocial cultural practices: practices that teach, promote, and richly reinforce behaviors and organizational actions that benefit others. The CBS community can take many steps to nurture such a movement. Below are some specific suggestions.

Promote prosociality. The significant changes in public opinion and public policy that the just described business advocacy movement achieved were accompanied by significant increases in the degree to which young Americans endorse materialistic values and by declines in their endorsement of altruistic, prosocial values (Biglan, 2015). Although it is impossible to sort out the causal relationships in these developments, it seems likely that there was a reciprocal process in which increased advocacy for the free market ideology (which says that when people pursue their own material well-being, it will necessarily benefit others) encouraged materialistic values and that increasing materialism garnered public support for business-friendly policies.

Much of the research and practice of the CBS community is relevant to these cultural changes. Some research suggests that psychological flexibility is associated with greater compassion and the embrace of values having to do with the well-being of others (Atkins & Parker, 2011). In addition, recent work has articulated a constellation of values and behaviors that have been labeled prosociality (Biglan & Embry, 2013; Wilson et al., 2014a; 2014b) and efforts are underway to assist groups in working effectively together in prosocial ways.

It would be valuable to evaluate whether clinical or community interventions that promote prosociality (in particular compassion for others and psychological flexibility) affects people's materialism and their support for advocacy organizations and public policies that would constrain deleterious business practices.

Cultivate a cadre of people working for societal well-being. The CBS community is increasing the number of people in poorer countries who are learning about contextual behavioral science through a system of scholarships. And there is a growing cadre of people doing research and practice with organizations. Moreover, there is increasing attention to how ACT interventions increase prosociality (Atkins & Parker, 2011; Wilson et al., 2014a). As these efforts expand, we might explore how we could cultivate a cadre of people who are skilled in working on the reform of capitalism. Research that showed that corporate practices could be influenced either by influencing the values and behavior of corporate leaders or by influencing policies that select better corporate practices would provide the scientific basis for such a cadre to expand and play an increasing role in societies' efforts to evolve a form of capitalism that maximizes human well-being.

Our society came under the thrall of free market ideology over the past 40 years thanks in part to the development of a cadre of well-educated and well-financed advocates for unfettered capitalism (Biglan, 2015). In the same way, it is possible to use the findings of behavioral science regarding what contributes to human well-being and create a cadre of sophisticated advocates for all of the policies, practices, and programs that are needed to ensure that a steadily growing proportion of people have the skills, interests, and values needed to live productive lives in caring relationships with other people. The reform of capitalism will not be the only facet of such a movement, but the movement will not succeed unless such reform is accomplished.

Research evaluating strategies to influence public policy. A science of how to influence public policy is developing. A recent book edited by Wagenaar & Burris (2013) analyzes how to affect public health through public policy and outlines ways to evaluate the impact of public policies empirically. However, thus far research on *strategies for bringing about changes in policies* that would influence corporate practices has not occurred. Empirical research on virtually any policy adoption would be useful. However, it might be efficient to start with a focus on policies that provide more funding, accountability, and influence for a class of nonprofit organizations that are working for societal benefit.

Among the policies that would strengthen advocacy organizations are those that (a) charge organizations to work on defining the public benefits involving public well-being; (b) require transparency regarding all activities and their impact; and (c) increase tax benefits for contributions to these organizations (Biglan, 2009).

A second set of policies that could leverage further progress would require assessment of the impact of corporate practices on societal well-being. Such policies would function like environmental impact statements; they would require that corporations assess and make public the benefits and harms of their practices.

Strengthen the flexibility of advocacy organizations. Chapter 22 in this volume discusses the flexibility of organizations, using a model that parallels the CBS model of individual psychological flexibility. They suggest that organizations will be more successful to the extent that they are clear about their purpose and goals, clearly define the projects needed to achieve their goals, are able to consider multiple alternatives and perspectives in the pursuit of their goals, design the work to be done in ways that allow organizational members flexibility in how they do their work, are open to the discomfort that inevitably comes up as the organization confronts obstacles to its progress, and effectively monitor the organization's environment to detect threats and opportunities for achieving their goals.

If research on this model concentrated on assisting advocacy organizations that are focused on the reform of capitalist practices it might function as a counterweight to the huge resources that the for-profit world has to maintain public opinion and the public policies that have provided advantages to corporate capitalism, often to the detriment of the society as a whole.

Increasing flexibility in public discussion. Much public discussion about policy issues suffers from vitriolic exchanges in which each side demonizes the other, with common ground seldom reached. In the United States at least, the for-profit contingencies partly explain this situation. In a cable news world, in which a network can reap profits by reaching a small, distinct segment of the total audience, getting that audience threatened and angry can work well. Thus, both so-called liberal and conservative news channels maintain an audience by demonizing the opposition. Meanwhile many citizens grow ever more disenchanted with such controversy and disengage from any civic involvement (Putnam, 1995).

Might contextual behavioral science help? The ACT analysis of psychological flexibility suggests that it might. First, it may help to advocate that public discussion remain centered around values. Considerable evidence indicates that people's motivation to take action grows when the advocated action includes a discussion of its contribution to important values. Anecdotal evidence from ACT work suggests that most people will embrace values that have to do with others' well-being, especially if they become more self-compassionate (Pettigrew, Christ, Wagner, & Stellmacher, 2007; Pettigrew & Tropp, 2008; Todd, Bodenhausen, Richeson, & Galinsky, 2011).

Second, it is important to increase the number of people who take committed action. An emphasis on values may help to do this.

Perspective-taking may be the most important thing to encourage when it comes to public discussion. We need to model and encourage others to support a norm that favors acknowledging others' points of view compassionately. The value of this flexible perspective-taking may be the thing least appreciated by the culture as a whole.

Defusion is closely related. Virtually every policy is advocated with assertions that it definitely will work. Indeed, to acknowledge otherwise is seen as undermining the efforts to get the policy adopted. We need to experiment with ways to encourage people to recognize that their ideas about what public policy should be are not verities, but simply ideas. One aspect of this that relates to our role as behavioral scientists involves advocating for empirical evaluation of the impact of policies and programs. Advocating that each proposed policy undergo empirical evaluation requires that we acknowledge our uncertainty of a policy's success. This is a form of defusion. The Coalition for Evidence-Based Policy (http://coalition4evidence.org/) has progressed in advocating for experimental evaluations of programs and policies.

Acceptance is also relevant. In particular, societal change is hard. Acknowledgments of the difficulties inherent in bringing about change should accompany our discussion of public policy issues. If accepting these difficulties became a societal norm, it might reduce the distress resulting from our failures and setbacks and result in fewer people simply abandoning any interest in public policy issues.

Lastly, there is the present moment. In the context of recognizing that our ideas are just ideas, that they need to be evaluated, that many of the things we try will fail, it may help to focus on what we are doing in the present moment that could help move our society forward and, at a minimum, will involve our taking action in favor of values that are important to us.

Research on each of these propositions could lead to the contextual behavioral science movement bringing about very significant changes in the way that our societies address their problems. In summary, these seem to be the key steps for generating the necessary public discussion:

1　Articulate a set of values regarding human well-being and make clear that these are values people choose, not values that need defending as the correct values.
2　Frame every discussion in terms of its implications for the well-being of all citizens.
　　a　How will it affect children and adolescents?
　　b　How will it affect public health?
3　Acknowledge the uncertainty of most of our claims about what public policies will be most beneficial.
4　Acknowledge the gaps in our knowledge and advocate for experimental evaluations of the impact of all of our policies and programs.

ACBS as an Action and Advocacy Organization

The contextual behavioral science community already has one organization working to "*change the world in a positive and intentional way*" (Hayes et al., 2012; emphasis added). It is the Association for Contextual Behavioral Science (ACBS). Traditionally, scientific and professional organizations (ACBS is both) have eschewed advocacy. However, a thoroughgoing analysis of the threats to human well-being and the massive cultural evolution that will be needed to prevent them (Biglan & Barnes-Holmes, 2015) calls for us to examine all of the ways that we can change the trajectory of cultural evolution.

Might ACBS articulate and advocate for policies that scientific evidence shows are likely to improve human well-being? Might the organization network with other organizations to create a social movement that uses the best available scientific findings and methods to increase the ability of societies to ensure that all of its component organizations (whether for-profit or nonprofit) are acting in the interest of well-being and minimizing practices that do harm to some members of the society?

References

Alterman, E. (2008). *What liberal media? The truth about bias and the news.* New York, NY: Basic Books.

Atkins, P., & Parker, S. (2011). Understanding individual compassion in organizations: The role of appraisals and psychological flexibility. *Academy of Management Review, 37,* 524–546.

Baker, E. A., Schootman, M., Barnidge, E., & Kelly, C. (2006). The role of race and poverty in access to foods that enable individuals to adhere to dietary guidelines. *Preventing Chronic Disease, 3,* 43–53.

Barnes-Holmes, Y., Hayes, S. C., Barnes-Holmes, D., & Roche, B. (2002). Relational frame theory: A post-Skinnerian account of human language and cognition. *Advances in Child Development and Behavior, 28,* 101–138.

Biglan, A. (2004). *Direct written testimony in the case of the U.S.A. vs. Phillip Morris et al.* Washington, DC: US Department of Justice.

Biglan, A. (2009). The role of advocacy organizations in reducing negative externalities. *Journal of Organizational Behavior Management, 29,* 215–230.

Biglan, A. (2011). Corporate externalities: a challenge to the further success of prevention science. *Prevention Science, 12,* 1–11.

Biglan, A. (2015). *The nurture effect: How the science of human behavior can improve our lives and our world.* Oakland, CA: New Harbinger.

Biglan, A., & Barnes-Holmes, Y. (2015). Acting in light of the future: How do future-oriented cultural practices evolve and how can we accelerate their evolution? *Journal of Contextual Behavioral Science* (2015). http://dx.doi.org/10.1016/j.jcbs.2015.06.002

Biglan, A., & Embry, D. D. (2013). A framework for intentional cultural change. *Journal of Contextual Behavioral Science, 2,* 95–104.

Bureau of Labor Statistics. (2014). Union Members Summary, USDL-14-0095. US Department of Labor, BLS. Retrieved from http://www.bls.gov/news.release/union2.nr0.htm

Chaloupka, F. J. (2013). Economic theory. In A. C. Wagenaar & S. C. Burris (Eds.), *Public health law research: Theory and methods* (pp. 147–168). New York, NY: Wiley.

Cray, C. (2007). Revisiting corporate charters. *2007 Summit on the future of the corporation, Paper no. 7,* 67–76.

Cray, C., & Drutman, L. (2005) Corporations and the public purpose: Restoring the balance. *Seattle Journal for Social Justice, 4*(1), Article 41. Retrieved from http://digitalcommons.law.seattleu.edu/sjsj/vol4/iss1/41

Frank, R. H. (2011). *The Darwin economy: Liberty, competition, and the common good.* Princeton, NY: Princeton University Press.

Friedman, M., & Friedman, R. (1990). *Free to choose: A personal statement.* New York, NY: Houghton Mifflin Harcourt.

Greenpeace. (n.d.). *Koch Industries backs California Proposition 23: A case study.* Retrieved from http://www.greenpeace.org/usa/en/campaigns/global-warming-and-energy/polluterwatch/koch-industries/CASE-STUDY-Koch-Industries-Backs-California-Proposition-23/

Grube, J. W., Madden, P. A., & Friese, B. (1996, June). *The effects of television alcohol advertising on adolescent drinking.* Poster presentation at the Annual Meeting of the Research Society on Alcoholism, Washington, DC.

Grube, J. W., & Nygaard, P. (2005). Alcohol policy and youth drinking: Overview of effective interventions for young people. In T. Stockwell, P. J. Gruenewald, J. Toumbourou, & W. Loxley (Eds.), *Preventing harmful substance use: The evidence base for policy and practice* (pp. 113–127). New York, NY: Wiley.

Hacker, J. S., & Pierson, P. (2011). *Winner-take-all politics: How Washington made the rich richer – and turned its back on the middle class.* New York, NY: Simon & Schuster.

Hayes, S. C., Barnes-Holmes, D., & Wilson, K. G. (2012). Contextual behavioral science: Creating a science more adequate to the challenge of the human condition. *Journal of Contextual Behavioral Science, 1,* 1–16.

Horowitz, C. R., Colson, K. A., Hebert, P. L., & Lancaster, K. (2004). Barriers to buying healthy foods for people with diabetes: Evidence of environmental disparities. *American Journal of Public Health, 94,* 1549–1554.

Hosler, A. S., Varadarajulu, D., Ronsani, A. E., Fredrick, B. L., & Fisher, B. D. (2006). Low-fat milk and high-fiber bread availability in food stores in urban and rural communities. *Journal of Public Health Management and Practice, 12,* 556–562.

Isidore, C. (2013). Buffett says he's still paying lower tax rate than his secretary. *CNN Money online.* Retrieved from http://money.cnn.com/2013/03/04/news/economy/buffett-secretary-taxes/

Jetter, K. M., & Cassady, D. L. (2006). The availability and cost of healthier food alternatives. *American Journal of Preventive Medicine, 30,* 38–44.

Kearns Goodwin, D. (2013). *The bully pulpit: Theodore Roosevelt, William Howard Taft, and the golden age of journalism.* New York, NY: Simon & Schuster.

Krebs-Smith, S. M., Cook, A., Subar, A. F., Cleveland, L., & Friday, J. (1995). US adults' fruit and vegetable intakes, 1989 to 1991: A revised baseline for the Healthy People 2000 objective. *American Journal of Public Health, 85,* 1623–1629.

Lapham, L. (2004, September). Tentacles of rage. *Harper's Magazine,* 31–41.

Lewis, M. (2010). *The big short: Inside the doomsday machine.* New York, NY: Norton.

Lewis, M. (2011). *Boomerang: Travels in the third world.* New York, NY: Norton.

Mantovani, R. E., Daft, L., Macaluso, T.F., Welsh, J., & Hoffman, K. (1997). *Authorized food retailer characteristics study technical report IV: Authorized food retailers' characteristic and access study.* Washington, DC: US Department of Agriculture, Food, and Consumer Service, Office of Analysis and Evaluation.

Master Settlement Agreement between 46 State Attorneys General and Participating Tobacco Manufacturers. November 23, 1998. Retrieved from http://www.naag.org/tobac/cigmsa.rtf

McLean, B., & Nocera, J. (2010). *All the devils are here: The hidden history of the financial crisis.* New York, NY: Penguin.

Morland, K., Diex Roux, A., & Wing, S. (2006). Supermarkets, other food stores, and obesity: The atherosclerosis risk in communities study. *American Journal of Preventive Medicine, 30,* 333–339.

Morton, L. W., & Blanchard, T. C. (2007). Starved for access: Life in rural America's food deserts. *Rural Realities, 1,* 1–10.

Moynihan, D. P. (1997). *Miles to go: A personal history of social policy.* Boston, MA: Harvard University Press.

Mulbrandon, C. (2007, November). Last 2000 years of growth in world income and population (revised). *Visualizing Economics.* Retrieved from http://visualizingeconomics.com/blog/2007/11/21/last-2000-of-growth-in-world-income-and-population-revised

National Aeronautics and Space Administration. (n.d.). *Consensus: 97% of climate scientist agree.* Retrieved from http://climate.nasa.gov/scientific-consensus/

National Cancer Institute (2008). *The role of the media in promoting and reducing tobacco use.* Tobacco Control Monograph no. 19 (Vol. NIH Pub. No. 07-6242). Bethesda, MD: US Department of Health and Human Services, National Institutes of Health, National Cancer Institute.

OpenSecrets. (2014). *Center for responsive politics.* Lobbying database. Retrieved from http://www.opensecrets.org/lobby/index.php

Pamuk, E., Makuk, D., Heck, K., Reuben, C. (1998). *Health, United States, 1998 with Socioeconomic Status and Health Chartbook.* Hyattsville, MD: National Center for Health Statistics.

Pechmann, C., Biglan, A., Grube, J. W., & Cody, C. (2012). Transformative consumer research for addressing tobacco and alcohol. In D. G. Mick, S. Pettigrew, C. C. Pechmann, & J. L. Ozanne (Eds.), *Transformative consumer research for personal and collective well-being* (pp. 353–389). New York, NY: Routledge.

Perino, M. (2010). *The hellhound of Wall Street: How Ferdinand Pecora's investigation of the great crash forever changed American finance.* New York, NY: Penguin.

Pettigrew, T. F., Christ, O., Wagner, U., & Stellmacher, J. (2007). Direct and indirect intergroup contact effects on prejudice: A normative interpretation. *International Journal of Intercultural Relations, 31,* 411–425.

Pettigrew, T. F., & Tropp, L. R. (2008). How does intergroup contact reduce prejudice? Meta-analytic tests of three mediators? *European Journal of Social Psychology, 38,* 922–934.

Pierce, J. P., Gilpin, E. A., & Choi, W. S. (1999). Sharing the blame: Smoking experimentation and future smoking-attributable mortality due to Joe Camel and Marlboro advertising and promotions. *Tobacco Control, 8,* 37–44.

Powell, L., Slater, S., Mirtcheva, D., Bao, Y., & Chaloupka, F. (2007). Food store availability and neighborhood characteristics in the United States. *American Journal of Preventive Medicine, 44,* 189–195.

Putnam, R. D. (1995). Bowling alone: America's declining social capital. *Journal of Democracy, 6,* 65–78.

Rosling, H. (2010). Hans Rosling shows you 200 years of global growth in four minutes. *Singularity Hub.* Retrieved from http://singularityhub.com/2010/12/09/hans-rosling-shows-you-200-years-of-global-growth-in-4-minutes-video/

Smith, H. (2012). *Who stole the American dream?* New York, NY: Random House.

Sober, E., & Wilson, D. S. (Eds.). (1999). *Unto others: The evolution and psychology of unselfish behavior.* Cambridge, MA: Harvard University Press.

Tax Foundation. (2013). *Federal individual income tax rates history: Income history 1913 to 2013.* Washington, DC: Author.

Todd, A. R., Bodenhausen, G. V., Richeson, J. A., & Galinsky, A. D. (2011). Perspective taking combats automatic expressions of racial bias. *Journal of Personality and Social Psychology, 100,* 1027–1042.

United States v. Philip Morris USA, Inc. (2006). Civil Action No. 99-2496 (D.D.C., 2012), Final Order.

Wagenaar A. C., & Burris, S. C. (Eds.). (2013). *Public health law research: Theory and methods.* New York, NY: Wiley.

Wagenaar, A. C., Erickson, D. J., Harwood, E. M., & O'Malley, P. M. (2006). Effects of state coalitions to reduce underage drinking: A national evaluation. *American Journal of Preventive Medicine, 31,* 307–315.

Wilson, D. S. (2007). *Evolution for everyone*. New York, NY: Delacorte.

Wilson, D. S., Hayes, S. C., Biglan, A., & Embry, D. D. (2014a). Evolving the future: Toward a science of intentional change. *Behavioral and Brain Sciences, 37*, 395–416.

Wilson, D. S., Hayes, S. C., Biglan, T., & Embry, D. (2014b). Collaborating on evolving the future. *Behavioral and Brain Sciences, 37*, 438–460.

Wood, E. M. (2002). *The origin of capitalism: A longer view*. New York, NY: Verso.

25

A Functional Contextualist Analysis of the Behavior and Organizational Practices Relevant to Climate Change

Mark Alavosius, Donny Newsome,
Ramona Houmanfar, and Anthony Biglan

The scientific community harbors no doubts about the seriousness of global climate change (Intergovernmental Panel on Climate Change [IPCC], 2007; 2014). According to the IPCC (2007), "Warming of the climate system is unequivocal, as is now evident from observations of increases in global average air and ocean temperatures, widespread melting of snow and ice, and rising global average sea level" (p. 30). Effects of global warming affect weather patterns that lead to extreme changes in precipitation, wind patterns, drought, heatwaves, and the intensity of tropical storms (IPCC, 2007). The 2014 IPCC report gives an even stronger warning, describing the impacts already observed, noting increased CO_2 emissions despite efforts to reduce them, and summarizing the effects these emissions have on populations around the globe. It states,

> Globally, economic and population growth continue to be the most important drivers of increases in CO_2 emissions from fossil fuel combustion. The contribution of population growth between 2000 and 2010 remained roughly identical to the previous three decades, while the contribution of economic growth has risen sharply. Between 2000 and 2010, both drivers outpaced emission reductions from improvements in energy intensity. (IPCC, 2014, p. 10)

Some popular media proclaim otherwise and the public disagrees in terms of how people understand climate change, its causes, and, more importantly, how it will affect humanity. Reactions range along a continuum from alarm and urgent calls for action to prevent further global warming, to preparations to adapt to changes, to disinterest and apathy, and to outright denial of climate change data (Maibach, Roser-Renouf, & Leiserowitz, 2009). The science involved in measuring the planet's temperature and climate patterns is complex and not readily understood by those not trained in the complexities of this endeavor. Scientific peer-reviewed reports provide accumulating

The Wiley Handbook of Contextual Behavioral Science, First Edition. Edited by Robert D. Zettle, Steven C. Hayes, Dermot Barnes-Holmes, and Anthony Biglan.
© 2016 John Wiley & Sons, Ltd. Published 2016 by John Wiley & Sons, Ltd.

evidence from a number of disciplines that converge to show climate change is happening now, the rate of change is accelerating (Hansen & Sato, 2011), and human activities (e.g., use of fossil fuels) following the Industrial Revolution are a major driver of that change. Thompson (2010) provides a very readable account of climate science findings and relates these findings to options humans have to address the crisis. The author (L. G. Thompson, personal communication, August 4, 2012) states that this publication in *The Behavior Analyst* is his most requested paper, as it provides his clearest communication of what future climates we can expect and how we must change our behavior to reduce their impact. He articulates three options – act to prevent climate change, adapt to new environments, or suffer.

Perhaps the best source of scientific information accessible to the public from across the many disciplines studying the problem is the IPCC, which summarizes research findings, interprets results, and issues periodic reports to communicate with policy-makers, business leaders, and the public. We urge readers of this chapter to study these reports when searching for reasoned information on climate change and for what it might mean for them. Becoming better informed is not just an academic exercise. Climate change will eventually affect all humans in some way, if it is not already having an impact. Climate changes are evident now and vary across geographic regions. Residents of coastal cities see rising seawaters affecting their communities. Agriculture worldwide is affected and the food supply has altered. Droughts increase wildfire risks and threaten water supplies. Heat taxes populations and threatens health and well-being. Floods from snowmelt and rains break records. Insurance companies worry about covering the losses. Catastrophic costs may overwhelm financial systems. The CNA Military Advisory Board (a group consisting of high-ranking retired US military leaders) identified climate change as a "threat multiplier" (Goodman & Sullivan, 2013): militaries accept the scientific evidence, and they are preparing for action. This likely entails a range of actions from combat, quelling armed conflict, police action to maintain security, and humanitarian aid to victims of climate-related disasters (United States Joint Forces Command, 2010; US Department of Defense, 2014). In its 2014 report, the US Department of Defense states it is collaborating with federal and local agencies and institutions to develop a comprehensive approach to the many challenges raised by climate change. In this same report, the US military describes the need to work with other nations to assess and manage climate change impacts and to help build their capacity to respond. Climate change is a global problem that the military recognizes: it accepts the scientific findings that others reject. Climate change does not respect national borders and those in the military realize that no nation can deal with it alone. It is quite compelling when an organization like the US military, with its global presence, states the need to work in harmony with other nations to build joint capabilities to deal with emerging threats.

The public sees climate changes through the lens of weather patterns and often confuses local conditions with global trends. Perhaps this explains variations in perspectives on the phenomena and reveals how the public response is likely to evolve. Residents of cities like New York, Venice, and New Orleans see firsthand the engineering of seawalls. Californians are experiencing severe or extreme drought conditions, facing water conservation proposals and paying fines, and observing firefighting year long. These serious challenges merit organized solutions, which many local governments are now enacting: Educating citizens and making changes.

Local problems occur within the context of *global* warming and the worldwide scale of complexity appears to exceed many national governments' ability to balance national with human interests. Most of the seemingly effective actions communities are putting into place to address immediate threats fail to address the interconnected events causing the global problem. The 2014 IPCC report concludes,

> Effective mitigation will not be achieved if individual agents advance their own interests independently. Climate change has the characteristics of a collective action problem at the global scale, because most greenhouse gases (GHGs) accumulate over time and mix globally and emissions by any agent (e.g., individual, community, company, and country) affect other agents. International cooperation is therefore required to effectively mitigate GHG emissions and address other climate change issues … International cooperation can play a constructive role in the development, diffusion, and transfer of knowledge and environmentally sound technologies. (p. 5)

Factors that shape daily behavior determine how humans respond collectively to prevent or adapt to climate change (Alavosius & Mattaini, 2011). Some responses to prevent climate change are easy, like adopting energy conservation practices, recycling, and other behaviors that reduce consumption of fossil fuels. Marketing practices of corporations shape these consumer behaviors under regulatory actions. For example, as corporate average fuel efficiency (CAFE) regulations increase mileage standards and manufacturers feel pressed to build and sell vehicles with greater fuel efficiency, consumers may shift from fuel-thirsty SUVs to more fuel-efficient transportation. Homeowners install energy-saving technologies and enjoy lower utility bills and tax offsets. People recycle waste formerly destined for landfills if community leaders adopt easy-to-use recycling practices and provide efficient services. These shifts in individual behavior are relatively easy and occur almost fad-like within established behavior-changing contexts like market forces, social pressure, and fashion trends.

These changes appear woefully inadequate to alter the course of accelerating global climate change. Perhaps they are small steps in a shaping process whereby populations relatively unaffected by changes now adopt lifestyles that are more sustainable. As people struggle to survive under extreme conditions (e.g., low-lying island nations, drought-ravaged communities, or famine-plagued countries), human responses are much more dramatic. Facing a collectively shared global warming crisis, the apparent dependence of prosocial action upon firsthand aversive contact is troubling for the social and behavioral sciences.

Even those who live in comfortable, secure environments can witness the effects of climate change and at some point will see others suffering from environmental degradation. A wide variety of solutions are emerging as scenarios for the future: technological gardens to feed the earth's growing population, urban designs that cool overheated cityscapes, alternative energies that power industries and communities, technologies that reduce future greenhouse gas production and sequester the already produced gases, and even fashion trends favorable to environmental stewardship. Geo-engineering (Biello, 2011) has produced ideas as fantastic sounding as global shields to reflect sunlight in the upper atmosphere for cooling the planet, whitewashing cities and roadways to reflect heat, and massive levees and dams that hold back the sea as options. In the end, if meaningful and measurable positive impacts are to occur, we will undoubtedly require advances like these and more.

We come then to the topic of this chapter – promoting positive human behavior in the context of a changing global climate. Can humans change deeply established life-style behaviors in time to halt or slow global warming? Can humans across the globe cooperate to address collectively the greatest threat to humanity and avert strife over limited resources? If not, will humans adapt to habitats created by climate change and learn to live within sustainable boundaries?

The Behavior of Individuals

Consider a fictional character, Joe, who is shopping for a new vehicle. Numerous factors influence his allocation of choice across a broad continuum ranging from full-sized sport utility to electric vehicle. He knows he will eventually save money on fuel if he chooses the electric, but he isn't sure if that is worth the extra cost now. A clean environment is important to him, but he isn't convinced his behavior has much direct impact on that. Joe's immediate considerations tend to guide behavior toward purchasing the SUV. Gasoline vehicles cost less than comparable electric or hybrid vehicles. His accountant says the SUV might be a better tax write-off. The SUV is more spacious and comfortable. The roaring powers of a V8 engine, complemented by its off-road prowess, are conditioned reinforcers for Joe irrespective of their necessity for his daily commute. The same driving experience and capabilities do not exist in an eco-friendly version at any price. He observes that SUVs line the streets of his neighborhood and worries about social disapproval from his hunting buddies who prize the masculinity and status of a 4×4 truck. Costs, utility, prevailing cultural attitudes and beliefs all impact Joe's vehicle choice.

In recent decades, most efforts by psychologists (Lehman & Geller, 2004) to analyze the behaviors and choices available to our friend Joe have focused on theories about attitudes toward environmental issues and choices of behavior. The approachability of the constructs applied within this school of thought (e.g., attitudes, beliefs, and values) likely contributes to the popularity of "social/environmental psychology." This way of speaking about causes of behavior, such as Joe's choice, has popular appeal, which mass media outlets commonly communicate. Familiar terms make these theories highly attractive to laypersons and policy-makers. This face validity might be one of the strengths of the social/environmental approach. If psychological inter-ventions were to enter mainstream culture, it would be best to frame the language describing them in terms broad audiences understand. Maibach and colleagues (2009) recommend this in their analysis of the segmented audiences interpreting information on climate change.

Although studies about the relationships between reported environmental attitudes and ecologically impactful behaviors have penetrated the cultural milieu, this subfield of environmental psychology has had very little influence on the problems associated with climate change (Lehman & Geller, 2004). It has become clear that research focused on the correlations between what people say and what they do is of little help for changing what they either say or do (Newsome & Alavosius, 2011). More useful are clear prescriptions for how to *change* environmentally relevant behaviors. That requires identifying manipulable environmental influences on behavior.

Direct Acting Contingencies

The behavior analytic intellectual tradition is the basis for contextual behavioral science. Critical foundations of the science of behavior include understanding the behavior of individuals and groups as being dynamic and adaptive. The notion of selection-by-consequences (Skinner, 1969; 1981) draws parallels between the phylogenic variation with environmental selection of genetic materials and the ontogenic selection of operant lineages. We can apply selection in the contingencies of reinforcement related to a given operant over time in much the same way as we relate it to the contingencies of survival critical to the evolution of species by the passing of genetic materials across generations. Applying the selection metaphor to study human action allows us to conceptualize the behavior of individuals as dynamic and adaptable in much the same way we view species because of adaptations to local ecology. Behavior is the outcome of a long lineage of organism–environment interactions. Behavior's susceptibility to change from environmental influence provides the basis for all operant psychology, including its application to environmental issues as described herein.

Behavioral science identifies functional relations between manipulable environmental variables and observable behaviors as the primary purpose of psychological investigation (Skinner, 1966). Applied behavior analysis (Baer, Wolf, & Risley, 1968) seeks to develop replicable behavioral technologies to alleviate human suffering and improve socially valid behaviors based on principles of behavior. In light of the above criticisms of the social/environmental approach, behavior analysis appears well positioned to inform practical solutions to the environmental problems that harmful human behaviors bring about. Indeed, behavioral interventions have been effective in influencing domestic and industrial energy consumption, litter control, recycling, transportation decisions, and consumer purchasing behavior (Lehman & Geller, 2004).

Herrnstein's (1961; 1970; 1974) *Matching Law*, derived from Thorndike (1911), succinctly states a predictable relationship between operants and consequent environmental changes. The Matching Law states that the probability of an individual behaving in one way or another changes as a function of the relative rate of reinforcing or punishing consequences for different behaviors. Thus, understanding the "reason" for a given behavior requires the identification of relevant contingencies. Similarly, manipulation of those contingencies can influence behavior. Behavior is lawful to the extent we can always attribute it to contingencies of reinforcement at play. The behaviorist tradition suggests that behaviors, which due to their destructive outcomes (e.g., those degrading the environment) might be "irrational," are in fact lawful and better understood as sensitivity to certain types of consequences and insensitivity to others. In this light, Joe's decision to buy a rugged, quasi-military vehicle with luxury appointments able to ford streams and climb sand dunes seems predictable. But why is he insensitive to the potential cost savings of a low/zero emissions vehicle and irreverent to the environmental impact of his choice?

The problem of delayed consequences. Among many available accounts of conditions sufficient to produce humans' insensitivities to contingencies, one particularly relevant to human-driven environmental problems is the decreasing strength of a reinforcer as its temporal distance from the correlated response increases (Fantino, 1969; Fantino, Preston, & Dunn, 1993; Skinner, 1938). The probability of a given response decreases as the time to reinforcement for that response increases. We can say the strength of a given reinforcer decays as a function of delay to delivery. The reinforcing strength of a given consequence in a direct acting contingency (see Malott, Shimamune, & Malott, 1992; Weatherly & Malott, 2008) can diminish markedly when the delay to delivery increases by just seconds (Skinner, 1938). This phenomenon has attracted much attention in the field of behavioral economics where applied to analysis of financial choices. Generally, the further a consequence occurs in the future, the less value or control the consequence maintains for the responding organism. The phrase for this line of research is delay discounting.

Delay discounting has been the subject of experimental investigation since the mid-1900s: a considerable body of evidence supports this analysis. Madden and Bickel (2010) define delay discounting as, "the process by which future events are subjectively devalued by the decision maker" (p. 3). Research suggests that sensitivity to delays in reinforcement is generalizable across a wide variety of complex human behaviors, as evidenced by studies of purchasing behavior in online shopping analogues (DiClemente & Hantula, 2003; Hantula, Brockman, & Smith, 2008; Rajala & Hantula, 2000), environmental stewardship (Hardistry & Weber, 2009), materialistic commodities (Weatherly, Terrell, & Derenne, 2010), workplace safety (Reynolds & Schiffbauer, 2004; Sigurdsson, Taylor, & Wirth, 2013) and social policies (Plumm, Borhart, & Weatherly, 2012). Our friend Joe, who chose a conventional SUV above an electric car, subjectively valued immediate consequences (including savings offered by an eager salesman) more than he valued what he might save on fuel in the long run.

Evidence of our insensitivity to delayed consequences is robust. Humans choose immediate rewards over larger but delayed ones. We consume immediately satisfying things at the expense of delayed negative consequences for doing so. More work can help to understand the phenomena and to better manage choices. The popular book *Nudge* (Thaler & Sunstein, 2009) describes applications of this research to decisions about health, investments, environmental issues, and more. One intriguing area for further research is the effect of language describing choices on how humans discount delayed consequences. Recent work shows that the words used to describe scenarios (e.g., varying the labeling of consequences) affect the rates at which humans discount these consequences.

Relational Responding

In addition to analyses of direct acting contingencies, contextual behavior scientists are equipped with the investigative constructs described by relational frame theory (RFT; Hayes, Barnes-Holmes, & Roche, 2001). This theory provides further understanding of why direct acting contingencies might fail to control behavior. Derived relational responding involves the apparently uniquely human ability to derive and apply relations among stimuli without any direct training. The emergence of such responses appears to be a function of other, directly trained relations. For example, a person trained to select B or C in the presence of A, will – without direct training – select A in the presence of B or C (called mutual entailment or symmetry) and B in the presence of C and vice versa (called combinatorial entailment or transitivity). Equivalence preparations (Sidman, 1994; Sidman & Tailby, 1982) clearly demonstrate this.

Further, if A acquires some discernible function, the functions obtaining among B and C will transform in accordance to the relation of them to A. For example, if people learn that A is the opposite of B and C, they will readily derive that B and C are the same without direct training. Moreover, given direct training for the relation A < B < C, any function bestowed by the environment upon A will transfer to B and C in accordance with the < relation. So if B is paired with an aversive stimulus that occasions an avoidance response, RFT predicts that the magnitude of the avoidance response will be greater for C and smaller for A, even though A and C have never been paired with the aversive stimulus directly. These predictions enjoy robust support from empirical investigations, and clearly distinguish "relational responding" from the narrower subset of "equivalencing" (Augustson, Dougher, & Markham, 2000; Barnes-Holmes, Barnes-Holmes, Smeets, Strand, & Friman, 2004; Berens & Hayes, 2007). Chapter 10 of this volume elaborates this analysis.

Let's apply this thinking to the example of Joe, the car shopper. After Joe listens to his peers say that large, powerful vehicles are great, we can see how he might automatically derive the rule that small, efficient cars are *not* great. This thought is likely to give rise to the aversive sensations associated with social disapproval, leading our potential hybrid owner to avoid visiting the hybrid showroom. But the avoidance comes at a cost. It may be in his financial best interest to buy a hybrid. Buying something other than a hybrid might be a disservice to his environmentalist values. He may also be entirely miscalculating his friends' reactions. Nonetheless, his rigid avoidance of the topic makes it unlikely he would even have a conversation to validate his peers' feelings, or be willing to accept some degree of social disapproval in the service of his environmental or fiscal values. The rules he derives artificially narrow his repertoire of potential value-directed responses to the present direct acting contingencies. Because of his relational abilities, the functional effects of most stimuli are a function of the relational responding, despite the direct contingency relations those stimuli might participate in.

Appreciating the role of derived verbal relations in regulating the functions of stimuli in Joe's environment, we suggest that manipulation of the direct acting contingencies for his purchasing behavior is necessary but insufficient (Newsome & Alavosius, 2011). His purchasing behaviors are not simply the result of rational decisions about costs and utility. Joe's choices are the products of the relational network that connects SUVs and hybrid vehicles to a myriad of other stimuli, which affect how much he values SUVs and hybrids. These networks are a function of his social interactions and his exposure to media.

Thus, the sweeping societal changes needed to combat and mitigate global warming must involve more than direct contingency manipulation. Providing subsidies to offset Joe's purchase price of high-efficiency vehicles is only part of the battle. It is necessary to consider Joe's behavior in the broader context of variables to scale up solutions to change the behaviors of large populations. Efforts to alter direct contingencies should accompany educational initiatives and savvy marketing and advocacy campaigns on a huge scale to influence the relevant relational networks of millions of people. Informed by an understanding of arbitrarily applicable relational responding, marketers can craft messages with consideration not only for what they say explicitly, but also for what rules, relations, and functions consumers are likely to derive. But to reach and influence millions of people will require influencing hundreds of thousands of organizations to change their practices (Luke & Alavosius, 2012). That in turn means that our science must have an effective analysis of the influences on organizations' practices.

The Prediction and Influence of Organization Practices

Types of Organizations

The massive changes needed to address the problem of climate change require that virtually every organization in society change some of its practices. In approaching what changes must occur, we consider the various types of organizations, by category, in search of a strategy for influencing the population of organizations.

One key category consists of for-profit organizations. These might be divided into (a) those that stand to lose if fossil fuel consumption is reduced; (b) those that might gain from reductions in fossil fuel use, either because they sell alternative products or because the adoption of practices that would reduce fossil fuel use would reduce the company's costs and improve its profits; and (c) companies that would neither benefit or be harmed by policies that reduce such fuel consumption. A precise analysis of which companies these changes would benefit or harm would be very helpful in planning, advocating for, and implementing strategies to reduce fossil fuel use. The structure of the organizations and their strategic plans likely reveal how the organizations defend their territories, intellectual property, talent, and other resources. Inspection might also reveal if leaders value environmental resources and potential for collaboration with other like-minded corporate leaders.

A second class of organizations consists of nonprofit organizations. There is a variety of organization types within this category making consideration of their potential fit to a pro-environment agenda more complex than is true of for-profit companies. One particularly important type consists of advocacy organizations that are working to reduce greenhouse gas emissions. There are, of course, also advocacy organizations that are working to prevent policies that would reduce the use of fossil fuels. The network of contingencies that link these organizations to others is likely complex. Clarification of these contingencies and the values of key members may reveal avenues to promote efforts to affect environmental issues.

Then there is a wide variety of other nonprofit organizations. They include churches, universities, foundations, and civic organizations. These entities could affect the problem by influencing their members and the individuals and organizations they reach to support efforts to affect greenhouse emissions.

Finally, there are governments. They range from the local city councils, school districts, and various service districts to county, state, and federal levels. These entities affect the problem in at least two ways. First, many of their practices involve the emissions of greenhouse gases. Second, they can set the contingencies for individuals and other organizations that both affect emissions and influence the norms that effect individual behavior (Luke & Alavosius, 2012). Governments set tax codes, rebates, emission standards, sanctions, education curricula, and more that establish the context for much behavior that we could label as "citizenship."

Influences on Organizational Practices

Houmanfar, Rodrigues, and Ward (2010) present a five-term analysis of the selection of practices of organizations that is useful for generating empirical research on how the actions of organizations affecting climate change might be changed. They argue that the interlocking behavior of organizational members results in products or services that are purchased (or not) by consumers. To the extent that consumers purchase these products and, as a result, what productive processes take place or grow, the contingency constitutes what Glenn (2004) has called a *metacontingency*. This same contingency can account for other actions of organizations. For example, a corporation presumably selects its marketing practices as a function of their success in generating sales. Similarly, a company chooses public relations and lobbying efforts based on their consequences or relation to the organization's profits.

Houmanfar et al. (2010) go on to suggest that this contingency occurs in the context of a "cultural-organizational milieu," "which consists of all of the antecedent factors" that function as the context affecting the production of a good, a service, or other organizational outcome. Examples include the resources available to the organization as well as aspects of the societal infrastructure, such as the regulatory schema within which the organization must operate. In addition, they suggest that organization leaders may conduct analyses of the results of the organizations' transactions with the environment that lead to the generation of rules that affect subsequent organizational actions.

In essence, metacontingencies are contingencies that select the interlocked behaviors of groups or organizations in the same way that operant consequences select the behavior of individuals (Houmanfar & Rodrigues, 2006; Houmanfar et al., 2010). A for-profit organization that creates a product that sells better than competitors' products is likely to achieve profits that maintain their production of the product as well as the practices that lead to the creation of the product. Elsewhere, we have described in detail the ways in which diverse practices of organizations are selected by their consequences (Biglan, 2009; Biglan & Embry, 2013). We can expect for-profit companies to maintain and strengthen practices that have proven benefit in generating profits. In the case of fossil fuel companies, it is understandable that they will work to prevent any public policy that threatens to reduce the use of fossil fuels, since it will reduce their profits. That in turn will motivate them to influence public opinion to support their policy objectives. Companies that face no harm from reductions in the use of fossil fuels will likely support policies that reduce their use, to the extent that such reductions will improve their profits. This highlights the value of seeking policies that will benefit many corporations. Cap and trade policies are examples of such policies. These policies limit ("cap") the pollution released by a company. Those companies limiting emissions below their cap can sell ("trade") permits to less effective companies who effectively buy a permit to pollute. The idea is that this policy promotes innovation in control of greenhouse gases and allows leading companies to profit from innovations and lagging companies to buy time to adopt solutions. This is not without controversy: many question execution of the policies as a limit on the effectiveness of this approach to reducing CO_2 emissions. Finally, some companies, such as manufacturers of photovoltaic cells, stand to gain from policies designed to reduce fossil fuels. We would expect these companies to work to garner support for such policies.

Metacontingencies affect nonprofit organizations just as much: their survival also depends on a flow of funds into them. They will likely engage in activities that ensure or expand their funding. With respect to climate change, we need to be concerned about flow of funds to organizations that advocate for or against climate-affecting policies. This is itself an issue for public policy. If our goal is to influence societies to adopt policies that curtail greenhouse gas emissions and advocacy organizations are a vehicle for doing so, we also need policies that advantage these organizations (see Biglan, 2009 for a more extensive discussion of policies that would strengthen these organizations).

Ultimately, governments adopt and enforce policies. One can analyze the actions of governments in terms of metacontingencies. A ruling coalition can lose office because of its policies, as happened recently in Australia. In 2011, its Labour government adopted a stringent carbon tax and plans to link with European cap and trade policy affecting the use of fossil fuels. However, the newly elected Liberal government repealed the policy in 2014 under pressure from the mining industry, which produces the coal fueling much of the Australian economy. At the time of writing this chapter (November 2014), the United States and China (world's number 1 and 2 carbon polluters) announced a joint plan to limit greenhouse gases. This is the first time China has agreed to commit to stop emissions. It will be instructive to see the trajectory of this agreement and view the political reactions this spawns in the United States, and whether other countries adopt similar protocols. Even major energy companies producing fossil fuels are seeing the negative impact of global warming as this threatens the value of their vast assets. We can expect to see some in the energy sector advocating for control of carbon emissions as this aligns with their survival too (Moorehead & Nixon, 2015).

The Interplay between Organizations and Individuals

One shortcoming of much behavioral literature on climate change is that it focuses on the influences affecting individual behavior, but ignores the way the larger social system affects individuals. It may be true that Joe might buy that electric vehicle if the relative cost of it versus an SUV becomes more favorable, if his friends look on his choice more favorably, or if his values shift toward less materialism (Biglan, 2015). But the problem for society is to bring such influences to bear on entire populations. This cannot happen unless organizations make it happen. And, as just discussed, harm will come to a panoply of organizations if such influences are brought to bear on large numbers of people. These organizations will put their considerable resources toward preventing this from happening.

Certainly, adopting policies that require or incentivize more green-relevant actions of organizations establish metacontingencies that will affect corporate action. The problem is how we get such policies adopted. Of course, *people* run organizations and it is possible that we can influence corporate leaders to take actions that run contrary to their pursuit of profits. One promising development is the creation of benefit corporations, which are required to pursue a "general public benefit," defined as "a material positive impact on society *and* the environment taken as a whole" (Ridgway, 2012). In this context, a corporate leader might be more likely to choose actions that have social benefit, even if these actions have a slightly negative impact.

As suggested above, we can conceptualize the values that people hold in terms of relational networks. Whether we are talking about your neighbor Joe or the CEOs of major corporations, what they value is presumably a function of their relational networks. Just as Joe may come to value an electric vehicle because he has come to relate climate change to harm to his children, it is conceivable that CEOs might come to value green practices because they have begun to think that such practices will reduce the company's costs, or because these actions will improve the company's reputation, or because they worry their children will suffer in a world in which climate change continues apace.

Such a scenario is at least plausible for the leader of a company that does not sell fossil fuels. But how likely is it that the CEO of an oil or coal company will endorse a policy that will lead to the value of the company reducing by half because it will not market half of its known oil or coal reserves? Such is the case with the Australian action to repeal its carbon tax and with North American companies' opposition to the Keystone XL pipeline.

In principle, this suggests that a strategy will be necessary in which we try to influence the values of corporate leaders in industries that stand to gain from curtailed fossil fuel use. But, even here, what do we know about how to achieve such an outcome?

A Summary of Necessary Actions

The preceding analysis suggests the specific things that must occur to influence entire populations to reduce fossil fuel consumption. Reducing fossil fuel use is admittedly only one facet of behavior that needs to change. But we believe this analysis applies to other aspects of individual behavior and organizational actions that must alter and to what people and organizations can do to mitigate the impact of climate change that we fail to prevent.

First, we must change the immediate consequences of individual behavior that involves consumption of fossil fuels. Consequences such as the cost of fuels, the cost of low versus high emission vehicles, and the approval or disapproval of an individual's social circle are prominent influences on this behavior.

Second, we have to motivate green choice by influencing people's relational networks about the problem in the direction we described above. Increasingly, people will need to understand and care about the long-term consequences of their consumption and the benefits to them, their children, and their community of adopting behaviors that lower their carbon footprint. However, we recognize that getting people to accept that their consumptive behavior has long-term harmful consequences runs the risk of influencing them to simply avoid any attention to the problem. For this reason, it may be as important to relate desired changes in their behavior to positive long-term consequences, such as the happiness of their children, the approval of their friends and neighbors, and recognition from their community. All of these considerations point to the likely value of media campaigns, entertainment media, education of our children, religious organizations that take a stand on this issue, and the cultivation of social circles that make this the "in" thing to do. In short, we need a mass movement.

Third, we need to change the practices of organizations that involve the consumption of fossil fuels and the things that they do that will promote or discourage individual behavior change and the adoption of relevant policies. As noted above, the two major ways in which we can affect these practices are through changes in the metacontingencies for organizations and changes in the relational networks of organization leaders.

Knowing what needs to be changed and changing it are not the same. The next section proposes strategies that could help to achieve these changes.

A Research Agenda for the Contextual Behavioral Science Community

The sad fact is that neither the behavior analytic community nor the CBS community (nor for that matter, any other wing of the behavioral science community) has made truly significant contributions to prevention or mitigation of climate change

(Newsome & Alavosius, 2011). The science of the behavior of individuals is relatively clear about the contingencies that could influence individuals to reduce their greenhouse gas emissions and behavior analysis has made significant contributions to our understanding. But, in the absence of strategies for influencing entire populations, this research is having little impact on the problem.

Behavior analysts (Glenn, 2004) have pointed out that the problem is one of the cumulative outputs of greenhouse gases and have articulated the concept of macro-contingencies to denote the relationship between the similar behavioral topographies of populations and the cumulative output of their behavior. Glenn's perspective holds that cultural practices are comprised of cumulative, noninterlocking behaviors, or IBCs, which can vary in complexity from the cumulative CO_2 emissions of several individuals, from our neighbor Joe's chrome-tipped tailpipes to cumulative IBCs of workers in several car factories producing the SUVs he craves (Glenn, 2004, p. 140). Although the IBCs of organized entities (e.g., car factories producing SUVs) may be maintained by a metacontingency, cumulative IBCs of a particular type (e.g., car-producing factories operating in relative isolation across a country) may constitute a cultural practice. When a cultural practice generates a cumulative product (e.g., CO_2 emission or pollution), the relation between the two is called a macrocontingency (Glenn, 2004; Malott & Glenn, 2006).

According to Houmanfar et al. (2010), consumer behavior captured by macro-contingencies affect the prevailing beliefs within the culture. In our example of Joe, the SUV pilot, consumers' beliefs associated with driving big, rugged, but luxurious SUVs in turn affects the cultural–organizational milieu and the rules generated by the corporate leaders regarding the purchasing behavior of consumers. The cultural–organizational milieu affected by consumers' purchasing patterns, state policies, government policies, and organizational resources (financial and human resources) influence the rules generated or modified by organizational leaders. These rules in turn modify the coordinated behavior of car factory employees that generate the aggregate product (e.g., SUVs) favored by consumers. In essence, communication networks frame the intricate relations among producers and consumers and may reveal or obscure the impacts these have on the environment. Many corporate leaders try to obscure the unsavory aspects of their production and supply chains from consumers and in so doing maintain unsustainable practices. Examples in the fashion and garment industry and computer manufacturing have made headline news. In their role as guides, leaders create new verbal relations between the current and future state of the organization, between the future organization and its niche in the future environment, and between current employees and the future organization. Corporate and community leaders effective in shaping conservation of natural resources take into consideration the ever evolving external environment and verbally evaluate the potential adaptations the organization can make to those possible futures. The basis of these relations is a verbally constructed future that, at least for the leader, bears some connection with the current situation (Houmanfar, Rodrigues, & Smith, 2009). The verbal networks that would motivate green choice by corporate leaders are pretty much the same as those described for individual consumers, plus other factors specific to the organization such as fiscal health, state and federal government policies, competitors' successes, and peer opinions. The role of advocacy organizations is evident here as a vital way to shape consumer beliefs and influence corporate actions.

Little empirical and only emerging theoretical work indicates how we can affect the behavior of populations by manipulating this complex network of contingencies. The analysis reveals how much we have to learn if we are going to make significant contributions to the solution to this problem. Here we enumerate the needed empirical research.

Increasing the Valuing of Green Behavior

Whether we are talking about influencing the green behavior of one person or the CEO of a company, we need research on the most effective ways to generate changes in peoples' relational networks related to climate change. Social psychological research on attitude change has much to offer in this area. Integrating that work with RFT could increase the efficacy of attitude and value change interventions. To the extent that the RFT analysis is useful, it should help to identify previously unseen methods of stimulating changes in attitudes and values.

However, even if laboratory studies can show major changes in attitudes and values and even if these studies prove to predict genuine behavior change, the problem will remain of translating this knowledge into changes in entire populations. To achieve this, research must take place to determine how to improve the reach and effectiveness of advocacy organizations.

Increasing the Effectiveness of Advocacy Organizations

To achieve the necessary massive cultural change, a huge number of organizations must become involved. The United Nations Climate Change Education Clearinghouse provides a list of organizations working on the problems of climate change (UNESCO, n.d.). We suggest that, at this stage of our knowledge, research at the local level is most likely to be practicable and productive of clear empirical results. If contextual behavioral scientists identify local organizations receptive to having research assistance in pursuing their goals, they could probably be of considerable help to them at the same time that they develop empirical findings that other organizations could adopt.

We believe that research could help these organizations refine their effectiveness in (a) functioning as organizations, (b) recruiting members, (c) influencing the values and behavior of populations, and (d) affecting policy change. In our view, two types of policies should have priority: (a) those that leverage support for advocacy organizations and (b) those that directly affect greenhouse gas emissions.

With respect to improving functioning, the Prosocial Movement, which ACBS is currently implementing through the leadership of David Sloan Wilson and Steven Hayes, is providing support to groups and organizations around the world in implementing the Ostrom principles. Elinor Ostrom (1990) identified these principles as the fundamental features of groups that successfully managed common pool resources, such as fisheries or water. Wilson, Ostrom, and Cox (2013) argued that the principles are key to supporting the cooperation vital to any group's success. Support in implementing these principles may be especially valuable for underresourced voluntary advocacy organizations. Research that showed that implementing these principles increased the success of such organizations in achieving their goals would contribute to strengthening the entire movement worldwide. The Prosocial Movement already has a protocol for helping groups and organizations adopt these principles and a system for evaluating the impact of the intervention. Published examples exist, including the cooperation of hundreds of Rhode Island companies to band together to effect policies promoting workers' health and safety, organizing financial contingencies to promote corporate investment in safety, and educating business owners on the value of workers' well-being (Alavosius, Getting, Dagen, Newsome, & Hopkins, 2009) and the formation of a citizen cooperative on Martha's Vineyard that established wind power as a source of energy for the island (Nevin, 2010). More published studies would promote systematic replication.

Recruitment of new members in this movement is vital. Only by activating a large and growing number of people across disciplines will significant cultural change occur. One way to think about it is that joining an organization working for green policies is itself a green behavior. Developing effective appeals for joining the group is itself research on how to influence attitudes, values, and behavior. The methods used for evaluating appeals to prospective members could be as simple as randomly alternating messages on the organization's website and finding out which messages recruit the most members.

Empirical Research on Policy Adoption

In the end, the most important work will involve identifying the effective ways to get policies adopted. We believe that this work should proceed at the local level, as getting the resources to advocate for policy change and the resources to evaluate strategies for getting policies adopted are much more tractable at this level. Global efforts like the 2014 China and United States agreement to limit emissions set the broad context for these local actions.

One thing that would help this effort would be to identify a suite of possible policies and obtain data on which ones are most likely to gain support (Luke & Alavosius, 2012). Those who feel that the organization should push for the best (even if not the most popular) policy might resist this move. However, many reform movements have foundered when the perfect became the enemy of the good. Getting any green policy adopted will have some benefit: It will change community norms and encourage more people to believe that change is possible (which should recruit more people to the next effort). For example, a state or local policy requiring an estimate of annual total greenhouse gas emissions would provide some leverage for advocates to motivate the populace to reduce emissions. It would help to identify the most important sources of greenhouse gas emissions and to recognize those who might feel more influence from further policy adoption. Vermont has already implemented a policy that requires monitoring of the state's emissions (Vermont Agency of Natural Resources, n.d.).

After identification of a target policy, we suggest evaluation of a well-defined strategy for getting it adopted in a series of communities or states (Biglan & Embry, 2013). The independent variable in such a study would be the strategy for getting the policy adopted. Such a strategy might involve creating a broad coalition of organizations to push for the policy, marshalling facts in support of the policy, and creating and implementing a campaign in support of the policy. Although it might seem more challenging initially, we suggest that a ballot initiative is the best vehicle for achieving policy change. Working through a city council or county government might be easier, but a citizen initiative to adopt a policy would require influencing many more people, and influencing the populations' relational networks and behavior is as important as implementing a single policy. Ultimately, affecting climate change will require many more policies, and if the norms and behaviors of the vast majority of people do not shift, it will be nearly impossible to achieve all the necessary changes.

We suggest the value of a multiple baseline design for empirically evaluating the strategy for achieving this policy change (Biglan, Ary, & Wagenaar, 2000). This would involve implementing the campaign in one judiciously chosen community and implementing it in a second and third community only based on the experience of working in the first. This would enable the concentration of resources in one community and the refinement of the advocacy campaign in that community. The intervention in the second community would benefit from the lessons learned in the first community.

A review of the introduction to this chapter underscores the dire consequences of human failure to address the problem of climate change. This chapter has laid out a theoretical account of the relevant behavior of individuals and the practices of organizations. The challenge for the contextual behavioral science community is to do the extensive and difficult research needed to pinpoint the variables that will bring about the massive, yet crucial, changes in individual behavior and organizational action. This challenge may seem to exceed the skill set and resources of the CBS community. But if the CBS community does not meet this challenge, who will? Certainly, the ideals, perseverance, and success that the community has shown in addressing all of the other problems discussed in this volume suggest that this community may be the last best hope for the behavioral sciences to address what may ultimately prove to be the biggest challenge to well-being that humans have ever faced.

Acknowledgments

Wade Brown shared his excitement with delay discounting research and the relevance of language to that topic. Ken Killingsworth contributed to consideration of corporate action as an engine for cultural change.

References

Alavosius, M., Getting, J., Dagen, J., Newsome, W., Hopkins, B. (2009). Use of a cooperative to interlock contingencies and balance the commonwealth. *Journal of Organizational Behavior Management, Special Issue, 29*, 193–211.

Alavosius, M. P., Mattaini, M. (2011). Editorial: Behavior analysis, sustainability, resilience, and adaptation. *Behavior and Social Issues, 18*, 1–5.

Augustson, E. M., Dougher, M. J., & Markham, M. R. (2000). Emergence of conditional stimulus relations and transfer of respondent eliciting functions among compound stimuli. *Psychological Record, 50*, 745–770.

Baer, D., Wolf, M., & Risley, T. (1968). Some dimensions of applied behavior analysis. *Journal of Applied Behavior Analysis, 1*, 91–97.

Barnes-Holmes, Y., Barnes-Holmes, D., Smeets, P. M., Strand, P., & Friman, P. (2004). Establishing relational responding in accordance with more-than and less-than as generalized operant behavior in young children. *International Journal of Psychology and Psychological Therapy, 4*, 531–558.

Berens, N. M., & Hayes, S. C. (2007). Arbitrarily applicable comparative relations: Experimental evidence for a relational operant. *Journal of Applied Behavior Analysis, 40*, 45–71.

Biello, J. (2011, February). Can geoengineering save the world from global warming? *Scientific American*. Retrieved from http://www.scientificamerican.com/article/geoengineering-to-save-the-world-from-global-warming/

Biglan, A. (2009). The role of advocacy organizations in reducing negative externalities. *Journal of Organizational Behavior Management, 29*, 215–230.

Biglan, A. (2015). *The nurture effect: How the science of human behavior can improve our lives and our world.* Oakland, CA: New Harbinger.

Biglan, A., Ary, D., & Wagenaar, A. C. (2000). The value of interrupted time-series experiments for community intervention research. *Prevention Science, 1*, 31–49.

Biglan, A., & Embry, D. D. (2013). A framework for intentional cultural change. *Journal of Contextual Behavioral Science, 2*, 95–104.

DiClemente, D., & Hantula, D. A. (2003). Optimal foraging online: Increasing sensitivity to delay. *Psychology & Marketing, 20*, 785–809.

Fantino, E. (1969). Choice and the rate of reinforcement. *Journal of the Experimental Analysis of Behavior, 12*, 723–730.

Fantino, E., Preston, R. A., & Dunn, R. (1993). Delay reduction: Current status. *Journal of the Experimental Analysis of Behavior, 60*, 159–169.

Glenn, S. S. (2004). Individual behavior, culture, and social change. *The Behavior Analyst, 27*, 133–151.

Goodman, S., & Sullivan, G. (2013, February). Climate change is "threat multiplier." *Politico*. Retrieved from http://www.politico.com/story/2013/02/climate-change-is-threat-multiplier-87338.html#ixzz3JSHeR7BJ

Hansen, J. E., & Sato, M. (2011). Paleoclimate implications for human-made climate change. In A. Berger, F. Mesinger, & D. Sijaci (Eds.), *Climate change at the eve of the second decade of the century: Inferences from paleoclimate and regional aspects: Proceedings of Milutin Milankovitch 130th Anniversary Symposium*. New York, NY: Springer. Retrieved from http://arxiv.org/abs/1105.0968

Hantula, D. A., Brockman, D. D., & Smith, C. L. (2008). Online shopping as foraging: The effects of increasing delays on purchasing and patch residence. *IEEE Transactions on Professional Communication, 51*, 147–154.

Hardisty, D. J., & Weber, E. U. (2009). Discounting future green: Money versus the environment. *Journal of Experimental Psychology: General, 3*, 329–340.

Hayes, S. C., Barnes-Holmes, D., & Roche, B. (2001). *Relational frame theory: A post-Skinnerian account of human language and cognition*. New York, NY: Kluwer/Plenum.

Herrnstein, R. J. (1961). Relative and absolute strength of responses as a function of frequency of reinforcement. *Journal of the Experimental Analysis of Behavior, 4*, 267–272.

Herrnstein, R. J. (1970). On the law of effect. *Journal of the Experimental Analysis of Behavior, 13*, 243–266.

Herrnstein, R. J. (1974). Formal properties of the Matching Law. *Journal of the Experimental Analysis of Behavior, 21*, 159–164.

Houmanfar, R., & Rodrigues, N. J. (2006). Behavior analysis & cultural analysis: Points of contact and departure. *Behavior and Social Issues, 15*, 13–30.

Houmanfar, R., Rodrigues, N. J., & Smith, G. S. (2009). Role of communication networks in behavioral systems analysis. *Journal of Organizational Behavior Management, 29*, 257–275.

Houmanfar, R. A., Rodrigues, N. J., & Ward, T. A., (2010). Emergence & metacontingency: Points of contact and departure. *Behavior and Social Issues, 19*, 78–103.

Intergovernmental Panel on Climate Change. (2007). Summary for policymakers. In *Climate change 2007: The physical science basis. Contribution of Working Group 1 to the Fourth Assessment Report of the Intergovernmental Panel on Climate Change*. Cambridge, England: Cambridge University Press.

Intergovernmental Panel on Climate Change. (2014). Summary for policymakers. In *Climate change 2014: Mitigation of climate change. Contribution of Working Group III to the Fifth*

Assessment Report of the Intergovernmental Panel on Climate Change. Cambridge, England: Cambridge University Press.

Lehman, P. K., & Geller, S.E. (2004). Behavior analysis and environmental protection: Accomplishments and potential for more. *Behavior and Social Issues, 13*, 13–32.

Luke, M. & Alavosius, M.P. (2012). Impacting community sustainability through behavior change. Behavior and Social Issues, *21*, 54–79.

Madden, G. J., & Bickel, W. K. (2010). *Impulsivity: The behavioral and neurological science of discounting*. Washington, DC: American Psychological Association.

Maibach, E., Roser-Renouf, C., & Leiserowitz, A. (2009). *Global warming's' 6 Americas: An audience segmentation analysis*. New Haven, CT: Yale Project on Climate Change and the George Mason University Center for Climate Change Communication.

Malott, M. E., & Glenn, S. S. (2006). Targets of intervention in cultural and behavioral change. *Behavior and Social Issues, 15*, 31–56.

Malott, R. W., Shimamune, S., & Malott, M. E. (1992). Rule-governed behavior and organizational behavior management: An analysis of interventions. *Journal of Organizational Behavior Management, 12*, 103–116.

Moorhead J. & Nixon, T. (2015). Global 500 greenhouse gas report: The fossil fuel energy sector. Thomson Reuters.

Newsome, W. D. & Alavosius, M. P. (2011). Toward the prediction and influence of green behavior: Seeking practical utility in research. *Behavior and Social Issues, 20*, 44–77.

Nevin, J. A. (2010). The power of cooperation. *The Behavior Analyst, 33*, 189–191.

Ostrom, E. (1990). *Governing the commons*. Cambridge, England: Cambridge University Press.

Plumm, K. M., Borhart, H., & Weatherly, J. N. (2012). Choose your words wisely: Delay discounting of differently titled social policy issues. *Behavior and Social Issues, 21*, 26–48.

Rajala, A. K., & Hantula, D. A. (2000). Towards a behavioral ecology of consumption: Delay-reduction effects on foraging in a simulated internet mall. *Managerial and Decision Economics, 21*, 145–158.

Reynolds, B., & Schiffbauer, R. M. (2004). Impulsive choice and workplace safety: A new area of inquiry for research in occupational settings. *The Behavior Analyst, 27*, 239–246.

Ridgway, D. (2012, September). Flexible purpose corporation vs. benefit corporation. *Hanson Bridgett Corporate Practice Group*. Retrieved from http://www.hansonbridgett.com/Publications/articles/2012-09-flexible-purpose.aspx

Sidman, M. (1994). *Equivalence relations and behavior: A research story*. Boston, MA: Authors Cooperative, Inc.

Sidman, M., & Tailby, W. (1982). Conditional discrimination vs. matching to sample: An expansion of the testing paradigm. *Journal of the Experimental Analysis of Behavior, 37*, 5–22.

Sigurdsson, S. O., Taylor, M. A., & Wirth, O. (2013). Discounting the value of safety: Effects of perceived risk and effort. *Journal of Safety Research, 46*, 127–134.

Skinner, B. F. (1938). *The behavior of organisms*. Englewood Cliffs, NJ: Prentice Hall.

Skinner, B. F. (1966). What is the experimental analysis of behavior? *Journal of the Experimental Analysis of Behavior, 9*, 213–218.

Skinner, B. F. (1969). *Contingencies of reinforcement*. Englewood Cliffs, NJ: Prentice Hall.

Skinner, B. F. (1981). Selection by consequences. *Science, 213*, 501–504.

Thaler, R. H., & Sunstein, C. R. (2009). *Nudge: Improving decisions about health, wealth, and happiness*. New York, NY: Penguin.

Thompson, L. G. (2010). Climate change: The evidence and our options. *The Behavior Analyst, 33*, 153–170.

Thorndike, E. L. (1911). *Animal intelligence: Experimental studies*. New York, NY: Macmillan.

UNESCO. (n.d.). *Climate change education clearing house*. Retrieved from http://www.unesco.org/new/en/education/themes/leading-the-international-agenda/education-for-sustainable-development/climate-change-education/cce-clearinghouse/

United States Joint Forces Command. (2010). *The JOE: Joint operating environment 2010.* Norfolk, VA: USJFCOM.

US Department of Defense. (2014). *Department of Defense 2014 climate change adaptation roadmap.* Alexandria, VA: Office of the Deputy under Secretary of Defense for Installations and Environment (Science & Technology Directorate). Retrieved from www.acq.osd.mil/ie/download/CCARprint_wForeword_c.pdf

Vermont Agency of Natural Resources. (n.d.). *Climate change team.* Retrieved from http://www.anr.state.vt.us/anr/climatechange/

Weatherly, J. N., Terrell, H. K., & Derenne, A. (2010). Delay discounting of different commodities. *The Journal of General Psychology, 137,* 273–286.

Weatherly, N. L., & Malott, R. W. (2008). An analysis of organizational behavior management research in terms of the three-contingency model of performance management. *Journal of Organizational Behavior Management, 28,* 260–285.

Wilson, D. S., Ostrom, E., & Cox, M. E. (2013). Generalizing the core design principles for the efficacy of groups. *Journal of Economic Behavior & Organization, 90,* S21–S32.

26

The Future of the Human Sciences and Society

Anthony Biglan, Robert D. Zettle,
Steven C. Hayes, and Dermot Barnes-Holmes

It is virtually impossible to predict where the contextual behavioral science (CBS) movement, or for that matter, the behavioral sciences in general will take us in the next 50 years. It is possible, however, to envision what might happen if recent progress in the human sciences were to continue on its current trajectory. In that spirit, we describe some of the developments that we hope will emerge if the findings and methods of the CBS movement continue to make significant progress and influence the human sciences in general over the next half century. One might think of these speculations as making concrete some of the aspirations of the CBS movement for building a science that is "more adequate to the challenge of the human condition" (Hayes, Barnes-Holmes, & Wilson, 2012).

We organize these speculations around two foci. First, we reflect on what might occur in the human sciences if the contextual behavioral science movement has a significant impact on scientific thinking and practice. Second, we consider how research and practice of the contextual behavioral science community might influence the further evolution of society.

Contextual Behavioral Science as a Paradigm

Thomas Kuhn (1962) made a significant contribution to our understanding of how science works with his concept of a *scientific paradigm*. A paradigm is a conceptual system that organizes research on a particular set of problems as well as the methods to be used in studying them. Darwin's (1859) theory of evolution is a good example. Prior to Darwin, the variation among species and their similarities and differences had been recognized. What Darwin brought to the enterprise was the insight that one could account for the features of species in terms of variation, selection, and reproduction. The articulation of a paradigm typically organizes a community of scientists to work on a phenomenon, asking the same questions and using the same methods. They do so because it provides more effective ways to deal with the world. For example, the discovery of the role of the weights of substances in their chemical combinations organized

The Wiley Handbook of Contextual Behavioral Science, First Edition. Edited by Robert D. Zettle, Steven C. Hayes, Dermot Barnes-Holmes, and Anthony Biglan.
© 2016 John Wiley & Sons, Ltd. Published 2016 by John Wiley & Sons, Ltd.

the study of chemistry around the periodic chart and led to enormous progress in this field (Scerri, 2006).

According to Kuhn, a field of study may be preparadigmatic in the sense that there are multiple ways of thinking about and studying the problem at hand, and consensus about the key questions and appropriate methods is lacking. Research conducted in the 1970s provided empirical evidence that psychology, as well as anthropology, economics, sociology, and political science, was preparadigmatic according to the judgment of scholars (Biglan, 1973). In these fields, there were multiple theories and methods, with different topics being studied according to different methods by different groups of people.

Skinner (1938; 1953; 1957) proposed a paradigm for the scientific study of human behavior that had the potential to organize such investigation within an evolutionary framework by incorporating contingencies of survival, reinforcement, and cultural evolution. The key insight was that all aspects of behavior (including emotions and cognitions) could be understood in terms of variation and selection. Moreover, the fact that behavior was selected by its consequences was itself seen as the result of the evolution of the genetic capacity to have behavior being influenced in this manner. Skinner proposed to organize all study of behavior around this selectionist agenda. This stood in contrast to much of psychology, which did and still does conceptualize the causes of behavior in terms of internal states such as traits, attitudes, intentions, and neural functioning. Even in areas of psychology that one might expect to be focused on noninternal causes, such as social psychology, the explanation of social behavior requires that internal mediating cognitive, emotional (and sometimes neural) mechanisms need to be specified (see De Houwer, Gawronski, & Barnes-Holmes, 2013).

It was certainly not the case that Skinner's view became the dominant paradigm in psychology, as documented by research in the 1970s on paradigmatic thinking in academia (Biglan, 1973). And it is unlikely that the majority of psychologists would agree that it is the dominant paradigm now. Sadly, even evolutionists did not readily recognize the link between contingencies of survival and reinforcement, and the historical alliance between behavioral science and evolution science did not occur during Skinner's lifetime. However, we would argue that developments in CBS, which have modified and extended the paradigm that Skinner originally proposed, now provide a framework for such an historical realignment. CBS research and development has shown itself to be so productive across such a broad range of problems that it is no longer odd to suppose that it has the potential to organize the productive study of virtually all aspects of human behavioral phenomena (Wilson, Hayes, Biglan, & Embry, 2014). At this point in the present volume, readers are in a good position to see if they themselves agree with that potential.

We see three key features of this paradigm shift. The first is the applicability of the pursuit of prediction-and-influence to all aspects of the human condition – biological, behavioral, and cultural. CBS is situated in an evolutionary framework that treats human phenomena in terms of evolution from genetic and epigenetic to the behavioral, symbolic, and cultural domains (Jablonka & Lamb, 2005). It encompasses multilevel selection at units ranging from genes to multicellular organisms, to nonverbal behaviors and symbolic relations in individual organisms, and to groups of organisms, such as couples, families, corporations, communities, and even entire societies. The study of all of these phenomena is organized around the goal of prediction-and-influence, with precision, scope, and depth.

The second key feature that has emerged from this work is a thoroughgoing analysis of multiple aspects of human language in terms of a fundamental unit – arbitrarily applicable derived relational responding – that is enabling the prediction-and-influence of multiple aspects of human behavior. As Hughes and Barnes-Holmes (chapter 9 in this volume) put it:

> Unlike many other theoretical enterprises in modern psychology (which tend to focus on specific features or aspects of a relevant domain), RFT operates with a relatively ambitious and extremely broad goal in mind: to develop an inductive, monistic, and functionally rooted account of language and cognition that can speak to topics as diverse as the origins of language and the emergence of self, to factors responsible for human suffering, intelligence, reasoning, and evaluation.

Furthermore, recent conceptual work on RFT has led to the development of a multidimensional, multilevel (MDML) conceptual framework that emphasizes the environmental selection of increasingly complex verbal operant units of analysis. This framework serves to clearly situate RFT within the paradigm of evolutionary science (chapter 8 in this volume).

A third key feature of the CBS framework or movement is the provision of strategies for addressing a very wide range of applied problems involving human behavior and culture. In principle, we seem to be converging on the ability to ensure that most problems involving human behavior can be understood in terms of the functional contextualist paradigm that identifies manipulable variables influencing human behavioral development and change as well as the evolution of the larger social system. This work seems to be rendering a science that can enable a growing proportion of the population to live productive lives in caring relationships with others.

The Human Sciences in the Future

We suspect that scientific research on human phenomena will increasingly focus on prediction-and-influence because of its empirical success and practical utility. It is perhaps not surprising from the standpoint of our functional contextualist framework that we would suggest that the proof of this strategy is ultimately measured by progress in the precision, scope, and depth of our ability to predict and influence contextually situated behavioral events. In a larger sense, however, an evolutionary perspective on knowledge and culture suggests that scientific methods and theories have always been adopted ultimately because they worked.

In particular, it may be that many, especially younger scientists, will embrace the goal of prediction-and-influence because they see empirical evidence that it is providing traction for the study of phenomena in which they are interested. That already seems to be happening in the study of human language and cognition (chapter 10 in this volume), clinical psychology (chapter 13 in this volume), and organizations (chapter 22 in this volume). The accumulation of examples of practical success in improving the human condition by focusing on function and context may influence other scientists to attend to the contextual processes and principles needed to create concrete positive outcomes.

Research That Better Contributes to Human Well-Being

Elsewhere (Biglan & Hayes, 1996) we have argued that embracing prediction and influence as the goal of research makes such endeavors particularly likely to yield practical strategies for influencing behavioral and cultural phenomena. In chapter 24 we have expanded this argument to suggest that a functional contextualist approach to the evolution of the practices of organizations is likely to lead to more effective ways to influence the further evolution of corporate capitalism.

We have to be careful here, however, because one cannot simply assume that an improved ability to influence phenomena will lead to their being moved in directions that enhance the well-being of the entire population. Although the stated values of the CBS movement have been to create a science that contributes to positive change in the world (Hayes, Barnes-Holmes, & Wilson, 2012), the findings of a science can be appropriated for the pursuit of other goals. For example, one of us (SCH) used the IRAP (Barnes-Holmes, Hayden, Barnes-Holmes, & Stewart, 2008) to help advertisers learn how to promote the enrollment website for the Affordable Care Act (aka "Obamacare") in a way that was attractive to the poor and to ethnic minorities. However, there would be nothing to prevent advertisers from doing the same thing to encourage, say, the purchase of tobacco products, or the consumption of alcohol. The CBS movement has the potential to shed light on what influences individuals and organizations to make use of this science for purposes that may do harm to some, but, like all scientific knowledge, there is nothing to guarantee that it will be used for prosocial purposes.

There is also a risk that a science of human behavior focused too narrowly on the immediate benefit of findings will so narrow our perspective that it stifles innovative ways of looking at problems. Nonetheless, there are several areas of biobehavioral research where embracing prediction-and-influence could enhance the chances that our research will contribute to human well-being. One of the most important may be a change in emphasis in the research funded by the National Institutes of Health (NIH) in the United States. For NIH the stated mission is "to seek fundamental knowledge about the nature and behavior of living systems and the application of that knowledge to enhance health, lengthen life, and reduce illness and disability" (National Institutes of Health, n.d.). Its $30 billion annual budget makes it the single biggest funder of research on human well-being in the world.

One thing to note about the NIH mission statement is that there is an implied relationship between basic and applied research: Fundamental knowledge is obtained and then it is applied in order to enhance well-being. It contrasts with a functional contextualist perspective, which does not assume that basic research derives knowledge, which is then applied to the solution of practical problems, but rather that knowledge with high precision and scope can be a goal for research programs in both areas.

Notice also that there is nothing in the NIH mission statement to ensure that "fundamental knowledge about the nature and behavior of living systems" involves knowing how to predict and influence events. For example, complex relationships among parts of the brain can be accurately and precisely mapped, even though none of the variables that are typically isolated are ones that would allow us to predict *and influence* any of the phenomena under study. Enormous knowledge is accumulating about how brains and bodies work, but because prediction-and-influence is not the explicit goal, we are not necessarily developing practical strategies for improving human well-being at the rate we otherwise might be.

One could hope that the success of the CBS movement would influence the direction of all research on human well-being. By including influence as a goal, CBS research returns constantly to the role of history and circumstance – that is to the manipulable context that produces events and their interrelationships. Indeed this strategy could even be applied to the choices that organizations like NIH make. Research that pinpointed the primary influences on NIH funding priorities could point to ways to influence those priorities in the direction of prediction-and-influence.

If the human sciences become more explicit about pursuing the goal of change in the service of improving human well-being, it will require greater clarity about what we mean by "human well-being." Human well-being can be operationally defined in terms of the incidence and prevalence of problems in populations, beginning with physical health, but it also encompasses psychological and behavioral well-being, if for no other reason than that they contribute to physical health (Biglan & Embry, 2013). And once we focus on these outcomes, it becomes clear that we must be concerned with the prevalence of environments that nurture versus fail to support these aspects of well-being (Biglan, Flay, Embry, & Sandler, 2012).

Advances in Our Understanding of Language

Advancing our understanding of symbolic processes and human language more generally presents numerous and, to be frank, enormous challenges for the CBS community. Cartesian dualism is the normal mode of discourse for most human beings. But even more problematically it is also well established inside scientific discourse as well. Nowhere is this more obvious than in mainstream psychological science, and, of course, particularly cognitive science. This way of speaking routinely locates the causes of action inside the mind (or brain) of the behaving actor, and thus the search for ways to change behavior involve first specifying the nature of how information is stored, represented, encoded and decoded, retrieved, and processed by the "mind-machine." And when it comes to a scientific analysis of human language and cognition, the gravity-well of dualistic thinking is almost impossible to escape. We should be clear that there is nothing intrinsically wrong with dualistic thinking, but from a CBS perspective we have, as a community, agreed that it is not the best way to achieve our overarching goals of prediction-and-influence with precision, scope, and depth so as to produce a science that is increasingly more adequate to the challenge of the human condition.

So, how might we begin to convince the wider scientific community of the value of studying human language and cognition from a nondualistic perspective? Developing a working theory of such an account, with a reasonable body of empirical evidence, is of course a good place to start. And we have, for all intents and purposes, achieved that objective in the form of RFT. However, as becomes clear upon reading the chapters that appear in the section on RFT in the current handbook, a great deal of *empirical* work remains to be done, particularly if the theory is going to continue to reticulate successfully with key areas of application.

Perhaps more importantly, however, RFT itself needs to be seen as a work-in-progress that is undergoing constant refinement and development, in much the same way as the theory of evolution, as articulated by Charles Darwin, is still being developed and refined over 130 years after his death. Given that CBS is situated firmly within evolutionary science itself, a critically important way in which RFT must develop conceptually is in specifying more clearly than it has thus far the units of language and cognition that are selected and modified by environmental contingencies, including the verbal contingencies provided by other speakers within a verbal community. It is here that real and steady progress is needed from the basic science wing of CBS.

The concept of the relational frame (as a relational operant) was of course pivotal in establishing a core unit of analysis, and a great deal has been achieved with that central concept over the past 25 years. However, there is a strong and increasingly demanding need to create a far more sophisticated framework for studying the selection of the units of human language and cognition as they occur "in flight" in the natural environment. When we have the conceptual and empirical basis for such a framework we will be in a better position to apply the evolutionary or selectionist approach to human symbolic processes in a genuinely convincing manner. This will be an enormous challenge, but it is one that we cannot avoid. The faint outline of what this framework might look like has been presented in the current handbook, but it is very much only the beginning of a long and difficult scientific journey that we hope CBS will take.

New Directions in the Treatment and Prevention of Psychological, Behavioral, and Health Problems

We envision accelerating progress in our ability to reduce the incidence and prevalence of psychological and behavioral problems in populations. One development that is already discernible is an increased focus on prevention research. To a great extent, prevention science is simply a shift in focus from providing effective services to people with psychological and behavioral problems to providing them soon enough to minimize the occurrence of such difficulties. It also represents a recognition that the ultimate achievement of human well-being requires affecting entire populations.

Work is also underway to develop more efficient methods of reaching populations through interventions relying on books, phones, and the Internet. There are already over 20 such studies in the CBS literature with generally good outcomes (e.g., Bricker, Wyszynski, Comstock, & Heffner, 2013; Jeffcoat & Hayes, 2012; Trompetter, Bohlmeijer, Veehof, & Schreurs, 2015) that in some investigations have produced effects even greater than in face-to-face interventions (Lappalainen et al., 2014).

Some humility is needed here in tempering our enthusiasm for CBS. CBS is one facet of a more general trend in the behavioral sciences to create environments that nurture well-being. In particular there is a strong and growing movement to improve the environments of young children (Heckman & Mosso, 2014; Shonkoff & Fisher, 2013). Moreover, CBS cannot claim sole credit for the advances that have been made in evidence-based approaches to virtually every psychological and behavioral problem and increasing use of behavioral methods to affect unhealthful behavior.

Research on the Environment

Nowhere is the need for a science of prediction-and-influence more needed than in the area of climate change (see Chapter 25 in this volume). Considerable research has been done by psychologists on this problem, but most recent work focuses on the prediction of environmentally relevant behaviors from psychological variables, such as attitudes;

manipulable environmental variables that might influence such behavior are seldom identified. Given the threat that climate change poses to human well-being, it is imperative that research be undertaken that identifies ways not simply to influence the behavior of individuals, but to change the contingencies for corporations. That, in turn will require the empirical evaluation of strategies for influencing policy adoption.

The Evolution of Society

In chapter 4 of this volume, we (Biglan and Hayes) suggested that embracing prediction-and-influence as a goal entails the valuing of values per se, and that research thus far suggests that psychological flexibility is, on empirical grounds, essential for living our values. If this is accurate, it suggests that both the scientific pursuit of prediction-and-influence and the applied work that is emerging could contribute to the evolution of societies where the behaviors of both individuals and organizations are more flexible and where the dominant values involve compassion and caring.

The Influence of Behavioral Science on People

We might first consider how other scientific advances have influenced cultural evolution and contrast these with how progress in the behavioral sciences might influence our societies over the next 50 years. We would argue that there is a major difference between behavioral science (as well as some key aspects of the biological sciences) and every other area of scientific progress. In every aspect of the physical sciences, scientific advances have been translated into changes in our world through experts. Only a tiny proportion of the people who make use of any of the scientific advances that have so improved our world understand the details of the science that underpins those advances. Most people who make daily use of the technologies that have so changed the world in the past century, need not understand the science that led to and underpins the efficacy of their computers, cell phones, televisions, automobiles, air conditioners, and so on. Even airline pilots who have extraordinary skills in operating aircraft, need not understand the details of the technologies that they employ in flying planes. Physicians who treat an infectious disease have critical knowledge for doing so, but may not understand the details of the biochemistry that underpins the efficacy of the antibiotics that they prescribe. Most scientific advances benefit society through the intercession of experts.

The situation is a little different when it comes to the behavioral sciences and the facets of the biological sciences that relate to health. In these areas, reaping the benefits of what we have learned very often depends on people understanding, at least in rough outline, the scientific principles that have been developed. Clients, for instance, who are helped by acceptance and commitment therapists must incorporate into their behavior the skills that research shows are involved in psychological flexibility. A mother who is helped by a program like the Nurse Family Partnership (Olds, 2010) to become more nurturing to her infant child, does not need to know about the biochemistry that underlies the importance of patient, noncoercive parenting, but she does need to know how to soothe her infant. The empirical relationship between a mother's soothing behavior and the development of an infant's self-regulation has to be translated into actions of the mother.

The implication is that to a much greater extent than has been true for translating scientific advances in the physical sciences into the dramatic changes in our societies over the past 150 years, translating the advances in scientific understanding of human development into comparable improvements in human well-being requires that we get most people in society to understand – at least in rough outline – what humans need to thrive. This may be particularly the case when we consider the implications of research on psychological flexibility.

The Spread of Psychological Flexibility

David Sloan Wilson (2002) has described how the early Christian religion grew because of the survival advantages it gave to adherents. When epidemics that frequently spread through Roman cities occurred, Christians had a greater likelihood of surviving because members of the group risked their lives nursing the sick. In short it was the advantages of Christianity that originally contributed to its spread. Perhaps a similar thing will happen with the CBS efforts to promote psychological flexibility.

Imagine a world in which the basic principles of psychological flexibility came to permeate societies. There is a genuine sense in which the philosophical framework of contextual behavioral science is instantiated in the clinical research that is described in Part III of this handbook. Psychological flexibility essentially involves living one's life according to the pursuit of one's values. As just mentioned, embracing the goal of prediction-and-influence implies that we have more generally embraced valuing.

One facet of the spread of psychological flexibility would be a greater emphasis on values in society. It is possible that the empirical progress that the CBS movement has been making could lead to an increase in the degree that people embrace an approach to living that is organized much more explicitly around the pursuit of values and goals. A greater emphasis on values in our daily lives could by itself promote psychological flexibility, because, as suggested above, people would increasingly ask themselves and others how well what they were doing was working to achieve or support their values. In essence, there may be a reciprocal relationship between the pursuit of values and the development of psychological flexibility. Thus we may also see the spread of a mindful, defused orientation in which people hold their beliefs lightly, are more compassionate, and more oriented toward nonmaterialist values. These developments could happen if the basic means of increasing psychological flexibility and reducing human suffering utilized within acceptance and commitment therapy (Hayes, Strosahl, & Wilson, 2012) seep into the culture via the spread of these ideas in self-help books (e.g., Hayes & Smith, 2005), expansion of the clinical community with this orientation, and ultimately by being depicted in entertainment media.

There are numerous cultural developments that could ensue from the spread of a values orientation and psychological flexibility. It could facilitate a coming together of secular and religious movements. Currently our society seems to be split between a segment that is religious and views secularism as alien and threatening. At the same time, there is a secular movement in which prominent atheists seem to feel that the improvement of society depends on getting religious people to admit the errors in their thinking (Harris, 2006). Moreover, the leaders of each side ostensibly benefit from keeping their followers hostile to those in the other camp. Yet ultimately both sides have values about the well-being of people in society that may not be as disparate as they think. Perhaps greater focus on the ultimate values that these groups have would lead to their finding common ground.

The same possibility should be explored with respect to the relationship among the major religions, as well as the relationship between science and religion. Perhaps rather than arguing about what is really true, in an ontological sense, human groups will benefit from focusing on the basic conditions that they want for all people and what it will take to achieve them.

The spread of psychological flexibility could also affect government. Currently, policy-making is dominated by ideological positions that make sparse use of empirical evidence and seldom articulate the values that underlie policy-making. If we could make progress in getting policy-makers to come together around the definition of human well-being articulated above, we would then have leverage to ask that policies be evaluated in terms of their contribution to these valued outcomes.

Conclusion

CBS is not a narrowly defined research program – it is a knowledge development strategy seeking a more unified and useful behavioral science. We cannot predict if CBS as an organized area will exist 50 years from now, but we can confidently predict that any approach that leads to the identification and dissemination of behavioral change principles that make a broad difference in improving the human condition will prosper. The history of humanity suggests that scientific knowledge, over time, has a net positive effect on human well-being. The behavioral sciences have lagged in their contributions as compared to, say, medical science or engineering, but part of that may be that it is just too easy to confuse mental correlates with causal processes when behavior is the subject matter of interest. CBS will not as readily make that error, but it remains to be seen whether new and demonstrably useful principles and models will consistently emerge from CBS thinking as a result. Looking at this volume, however, we can say, "so far, so good."

References

Barnes-Holmes, D., Hayden, E., Barnes-Holmes, Y., Stewart, I. (2008). The Implicit Relational Assessment Procedure (IRAP) as a response-time and event-related-potentials methodology for testing natural verbal relations. A preliminary study. *The Psychological Record, 58,* 497–516.

Biglan, A. (1973). The characteristics of subject matter in different academic areas. *Journal of Applied Psychology, 57,* 195–203.

Biglan, A., & Embry, D. D. (2013). A framework for intentional cultural change. *Journal of Contexual Behavioral Science, 2,* 95–104.

Biglan, A., Flay, B. R., Embry, D. D., & Sandler, I. N. (2012). The critical role of nurturing environments for promoting human well-being. *American Psychologist, 67,* 257–271.

Biglan, A., & Hayes, S. C. (1996). Should the behavioral sciences become more pragmatic? The case for functional contextualism in research on human behavior. *Applied and Preventive Psychology: Current Scientific Perspectives, 5,* 47–57.

Bricker, J., Wyszynski, C., Comstock, B., & Heffner, J. L. (2013). Pilot randomized controlled trial of web-based acceptance and commitment therapy for smoking cessation. *Nicotine & Tobacco Research, 15,* 1756–1764.

Darwin, C. (1859). *On the origin of species.* London, England: John Murray.

De Houwer, J., Gawronski, B., & Barnes-Holmes, D. (2013). A functional-cognitive framework for attitude research. *European Journal of Social Psychology, 24,* 252–287.

Harris, S. (2006). *Letter to a Christian nation.* New York, NY: Knopf.

Hayes, S. C., Barnes-Holmes, D., & Wilson, K. G. (2012). Contextual behavioral science: Creating a science more adequate to the challenge of the human condition. *Journal of Contextual Behavioral Science, 1,* 1–16.

Hayes, S. C., & Smith, S. (2005). *Get out of your mind and into your life: The new acceptance and commitment therapy.* Oakland, CA: New Harbinger.

Hayes, S. C., Strosahl, K. D., & Wilson, K. G. (2012). *Acceptance and commitment therapy: The process and practice of mindful change* (2nd ed.). New York, NY: Guilford.

Heckman, J., & Mosso, S. (2014). The economics of human development and social mobility. *Annual Review of Economics, 6,* 689–733.

Jablonka, E., & Lamb, M. J. (2005). *Evolution in four dimensions.* Cambridge, MA: MIT Press.

Jeffcoat, T., & Hayes, S. C. (2012). A randomized trial of ACT bibliotherapy on the mental health of K-12 teachers and staff. *Behaviour Research and Therapy, 50,* 571–579.

Kuhn, T. S. (1962). *The structure of scientific revolutions.* Chicago, IL: University of Chicago Press.

Lappalainen, P., Granlund, A., Siltanen, S., Ahonen, S., Vitikainen, M., Tolvanen, A., & Lappalainen, R. (2014). ACT internet-based vs face-to-face? A randomized controlled trial of two ways to deliver acceptance and commitment therapy for depressive symptoms: An 18-month follow-up. *Behaviour Research and Therapy, 61,* 43–54.

National Institutes of Health. (n.d.). *Mission.* Retrieved from http://www.nih.gov/about/mission.htm

Olds, D. L. (2010). The nurse–family partnership: From trials to practice. In A. J. Reynolds, A. J. Rolnick, M. M. Englund, & J. A. Temple (Eds.), *Childhood programs and practices in the first decade of life: A human capital integration* (pp. 49–75). New York, NY: Cambridge University Press.

Scerri, E. R. (2006). *The periodic table: Its story and its significance.* New York, NY: Oxford University Press.

Shonkoff, J. P, & Fisher, P. A. (2013). Rethinking evidence-based practice and two-generation programs to create the future of early childhood policy. *Development and Psychopathology, 25,* 1635–1653.

Skinner, B. F. (1938). *The behavior of organisms.* New York, NY: Appleton-Century-Crofts.

Skinner, B. F. (1953). *Science and human behavior.* New York, NY: Free Press.

Skinner, B. F. (1957). *Verbal behavior.* New York, NY: Appleton-Century-Crofts.

Trompetter, H. R., Bohlmeijer, E. T., Veehof, M. M., & Schreurs, K. M. (2015). Internet-based guided self-help intervention for chronic pain based on acceptance and commitment therapy: A randomized controlled trial. *Journal of Behavioral Medicine, 38,* 66–80.

Wilson, D. S. (2002). *Darwin's cathedral: Evolution, religion, and the nature of society.* Chicago, IL: University of Chicago Press.

Wilson, D. S., Hayes, S. C., Biglan, A., & Embry, D. D. (2014). Evolving the future: Toward a science of intentional change. *Behavioral and Brain Sciences, 37,* 395–416.

Index

Note: Page numbers in *italics* refer to Figures; those in **bold** to Tables.

The Wiley Handbook of Contextual Behavioral Science, First Edition. Edited by Robert D. Zettle,
Steven C. Hayes, Dermot Barnes-Holmes, and Anthony Biglan.
© 2016 John Wiley & Sons, Ltd. Published 2016 by John Wiley & Sons, Ltd.